THE OSS AND HO CHI MINH

THE OSS AND HO CHI MINH

Unexpected Allies in the
War against Japan

DIXEE R. BARTHOLOMEW-FEIS

UNIVERSITY PRESS OF KANSAS

Published by the University Press of Kansas (Lawrence, Kansas 66045),
which was organized by the Kansas Board of Regents and
is operated and funded by Emporia State University,
Fort Hays State University, Kansas State University,
Pittsburg State University, the University of Kansas,
and Wichita State University

Library of Congress Cataloging-in-Publication Data
Bartholomew-Feis, Dixee R.
  The OSS and Ho Chi Minh : unexpected allies in the war against Japan
/ Dixee R. Bartholomew-Feis.
    p.   cm. — (Modern war studies)
  Includes bibliographical references and index.
  ISBN 978-0-7006-1431-8 (cloth : alk. paper)
  ISBN 978-0-7006-1652-7 (pbk. : alk. paper)
    1. World War, 1939-1945—Secret service—United States. 2. United
States. Office of Strategic Services. 3. World War, 1939-1945—Vietnam.
4. Ho__, Chí Minh, 1890-1969. 5. United States—Foreign Relations—
Vietnam. 6. Vietnam—Foreign Relations—United States. 7. United
States—Foreign relations—1933-1945. I. Title. II. Series.
  D810.S7.B336 2006
  940.54'867309597—dc22   2005033649

British Library Cataloguing-in-Publication Data is available.

Printed in the United States of America

10 9 8 7 6 5 4 3 2

In loving memory of my grandparents
Philip O. and Fern T. White

Contents

Acknowledgments

Many people played an indispensable role in helping to complete this book. I give full credit to the people mentioned below, and apologize to anyone inadvertently left out, but I alone am to blame for all errors. First, I express my deepest gratitude to the men of the OSS who served in Vietnam in the 1940s. In particular I would like to thank René Défourneaux, Carleton Swift, and the late Charles Fenn for opening up their lives, their archives, and their homes to me. Frank Tan, Allison Thomas, and Frank White (all since deceased) and Henry Prunier were consistently generous with their time, spending many hours over the telephone being interviewed and answering the myriad questions that emerged with each step of this work. I also owe a special thanks to George Wickes, as well as the others, who shared with me their own written recollections of those turbulent months in Southeast Asia. For their help in procuring photographs for this work, I extend my gratitude to Charles Miles, Alyn Fenn, John Nordlinger, and Samuel Chu.

I owe a special debt to my colleague and mentor, John F. Guilmartin, who taught me a tremendous amount about Vietnam, military history, and the intricacies of weaving together oral interviews and primary documentation. I am especially appreciative of the many fine evenings spent with him and Lore Guilmartin and of the fine food and conversation that came with each one. I also thank William Duiker, who kindly read my manuscript, provided suggestions, and opened up his own "archive" to me.

I would also like to thank John Taylor and Lawrence McDonald at the National Archives and Records Administration for providing invaluable guidance through the OSS records, Kate O'Brien at the Liddell Hart Centre for Military Archives for her help with the Sir Douglas Gracey Papers, and Elizabeth Konzak and Robert Bledsoe for providing access and guidance with the Archimedes Patti Collection at the University of Central Florida. A special thank you goes to my map designer Josh Weitzel, who remained good-natured even when I wanted to add or change something to every draft of every map he presented to me. I extend deep gratitude to my dean and colleague Jeanne Tinsley at Buena Vista University for her support, which manifested itself in so many ways.

I could never repay the enormous debt of gratitude that I owe my parents, Richard and Sharon Bartholomew, for their unwavering support and faith in me. I would also like to thank my mother- and father-in-law, Polly and Gil Feis, and my grandparents-in-law, Dr. Bill and Anne Doering, for their encouragement. Without my dear friends Lisa Tuttle, Liz Repka, David Hogan, Joyce Grimes, Suzanne Studer, Joyce Bettin, and Karen Grieme, the writing process would have been a weary one—thank you for the many pick-me-ups as I confined myself to the office.

Finally, to my husband and best friend, Bill Feis, and my sweet daughters, Phoebe Elizabeth and Lydia Anne, I owe the greatest debts of all. They both spent too many nights and weekends waiting for me to lift my eyes from a computer screen, and Bill patiently read and critiqued each page without complaint, even when working on his own books. This book simply would not have been possible without him. As we close this chapter, we begin the next adventure.

Introduction

The explosions that rocked Pearl Harbor on December 7, 1941, resulted in enormous changes worldwide. The Japanese attack brought the United States into the war alongside Great Britain, the Soviet Union, and China in their efforts to defeat the military power of Germany, Italy, and Japan. As the war raged across the European and Pacific theaters, few nations escaped the economic, military, political, and social devastation of the conflagration. The war also brought together peoples and nations whose paths had barely crossed in times of peace. One such "accidental" relationship emerged between Americans and Vietnamese. Known at that time as Annamese or Indochinese, the people of Vietnam languished under decades-old colonial rule in Southeast Asia as part of French Indochina, which was composed of Tonkin (northern Vietnam), Annam (central Vietnam), Cochinchina (southern Vietnam), Laos, and Cambodia.

Relations between the Vietnamese and Americans would have many twists and turns and would eventually lead to another war some twenty years later. But in 1941 neither Americans nor Vietnamese knew of this future. In fact, while Americans were still reeling from the attack on Pearl Harbor and only beginning to gear up for the long war ahead, some Vietnamese were already analyzing what the American entrance into the war might mean for them and their struggle for freedom from colonial control. "We should guard against the illusion that the Chiang Kai-shek and Anglo-American troops will bring us our freedom," warned Truong Chinh, general secretary of the Indochinese Communist Party. "In our struggle for national liberation," he continued, "we must obviously seek allies—even if they are temporary, vacillating, or conditional—but the struggle must no less be the fruit of our own efforts."[1] It would have surprised the stern communist Truong Chinh to learn that one of the most prominent capitalists in the United States, millionaire attorney William J. Donovan, who would later head an

maps©Josh Weitzel

organization that would play a key role in "introducing" the two nations, shared his philosophy on the use of allies.

Donovan, director of the Office of Strategic Services (OSS), a wartime agency within the U.S. Army tasked with intelligence and counterintelligence operations, also recognized the need to use a broad range of allies—whether "temporary, vacillating, or conditional." Although he was personally opposed to communism, during the course of the war Donovan's OSS worked with the communist underground throughout Europe. "OSS was not a policy-making organization, [Donovan] stressed repeatedly, and with Russia as a co-belligerent it was his duty to cooperate in the common objective—the earliest possible defeat of the Axis."[2] The same considerations obliged Donovan's agents to work with communists, both known and suspected, in

Asia, for at times it was they who most clearly understood the political and military situation on the ground. Simply stated, the mission of the OSS in Asia was to aid in the defeat of the Japanese and end the brutal oppression of their Greater East Asia Co-Prosperity Sphere. And that meant addressing the needs of the U.S. armed forces for intelligence on the Japanese occupying Vietnam, an area remote from prewar American concerns but strikingly important because of its proximity to both China and the Japanese home islands. OSS officers were thus impelled to recruit intelligence agents and, later, armed military missions under the aegis of the OSS and to dispatch them into that region. Thus two peoples' paths converged for one brief moment—a moment both perilous and promising for the future of both nations.

In its short three years of existence, the OSS engaged in a variety of covert operations and intelligence activities, and the agency recruited men and women suited for these tasks. Edmond Taylor, a former member of the OSS, offered his view of the rationale behind the organization: "Donovan, I think, hoped to demonstrate through OSS that the normally untapped reserves of individual courage and resource, and the dynamism of the individual will to win constitute the basic raw materials of victory, and that in an increasingly mechanized world, human dignity is still not only a moral but a strategic quality."[3] Perhaps it was the presence of just such men on the ground in Vietnam that made the situation they encountered so complex and, at times, so disturbing to them. For not only did these Americans encounter Japanese brutality, but they also came face-to-face with the stark reality of French colonialism from a Vietnamese perspective.

Perhaps this reality is best summarized by a Vietnamese refrain popular in the 1930s: "Ill fortune, indeed, for power has been seized by the French invaders, who are bent on barbarous deeds, as is their wont. It's criminal, criminal, criminal to set out the food tray and find that one has nothing but roots and greens to eat; it's misery, misery, misery to take up the chopsticks and have one's meal cry out beseechingly because of a lack of salt."[4]

This description of the dire condition and dismal future of most peasants in rural Vietnam clearly places the blame at the feet of the French—the "barbarous invaders." Indeed, most Vietnamese had gained little but suffered much from the previous fifty years of colonial domination. While the French extolled the benefits of their *mission civilisatrice*, or "civilizing mission," the peasants' situation continued to worsen. But the French, and the Vietnamese and Chinese elite who collaborated with them, enjoyed the fruits of peasant labor. Contemporary Vietnamese accounts such as *The Red Earth*, Tran Tu Binh's memoir subtitled *A Vietnamese Memoir of Life on a*

Colonial Rubber Plantation, and Tran Van Mai's "Who Committed This Crime?" clearly illustrate the chant's claim that French rule was oppressive and that the average peasant suffered heavily under its yoke. If one were French, Cochinchina in general and Saigon specifically fulfilled the image implied in the appellation "Pearl of the Orient." But few Vietnamese were allowed to bask in the luster of that French gem.

From the roots of such despair, Vietnamese nationalist leaders and movements arose. There were numerous competitors with a variety of ideological bents vying to lead the discontented, including pro-Japanese monarchists; the Viet Nam Nationalist [Revolutionary] Party, better known as the VNQDD (nationalists modeled after the Chinese Nationalist Kuomintang Party); revolutionary Marxist groups, most notably the Indochinese Communist Party (ICP), who dominated the League for the Independence of Viet Nam (best known as the Viet Minh); and the lesser-known Trotskyites. All tried to tap into and ride into power on the pervasive anti-French sentiment. Ultimately, the communists prevailed, but only after aiding in the liquidation of the VNQDD and co-opting many of their rivals into the Viet Minh. By 1945 the Viet Minh had begun to attract ever-increasing numbers and was clearly emerging as the most prominent of the Vietnamese groups struggling for power and asserting Vietnam's independence. At that time it was primarily viewed as an anticolonialist, pro-independence, and perhaps nationalist movement, not as a communist organ. In fact, very few Vietnamese at that time understood what communism stood for, but most were painfully aware of what French colonialism meant in their lives.[5] By late 1945 the Viet Minh seemed to understand, better than any of the other groups, how to use for their own ends the intense desire of most Vietnamese to throw off the colonial yoke. Historian Huynh Kim Khanh argued that key to the Viet Minh's rise to power were their "skills in revolutionary analysis, organization, propaganda, and leadership [which] were undoubtedly superior to *all*, save none, of the Vietnamese political parties." As Khanh pointed out, however, "these skills would have been useless, if there had not been a favorable 'revolutionary environment.'"[6]

One of the first to sense the "favorable 'revolutionary environment'" was the man who would emerge by the end of the war as the leader of the Viet Minh and who would eventually become the most recognized Vietnamese in the world. Born in 1890 in Nghe An, historically a province given to revolutionary activity, Ho Chi Minh traveled the world for much of his early maturity, working at a variety of odd jobs and experimenting with an array of political philosophies. Soon after the conclusion of World War I, Ho, known as Nguyen Ai Quoc, "Nguyen the Patriot," concluded that communism offered the most clearly defined arguments against colonialism and the best prospect for unifying and governing an independent Vietnam. Although Ho was a persuasive writer and strong patriot, he spent most of his early years outside the country and did not return to Vietnam until early in World War II—a time that became a most propitious moment in Vietnamese history.

World War II brought together a variety of actors and situations that combined to create a golden opportunity for Ho Chi Minh and the Viet Minh. Japan's five-year occupation of the French Pearl of the Orient worsened the poverty of most Vietnamese and substantially weakened the French position in the eyes of both its colonial subjects and the Allies. In addition to being able to champion an anticolonialist stance, the Viet Minh would also claim a partnership with the Allies in the fight against the Japanese. Although Viet Minh activities against the Japanese were little more than a nuisance to the emperor's forces, they provided excellent propaganda for the movement. Furthermore, the Viet Minh reaped significant benefits from the Japanese coup de main in March 1945, which effectively ended French colonial rule for a brief period and, following Japan's defeat, created a power vacuum into which stepped Ho Chi Minh and the Viet Minh.[7]

Into this wartime situation also walked (sometimes quite literally) American soldiers of the OSS. As part of their mission, those chosen for OSS often worked covertly with a variety of resistance groups in Europe and the Pacific. In the years since World War II, the decisions to work with many of these groups have been questioned. The brief partnership between the OSS and the Viet Minh in particular became the subject of great debate, especially after the unhappy U.S. involvement in Vietnam from 1965 to 1975. The disagreements over whether Ho Chi Minh could have become an "Asian Tito" or would have settled steadfastly in the Soviet camp have absorbed the attention of numerous scholars. These arguments have even emerged among members of the OSS who knew Ho in the 1940s. One former OSS operative contended that Ho was "totally intractable," adding, "I doubt that there was ever any way in which Ho could be dealt with."[8] Another described the situation a bit differently:

> You've got to judge someone on the basis of what he wants. Ho couldn't be French, and he knew he could fight the French on his terms. He was afraid of the Chinese, and he couldn't deal with them because they'd always demand their pound of flesh. Moscow, so far away, was good at blowing up bridges, but not much good at building them again. If it weren't for the war, of course, Ho wouldn't have had a chance against the long background of French colonialism. But now he was in the

saddle, although it wasn't clear what horse he was riding. For the moment, surely, he was helping us, on the ground. We and the French were in a position to help him in the future. I think he was ready to remain pro-West.[9]

Yet the fact remains that in the last years of the war members of the OSS in Vietnam saw these debates as mostly beside the point, if indeed they were aware of them at all. The OSS, like other wartime agencies, was concerned with winning the war and finding allies to aid in that mission—including communists and little-known indigenous nationalist groups of all stripes. And although the director of the OSS and the leader of the Viet Minh would never meet, some similarities between the two men and their philosophies enlighten the relationships between William Donovan's men and those of Ho Chi Minh.

Ho, like Donovan, believed in the intrinsic value of the "untapped reserves of individual courage and resource" and the importance of human dignity as a "strategic quality" for victory. Both recognized talent, intelligence, and that certain indescribable but necessary quality—what historian Robin Winks called "the right stuff"—in others. They also understood the need to empower those with the "right stuff" to foment change, whether to broaden participation in the Viet Minh and liberate Vietnam from French control or, in the American case, to gather a wide range of intelligence resources for the ultimate defeat of Japan and liberation of those enduring its brutal occupation.[10] Initially both Ho and Donovan recruited large numbers of scholars into their organizations—in particular, Ho in the formation of the Revolutionary Youth League in the mid-1920s and Donovan in his all-important Research and Analysis Branch of the OSS. With time the organizations of both men would expand to include a broad array of members with myriad backgrounds.

Regardless of their operatives' educational achievements, both Ho and Donovan had high expectations of those they worked with as well as of themselves, believing that the men and women who fought alongside them should be "courageous, bold, and persevering," and should subordinate their own needs to the "requirements" of the "cause."[11] Faced with such high standards, it was fortunate for both the Viet Minh and the OSS that their chiefs were blessed with the charismatic personalities that made them famous. Both were described as gentle and slow to anger, as persuasive and open to ideas, and above all as undeniably patriotic with a firm determination to serve the needs of their countries. And no doubt Ho would have agreed with Donovan's 1941 pronouncement that "there is a moral force in wars, that, in the long run, is stronger than any machine."[12] Ho looked to the ultimate victory—independence from France—while Donovan had his eye on the more immediate goal of defeating the Axis. But both believed they fought a moral and just war and that they would, in due course, prevail.

Certainly Donovan's men believed they were participating in a just war to free the world from the claws of the German Reich and the Japanese Empire. But at war's end most wanted simply to return home. For OSS operatives in French Indochina, however, their mission remained unfinished even after Japan's defeat: They had yet to arrange the formal surrender and repatriation of the Japanese and investigate alleged war crimes. In order to achieve their goals, the Americans on the ground by necessity had to work with the Vietnamese, French, British, and Chinese, and they found their mission severely hampered by these groups' often-conflicting goals and ideals. In addition, as unbiased as they may have thought themselves, many of these young Americans were committed to an idealism that led them to conclude, especially after witnessing the living conditions in Vietnam, that French colonialism should also become a casualty of the war. Many in the OSS believed they were acting on the wishes of President Franklin Roosevelt, who was on record as opposing French colonialism and had even gone so far as to mention the situation in Indochina specifically. Moreover, his rhetoric throughout the war and formal proclamations, such as the Atlantic Charter, only added to this perception. Although all felt justified in their sympathy with the Vietnamese, many of the OSS personnel in Vietnam became the targets of harsh criticism, especially from the French colons.

The profits and lifestyle the French enjoyed, especially in Saigon and the southern region, made them reluctant to change their ways and hostile toward suggestions that they should relinquish control over the Pearl of the Orient. Jean Sainteny, the French representative in Hanoi, was especially outspoken in his criticism of the OSS, describing the men who served in Vietnam in 1945 as "absolutely ignorant" of the situation in Indochina and, indeed, of the circumstances in all of Asia. In his view, these men naively believed they stood for the concept of anticolonialism but, instead, were playing into both the Japanese and Vietnamese "anti-white" game and preparing Vietnam to fall prey to "Asiatic communism."[13] But the views of those working for the OSS in 1945 were not colored by the rhetoric of the cold war that was yet to come. Instead, they evaluated the situation as they saw it on the ground in 1945. OSS officer Austin Glass, for one, would have disagreed with Sainteny. He based his assessment on thirty years of experience in Indochina prior to the war as well as on his wartime experience. In July 1945 he wrote his final report for OSS:

> I do not believe that the French have ever understood the Annamese mentality, because they have been, for the most part, too egotistical and avaricious to comprehend the aspirations of other peoples. The liberty which they claim for themselves, they deny to others. They talk much of French "dignity," but they frequently treat the people under them with a callous disregard for human rights and dignity. The semi-slavery of the plantation coolies, the corralling of peasants for forced labor on dykes, roads, etc., or their induction into the native army for slave labor, are all cases in point. The world has recently been horrified by the French in their attempt to dominate the Syrians—but that is what they have been doing in Indo-China for nearly one hundred years.[14]

Like Glass, many other members of the OSS spoke or wrote about their concerns regarding the return of French rule to Indochina. Their reports were read, filed, and forgotten, for the "Indochinese" were politically unimportant for the United States at that time. When debates over American involvement in Vietnam emerged, especially in the 1960s and 1970s, some politicians and journalists returned to the reports of the OSS and personnel who served there, but by that time the "intelligence" was cold. As early as 1946 William Donovan was urging his listeners to consider the work of his agents and its implications for the future. "There are many young men and women whose patriotism and skill in this kind of [intelligence] work have been tested and trained in war, and who are eager to be used if our government will only have sense enough to use them." But it was his final statement that seemed to set his blue eyes aflame and that the postwar audience might have taken most to heart: "These young men and women can well be the saviors of the peace."[15]

Whether or not his statement might have held true in regard to Vietnam is beyond the scope of this work. However, it is the actions and interactions of the OSS men on the ground and of the individuals and groups with whom they worked that point to the importance of time, place, and actor, or in other words, the importance of contingency, in understanding the tortured relationship that did develop between the United States and Vietnam. We can only speculate as to whether their insights might have averted further warfare in that region had they been heeded rather than filed.

1

The Situation on the Ground: Vietnam

"Misery, misery, misery"[1] has summed up the life of the Vietnamese peasant since the beginning of Vietnam's history as a state. Conquered by the Han Empire in III B.C.E., Vietnam struggled to regain its freedom for over 1,000 years, finally defeating the Chinese and declaring the independent Dai Viet state in 939 C.E. Stability was difficult to ensure, however. The Chinese reconquered Vietnam briefly in the fifteenth century, and the seventeenth and eighteenth centuries witnessed frequent internecine warfare as rival families struggled for dominance. This dynastic instability paved the way for interference by foreigners. The Portuguese were the first to arrive, followed by the Dutch and the English, but the French emerged as the dominant European power on the Indochinese peninsula. By the late nineteenth century the French had established a firm presence and asserted their dominance in the area, having captured the major cities of Da Nang, Saigon, Hue, and Hanoi and having forced the Vietnamese emperor Tu Duc to cede territory. A French and Spanish contingent captured Saigon in 1859, and a decade later southern Vietnam, or Cochinchina, with its capital at Saigon, had become a critical French colony, hailed as the Pearl of the Orient.

For a time, Cochinchina was France's only Vietnamese colony, but the remainder of the country fared little better. By 1884 the French had conquered the northern Red River delta region and the central provinces and had transformed them into protectorates, renamed Tonkin and Annam, respectively. Although the Nguyen Dynasty emperor continued to sit on the throne in Hue, the French held the power. By 1893 the French had completed their conquests of Laos and proceeded to organize the five regions—Tonkin, Annam, Cochinchina, Laos, and Cambodia—into the Indochinese Union under French control.

Cochinchina boasted a tropical climate and fertile soil, and the French first set about developing the south for economic profit. They would soon

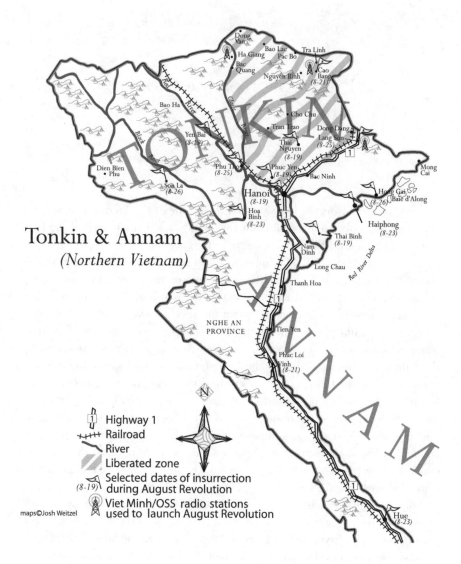

Tonkin & Annam
(Northern Vietnam)

maps©Josh Weitzel

1 Highway 1
Railroad
River
Liberated zone
(8-19) Selected dates of insurrection during August Revolution
Viet Minh/OSS radio stations used to launch August Revolution

turn to the north, where life had traditionally been more difficult because of a substantially higher population density and a more intense climate, which made growing rice more difficult. Neither area brought immediate profits. In *The Development of Capitalism in Colonial Indochina (1870–1940)*, Martin Murray noted that the French "inherited vast territories in Indochina that were characterized by subsistence agricultural production, relative technological backwardness, and low levels of social and economic differentiation," which meant that "the initial costs of occupation and administration in these new overseas possessions far exceeded any economic advantages that were able to be immediately exploited."[2] In order to remedy this situation, the French worked to redistribute landholdings and improve agricultural production.

The French eventually achieved their economic goals, but the process significantly changed the patterns of traditional Vietnamese village life. Typically, each family farmed a plot for subsistence and worked village communal lands to pay communal expenses. Under the French, however, the land was expropriated and reapportioned to allow the French and their supporters the largest and most fertile or strategic holdings. In addition, the relatively low taxes paid by Vietnamese before the French arrived, at most 6 percent of the crop, skyrocketed to 70 percent or more under the colonial administration. As a result, the overabundance of landless peasants competing for work allowed landlords to pay their tenants even less and treat them with minimal regard. Landlords soon found that great profits could be made by loaning money to these desperate farmers, who could not support themselves on what was left after taxation. To compound matters and heighten the peasants' sense of exploitation, many of the money lenders who profited under the French were ethnic Chinese who had settled in Vietnam over the centuries—as refugees during periods of domestic unrest or often at some stage in the Chinese conquest of the country. Needless to say, the rates on both long- and short-term loans were very high, and once in debt, peasant farmers had few options.[3] In desperation, some landless peasants headed for the few cities in Vietnam. This influx created fierce competition for jobs, driving wages lower and increasing the poverty level in urban areas.[4] Overall, the French colonial system, imposed from above with little sensitivity to the realities of life on the ground, intensified the existing poverty throughout Vietnam and deepened the misery and discontent of most Vietnamese.

Under Governor-General Paul Doumer, who ruled French Indochina from 1897 to 1902, the French succeeded in turning losses into profits by shifting the tax burden for support of the colony and protectorates away from the French populace, placing it squarely on the shoulders of the Vietnamese. Doumer not only gained the necessary capital for his construction projects from the Vietnamese, but he also improved French revenues by initiating a state monopoly on the production and sale of alcohol, opium, and salt. Naturally, French gains meant corresponding Vietnamese losses. Cheap opium and a desire among some of the poorest segments of Vietnamese society to escape their painful reality resulted in a rapid increase in the number of

Vietnamese opium addicts. Journalist Tam Lang provided a painful look at opium addiction among Hanoi's rickshaw drivers in his 1932 "I Pulled a Rickshaw," written for the *Hanoi Midday News* and published in book form in 1935. The words of Tu, the author's "teacher" in matters regarding life among Hanoi's poor drivers, encapsulated the situation for far too many of Vietnam's most desperate: "'Working a rickshaw, you toil all day, eat hastily, and the only leisure you get is when you lie beside the opium tray.'"[5] Still, it was the wealthy Vietnamese and Chinese who contributed most to the colonial coffers through the purchase of opium. Monies from the monopolies on opium, alcohol, and salt eventually provided about 70 percent of the French colonial budget.[6]

By the turn of the century southern Vietnam was exporting large quantities of both rice and rubber. Hundreds of thousands of hectares of new rice land came under cultivation, and the exploitation of resident tenant farmers and sharecroppers intensified correspondingly. In 1860, 57,000 tons of rice were exported from Cochinchina; by 1929, the number had risen to 1,223,000 tons.[7] As expected, French profits soared, and the Vietnamese and Chinese elite lived well, but the peasant majority continued to suffer.

Perhaps the most infamous example of peasant exploitation and suffering was the French rubber plantation. "For the European capitalists who sought easy profits through investments in colonial rubber production, the latex which oozed from the rubber trees became known as 'white gold.'"[8] To make sure that profits continued to ooze, the colonial administration worked with plantation owners to prevent and when necessary break up or settle labor disputes. In the 1930s the French administration encouraged some improvements in the circumstance of the workers, such as the construction of clinics and schools, but these came at a price. Under continuous pressure to maximize profits and minimize expenses, plantation managers often resented state interference in what they perceived as their private domains. "Under these circumstances," noted Martin Murray, "these European managers considered state regulations and reformist-minded policies as a nagging inconvenience and treated workers' grievances as the consequence of an inherent 'native' laziness and ingratitude. If the European capitalists called the latex 'white gold,' the plantation workers found a different name to describe it: 'white blood.'"[9]

Tran Tu Binh, one of our best Vietnamese sources for this aspect of colonialism, would surely have agreed with that description. After being expelled from a seminary in northern Vietnam, Tran Tu Binh boarded a French ship bound for the south. He had signed up to work on a southern rubber plantation even though, given his knowledge of both spoken and written French, he could have obtained other work. "He was determined to break away, to seek adventure, to test his physical and spiritual powers on totally unfamiliar terrain."[10] On the Phu Rieng rubber plantation both his physical and spiritual powers would be sorely tested. At Phu Rieng, workers ceased to be individuals and became property to be accounted for but not necessarily cared for:

> Each person was issued a numbered piece of wood to hang around his neck like a prison number. . . . Every morning we had to get up at four o'clock to cook our food. At five-thirty we all had to form ranks in the village courtyard so the overseers could check the roll. As they did this, some of the overseers would use their batons, whacking the workers' heads as they counted them. There was not one of them who did not play that game. . . .
>
> After roll call, the overseers took us out to the work area from six in the morning until six in the evening. We had to toil steadily under the sun, hot as fire, except for fifteen minutes at noon to eat, drink, and relieve ourselves. . . .
>
> At the end of the day a person really had no enthusiasm left, but wanted nothing more than to slip into the barracks and fall asleep so that the next day, when the overseer's siren sounded again, he could get up, eat, and begin another day of backbreaking work. One's strength today was never what it had been the day before. Every day one was worn down a bit more, cheeks sunken, teeth gone crooked, eyes hollow with dark circles around them, clothes hanging from collarbones. Everyone appeared almost dead, and in fact in the end about all did die.[11]

Whereas the plantation dominated the south, the most notorious abuse of peasants in the north occurred on the mining estates. Although the northern mines never reached the level of efficiency in the use of peasant labor that the southern plantations did, mine employees suffered the same types of injustices. As on the rubber plantations, laborers had an inadequate diet and insufficient clothing and housing, and they worked long hours, in poor conditions with frequent abuse, for wages far below the poverty level.[12]

The lives of the plantation owner and his functionaries were much different. Even the Vietnamese overseer enjoyed a virtual paradise compared to the workers. He had a private house with modest furnishings and sufficient clothing and food to live in comfort. The plantation and estate homes sported all the luxuries available in Vietnam and imported others from the *métropole* (France). The discrepancies between the standard of living of the worker and that of the owner and overseer fed the growing anger and resentment of the lower class. The plight of the peasant and the bitterness it engendered would eventually fuel the growing nationalist movements throughout the region.

Appearances to the contrary, the French presence was not geared entirely toward profit. The self-proclaimed goals of France's *mission civilisatrice*, "civilizing mission," were to improve the Vietnamese through a Western education (especially in French history, language, and culture), conversion to Catholicism, and incorporation into the world capitalist system—but as a colony beholden to and exclusively for the profit of France. From the moment they set foot in Indochina, the French presumed the Vietnamese were backward and in need of significant growth before they could ever hope to function as a "modern" people on the world stage. As historian Jacques Dalloz observed:

> For the colonizer, domination was largely justified in terms of what was achieved, and this was ritually extolled by the administration. The *pax gallica* brought order and security, although the only inhabitants who could appreciate this at all were the very old who could remember the robber bands who had once roamed the countryside. France saw herself as a conduit of enlightenment and prided herself on her achievements in education.[13]

The French educational system discouraged the study of Chinese characters and encouraged the study of French. To a certain degree the study of Vietnamese became easier with an increased use of the *quoc ngu* alphabet. Designed by Portuguese Jesuit missionaries as a means of teaching their colleagues Vietnamese, the *quoc ngu* alphabet was perfected by French Jesuits. Nonetheless, the Vietnamese basic literacy rate, nearly 80 percent at the outset of French colonialism, plummeted. Many young Vietnamese whose families could afford schooling resisted colonial education. An even larger number remained uneducated because their families needed all hands to work in order to pay the myriad taxes imposed under the French system. By the start of World War II, less than 20 percent of Vietnam's school-age boys were attending school at the lowest levels, and only about 1 percent was enrolled in a school above the elementary level.[14]

The development of a working infrastructure was a more tangible sign of French development in Vietnam. The French administration concentrated on building roads and bridges to expedite the transportation of both people and supplies throughout the country. In the five years of Doumer's tenure, he transformed Vietnam by building opera houses, roads, railroads, and a bridge spanning the Red River in Hanoi, known as the Doumer Bridge until 1954. In his memoir, however, Tran Tu Binh recalled that the building surge did little for workers. "Projects in construction, highways, bridges, and locks developed rapidly. All the capital, talent, and materiel that were flung into this period of exploitation had been drawn from the blood and bones of our people. . . . Who knows how many cruel and senseless taxes were proclaimed and dumped on the heads and shoulders of our already impoverished people, making them poorer still."[15] New construction continued in the early twentieth century, but new schools and hospitals "were too few and were designed for the urban population. The real benefits to the peasants were nil."[16]

The monopolies, as well as conditions on the rubber plantations, in the mines, and in the cities, increasingly fueled the existing Vietnamese resistance to French rule, especially among the intelligentsia of the 1920s. Historian David Marr, in his acclaimed *Vietnamese Tradition on Trial, 1920–1945*, noted:

> Looked at from the perspective of eighty years of French colonial activity, the only period when truly favourable conditions existed for full-scale capitalist economic exploitation of Indochina was from 1922 to 1929—a mere eight years. Economic fragility combined with administrative uncertainty underlay the entire colonial operation. Projects were begun and left uncompleted, or altered in such a way that profits survived but not the ameliorative social trimmings. This fundamental weakness of French colonialism, hardly sensed previously by even the most astute Vietnamese observers, was to become a subject of serious analysis among the new generation of intellectuals.[17]

The most famous of the new generation to emerge on the scene was Nguyen Tat Thanh—better known as Nguyen Ai Quoc and later as Ho Chi Minh. Nguyen Tat Thanh was born in 1890 in Nghe An Province in central Vietnam. William Duiker, author of the preeminent biography on Ho, describes the area and its significance:

> A land of placid beaches and purple mountains, of apple green rice fields and dark green forests, Nghe An . . . is a land of hot dry winds and of torrential autumn rains that flatten the rice stalks and flood the paddy fields of the peasants. The soil is thin in depth and weak in nutrients,

and frequently the land is flooded by seawater. The threat of disaster is
never far away, and when it occurs, it sometimes drives the farmer to
desperate measures. Perhaps that explains why the inhabitants of Nghe
An have historically been known as the most obdurate and rebellious of
Vietnamese, richly earning their traditional sobriquet among their
compatriots as "the buffalos of Nghe An."[18]

Many of Nguyen Tat Thanh's ancestors were among the diligent farmers
who worked this beautiful but difficult land in central Vietnam. His father,
Nguyen Sinh Sac, however, exhibited a talent for learning as a boy and was
lucky enough to find a sponsor to support his studies. During the course of
his career, Sac attained one of the highest degrees available under the imperial court system and could have, according to the tradition of the time, applied for a lucrative position within the imperial court bureaucracy. But he
did not. Sac remained a relatively low-level administrator and teacher and
faced continual financial strains throughout his career. No doubt many of his
contemporaries were shocked at his decision, but Sac was disenchanted with
the ineffectual court and "had no desire to pursue a career in the bureaucracy, especially in a time of national humiliation."[19]

Neither Nguyen Sinh Sac's talents nor his attitude toward the governments (both Vietnamese imperial and French colonial) was lost on Nguyen
Tat Thanh. In his education Thanh was atypical of most mandarins' sons.
His first important mentor—one of his father's scholar friends—"rejected
the traditional pedantic method of forcing his students to memorize texts,
but took great care to instruct them in the humanitarian inner core of Con-
fucian classical writings while simultaneously instilling in their minds a
fierce patriotic spirit for the survival of an independent Vietnam."[20] By the
time Thanh was sixteen years old he had begun to study French language
and culture as well as *quoc ngu*. Thanh was well aware of the writings of the
leading nationalist intellectuals of the day, including those of Phan Boi
Chau, who wrote that only violent resistance could free the country from
French oppression. In 1908 Thanh became directly involved in an unsuc-
cessful peasant rebellion against high taxes and corvée labor when he volunteered to translate the peasants' demands to the resident superior (the representative of France). The talks failed, French troops were called in to quell
the uprising, and the next day Thanh was dismissed from school.[21]

With his career as a student at an end, Thanh began his travels southward.
To support himself, he worked as a teacher for a year, and in doing so he demonstrated both his nationalist ardor and a natural talent for persuading others

to his views—both of which would increase in the years to come. On June 5, 1911, Thanh left Vietnam to discover the world outside of French colonial domination by taking a job on a French ship. His duties aboard the *Admiral Latouche-Treville* were arduous—washing dishes and floors and shoveling coal—but his two years at sea allowed him to see many areas of the world, including other colonial possessions such as Singapore, India, and Algeria. He also visited France, Great Britain, and the United States.[22] Long after Thanh was known to the world as Ho Chi Minh, he explained his decision to leave home to American journalist Anna Louise Strong: "The people of Vietnam, including my own father, often wondered who would help them to remove the yoke of French control. Some said Japan, others Great Britain, and some said the United States. I saw that I must go abroad to see for myself. After I had found out how they lived, I would return to help my countrymen."[23]

As Thanh became increasingly familiar with the circumstances under which most colonized peoples lived, his anticolonial sentiments grew stronger and his political activism more concentrated. After watching a group of Africans drown in the stormy sea off Dakar, as the colons who had sent them out to contact the ship on which he worked looked on unmoved, Thanh wrote: "The French in France are all good. But the French colonialists are very cruel and inhuman. It is the same everywhere. At home I have seen such things happening in Phanrang. The French burst out laughing while our compatriots drowned for their own sake. To the colonialists, the life of an Asian or an African is not worth a penny."[24]

Thanh soon left life at sea and spent the early years of World War I in Great Britain studying English and working at various odd jobs—from sweeping snow to working in the kitchen of the famed chef Auguste Escoffier. By late 1917 he was in Paris, where he attended meetings of the French Socialist Party and became acquainted with members of the French intellectual community as well as Vietnamese émigrés of all social ranks. Although his name was gaining recognition within the socialist and expatriate communities in Paris, Nguyen Tat Thanh was still basically an unknown. But with the Allied victory and the coming of the peace conference in June 1919, that began to change. With aid from a Vietnamese nationalist lawyer more fluent in French, Thanh drafted a petition for the leaders converging at Versailles that demanded the application of President Woodrow Wilson's Fourteen Points to Vietnam, particularly the provision regarding the self-determination of peoples. In the petition, the "Demands of the Annamite People," he called for Vietnamese autonomy; freedom of association, religion, press, and movement; amnesty for political prisoners; equal rights between Vietnamese and French; and the abolition of the salt tax, corvée labor, and French policies "forcing" the consumption of alcohol and opium for colonial profit. He signed the petition with the sobriquet that would initially make him famous: Nguyen Ai Quoc, or "Nguyen the Patriot."[25]

Despite the eloquence and idealism of Wilson's Fourteen Points, in practice the ideal of self-determination held little appeal for colonizer nations, especially the French and British, who fought the notion at every turn and saw that it faded from view. Nguyen the Patriot's petition gained little attention—except from the French police, the Colonial Office, and those Vietnamese in Paris and Hanoi who read it. After Versailles Nguyen Tat Thanh—now known as Nguyen Ai Quoc—"understood that declarations about freedom made by the politicians during war time were catchwords, used to deceive the peoples." "If they want to be liberated," he observed, "the people must rely on themselves, on their own strength."[26]

Although disenchanted with world leaders at Versailles, Nguyen Ai Quoc was only beginning his pursuit of Vietnamese liberation. In 1920 he continued to press his points regarding the situation in Vietnam at a meeting of the French Socialist Party. Reiterating the Vietnamese lack of basic freedoms, he added: "We are forced to live in utter ignorance and obscurity because we have no right to study. In Indochina the colonialists find all ways and means to force us to smoke opium and drink alcohol to poison and beset us. Thousands of Vietnamese have been led to a slow death or massacred to protect other people's interests."[27]

Although his speech was greeted with applause from the assembled delegates, Quoc was becoming more frustrated by his comrades' failure to seriously address the colonial situation. This aggravation, combined with his introduction to Vladimir Ilyich Lenin's "Theses on the National and Colonial Questions," motivated him to participate with fellow radicals in breaking away from the existing Socialist Party to form the French Communist Party. William Duiker wrote that Lenin's theses, which connected the destruction of capitalism with the end of the colonial relationship that helped sustain it, "set Nguyen Ai Quoc on a course that transformed him from a simple patriot with socialist leanings into a Marxist revolutionary."[28]

Over the next few years Nguyen Ai Quoc continued to write and speak on behalf of the oppressed, primarily those in the colonies, but he also published an article on the lynching of blacks in the United States. The French police kept him under surveillance as a subversive, but he managed to avoid prison. In 1923 he left France to study and work for the Communist International

(Comintern) in the Soviet Union. He was anxious to return home, however, and take the revolution to Vietnam. But in 1924 he was dispatched by the Comintern to China to begin work with the growing Chinese revolution as well as with the large number of Vietnamese émigrés in the south.

Nguyen Ai Quoc's work in China was both fulfilling and successful. By mid-1925 he had succeeded in forming the Vietnamese Revolutionary Youth League, which aspired to bring about both freedom from French colonial rule and a social revolution. While in China he also taught at the Special Political Institute for the Vietnamese Revolution and, by all indications, exhibited the same special talents for working with students that he had demonstrated earlier in Vietnam. And Lenin's message, as interpreted by Nguyen Ai Quoc, was a powerful draw for most of the young people attracted to the league. In "Lenin and the East" Quoc praised the recently deceased Lenin as "the first man determinedly to denounce all prejudices against colonial peoples" and "the first to realize and emphasize the full importance of a correct solution to the colonial question as a contribution to the world revolution." And perhaps more importantly, for Quoc and his students Lenin's agenda for carrying out revolution fit with their own goals for Vietnam: "With his inborn clearsightedness," Quoc wrote, "Lenin realized that in order to carry out work in the colonies successfully, it was necessary to know how to take full advantage of the national liberation movement which was gaining ground in these countries, he realized that with the support of the world proletariat for his movement we will have new strong allies in the struggle for the socialist revolution."[29] Buoyed by the powerful rhetoric at the Special Political Institute, most of Quoc's students went on to join the Revolutionary Youth League, which by 1929 had over 1,700 members working inside Indochina.[30]

The success of the Revolutionary Youth League came with a price, however. Nguyen Ai Quoc's radical activities attracted the attention of Chinese authorities, and he was frequently under surveillance. Forced to leave south China, he escaped to Hong Kong. Quoc was instructed by Comintern headquarters to return to France, but he found work there impossible because the Sûreté kept a watchful eye on him, hoping to silence the outspoken critic of French rule. Anxious to return to work in Asia, he was dispatched to Siam. In July 1928 he began work among the well-established Vietnamese communities there. Although Quoc and his message were generally well received, by this time his Revolutionary Youth League had two serious problems. First, a new political party—the VNQDD, or Viet Nam Nationalist [Revolutionary]

Party (modeled on the Nationalist Kuomintang Party in China)—now competed with the league for members. Second, dissent among the league leadership over its primary goal—social revolution or national independence—threatened the continued existence of the organization.[31]

In an effort to quell dissent, a new organization was formed in 1930 called the Vietnamese Communist Party (VCP), which incorporated remnants of the Revolutionary Youth League as well as members of the dissident Indochinese Communist League. But the role that the struggle to gain national independence was to play within the VCP continued to be problematic, and in 1930 Nguyen Ai Quoc seemed to be on the wrong side of the debate. Competing communists criticized him for failing to focus on recruiting among the proletariat, for making alliances among the petty bourgeoisie—most of whom were deemed inherently untrustworthy—and for overemphasizing the nationalist aspect of the struggle. One clear example of Moscow's rejection of the nationalist cause was the Comintern's insistence that the Vietnamese Communist Party become the Indochinese Communist Party because, among other reasons, "dropping the reference to 'Vietnam' shifted attention away from the cause of national independence—now viewed in Moscow as a 'petty bourgeois' concern—to class struggle."[32]

Although the new Comintern policies renounced what Nguyen Ai Quoc did best—rally individuals from a wide variety of backgrounds to the cause of independence and subsequently to "Leninist" ideals—he marched forward with the new directive and announced the formation of the Indochinese Communist Party (ICP). In his concluding remarks he stressed the party line, declaring the new ICP "the party of the working class." "It will," Quoc avowed, "help the proletarian class to lead the revolution in order to struggle for all the oppressed and exploited people." Yet his remarks betrayed his inner conviction that national independence could and should be tied to the communist call for world revolution. He enjoined his listeners to follow ten principles to help the party; number two on that list, second only to "overthrowing French imperialism, feudalism, and the reactionary Vietnamese capitalist class," was "to make Indochina completely independent."[33]

Nguyen Ai Quoc remained in Hong Kong, frustrated both by his inability to do significant work from that location and by ongoing disputes with younger party members, who contended that they possessed a more correct understanding of communist policies in their current form. In 1931, while still pleading with Comintern authorities to be sent elsewhere to work, he was arrested by the British police as a subversive. He spent nearly eighteen months in British custody (either in prison or in the hospital) before allies managed to have him set free on the condition that he leave the colony. After several false starts Quoc made his way to China and then on to the Soviet Union, where he recovered his health, attended and gave lectures, and mentored young Vietnamese studying in Moscow. However successful Quoc's work in Moscow seemed to be by most standards, prominent and competing ICP leaders continued to criticize his views. One particularly harsh critic bemoaned "the nationalist legacy of Nguyen Ai Quoc and his erroneous instructions on the fundamental questions of the bourgeois democratic revolutionary movement in Indochina, as well as his opportunist theories" and pronounced that "Nguyen Ai Quoc did not understand the directives of the Communist International."[34]

But as early as the last quarter of 1934 the Comintern was altering its official views to again favor more-widespread cooperation and the use of national independence slogans to further party goals. Yet Nguyen Ai Quoc, a revolutionary who was a veteran in using just such tactics, remained in the Soviet Union throughout the mid-1930s and kept a low profile. Meanwhile, the situation in Vietnam seemed to beg for his presence. The vibrant economy of the 1920s had ended, and by the early 1930s French Indochina was suffering under the weight of the worldwide Great Depression. "When world market prices dipped even below the lowest cost producers (despite massive state subsidies, particularly in rubber production), export-oriented production was virtually brought to a standstill."[35] The colossal failure of the French economic system only highlighted other failings of the *mission civilisatrice*. Capitalism seemed to be collapsing just as the communists had predicted. Despite all this, the ICP in Vietnam had trouble gaining traction.

The deteriorating economic situation brought on by the depression had aroused the anger and frustration of the workers and peasants. While many feared that further hardship would result from aligning themselves with the communists, distressed peasants in Nghe-Tinh Province, supported by the local party, revolted. Although they managed to oust the local authorities and organize themselves into "soviets," their success was brief, and French repression was swift and sure. For the long term, a more devastating result than the destruction of the Nghe-Tinh soviets was the concentrated effort of the French to root out senior communist cadres. In Saigon—where the ICP originally had its headquarters in Indochina—the leadership was decimated in successful raids by the Sûreté in summer 1931 and was not rejuvenated until the arrival of the young communist Tran Van Giau in 1933. With both Cochinchina and Annam temporarily silenced and with no real ICP activity in Tonkin until well into 1934, Indochina seemed to its colonial masters to once again be peaceful.

Even more important than the brief rebellions brought on by the economic crisis of the early 1930s were the important—yet brief—changes in French politics ushered in by the Great Depression. By 1936 economic recovery had begun, and the newly elected Popular Front government in France was allowing intellectuals, both at home and to a more limited extent in Indochina, to more openly criticize the colonial situation. Nguyen Ai Quoc, still on the sidelines in the Soviet Union, urged his ICP colleagues to seize the opportunity offered by the new socialist government of Léon Blum. "The Popular Front victory in France is a rare chance, and we must not fail to use it," he advised. "The main thing now is to secure complete unity inside the party, especially between its homeside and overseas units." His optimism about the opportunity presented by the election of socialists in France was also colored by the growth of Nazism in Germany. "Every effort must be made to form an antifascist and antiwar democratic front," he counseled, adding that "it must embrace all patriotic forces, all those who want to fight for the country's salvation."[36] In "The Party's Line in the Period of the Democratic Front (1936–1939)," Nguyen Ai Quoc again made clear his belief in the need for a broad base of support. In his report to the Comintern he wrote:

> This Front does not embrace only Indochinese people but also
> Progressive French residing in Indo-China, not only toiling people but
> also the national bourgeoisie. The Party must assume a wise, flexible
> attitude with the bourgeoisie, strive to draw it into the Front, win over
> the elements that can be won over and neutralize those who can be
> neutralized. We must by all means avoid leaving them outside the Front,
> lest they should fall into the hands of the enemy of the revolution and
> increase the strength of the reactionaries.[37]

While the ICP in Vietnam did grow during the era of the Popular Front, the rumblings of another world war, as Nguyen Ai Quoc noted, could clearly be heard in the distance. When the socialists fell from power in 1939, the Vietnamese soon lost the new freedoms they had brought about, but the onset of World War II resulted in an entirely new set of opportunities—and challenges. One of these was the return of Nguyen Ai Quoc to Asia. After repeated requests for an active assignment, Quoc was finally sent back to China in 1938 to work with the growing Chinese Communist Party (CCP). The situation for the CCP was difficult. They faced two powerful enemies, Chiang Kai-shek and his nationalist forces (who continued to harass the communists regardless of their temporary truce) and the Japanese Imperial Army. They had few allies. But Nguyen Ai Quoc was well received as an important revolutionary, and he set to work as a journalist writing about the situation in China. Perhaps even more importantly, Quoc could now make direct contact with his fellow Vietnamese revolutionaries operating from southern China and could return to the heart of his life's work: freeing Vietnam from French control. This was greatly facilitated when he at last made contact with the ICP's "overseas Party branch" in Kunming in 1940. With the coming of World War II, finally both location and historical timing were on Quoc's side.

Everything seemed to be coming together for Nguyen Ai Quoc. He was joined in late spring by Vo Nguyen Giap and Pham Van Dong, two long-term party members who had come to China for "further training in revolutionary operations." A strong core group of the ICP was emerging, but the situation in southern China was not favorable to communists of any nationality. In order to increase their chances of success and allay the suspicions of anticommunist leaders, Quoc "proposed the formation of a broad organization that would unite all patriotic forces in a common struggle to evict the French colonial power." The new united front, known as the League for the Independence of Viet Nam, or Viet Minh, was carefully crafted to be "susceptible to strong ICP influence and direction," though "the Party's role would have to be carefully disguised in order to alleviate the concerns of non-Communist elements in Indochina and abroad as to the front's political leanings." The new organization gained formal recognition in China, and Nguyen Ai Quoc and the others set about building the Viet Minh into a going concern.[38]

By January 1941 Nguyen Ai Quoc was once again training students and recruiting members—this time at a "Party training program" in Jingxi, China—and preparing for the ICP's upcoming Central Committee meeting.[39] The meeting, convened in mid-May, was held in a cave near the village of Pac Bo in Tonkin, not far from the Chinese border. Although surrounded by other committed revolutionaries, Nguyen Ai Quoc clearly emerged as the leader of what was becoming Vietnam's most important political movement at what was plainly a propitious moment. Quoc and his colleagues quickly moved forward to broaden and strengthen both the ICP and the Viet Minh. Historian Huynh Kim Khanh noted that the conference "set forth a radical redefinition of the nature and tasks of the Vietnamese revolution," calling for a "national liberation revolution" and "temporary postponement of the class struggle."[40] After the meeting dispersed, Nguyen Ai Quoc stayed in Pac Bo writing for the Viet Minh journal, creating a brief instruction manual on guerrilla warfare, sponsoring literacy programs, and teaching. In his "Letter from Abroad," written after the Central Committee meeting, Quoc beckoned his countrymen to join the struggle: "National Salvation is the common cause to the whole of our people. Every Vietnamese must take a part in it. He who has money will contribute his money, he who has strength will contribute his strength, he who has talent will contribute his talent. I pledge to use all my modest abilities to follow you, and am ready for the last sacrifice."[41]

Nguyen Ai Quoc stayed in Tonkin working at Pac Bo and later at the new Viet Minh base, Lam Son, located west of Cao Bang, until summer 1942. His work, and that of all the other cadres working in the area, developing both propaganda and guerrilla war tactics, was crucial for the ultimate success of the movement. From his research on the formation of the first guerrilla bases in Vietnam, Greg Lockhart wrote convincingly: "With guerrilla tactics and armed propaganda to project the ideal of strength and a better life in the modern world the Viet Minh had begun to mobilize the force of the nation."[42] By August Quoc felt confident that the situation in the Viet Bac, the liberated zone in the mountains of northern Vietnam, was progressing and set out for China to try to gain outside support for his cause. Supplied with a cache of false travel documents, he traveled as an overseas Chinese reporter under a new alias: Ho Chi Minh. Unfortunately for him, the sheer volume of false documents convinced local Chinese authorities that Ho Chi Minh "must be not only dangerous but also someone of considerable political importance."[43] Tossed into a Kuomintang (KMT) jail on August 29, he remained in prison for the next year. As Ho Chi Minh's friends and colleagues endeavored to secure his release, they also continued to work both inside and outside Vietnam for the common cause of building the Viet Minh base. By 1942 many of them realized the historical significance of the time and looked to the opportunities brought on by the world war, even if their most famous member remained indefinitely detained in China.

Initially, it seemed that World War II would not directly affect Vietnam itself, although Japanese aggression against China in 1937 and the rhetoric of the Greater East Asia Co-Prosperity Sphere (GEACPS) put many on alert to the ever-growing power and ruthless imperial aspirations of the Nation of the Rising Sun. By 1939, however, the Japanese had failed to crush Chinese resistance and were increasingly bogged down in efforts to defeat the government of Chiang Kai-shek. In the European theater Adolf Hitler's Germany (Japan's Axis partner) had begun its quest for Lebensraum in the Rhineland, Austria, and the Sudetenland. In the autumn of 1939 Hitler invaded Poland, which brought both Great Britain and France into the war.

Though Britain managed to hold out in the face of German air attacks, France quickly fell before the might of German air and land forces. In June 1940 France capitulated, and nearly two-thirds of the country came under Nazi rule. The remaining unoccupied area was administered by the collaborationist French Vichy government under Marshall Henri-Philippe Pétain. General Charles de Gaulle declared the existence of "Free France," with himself at the helm, and established a French government-in-exile in London. In mid-1940, however, both French governments were essentially isolated from their Indochinese colony.

Even prior to the German invasion, France had had difficulties handling its affairs in Indochina. Japan had repeatedly complained to the French about the supplies that continued to reach Chiang Kai-shek's KMT forces via the Haiphong-Yunnan railroad.[44] The railroad had become a lifeline to Chiang Kai-shek, with the line connecting Haiphong and Kunming carrying 48 percent of the much-needed supplies to Nationalist Chinese forces.[45] When, in 1939, Japan again demanded that the French colonial government in Vietnam halt the flow of supplies to Chiang Kai-shek, the *métropole* could offer the colons little tangible protection. Japan's military leadership believed that severing Chiang Kai-shek's access to supplies would hasten Japanese victory, and they were irritated by then governor-general Georges Catroux's failure to do so. Recognizing France's de facto impotence in protecting its Southeast Asian empire, Catroux, in an attempt to prevent an outright military occupation by the more powerful Japanese army, did accede to some of Japan's demands. Within a few months, the shipment of weapons to Chungking had virtually ceased, but important food and medical supplies continued to reach the Nationalist Chinese. In an effort to cut that supply line, the Japanese bombed the railroad, but with little effect.[46] Throughout the remaining months of 1939 the Japanese continued to demand the closing of the railway into southern China, and Catroux continued to sidestep their requests.

After the French collapse in June 1940, however, Catroux found himself working for the Vichy government and decided that additional limited concessions to Japan were a far better option than losing the colony entirely. Believing that if he bargained wisely he could keep Indochina as the last bastion of independent French territory, Catroux allowed Japanese inspectors to oversee the embargo of materiel into China. By June 29, a mere seven days after the fall of France, Japanese checkpoints had been established at Haiphong, Ha Giang, Lao Cai, Cao Bang, Lang Son, and Fort Bayard.[47] Though this seemed a relatively minor concession to the Japanese, the Vichy government was

clearly unhappy that Catroux had failed to get official approval before he
acted. On June 25 Vichy president Albert Lebrun replaced Catroux with Vice
Admiral Jean Decoux, commander of French naval forces in Asia.

While awaiting Decoux's arrival from his headquarters in Saigon, Catroux continued negotiating with the Japanese mission headed by Major
General Nishihara Issaku. Negotiations seemed productive from the standpoint of both. The French kept Indochina firmly under their control. The
Japanese were at least temporarily satisfied with their position as well. As
historian Minami Yoshizawa noted: "Because French Indochina permitted
the Nishihara Mission to engage in activities that far exceeded surveillance
functions, it was natural for the authorities in Tokyo to regard Governor
General Catroux and his colonial administration as cooperative and conciliatory." One Japanese Foreign Ministry document even described colonial
authorities as "intent on showing as much goodwill as possible" and as "very
cooperative."[48] They did not know what to expect from Decoux. On July 20
Vice Admiral Decoux arrived and assumed the post of governor-general. But
Decoux's position was never an easy one, and his tenure as governor-general
would forever sully his reputation because of his position as a Vichy appointee and his cooperation, however hesitant at times, with the Japanese.

By the end of summer 1940, the Vichy government had agreed to "recognize the supreme interests of Japan in the economic and political spheres in
the Far East" in the hope that Japan's occupation would be both temporary
and confined to Tonkin.[49] And the Japanese continued to assure the Vichy
government of its sovereignty over Indochina. In late August 1940 the Japanese foreign minister, Matsuoka Yosuke, wrote to Vichy's ambassador to
Japan, Charles Arsene-Henry, informing him that "the Japanese Government
has every intention of respecting the rights and interests of France in the Far
East, particularly the territorial integrity of Indochina and the sovereignty of
France over the entire area of the Indochinese Union."[50] The Japanese had
determined early on that the most fruitful and least tedious method of administering their newest "acquisition" was to permit Decoux's government to
continue its administrative functions. Thus, few Japanese troops were needed
to control Vietnam, and the Japanese army was free to pursue other territorial
goals in Asia. Even in late 1944, only 40,000 Japanese soldiers were stationed
throughout all of Indochina.[51] French administrators, police, and businessmen were in effect charged with maintaining order and running Vietnam as
an efficient supply and logistical base for the emperor's army.

After the signing of the Tripartite Pact with Germany and Italy in September 1940, however, Japan was in an even stronger position to make demands

on France. On September 22, the Vichy government acceded to Japanese demands for four airbases in northern Vietnam. To protect the newly acquired airfields, between 5,000 and 6,000 Japanese troops would also be stationed in Tonkin. In addition, the Japanese army gained nearly exclusive transit rights on the Tonkin rail system, thus denying Chiang's troops supplies via Haiphong Harbor and simultaneously guaranteeing (at least at the outset) the flow of war materiel to the Japanese army fighting in southern China.

As Decoux's negotiators were finalizing the terms for the uncontested entry of Japan's military forces, Japanese forces crossed into Vietnam from southern China. On September 22, the same day the French and Japanese reached an agreement, Japanese forces attacked French garrisons in Tonkin. Local Japanese commanders, greatly frustrated by French reluctance to grant them free passage through the colony, quickly overran two garrisons, at Lang Son and Dong Dang, defeating combined French and Vietnamese colonial forces in some of the fiercest fighting the Japanese would encounter in Vietnam. The surrenders of Lang Son and Dong Dang showed French authorities, in both Indochina and in the *métropole*, that despite their claims to the contrary, they could not withstand the might of the Japanese military. Collaboration and compromise remained their only viable alternative if France was to retain its hold on Indochina. The combined effects of the loss of the French outposts, the September 26 bombing of Haiphong, and the final acquiescence of Decoux to all Japanese demands squelched effective French resistance to the new rulers of Indochina.[52]

Strategically, Vietnam proved an ideal location for the Japanese advance. By July 1941 the Japanese had moved into southern Vietnam without resistance, acquiring control of airports and port facilities, including the area around Cam Ranh Bay and the airfields around Saigon. The Japanese used the Indochinese bases to support their drive to expand the Empire of the Sun into Southeast Asia. In fact, Japanese aircraft based in southern Vietnam played a vital role in the successful Japanese invasion of British Malaya. By early 1942 Emperor Hirohito's forces had conquered not only British holdings but also the U.S. colony in the Philippines and the Dutch East Indies. By that time, Singapore had also fallen, and the Japanese Fifteenth Army had thrust into Burma, threatening India, the pride of the British Empire.[53]

Consumed by this drive for territory and determined to avoid having to commit too many forces to holding its expanding empire, Japan continued to permit the French a high degree of autonomy in running Vietnam. During the course of the war, French and Japanese officers often interacted as colleagues, inviting one another to tea or for drinks. In an effort to achieve a semblance of working harmony, the General Commission for Franco-Japanese Relations was created to solve the "many difficulties created by the uneasy cohabitation of the two imperial powers."[54] This superficial cordiality did not create genuine friendship, nor did it mask the facts of the situation: The Japanese were in charge, and when push came to shove, the French obeyed them. Conversely, the French assured themselves of their superiority by continuing to dominate the Vietnamese, who remained on the bottom rung of the colonial ladder. Perhaps Ho Chi Minh explained the situation best: "The Japanese become the real masters. The French become kind of respectable slaves. And upon the Indo-Chinese falls the double honor of being not only slaves to the Japanese, but also slaves of the slaves—the French."[55]

However, the situation was subject to different interpretations. Certainly, the French continued to regard the Vietnamese as no more than their colonial subjects. The Japanese, on the other hand, at least theoretically offered some hope for the Vietnamese. There were a few instances in which the Japanese showed preferential treatment to their fellow Asians. Interestingly, the Vietnamese soldiers who fought alongside the French and were also captured at Lang Son and Dong Dang were surprised at how the Japanese differentiated between them and their French commanders. In a 1945 report from the Annamite Communistic Group (better known as the Viet Minh) to the OSS, the writer commented that "during the Langson[56] affair, the Japanese treated well the Indo-Chinese soldiers while they forced the French officers and soldiers to take off their shoes and caps [and] to do hard labor."[57] Of course, that situation lasted only briefly; within a month all prisoners were released and the garrisons were returned to the French. But the Japanese continued to promote the ideal of a shared Asian "identity." This paradigm of "pan-Asianism" ostensibly meant Vietnamese participation in the GEACPS under the slogan "Asia for the Asians." Most Vietnamese, and indeed most of the world community, viewed both the GEACPS and the idea of "Asia for the Asians" with skepticism and distrust. The GEACPS, perhaps more suitably called the Greater Japanese Prosperity Sphere, aimed at economic cooperation among the Asian nations for the primary benefit of Japan. In a classic colonial relationship, China, Manchuria, the Dutch East Indies, and French Indochina would contribute their raw materials to Japan's industrial machine, which would in turn produce finished merchandise for sale to the Asian nations. Japan would also import the foodstuffs grown throughout East and Southeast Asia to feed its home islands. Japan professed that within the GEACPS all Asians would profit, both financially and from Japanese guidance. Ironically, Foreign Minister Matsuoka was the first to publicly use the term "Greater East Asian Co-Prosperity Sphere"; in the same month, he promised to "respect the rights and interests" of France, "particularly in Indochina."[58]

The projected GEACPS was a basic colonial relationship masked by pan-Asian rhetoric, and—perhaps most significantly for the Vietnamese—it differed little from French mercantilism. Although some Vietnamese groups, such as the Cao Dai and Hoa Hao religious sects and the entourage of Prince Cuong De (a dissenting member of the imperial family and aspirant to the throne), at least initially supported the Japanese, an alliance along the lines of "Asia for the Asians" never emerged. There were members of the Japanese government, such as Nagata Yasukichi of the Foreign Ministry, who "advocated gathering together pro-independence patriots, inciting an independence movement, and incorporating an independent Vietnam in the Greater East Asia Co-Prosperity Sphere." But the ultimate goal, even for someone like Nagata who had served as consul general in Hanoi from 1930 to 1933 and was relatively well versed on the country, was not to liberate the Vietnamese for their own sake but to "foster a pro-Japanese independence movement, and thus to twist Vietnam's indigenous nationalist movement to Japanese ends."[59] The dominant attitude of the Japanese was formed by their greater mission: a successful conclusion to the Pacific war. Minutes from the November 1941 meeting of Japan's Supreme War Council summed up Japan's attitude toward administration of the occupied territories: "First, secure raw materials; second, ensure freedom of transport for raw materials and personnel; third, in accomplishing these two objectives, we must not hesitate, as we did in China, to oppress the natives. On the other hand, we will not interfere in the details of government, as we did in China, but will make use of existing organizations and show respect for native customs."[60]

The Japanese pursued the first two goals with the most vigor, for Vietnam had much to contribute to Japan's overall economic plan. In particular, Vietnam was a source of agricultural products, especially rice and rubber, that were vital to the Japanese war economy. Vietnamese rice was used to feed Japanese soldiers and was exported to the home islands. Rice and corn were also distilled into alcohol to compensate for gasoline shortages. In time, however, rice and corn were supplanted as the primary agricultural products. Peasants were ordered to plant increasing amounts of jute and oil-seed crops, such as peanuts, to help offset shortages in cloth and in oils and lubricants for vehicles and machinery.

The first two years of Japan's hegemony over Vietnam were relatively uneventful, and the burden of Japanese rule was comparatively mild, especially when compared to the situation in the Philippines, where resistance to Japanese rule produced a spiral of brutal repression and atrocity. However, as the war progressed, the Japanese encountered increasing difficulties in their pursuit of victory. Prices had already begun to rise dramatically by late 1942 as Japanese demands for rubber, rice, and minerals increased. In 1943 the flow of goods to Japan began to grind to a halt as American submarines wreaked havoc on the Japanese merchant marine. In addition, Allied bombing of the north-south railways, coastal shipping lanes, and roads destroyed much of the Indochinese transportation network. In the process, American and British bombs also destroyed many of Vietnam's few industrial and commercial centers. Although most French and Vietnamese were unconcerned by the disruption of the flow of supplies to Japan, they were greatly disturbed by the interruption of rice shipments from the rich Mekong Delta to the north.[61]

The Mekong and Red River deltas were of particular significance as the principal wet rice-growing areas of Vietnam. As such, those regions were also the major demographic and political centers. This was particularly true of the Red River delta, where the population density was highest and the demand for rice greatest. Thus, the Japanese exactions on the rice crop carried out by the French authorities and the destruction inflicted on the railroads and coastal shipping routes combined to increase the misery of Vietnamese peasants. In the north, where the bulk of the peasantry lived on the ragged edge of subsistence at the best of times, monsoon rains had caused destructive flooding, and famine was endemic. In addition, Japanese requirements that the peasants in Tonkin plant oil seeds, cotton, peanuts, and jute further reduced the traditional rice crop, making northerners dependent upon the rice from Cochinchina for their daily diet. By autumn 1943 areas of Tonkin and northern Annam were already experiencing famine. In early 1944 the problem was compounded when Cochinchina was also subjected to the new planting requirements, reducing the rice crop even further. In the more fertile south, most families were able to survive. The Vietnamese in Tonkin and northern Annam were especially hard hit in late 1944 and early 1945, when violent storms resulted in a poor harvest for most of the northern region. Official estimates of the number of victims vary; however, it is generally accepted that between 1 million and 2 million Vietnamese died as a result of the famine of 1944–1945.[62] To the Vietnamese, this was perhaps the most obvious sign of the high costs of answering the demands of two masters who cared little for their needs.

The famine can be attributed to the combination of Japanese and French policies, poor harvests, and Allied bombing. But most Vietnamese primarily

This Vietnamese woman and her child were among the 2 million victims of the famine of 1944–1945. This photograph, one of a series given to Archimedes Patti by Ho Chi Minh, graphically illustrates the horrors of French and Japanese colonialism. *Archimedes L. Patti, Papers, Special Collections, University of Central Florida, Orlando.*

blamed the French. In "Who Committed This Crime?" Tran Van Mai wrote, "to make sure the people would not revolt, the colonizers used extremely 'scientific' methods to create a severe and long-lasting famine."[63] Ngo Vinh Long added, "At best one might discover that the French were very uncertain about their own future and were hoarding rice and taking other 'precautionary' measures, which led, along with other factors, to famine."[64]

Despite the effects of the Allied bombing campaign on transportation networks vital to the transfer of southern rice to Tonkin, few French or Vietnamese blamed the Allies for the famine. Indeed, most Vietnamese who thought about the situation placed the blame squarely upon the shoulders of the French and, to a degree, the Japanese; they looked to the Allies as fellow combatants. Undoubtedly Ho Chi Minh and the Viet Minh saw themselves as part of the greater struggle against Japan, though the ICP's view of victory in terms of world revolution certainly would not have corresponded to the view of most of the Allies. But to encourage his fellow countrymen to unite in the struggle for national liberation, Ho Chi Minh noted that "on the one hand [the Japanese] are bogged down in China, on the other, [they] are hamstrung by the British and American forces, and certainly cannot use all their forces to contend with us."[65] But rhetoric aside, the Viet Minh could do little against the Japanese. Throughout most of 1943 Ho Chi Minh was still in jail, and the Viet Minh, although growing, had nothing in the way of arms or trained soldiers.

But luck was about to change for Ho Chi Minh. In September 1943 he was released from prison on the orders of the KMT's General Zhang Fakui, who hoped to utilize Ho Chi Minh and his reputation to organize Vietnamese nationalists in southern China into an organization dominated by his interests and for possible use against Japanese forces inside Indochina. In the following months, Zhang's organization, the Vietnamese Revolutionary League (Dong Minh Hoi), did substantially better under Ho Chi Minh's guidance. Utilizing his hallmarks of hard work, persuasion, and carefully crafted argument, Ho Chi Minh convinced many Vietnamese to join the league and showed Zhang that he was the best hope for the success of the Dong Minh Hoi. In August 1944 he asked to be given the necessary permits and resources to allow him to return to Vietnam to set up guerrilla bases. Zhang agreed and provided him with medicines and funds but was unable, and perhaps unwilling, to give him weapons for his guerrillas. In late summer 1944 Ho Chi Minh returned to Tonkin and the increasingly difficult economic situation there.[66]

Although by late 1944 Japan was clearly losing the war, the Viet Minh were far from the victories over both Japan and France that they had hoped to achieve. Indeed, the French and the Japanese appeared to have settled comfortably into their wartime relationship in the colony. The Japanese allowed the Vichy regime to remain in theoretical possession and control of the jewel of the French empire. And the French, for the most part, kept the Vietnamese in check—docile, subservient, and productive, just as the emperor's forces required. Relations between the French and the Japanese might best be described as a diplomatic model of the classical minuet, with each side stepping to its own tempo as the music played on.

But it was by now clear to most colons that the Japanese would ultimately lose the war, and public opinion among the French in Indochina had perceptibly shifted in favor of the Allies. However, one American observer, Major Austin Glass, who had lived three decades in Indochina, noted that "French public opinion is capricious and may swing overnight from one extreme to another."[67] Many factors influenced public opinion among the colons, including the turning of the tide in the Allied war against Germany, Japanese losses in the Pacific, and the long-held resentment toward the Japanese in Indochina and their attitude of superiority, which never failed to annoy the colonial elite. But even as logic seemed to dictate that the colons would favor the Allies, many were reticent to give their allegiance to that cause without some clarification of the position of the Allies on the postwar status of colonial territories. Specifically, the rhetoric of President Roosevelt concerning the future of European imperialism disturbed many Frenchmen. But that same anti-imperialist rhetoric also caught the attention of observant Vietnamese such as Ho Chi Minh, who wondered if the Allied cause could be linked to his own.

2

The Situation on the Ground:
The United States

Franklin D. Roosevelt, like most Americans, had little specific interest in or knowledge of French Indochina prior to the onset of World War II. At the turn of the century, even highly educated Americans with ample international experience, such as Roosevelt, concerned themselves primarily with Europe—still viewed by many as the true heart of aristocratic society—or neighboring Latin America. Roosevelt's interest in world issues was instilled early on by his parents, who were "Hudson River Valley aristocrats who habitually lived and traveled abroad," and in his schooling at Groton, where the headmaster taught the boys that "privileged Americans should take a part in relieving national and international ills."[1] The headmaster's lessons fit nicely into the worldview of young Franklin, who was raised in a family known for their innate sense of noblesse oblige; in particular, Franklin's cousin Theodore Roosevelt championed progressive causes throughout his career.

Although Franklin Roosevelt's experience abroad was mainly within western European elite society, he participated in debates at Groton that focused on the "annexation of Hawaii, British and American responsibility for the integrity of China, Philippine independence, and the Boer War."[2] Roosevelt and his contemporaries were certainly aware of the arguments about imperialism and dependent peoples that raged about them in their youth. Opinions varied from Mark Twain's view that imperialism would leave the United States with "her soul full of meanness, her pocket full of boodle, and her mouth full of hypocrisy"[3] to Indiana senator Albert Beveridge's claim that Americans were "a chosen people" destined by providence "to lead in the regeneration of the world,"[4] and the debates that blew through turn-of-the-century American society exposed Roosevelt to two sides of an issue he would have to deal with during his presidency.

After his graduation from Groton, Franklin went on to Harvard and Columbia Law School. By 1907 he was practicing law on Wall Street and dreaming of a career in politics on the model of his cousin Theodore. His aspirations quickly materialized: He was elected to a seat in the New York State Senate in 1910 and, following that, was appointed assistant secretary of the navy in the administration of Woodrow Wilson. An avid navy man, Roosevelt argued for a much expanded fleet and pushed the new president to assert American power with both Japan and Mexico. "Roosevelt's militancy," wrote presidential historian Robert Dallek,

> was the product not only of his desire to win a reputation and advance his political career but also of his sincere commitment to ideas he had learned in earlier years and now shared with the diplomatic, military, and political elites he associated with in Washington. Like them, he believed that a major American role in world affairs would serve both the national well-being and the needs of backward peoples around the globe.[5]

The commencement of World War I only heightened Roosevelt's desire for active involvement in the international realm. Although he initially hoped to participate in the fighting, circumstances kept him out of military service, and thus, the lessons he drew from the era came more from the efforts to end the fighting than from the war itself. Watching and listening to the president and the public's response as Wilson appealed to American idealism with his Fourteen Points, Roosevelt became a pragmatic Wilsonian. Persuaded by circumstance, Roosevelt understood that "an aspiring politician with internationalist commitments could not now make his way with the kind of martial deeds and rhetoric" his cousin had used so effectively. The "watchwords" for the post–World War I public were "disarmament and peace." For the next ten years Roosevelt continued to build his political reputation; he had his sights set on the nation's highest office. A good politician, he kept a close eye on the public mood and incorporated popular opinion into his own foreign policy goals. Thus, when international issues emerged during Roosevelt's campaigning, he focused on the pacifism that "dominated public thinking everywhere," and he believed it was a "simple political realism to back the international drive for peace." Roosevelt understood Americans' overall desire to avoid becoming entangled in the European wars that were assumed to be part of empire building. As he noted, "The whole trend of the times is against wars for colonial expansion."[6]

With the onset of the Great Depression, Roosevelt fixated on America's economic ills, and, acknowledging public sentiment for avoiding costly international entanglements, he remained as silent as possible on foreign

policy issues. This silence belied in many ways his true feelings about the ultimate interdependency of nations and alienated some who felt he had abandoned his internationalist views. But his campaign strategy of focusing on
national, instead of international, ills worked, and he was elected president
in 1932. By necessity, he focused his first term on conquering the dire domestic problems of the era. Although the prescient might have predicted the
coming global maelstrom, Roosevelt was in no position to act on his suspicions, even if he had them.

Among the early warning signals of the war to come was Japanese aggression in northern China. Anyone looking for the warning shots of World War
II need look no further than Japan's violent seizure of Manchuria in 1931. Although Roosevelt, like most politicians worldwide, condemned Japan's con-
fiscation and subsequent annexation of Manchuria, renamed Manchukuo by
the Japanese, he had no intention of becoming entangled in this far-off dispute. Early in his second term (1936–1940), however, Japanese actions once
more became a cause for concern. When war began between China and
Japan in 1937, the president once more condemned Japanese military action
but did not attempt to stop the emperor's forces, which were poised to overrun China's most populous and productive regions. Roosevelt's inaction was
founded in large part on a political pragmatism driven by domestic concerns, for certainly the American public would not have backed armed U.S.
action to save China—although most Americans aware of the situation favored a Japanese defeat. Roosevelt's sympathies also clearly lay with the
Chinese. His early education, at home and at school (which stressed a need
to respect Chinese territorial integrity as well as U.S. trade interests in the
area), a desire to promote international peace, and, of course, a degree of
trepidation about what Japan might do next—all persuaded him to help
China if possible, but in ways that would antagonize neither the Japanese
nor the American isolationists.

A host of other nations were also watching the Sino-Japanese conflict,
but western European countries with colonial holdings in Asia were particularly anxious. Both the British and the French had good cause to be
worried. By early 1938, British Hong Kong and French Indochina were two
of the few remaining points from which war materials could be transferred
into China. These supplies were desperately needed for the survival of Chiang Kai-shek's government, and the Japanese were well aware of that fact.
The French in particular feared the Japanese would attack Tonkin, where
vital equipment was brought by ship to Haiphong and transported via rail
to either Yunnan or Lang Son and then by highway into central China.

Governor-General Catroux was thus understandably "reluctant" to permit munitions shipments to Chiang via Haiphong "for fear of Japanese reprisals"; in particular, he worried that the Japanese would bomb the railroad with planes based on carriers off the island of Hainan. As noted earlier, Catroux, realizing that he was "on his own," walked a tightrope, making some concessions to the Japanese but still allowing some aid to reach China.[7]

As he monitored the situation in Asia, Roosevelt urged his advisers to find peaceful ways of helping keep open the supply lines into central China, but he was in no position—politically or militarily—to send forces to defend Indochina or any other European colony. Concerns regarding possible Japanese expansion continued into 1939, with added disputes between France and Japan over ownership of the Spratly Islands (located between Vietnam and the Philippines in the South China Sea). At that time, the Roosevelt administration made a careful distinction between France's claims to Indochina and its claims to the Spratlys. In a conversation with Ambassador René Doynel de Saint-Quentin of France regarding the Japanese threat, Maxwell Hamilton, a U.S. Foreign Service officer, stated: "The same considerations which would influence this Government in regard to forceful acquisition of territory in Europe would apply to the forceful acquisition of territory by Japan such as Hong Kong or French Indochina." When asked by the ambassador whether the same considerations applied to a Japanese seizure of the Spratlys, Hamilton outlined the American view: "There might be a distinction in that there was no question as to British ownership of Hong Kong or as to French ownership of French Indochina, whereas there were two claims, a French claim and a Japanese claim, to ownership of the Spratly Islands."[8] Clearly, French Indochina had entered the mental framework of the president and personnel within the State Department, but as a geographic area indisputably under French control and important for the perseverance of Chiang Kai-shek's government, not as a land with an indigenous people with rights and desires of their own.

The situation became considerably more complex in 1940. As Roosevelt campaigned for reelection to a third term, he walked a difficult tightrope: balancing the isolationists' demands to stay out of both the mess in China and the increasingly dire European war and his own belief that the United States would have to become involved in order to safeguard the democratic and trade freedoms so dear to America and so critical in establishing and maintaining world peace. Comforted to some degree that Roosevelt's own beliefs might in the end hold sway but acknowledging his difficulties with American public opinion, both Great Britain and France feared that American intervention simply would not come. On June 16, 1940, in one of his last appeals for help from the United States, as German forces rolled across France, Premier Paul Reynaud of France avowed: "I must tell you . . . that if you cannot give to France in the hours to come the certainty that the United States will come into the war within a very short time, the fate of the world will change. Then you will see France go under like a drowning man and disappear, after having cast a long look towards the land of liberty from which she awaited salvation."9 Although Roosevelt provided as much materiel as he could within the confines of U.S. law and congressional approval, he could not offer American military intervention, and he could not prevent France's surrender.

With the fall of France to the Nazis the eventual fall of Indochina to their Axis partner seemed inevitable. Japan continued to press the Vichy French for more concessions, and the United States continued to protest its actions. It was not until the beginning of the Japanese occupation of northern Vietnam in September, however, that American economic pressure was brought to bear with a full embargo on iron and steel scrap. But despite the best efforts of the Roosevelt administration, neither economic sanctions nor diplomacy seemed to be working in 1940 and certainly not in 1941; the Japanese and American governments were dancing to different scores.

Roosevelt attempted to prevent the spread of Japanese forces into the rest of Vietnam and further expansion of the Pacific war by proposing the neutralization of French Indochina as a Switzerland-like country with open access to trade.10 The Japanese rejected that offer, and by the end of summer 1941 they had moved into southern Vietnam; in response, the United States had frozen their assets. This in no way indicated, however, a solid intention to "save" Vietnam, or even China, from the Japanese. American diplomats continued discussions with Tokyo in hopes of postponing, perhaps even avoiding, a war in the Pacific based on Roosevelt's "continuing concern" that "scarce resources be marshaled to fight Hitler." But as summer turned into autumn, "newspaper, public, and official opinion was uniformly opposed to any appeasement of Japan."11 And with the failure of diplomacy on both sides, the attack on Pearl Harbor in December brought the United States into the world war with all three of the Axis powers, stretching U.S. resources between the two theaters.

As the United States became a full participant in World War II, Roosevelt's views regarding the French and French Indochina gradually shifted. Initially the president and his aides continued to assure the French that their world status, both in Europe and as a colonial power, would be secure in the postwar era. In January 1942, for example, in an effort to stem

Vichy collaboration with the Axis powers, Roosevelt conveyed a five-point message to the U.S. ambassador to France, Admiral William Leahy, to "use if the occasion offered—either with Marshal Pétain or General Weygand." Point number two dealt directly with French possessions, affirming that "the word 'France' in the mind of the President includes the French Colonial Empire." In the same message, the president warned Vichy against any possible submission should Germany attack either unoccupied France or any of the French colonies, cautioning that their "acquiescence to such an attack" could only be regarded as "playing the German game."[12]

Although the Vichy government would undoubtedly have liked to avoid any further conflict with either their German occupiers or the Americans, they were not wholly cooperative with either. That same month, Ambassador Leahy relayed the contents of his conversation with France's Admiral Jean François Darlan and his overall impressions regarding the Vichy as allies. In regard to French Indochina, Leahy wrote: "I referred to newspaper reports of an Allied attack on the Japanese occupied aerodrome at Hanoi and expressed an opinion that we in France must be prepared for military action by the Allies against Japanese occupied Indochina, particularly the bases and ports used by Japan. Darlan replied that there are no bases in Indochina and the ports are not useful." Darlan's assertion, of course, was little better than a bald-faced lie that did nothing to allay American suspicions. "My general impression as a result of this interview," concluded Leahy, "is that America cannot expect any cooperation whatever by Vichy."[13]

In his January 1942 dealings with the British, Roosevelt took a slightly different angle with regard to colonial holdings. Although his foremost goal was the firm establishment of a wartime partnership between the two nations, Roosevelt sought to impress upon the British leader, Winston Churchill, some understanding of American public opinion toward imperialism and the need for British "identification with idealistic post-war aims." India, in particular, was a point of disagreement. With the Japanese advance toward the British Empire's crown jewel, "an outcry went up in the United States for a change in Britain's imperial policy." For their part, the British were neither moved nor amused by American meddling in their national affairs. In a telling statement, Roosevelt lamented to the wife of author Louis Adamic that Churchill did not "understand how most of our people feel about Britain and her role in the life of other peoples. . . . There are many kinds of Americans of course, but as a people, as a country, we're opposed to imperialism—we can't stomach it."[14]

Although Roosevelt's impression of the views of the American public may have had much truth in it, there certainly was no grand push to end imperialism worldwide. For example, the empathy, however arrogant at times, exhibited toward Indians and their nationalist aspirations was certainly not extended to neighboring Burma, also a British colony with avid patriots. As part of a memo sent to Churchill in 1942 on Burmese collaborators, Roosevelt clearly exhibited a lack of genuine identification with those oppressed by colonialism:

> I have never liked Burma or the Burmese! And you people must have had a terrible time with them for the last fifty years. Thank the Lord you have HE-SAW, WE-SAW, YOU-SAW [the reference is to the controversial Burmese politician U Saw] under lock and key. I wish you could put the whole bunch of them into a frying pan with a wall around it and let them stew in their own juice.[15]

To keep American public opinion pro-British, the president delicately pushed Churchill for some measure of change in India but blatantly disregarded Burma. The French colonies fell into basically the same category as Burma. Since few Americans knew much about the countries in particular, let alone about their nationalist aspirations, Roosevelt could afford to deal with the French and their empire as best suited wartime military and diplomatic needs, not according to the lofty sentiments of the anti-imperialists or the desires of the colonies' peoples. For example, when the United States sought to establish a U.S. consulate in French Equatorial Africa at Brazzaville, Undersecretary of State Sumner Welles once again sought to allay French nervousness regarding the postwar world: "As this Government has informed Your Excellency's Government upon several occasions, the Government of the United States recognizes the sovereign jurisdiction of the people of France over the territory of France and over French possessions overseas. The Government of the United States fervently hopes that it may see the reestablishment of the independence of France and of the integrity of French territory."[16]

These comforting statements were repeated less often in the following year as Roosevelt became more disenchanted with the conduct of both the Vichy French and the Free French under de Gaulle, a man the president neither trusted nor liked. In an effort to create a peaceful postwar world, tap the idealism and gain the approval of the American public, and create a positive feeling among Americans for the Allies, Roosevelt began to talk about, among other things, the possibility of international trusteeships in the post-war era. In a mid-1942 conversation with Russia's foreign minister, Vyacheslav Molotov, Roosevelt "stated his belief that an end to colonial possessions would serve world peace by preventing postwar struggles for independence and that international trusteeships should be set up for former colonies until they were ready for self-government." In Roosevelt's vision of the postwar world, the United States, Russia, Britain, and potentially China would be the world's "policemen" responsible for international security, including overseeing trustee nations.[17] Although the trusteeship plan, if put into practice, might have had enormous appeal among Americans uneasy with colonialism, it also brought a great deal of consternation to the holders of empires—in particular the British and the French. As will be seen, Roosevelt tended to soft-pedal the issue with the British, emphasizing that enemy-held colonies such as Korea would be the first to come under trusteeship rule, but he became quite hostile toward the French empire.

Throughout 1943 Roosevelt made multiple statements regarding his loosely formulated trusteeship plan and the colonial situation in general, stressing the connection between imperialism and war. In a conversation with his son Elliott, Roosevelt articulated his theory that without a change in the prewar colonial system, the world would find itself in yet another war at the conclusion of the current one. He was, of course, not far off the mark. "The thing is," he declared, "the colonial system means war. Exploit the resources of an India, Burma, a Java; take all the wealth out of those countries, but never put anything back into them, things like education, decent standards of living, minimum health requirements—all you're doing is storing up the kind of trouble that leads to war."[18] Interestingly, by 1943 Burma, which he had dismissed so sarcastically in his note to Churchill only a year earlier, had become one of his examples of an oppressed nation deserving change. But this statement and others like it concerning the British and Dutch colonies seemed perfectly benign when compared to Roosevelt's comments on the French. In particular, he put an unusual emphasis on French Indochina—unusual because although French imperial domination had resulted in significant misery among the Vietnamese peasantry, that was certainly not an atypical situation within the colonized world. In a conversation with Elliott he denounced French rule:

The Japanese control that colony now. Why was it a cinch for the Japanese to conquer that land? The native Indo-Chinese have been so flagrantly downtrodden that they thought to themselves: Anything must be better than to live under French colonial rule! Should a land belong to France? By what logic and by what custom and by what historical rule? . . . I'm talking about another war, Elliott, . . . I'm talking about what will happen to our world, if after *this* war we allow millions of people to slide back into the same semi-slavery![19]

As an alternative to French colonial rule, the president proposed to the British that French Indochina, as well as Korea, should become trustee nations under the United States, the Soviet Union, and possibly China. The British government was not supportive of the idea, pointing out, among other problems, that China was not and could not be classified as a world power alongside Britain, the United States, or the Soviet Union. For Roosevelt, however, the suggestion made perfect sense. China was for many Americans the "favorite ally" because it was "untainted by Communism or imperialism, a victim rather than a practitioner of power politics, China above all was seen as America's natural democratic ally."[20] And it seemed logical that China, sharing geographic proximity to both nations, should have a strong hand in leading the two colonies toward democratic self-government. China was riddled with internal corruption and strife and so would have been a poor choice as an international trustee. However, if a politically secure government friendly to the United States were to emerge there, Roosevelt's trusteeship plan as a whole would have had potential.

Assuming that the status of the colonies was indeed key to a lasting postwar peace and looking to build U.S. military and economic strength, Roosevelt "hoped the trusteeship system would allow the United States to establish long-term naval and air bases at strategic points in the Pacific and elsewhere without confronting traditional American antipathy for power politics." In Roosevelt's judgment, "a system of collective rule for the benefit of emerging nations would effectively de-emphasize American military control" and "could provide a means of both aiding exploited peoples and creating a workable Pacific security system for at least twenty years."[21] Roosevelt identified Indochina as an important element in ensuring the postwar security of Asia, so it was only fitting that he should give that colony a starring role in the trusteeship plan. China and the Soviet Union, both with their own agendas, were for the most part amenable to the American plan. In fact, Joseph Stalin's comments about the French were distinctly similar to Roosevelt's. Concluding that the "entire French ruling class was rotten to the core" and "actively helping our enemies," Stalin had determined that "it would be not only unjust but dangerous to leave in French hands any important strategic points after the war," and French Indochina fell into that category. Suspicions of the intent and scope of the trusteeship plan only increased British opposition to discussions on the postwar status of Indochina. Churchill's heated objections at the 1943 Tehran Conference prompted a sharp response from Roosevelt. "Now look here Winston," he retorted, "[in the matter of French Indochina] you are outvoted three to one."[22]

Even after the 1943 conferences at Cairo and Tehran, Roosevelt continued to speak about ending French colonial rule, specifically in Indochina and in the African colony of Dakar, both of which were deemed necessary for American military bases to help ensure postwar security. And the British continued to oppose the plan, in part because of its implications for the fate of the British Empire. Although Churchill was adamant that the demise of the empire would not take place on his watch, by signing the Atlantic Charter alongside Roosevelt in August 1941, he had opened the door for discussion on the meaning of liberation and self-determination and to whom those terms would apply. Indeed, Point Three of the charter caused quite a stir among the French and brought hope to many nationalists worldwide, including those in Vietnam.[23] It read: "They respect the right of all peoples to choose the form of government under which they will live; and they wish to see sovereign rights and self-government restored to those who have been forcibly deprived of them."[24]

In the context of World War II, this statement can be interpreted in different ways. On the one hand, a conservative reading implies a desire only for the liberation of Nazi- and Japanese-occupied territories. On the other hand, a more liberal reading suggests a commitment to an end to all colonialism, for the subject peoples had undeniably been "forcibly deprived" of their rights. Both Roosevelt and Churchill hoped that the broad aims expressed in the Atlantic Charter, including Point Three, would help cement American public opinion behind the British war effort and would lay the foundations for increased U.S. aid in the fight against the Nazis. After the United States formally entered the war, the Atlantic Charter became even more important as one of the crucial ties that bound this war to a more idealistic postwar world.

Until late 1944, Franklin Roosevelt's statements indicated that at least in selected instances, he ascribed to the more disputatious version of Point Three. In advocating a change in the colonial system, the president continually singled out France for criticism, placing special emphasis on the situation in Indochina. In his view, France had failed throughout their tenure in Vietnam to improve the standard of living of the people and had, by virtue of their failings, relinquished their right to rule. In addition, Secretary of State Cordell Hull believed that one of the reasons Roosevelt was so concerned with Indochina was that it had been the "springboard for the Japanese attack on the Philippines, Malaya, and the Dutch East Indies."[25] In January, Roosevelt sent a memorandum to Hull stating:

> I had, for over a year, expressed the opinion that Indo-China should not go back to France but that it should be administered by an international trusteeship. France has had that country—thirty million inhabitants— for nearly one hundred years, and the people are worse off than they were at the beginning. . . . the case of Indo-China is perfectly clear. France has milked it for one hundred years. The people of Indo-China are entitled to something better than that.[26]

Given Roosevelt's upbringing and fondness for France during his youth, many have speculated on his singling out of the French colonial situation for special damnation. Historian Mark Philip Bradley provided an important context for understanding the issue:

> Embedded in the harsh judgments of World War II–era American policy makers was a broader discourse on the proper relationship between what was seen as the backward character of nonwhite peoples and the more progressive West. American images of Vietnamese society reflected a fundamental belief in racialized cultural hierarchies that had underlain the American encounter with nonwhite peoples at home and abroad since the mid-nineteenth century. Much of the vociferous critique of French colonialism rested on the widespread notion of the unique success of the American colonial project in the Philippines and the superior claims of American models to reshape the lives of backward peoples.[27]

Hence, for Roosevelt and for many in his administration, the French were simply not "good colonizers" and had failed at their moral obligation to properly take up the "white man's burden." Steeped in the notion of American exceptionalism, they believed that the Philippines—set to receive its independence in 1945—was the shining example that American cultural, political, and economic models could and should be utilized for the new trustee nations. In a March 1943 meeting with his Pacific War Council, Roosevelt suggested that "French conduct in Indochina was at considerable variance with [the] general practice of Great Britain and the United States to encourage natives to participate in self-government to the limit of their abilities."[28]

Although placing the United States alongside Great Britain as "good colonizers," Roosevelt still looked at Britain's long history of colonialism as distinct from America's relatively short run as an imperial power. In May 1943, in an exchange with Churchill over whether or not the Chinese might lay claim to Indochina, Roosevelt asserted that China would have no interest in the territory. Churchill disagreed. Roosevelt's rejoinder is telling: "Well, you are speaking for Britain which has been for centuries an imperialistic power and you have several generations of imperialist ancestors behind you. You have never refused a square mile anywhere you could lay your hands on."[29] Nevertheless, although trusteeship—based on the American colonial model and under a new international administrative body—was deemed the proper solution for French Indochina, pushing the British, the "good colonizers," toward this goal was considered unnecessary for the time being. Needless to say, the French did not agree with Roosevelt's assessment of their colonial behavior.

Prior to World War II, the French had believed that "Indo-china could not wish for a better destiny. Half a century of French peace has brought its nations a miraculous degree of economic prosperity and political security."[30] Given these conflicting views, it was only natural that French postwar plans for Indochina would collide with those of Roosevelt. In the same month that Roosevelt was declaring that "Indo-China should not go back to France," the French Committee for National Liberation declared that "the aims of the work of civilization which France is accomplishing in her possessions exclude any idea of autonomy and any possibility of development outside the French Empire bloc. The attainment of 'self-government' in the colonies even in the most distant future, must be excluded."[31] Ralph Bunche, a former Howard University professor, reported for the State Department: "There was no recognition that France owed any accountability to the international community in the conduct of their international affairs nor that the international community had any valid interest in such affairs."[32]

Obviously the French were strongly opposed to any type of international trusteeship over their colonial holdings. Robert Murphy, Roosevelt's handpicked agent in dealings with the French, first heard of the president's ideas concerning trusteeship at the Casablanca Conference in 1943. "He [Roosevelt] discussed with several people, including Eisenhower and me, the transfer of control of Dakar, Indochina, and other French possessions, and he did not seem fully aware how abhorrent his attitude would be to all imperialist-minded Frenchmen including De Gaulle and also those with whom I had negotiated agreements."[33] It was not long before word reached Secretary of State Hull that the president had been spreading his ideas about French colonialism even further. By January 1, the British ambassador to the United States, Edward Halifax, had reported to Hull that Roosevelt, "during his visit to the Near East for the Cairo and Tehran Conferences, had rather definitively stated to the Turks, Egyptians, and perhaps others his views to the effect that Indo-China should be taken from the French and put under an international trusteeship."[34]

French historian Bernard Fall asserted that "President Roosevelt accorded Indochina—and, in particular, French activities there—an importance far out of proportion to its actual position within the scheme of things" and that "his pre-occupation amounted almost to a fixation."[35] Historian Gary Hess is perhaps more objective: "To Roosevelt, the French had behaved as shamefully against Japan as against Germany. As this pattern of thinking crystallized, Roosevelt came to attribute the worst characteristics to the French administration of Indochina."[36] Hence, in addition to his desire to see French Indochina become a trustee nation moving toward independence—reflecting a sense of the American noblesse oblige—Roosevelt also "appeared to have been equally motivated by his desire to see the French punished for what he regarded as their moral turpitude in the face of danger."[37]

Although Roosevelt spoke compellingly for an end to French colonialism in Indochina, he did not develop a concrete policy for removing territories from French control or for establishing an international trusteeship. Although some analysts have argued that this evinced a lack of commitment to the ideal, in part to avoid a "rupture in the wartime coalition,"[38] Joseph Siracusa provided an alternate hypothesis: "FDR's apparent diplomatic weakness *and*, at least in this instance, principal strength lay in his ostensible vacillation [on this issue of trusteeships]; for until the Axis powers were completely defeated it would surely have been unreasonable on his part, a possibility perhaps overlooked by his critics, to take a fixed position on such peripheral issues."[39]

Roosevelt's aides often had to reassure the French and the British regarding U.S. postwar intentions in order to avoid a serious split with America's wartime allies. Although Roosevelt occasionally chided Churchill about British imperialism, he avoided pinning the British down on postwar policy regarding the colonial powers and their possessions. In fact, Robert Dallek reported, in February 1945 Secretary of State Edward Stettinius calmed an incensed Churchill by explaining that "trusteeships were only intended for existing League of Nations mandates, territory detached from the enemy, and any other territory *voluntarily* put under United Nations control." His formulation pointedly omitted the British Empire from any discussion on trusteeships. "This trusteeship plan, less ambitious than any Roosevelt had favored in the past," wrote Dallek, "largely resulted from Churchill's resistance and the changed position of the French."[40] Indeed, much to Roosevelt's chagrin, in was clear that de Gaulle would not only lead the Free French but would also play an important role in postwar Europe. And de Gaulle was determined to lead not only France but its empire as well. Thus, by early 1945 Roosevelt seems to have concluded that a final policy decision on French Indochina could and should be postponed until after victory in both theaters. Although he did tame his rhetoric on Indochina, he had not abandoned the idea of a trusteeship. At Yalta he told Stalin that he still "had in mind a trusteeship for Indochina," adding his familiar refrain that the French "had done nothing to improve the natives since she had the colony."[41]

Whether Roosevelt's interest in French Indochina derived from a desire to punish the French primarily for being "bad" colonizers or primarily for their failure to "stand up" to the Germans and Japanese, it was still clear that Indochina had become an important element of Roosevelt's thinking on colonialism. In addition to looking at what the French had or had not done, Roosevelt also fixed on what the colonial situation meant for the United States "in the context of his concern that failure to support nationalist aspirations in Asia would discredit the United States in the eyes of a billion people." An international trusteeship plan "would have helped elevate the Allied cause among the colonial peoples because it would have shown that the war's goal was not to reestablish the European empires."[42] And the plan's emphasis on multinational rather than U.S. oversight of former colonies and its "outward adherence to national self-determination" would have helped bring domestic public opinion "firmly behind a continuing American part in overseas affairs."[43]

Roosevelt's anticolonialist feelings were for the most part an expression of educated public opinion, but they were not always shared by the key military figures who would probably have become responsible for handling the detachment of former European colonies. In the China theater, however, General Joseph Stilwell and General Albert Wedemeyer were anti-imperialist and "opposed in principle to European possession of Asian territory as formal colonies. They simply believed colonialism wrong and furthermore thought the colonial powers—Britain, France, and the Netherlands—and Nationalist China too weak in Asia to do much of the real fighting against Japan." Watching the machinations of the colonial powers,

Wedemeyer reported in 1944 that the British, the Dutch, and the French had every intention of retaining their colonies, and he felt, as summarized by historian Bradley Smith, "sure that those three Governments have definitely reached an agreement on these matters among themselves."[44] As an example, Wedemeyer cited the French training in India of paratroopers who would be dropped into Indochina. He was convinced that the imperialist nations intended to reassert their colonial dominion after the expulsion of the Japanese, with help from the United States, and he firmly recommended that the Americans look "carefully at all requests for materials" to make sure they would "further the war effort rather than post-war ends."[45] Perhaps John Davies, Stilwell's political adviser, best summed up what was in the minds of many Americans who, in Roosevelt's words, "[couldn't] stomach" imperialism: "Why should American boys die to recreate the colonial empires of the British and their Dutch and French satellites?"[46]

There were, of course, those in both the military and the administration who were not anti-imperialists and who maintained a relatively good rapport with their European counterparts, including the French. OSS director William J. Donovan was one of those people. Although both Roosevelt and Donovan were New Yorkers and both were bound for national and international renown, their early backgrounds were quite different. Whereas the Roosevelts cavorted with the European elite, Donovan socialized with other working-class children in the Irish section of Buffalo and earned the moniker "Wild Bill," which would follow him throughout his career.

Born in 1883 to a first-generation Irish Catholic railroad worker, William Joseph Donovan was well versed in the necessity of hard work and in the sacrifices his Irish immigrant grandparents had made to come to the United States. He worked nights and summers to earn his college tuition money and served as his fraternity house manager in exchange for room and board. Donovan excelled on the football field but performed poorly in the classroom, yet his personality and drive brought him eventual success at both. He went on to graduate from Columbia Law School, as did Franklin Roosevelt, although the two men moved in very different social circles while there.

After graduation Donovan began practicing law and soon joined a group of young men seeking to form a local National Guard unit. In May 1912 he became a proud member of Troop I of the First New York Cavalry and by October had been elected captain. Donovan's upward spiral continued with his marriage into a wealthy Buffalo family and a 1916 invitation by the John D. Rockefeller Foundation to travel to Europe, which was deep in the throes of World War I, in an effort to gain permission from the belligerents to provide war relief to the Poles—then being trampled by German armies intent on the destruction of tsarist Russia.

While Donovan was becoming acquainted with London and Europe as part of his mission, military duty demanded he return home. In 1916 Donovan and the First New York Cavalry were promptly sent to Texas to help settle troubles with the Mexican revolutionary Pancho Villa, who had raided the small town of Columbus in New Mexico. Donovan spent six months riding after Villa and training his men to be tough soldiers, for he, like Roosevelt and many others, believed that the United States would not be able to avoid entrance into the ongoing world war.

On March 15, 1917, only three days after Donovan returned home from Mexico, he again reported for duty, this time becoming commander of the First Battalion of the Sixty-ninth Infantry Regiment. With the American entrance into World War I, the Sixty-ninth, known as the Fighting Irish and attached to the 165th Infantry, Forty-second Rainbow Division, soon shipped out, bound for the bloody trenches of France. There Donovan and his men gained the military experience that Roosevelt had been denied. Donovan, now a major, and his men fought well, and his reputation grew. Although known for his strict rules on alcohol and his continuous drilling, the major was admired by his men. One of his most ardent supporters, Father Patrick Duffy, the regimental chaplain, wrote: "As a result of watching him through six days of battle—his coolness, cheerfulness, resourcefulness—there is now no limit to [his men's] admiration of him." Never content to sit in safety while his men were in harm's way, Donovan fought alongside the men of the Fighting Irish, suffering a series of minor wounds and earning the Purple Heart with two Oak Leaf Clusters. He received the Distinguished Service Cross for his conduct in the second Battle of the Marne and was promoted to lieutenant colonel. It was the major's "usual disregard of danger"[47] and success in routing the enemy at Landres-et-St. Georges that earned him the Medal of Honor and promotion to full colonel.[48]

William Donovan returned to New York a famous and honored son with plenty of opportunities. His strict adherence to a philosophy of matching word and deed would soon turn his high reputation, associated with heroism on the battlefield, to that of an outcast. His battlefield fame had resulted in an invitation to join one of Buffalo's most exclusive men's clubs, where the city's most important and influential leaders enjoyed a steady supply of premium whiskeys—then banned under Prohibition. But Donovan's legal star

had also risen, and by 1922 he was a U.S. attorney, bound by his vocation to
enforce the unpopular amendment. The raid he ordered on his own club and
the arrest of many of its members resulted in his being ostracized for a time
from the highest reaches of Buffalo society and put a serious damper on his
once-promising political career. Donovan's bid for the governorship of New
York in 1932 failed, but his legal career continued to do well throughout the
1920s and 1930s, and he maintained ties with numerous political leaders,
most notably Herbert Hoover during his successful candidacy for president
in 1928.

In addition to keeping a keen eye on the domestic scene, Donovan also
made frequent trips abroad and he, like Roosevelt, viewed the growing turmoil in both Europe and Asia as bound to lead to a war that the United
States would not be able to avoid. Donovan, biographer Richard Dunlap explained, would "come to play the leading role in the community of American
citizens who, for patriotic reasons, kept abreast of crucial developments
abroad. At the same time he enjoyed the excitement and danger that a close
look at war represented."[49] Billing himself as an affluent lawyer representing
some of his country's largest corporations and playing on his military reputation, Donovan talked Italian dictator Benito Mussolini into allowing him to
visit and evaluate the status of the Italian army in Africa.

Donovan landed in Ethiopia in December 1935 as a representative of Il
Duce himself, was given access to all he wished to evaluate—weapons, de-
ployments, the morale and health of the soldiers, the status of roads—and
left the continent forecasting a swift Italian victory and the subsequent establishment of an Italian colony. Donovan, whose report contradicted the information held by the League of Nations and others in both Europe and
America who wishfully predicted Italian failure, reported back to Mussolini
and then to the League of Nation's American representative in Geneva. Back
in the United States, he conveyed his appraisal of the Italian situation to the
War Department and made a personal report to President Roosevelt. Within
a few weeks, just as Donovan had said it would, Ethiopia fell to the Italians.
But Donovan's new career, watching and assessing the growing chaos
abroad, had not quite begun.[50]

As he pursued his flourishing legal career, Donovan continued his extensive travels in Europe as a private citizen. In the spring of 1937 he visited
Germany, Czechoslovakia, the Balkans, Italy, and Spain—always assessing
the political, economic, and military scene as carefully as if he were already
planning for war. His address to the Army War College upon his return
could have come from a postwar text: "We are facing a new kind of war," he

pronounced, "not so much in point of principle, because in war the fundamental principles remain the same, but new in respect to machines and
weapons. More than that, this war is moving to a new tempo. . . . The second characteristic of the new warfare is more perfect coordination between
the air arm and the land arm."[51] But even though he was an "old" war hero
and as accurate as we now know his words to have been, at that time many
disregarded and even resented the affluent republican attorney's intrusion
into the realm of the democratic Roosevelt administration—a place in
which he did not yet belong. However, the president did listen to Donovan's
report, and much of what he said fit with Roosevelt's own fears regarding
the international situation. And that October, when Roosevelt made his so-
called Quarantine speech in Chicago, Donovan was one of the few important Republicans to both agree with and speak out in favor of the president's warning:

> If we are to have a world in which we can breathe freely and live in
> amity without fear, the peace-loving nations must make a concerted
> effort to uphold laws and principles on which peace can rest secure. War
> is a contagion, whether it be declared or undeclared. It can engulf states
> and peoples remote from the original scene of hostilities. We are
> determined to keep out of war, yet we cannot insure ourselves against
> the disastrous effects of war and the dangers of involvement. We are
> adopting such measures as will minimize the risk of involvement, but we
> cannot have complete protection in a world of disorder in which
> confidence and security have broken down.[52]

The rapid victories of Hitler's armies in Europe in 1939 and 1940 brought
Donovan and Roosevelt into closer communication. Concerned about the
role of fifth-column subversives in the rapid collapse of the western European countries and plagued by growing pessimism regarding Britain's ability to withstand the German assault, Roosevelt sent Donovan to London in
the summer of 1940 to join *Chicago Daily News* correspondent Edgar
Mowrer in evaluating the situation. The mission was to be strictly unofficial,
with Donovan purporting to be a private citizen on business. However, important persons, including the king and queen, Churchill, and Colonel Steward Menzies, "Britain's chief spymaster," had been informed of the true situation and opened their doors to him. Soon after his return to the United
States, the president invited Donovan to join him on a brief vacation in New
England, and for those two days in August that Donovan "had the

President's ear," he "continued to tell the President what he wanted to hear, reversing the gloom and doom prophecies of [American ambassador to Britain Joseph] Kennedy."[53] The attributes that Donovan brought to the table were many: his numerous connections, both domestic and international; his ability to carefully assess the international situation based on military, economic, political, and societal considerations; and the fact that his message fit with Roosevelt's developing agenda. All of these, combined with a little help from a well-placed friend, Frank Knox, would soon result in a place for Donovan in Roosevelt's administration.

Knox had become Roosevelt's secretary of the navy in June 1940. A staunchly pro-Allied Republican, Knox brought both bipartisanship to the president's cabinet and a multitude of ideas designed to support Britain's war effort. One of Knox's ideas was to bring his good friend and fellow Republican, Bill Donovan, into the Roosevelt administration. Although his initial placement efforts failed, it was Knox's prompting of the president that resulted in a second "secret" mission abroad for Donovan. In December 1940 Donovan left the United States with William Stephenson, the operations chief in the United States of the British Intelligence Agency (MI6). The two men were already acquainted—in fact, it was Stephenson who had paved the way for Donovan's visit with Menzies during his first "mission"—and they rapidly became good friends, with a mutual belief in the primacy of intelligence. Donovan spent more than two months traveling; from England he went to Spain, North Africa, Eastern Europe, and the Middle East, listening as he went to leaders of lands, armies, navies, and parties and forming evaluative impressions of them and of the ongoing conflagration.

With this trip Donovan's reputation also grew. Met by members of the press on his return, the reporters found that Donovan "'had nothing to say' after traveling 30,000 miles in fourteen weeks." The disbelieving journalists duly dubbed him "the Man of Mystery, the Akhoond of Hush."[54] Donovan clearly enjoyed the titles and the notability and used his "fame" to take his message to the American people. Convinced that the United States would have to enter the war alongside Britain and sure of the Nazis' strength and sense of purpose, Donovan addressed the listening audience of the Columbia Broadcasting System in June. He admonished his listeners not to be fooled by Nazi propaganda and isolationist sentiment at home, which encouraged Americans to believe that the United States was safe from the war in Europe. Donovan cautioned:

William Donovan, returning in 1941 from a fact-finding mission abroad, was dubbed "the Man of Mystery, the Akhoond of Hush" by the local media (Walter Karig, "The Most Mysterious Office in Washington," *Liberty*, January 3, 1942, 46). *Courtesy of the Buffalo and Erie County Historical Society.*

Christian democracy can never love war, but we must not lose sight of the fact that we may be forced to accept war in order to survive. If Hitler wins, our vital interests will be affected. We will have to redraft our plans for the future; our trade, our standard of living, our concept of human life, will all be placed in jeopardy. We shall have to match Germany's military and sea power merely to live. For the conflict between the two systems is irreconcilable and inevitable. . . . Hitler strikes at everything that affects our will, yours and mine. He tries to place a fifth columnist in the hearts of each of us—a fifth columnist of doubt and discord. If these weapons prove successful and he can hold us out of the Atlantic, or if he can prevent us from giving essential aid, then the battle of the Atlantic is lost to Britain and to us. With that battle lost, the last obstacle to European domination by Germany is removed. The shield behind which we could prepare and get strong is beaten down; Nazism and Americanism will be face to face. A Germany strong and self-confident, feeling the urge for new conquests and an America without an ally, unready to meet so strong an enemy *alone*. . . . No one can reasonably deny that danger threatens our republic. Will we go to meet danger in the spirit of the American generations who came before us, or will we wait until it has crossed the doorstep of our homes and touches our families and our altars?[55]

Upon his return Donovan had also gone to see the president, but with minimal results. Although Roosevelt was beginning to think about a solution for the "muddled state of U.S. intelligence," he had not come to the conclusion that Donovan was a part of the answer. But others had. Knox, who encouraged Donovan to write out his ideas about the formation of a centralized intelligence agency, and those closely associated with Stephenson and British Intelligence believed that Donovan was the man to remedy America's intelligence shortcomings. In a fact-finding mission designed ultimately to "draw America into Britain's intelligence web," Admiral John Godfrey, director of British Naval Intelligence, and Commander Ian Fleming (later of James Bond fame) met with intelligence agents representing the U.S. Army, Navy, State Department, and FBI. Although Godfrey and Fleming found the various departments eminently cooperative, they marveled at both the lack of interagency cooperation and the high degree of competition among them. The admiral concluded:

There is no U.S. Secret Intelligence Service. Americans are inclined to refer to their "S.I.S.," but by this they mean the small and uncoordinated force of "Special Agents" who travel abroad on behalf of one or another of the Governmental Departments. These "Agents" are, for the most part, amateurs without special qualifications and without training in Observation. They have no special means of communication or other facilities and they seldom have clearer brief than "to go and have a look."[56]

Donovan's intelligence plan certainly aimed to remedy this situation. Modeled on the British intelligence system and in large part the product of his many fruitful conversations with Stephenson, Donovan proposed an agency with "sole charge of intelligence work abroad" whose director would be above partisan politics and responsible only to the president. Although the secretary of the navy was pleased with his friend's draft, others within Roosevelt's administration were not. For example, the War Department's response, that the proposed "super agency controlling *all* intelligence" and "no doubt under Col. Donovan" would "appear to be very disadvantageous, if not calamitous," reflected the views of the FBI and others who had no desire to see their control of information diminished. For although the coordination of information could be helpful to all, "jealous and competitive, the Americans operated on the premise that knowledge is power, but that knowledge shared is power diluted."[57] However, convinced of the need to remedy his lack of coordinated intelligence, in a July 11, 1941, presidential directive Roosevelt created the Office of the Coordinator of Intelligence designed to effectively inform him "about events on the international scene that might threaten the safety, or at least the foreign interests," of the United States.[58] Much to the consternation of the War Department and others who feared their power would soon be diminished, Roosevelt officially appointed Donovan as his coordinator of information.

When Donovan's office, collectively known as the COI, was established, there were eight separate intelligence gathering entities within the U.S. government: Army G-2, the Office of Naval Intelligence (ONI), the FBI in the Justice Department, the State Department's representatives abroad, customs inspectors for the Department of Commerce, Treasury's Secret Service, the Labor Department's Immigration and Naturalization inspectors, and the agents for the Federal Communications Commission. The problems with such a system were obvious: Although an enormous amount of raw material could be gathered, it was subject to at least eight different interpretations. Even given the best intentions, the time and effort necessary to sort, evaluate, and pass on information often precluded one unit's discoveries from being shared with another. At worst, guarding each individual agency's interests often prevented valuable interagency sharing and left everyone deafened by the white noise of information and misinformation. There were other problems as well. Until the development of COI there was no centralized head, no clearinghouse for the information, and no direct link to the ultimate decision maker, Roosevelt. In the best-case scenario, the agents working for COI would "synthesize and disseminate intelligence" acquired from all eight agencies and pass it on to those responsible for the nation's defense.[59] Donovan would act as the direct link to the president.

The COI's business was in theory secret, but COI and Donovan made headlines not long after the agency's establishment. In January 1942 journalist Walter Karig's article "The Most Mysterious Office in Washington" appeared in *Liberty* magazine and roundly applauded both Donovan and COI. "COI," Karig wrote, "is the super-spy and counter-espionage agency of the government. On its staff is the greatest aggregation of bulging brains and nimble wits that ever a government drafted from its nation's college faculties, military establishment, diplomatic corps, and newspaper offices." The "bulging brains" of COI correlated "the confidential information acquired by all the other federal sleuthing agencies" and put "the compilation on the President's desk," prepared propaganda and counterpropaganda through the Foreign Information Service, and staffed the Bureau of Research and Analysis, COI's intellectual heart.[60]

COI, however, had opponents from its very beginning. J. Edgar Hoover, director of the FBI, described COI as "Roosevelt's folly" and deliberately ruined at least one COI mission to protect his own turf, while the ONI and G-2 "offered little cooperation and, in some cases, deliberately withheld information" from Donovan's team.[61] Even within COI there was dissention—over procedures, interpretations, and Donovan's role. COI's problems prompted Roosevelt to abolish the office on June 13, 1942.

For a variety of reasons COI had failed, but the concept of centralized intelligence gathering under the auspices of William Donovan had taken firm hold. On the same day that COI was collapsed, Donovan became the director of its successor, the Office of Strategic Services (OSS), established by military order under the jurisdiction of the Joint Chiefs of Staff (JCS). The new placement under the JCS had not come easily. "From the beginning the military had opposed Donovan; he was a civilian dabbling in a military preserve or proposing operations upon which they frowned. In both cases he was an inexperienced interloper whose schemes were a threat to security, efficiency, and military success." However, the JCS reluctantly agreed to accept Donovan and the OSS in hopes of controlling both the man and the organization.[62]

The OSS emblem represented the global nature of its missions, which touched almost every nation in the world during the war. *Courtesy of H. Keith Melton.*

Regardless of JCS fears, the OSS quickly developed its major branches and hired personnel. One of the five major branches, the Research and Analysis (R&A) Branch was much like COI; it employed some of the finest minds in the United States; for example, Ralph Bunche was hired to "handle the subjects of colonial policy and administration, native problems, and race relations within the British Empire."[63] R&A experts sorted and analyzed data and prepared intelligence reports for the agency and the president. The other branches included the Secret Intelligence Branch (SI), which engaged in the covert collection of intelligence; the Counterintelligence Branch (X-2), which dealt primarily with enemy espionage; the Special Operations Branch (SO), which worked behind enemy lines, training and assisting resistance groups across Europe and Asia, supplying target information, and aiding downed airmen; and the Morale Operations Branch (MO), which created and distributed "black" propaganda, or propaganda that "deliberately falsifies its source."[64] By the time the OSS was abolished on October 1, 1945, it had developed "more than 40 branches and units with a well-chosen staff of almost 13,000 men and women."[65]

Over the course of World War II, the men and women of the OSS operated in some way—everything from fighting with the French Resistance behind enemy lines to preparing statistical reports on the population of Burma—in almost every nation in the world. Officers were selected by the OSS, and

those not recruited by Donovan or his staff were required to apply for the
privilege of serving. "Most of the top appointments in OSS tended to go to
Waspish candidates, especially to those from Ivy League schools," wrote historian Lawrence McDonald, "provoking critics to gibe that the agency's ac-
ronym actually stood for 'Oh So Social' and 'Oh Such Snobs.'"[66] Gaining a
place within the OSS—especially at the Research and Analysis Branch—was
for some an effective place to serve the country without placing one's body in
mortal danger. Barry Katz wrote:

> The Research and Analysis Branch mobilized a formidable battalion of
> progressive scholars whose vocation was to manipulate ideas, who
> understood the war in political terms, and who wanted to help. Wartime
> Washington was not Periclean Athens, Florence under the Medici, or
> Goethe's Weimar, but there remains something inspiring about it; even if
> the motives of particular individuals were often more pragmatic:
> transfers to the OSS were known in the army as "cellophane
> commissions"—you could see right through them, but they protected
> you from the draft.[67]

The R&A Branch was not the only one to receive criticism. Robert Sherwood, who was the chief of COI's Foreign Information Service, a speech writer
for Roosevelt, and a playwright (he won four Pulitzer Prizes between 1936 and
1949), disliked MO and disagreed with Donovan's affinity for the use of black
propaganda. Sherwood and others contended that propaganda emanating
from the United States should be based primarily on truth, not lies. Although
some believed that by its very nature MO work was immoral, the importance
of using secret agents who spread rumors and misleading information to
create and exacerbate internal discord had been acknowledged for centuries,[68]
and Donovan's views clearly prevailed in the disagreement.[69] Within the OSS,
MO became an important part of operations around the globe.

Aside from those who opposed the use of black propaganda, there were
critics of Donovan himself, some of whom employed his old nickname "Wild
Bill" against him, "depicting both Donovan and his agency as trigger happy
and irresponsible."[70] Looking back at the OSS and Donovan, former director of the CIA Ray S. Cline noted:

> "Wild Bill" deserves his sobriquet mainly for two reasons. First, he
> permitted the "wildest," loosest kind of administrative and procedural
> chaos to develop while he concentrated on recruiting talent wherever he

could find it—in universities, businesses, law firms, in the armed services, at Georgetown cocktail parties, in fact anywhere he happened to meet or hear about bright and eager young men and women who wanted to help. His immediate lieutenants and their assistants were all at work on the same task, and it was a long time before any systematic method of structuring the polyglot staff complement was worked out. Donovan really did not care. He counted on some able young men from his law firm in New York to straighten out the worst administrative messes, arguing that the record would justify his agency if it was good and excuse all waste and confusion.[71]

Donovan and his subordinates were for the most part very lucky in recruiting able young Americans to serve in the OSS. Indeed, it was the charisma and personal legend of Donovan that drew some to the organization. Journalist and OSS agent Edmond Taylor recalled his occasional frustration with OSS policies and his relationship with Donovan. "I stayed in OSS," Taylor remembered,

> though sometimes attached to it by nothing more tangible than the invisible presence of Donovan in my mind. . . . [Donovan] was a great believer in learning by doing, and his inspired amateurism helped create an atmosphere in OSS that sometimes recalled the satiric writings of Compton Mackenzie or Evelyn Waugh; on the other hand the fact that so many untrained, or undertrained, young Americans survived the hair-raising missions on which they were launched by OSS, achieving creditable or even impressive results in the process, suggests that the Donovan philosophy was not completely unsound.[72]

Certainly there were many agents, missions, and areas of operation in which the OSS failed to achieve its intended goals. In his article on the "Birth of Special Ops," Noel Poirier noted that the "OSS's shortcomings were the result of inexperience and insufficient resources," and historian Ian Sutherland stated that "OSS operations in North Africa were not strategically valuable."[73] Yet particularly in Europe, the contributions of the OSS were many. For example, during the Italian campaign, "the various divisions of the OSS, from the single individual in the field to the policymakers in the White House" played a role in the ultimate Allied victory.[74] Moreover, the Jedburgh teams (three-man Special Operations units that were parachuted behind enemy lines to work with resistance groups) in France, who sabotaged critical infrastructure utilized by the enemy, are credited with having delayed the German response to the D-day invasion by forty-eight hours.[75]

OSS work in Asia was more difficult than in Europe for a number of reasons, including the greater racial, linguistic, and cultural differences that had to be dealt with by agents on the ground. However, there were also philosophical issues concerning the reestablishment of European colonial empires. Donovan, with his proximity to the president, no doubt heard the rumblings regarding American participation in or opposition to returning Asian colonies to their former European masters, specifically the French. However, Donovan's personal position on the matter is unclear. Without doubt Donovan was (and had been throughout his career) a strong supporter of the British and the British war effort. But Donovan may have been critical of British colonial policy. Author Anthony Cave Brown, who had extensive access to Donovan's private papers and to those of his friend and colleague Otto C. Doering Jr., wrote: "His [Donovan's] papers show that he had deplored certain aspects of British capitalism and imperialism after World War I, especially in regard to British rule in India." Historian Stein Tønnesson reached different conclusions, specifically regarding French colonialism: "Since the OSS Director did not personally share Roosevelt's anti-French and anti-colonialist attitude," wrote Tønnesson, "he was perhaps a poor choice for carrying out the President's anti-French ambitions."[76]

Although the exact nature of Donovan's opinions on colonialism is uncertain, what is clear is that Donovan successfully maintained good relations with numerous Europeans. For example, Brown, like others, marveled at the close friendship between Donovan and Stephenson of MI6 and his good working relationship with Lord Louis Mountbatten—both of which clearly demonstrated that Donovan had amicable working relationships with Englishmen in their mutual quest for an Allied victory.[77] Donovan also had "a deep love of France," and he maintained cordial relationships with de Gaulle and with his chief of intelligence, Colonel André Dewavrin, as well as other Frenchmen.[78] Although Tønnesson agreed that Donovan's attitude was pro-French, he countered that with regard to French Indochina, "Donovan's loyalty to Roosevelt probably outweighed his Francophilia."[79]

There is no doubt that Donovan was loyal to the president and followed official directives that came his way. But Donovan was also clearly an independent thinker and a man of action, as his sobriquet Wild Bill indicated. Loyalty to Roosevelt in this context implied that Donovan would avoid aiding the French in their ultimate endeavor to regain their colony. But Donovan was a man deeply enamored of the role of intelligence and of the idea of

winning the war. In the absence of clear policies regarding America's position on European empires, Donovan and the OSS were mostly free to pursue
intelligence where and with whom they saw fit—including the French, who
were as eager to regain their colony as they were to defeat the enemy.

However, as discussed in chapter 1, for most of World War II French Indochina was one of the quieter sectors of the Pacific theater. By 1944, although
the drive to take back Japanese-held territory was well under way, no major
Allied operations had taken place in Indochina, and it was not at the top of
the list of strategic ground on which to stage an offensive. Yet it was not altogether unimportant. There was some consideration of an invasion of Indochina to establish a southern front against the Japanese in China, and reports on weather and the movement of troops and supplies were important
to American forces based in China, especially General Claire Chennault's
Fourteenth Air Force. How much Donovan knew specifically about the situation in French Indochina is "difficult to ascertain,"[80] but for him it was
simply not as important as China or the Philippines in the Pacific theater
and certainly did not equal the significance of the European theater.

However, in the possible event of an Allied invasion of French Indochina,
in 1944 the French Resistance seemed to be the best source of information for
the United States and its most likely ally. Donovan reported in a memorandum to President Roosevelt in July that both General de Gaulle and General
Antoine Bethouart had spoken to him about the Resistance movement in Indochina. The OSS was at that time working with General Zinovi Petchkoff
(whom Chiang Kai-shek called the French "ambassador" to China) on "the
question of some 500 French soldiers" who had been "trained for special operations and would, at the appropriate time, be dropped into Indo-China by
parachute."[81] Had they been dropped in, the French operatives might have
provided valuable services to the Allied war effort. On the other hand, they
might well have concentrated on preparations for France's postwar reclama-
tion of Indochina. Nevertheless, Donovan's concern in using the French paratroopers was over the question of theater jurisdiction (whether the operation fell within the theater of Britain's Admiral Mountbatten in India or
America's General Stilwell in China), not over philosophical quibbles about
the possible imperialist nature of this particular operation.[82]

In the summer of 1944 Donovan's most important mission was providing
the president, the JCS, and the military commanders with the intelligence
needed to achieve victory. Donovan's stance on imperialism aside, many of
the OSS hierarchy were well aware of Roosevelt's views on French imperialism and agreed with him. And through them, and possibly through Donovan,

"the OSS became one of the main instruments of [Roosevelt's] attitude and policy."[83] Bradley Smith wrote: "The senior American authorities were also uneasy and embarrassed that 'democratic America' was allied with exploitive yet impotent imperialists in Asia." But even those of "Donovan's people" who "were seriously upset by the prospect of aligning with European imperialism" worked well together, especially with the British, for the larger cause.[84] The OSS operatives most likely to be exposed to colonialism were outside the organization's hierarchy and probably would have grouped themselves into that portion of the American public whom Roosevelt believed "[couldn't] stomach" imperialism. But these men and women were also focused on their main goal, winning the war. And achieving that pragmatic objective left little room for ideological debate about the creation of a "free world" devoid of the uglier trappings of imperialism envisioned by Roosevelt in his finer moments.

In Indochina, trying to provide the French with support in the war against Japan while at the same time avoiding French efforts to reclaim colonial territory proved a difficult task for all involved—from the highest decision makers to the men on the ground in French Indochina. It certainly could in no way be guaranteed that support provided to fight Japan would not subsequently (or even simultaneously) be used against the Vietnamese. Yet the United States required information about the situation on the ground in Indochina and needed someone to gather it for them. While the OSS was struggling to find its place in French Indochina, others had already broken ground on intelligence gathering in the area, and the OSS would later attempt to capitalize on their successes, especially the work of Captain Milton Miles of the U.S. Navy and the highly effective international trio of men known as the GBT.

3

The First on the Ground: Miles, Meynier, and the GBT

The United States was not the only nation interested in acquiring intelligence on French Indochina. The British, Free French, and Chinese also sought information concerning Japanese troop strength and movements in hopes of gaining clues to their future plans. The British watched closely lest Japan succeed in bringing India into the GEACPS. The Free French under de Gaulle tried to assert their status as the legitimate government of France, but without endangering the nation's claim to sovereignty over Indochina. The Chinese feared that an assault on their southern flank might force Chiang Kai-shek and his ministers to flee even deeper into the interior of China. All four nations were enemies of the Japanese and of the Vichy French by virtue of circumstance, but none was in a position to get firsthand information from Vietnam. Thus, the critical question for all of them was how to obtain this needed intelligence. The answer came in the form of a unique trio of operatives known as the GBT.

"GBT" was made up of the initials of the surnames of three exceptional individuals: Laurence "Laurie" Gordon, Harry Bernard, and Frank "Frankie" Tan. In the years before the GBT network's collapse, Gordon provided information to the British, Bernard to the Americans, and Tan to the Chinese in what one OSS veteran described as "a really splendid example of international co-operation."[1] Gordon was the acknowledged leader of the group, and many simply referred to the three, and the information network that the GBT established, as the Gordon Group. Gordon was a man of wide-ranging background. Born in Canada, he was a British subject with a home in California, but his many business ventures took him around the world. After selling his coffee plantation in Kenya, he tried his hand in the highly lucrative oil business, managing drilling operations in Egypt, China, and Madagascar. In 1938 he was in Haiphong, French Indochina, directing oil operations for the Cal-Texaco Corporation, headquartered in Beaumont, Texas.[2]

When Japanese troops moved into the area in the fall of 1940, he chose to leave northern Vietnam for the United States. After establishing himself and his family in California in early 1941, he notified his employers of his change of residence, but Cal-Texaco was more interested in having him return to Southeast Asia to "look after the firm's interests." Gordon agreed and began making arrangements for his return, but the events of December 1941 changed his plans significantly. With the Japanese attack on Pearl Harbor and the mutual declarations of war, trekking to Indochina involved travel to a country occupied by the enemy—no easy feat from either side of the ocean. Thus, Cal-Texaco devised a plan to infiltrate Gordon into Indochina under "semiofficial cover."[3]

Coincidentally it was Bill Donovan's close associate Sir William Stephenson who provided the cover for Gordon. Stephenson, Winston Churchill's "man called Intrepid," helped Gordon join the British Secret Service, and Gordon was "secretly commissioned a captain in military intelligence." His assignment was to set up an intelligence network in Indochina in conjunction with the Free French Military Mission (FMM) stationed with Chiang Kai-shek's government in Chungking, but the task assigned Gordon was far easier said than done.[4]

Regardless of one's nationality, gathering intelligence in the China theater was difficult. General Tai Li, the head of Chiang Kai-shek's secret service organizations, attempted to control everything and everyone in China, especially with regard to information procurement. Where Tai Li ruled, he did so with an iron fist under the personal protection of the generalissimo himself. Tai Li's reputation was widespread: He was well known throughout China and within the U.S. intelligence community, as well as among the British and the French. In Washington he was known as an assassin (supposedly, he even murdered his own mother) who created concentration camps to incarcerate his political enemies. He disliked and distrusted both the French and the British, and they found him very difficult to work with under the best of circumstances. Within China it was difficult to move without the express permission of Tai Li's organization, and it was nearly impossible to get anything accomplished without the all-important "connections." Obtaining the necessary passes for travel and making the necessary introductions required a complicated procedure that few mastered. Hence, when Gordon stepped off the plane from New Delhi in June 1942 with two portable radios he had acquired from a friend there, he was entering a complicated world of both Chinese and French politics.[5]

Gordon quickly discovered the difficulties of trying to work within Tai Li's guidelines and the more formidable hurdles involved in working with the French Military Mission in Chungking. In 1942 de Gaulle was not the un-disputed leader of the Free French. Although he certainly had his support-ers, many also looked to the leadership of General Henri Giraud, a popular Resistance figure. There were also rivalries among the officers of the French mission, and trying to work with any one group only produced opposition from another. Gordon found himself unable to maneuver within the FMM, and he began looking elsewhere for official backing. U.S. military attaché Colonel Morris B. DePass Jr. introduced him to the influential Chinese admi-ral Yang Hsuan-cheng who "authorized Gordon to operate in the province of Kwangsi, with the understanding that he would not cooperate with the French intelligence services."[6]

Kwangsi, on the northeast border of Tonkin, was an excellent base of op-erations. In order to protect company interests, Gordon began by quietly re-connecting with Cal-Texaco employees still in the region,[7] but his work soon took on a different cast. Captain Archimedes Patti, an OSS operative who investigated the GBT as part of his own work in Indochina in February 1945, discovered that

> later, under the guise of a free-lancing agent, he [Gordon] traveled
> through Tonkin, Annam, and Cochinchina, renewing old contacts,
> regrouping loyal Frenchmen and Vietnamese, and purchasing quantities
> of gasoline and other commodities for the Chinese black market, while
> at the same time organizing a network of informers in the interest of
> salvaging company assets. What at first may have been a casual
> arrangement soon began to assume the characteristics of an amateur
> intelligence organization.[8]

In his first year of activity, in return for providing them information, Gor-don managed to obtain funds and equipment from the British and personnel from the Chinese. More importantly, he gained two American partners, Harry Bernard and Frank "Frankie" Tan. Bernard was an official of the British-owned Asian Tobacco Monopoly and an ex-employee of Cal-Texaco.[9] Described as "short on words and long on know-how," Bernard was an enig-matic and interesting figure.[10] The cool head, strong sense of efficiency, and willingness to be low profile that had made Bernard a model executive in peacetime now made him an invaluable asset to Gordon. In the early years of the GBT his role was usually overshadowed by that of the energetic Gordon. Yet it was Bernard's presence that assured the trio that the less-glamorous tasks of the network would be accomplished. OSS and French reports tended to list both Bernard and Tan as subordinate members of the GBT until early 1945. Tan's activities at that time, however, provided him with sufficient fame to make his the best-known story.

The youngest member of the group, Tan was a Chinese American, born in the United States and educated at the Boston Latin School. He came from a Cantonese family well versed in revolution: His father had been involved in the 1911 Revolution that brought down China's Ching Dynasty. After immigrating to the United States, the senior Tan became a successful doctor, but he still sensed a barrier between himself and his peers and felt "discriminated against by whites." Thus, with new opportunities seemingly opening up in China in the early 1930s, the Tan family chose to return to their homeland to try and help the Nationalist Chinese construct a stable and successful nation. After completing his college degree in engineering, Frank Tan went to work for General Small at Chiang Kai-shek's personal headquarters and, in so doing, cultivated numerous contacts among the Chinese. Conversant in both English and Chinese, he could function effectively in many settings and with many different nationalities. Tan also became involved with the British. While his training as an engineer had proven helpful in his work with General Small, it did not prepare him for the myriad roles he would come to play as a member of Gordon's group. Tan, like Gordon, received aid from the British—the British Security Service (MI5) provided Tan with some training in covert operations, and he also trained with the Tenth Rajputana Lancers. By 1938 he was in French Indochina, where he would remain directly involved for the next seven years.[11]

Tan was just twenty-six years-old when he met Gordon in Hanoi in 1938. Although he and Gordon became good friends early on, they were not involved together in intelligence work until Gordon's undercover return to Indochina in 1942. Tan was far from idle in the intervening years, however. His early exploits provided him with innumerable skills that made the GBT successful and that, after the Japanese coup de main in March 1945, made Tan the perfect candidate to be the first American to walk into Indochina with Ho Chi Minh.

In the early phases of Japan's war with China, Tan smuggled U.S. military goods into China, a task that required not only covert skills but also courage and common sense. All of these attributes were tested early on when he was captured by the Japanese in 1941 after boarding a ship scheduled to depart for Hong Kong. Tan had been using his many connections throughout Vietnam to facilitate his movement as a courier of secret documents between China and Indochina, and a Japanese patrol boat, suspicious of Tan's activities, pulled alongside the docked ship and seized Tan for questioning. Sensing his dire circumstances, Tan looked around the small interrogation room for any possible means of escape, but found none. Thinking on his feet, Tan complained to the Japanese that he had a serious case of dysentery and needed to go to the bathroom. The Japanese, suspecting a ruse, refused his request. Tan was not to be put off that easily, however. He made the complaint again and began taking his pants down as if to relieve himself on the spot. The disgusted Japanese officers sent him on to the bathroom, locked the door, and posted a guard outside. Tan went out the window and fled to the safety of the American-owned "Texaco House."

Because Japan and the United States were not yet at war, the Japanese could not forcibly arrest a U.S. citizen on U.S. property. In the middle of the night, Tan was stuffed into the trunk of a car and driven to the harbor, where the captain of a Norwegian ship bound for Hong Kong let him on board.[12] The Japanese continued their pursuit, but once the neutral ship was under way they could not force it to halt. Greatly frustrated, the Japanese patrol boat traveled alongside Tan's ship hoping to obtain authorization to take him off. Luckily, they failed to receive it, and Tan reached Hong Kong safely. From there his exploits continued with a British military mission to the Burma Road.[13]

Tan's escape on the neutral Norwegian ship would not be his last, for after the bombing of Pearl Harbor Norwegian ships and their captains became even more useful to Tan and the GBT. The network chartered neutral ships to transport military goods from warehouses in French Indochina to Shanghai. The stock passed right under the noses of the Japanese as the GBT slipped it out of Haiphong Harbor on the way to Rangoon and the Burma Road. On just such a mission, Tan was again captured by the Japanese. He had just completed a deal selling aviation fuel to the French to keep it out of Japanese hands and was preparing to depart Vietnam when he was arrested by the Japanese a second time.[14] The evidence of his recent activities, a check from the French worth $400,000, was in his wallet. The Japanese interrogated and searched him, but they failed to examine the contents of his wallet. He was released and quickly made his way to a Norwegian ship. Once again Tan, and in this case substantial funds as well, made it back to Allied territory unscathed.[15]

Tan attributes his success and that of the GBT to their ability to "start at the bottom." Each member of the group started with the simplest of covert tasks and then developed his talents over time. Almost immediately all three men could provide the Allies with what Tan termed "the first part of intelligence," or general knowledge such as information on the countryside and "how to get from A to B with nobody seeing you." "General knowledge," Tan correctly pointed out, "is not acquired overnight. It takes a legit business that takes you into the country so you know the country and the people. You know who can be trusted."[16] All three men had legitimate business in the country. Since they had conducted official business in Vietnam prior to the outbreak of the war, they could continue to move in the same official social circles, bringing their closest friends and colleagues from before World War II into their network.

These innumerable connections provided them a very broad base of support. Gordon reported that he was "in a position to call on a readymade circle of loyal French friends who knew and trusted me."[17] His "number two" agent within the French network was his secretary, Helen Tong, an ethnic Chinese refugee from Vietnam. Helen's sister Janet also worked in the GBT office, and their mother, Madame Tong, ran the GBT "household." All three were valuable employees—as much for their ability to translate from Chinese into both French and English as for their office and organizational skills. Gordon's "number one," or most important, agent, however, was André Lan, known under the code designation "agent No. 22," a French citizen and longtime resident of Indochina who directed the actions of many of the French civilians in the network. Lan later received the Legion d'Honneur for his work.[18]

Bernard functioned with equal ease in the period before the Japanese coup. Indeed, American civilians repatriated from Vietnam in early 1943 reported to OSS officials in China that they had moved "freely" about the city and had also been able to obtain passes to travel outside the city.[19] Tan's Chinese contacts were also indispensable. When the group needed to enter Saigon covertly, they went to a Chinese Texaco agent, one of Tan's contacts, for help and got results. All in all, the network of the GBT was formed by a "family of volunteers" of many nationalities: Canadian, British, American, French, Chinese, Vietnamese, and Norwegian.

None of the three principals made any money for his efforts, although their expenses were usually covered by different individuals or organizations. The GBT eventually represented the interests of and received funding from the Chinese, especially Admiral Yang, the head of intelligence for the Chinese National Military Council (under Tai Li), and General Chang Fa-kwei, commander of the Nationalist troops in southern Kwangsi and Kwangtung provinces; the British MI5; the Free French; and a diverse array of Americans, including Generals Stilwell and Wedemeyer and General

Chennault, commander of the Fourteenth Air Force in China. Gordon, Bernard, and Tan considered themselves to be the personal representatives of Chennault and had a pass to act on his behalf anywhere the Fourteenth Air Force had facilities. Because of the premium placed upon intelligence from Vietnam, all of these groups wanted to control GBT activities and wanted access to the personnel in their network. However, their success by mid-1942 can be attributed to their willingness to work with everyone while being subservient to no one. Although many looked to the Gordon Group for intelligence on Indochina, the GBT was not the only organization struggling to develop an effective network.

The OSS worked diligently from the outbreak of the Pacific war to establish a presence in that theater, but with little success. General Douglas MacArthur had his own intelligence service and saw no need for the OSS within his area of operations. But as historian R. Harris Smith noted: "The complete exclusion of OSS from the South Pacific had one important organizational side-effect—Donovan was forced to maintain a Chinese base for Asian operations."[20] The founding of the "China base" soon pushed the OSS into Indochinese affairs as well. Nevertheless, as with anything in China in the 1940s, establishing a base of operations was no easy task. Donovan was thus forced to look for a man who had knowledge of the Chinese and who might achieve some success working within and around the limits established by Tai Li and Chiang Kai-shek. The man chosen for the job was U.S. Naval Captain Milton "Mary" Miles.

President Roosevelt had given primary responsibility for collecting intelligence in China to the navy early in the war, and in March 1942 Miles was sent to Chungking to head Naval Group China. His main tasks were to develop weather stations and a system of coast watchers to support the Pacific Fleet. Miles was in many ways an excellent choice for this post. After graduating from the Naval Academy in 1922, he began a five-year tour of duty at the China Station. As a result of this posting, Miles became familiar with the numerous ports of China's coastline, as well as with the rivers flowing out of China. He was interested in Chinese culture and history and managed to learn a bit of both Cantonese and Mandarin. It was his appreciation of Chinese cuisine and language that first favorably impressed the all-important Tai Li.[21]

Miles and Tai Li quickly developed a good working relationship, and Tai Li agreed to help Miles pursue his intelligence goals. Because Naval Group China functioned at the pleasure of the Chinese government, Miles concluded that the best way to accomplish his mission was to establish a "friendship

Commodore Milton "Mary" Miles and Tai Li worked well together throughout the war, becoming friends in addition to professional colleagues. *Courtesy of Charles Miles.*

plan" to coordinate an American and Chinese intelligence network. It appeared that with the proper signatures from their respective governments, the friendship plan would proceed, with the U.S. Navy as the front-runner in intelligence collection in China and in neighboring Indochina.

In the fall of 1942, Donovan, "desperately eager to carry out large O.S.S. activities somewhere," looked to Miles's relationship with the Chinese as an opportunity for the OSS as well. The agent Donovan sent to evaluate the Miles–Tai Li connection reported back that Miles "had subversive warfare prospects sewn up, and OSS could either accept his offer and be cut into a position of action or reject it and stand little chance of developing any operational base there." Accepting the navy's monopoly on intelligence in the region, at least for the time, Donovan appointed Miles chief of the OSS for the Far East that December.[22]

The friendship plan was formalized and given final government approval in April 1943 as the Sino-American Cooperative Organization (SACO), with Tai Li as director and Miles as deputy director. SACO would engage in guerrilla training, espionage, sabotage, and radio interception. The Chinese supplied the manpower, and the Americans, the training, arms, facilities, and other equipment. Miles had worked hard to forge the necessary ties to make SACO work for the U.S. Navy and for the Chinese, and he was not especially happy at his OSS appointment. An agent sent by Donovan to evaluate Miles and the friendship plan reported back that Miles was "'100 percent Navy and oo percent OSS.'" Furthermore, Miles stated to the agent that he would not tolerate any "interference" from the OSS, would not accept "any personnel not selected by himself," and would not act upon any "directive which he did not deem wise." Miles even threatened to "sever all connections" with the OSS if his conditions were not accepted.[23]

Miles's relationship with the OSS was strained before SACO even got off the ground. In Washington in early 1943, Miles met with Donovan and the OSS General Planning Board and was disturbed by what he saw and heard. For Miles, who considered himself to be a close friend of the Chinese, the attitudes among the men present were intolerable. He wrote: "What bothered me most was that among those present were some before-the-war businessmen of Asia who still hewed to the 'white supremacy' line, as well as some others who were 'follow-the-British-Imperial-line' chaps, and even one or two 'let's-make-poor-old-China-over' gentlemen. . . . About the Washington offices of the O.S.S. there were some who had little regard for China's sovereignty and who also had a positive dislike of Chiang Kai-shek's government."[24]

Thus, from the very beginning Miles's pairing with the OSS was not a happy match. Bradley Smith, author of *The Shadow Warriors: O.S.S. and the Origins of the C.I.A.*, has concluded that "since neither Tai Li nor Miles was anxious to see O.S.S. develop and prosper, the SACO agreement was a straightjacket that long restricted and constrained O.S.S. operations in the Far East."[25]

Miles's intelligence group did have its share of successes in China. General Chennault commanded a "sizeable group of Miles' Naval officers" who provided the Fourteenth Air Force with "shipping intelligence, did photo-interpretation and kept us in constant communication with the Pacific Fleet." "This effective liaison," Chennault stated, "paid enormous dividends in attacks on enemy shipping."[26] His praise carried a great deal of weight in the China theater, and, much as in the case of the GBT, his approval allowed SACO a great deal of freedom of movement. As SACO was being formalized in Washington and Chungking, Miles discovered that Indochina also fell within his purview.

In his initial study of the situation in northern Vietnam, Miles found that in terms of intelligence, "there were no such activities" going on and that furthermore, "General Tai could do almost nothing so far as Indo-China was concerned." Thus, Miles would have to look elsewhere to fulfill his Indochina obligations. Miles's first obstacle in extending his coast watchers along the shores of Tonkin involved determining who to work with in Vietnam. General Tai explained to him that there were "French, British, and Chinese groups, as well as several different native stocks, each of whom had its individual aims and ideas" and that among the French there were numerous groups contesting for power. In the spring of 1943, Miles requested Donovan's help in sorting out this situation. Donovan sent him back to China, but had him make an important stop in North Africa on the way.[27]

In the spring of 1943, General Henri Honoré Giraud had assumed control over French North Africa, now free from Vichy and German control, and was happy to meet with Miles at Donovan's request. Giraud recommended that Miles contact a young hero of the French navy, Commander Robert Meynier, temporarily unassigned after having just received the Croix de Guerre for incapacitating and boarding both a German and an Italian submarine. Miles and Meynier liked each other immediately, and Miles concluded that he had found the man to help him. There was, however, a catch: If Miles wanted to hire Meynier, he also had to accept Meynier's wife as part of the deal. Upon hearing about the young woman who would become known as the "Princess of SACO," Miles was eager to have her join the mission.

Katiou Meynier, a lovely Eurasian, came from an influential Vietnamese family. According to Miles's sources, her uncle, Hoang Trong Phu, was the viceroy of Tonkin and a member of Emperor Bao Dai's Privy Council. His influence, it was reported, extended throughout the country, including control over the largest group of political appointees in all of Indochina. Her father, Do Huu Thinh, was a powerful man in his own right. He reportedly controlled the major groups of political appointees in Cochinchina. In his diary, Miles made the following entry regarding Madame Meynier and her father:

> Her father was the leader of the biggest group of revolutionary
> nationalists in Cochin China. They are commonly called Communists,
> Reds, Revolutionaries and Bolsheviks. Actually most of these
> revolutionary nationalists are concerned, not with over-throwing the
> Government, but with obtaining greater representation for the native
> element in the French-run Government. They do not in any way
> consider themselves fully capable of throwing the French out nor [of]
> running the Government if the French were thrown out. I do not believe,

Robert Meynier, seen here at a banquet with Madame Tai Li, continually ran into difficulties with French officials in China, eventually resulting in his withdrawal from the theater. *Courtesy of Charles Miles.*

from all that I have heard, that they are even generally anxious for the French to leave, although there has been some incitement toward this goal. The most prominent part they play is to obtain a greater native representation in the National Government. A few years ago, when this large group, of which Mme. Meynier's father was the leader, became appeased by the French Government, they split off from more radical

Reds and became what is known as the Democratic-wing or the Indo-China Democratic Party. Mme. Meynier's father was the leader of this group and brought with him most of his followers. They seem to change their name at random to fit the occasion. Some people believe they are anti-French. Mme. Meynier, having lived with them all of her life may be considered as being an expert on the subject.[28]

Madame Meynier, Miles concluded, was "particularly anxious to guard her countrymen both from the Japanese and from other foreign nationalities," a sentiment that fit Miles's needs as well her own.[29] Thus, Miles concluded that there were numerous benefits to be gained from Madame Meynier and her family's influence. However, General Giraud informed him that bringing the Meyniers on board might pose, as he stated, "a difficulty of the slightest."[30]

The "difficulty" was Katiou Meynier's detention in a German internment camp in occupied France. Miles agreed to the condition of freeing her, leaving the OSS to arrange her escape. The OSS called on the British Special Operations Executive (SOE) and both Generals Giraud and de Gaulle to help set up her rescue. Although a French "commando unit" managed to stage a successful "prison break," three British and seven French agents reportedly lost their lives freeing the woman who would come to be called the Princess of SACO. Although saddened at the deaths of the Frenchmen, General Giraud reportedly considered the raid "worth the loss because of her [Katiou Meynier's] standing in Indo-China. [Because] it is apparent that the Annamites worship the ground on which she walks both because she is a Princess and a Priestess."[31]

According to Madame Meynier, after her liberation she was passed around France like a "letter with a stamp" until she could be flown out to London, where she was received by Dr. Wellington Ku, Chinese ambassador to England. Unfortunately for Madame Meynier, upon her arrival the British government had a few questions for her.[32] The SOE had been misled as to the actual nature of the operation to rescue Madame Meynier. Again, the division in French politics came into play: The SOE supported de Gaulle, and the plan to bring Miles and Meynier together was backed primarily by Giraud. Nevertheless, Miles had already arranged to keep Katiou Meynier undercover in London. Commander Junius Morgan of the OSS sidestepped the British and checked her into the Ritz Hotel as Miss Paula Martin, a member of the U.S. Army Women's Auxiliary Corps (WAC). She was instructed to pretend that she had a sore throat and could not speak, and her

English-speaking companion would respond for her as necessary. Katiou played her part well, and, with her refined features and mannerisms, she passed the time in London uneventfully. A few days later she was flown out to Calcutta, where she was reunited with her anxious husband.[33]

There was yet another difficulty involved in establishing the Meynier mission in Indochina. To facilitate the creation of the network in Indochina, Robert Meynier had managed to "spring" a group of "young Annamites, French officers, and priests" from a German prisoner of war (POW) camp in North Africa. The British had a few questions for this group as well. In order to evade the authorities, the group had assumed the label "Philippine Army troops of liberation" and boarded a British freighter to Bombay. They arrived without incident because, according to Miles, "no one they had to deal with knew the difference between the language and appearance of Filipinos and Annamites." The entire group, including the Meyniers, hid in Calcutta in a house rented by "U.S. WACs" and "Filipinos" until Miles could make arrangements to get them to Chungking.[34]

With these tasks behind them, Miles and Meynier could focus on their plans for their mission: developing an intelligence network in Indochina. Miles reported on October 15, 1943, that "for over a year I have been investigating the political activities in Indo-China, have talked to various nationalists on the subject, and at the present time have under my command a unit of French and Annamite people who are fully cognizant of conditions in their home land, both in the past and at the present time."[35] However optimistic Miles might have been, the situation would not proceed as he had hoped. The Meyniers and the "Filipinos" encountered problems from the moment they arrived in China.

Robert Meynier's papers, signed by both Giraud and de Gaulle, dictated that he would report to General Zinovi Petchkoff and his chief of staff, Colonel Emblanc of the FMM in Chungking. Both Petchkoff and Emblanc were unhappy that they had not been included in any of the arrangements for the Meynier group and that they did not "have complete control" of the group. Initial meetings with both men were a disaster. In a burst of anger, Colonel Emblanc said that he would deny them all entrance into Indochina. General Petchkoff threatened to leave immediately for North Africa and "take his fighting French with him." Using his considerable charm, Meynier managed to reassure the general that the Meynier mission was in no way threatening to either Petchkoff's position or the FMM as a whole. Even so, Petchkoff once again became "very much disturbed when he heard that Mrs. Meynier accompanied the party" because, he contended, "since she is an Annamite it will help to build up the Annamite's [*sic*] strength in Indo-China against the Frenchmen." Luckily, Meynier found a way to pacify the FMM, at least for a brief time. Commander Meynier discovered that the FMM had not received any funds from the British (on whom they were dependent) in several months, and he "was able to smooth things out a little by turning over two or three thousand dollars of O.S.S. funds to 'keep them from starving.'" As a result the FMM let Miles and the OSS in on some of their intelligence from Indochina. Petchkoff agreed to detach Meynier for temporary duty with SACO, and he and the "Filipinos" began to plan in earnest. Optimistic about the success of this new venture, Miles reported to Donovan, who had become a brigadier general in March, that "within a few months we can have 200,000 to 300,000 agents working for us in Indo-China if we want them."[36]

Had the Meynier mission succeeded in full, the OSS would have had an excellent covert network in Vietnam. Meynier planned to develop a system of informers and agents who would "propagandize the natives and encourage their resistance to the Japanese"; "damage" and "annoy" Japanese shipping; smuggle contraband materials into China; and "persuade French naval officers and enlisted men to scuttle their ships at the proper time if they could not bring them out to fight beside us."[37] And by mid-October Miles had already ascertained much from his study of Indochina. In a memo requesting permission to have propaganda leaflets dropped in Vietnam, Miles noted that there were "certain revolutionary parties which exist in great numbers to the west of the city [Saigon]." "These revolutionary parties are not," Miles added, "pro-Japanese. In general, they are pro-native."[38] Miles believed that the leaflets, prepared in both Vietnamese and French, would be very effective in convincing these groups, as well as others in Cochinchina, to support the Allied cause. One reason for Miles's optimism was that he believed Katiou Meynier would have great success propagandizing to the Vietnamese on behalf of the United States. He boasted in his diary that "she has the greatest respect for Americans and has become aware of the fact that of all the nationalities involved in Indo-China, the Americans are not out after territorial gains."[39] In addition, he considered her a "natural" in dealing with the "natives," in part because she traveled with official sanction but also because "she was a princess in her own right, as well as a priestess of Annam."[40]

Her pedigree aside, Katiou Meynier was a quick study at both English and Chinese and was listed under her alias Paula Martin as the author of Miles's propaganda plan for Cochinchina. The plan was to be directed at, among others, the "Indo Chinese Democratic Party"—no doubt because of her father's participation in it. The party was described as being "comprised of all Indo-Chinese naturalized or born French," but, contended Madame Meynier, it was erroneously classed as "anti-French" because its members desired the eventual independence of Vietnam. In working on the report, she took pains to establish the "Indo Chinese Democratic Party" and the "7 or 8 groups of so-called 'revolutionary Nationalists'" as both nationalistic and anti-Japanese. Section C of the plan clarified: "Do not forget that for the Cochin Chinese, it is not only the 'revolutionary Nationalists' who enjoy the armed protection of the Japanese, but also the administration, the civilians & the French Army (uprising 1940). As Governor General Decoux has so often said, the Japanese are helping us to defend Indo China and to preserve French sovereignty there."[41]

Katiou Meynier, described as "half-pint size, cute, curvaceous and once the winner of a beauty contest," had clearly impressed and charmed Miles and many others around her, but she was not without her detractors.[42] Naval Lieutenant Robert Larson declared that he would not "care to make a habit of traveling with a spoiled woman." Upon arriving in Nanning with the Meynier group, Larson wrote to Miles regarding the trip and their new location and could not refrain from including in his report a brief tirade regarding Madame Meynier. His exasperation reflected both her upbringing as a "princess," and the fact that Larson was on a military mission with a job to do and certainly had not expected to cater to a "princess" along the way. His missive regarding Madame Meynier unintentionally added a degree of humor to the daily report. He huffed,

> If she wanted to make pee-pee in the middle of the night, she woke him [Meynier] up, and therefore me too, in order that he might accompany her. One of her cats got lost, and everything stopped at 0530 in the morning to find the animal. As for shopping, I'm surprised that the commander has any money to his name, and what she wanted, she kept after till she got it.

Undoubtedly aware of Miles's growing fondness for the Meyniers, Larson softened his tone and added, "I continue to think Madame is very charming, very likeable and everything a woman should be."[43]

Once installed in Nanning, the Meynier group, including Katiou, set up shop quickly, securing housing for themselves and the Vietnamese working with them and setting up a radio in the country outside the city. Problems for the group were already developing, however. OSS agents were angling for more direct control over the production and use of propaganda and the use

A portrait of President Franklin Roosevelt looks on as Katiou Meynier (the "Princess of SACO"), Tai Li, and Milton Miles raise their glasses in a toast. *Courtesy of Charles Miles.*

of "psychological warfare." The OSS appointed Major Jack de Sibour to head the "Indo-China Mission" under Miles. Meynier, it was proposed, would work directly with de Sibour although still technically under Miles and SACO and officially tied to the FMM. The cable to Miles announcing the addition of de Sibour clearly separated men trained by the OSS from those who were not. "Morale Operations (Subversive Propaganda), known here as MO, is responsibility which rests entirely on OSS," read the cable; "the over-all plans must be fully coordinated as it is a field which must be fully understood and carefully handled by trained men."[44] De Sibour was, it noted, one of these men. The memo announcing de Sibour's appointment also noted, in what could be construed as an anti–Meynier mission comment, that the Chinese might "look with disfavor at a too close open relationship between U.S. and French interests as far as Indo-China is concerned."[45]

De Sibour, for his part, was also ready to make solid plans for MO work in Vietnam. He expressed his conviction that since "nothing on the MO side" had been done "outside the French SO Mission," an American MO section should be set up as soon as possible. And although clearly connected to Miles and SACO, the Meynier group was viewed as a French mission with obvious difficulties. For example, although the MO plan acknowledged that Katiou Meynier operated officially with the group, her family connections were described as having been "at one time anti-French" but as having since "come over to the French way of thinking" and as "cooperating with them." Additionally, de Sibour pointed out the myriad problems associated with the political tug-of-war that Giraud and de Gaulle seemed to be having over control of the FMM and the Meynier crowd. But putting all of this aside, de Sibour concluded that the assets of Meynier's group—"their perfect knowledge of the country" and language skills, and the "scarcity of reliable agents" as compared to "those available under their control"—made them the Americans' best option for successfully penetrating Vietnam through "rumors, counterfeiting and forgery, bribery and blackmail and 'black' radio."[46] Nevertheless, no matter what de Sibour and the OSS might have concluded, the French situation in Chungking at that time prevented Miles, Meynier, and de Sibour from accomplishing their goals in Vietnam. The split between the Gaullists and the Giraudists made Meynier's position untenable: Meynier was increasingly considered the appointee of Giraud, whereas the FMM in Chungking was backed by de Gaulle. The fact that Tai Li supported the Meynier mission (as sanctioned by Miles) did little to help their position. Tai Li accused the FMM in Chungking of spying on the Chinese government, and the French countered by charging Tai Li with murdering French nationals "to insure unimpeded Chinese subversion of the Vietnamese in Tonkin."[47]

As a result of the ongoing power politics, the Meyniers were not permitted to enter Indochina. A number of the "Filipinos" however, did gain entry. In particular, a Vietnamese priest, Father Bec, made contact with other Catholic clergy in Indochina and, along with others from the Meynier mission, brought news and information out of Vietnam. Father Bec took a special interest in downed American fliers. He was able to bring back the names of American pilots whose planes had been shot down and information on their fate. He also distributed leaflets telling friendly Indochinese how to identify themselves and be helpful to downed American aviators. Miles reported that Chennault and his men "were enthusiastic" and that they "even offered to help put representatives of the Meynier group into the country by parachute." However, according to Miles, "the more the Meyniers accomplished, the more enmity they encountered from the French Mission in Chungking. Father Bec bore the brunt of this for a long time because he was so outstanding a worker."[48]

Evaluations of the accomplishments of the Meynier group differ. Historian Ronald Spector stated that Meynier established a successful network of agents in Indochina, many of whom "operated inside French government agencies and even inside the French intelligence office." "They sent back," he continued, "a steady stream of information on field fortifications, troop movements, bombing targets, and local political developments."[49] Miles contended that for the rest of the war, he "received a continuous stream of information—weather, prisoners, status of wounded men, intelligence on shipping, reports about Japanese planes—and an amazing amount of port and maritime information."[50] Certainly the arrangement paid off in October 1943 when coast watchers reported a Japanese convoy of nine to ten ships on the way to Haiphong. The relevant information was passed on to Chennault, who succeeded in dropping mines in the harbor while other aircraft diverted attention by bombing the Japanese at Haiphong airbase. Miles reported the mission to be a complete success: "As the planes came over, the ships in the harbor panicked. A three-thousand-ton freighter, hurrying out, struck one of the newly laid mines and blew up at just the right spot to put a cork tightly in the bottle. The entrance to Haiphong Harbor was never completely open again during all the rest of the war."[51]

In addition, Admiral William F. Halsey Jr. also found the Meynier net quite effective. As Miles noted:

On January 11, 1945, the Indo-Chinese coast watchers whom Captain Meynier and his princess wife had succeeded in putting to work, paid in full for all the cost and effort of our work with them. This came about because Admiral William F. Halsey, Jr., preparing for an attack about which we knew nothing, asked us for targets in Indo-Chinese waters.

With this request before us, we promptly alerted such port officials, lighthouse keepers, customs officials, and others who had orders to come on the air in special emergencies "by the order of Commodore Miles." Though Meynier himself had been gone for months, the net he and his wife had established responded instantly. Within a few hours we in Chungking had a wonderfully complete list of ships in Camranh Bay, Saigon, and other ports under Japanese control. We even knew a good deal about their sizes, speeds, and cargoes. One lighthouse keeper reported a twenty-six-ship convoy that had passed that morning, and he gave its course and speed. So many messages gave us information for Admiral Halsey that he told me later that it was embarrassing, in a way. With so much information on which to work, he was compelled to change many of his designations. As it was, he detailed just enough planes for each target and as a result he managed to "cover the waterfront." In fact, his fliers were so successful that they sank forty ships that day, for a total of 120,000 tons, and among them were a Japanese cruiser and eleven other naval craft.[52]

OSS officer Archimedes Patti was not as charitable. "The Meynier mission, which took on so much importance in splitting the French, was a disappointing failure to O.S.S.," he wrote. "It made little progress in penetrating Indochina and OSS did not receive the military information Donovan had anticipated and Miles had promised."[53] The most realistic evaluation of their efforts, however, is more mixed. Certainly the Meynier network never produced the spine-tingling intelligence for which Donovan had hoped. But as is clearly indicated by both Chennault and Halsey, the Meynier group did provide valuable information on bombing targets and shipping information.

In addition to the Meynier network, Miles had one other plan in the works with regard to Vietnam. He planned to utilize the "mountain tribesmen" of the highlands for "guerrilla warfare and espionage against the Japanese." This "Special Military Plan for Indochina" was suggested by a member of Miles's staff, Lieutenant George Devereaux, who, prior to the war, had researched the ethnic Meo. According to the plan, specially trained agents would be parachuted in to establish friendly relations with the mountain tribesmen. They would then organize and train them for guerrilla warfare and would parachute arms, medicines, and other supplies into their base camps. The plan was approved by the OSS, the U.S. Navy, and the Fourteenth Air Force, and Chennault even "promised to launch diversionary air raids to cover the parachute drop."[54] Regardless of the support from many quarters, nothing came of Miles's Special Military Plan for Indochina.

In fact, Miles's endeavors in the area were quickly coming to a halt. Added to his disappointment that the promise of the Meynier mission was only partially fulfilled were the incessant, and mutual, difficulties with the OSS. Donovan and others frequently complained that although in name an OSS officer, Miles demonstrated no loyalty to the organization and provided all of the first-rate intelligence to the navy first. For his part, Miles was continually irritated by what he perceived as the OSS's drive for control of everything intelligence-related in China. In addition, whereas the OSS viewed itself as openly friendly to the Chinese Nationalist government, Miles was disgusted by the preponderance of "old China hands" within the OSS; they were, in his view, incapable of working with the Chinese as equals. The mutual dissatisfaction resulted in Miles's quitting as chief of the OSS for the Far East and in Donovan's firing him during a most unproductive conversation in December 1943.[55] Nevertheless, even after the conclusion of Miles's duties with the OSS in the Far East, the Meynier operation continued to function throughout 1944. Lieutenant Larson became the chief liaison officer with Robert Meynier in Nanning.

Lieutenant Larson's reports demonstrate his research on and growing understanding of Vietnam. "The adage, 'when in Rome, do as the Romans do' is nowhere of more significance than it is in Indo-China at the present time," wrote Larson. "The Japanese occupation of the country has been carried on in an intelligent fashion. The government has been left for the most part in the hands of the people—or at least of the 'functionnaires' and mandarins who exercised authority before the war." Unfortunately, Larson had more good things to say about the effectiveness of Japanese rule than about the efficiency of OSS propaganda efforts, which he described as "sadly inadequate" and "more detrimental than otherwise."[56]

American propaganda efforts, asserted Larson, showed "a lack of understanding of the country. This is not a primitive people. Indeed, upon undertaking the conquest of this country in 1858, the French found there a political and social organization which has continued to serve as the basis for their administration." In subsequent pages, Larson utilized the words of numerous French officers—such as Captain H. Rieunier of the French navy, who cited the "intelligence of the race" in prophesizing Vietnamese leadership of the "entire kingdom" in years to come—to demonstrate his earlier point that the Vietnamese should be approached as an evolved society. Larson also pointed out the inefficiencies of colonial rule and the French habit of simultaneously praising yet brutally oppressing the Indochinese, who righteously demanded a voice in their own country.[57]

Although Larson had clearly done his homework on the situation, the influence of Katiou Meynier on the young lieutenant can still be detected:

> If many Annamites have clamored for a greater voice in their
> government, it is not a new development, and it is not in the guise of the
> literal implications of the title they bear "Revolutionary Nationalists." It
> is evident that they desire eventual independence of their country, but
> they admit that it is not an immediate possibility. An important phase of
> the propaganda directed towards Indo-China should emphasize the
> willingness of the United Nations to prepare gradually for the freedom of
> the country. . . . The example of the Philippines has already endeared us

to the Annamites because they want and deserve a similar policy to be followed in their country. They also consider our treatment of Cuba as proof of our lack of colonial ambition and of our belief in the right of self-government.[58]

His reports between February and September 1944 reflect both his own and Robert Meynier's escalating frustration with the situation. Larson blamed Miles's OSS successor, Lieutenant Colonel John Coughlin, as well as the French for the group's failed efforts. In March 1944 Larson protested that the "OSS has at least 20 portable radio sets and has had them for some time. I have been screaming for some time to no avail, and it makes me more than disgusted to see Coughlin not only complaining about the lack of results from here, but also siding with Emblanc and not sending us the materiel we need." He went on to say that "the thing which angers me more than anything else is the attempt [by the OSS] to place the Meynier group in the category of agents [provocateurs] and to scare them. None of us will scare." When visited by OSS agent Austin Glass, who was charged with developing SI work for Indochina, Larson's ire was piqued even more by what he considered to be an extremely personal attack. Larson wrote to Naval Commander D. D. Wight:

Glass admits that, among other things, Coughlin had ordered him to investigate the rumors that I have been sleeping with Madame [Meynier]. Rumors to that effect are probably to be expected in a job like this, and I can shrug them off when they come from outsiders. However, when someone like Coughlin takes stock in them and doesn't come to me about it, I am darned disgusted.[59]

At the conclusion of Glass's visit, Larson felt relatively positive about Glass and the report he would write for the OSS, and he was more hopeful that he would receive the radios and other equipment he had requested, but he was still quite hostile toward Coughlin. In a confidential letter to Wight he explained:

Glass has left convinced of the potential value of the Meynier organization, amazed at what has gone on in the past, and with a high personal regard for us. I think he will try, but with Coughlin, I don't think he will meet with much success. Coughlin is only about seven years older than I am. There are many times when I think he acts even younger and less experienced than I.[60]

In fact, Larson appeared to be insulted by the inference that he was a part of the OSS at all. "Coughlin informed Glass that I am an OSS officer," huffed Larson; "I have not been consulted on the matter and I have not been informed that such is the case. I have not the slightest desire to become one of his officers or to become a part of the OSS organization."[61] Larson continued to say that he considered himself "a Naval officer and under the orders of Captain Miles" and not subservient to Coughlin. He promised to do "everything in his power" to bring about cooperation between the OSS and the Meynier mission, but he contended hotly to both Glass and Wight that he would "need a little more than throat cutting from the other side" to make it happen. Meynier, Larson made clear, was equally unhappy with the OSS and with the FMM and continually threatened to "pack up and go."[62]

Although sympathetic to Larson's complaints and Meynier's frustrations, Wight encouraged the two to continue their work. In response to Larson's letter of March 26, Wight wrote: "I hope that you will do your best to keep the Commander [Meynier] from kicking over the traces. Even though it may not look like it from Nanning, there is, I think, some progress being made and this progress might well be entirely counteracted if Cdr. Meynier throws up the sponge."[63] Perhaps it was the OSS connection with Emblanc and the FMM that colored Larson's and the Meyniers' view of the OSS and vice versa; however, regardless of the reason, relations between the parties mostly failed to improve. Larson's protests continued for the next several months, and by June they indicated the growing disfavor of yet another organization, which Larson believed had been influenced by the OSS.[64]

Captain Mullens of what Larson called the "Air Ground Rescue Forces" based in Kunming further curtailed Meynier's and Larson's activities.[65] Mullens asked Larson and Meynier "to keep hands off" of rescue operations in Indochina. Both men believed this to be a rather strange request since "nothing had been done [by the United States] in Indo-China [for downed pilots]," "an impression which had been emphasized time and time again by the very pilots who fly over the country." Larson reiterated what he believed to be myriad possibilities for rescue operations and demanded Mullens provide some explanation. Mullens informed him that the issue was simply "a matter of a lack of trust" between his organization and the Meynier group. Although Larson restated the backgrounds and training (done mostly by Americans) of the members of the organization, he met with little success. Apparently, neither the French nor the Americans trusted the Meynier group. Larson believed that their soiled reputation resulted from the maneuverings of the GBT's Gordon and the French. In his June 1944 report, Larson laid out his conversation with Mullens and stated: "I saw the workings of Gordon in there again."[66]

Given the time frame, Larson was probably reacting to the ready availability of funds for and praise heaped upon the GBT by the same organizations and individuals who offered his own group little more than criticism. With regard to the French, Larson summarized two main points. First, the "official French attitude of mistrust for the Americans," certainly came as no surprise. The second point, however, was more disturbing. Larson believed that the French were trying "to play OSS against the Navy" to hinder any coordination between the two services, especially in their dealings with the Chinese. Tai Li's cooperation with Miles and the Meynier group had further aggravated the tense relationship between the Americans and the French. Perhaps it was only natural for the French to assume that a break in Sino-American relations would help their own cause. Larson, however, vowed that "if the French felt they could use the Americans to play tricks on the Chinese, they were sadly mistaken and would find themselves in trouble."[67] As resistance to Miles's Meynier operation escalated, so did the hostility between Tai Li, Miles's friend and superior in SACO, and the FMM. As a result, Tai Li ordered the FMM to close down its China-based facilities communicating with Indochina. Patti concluded that this "crippled the operations of the gaullistes until the very end of the war."[68] As a result of the mutual mistrust, in summer 1944 Robert Meynier was relieved of his post and the Meyniers left China.[69]

Overall, Miles was sorely disappointed in the collapse of the Meynier mission, in the OSS, and, finally, in the role the United States came to play in Vietnam's history. In regard to the first, he stated: "With the departure of the Meyniers we, in effect at least, had pulled out of Indo-China, leaving a vacuum for the Japanese to fill." In looking back at the situation of 1943, he was even more disturbed by his government and by the leader of the OSS:

> With more pressure from U.S. higher-ups to keep French squabbles in their place we might, in the Indo-Chinese business, have produced some miracles. But despite the fine principles that had been enunciated in the Atlantic Charter we failed to follow our star of freedom. Instead of leading, we played follow-the-leader in the Far East. Intentionally or unwittingly—I do not know which—we permitted ourselves to be too much influenced by Great Britain and France, whose interests and history had long been bound up with the subjugation—not the liberation—of Far Eastern peoples. That day was finished, as most

observant people knew, but Donovan, for reasons I shall never
understand, aligned himself firmly with those who wished to preserve
the prewar Asian status quo.[70]

Miles echoed the oft-expressed anti-imperialist sentiments of Roosevelt in
the two years before the president's death. Although Miles gave no indication
that he was familiar with Roosevelt's trusteeship plan, he clearly believed
that the United States should play an instrumental role in supporting "nationalism" in Asia. Although he was most concerned with the preservation
and strengthening of Chiang Kai-shek's government, his idealism reached
beyond that nation. His experience with Robert Meynier, the Princess of
SACO, and the "Filipinos" convinced him that certainly the elite Vietnamese, such as the Princess, her family, and the Vietnamese soldiers and
priests on their mission, were fully capable of leading a nation. Miles's approval of Vietnamese wishes to have a stronger say in their government is
clearly shown in his diary entries.

As noted earlier, Larson, Miles's subordinate, also reached this conclusion
through his own work with the Meynier mission. In some ways, Larson's
views on how to work effectively in French Indochina are even more sophisticated. Although Robert Meynier's connections were largely French and
thus Larson's interactions were most frequently with Frenchmen, he concluded early on that "no activity of any sort whatsoever will be successful in
Indo-China without local support." Larson firmly believed that Americans
had the upper hand in gaining local support in Indochina because the
United States was viewed as "the apex of democracy and self-government"
with "no colonial ambitions" in Asia. However, Larson contended that the
people should be frequently reassured that American war aims were not
merely "empty phrases" and insisted that the people should be referred to as
the Vietnamese. "We should be farsighted [enough] not to refer to the term
'Annam', but rather to "Viet Nam," wrote Larson. "Literally, 'Annam'
means 'the south pacified', and reminds the Annamites of their history of
subjugation to the Chinese, whereas "Viet Nam" is the name they, themselves, have given to their country."[71]

In addition to Miles and Larson, and perhaps to their surprise, many
young OSS officers would also condemn French imperialism in Southeast
Asia and support Vietnamese nationalism. The World War II experiences of
these OSS officers paralleled those of Miles and Larson, for they often met
and worked with the best and the brightest, not to mention some of the most
pro-American, Vietnamese. They would also encounter a number of the

same frustrations as they, too, attempted to work within, and circumvent when necessary, the complicated world of French politics. Regardless of Miles's commentary on U.S. policy, the departure of the Meyniers did not create "a vacuum for the Japanese to fill." Although losing the accumulated knowledge and contacts of Miles, Larson, and the entire Meynier organization amounted to a substantial blow, the GBT, still firmly in place in 1944, was more active than ever.

Throughout the first several years of the war, the GBT continued passing information from their extensive network in Vietnam on to the Chinese, British, Free French, and a number of different American groups, most notably Chennault's Fourteenth Air Force. One example of information the GBT network provided to all services was a series of reports, consisting of both present and expected troop movements, over a three-day period in November 1944. Although simple, the transmissions presented a remarkable degree of detail on Japanese activities. On November 25, agents reported that 800 troops were "scheduled to leave Bac Ninh for Langson." The following night they reported that Japanese troops "from Sept Pagodas and Vinh Yen left by train and trucks for Langson," and on the twenty-seventh, that Japanese "troop train no. 3048 is scheduled to be at Phulangthuong at 1:15 AM; Langson 6:22 AM; & Nacham 9:44 AM."[72] Such information allowed the Fourteenth Air Force, for example, to coordinate bombing raids of the railroads; it also had the side benefit of enhancing the Allied image in Vietnamese eyes. One field agent reported that "everyone would have believed that strafing these two trains [filled with Japanese soldiers, arms and horses] was well done and would have rejoiced over it."[73]

The Fourteenth Air Force consistently received valuable information from the GBT and respected their network. Colonel Jesse Williams of Chennault's Flying Tigers reported to Coughlin that the GBT "furnished the best information coming out of Indo-China." Williams stated that many missions had been based on GBT information and that in comparison to intelligence furnished by the FMM and the Meynier network, he rated GBT intelligence "superior to all other sources combined." As a result of Williams's excellent recommendation, the OSS furnished the GBT with "several radio receivers, a transmitter, and two small generators, also approximately 1,000,000 dollars" in Chinese currency.[74] Although the OSS clearly knew about GBT, it was not until Miles's dismissal from the OSS and the subsequent collapse of all hopes for the Meynier network that Donovan's group began to seriously investigate Gordon, Bernard, and Tan and the information web they had created.

Using radio transmitters provided by the British, the OSS, and Chennault, the GBT had managed to establish a web of informants and couriers who delivered information both to and from the GBT's series of clandestine radio posts.[75] The network involved a wide array of agents, including both French and Vietnamese personnel who staffed the radio stations and listening posts. Additional aid came in other forms. For example, historian David Marr wrote that a French priest was a "key" GBT participant who helped to finance their efforts by tapping "the wealth of the Catholic mission in Indochina."[76] All of this intelligence activity was coordinated from Gordon's headquarters at Lungchow (in strategic Kwangsi Province) and distributed among their various sponsors. Historian Bernard Fall emphasized the role of the French in aiding both the British and Americans, using information provided by way of Gordon as an example. He wrote in "La politique americaine au Viet-Nam" that the French Resistance had provided critical information on Japanese troop and naval movements to Gordon, who in turn gave it to Chennault. Fall claims that this information allowed the Fourteenth Air Force to execute "very precise raids on Japanese military targets."[77]

Other scholars emphasized the Vietnamese role in the GBT. According to Cecil B. Currey, since 1942 Viet Minh cadres "carefully monitored by Ho, Pham Van Dong, and Giap . . . had provided helpful information to an Allied intelligence operation, the GBT group."[78] Reporter Robert Shaplen put a slightly different slant on the cooperation. He emphasized the GBT's cooperation with the Viet Minh, rather than the reverse. He noted: "With him [Ho Chi Minh] came a representative of the civilian group of former American businessmen in Indochina who had for some time been co-operating with Ho's men."[79] Since the Gordon-Bernard-Tan network had such an apparent wealth of contacts, the OSS knew it needed to find out more about them, as well as about the overall situation in French Indochina.

The man tasked with unraveling the secrets of the GBT was army Major Austin Glass, whom Coughlin had also sent to investigate Larson and the Meynier organization. Glass left Washington for the China theater in January 1944 and spent the next year doing secret intelligence (SI) work in and around Indochina. He was in most respects an excellent choice for the position. After studying at the University of Michigan for four years, Glass moved to Vietnam in his early twenties. He worked for the Standard Oil Company for the next twenty-five years, married a Vietnamese woman, and retired in 1937 to a life of relative leisure as "a horticulturalist and rice planter" near Haiphong. In the spring of 1942 he was repatriated in the first exchange of civilians and diplomatic prisoners with Japan. He returned to the United States on the Swedish ship *The Gripsholm* and entered the army. Later that same year he joined the OSS. Having lived in Indochina for thirty years, Glass was fluent in French as well as the "native languages." He was described as "exceptionally well liked by the French and natives" and as having a range of knowledge "of the country and the people of this area" that was "not equalled by any other American." Thus, he was well suited for his SI assignment, which was "to procure agents in the field to enter Indo-China and keep in close contact with French and native underground organizations."[80]

During Glass's year in the China theater, he worked closely with the FMM, several Vietnamese, and various other personal contacts, reporting back on everything from the economic situation to the number of Japanese aircraft on the ground at Gia Lam and Tan Son Nhut. In his quest to obtain reliable and accurate information, he discovered the GBT. In his report to the OSS, Glass stated that he had seen enough to "prove without doubt" that the GBT was the "best equipped both in and outside of FIC [French Indochina] to obtain information from that important area." He described Gordon, Bernard, and Tan as "live wires, hard workers and capable." He continued:

> They have been most instrumental in obtaining information of a highly tactical value as well as that of both a political and economic nature. They have also obtained many current copies of "L'ACTION," the Hanoi daily paper, "L'INDOCHINE," a weekly illustrated magazine published in Hanoi, and the official gazette of the French Indochina government. Much useful information of a general nature has been obtained from a perusal of this material. It is surprising that in both volume and value the information received from this group exceeds that obtained from the French Military Mission.[81]

Although he gave the GBT a glowing recommendation, Glass was certainly not alone in his investigations of the group. Other OSS members had also become aware of the group and had made similar reports, although with slightly different emphases. Colonel Robert B. Hall characterized the OSS's connection with the GBT as "a very indirect one." He de-emphasized the group's French connections, which was clearly Gordon's strong point, in favor of their ties to the Chinese. Hall viewed this, in general, as a positive attribute:

> The Bernard-Gordon Group do not dare cooperate with the French as they have strong Chinese support and assistance (not financial). . . . Their main support has been from the British, but the 14th has also

helped over a long period of time. They are doing a great job and are pretty autonomous. Their interests are not always those of the French Empire. Consequently, their reports are often without that particular bias. The F.M.M. would like to get them out of the picture or at least get at their sources.[82]

Although Hall described the OSS-GBT relationship as an "indirect one" they did have one relatively strong, albeit covert, tie: Hall reported that "for certain assistance," the GBT did "give their findings to AGFRTS." AGFRTS stood for the 5329th Air and Ground Forces Resources Technical Staff, christened in April 1944 by General Donovan as an OSS cover group. In early 1944 Donovan was still struggling to circumvent the Chinese network, but Miles's agreement with Tai Li continued in force, and SACO was technically *the* intelligence-gathering agency in the China theater. The cover group AGFRTS was established to assume "all of the intelligence duties for Chennault's Fourteenth Air Force" and thus to break free of SACO's control.[83] Needless to say, a flow of information from the GBT to AGFRTS was very important, not only to the Fourteenth Air Force but to the OSS as a whole.

Gordon had been working on a number of plans for increased intelligence gathering in Indochina, one of which he presented to Coughlin on September 11, 1944. In his meeting with Coughlin, Gordon outlined an overall plan for civilian French resistance in Vietnam. Gordon informed Coughlin that the French underground had contacted him and that "French civilians in F.I.C. feel that the time has come" for them to "take a more active part in the war against Japan." Gordon explained that except in "one isolated area, the resistance group was entirely French; and it was most highly organized in the north and central regions, with seventeen resistance groups, totaling 412 members in Tonkin, and eight resistance groups in Annam, with an additional 94 members."[84] According to Gordon, the French Resistance did not need money but was desperately in need of supplies and equipment, especially arms.[85] It was for that reason that he approached the OSS. Coughlin outlined and commented on "The Gordon Plan" and on September 20 forwarded it and his assessment to Washington.

Gordon's plan first sought to provide concrete assurance to the Resistance that the American government would be willing to supply and equip them as well as provide them with "directives that are coordinated with Allied strategy." The Resistance wanted American personnel to come and meet them, assess their needs and capabilities, and help them establish additional radio communications. In return, the Resistance would continue to aid American pilots and POWs, and Gordon even "felt certain" that the combined opera-tions of the OSS and the Resistance could "spring the entire camp [a large POW camp in Saigon] or only certain members which ever the planners wanted."[86] The Resistance also proposed to utilize their radios, "with the necessary frequencies, codes, and schedules," to contact submarines off-shore. The subs could be used "for the safe entry or departure of individu-als" or even for "kidnapping certain individuals and delivering them to the Allies." Coughlin commented that the civilian resistance groups were "or-ganized with a view to sabotage acts of all descriptions" and furthermore that although "as far as Gordon and the French themselves are concerned this plan is primarily concerned with resistance, a very natural by-product of such a plan would be intelligence."[87]

Coughlin's interest in the possibilities for intelligence collection prompted him to endorse Gordon's plan for consideration. He recommended that the OSS "take advantage of this organization," with the added injunction that it was "essential that the work be conducted through Gordon, at least initially." Coughlin stressed Gordon's positive relationship with the Chinese and the fact that they allowed the GBT to "operate without hindrance" within their theater, as ample reason to continue using Gordon as the primary liaison. As evidence, he sent Gordon's chart of "The Disposition of Combat and Sabo-tage Groups" throughout Tonkin and Annam, as of September 1, 1944, and also attached a GBT map of Indochina identifying sites suitable for parachute drops or the landing of Americans, airfields that would be "immediately available," and radio-communication positions. Coughlin concluded his comments with a brief summary of the GBT position:

> The French Indo-China theatre presents problems quite different from those of China proper. For this reason the G.B.T.B. [sic] does not specialise on any one subject. They are handling intelligence, air ground aid, air force target work, and combat and sabotage. They wish to retain an active interest but to make sure that each feature is properly handled and that any action of a large scale nature will be completely synchronised. To this end they wish to receive directives and specialist assistance and to be consulted so that their experience and capabilities may be exploited to the full.[88]

While Gordon and the GBT were obviously very careful to include all nec-essary personnel so as not to compromise either the mission or their network, they were just as cautious regarding their independence. Coughlin clarified,

"Gordon has not invited us to participate in the [GBT] intelligence service, and has stated that he needed no assistance to continue that service. He would not divulge his agents or his set-up to any outsider." Nonetheless, Coughlin remained optimistic about the future of OSS-GBT cooperation. "I believe that closer liaison and association with him [Gordon] may permit our becoming fully acquainted with his intelligence organization and at the same time allow us to set up one of our own."[89]

In November 1944, the GBT group submitted a "French Indochina Report" discussing, among other topics, the need for civilian resistance and the current status of such resistance. The GBT pointed out that although "the French Army in Indochina is the most competent body to offer serious resistance to the Japs," it obviously had serious limitations, such as the "constant fear that the Japs will disarm them." Thus, it seemed obvious to Gordon that "a group of able-bodied civilians, organized into combat and sabotage units, would be of great value." The GBT believed the most reliable members of the French Resistance were those known as Group 22. Group 22 was sponsored by the GBT and was the only sizable civilian organization in existence in Vietnam prior to the liberation of France. Gordon held the members of Group 22 in high esteem: "Having been selected in the early days when friends were rare and having proved their loyalty, ability and steadfast purpose," he wrote, "they are in my opinion not only the best group but probably the only reliable one in the country." Gordon expressed grave concern that Group 22 was being undermined by a combination of French politics and a failure on the part of the Allies, the Americans in particular, to recognize and back them. He warned the Americans that since the liberation of Paris in August, pro-Allied resistance groups had been "mushrooming all over the country," mostly to "attempt to establish favor in Allied eyes."[90]

Now that the *métropole* was liberated, French attentions centered on the liberation and preservation of its empire. In an effort to establish some form of legitimacy with the Allies, France's General Gabriel Sabattier, commander of the Colonial Army in Tonkin, sent messages to Gordon, through Group 22, urging him to establish official relations for the Resistance through the FMM in Chungking. This had become even more difficult with the appointment of General Eugene Mordant as *chef de la Résistance* (head of the Resistance). Mordant began campaigning for the formation of his own civil resistance group immediately after assuming his new post. He advised Group 22 that they would be incorporated into his larger resistance framework and would be offered a choice of "certain duties." Group 22 expressed their unhappiness to Gordon, emphasizing their desire for a leader with "a clear-cut plan and Allied support." They detailed for him the reasons for their objection to Mordant and his clique in three main points:

1. They represent past failures in ability.
2. They are not only turncoats seeking their own safety but they brand Group 22 as anti-French because of their insistence on Allied directives and cooperation.
3. Two immediate examples of Mordant's command reported by a good source, speak for themselves:—
   a. In a leaflet prepared in October 1944, as a recruiting device the need is stressed for Civil Resistance as a weapon against *"American Imperialism."* This is so disgusting as to be almost comical but it fully illustrates the wavering policy of this clique.
   b. As a first step towards training civilians they are being collected in Military trucks in Hanoi and driven in daylight several miles out of Hanoi to French Barracks for their training. It is plain to all observers what is taking place. The Japs are thereby given ample opportunity to check on the individuals recruited and the surprise element of a Civilian Movement is being hopelessly compromised.[91]

The future would prove Group 22 correct in many ways. The liberation of France had encouraged many of the French in Indochina to look for an Allied victory in the Pacific in the near future, and the Japanese were watching the colons' increased pro-Allied activity. Certainly, the GBT's encouragement of civilian resistance to the Japanese had moved them beyond the collection and dispersal of information to what historian David Marr described as the "evaluation of political attitudes and the encouragement of an armed anti-Japanese underground."[92] As is evident, Gordon's ability to evaluate his sources and report on them was clear to many, including the OSS and the Fourteenth Air Force. However, the OSS was not completely sold on the use of the GBT, as certain attributes concerned both Coughlin and his superior, Donovan.

In his comments on "The Gordon Plan," Coughlin included his personal observations on each of the three principal members of the GBT. Coughlin confessed that he had not yet met Frankie Tan, but said he accepted Gordon's characterization of Tan as "an entirely trustworthy Chinese." He also added that Tan was "dependent upon him [Gordon] for his position in the post war world." Coughlin commented that in comparison to Gordon,

Harry Bernard was "not as shrewd," and did not possess the same "drive." Coughlin pointed out, however, that "Bernard strongly desires helping Americans in every way he can." This was in contrast to Gordon, whom Coughlin described as "strongly pro-British" and as "thinking in terms of preserving the Empire." He added, "I do not think that we get all of the intelligence that he obtains but the part that we have gotten to date has more than paid for the help we can render."[93]

Donovan also questioned Gordon's loyalties. In conversations with General Petchkoff in Chungking, Donovan blamed the GBT for misunderstandings between the Americans and the French.[94] In his investigations of Gordon, Colonel Paul Helliwell, SI chief at OSS headquarters in Kunming, found quite the opposite. Helliwell reported that Gordon characterized the British as going "into FIC on their own hook, without Theater coordination" and the French as "completely unreliable."[95] Even without these reservations regarding Gordon's loyalties, Donovan would have found it difficult to move on Gordon's plan. The OSS proposal to aid French Resistance groups had encountered difficulties in Washington. President Roosevelt responded to the idea in a memorandum to Secretary of State Hull. He wrote: "In regard to the Indo-China matter, it is my judgment on this date that we should do nothing in regard to resistance groups or in any other way in relation to Indo-China."[96] Although the Gordon Plan languished, the OSS remained anxious to increase its intelligence role in French Indochina, in part by gaining greater access to the existing GBT network. In order to do so, as well as to keep an eye on Gordon, the OSS assigned Lieutenant Charles Fenn as its liaison to the GBT. Fenn, Coughlin declared, "was the only person he would care to trust with this assignment."[97]

For the last three months of 1944, Charles Fenn was the only OSS officer working with and reporting on GBT activities, and as 1945 approached, Fenn had every reason to expect that the OSS's good relations with the GBT would continue. However, the OSS relationship with the GBT would soon change. Having assured himself of the nearly unlimited potential of the group, Donovan had determined to try and bring it fully under OSS control. As much of the success of the GBT could be attributed to its relative autonomy, it is easy to guess at the reactions of Gordon, Bernard, and Tan to any attempt at a takeover. Thus, while Gordon was off in Washington to deal with this new difficulty, Fenn became more involved with the other two members of the group. It was in the company of Bernard and Tan that Fenn met a new Vietnamese agent, introduced under his alias, Ho Chi Minh.

4

The Chameleon: Charles Fenn

In the introductory chapter to his 1973 book, *Ho Chi Minh: A Biographical Introduction*, former OSS agent Charles Fenn wrote:

> Under colonialism, rulers and ruled alike seem fated to get tarnished. The rulers become mercenary, arrogant, contemptuous, intolerant, and some become ruthless. The ruled become servile, indolent, crafty, treacherous; and some become rebellious. It is when the rulers become particularly ruthless that the ruled become particularly rebellious. Those of us old enough to look back at the colonial era remember with a kind of bewildered unease that for the most part we accepted this muzzling of Vietnamese, Africans, Indians, Burmese, Indonesians and other subject races as part of the general pattern of organized society. If we happened to be Englishmen, Frenchmen, Germans, Dutch, Belgians or Italians, we took as much pride in boasting of our "possessions" as we take today in boasting of our "gross national product." We were satisfied that Africans, for instance, were lower in the evolutionary scale; and that Asiatics, although entitled to be called *homo,* could scarcely be described as *sapiens.* One has only to remember the names applied to the rulers (baas, master, sahib) as against the single pejorative given to the ruled (native). Originally a useful term to describe an indigenous person, this finally classified its recipient with a status only one step up from a dog.[1]

Fenn's conclusions in 1973 were founded on his World War II experiences, initially as a reporter covering the first years of the war and later as a Marine lieutenant working with the OSS and the GBT. The diversity of Fenn's adventures convinced him early on that working with some of the most "rebellious"—at least in the eyes of the French—Indochinese would produce the intelligence results that the Americans needed. His subsequent conclusions would get him into trouble with the leader of the GBT, some members of the OSS, and eventually both the American and British governments. However that may be, he had an impact on events out of proportion to his nominally modest role; both critics and admirers alike credit Fenn with helping to make Ho Chi Minh the undisputed leader of the Viet Minh in 1945. His detractors blame him, at least in part, for the emergent strength of the Viet Minh, the subsequent loss of the French Empire to the communists, and even the difficulties the United States encountered in that country. Supporters see Fenn as a bit of a visionary who recognized the strength and character of Ho Chi Minh and "his" Viet Minh early on and who, had his arguments been heeded, might have prevented the colossal loss of life on all sides between 1946 and 1975.

Charles Fenn was born in 1909 in the United Kingdom. At seventeen he set out to sea working as chief steward in the tourist class on the British cruise ship the R.M.S. *Aquitania.* After five years of this work, he emigrated to the United States, settling in Philadelphia. He soon acquired U.S. citizenship and began work as a textile salesman. Although successful in that occupation, his marriage to a prominent painter, Marion Greenwood, encouraged him to explore his more artistic side. He became a news photographer for the picture magazine *Friday,* and by 1940 he was off to China to photograph the effects of the Japanese occupation. *Friday'*s format paralleled that of *Life* magazine, but *Life'*s popularity and *Friday'*s left-wing politics prevented *Friday* from gaining more than a limited circulation. Although fond of the magazine in many ways, Fenn soon found himself searching for steadier (and more profitable) work. In mid-1941 he became a war correspondent and photographer for the Associated Press (AP). Over the next two years he covered the war in North Africa and in Asia, including the 1942 Japanese campaign into Burma. In the early 1940s new reporters and photographers were paid by the piece, without a per diem, and Fenn soon found his resources painfully stretched. In 1943 he returned to New York City, looking for work. At a party he met Buckminster Fuller, an acting adviser to the OSS, and was invited to Washington to be interviewed.

Fuller had identified Fenn's talent as a photographer and journalist as potential assets for the OSS, but Fenn's experience in China and modest ability to speak Mandarin Chinese interested him more. Thus, Fenn became one of the organization's "specialists." From the beginning, it seemed that Fenn would have difficulty fitting in. The OSS was "distinctly elite, selective, right-wing and university educated," he recalled, and "it was realised that 'specialists' like myself might not have all these otherwise-desirable attributes." Indeed, Fenn

Charles Fenn, often referred to as "Troublesome Fenn" by
fellow officers, found himself an outcast within the
organization because of his failure to bring the GBT under
OSS control. *Courtesy of Alyn Fenn.*

seemed to have none of them. As an immigrant from a working-class British
family, he could not be considered elite, and his departure from high school
prior to graduation fell far short of a university education. Perhaps most problematic, in a "right-wing" organization, he was distinctly left-wing. Clearly
these essential differences were in part responsible for setting Fenn apart from
most of his superiors and for driving a solid wedge between Fenn and the OSS
in 1945.[2]

After joining the OSS in 1943, Fenn, who had not yet been drafted, enlisted in the Marine Corps and, probably to afford him cover in his OSS
work, was commissioned a first lieutenant. After basic training, he attended
the OSS training school, where he became acquainted with the five branches
of the OSS (Special Operations [SO], Secret Intelligence [SI], Research and
Analysis [R&A], Counter Intelligence [CI], and Morale Operations [MO]).

Fenn excelled in the final category and was assigned to MO for the Far East. His job was to "devise all possible ways to deceive the enemy as to one's intentions or capabilities or timing" and to "reproduce enemy handouts, leaflets, magazines, newspapers and photographs in exact facsimile but with subtle changes that were damaging to the enemy." Although technically assigned to MO, Fenn's job would soon call for him to engage in SO and SI as well.[3]

Fenn's first assignment was to develop, with Lieutenant Colonel Herbert Little, an MO scheme in support of military plans to regain Burma. After working in Burma for three months, he was sent to China with orders from the U.S. Navy enabling him to travel "anywhere" in the China-Burma-India theater that "duty required." These orders provided Fenn with a high degree of freedom of movement. That freedom of movement allowed him to perform his job to the fullest. It also gave him full opportunity to earn the resentment of many superior officers who objected to his unrestricted "jaunts," taken without their approval. Upon his arrival in Kunming in June 1944, Fenn's OSS superior, John Coughlin, directed him to commence operations under the cover of AGFRTS with approval from General Chennault, the commander of the Fourteenth Air Force.[4]

Fenn's visit with Chennault was both pleasant and productive. He knew the general "quite well" from having covered the Fourteenth during his years with the Associated Press, and Chennault readily endorsed Fenn's MO plans, including the use of a number of Fenn's Chinese friends as agents. Chennault wanted MO agents to "help him in the psychological briefing of his pilots." He believed that these agents could train his pilots to counteract "the effects and reaction to the bombings of the people of the occupied territories." Chennault was particularly concerned with regions such as French Indochina, which he identified as "populated by white people, though under Jap control." Although Fenn had clearance to use Chinese agents, there was little time to do so at the start. With the commencement of the Japanese drive across southeast China from Hankou to Canton in 1944, Fenn was forced by circumstances to operate alone. His duty was to spread rumors to "counteract the deceptive and subversive rumors which the Japanese on the Hengyan and Kwellan [Kweilin] fronts and other places had planted in advance of their drive." Because of the rapidity of the Japanese offensive, he was "operating almost single handed . . . spread[ing] these rumors more or less personally."[5]

Fenn was commended for his rapid and courageous MO work but was urged to expand his work beyond MO and engage in SI work for the Air Force. The Fourteenth needed information on targets, Japanese defenses and troop movements, and, most of all, weather conditions. Thus, it was made clear from the start of his term in China that SI was "far more essential" than morale operations. The network grew quickly, and Fenn's Chinese agents provided valuable intelligence to Chennault, the OSS, and the GBT throughout the war.[6]

Fenn's work took an unexpected turn at an unexpected place in the summer of 1944. While in Kweilin awaiting a flight to Kunming, Fenn went to the OSS dining room for a cup of coffee. There he struck up a conversation with two strangers, an "oddly dissimilar pair" he remembers, "one a tall Westerner, the other an exceptionally short Chinese, both wearing civilian khaki." The two were Laurie Gordon and Frankie Tan. Although their initial conversation was guarded due to the nature of their occupations, this pleasant encounter would later amount to much more than it seemed at the time. In September, Coughlin again called Charles Fenn to his office—this time to discuss the GBT.

When Coughlin broached the idea of working with the Gordon Group, Fenn's initial reaction was positive, although he did caution that he knew "nothing about Indochina." As Fenn's work to that point, primarily in MO, had been limited to Burma and China, he might have felt unqualified; however, given the limited knowledge of Indochina throughout the OSS, Fenn was the best they had, and he proved an excellent choice.[7] Coughlin further explained that the OSS wanted to "take over the whole [GBT] operation, full stop," but that Gordon "wouldn't buy it," insisting that the success of his operation "depends upon him staying independent." Coughlin indicated that after a bit of wrangling, both the OSS and Gordon had compromised: the OSS would provide funding but Gordon had to "take an OSS officer into his group." It proved quite convenient that Coughlin considered Fenn to be "the only person he would care to trust with this assignment," because Gordon had also laid out a condition: Fenn's "was the only name he'd agree to."[8]

The OSS was intrigued by the GBT's accomplishments, but Gordon's secrecy both frustrated and annoyed many in the organization who wanted access to his network. Fenn's role was to work with the GBT but also to find out for the OSS "how Gordon really stands with the other outfits he's hooked up with" and whether he was a "British agent, or working for the FMM, or even Tai Li." Thus directed, Fenn set out with Gordon for the GBT headquarters at Lungchow, an important point in the trading network between China and northern Vietnam, approximately 100 miles southwest of Nanning, near the Indochina border.[9] Fenn was cautioned that the journey to the GBT compound would take a week, traveling by sampan—acquired through "'Fatty,' one of Gordon's Chinese business associates of former times"—up a fast-flowing river. With coolies to pole the boat and the owner's wife to see to meals, Gordon and Fenn had many hours to talk and get to know each other. Gordon used the time to explain the details of his operation. Gordon boasted that by that time (the summer of 1944), he had a "dozen friends [all French, but "strictly pro-Ally"] in Indochina sending reports: two by radio contact, the others by courier."[10]

Although Fenn and Gordon became close friends, Fenn maintained frequent contact with the OSS through Colonel Robert Hall and Majors Glass and de Sibour. When he and Gordon were under way, Fenn immediately began to follow his OSS directive to probe for the roots of Gordon's allegiances. Fenn found him to be "generally pro-French," but not working *for* the FMM any more than he worked *for* the British, Americans, or Chinese. Fenn characterized Gordon as "in tune with the British and Americans," but he qualified this by stating that if Gordon "was rather more friendly with the former [the British], this was largely because they were more friendly to him."[11]

From Gordon's point of view, this was certainly the case. The British, especially MI5, provided what assistance they could with only one string attached: that the GBT give them all pertinent intelligence. The Americans demanded a bit more. Clearly Chennault and Air Ground Aid Service (AGAS) appreciated the GBT's work and were generally supportive of their efforts. After witnessing conversations between Gordon and Chennault's men who had come to discuss "targets and possible operations in Indo-China," Fenn reported back: "Obviously Gordon has excellent relations with these people as well as Hsiu [Hsiu Kwang-yin, one of Tai Li's men in charge in Nanning]."[12] The OSS was less content to be a simple recipient of GBT information, and from the very beginning it endeavored to subsume the group, a move Gordon both resisted and resented.

For his part, Gordon was quite clear on the rationale of the OSS and on the reason that Fenn had been assigned to work with the GBT: "With the U.S. fleet moving up into the China Sea, [American involvement in Indochina] is inevitable. When they get carriers near enough to the coast of Indochina they'll need to know weather, targets and Jap defences. That's why Coughlin was told to get into this show and get in fast. The only effective way he could do this was through our set-up. Hence his anxiety to bring us together."[13]

As Gordon and Fenn continued upriver, they picked up Frankie Tan. Fenn and Tan also got along quite well, and the journey to Lungchow was generally pleasant. Upon arrival at the GBT's headquarters, "a well-built brick house of about ten rooms," Fenn met the third member of the group, Harry Bernard, as well as Gordon's immediate staff, Madame Tong and her

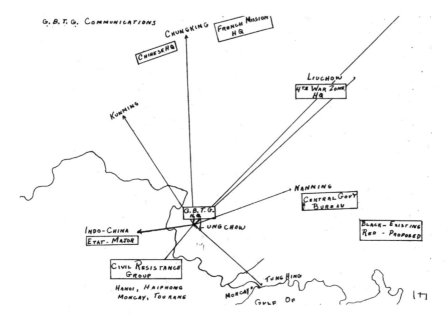

Charles Fenn's sketch map of GBT headquarters in its larger geographic context was one
of the many items of information he passed on to OSS headquarters in Kunming.
National Archives and Records Administration.

daughters Helen and Janet. Over time, Fenn developed a deep appreciation
of Bernard's character and abilities and became close friends with him and
with Gordon's secretary, Helen Tong.[14]

For a brief time, Lungchow, China, proved an ideal working environment
for Fenn and the GBT. Because the Americans and the British were working
with and supportive of the Nationalist Chinese, the members of the GBT
could work openly and without fear of reprisal. Yet Lungchow's proximity to
Indochina allowed them to communicate with agents inside Vietnam with
relative frequency and to plan and initiate new operations. Within a few
days, Fenn even began to utilize his own Chinese agents as part of the GBT
operations. The more involved Fenn became with the GBT, the more he
came to appreciate their efforts on behalf of the Allies. Luckily the feelings
were mutual, and the trio's relationship with Fenn developed into one of mutual trust and camaraderie. For example, Gordon allowed Fenn to accompany him to a border meeting with André Lan, his chief agent inside Vietnam—a considerable act of trust, considering Gordon's reluctance to expose
the members of his network to outsiders.[15]

In subsequent meetings with Lan, a colon with strong local ties, Fenn learned a great deal more about the situation in Indochina. Although a Frenchman, Lan's loyalty to the Allies and to Gordon was unquestioned, and as time would soon tell, Lan's endeavors at objectivity usually outweighed his prejudices. In his statements to Fenn, Lan confirmed much of the information known to the OSS at the time, especially with respect to the continuing French administration of the area, and he inadvertently indicated a bit of the danger that he himself faced simply by his involvement with the GBT. In his discussion of Franco-Japanese relations, Lan verified that the Japanese did not "interfere between the natives and the French except in freeing the political prisoners," which they did only because "they need[ed] the prison space for what they consider[ed] more important offences, such as anti-Japanese behavior or trouble-making, non-co-operation and minor espionage"; he added that "major spies" were executed immediately.[16] Given his position as Gordon's most important agent in Indochina, had he been caught, Lan would have been executed by the Japanese. Although he was in more danger than any other member of the group, Lan worked tirelessly to provide Gordon with information from Hanoi, and on numerous occasions he escorted Frenchmen fleeing Indochina to safety in China.

Lan also provided the GBT with firsthand accounts of the Japanese impact on the Indochinese economy and of the way the Japanese were viewed by the Vietnamese populace—from his perspective. Regarding the Vietnamese perception of the Japanese, Lan reported that one thing that worked to the benefit of the latter was their behavior. He told Fenn that Japanese troops behaved "better than Western troops, whether French, British or American," adding that "the Officers are always strict in enforcing discipline." In his opinion, "the Annamites prefer[red] the Japanese to the French merely because they so much hate the French."[17] Although the situation might certainly have appeared this way to Lan, others viewed the Vietnamese attitude differently. A report from the British Ministry of Information and Political Warfare Executive, while acknowledging that the Japanese had "behaved with considerable correctness in Indo-China," reached a conclusion quite opposite from Lan's and also noted the pro-Allied feelings among the people:

> It is in fact rather remarkable how rapidly the native discovered and understood the Japanese mixture of arrogance and "bonhommie," and loathed them for it. This partly explained the kindness of poor native people to the British prisoners of war, where the Annamites and others

took great risks in passing on money, food, etc., to the prisoners. The native attitude toward the French has possibly turned to one of indifference. The previous dislike of the natives for the French is now focussed on the Japanese, and for this the French may be thankful. But for probably the first time the native has become conscious of the British and the Americans whom he admires for fighting the Japanese.[18]

Most 1944 OSS reports regarding the support of the Indochinese population for the Allies were similar to that of the British Ministry of Information and Political Warfare Executive. In October, in his brief on cooperating with the FMM for work in Indochina, Major Harold Faxon of the OSS optimistically declared: "Practically the entire native population is anti-Japanese and would welcome the opportunity to take part in the proposed [Allied] training and subsequent operations."[19] Yet distinct differences in opinion about the "psychological makeup" of the Vietnamese and about the viability of using them as part of operations began to emerge among members of the OSS.

Early reports from 1944 failed to capitalize on the information gleaned by Milton Miles and Robert Larson (who had clearly stated that the Vietnamese were not and should not be considered inferior) and discussed the Vietnamese in primarily pejorative terms. A mid-May report on the "Proposed Means of Disseminating Propaganda in Indo-China" stated that the "receptivity of the Annamites to propaganda" should be based on two factors: first, that "Annamites" were basically incapable of working toward long-term goals and were interested only in "short range considerations," and second, that "the Annamites have been a subject race for so many years that they respond more readily to foreign advice or instructions than to such as supposedly emanates from among themselves." The same report also characterized the Vietnamese as "used to obeying" and as having "no organizing ability or initiative."[20] As the MO office continued to work on plans for French Indochina, comments about the people gained more "depth" and became more insulting. MO officer R. P. Leonard wrote:

The subservience of the natives and their mercenary proclivities, considering the Annamites particularly since they are predominant of all Indochinese races, have an important bearing in consideration of MO operations. They are quite incapable of developing an organization of any kind, certainly not an underground. Being suspicious of each other and practicing trickery among themselves, any organization they have ever attempted to create, has always broken down from the incapacity of its members to pull together. . . . [Because they] have become mercenary to an extraordinary extent . . . they will do anything for money but they cannot be expected to take risks from ideological motives.[21]

Although Leonard did concede that there were exceptions to this "rule of thumb"—individuals who were "courageous and idealists"—he concluded that "such an Annamite" would not be useful since he "would not be credited by other Annamites of responding to an ideal." In Leonard's view, OSS efforts should concentrate on utilizing the French colons, since they "have more at stake in Indochina than do the natives" and "have a basic psychology similar to ours."[22]

Although comments on Leonard's reports were essentially positive and did not contradict the deprecatory remarks about the Vietnamese, qualifying statements did at least recognize more than one category of "Annamites." In his assessment of the proposal, Major B. M. Turner characterized the evaluation of the Vietnamese as a "typical new comer's reaction" and pointed out that "the Nationalists and Communists have had strong organizations within Indo-China"; he suggested that operating through them would be "a splendid way to catch the attention and belief of the higher class educated Annamites."[23] Turner advocated an economic approach to gain the attention and garner the allegiance of the people. Propaganda related to the economic situation in French Indochina hoped to discourage the Vietnamese and others from "aiding" Japan through work. For example, one proposed MO theme—"The wooden ships we build for Japan will carry our food to Japan and to the Southern Regions while we go hungry"—hoped to "aid in the break-up of Indo-China as a military and economic base for Japan" by persuading the Vietnamese to cease work on wooden transport ships used by Japan. Whereas propaganda designed to create anti-Japanese feelings by showing that Japan was "the cause of shortages, [the] high cost of living, [and] inflation" had a high probability of success, efforts to rouse the population to "cease work in factories, mines, railroads, etc." did not— the price for such action was simply too high. To promote his MO messages Turner recommended producing "leaflets and pamphlets" to circulate among the people, noting that the OSS possessed an "excellent little pamphlet produced by the Annamite Independence League which gives us a well-nigh perfect example to follow in the format for all kinds of leaflets and pamphlets and gives an excellent outline to follow in pamphlet writing."[24]

MO operative Turner was not the only person to acknowledge the existence of effective Vietnamese organizations. Reports written almost a year earlier exhibited many of the same prejudices as Leonard's yet managed to admit the existence of more than one "type" of "Annamite." In identifying rumor themes, then major Herbert Little selected the Vietnamese Catholics for special attention, noting that they had "one of the most powerful political organizations in the country."[25] A separate outline of MO objectives written in late 1943 not only acknowledged the existence of two organized and "rival Anti-Japanese groups operating in Indo-China" but also considered Vietnamese agents, as compared to both French and Chinese agents, to "be the most valuable contact[s]" in distributing propaganda through a courier system. Overall, the outline's author considered the Chinese to be the "most dependable and useful agents," in part because they moved "in and out of Indo-China without restriction," but had serious reservations about using the French because of the rivalry among the French political factions and because of "our own statements against imperialism." Quite simply, the French "desire for complete postwar restoration of Indochina" was viewed as "not compatible with American policy." Thus, the author concluded, "there should be that minimum of cooperation and exchange of information [with the French groups in Kunming] which would avoid outright conflict and confusion . . . without compromising American post-war policy toward Indo-China."[26]

While various OSS officers discussed the issues of whether and how Vietnamese or French agents might be used, Fenn continued his work with the GBT. His connection to numerous Frenchmen within Gordon's net was already established. Soon, however, Fenn would have to take up the question of whether or not to work with the Vietnamese. It was Frank Tan who inadvertently brought the issue to light. Tan, like Gordon, introduced Fenn to a host of GBT contacts and even permitted him to join a number of meetings with Chinese officers to draw up plans for a radio network along the coast connecting Kwangsi and French Indochina. Meetings with the Chinese were always cordial although they, like the French, were concerned about GBT activity in Indochina. Marshall Chang Fa-kwei of the Fourth War Area (comprising all of Kwangsi Province and the western portion of Kwangtung Province) sent one of his top men, General Chen, to visit with Gordon, Bernard, and Tan. Officially Chen came to assess the political and military situation in and around Lungchow. However, his special concern centered on whether or not the GBT was using Vietnamese agents. In the fall of 1944, the GBT could honestly answer that they were not working with the Indochinese, but Fenn, always looking to delve deeper and discover more of the situation, queried Chen for the reason behind the Chinese objection to using

Vietnamese agents. Chen's response was instructive, further illuminating the
Chinese view of world affairs:

> They [Vietnamese] aren't to be trusted. For one thing, they aren't really
> interested in the war against the Japanese. It's true they're anti-
> Japanese, but they're equally anti-French. To a lesser degree they're
> anti-Chinese. So they'd hardly make a loyal ally. I suppose you've
> already discovered they profess to be pro-American. This is because they
> hope you'll help them to gain independence when the war is over and we
> kick the Japanese out. You may be approached by a group known as the
> Vietminh, which is more or less communist although they pretend to be
> strictly nationalist. They offered help to Marshall Chang against the
> Japanese if in turn China would help them gain independence after the
> war. In this instance, the Marshall consulted with the Generalissimo. But
> His Excellency was dead against it. Although France is at present a dead
> duck, it's possible she may stage a come-back. So it wasn't worth
> offending her for the sake of helping an insignificant group like the
> Vietminh who'll probably never amount to anything. But if they should
> approach you—they claim to be strongly pro-American—don't get taken
> in, if you'll forgive my saying so. They have a big sales talk but nothing
> much to sell.[27]

Gordon's reaction to the dialogue between Fenn and Chen foreshadowed
much of what was to come. Gordon assured Chen that the GBT was not then
working with any Vietnamese and had no intention of working with them in
the future. He stated emphatically, "I agree with you they're all anti-French
and quite untrustworthy."[28] In the next several months, as circumstances
changed, Gordon's refusal to work with any Vietnamese would cause a serious rupture between Gordon and Fenn and within the GBT itself.

Nevertheless, in the last months of 1944 Fenn became an active member
of the GBT network. He even began to participate in the future plans for the
group, contributing advice and advocating for OSS financial and logistical
support. The group hoped to provide SO training to the 1,500 French civilians connected with the GBT, as well as to conduct a "widespread MO campaign." Given Fenn's earlier MO activities in the China-Burma-India theater, he was obviously well prepared to train agents and put out "black
leaflets"—counterfeit copies of printed matter produced by the Japanese
that were superficially pro-Japanese but contained material insidiously anti-
Japanese in effect—in Indochina.[29]

Fenn's end-of-month reports wholeheartedly supported the GBT. In November Fenn commented on the general increase in GBT security precautions as the Japanese watched the increasingly open pro-Allied activities of many Frenchmen in Vietnam. Fenn observed that with three highly efficient radio/observation sites in Tonkin, "around twenty messages were being handled daily, covering target information, weather reports, Jap OB [Order of Battle], and special intelligence for various organizations like AGAS." Furthermore, he concluded that it was "clear from raid-response" that the Fourteenth Air Force was "relying almost entirely on GBT target information." Fenn added that the extra site at Hanoi and the two new sites in Saigon and Tourane (now Da Nang) were expected to increase net productivity within a brief period of time.[30]

True to his original specialty, Fenn also provided an intelligence report on Indochina "of special interest to MO." His report covered the morale and living conditions of both Japanese and French troops and civilians as well as the disposition of the Vietnamese toward the Japanese and Allies.[31] Fenn also indicated that the GBT was undertaking more forays into relief and rescue work. By late 1944 the GBT had a well-developed system in place to aid Allied pilots shot down over Indochina and had, in several instances, acquired the gratitude of both AGAS and the Fourteenth Air Force. AGAS gave "Gordon warm support," Fenn reported, "mainly with radio equipment, in return for such operations as bringing out Allied prisoners from the POW camp and U.S. pilots who have been downed" in French Indochina.[32]

Lan, Gordon's agent in Vietnam, reported on his efforts to aid POWs in Tonkin:

Inside various detention camps are a few thousand mixed Australian, British, Dutch and American prisoners-of-war—a very few of the latter. I always carry in my car a few tins, packages and oddments of clothing, and whenever I pass a truckful I manage to throw them something. These prisoners have recognized my car by now so they elbow the guards aside, and usually manage to grab and hide what I throw them. By using the van that delivers rice to the camps one of my contact men managed to smuggle into one camp a whole machine gun with ammunition, and they're keeping this weapon for an organized getaway. One day when the Japanese guards were searching for letters reported to have been smuggled into the camp they came upon several rounds of ammunition. But their one-track minds were fixed upon the letters so they merely commandeered these bullets without comment![33]

Although his story is most probably an exaggeration of actual events, Lan and his contacts certainly aided the prisoners at considerable risk to themselves. If the prisoners had indeed learned to recognize Lan's car, the guards certainly had as well. It is conceivable that Lan's throwing food to prisoners did not significantly irritate their escorts, but had the gun been found on board the rice truck, the delivery men would surely have been executed on the spot. Furthermore, as this episode demonstrates, the GBT network was by late 1944 fully developed, and any agent caught would have seriously compromised the safety of a wide range of loyal friends and colleagues of Gordon, Bernard, and Tan. The covert nature of the GBT network and their careful maneuvering offered them a high degree of protection, but it is also possible that the ever-prying eyes of the Japanese were in part diverted by the increasingly open activity of the French Resistance in Indochina.[34] As will be seen, the Japanese were carefully watching the overt pro-Allied activity among the French, which seems to have shielded many of the GBT agents from Japanese detection.

Gordon's system for bringing out downed pilots was also quite sophisticated. The network provided pilots with a list of designated "safe areas" where, if it was possible to land the plane, pilots could put down safely. Pilots were instructed that if they were forced to bail out over hostile terrain, they should travel at night toward the safe areas. As soon as the GBT was notified that a pilot had gone down, their local French agents would organize signal fires on the hillsides to help the pilot find his way to protected positions. Gordon's resolve not to use Vietnamese as part of GBT operations is demonstrated in his warning that pilots should "avoid the natives, who are offered a reward for turning the fliers over, dead or alive." As Indochina had not been a principal area of activity up to this time, there had been relatively few bombing runs, and only two downed pilots were rescued in the summer of 1944. One of the men had been picked up by the GBT, the other by Fenn's Chinese agents.[35]

As the course of the war continued, however, there would be more downed pilots, and whenever possible, members of the GBT network provided aid in search and rescue. In October, only a few weeks after Fenn's arrival at the GBT headquarters, they were informed that a pilot named Ray Marshall had been shot down near Haiphong. The young man had survived the crash with only minor injuries and had been rescued by an ethnic Chinese farmer. It took nearly two weeks, and several close calls, for the Chinese farmer, whom Marshall nicknamed "Pop," to escort the pilot from Haiphong across the Indochina border to the GBT compound at Lungchow. One of the difficulties the two men faced was procuring food, as both Marshall and Pop were short on cash and valuables; although Marshall had to give up his watch in exchange for rice, he did manage to keep his .45. On their journey, Pop guided the young man through a number of villages where he had acquaintances and through others where he managed to convince the peasants to help them. In his testimony, Marshall commented: "I never could figure out how Pop could have all these friends far and wide, or why they risked their lives helping us." Both Fenn and Gordon's secretary Helen Tong recorded Marshall's story as well as Pop's statements. In his memoirs, Fenn offers his own opinion on why Pop's friends helped the American pilot. He concluded that "some of them, no doubt discovered that the Japs were worse masters than the French."[36]

Not all villages were willing to receive the pair, especially given that the Japanese had threatened both the Vietnamese peasants and the French with dire consequences should they aid Allied pilots. Furthermore, Pop informed Fenn and the GBT that in the case of one village, the hostile reception they received was due more to the villagers' negative prior experience with an American pilot than to Japanese threats. As Pop and Marshall came closer to the border with China, they skirted the one and only truly hostile village that they would encounter on their trek. Marshall recounted the story to Fenn and the GBT:

> While Pop went off to find them [two young boys who had taken Marshall's few remaining piasters] I fell asleep. When I woke up it was already pitch dark. I suddenly realised that the jungle all around was twinkling with the torches of a search party and they were slowly closing in on me! I lay there in the brush with my pistol cocked, thinking this was it. The lights crossed and re-crossed, some within a few feet while I held my breath! I'd fixed it with Pop that the signal between us would be a grunt from him followed by three claps, and I was to reply with three claps. So during the blackness when I heard a grunt I waited for the claps but there was only another grunt. The fact was, Pop hadn't dared to clap because the searchers were too near. Anyway, the next thing I knew Pop was tugging at my leg and gesturing for me to take my shoes off, otherwise the villagers would track me by the marks of the shoes.
>
> Then we climbed higher and higher up the mountains until we could see the whole valley honeycombed with moving lights. By running hard we got something of a start, but I suffered not only from my shoeless feet, pretty tough! But even worse from banging into trees and such, one caught my face—a real shiner. So rather than knock myself out I insisted

on lighting a torch, feeling that one more amongst all those already burning could scarcely matter. But to be on the safe side I sent Pop a few steps ahead so that if we ran into anyone it would be Pop who got shot and not me.[37]

Pop explained to Fenn and Helen that the village was particularly hostile because earlier, a downed pilot named Norton had shot a village elder.[38] Thus, the villagers' prior experience with American pilots was less than favorable. Although his story cannot be verified, Pop's understanding of the potential dangers in aiding an American pilot affirms his bravery in conducting Marshall to safety. Pop went on to explain the reason that he had taken such huge personal risks to save Marshall:

> As soon as the plane came down, word spread like wildfire that the Japanese were offering huge sums to catch the pilot. So everyone— Japanese, French and Annamites—was madly looking for him. But the fact is, a lot of the Annamites are pro-American and almost all those like me who are of Chinese origin know that America is helping China against the Japanese so we want to help them. Well, about a year ago some leaflets written in Chinese were dropped where I live, and they said everyone should help American airmen if they got shot down. So I knew it was my duty to do that, no matter what.[39]

Gordon reiterated his warning that pilots should avoid the Vietnamese villagers since they had "all been offered high rewards by the Japs for turning in pilots whether dead or alive." Pop, in his view, was an exception, not the rule. The Allies, of course, also offered such rewards, Gordon clarified, but "the Jap reward is on the spot while the Allied reward is a nebulous 500 miles away!" For his act of bravery, Pop did receive a reward, although much smaller than that offered by the Japanese and considerably less than Marshall was considered to be "worth." The Japanese offered up to 100,000 piastres for him; in their propaganda, the Fourteenth Air Force touted a pilot's "worth" at $50,000, or 1,250,000 piastres. Fenn reported that Pop seemed pleased to receive the meager 5,000 piastres that the GBT paid him, but he declined a copy of the picture Fenn took of him, stating, "To receive a photograph from the Americans would be to receive a bullet from the Japanese."[40]

Soon after Marshall's safe return to the Fourteenth Air Force's base at Nanning, one of Gordon's agents, Simon Yu, brought news of the consequences of Pop's good deed. Yu was a complicated character who fit in perfectly with

Gordon's organization. His family background alone allowed him to conform to many different situations: his mother was Belgian, his father half Chinese and half Vietnamese. Based near Hanoi, he had the distinct advantage of speaking French, Chinese, Vietnamese, and English fluently, making him a nearly perfect agent. Yu was characterized as exceptionally intelligent and knowledgeable, as well as a bit temperamental and oversensitive. He expected as much of others as he did of himself and did not suffer fools gladly. Fenn remembered Yu's favorite English expression to be "balloon man," to describe "someone out of whose mouth comes meaningless words."[41] In his future dealings with the OSS, Yu would discover many balloon men among the hierarchy in Kunming. However, on this first meeting with Fenn, Yu was on his best behavior, bringing news of Japanese-Chinese trade along the border as well as of the unfortunate consequences of the Japanese reaction to Marshall's escape.

Although Fenn had tried to "throw a false scent across the trail of the Chinese who actually helped Marshall" by asking MO to place an "inside" story in a Kunming newspaper of Marshall's dramatic rescue by "certain Annamites who arrived in Yunnan and were richly rewarded," the propaganda work was not completed in time.[42] After Marshall's successful escape, the Japanese accused all Chinese living in the area north of Haiphong of being pro-Allied. Yu and General George Wou of the Fourth War Area reported that the consequent harassment was "driving [the refugees] into China," where they expected both food and housing. Both men emphasized the need to stop the flow of refugees across the border. Yu contended that most were not desperate refugees at all but were "really spies and fifth columnists preparing the way for a Japanese invasion." Wou added that to stop the influx would be "hard on them [the refugees]," which both Fenn and Bernard translated as meaning "in the process of stopping them, we would have to shoot them." Bernard cut to the point: "If a few genuine refugees do get shot, it will discourage both genuine and false from coming in. And I gather you don't really want either."[43] Both Yu and Wou agreed with Bernard's summary. Obviously, the lack of a warm reception from the Chinese, the perils of angering the Japanese, and the temptation of the immediately available Japanese reward money highlight the exceptional nature of those, like Pop, who chose to aid Allied pilots regardless of the numerous hazards they might encounter.

As time would tell, the GBT also underestimated the willingness of the Vietnamese to aid American servicemen in distress. In late 1944 a little-known local group rescued Lieutenant Rudolph Shaw when his plane was shot down near Cao Bang. The leader of the group, known to history as Ho Chi Minh, escorted Shaw to the American base at Kunming, refusing the

proffered reward and asking only for the privilege of meeting the famous
general of the Flying Tigers, Claire Chennault. Ho's request was denied at
that time, Shaw was shipped home, and the event seemingly slipped into the
footnotes of wartime history. As will be shown later, the rescue, so easily
brushed aside in late 1944, would come to Fenn's attention in early 1945. In
the intervening months, Fenn would become more immersed in the activities
of the GBT, assuming for all intents and purposes the position of fourth partner to Gordon, Bernard, and Tan.

All four members of the team enjoyed their safe haven at headquarters at
Lungchow, although there were repercussions from Marshall's rescue.
French agents inside Vietnam reported to Fenn that the Japanese were "fu-
rious because a plane had picked up Marshall at Lungchow." Fenn warned
his superiors that "if the Japs get too irritated they can come over in half a
day and clean us up."[44] Luckily, the Japanese did not choose to retaliate directly. For Fenn, Gordon, Bernard, and Tan, the days passed swiftly. Their
work was challenging, their accommodations comfortable, and their company enjoyable. All of this came to an end, however, with the November and
December operations of the Japanese.

The Japanese had begun Operation ICHIGO in April in an effort to seize the
air bases of the Fourteenth Air Force located in southeastern China. In the
Japanese northern drive from the Vietnamese border to the U.S. air base at
Nanning, Lungchow was overrun. The GBT, like most Allies in the area, had
assumed that the Chinese forces guarding the air bases, as well as the Americans on base, would be able to hold their positions. This was not the case.
The Chinese military folded, and the GBT establishment was forced to flee,
first from their idyllic headquarters, then from a temporary setup at Ching-
hsi. In an effort to stay close to Indochina, the group headed for Kweilin, the
main base of the Fourteenth, but Kweilin was also overwhelmed in November. All in all, Operation ICHIGO seized six U.S.-Chinese air bases (Nanning,
Liuchow, Kweilin, Lingling, Hengyang, and Suichuan) and made it much
harder for members of the GBT to reconnoiter with their agents on the Indochinese border.[45]

Because of their desire to remain close to the Fourteenth Air Force and
AGAS, the GBT chose as their new headquarters the bustling city of Kunming. Once a relatively quiet Chinese city, by 1944 Kunming was the major
terminus for supplies flown over "the Hump" (the Himalayas) to the Nationalist Chinese. After ICHIGO, the city also housed a large contingent of the
American military, including members of the Fourteenth Air Force, the OSS,
and AGAS, as well as the FMM and various civilian organizations such as the

This lovely country home, which housed SO headquarters, was one of many buildings used to lodge branches of the OSS in and outside Kunming, China. *National Archives and Records Administration.*

Red Cross. Now deprived of their remote headquarters and the freedom that its isolation had brought, Fenn and the GBT found themselves in the eye of another storm and experienced ever-increasing pressure to formally put their organization under the direction of the OSS.

Gordon's frustrations with the OSS had begun mounting even prior to the group's move to Kunming. He and Fenn concurred that many within the OSS were basically "anti-French"; however, Fenn, still an OSS officer, censored his own comments regarding the organization. Gordon felt no such need to hide his growing resentment. With funds available from AGAS, Chennault, and the British, he stated flatly that although he appreciated OSS resources, he was not in desperate need of them. In Gordon's opinion the OSS was "anti-everything except feathering their own nest." He went on to complain to Fenn that, so far, the OSS had "taken everything and given almost nothing except back-stabbing, with men like [Major Austin] Glass sent down to compete or even spy on us and subvert our agents." "Frankly," he continued, "I've had enough of such double-dealing. If OSS won't play ball, I intend throwing in my lot with AGAS who are only too keen to take us on, while allowing us full independence."[46]

Gordon's analysis of the situation was in many ways not far off the mark. AGAS had repeatedly demonstrated its appreciation of the GBT network's pilot and POW rescue efforts, and all members of the team enjoyed good relations with AGAS officials. Meanwhile, the OSS continually expressed its frustration with Gordon's unwillingness to submit his group to OSS direction or to divulge the names of his agents. However, for all of Gordon's disappointment (and Fenn's, for that matter) with Glass, Glass's reports to his OSS superiors consistently praised the GBT.[47] Given his own long experience in Indochina, it is possible that Glass already knew many of Gordon's French contacts in the Hanoi-Haiphong area. It is equally plausible that Glass sensed the pro-Allied leanings of their mutual friends and acquaintances and tried to recruit them for the OSS, perhaps without knowing of their connection to the GBT. Nevertheless, Glass's investigation of the GBT only served to heighten Gordon's disdain for the OSS, while his reports to the OSS intensified the OSS's desire to acquire control over the entire GBT organization.[48]

In an effort to preserve his network's independence while still benefiting from the supplies and cash available through his various sponsors, Gordon traveled to Chungking to meet with the Americans, French, British, and Chinese. But these meetings proved frustrating. He reported back to Fenn that "the Americans and the French vied with each other in giving me the run around. I was reported to Wedemeyer as a British agent, to the French as an American agent, and to the British as a Chinese agent. Only the British disbelieved the nonsense." No doubt the very fact that he was meeting with so many representatives only increased the OSS's determination to bring Gordon under its direction. Gordon also complained about the situation at the Texaco House in Chungking, in particular about an "insufferable" American colonel who engaged in drunken brawls on a daily basis. His vehement reaction to the situation prompted Fenn to query Bernard about Gordon's attitudes vis-à-vis the Americans. Bernard, whom all reports characterize as staunchly pro-American, countered Fenn's characterization of Gordon as "anti-American," but with a qualifier. He stated that Gordon was not anti-American when it came "to the AGAS crowd or State Department men like [John] Davies." The obvious inference here was that Gordon was distinctly anti-American when it came to the OSS. This statement may have also reflected Bernard's attitude, for while he was certainly pro-American, he was against involving the GBT any further with the OSS.[49]

By the end of the year, Fenn reported that he had accomplished all of his earlier objectives as outlined to Colonel Coughlin. More significantly, he stated in his report that he had brought "[the] OSS more closely into the GBT-group picture" and had satisfied them as to the ability of the OSS to "handle their problems." Conversely, he stated that he had given "full reports on the activities of the GBT-group and their ability to serve" the OSS. Fenn declared that he had also managed to "put into operation a full MO program within FIC" and to meet with "FIC agents to arrange the delivery and use of SO material within FIC."[50]

Fenn's report was clearly overly optimistic in the long view. Fenn could easily claim that he had brought "[the] OSS more closely into the GBT-group picture" since *he was* an OSS officer and was participating as a full member with Gordon, Bernard, and Tan. Similarly, on several occasions, such as after John Davies's glowing report about the GBT to the State Department, the OSS was forthcoming with both cash and supplies. However, the members of the group, including Fenn, were unanimous in their desire to distance themselves from what they saw as the prying eyes and vice-like grip of the OSS, and in any event, the GBT had other means of support. Both AGAS and the British were ready to provide what funds they could without evidencing the need for control over the group. Indeed, as the year came to a close, Willis Bird, OSS deputy chief, advised Fenn confidentially to "transfer the GBT outfit to AGAS, yourself included."[51] While Fenn and the leaders of the GBT were willing to do so, other members of the OSS were not as willing to see this active group leave OSS control.

As 1944 ended, Gordon traveled to Washington, D.C., to visit and meet with OSS representatives, leaving Fenn and Bernard in control of the group. While Bernard managed the GBT compound in Kunming, Fenn spent New Year's Eve in India cementing the GBT's relationship with the British and collecting £3,000 for operating expenses. This task put Fenn in a potentially precarious position. Though an American officer of the OSS, Fenn was taking his marching orders from Gordon, a British subject, and attempting—without official U.S. sanction—to strengthen ties between the British and the GBT, not to bring the GBT closer to the OSS. Nonetheless, Fenn made no secret of his presence in India, inspiring comments from both British intelligence and the OSS. MI5 expressed its regret at not being able to provide more funds for Gordon, lamenting what it supposed was an imminent OSS takeover of the network and praising the benefits of Gordon's independence. Meanwhile, OSS colleagues assailed Fenn with questions as to the purpose of his trip and as to his organizational loyalty.

The new year would bring many changes to both the OSS and the GBT. In January Chiang Kai-shek authorized the OSS to set up networks of its own, free from the oversight and control of General Tai Li. As OSS opportunity increased, so did OSS desire to acquire the GBT network. In early February Major Duncan Lee, SI chief of the Japan-China Section of the OSS's Far East Division, reported that the commanding general of U.S. forces in the China theater, Albert Wedemeyer, had decided to "transfer the Gordon-Bernard unit to OSS" and that the OSS would "apparently have the principal responsibility for SI operations."[52]

But this move encountered serious obstacles. With the exception of Fenn's Chinese agents, the GBT network was almost exclusively made up of pro-Allied Frenchmen. And, as discussed previously, only a few months earlier Roosevelt had prohibited aiding and working with the French in Indochina. While Lee and Colonel Richard Heppner, who oversaw OSS activities for Wedemeyer, explored the possibilities of utilizing the GBT network, Donovan, in Kunming, advocated closer cooperation between the French and the OSS. Thus, it seemed that the OSS's two best opportunities for collecting intelligence in Indochina involved working directly with the French, in violation of presidential orders. Historian Stein Tønnesson has concluded that "since Donovan had certainly been informed of this prohibition which he cannot simply have disregarded, the only plausible explanation is that he was exempted from the presidential directive through some special arrangement with the President."[53]

Even assuming this to be the case, relations between the French and the Americans in China were tense. The French resented any implication that their colony should be stripped from them and were both angry at and embarrassed by their inert status in China, especially since they had neither cachet nor resources. It was perhaps inevitable that the French working with Gordon soon felt the same. In January Bernard and Fenn received a frantic message from André Lan saying that he was being "harassed by the French authorities because he had been reported to be working for the Americans!" According to Lan, even the Free French were becoming anti-American because Roosevelt would not recognize French rights to Indochina, and as a result GBT agents "found it difficult to get information and even more difficult to keep up radio schedules."[54]

After discussing the situation, Bernard and Fenn decided that one of them should go to the border to meet with a small group of Lan's unhappy French officers to assuage their fears. After a cold and difficult journey, Fenn arrived on the Vietnamese border carrying much-needed supplies for the French agents, including a portable radio. Although neither Fenn nor Bernard could be sure that the French were convinced of GBT sincerity, the gifts, especially the radio, had made a favorable impression. Although the GBT network was still a bit weakened by the rift in relations with the Free French, it nevertheless managed to report on an Allied bombing mission over Saigon and on the nine pilots who had been shot down. Sadly, they reported, three of the men were captured by the Japanese, though André Lan and his contacts among the French Resistance managed to rescue the others.[55] Frank Tan, who had been meeting with agents in the field, reported on the safe return to China of two of the pilots. One of the young pilots, named Knight, was relatively uninjured and told the GBT his story. Knight credited both Lan and "natives" for his rescue:

> My vision and thoughts began to clear and I suddenly saw the whole shebang—our plane in flames, big crowds converging in all round and a Japanese truck hurtling towards me on the road. So I swiftly turned to bury my chute, but to my amazement some natives were already doing this! Then I remembered I must clear my pockets; and when I started pulling things out a native grabbed my silk map and buried it in the soft mud with a single movement. . . . Already the others were hurrying me off and they hid me in a nearby hut. About fifteen minutes later several Frenchmen appeared. They offered the natives a wad of money but they wouldn't accept it and finally went off bowing to me. . . . Then this man André took over and I learned later that he'd directed the whole deal.[56]

Thus, whether acknowledged as "agents" or not, the Vietnamese were participating in the rescue of American pilots. This example gave credence to earlier claims that many Vietnamese were at the very least anti-Japanese, and were perhaps even pro-Allied.

Little did Fenn realize in January of 1945 how soon he would be forced to reconsider all that he had heard about the Vietnamese. For the moment, he was too wrapped up in trying to calm the increasingly heated dispute between himself and the OSS and between the OSS and the GBT. From the OSS perspective, ultimate control of the GBT seemed just around the corner. An OSS report written in February stated optimistically that the GBT had been placed under OSS control and that Gordon, then in Washington, would soon meet with OSS representatives to determine how his group would be used. With the difficulty regarding the GBT network's desire for independence apparently solved, according to the report, the only problem lay with the region itself. The author undoubtedly referred to the president's prohibition on working with French Resistance groups in his concluding remarks: "The whole question of French-Indochina [was] complicated by a number of high level policy decisions," which still needed to be addressed.[57]

The report's confidence was unwarranted. In both Washington and Kunming, OSS-GBT relations went steadily downhill. As far as Gordon was concerned, OSS methods were "autocratic." He maintained that the level of control desired by the OSS would destroy the very independence that had made his group so successful and hence so desirable. In Kunming, Bernard and Tan found getting supplies from the OSS to be a continual chore.[58] OSS Supply thought Bernard and Tan arrogant and considered Fenn untrustworthy. Only SI managed to retain cordial relations, mostly because the GBT continued to feed SI important information from their agents in southern China and Indochina. However, Wedemeyer insisted that all intelligence groups in his theater be brought under his command, meaning that the GBT could not continue to operate as an independent unit. In February, Wedemeyer and the GBT reached a compromise. The combined efforts of Gordon in Washington and Fenn in Kunming resulted in a transfer to AGAS of the GBT and Fenn, although technically Fenn became the OSS liaison to AGAS.[59]

Although the OSS did not achieve the monopoly on the GBT that it desired, it did manage to preserve its access to the GBT's information network. AGAS had long benefited from the GBT's sources and information and was more than happy to acquire Fenn and the group. Fenn, Bernard, and Tan settled into their new position with AGAS, while Gordon remained in the United States for an additional month. The first few days in March 1945 were uneventful. Messages continued to arrive, Helen decoded them, and Fenn and Tan analyzed and dispersed them as necessary.

On March 9, the wires went strangely silent. Bernard and Fenn were puzzled at the absence of news but were relatively unconcerned. The next day, March 10, one cryptic message got through from a GBT agent in Mengkai. It consisted of six words: "Japanese seized all posts throughout Indochina." Bernard and Fenn waited for more but got only silence from their usually busy wires. They would soon discover that the network they had worked so hard to establish, and of which they were so proud, was all but nonexistent. The Japanese had initiated Operation MEIGO (Operation Bright Moon) and were now in complete control of Vietnam. The GBT network was gone. *French* Indochina was no more.

5

Endings and Beginnings

As Fenn and Bernard waited by their silent radio, they did not yet realize the full impact of the dispatch they had received earlier in the day. The cryptic message of March 10 stated simply: "Japanese seized all posts throughout Indochina." The words were ominous, yet neither man could comprehend their full impact—the sudden demise of the GBT as an organized net or of French dominance in Vietnam. The two men, along with many others worldwide, would soon discover that on March 9, 1945, at 9:00 PM local time the Japanese had initiated a coup de main, code-named Operation MEIGO.

Although MEIGO surprised both Americans, the possibility of a coup had existed since the very beginning of the Japanese occupation of Vietnam. Based on his study of the *Official Japanese History of the Pacific War*, historian Louis Allen has concluded that the Japanese Imperial General Staff had begun to contemplate the possibility of a coup following the British and American landings in North Africa in early November 1942. Although the Japanese certainly preferred to maintain the status quo in Indochina, freeing their armies for engagements elsewhere, the possibility that the French colons might join the Allied cause remained. Should this occur, the Japanese would be forced to "block hostile movements within the country [Indochina] itself."[1]

From November 1942 until summer 1943 little time was spent on planning for the potential overthrow of the French. However, in late summer 1943 officers of the Japanese Southern Army (then based in Singapore) discussed the need to study the various options available should the need for military action in Indochina arise. By December the planning of Operation MA (the name would later be changed to MEIGO) was under way. The War Plans Section at Army General Headquarters noted a number of potential obstacles—one of which would be the difficulty in getting the Vietnamese to support the Japanese. Operation MA called for the expansion of military forces in Vietnam, including an increase in the number of *kempeitai* (military police), the deployment of a tank regiment, and the movement of the Thirty-fourth Independent Mixed Brigade and the Fifty-third Division to Indochina. With the rapid downturn of Japanese military fortunes after June 1942 and increasing difficulties during 1943, no one within the Japanese military hierarchy was anxious to divert much-needed resources to Vietnam unless the situation worsened dramatically. And in 1942–1943 the Japanese had little to fear in Indochina. Allied forces were still far away from Vietnam, and although not necessarily friendly, relations between the Japanese and French remained, for the most part, cordial.[2]

The dynamics of the Franco-Japanese relationship began to shift, however, as Allied victories in Europe mounted. The repeated bombing of German cities throughout the spring of 1944, the liberation of Rome and the D-day invasion in June, and finally the liberation of Paris in August altered the attitudes of both the French and the Japanese. Whereas the French openly celebrated the end of the Nazi puppet government and the liberation of their capital, the Japanese grew increasingly wary of how this "joy" might manifest itself in the colony. "A series of unfortunate incidents compounded Japanese suspicion, according to a former *Kempei*'s recollection: contempt shown toward Japanese flags in Hanoi, the deliberate wrecking of a Japanese army transport truck, discrimination against Japanese commercial firms, and the coercion and arrest of pro-Japanese Vietnamese."[3] By the autumn of 1944 the Japanese Foreign Ministry, military officials stationed in Indochina, and the Southern Army favored a military takeover. In preparation for this eventuality, a joint Army-Navy agreement had been in place since January. It emphasized that stability had to be preserved, "while overthrowing the military and political force of the French, and compelling their surrender by prompt and resolute action to destroy any war-like spirit they might show. Lines of communication, airfields and shipping, must all be seized and the existing administrative structure must be maintained. Plans should be secret, espionage increased, and forces trained and re-distributed."[4]

One major stumbling block to the coup remained, however. The authorities in Tokyo were not yet convinced that a military takeover was either necessary or advisable. From the Japanese perspective, Indochina, Vietnam in particular, had (since 1940) become an important logistical and supply base. As the Americans crept closer, invading the southern Philippines in October 1944 and liberating Manila and central Luzon in early 1945, the Japanese command became increasingly anxious about the possibility of an Allied landing on the Indochinese coast, particularly since the number of Japanese troops stationed there was "inadequate."[5] The Japanese could not afford to risk having an enemy in the rear. The hopeful anticipation of this event demonstrated by the French did not help matters.

The French had good reason to expect an Allied invasion of Vietnam. Operation BETA, developed by General Albert Wedemeyer, the commander of U.S. Army forces in the China theater, envisioned a two-pronged attack with the main thrust toward Canton, China. The Allies hoped to open a southern Chinese port that would provide a "short, large-scale supply line to Chungking."[6] The second, or "Indochinese" phase of BETA, called for a diversionary operation into Tonkin. In February 1945 Wedemeyer stated that he had "evolved a plan for advance into Indo-China," which was kept top secret and discussed with only a few people outside his immediate staff. The general had, however, broached the idea to the French military attaché, who had "requested that as many Americans as possible be placed with the Chinese advance units." The invasion failed to materialize, as Allied strategy "decided to move from the Philippines directly to Okinawa, without troubling to land forces on the Asian mainland," and Indochina again took a back seat in wartime planning.[7] Nevertheless, historian Stein Tønnesson has concluded that the proposed landing had important long-term consequences: "By fueling French and Japanese expectations of a US invasion, Roosevelt, Wedemeyer and the OSS prompted a Franco-Japanese confrontation, which in turn paved the way for revolution."[8]

The potential for revolution was not, however, on the minds of the colonial French in early 1945. Encouraged by Allied victories in both Europe and the Pacific, the French in Indochina had been predicting a victory over the Axis powers for several months, and by early 1945 the French Resistance was becoming progressively more blatant in its anti-Axis behavior.[9] Japanese authorities were not blind to this, and although the activities of the French Resistance did not *cause* the March coup de main, they certainly added fuel to the fire. The Japanese expressed distinct displeasure with Frenchmen, not unlike the members of André Lan's network and agents of the GBT, who "hid American aviators who had crashed in Indo-China and refused to give them over to the Japanese unless given formal assurance that the prisoners would be treated according to the Geneva Convention. The Japanese gave no assurance and the French did not release the Americans." The Japanese irritation increased when Frenchmen blamed the Japanese for "a good many" casualties among the French after thirty American B-29s bombed Saigon.[10] On February 2, the decision to carry out the coup de main and plans related to it were transmitted to Emperor Hirohito, but an exact date for the takeover had yet to be set. "The Japanese Army customarily initiated actions on certain historic days," noted Louis Allen; "8 March was Observance Day for the Handing down of the Imperial Rescript; 10 March was Army Remembrance Day. 9 March neatly avoided these two dates."[11]

On March 9 the Japanese initiated Operation MEIGO in the interests of maintaining the secrecy surrounding its planning and execution. At 6:00 PM Governor-General Jean Decoux and Japan's Ambassador Matsumoto Shuni-chi met in Decoux's offices in Saigon for the official signing of the annual rice-supply agreement. The meeting seemed a routine formality to Decoux, although he had been worried about the Japanese reaction to the frequently overt actions of the French Resistance.[12] When he left Hanoi in February for his annual trip to Saigon, Decoux had no idea of what would transpire on the ninth. With the end of World War II in sight, he remained confident that France's colonial status in Vietnam would remain unchallenged. He remembered looking with delight at the French flag floating on the breeze in Saigon—a symbol of French pride and power in an era of French humiliation in Europe.[13] As he prepared for what he believed would be a routine meeting with the ambassador, he sensed no significant changes in the mood of the Japanese in Saigon during those first few days of March. He recalls that on March 7 nothing seemed out of the ordinary, even as the Japanese prepared for the execution of their *"acte abominable contre l'Indochine."*[14]

Nonetheless, Decoux was not looking forward to his meeting with Matsumoto. He did not like the ambassador and found him to be crude and lacking the sophistication of his predecessor, Ambassador Yoshizawa Kenkichi. At the meeting on the ninth Decoux noted that the ambassador continually looked at his watch and seemed preoccupied and nervous as they discussed the rice-supply agreement.[15]

With the conclusion of the agreement, Matsumoto began probing Decoux as to the intentions of his government vis-à-vis de Gaulle, the Allies, and the Japanese. Decoux attempted to sidestep the questioning without further antagonizing the Japanese, but the die had already been cast. There were no answers that would satisfactorily answer the Japanese questions at that point. The Japanese charged Decoux's administration with aiding Allied airmen brought down over Indochina, with failing to recognize the Japanese puppet regime in Nanking, with failing to provide adequate corvée labor and funds to the Japanese military, and with tolerating the American bombing missions over Indochina without "serious protests." Historian F. C. Jones declared that "all these charges were true enough and the recital of them shows that the Japanese were under no illusions as to Decoux's real attitude towards them."[16] Nothing the governor-general could say at that moment would have changed the situation: The ultimatum was in hand and Matsumoto would present it regardless of Decoux's responses. At precisely 7:00 PM Matsumoto presented Decoux with the newest demands of the Japanese government.[17]

The aide-mémoire Matsumoto passed to Decoux noted Japanese displeasure with the "recent situation," calling special attention to "the repeated attacks of the Americans against Indochina and the possibility of an imminent invasion by the enemies of the Japanese government." It urged Decoux to show proof of his intention to participate in the joint defense of Indochina should an Allied invasion occur. Decoux was given two hours—until 9:00 PM—to agree to place under Japanese control all French forces, munitions, railways, maritime and river transport, internal and external communications, and other assets deemed necessary for military operations. The note also stated that all administrative apparatuses of the Indochinese government would be expected to give immediate consent to Japanese demands. The governor-general expressed his dismay at both the contents of the message and the two-hour time limit in which he was to deliver a decision.

The weight of the situation was obvious to all concerned. Decoux could not agree to the Japanese demands without forfeiting any credibility he might have with the new French government of Charles de Gaulle. In capitulating, he would appear to be a collaborator and possibly even a traitor in the eyes of both the colons and the mainland French. Yet if he did not acquiesce he would forfeit the one goal he had worked diligently for since taking over from Catroux in 1940: the maintenance of *French* Indochina. Decoux replied that he would have to consult with the French military commanders before tendering a reply. Both Decoux and Matsumoto knew that he was only attempting to gain more time. By 8:15 Matsumoto, relatively confident about the impending coup, had left the governor-general. As the sun set on March 9, in the "deathly silence" following the ambassador's departure, Jean Decoux watched the daily ceremonial lowering of the French flag and worried what the next morning would bring.[18]

Given Decoux's predicament, there was little he could do. He quickly convened his senior staff members and the available high-ranking civilian and military authorities in Saigon to bring them up to speed on the situation, and all judged the Japanese demands unacceptable.[19] At 8:45 Decoux finished preparing his reply, which neither accepted nor rejected the Japanese memorandum. He reiterated that he could not accede to the Japanese memo without consultation with the French high command in Hanoi but said he was certainly ready to pursue further talks with the Japanese. Decoux had already concluded that he "would never sign an agreement contrary to his personal honor or to that of the French military."[20] Although the two-hour time limit was not yet up at 8:45, Decoux learned that French citizens had already been "arrested and molested" and that Japanese forces had cut the roads between Saigon and Cholon.[21]

By 9:00 the French message was on its way but had not yet arrived at Japanese army headquarters, though the Japanese had been notified that it was en route. Earlier, when Ambassador Matsumoto had departed the governor-general's office, he had left a Japanese officer at the Palais du Gouvernement Général to act as a guide and "safeguard" for the French officer, Captain Robin, charged with delivering Decoux's response. However, as Robin prepared to leave, he discovered that his Japanese escort had vanished. Nevertheless, Robin departed, accompanied by Lieutenant d'Aiguilhon. Apparently unfamiliar with the exact location of Japanese headquarters—hardly an advertisement for French competence—Robin and his escort got lost, which delayed delivery of the message.[22]

The Japanese waited for fifteen more minutes. At 9:18 General Tsuchihashi Yuitsu, Thirty-eighth Imperial Army in Saigon, gave the verbal order for the 67,000 troops in Vietnam to begin the coup de main.[23] At 9:21 the code "7 7 7" was signaled to Japanese officers throughout Indochina. To its recipients, this coded message meant that the governor-general had rejected the Japanese demands and that all units were to begin operations at once.[24] Shortly thereafter Captain Robin entered Japanese army headquarters. It was only after Robin and d'Aiguilhon had spotted an arriving automobile displaying an immense Japanese flag that they managed to locate their destination.[25]

Luckily for Tsuchihashi, the French reply could easily be interpreted as a rejection of Japanese demands. If for some unforeseeable reason Decoux had agreed to the new set of Japanese demands, Tsuchihashi would have been guilty of ordering an attack on a cooperative and valuable ally in Indochina. However, the governor-general had not accepted the Japanese demands, and the Palais du Gouvernement Général was occupied by Japanese forces without bloodshed. At roughly the same time, Japanese troops took possession of administrative offices, radio stations, the central telephone and telegraph offices, banks, and the main industrial enterprises. They also attacked the police forces and arrested French civilian and military authorities.[26]

The next morning, Major General Kawamura, chief of staff of the Thirty-eighth Army, demanded an interview with Decoux. Kawamura expressed his regret that the French lack of cooperation had necessitated the coup and assured Decoux of the continued protection of French lives and property. Yet the governor-general himself soon became a prisoner of the Japanese in Loc Ninh, eighty miles north of Saigon.[27] Although confined, Decoux and "high French officials" were, the Japanese assured, to be treated "as liberally as possible."[28] The French certainly did not agree that Japanese treatment was "liberal." An estimated 500 French civilians, "starting with anyone suspected of aiding the Allies, and followed by Sûreté officers who had previously maltreated natives sympathetic to the Japanese," were jailed, and over 200 were killed or disappeared.[29]

In an attempt to justify the coup, the Japanese addressed the public via the radio stations, placing the blame for necessitating the coup on the activities of the French Resistance working in collaboration with the Allies and on the lack of French cooperation.[30] At home, in his speech before the Diet, the Japanese premier, General Koiso Kuniaki, accused the French administration of "acts of treachery" that had "necessitated" the coup.[31] Foreign Minister Shigemitsu Mamoru clarified the matter from the Japanese perspective:

> When the German Army withdrew from France, the new de Gaulle
> Government revived the original declaration of war against Japan. De
> Coux [*sic*] then proclaimed his allegiance and made it clear that Indo-
> China was at war with us. Indo-China was the base for Japan's
> expeditionary forces in Malaya, Burma, Java and Sumatra and had to be
> held secure at all costs. Nor could Japan tamely submit to a declaration
> of hostility. . . . Japan had no option but to make an end of it.[32]

Although the first signs of the coup appeared in Saigon, March 9 witnessed the demise of French control throughout the colony. The first attack and the strongest resistance were in Tonkin, where 32,000 French Indochinese troops fought the Japanese.[33] In numerous instances, French officers and senior staff had been invited to dinner with their Japanese counterparts. Many accepted the invitations only to be arrested at the appointed hour. Some Frenchmen did not survive the arrest. At Lang Son, site of the 1940 Franco-Japanese skirmish, General Emile Lemonnier and the French resident, Camille Auphelle, as well as three senior staff officers, were beheaded after refusing to sign the surrender document. One hundred legionnaires at Fort Brière de L'Isle (Lang Son) fought the Japanese for twenty-four hours, at times in hand-to-hand combat. The Japanese killed most of the garrison, many of whom reportedly sang "The Marseillaise" as they died. The garrisons at Ha Giang and Hanoi were also overwhelmed, and thousands were taken prisoner. The last French position to surrender was Dong Dang, where colonial troops and their French officer (only one survived) held out until March 12.[34]

Historian David Marr concluded that "2,100 European officers and enlisted men were killed or disappeared" during the coup and that Vietnamese casualties numbered even more. He estimated that "about 15,000 members of the Indochina armed forces were interned by the Japanese, 12,000 of them European."[35] Although most garrisons collapsed quickly, two commanders, Generals Gabriel Sabattier and Marcel Alessandri, managed to flee Indochina with their men.

French historian André Gaudel wrote that in late February General Sabattier, commander of the Tonkin division and leader of the northern Resistance, had given precise verbal instructions to the province heads to stand firm against any impending Japanese aggression. Based on Sûreté information, Sabattier alerted the garrisons in Tonkin and northern Laos of the possibility of a coup and secretly left Hanoi on March 8 to join his forces positioned northwest of the city.[36] The largest force in the area, located just west of the Red River, was the Foreign Legion Fifth Regiment. The legion's approximately 2,000 men were under the control of General Alessandri.[37] Engaged elsewhere, the Japanese did not attack on the evening of March 9, allowing Alessandri and his men time to evacuate and begin the march north. Their reprieve did not last long, however; the Japanese pursued the escaping soldiers, cutting off access to the two most important border exits, at Lao Cai and Ha Giang.[38]

The terrain and circumstances were trying for both Sabattier and Alessandri. Sabattier quickly lost contact with most of his units and was forced to walk along the Black River to Lai Chau, accompanied by a small band of survivors: three officers, an interpreter, his driver, and two soldiers of a T'ai minority.[39] Meanwhile, Alessandri considered the plausibility of a successful escape into Allied territory. The average age of Alessandri's men was forty, and they were unaccustomed to physical hardship, which meant many would be unable to survive the treacherous journey across miles of dense, mountainous jungle to the Chinese border.[40]

Alessandri also had a few companies of Indochinese soldiers in his ranks. When contemplating his next move after the coup, he decided to separate from the Indochinese troops.[41] This move has been interpreted in different ways. Historian J. Lee Ready stated that the Indochinese were ordered to "leave their equipment and uniforms with the Europeans and try to escape home" in the hopes that they might be able to survive by "going bush."[42]

Likewise, Gaudel wrote that Alessandri "gave them their freedom."[43] French agent and Asian religious scholar Paul Mus recalled that some of the Vietnamese contingents wept as they left. According to Mus, these men "went back to their villages, still in their French uniforms, and some were killed by Japanese whom they refused to salute."[44] David Marr pointed out, however, that these men were "left to their own devices . . . alone, without weapons, vulnerable to retaliation." He observed that being demobilized may have "relieved some of them, but it undoubtedly hurt others deeply, and it was soon being used by Vietnamese nationalists to symbolize the perfidiousness of French colonialism."[45]

We can reasonably hypothesize that this "perfidious" behavior had significant long-term effects. When Americans arrived in Indochina later the same year, they befriended and operated *alongside* the Viet Minh, which among some Vietnamese further enhanced the positive image of Americans and deepened Vietnamese disgust for Alessandri and the French. Set side by side for propaganda purposes, these two incidents would have only further disgraced the French for their behavior and discredited their claim to an inherent right to rule Vietnam. For although Alessandri's troops would encounter numerous hardships over the next three months, the Indochinese troops, stripped of their uniforms and weapons, certainly had every right to feel humiliated and abandoned.

By March 10 Alessandri's column of men, horses, and mules crossed the Black River, harassed by the Japanese as they fled. The men of the Third Foreign Legion lost seventy-five men fighting a rearguard action and continued to deal with attacks by the Japanese over the next several weeks. In some cases, they were also attacked by Indochinese. An Ultra report from April 27, 1945, noted that "a French unit of 56 men, trying to reach Chinese territory," was "attacked along the way by the populace and lost 30 men." Another French detachment was "betrayed by the Annamese and was forced to abandon its equipment in order to escape the Japanese."[46] The experience of Mus, however, does not substantiate this.[47] He recalled that "the day before the coup the French were the respected masters of the country, the day after it they were uninvited guests with the worst of reputations."[48] But in his flight from Hanoi in March 1945, he "was given every possible help" by the Vietnamese. According to Mus, the coup was simply the "instant when their eyes were opened and the feeling of dependence lost."[49]

It was exactly this loss of control that the French were trying to prevent. On March 28, General Alessandri established his headquarters in what would become the most famous valley of the Vietnamese War for Independence,

Dien Bien Phu.[50] On March 29, General Sabattier joined him in the highland garrison. On that day a British plane landed, bringing François de Langlade, a messenger from de Gaulle, and Colonel Dewavrin (better known by his alias, "Passy"), head of de Gaulle's intelligence service, the Direction Générale des Etudes et Recherches (DGER). De Langlade arrived with two messages for Sabattier. The first notified Sabattier that de Gaulle had appointed him *délégué général*, granting him both civilian and military powers. As the commander of all French forces in Indochina, Sabattier established his temporary "capital" at Dien Bien Phu. In the second, de Gaulle ordered Sabattier to maintain his position in Indochina as a tangible symbol of uninterrupted French sovereignty over the colony.[51]

However, after less than a week in Dien Bien Phu, the Japanese forced the French to flee. Sabattier and Alessandri had comforted themselves early on with the belief that the Japanese would be content to hold the fertile lowlands and that the escaped French soldiers would be safe in the highland region. But their brief stay at Dien Bien Phu was marked by daily skirmishes with superior Japanese forces. With little respite, the French conducted a fighting retreat from Dien Bien Phu in the direction of Lai Chau. By the last day of the month, the Japanese had forced them from Tuan Giai. The emperor's forces continued to push the French past Luang Prabang to Phong Saly and on to Lai Chau, where the men resisted until April 9.[52] By late May the Japanese had pushed the French out of Indochina entirely. On May 20 the French crossed the border into China. For seventy-two days they had been in a running fight over difficult terrain, in adverse weather, and without adequate supplies. By June nearly 5,700 stragglers, including 2,469 Europeans, crossed the Chinese frontier at various locations, only to be "disarmed, and treated with ill-disguised contempt" by their hosts.[53]

Sabattier failed in his mission to maintain a fighting French position in the colony. And although he—and many others—blamed the Japanese for their "treachery," they also blamed the United States for denying them the support necessary to withstand the Japanese onslaught.[54] David Marr, as well as numerous other historians, contended that "substantial American and Chinese assistance could have enabled Sabattier to defend several mountain redoubts."[55] The French hoped, in particular, for air support from the Fourteenth Air Force operating from bases in China.

The Fourteenth's commander, General Claire Chennault, found himself in a difficult position with regard to the Japanese coup. After the coup, reports of the siege of Lang Son reached Chennault's desk. The French reported heavy losses and requested Allied air strikes against the enemy. When

Chennault requested clearance from China theater headquarters to undertake an immediate bombing mission in support of the garrison, the affirmative reply was brief and clear: "Give them hell."[56] Although it was too late to save the garrison at Lang Son, Chennault's inclination to aid the French seems apparent. On March 10 he met with Chiang Kai-shek to discuss the Chinese policy on the fleeing French.

Cognizant of the Chinese disdain for the French, Chennault hinged his questions on whether or not the French resisted the attacks of their mutual enemy. He asked: *If* the French put up a stiff resistance to the Japanese, would they be abandoned to their own fate or would the Allies, specifically the Americans and Chinese, send troops to assist them? *If* they put up little serious resistance, would they be disarmed upon entering China? Chiang's answer to the latter query was vague; he stated that the French might be "permitted to remain in China at a specified area." His response regarding assistance seemed a bit clearer. "If stiff resistance is put up," he declared, "assistance may be rendered."[57] Given this "authorization," between March 12 and March 28 the Fourteenth Air Force flew ninety-eight sorties over Indochina, including bombing and reconnaissance missions. Twenty-eight of these were "in response to direct request by the French." Chennault maintained that the number of missions would have been even greater if not for "bad weather, non-availability of supplies [and] surplus equipment, and the fluidity of the situation."[58]

In his memoirs, Chennault recalled:

Soon after the Japanese struck, I sent Fourteenth Air Force intelligence officers into Indo-China to make contact with the French troops. Flying in tiny grasshopper planes, they landed in cleared jungle strips and had made arrangements for air drop of ammunition, medical supplies, and food to the retreating French when orders arrived from theater headquarters stating that no arms and ammunition would be provided to French troops under any circumstances. The Fourteenth did the best it could to relieve pressure on the fleeing French by strafing and bombing attacks on Japanese columns. Eventually we were also allowed to evacuate French women and children by air.[59]

As discussed previously, the ambiguities of American policy regarding the continued French possession of Indochina had yet to be settled by early 1945. However, a reluctance to *help* the French *keep* Indochina seems to have been articulated at the presidential level and passed to lower echelons through the chain of command. This was certainly clear by the last of April, for although the president had died on the twelfth, China theater command continued to follow Roosevelt's directives concerning French Indochina. General Wedemeyer held a staff conference on the morning of April 25, 1945. In attendance was the deputy OSS chief of China theater, Colonel Willis Bird. In reporting to his superior Bird noted clear directives from Wedemeyer concerning French Indochina: "No equipment or arms will be given FIC [French Indochina] under any circumstances. Food and medical supplies may be furnished on humanitarian grounds but it was not indicated that we should supply those. OSS may do as much as they can in FIC for intelligence purposes only and may only take in such equipment and arms as necessary for teams own protection, no sabotage work to be done."[60]

On March 7, 1945, General Wedemeyer received additional information on policy regarding the French colony when he and Patrick Hurley, U.S. ambassador to China, met with President Roosevelt.[61] Both men left with "clear instructions as to what they *could not do* in Indochina." Yet what they *could do* was left undefined. Historian Stein Tønnesson posed the difficult question: "Should this be ascribed solely to Roosevelt's weak condition, or did the President also deliberately leave the initiative in Indochina to the Japanese? Since Roosevelt's goal was to place Indochina under international trusteeship it must have been tempting to let the Japanese do the job of removing the colonial regime."[62]

Whether or not Roosevelt deliberately left the "initiative" to the Japanese will remain open to speculation. But regardless of Roosevelt's intent, in reality his actions did leave the door open for the Japanese to remove the French from power. Certainly Chennault's understanding of presidential policy regarding Indochina, as directed to him through orders from Wedemeyer, gave him few options regarding the French, which in essence left them twisting in the wind. "I carried out my orders to the letter," recalled Chennault, "but I did not relish the idea of leaving Frenchmen to be slaughtered in the jungle while I was forced officially to ignore their plight." He concluded, "The American government was interested in seeing the French forcibly ejected from Indo-China so the problem of postwar separation from their colony would be easier."[63] However, although they did not receive the American aid they hoped for, the French were not without options. American transports bypassed the French, but British supplies flown from Calcutta reached some of the fleeing soldiers. British aerial supply missions dropped in guns, grenades, and mortars. Although undoubtedly a psychological asset, these airdrops turned out to be of very little use to some escapees who, because of their diminishing physical strength, discarded the heavy burden. Others, who were in perhaps better condition to fight, had to abandon guerrilla warfare because of their lack of supplies.[64]

Initially, the OSS had planned to aid the remaining French Resistance forces. On March 12, 1945, the "Gorrilla Team," headed by Major John W. Summers, was alerted about a mission near Mong Cai, on the northern coast of Vietnam. Lieutenant Robert Ettinger of the OSS was assigned to the team for special SI work. Five men (not including Ettinger) were to organize and arm "any French resistance forces in the area" and perform "regular SO and demolition work." Although this was seemingly in clear violation of Wedemeyer's earlier briefing, it can be assumed that the Summers mission was operating according to the March 20 directive authorizing the OSS to provide military aid "in the form of supplies and/or U.S. controlled military personnel to any and all groups opposing the Japanese forces."[65]

This first Summers mission was canceled, as were several "new" missions to be carried out in Vietnam by the Gorrilla Team between March 12 and April 23. It was not until April 24 that the men of the Summers mission finally jumped into French Indochina. Summers recorded some apprehension as to what they would discover on the ground: "All this time since March 12 the Japanese had been pushing steadily North and Northwest and we were becoming increasingly unsure as to just what the situation was at the time." Upon landing and locating the retreating soldiers, the Gorrilla Team reported on the French situation:

> The French forces we saw had no intention of doing any more fighting and were merely moving toward China the best they could. They carried only the bare essentials of equipment. Many were armed with American carbines which they said were dropped [to] them by the British. They said they had received considerable small arms and ammunition from the British, but they destroyed it. None of us remember seeing a wounded Frenchman. None of the French we saw or talked to had any Jap insignia, equipment, souvenirs, etc. Our impression was that the French did very little actual fighting. No Frenchman could tell us of any place where they made a determined stand. We are of the opinion that the fighting mainly consisted of rear-guard action when leading Jap patrols caught up with the retreating French. . . . Our opinion, and it is only an impression received in talking with the French officers, is that they only desired to get out of FIC to China and try to get into the present French Government graces. . . . From what we saw, the

American officials were right in not sending the French supplies as they probably would have only destroyed them as they did much of the equipment sent in by [the] British.[66]

The French moved on toward the Chinese border, leaving the five men of the Summers mission as their rear guard. On the morning of April 28, a Japanese force, estimated to number sixty-five men, attacked. Luckily, all members of the Gorrilla Team escaped the trap, but their intelligence-collecting mission in French Indochina had come to an abrupt end.[67]

The experience of Lieutenant Ettinger was quite different from that of the Gorrilla Team. Although the OSS had originally assigned Ettinger to the Summers mission, he arrived in French Indochina separately, joining Sabattier's forces on March 28 at Dien Bien Phu. Ettinger, a French American, joined Sabattier's troops as they began their difficult trek through Tonkin to China. On March 29, OSS headquarters in Kunming received the first messages from Ettinger, which stated that the French were "very badly pressed" and that he had had "to move three times in twenty-four hours to avoid capture." Between March 29 and April 4 Ettinger sent out intelligence information to theater headquarters and to the Fourteenth Air Force, calling in "certain bombing missions."[68] It was allegedly in response to Ettinger's requests that General Chennault was "allowed to strafe hostile Japanese columns along the line of retreat."[69] As will be seen, the experience with Sabattier's troops was the first in a long line of often-controversial interactions between Lieutenant Ettinger and the French regarding Indochina.

Nevertheless, neither Ettinger's stint with Sabattier nor the brief stay of the Gorrilla Team in northern Vietnam satisfied the U.S. need for intelligence on the Japanese in Indochina. As the main information collection agency for the United States in the area, the OSS was now, more than ever, in need of reliable sources. Prior to the coup, the OSS had been attempting to gain a place in the intelligence-collection networks in the area or, even better, to establish its own. But the OSS had been frustrated in its efforts to bring the GBT under its control and had not succeeded in establishing a strong working relationship with the French in the area. As the OSS looked to expand its options, a March 1, 1945, memorandum to Wedemeyer from Lieutenant Colonel Paul Helliwell, SI chief of the OSS in the China theater, raised a different possibility. Helliwell wrote:

As you know, besides the French, who cooperate to a greater or lesser extent as circumstances develop, there are a number of revolutionary native groups of widely varying political connections and of widely varying strengths. Practically all are anti-French as well as anti-Japanese. Many of these groups have made efforts to contact this organization in order to trade information or to do MO work in return for monetary advances, or, in some cases, arms and ammunition.[70]

Helliwell believed that the timing for OSS activities was critical. He stated: "I have reason to believe that the French Military Mission takes a somewhat dim view of the GBT activities, and if they suddenly clamp down on them, we may find our presently limited coverage of FIC cut down to nothing. I, therefore, feel it is quite important that we get to work on straight OSS activities in that country." Helliwell clearly believed that the OSS needed a U.S.-directed net instead of relying on others to share their information. In order to accomplish this, he requested specific directives from theater headquarters on the use of indigenous agents. In particular he wanted to know: "To what extent can we deal with native individuals or revolutionary groups to secure information and to secure physical cover for our agents?" And further, "In the event we can deal with these native groups, are we authorized to give them arms and other supplies, or are we limited to paying them off in money?" He emphasized that the OSS was "on the fence" with "certain native groups" and could not move forward without direction from theater headquarters.[71] The urgency Helliwell alluded to in his memo was compounded eight days later by the Japanese coup.

The events of March 9, 1945, changed the situation for everyone involved, certainly for the major powers also involved in the world war: the Americans, the French, and the Japanese. The Americans, at least temporarily, experienced a shortage of information on such things as weather and Japanese troop and ship movements. The French lost not only their colony but also status in the eyes of their colonial subjects. After March 9 the Japanese had added responsibilities in administering—or at least in overseeing the administration of—Indochina. However, the most crucial change in the wake of MEIGO did not involve Franco-Japanese relations or seriously affect the war effort. With the coup de main the Vietnamese and the Japanese entered into a new phase of their relationship, a phase that would completely change the dynamics of the situation.

In their planning for the coup, the Japanese military and civilian authorities had frequently disagreed—on timing, on their relationship with the French, and most significantly on the policy to be followed regarding the Indochinese "kingdoms." Members of the Japanese Foreign Ministry, especially

Foreign Minister Shigemitsu, preferred to declare the kingdoms independent prior to any military action against the French. Messages decoded by Ultra in February 1945 indicated that Shigemitsu had "taken up the cudgels" on the issue of sovereignty for the Indochinese and that the "[Foreign] Ministry's opinion on the independence question" was "at least partly attributable to fear of offending Soviet Russia." Another message decoded by Ultra provided the more exact nature of Japanese concerns. In its four points, the message set forth solid arguments for granting Indochinese independence sooner rather than later. It read:

a. Russia has already called Japan an aggressor,
b. The opening date of the San Francisco Conference is 25 April [where purportedly the Allies would work on a charter for the envisioned United Nations and set forth policy on Indochina],
c. De Gaulle has already made preparations to grant Indo-China self-government,
d. The rising local Communist Party in Indo-China opposes the replacement of France by Japan and advocates real national independence.

The Japanese army, however, disagreed with the Foreign Ministry's assessment and considered it "absolutely essential to deal with the French Indo-China forces before anything else is done."[72] Furthermore, Shigemitsu's insistence that one of the objectives of the coup should be *minzoku kaihoo* (the liberation of people) also met with fierce opposition within the highest military and governmental circles. At the Supreme War Leadership Conference, Shigemitsu emphasized that *minzoku kaihoo* would look better to the Soviets than claiming only the "self-defense of Japan as a pretext" for MEIGO and would surely "please" the Soviet Union. Other members of the conference expressed grave reservations, fearing that the ideology of *minzoku kaihoo* would run the risk of turning the coup into a "racial war."[73]

Ironically, according to Stein Tønnesson, there was a "remarkable similarity" between the attitudes of Foreign Minister Shigemitsu and Roosevelt. Both men were highly critical of French colonialism, and Roosevelt's condemnation of French rule sounded remarkably like Shigemitsu's—although neither man would have appreciated the comparison. Roosevelt characterized French rule as "milking" the Indochinese, and he declared the Indochinese "entitled to something better than that,"[74] while Shigemitsu termed French colonial policy "violently reactionary."[75] Both Shigemitsu and Roosevelt "felt that the days of European colonialism were numbered and wanted to gain popularity among the Asian peoples by contributing to their liberation. Both were at great pains to convince the military commanders of their respective countries that something should be done to end the reactionary French rule."[76] Roosevelt died before the end of the war, and nothing came of his trusteeship plan for French Indochina. Shigemitsu was perhaps luckier.

Although the foreign minister would lose the debate and independence would not predate MEIGO, the Japanese would grant Indochina "independence" before the conclusion of the Pacific war. Shigemitsu remembered that "it was a basic part of Japan's new G.E.A. [Greater East Asia] policy that, should the Japanese Army, for its own security, throw out the French authorities, racial aspirations should be recognized and an independent government set up."[77] Indeed, historian Kiyoko Kurusu Nitz has found that "senior officers and commanders in Indochina seemed to have persuaded themselves that they were taking action for the benefit of the Indochinese peoples as well as of Japan. They were looking forward to the day when they could fully give themselves to the cause and assist the Indochinese people."[78] Indeed, in the last week before the coup the Japanese continued to assert their interest in the well-being of the Indochinese. The foreign minister issued a proclamation to the embassy in Saigon stating:

> It is to be taken for granted that our Empire has no territorial designs whatever upon Indo-China, and it hereby declares that it will not refuse any aid to the people of Indo-China who are trying to defend their native land from the aggressive powers in East Asia, and that it strongly desires the realization of independence on the part of these people who have long been oppressed and to that end will render every possible assistance on the basis of the Greater East Asia Joint Declaration.[79]

While espousing the desire to aid the peoples of Indochina, the Japanese Army maintained a practical view—independence for each area of Indochina would be decided upon "separately" and only "insofar as they do not interfere with military operations."[80]

In Hue, the Yasutai, a small secret agency that conducted intelligence work for the Japanese,[81] was responsible for the MEIGO action and for the "rescue" of Emperor Bao Dai and his wife from the French authorities. The imperial couple were identified and detained on their way home from a hunting trip and were brought "safely back to the palace." The Japanese "seemed to worry that Bao Dai would be taken by other groups who then would organize a strong anti-Japanese organization with him as a symbolic head of state."[82] The Japanese, of course, were unwilling to allow that to happen. With the emperor "safe" from the French, they encouraged him to proclaim the "independence of Annam," including both Tonkin and Annam, but not the highly profitable southern colony, Cochinchina. This surprised many of the relatively few pro-Japanese Vietnamese, who expected that Bao Dai's uncle, Prince Cuong De, would be invited to assume the throne.[83] Vietnamese nationalists allied with the Japanese opposed the selection of Bao Dai and charged him with subservience to the French. However true that claim might have been, proponents of Bao Dai could also counter by charging Prince Cuong De with subservience to his Japanese patrons.

The prince, the "leading pretender to the throne," had emigrated to Japan in the early 1900s. His ties to Japan were indeed unique. While in Tokyo, he allegedly adopted a Vietnamese boy born in Japan. This adopted son later "became Colonel Sibata in the Japanese Army and was one of the leaders of the Japanese invasion of Indo-China."[84] In Japan, Cuong De assumed the leadership of the Phuc Quoc (Viet Nam Phuc Quoc Dong Minh Hoi), or Viet Nam Restoration League, at the invitation of the Vietnamese patriot Phan Boi Chau. The Phuc Quoc was founded by Phan Boi Chau in 1912 as a "pro-monarchical nationalist movement" and became the "principal organizing agency of pro-Japanese Vietnamese" during the World War II years. In 1943 the *kempeitai* used the Phuc Quoc to recruit Vietnamese soldiers for their puppet military force.[85] If indeed Cuong De's son was a colonel in the Japanese army, this task might have been greatly facilitated. In mid-1944, OSS intelligence reported that Cuong De had seven followers with him in Japan and fifty more in Taiwan.[86]

Regardless of Cuong De's potential, he also had distinct liabilities: He was already an old man and had lived away from Vietnam most of his adult life. In hopes of gaining popular support and stability for the newly "independent" government of Bao Dai, the Japanese decided not to bring the prince from Tokyo to Annam in March 1945 because they felt there was the "danger of an outbreak of local unrest over nothing."[87]

As in Vietnam, the other Indochinese rulers were also "encouraged" to declare their kingdoms "independent." Japanese so-called advisers offered "secret guidance" to the Cambodian and Laotian monarchs, as they had to Emperor Bao Dai. In each case a Japanese "adviser" visited the leader and presented him with the "proclamation of independence" accompanied by the following statement: "We are by no means employing compulsion in this matter (declaring independence) but compliance will minimize the shedding of blood."[88] Not surprisingly, shortly after the visits of the "advisers," each of the sovereigns announced the proclamation. On March 13, 1945, King Norodom Sihanouk declared Cambodian independence.[89] Three weeks later, King Sisavang Vong declared Laos free of French rule. With these two announcements, and Bao Dai's on March 11, more than seventy years of French colonialism in Indochina had come to a formal end.

In Vietnam, although Bao Dai's government has been widely assailed as nothing more than a puppet regime, its few months of existence under the Japanese were highly significant. With the establishment of local government, the name "Vietnam" also returned. In his declaration of independence, Bao Dai abrogated the Franco-Annamese treaty of protectorate and announced that the Government of Vietnam "resumed its right to independence."[90] Henceforth, the French terms "Annam" and "Tonkin" would be replaced with "Viet Nam," and "Vietnamese" would supplant "Annamite," a designation long considered to be derogatory. This simple gesture, one of Bao Dai's few accomplishments, signaled his own reawakened sense of the Vietnamese national identity.

Nevertheless, it was widely recognized that although Bao Dai had rejected dependence on the French, he had accepted dependence on the Japanese. This perception seriously undermined the imperial court's credibility. Bao Dai's independence address did not ameliorate the situation. He proclaimed:

Indochina will try to develop itself to deserve its place as an independent nation. According to the declaration of Greater Asia, Indochina is part of Greater Asia therefore she must muster her strength to help the common prosperity. The government of Indochina truly believes in the sincerity of the Nippon Empire and has decided to cooperate with Japan, offering all the wealth of the nation in order to arrive at the common end.[91]

In researching the Bao Dai government, scholar Bui Minh Dung has concluded that for Bao Dai, "even nominal independence was more exploitable than no independence at all."[92] In his 1980 memoir, Bao Dai asserted that he "accepted independence" without believing in the rhetoric of GEACPS.[93]

Perhaps no one realized the truth of the situation more than the Japanese themselves. Although they fully intended to use the new government for the good of the Empire of the Sun, the Japanese supreme adviser, Yokoyama Masayuki, among others, concluded that they must reshape Bao Dai's image to make him appear more a Vietnamese leader than a Japanese puppet. The Japanese were, in part, preparing for the possibility of an Allied invasion. On

March 12, Japanese diplomats and army officials met in Bangkok and cabled Tokyo an "Emergency Policy for Burma, Thailand and Indo-China." "If the worst happens," it read, "we plan to foster revolts by the various local races as much as possible and to develop this area to the maximum extent as a peripheral fighting base, thus reducing our own burden of defense. To that end, we must make increasing efforts to get control of the mental attitude of the local inhabitants and to develop pro-Japanese sentiment."[94]

Although Bao Dai was now the undisputed imperial head of the new "nation," the Japanese encouraged him to form a new cabinet with Tran Trong Kim, whom they had already chosen for the position, as the leader.[95] Even though Tran Trong Kim was "widely respected for his scholarship and for the way he had directed the public schools in Hanoi," he had little practical experience in politics.[96] Known for his strong sense of nationalism, in another time and place he might have been able to grow into his position; however, in March 1945 Tran Trong Kim was faced with an extremely difficult situation. Reportedly, Emperor Bao Dai told him, "Before we were not independent. Now we have the opportunity, though not complete independence. But we should prove ourselves qualified for independence. If we fail to form a Cabinet the Japanese will say that we are incapable and they will certainly establish military rule which will be very detrimental to our country."[97]

Although maintaining only nominal independence, Tran Trong Kim's government did take important first steps toward Vietnamese national independence. Its accomplishments included a partial Vietnamization of the French colonial administration, the negotiation of the formal territorial unification of the country to include Cochinchina as part of Vietnam, stimulating mass political participation, launching educational reforms, and the elevation of Vietnamese to the official language in classrooms and offices. During the Tran Trong Kim government, public participation in all types of gatherings, whether political, cultural, or religious, was encouraged—a dramatic change considering the draconian restrictions on public gatherings under the French.[98] Although the Japanese allowed comparatively modest improvements, Tran Trong Kim certainly understood the implications of Japanese support for his rule and accepted that his government would collapse with an Allied victory. In 1949, looking back at his brief five-month tenure in office, his evaluation of the Japanese during World War II was less than positive:

Japan used to be a country of [our] same East Asian culture, but later had followed Europeanization, using malicious means to expand its imperialism. Japan had earlier annexed Korea and Manchuria, [and] later also wanted to invade China and other Asian countries, occupied by the Europeans. Though using slogans such as "allies and the same race" and the name of "liberating the oppressed people," the dark designs of the Japanese were to draw all benefits to them. Their politics were, therefore, full of contradictions. Their deeds did not match their words. They used humanitarian words to lure people into their trap, making it easy for them to rule. What they did, in fact was for their own interests, not at all for justice.[99]

For most Vietnamese, life under the new Bao Dai–Tran Trong Kim government improved little. Most lower-echelon French and Vietnamese employees appeared for work in the days following Operation MEIGO. Businesses and municipal offices reopened, and life in both the cities and the countryside carried on. Although "liberated," many Vietnamese continued to dislike and fear the Japanese, who were, after all, another in a long line of oppressors. In fact, Hoang Xuan Han, the minister of national education in the Tran Trong Kim government, recalled telling General Mordant in mid-1944 that "the Vietnamese people would rather be granted their independence by the French than by the Japanese."[100]

However, as the situation had transpired, the Japanese moved on the issue first, and many Vietnamese saw the French in new ways. In her family history, *The Sacred Willow: Four Generations in the Life of a Vietnamese Family*, Duong Van Mai Elliott recalled her father's experience on the day after the coup. Elliott's father, Duong Thieu Chi, a successful mandarin working for the French colonial government, "had never thought the time would come when an Asian could strike down a Frenchman and get away with it." Duong Thieu Chi had been in the middle of a meeting with the provincial governor when the French resident "burst into the room," saying that the Japanese were pursuing him and begging for help. Elliott wrote that before her father "could recover from the shock of seeing a frightened Frenchman pleading for help," a Japanese captain arrived. "The Japanese bowed to them very politely, and then went straight for the Frenchman." The two Vietnamese officials "dared not intervene" as the captain "hit the deputy *resident* of the province over and over again on the head with the hilt of his sword."[101]

Although many undoubtedly rejoiced at the French humiliation at the hands of the Japanese, some of the elite, like Duong Thieu Chi, felt that their position became more difficult. "With the French no longer acting as a buffer," Elliott described, "my father was thrust face to face with them [the Japanese]. He found the officials he dealt with educated and courteous, but also ruthless in enforcing their demands for food and labor and callous to the impact these demands had on the Vietnamese."[102]

It was the continuous requisitioning of rice by the Japanese in Vietnam that, in combination with other factors, created one of the worst famines in Vietnamese modern history. Japanese exactions on the rice crop and the destruction inflicted on the railroads and coastal shipping by Allied bombing, combined with heavy flooding and violent storms, had already reduced the peasantry to misery. The famine, which began in 1944, continued to worsen after the coup. Although Japanese officials in Vietnam advised Tokyo that "prices on the whole have not made a conspicuous rise and the economic life of the people has hardly changed at all," they did not relay the ugly truth of the situation.[103] With the severe rice shortage, prices had risen dramatically. By the time of the coup, prices in Hanoi were five times what they had been when the Japanese had arrived in Vietnam five years earlier.[104] Thus, to say that the "economic life of the people" had "hardly changed at all" was painfully correct: Vietnamese were still dying daily of hunger and malnutrition. And yet, as Elliot so eloquently described, "every day, Japanese officials would come in to press their demands. They wanted more rice, at a time when people were dying of famine."[105]

As the Vietnamese surveyed their lives in the early spring of 1945, life without the French seemed no better than it had been with them. The poor remained poor, and many became destitute as the effects of the famine continued to take the lives of society's weakest members. The peasants continued to pay exorbitant taxes in rice that had become more precious than gold. They continued to obey a haughty and often cruel master. Only the face of the master had changed. Very few among the middle class or elite found their lot in life improving after the coup. Like Duong Thieu Chi, most mandarins fulfilled the same functions they had under the French. There were a few pro-Japanese Vietnamese, such as some members of the Phuc Quoc, who benefited. It can even be argued that the government of Bao Dai and Tran Trong Kim failed to benefit. With the Japanese defeat, these men would be branded as collaborators, and few would enjoy a prestigious career in Vietnam.

There are, of course, differing views of the contributions of the Tran Trong Kim government and the significance of "independence" under the Japanese. Vu Ngu Chieu concluded that after the coup de main there was a "burst of independence fever," when the word "*doc lap* (independence) had a magical effect, which altered the attitude of everyone." As evidence he cited a Vietnamese language newspaper in Hanoi whose editor wrote, "We are entering into a new historical phase. The Japanese troops' gunshots here on the night of March 9, 1945, destroyed the life of enslavement which had lasted for almost a century under cruel French domination. From now on, we are allowed to conduct our own true life."[106] Historian David Marr concluded that between March and September 1945, "there was an upsurge of patriotic fervor and social commitment unparalleled in the history of Vietnam. . . . it was as if both individuals and the nation had been born anew."[107] American intelligence reports in 1945 sustained a more pessimistic view: "Most people," one report read, remained "completely indifferent to their new liberation, [and] followed the same kind of life accorded them under French domination. But others (mostly Annamese) became disillusioned about the extent of independence offered by the Japanese."[108] Perhaps historian Bui Minh Dung summed up the situation best. "In Vietnam," he wrote, "a regime which accepted, succumbed to, or owed its survival to the presence of foreign garrisons of an occupation nature in the country was practically not considered, either consciously or unconsciously, as genuinely independent by the majority of the population."[109]

In the days and weeks following the coup de main the Japanese settled into a new level of control. The French in Indochina seethed with indignation over their treatment at the hands of the Japanese and over the attitudes of the Vietnamese they had long regarded as no more than servants. The French Resistance, especially those regrouped in China, looked for a way to reenter their colony under an Allied flag and the force of arms. The Vietnamese looked for a way out of a miserable situation, and in the north, one possible savior, the Viet Minh, seemed to be gaining momentum. Finally, the Americans continued to wage the war in the Pacific. Toward that end, the OSS in the China theater searched for a new, effective means to gather intelligence and aid the war effort. And Harry Bernard and OSS agent Charles Fenn tried to recover anything that might still exist of the GBT intelligence network and to rebuild it using whatever means necessary. The results of the Japanese coup forced the last three actors—the Viet Minh, the OSS, and the GBT—to work together to defeat a common enemy and remove them from Indochina. The question that remained, however, was whether or not they would be permitted to do so.

6

After the Coup de Main: March and April 1945

In the aftermath of the Japanese coup de main, the OSS and the GBT found themselves scrambling for new ways to gain intelligence on Indochina. Although the OSS and the GBT had had a strained relationship since the moment of their acquaintance, Charles Fenn's participation in the GBT had provided an important link between the two, if not the results anticipated by either party. The OSS remained frustrated over its lack of access to GBT personnel and its inability to gain control over the group. Lawrence Gordon and Harry Bernard, specifically, continued to be irritated by the sustained attempts of the OSS to take them over and by the paucity of supplies "allotted" them by Bill Donovan's organization. Although the GBT and the OSS were mutually aggravated, both experienced a decided jolt of urgency to gain new sources of information as the impact of Operation MEIGO became more fully understood. In the days following the coup both organizations quickly reexamined their options. Appearances to the contrary, the GBT network had not completely collapsed, although Bernard and Fenn had to set about rebuilding it with little knowledge of the status of their agents in Vietnam.[1] As for the OSS, French agents still seemed a possible option. The Gorrilla Team had already parachuted into the position of the retreating French, and Lieutenant Ettinger had walked out with Sabattier's forces. But with the French clearly pushed further out of the picture, the OSS had to find other sources of information from within Vietnam.

In his biography of Ho Chi Minh and in his own memoir, Charles Fenn recalled the urgent "pleas" of both Wedemeyer and the U.S. Navy the day after the coup. Both Wedemeyer and the navy reiterated their need for weather reports and for information on Japanese targets, air defenses, and troop movements. Fenn was then directed to get a new intelligence net operating using "natives if necessary!" Fenn contemplated this option, but for him the dilemma was not *whether* to use "natives" but *which* "natives" to use: "Nobody knew any they felt could be trusted," he stated.[2]

Certainly the GBT was not the first group to claim that the Indochinese could not be trusted, and it would not be the last. But Fenn had come to this conclusion through his earlier intelligence-gathering experience. In November 1944 Fenn produced a document for the OSS entitled "French Indo-China—Intelligence of Special Interest to M.O." In that report Fenn concentrated primarily upon the Japanese, the French, and the overall situation on the ground, but he did comment on the Vietnamese as well. In his opinion, at that time, "the natives" were "not especially anti-Jap." But they did realize that the Japanese were "to blame for shortages, high taxes, and Allied raids, in spite of clever manipulations by the Japs to pass the buck to the French." Furthermore, Fenn reported, "it has not escaped the notice of the French and Annamites that everything Japanese is inferior both in material and construction to American products. This has given rise to the attitude 'How could the Japs win, having such inferior ability?'"[3] Although this might provide one explanation for the low success rate achieved by the Japanese in attempting to recruit Indochinese to their cause, Fenn had reached a different conclusion. He stated simply that the Japanese had failed because "the Annamites don't like to have anything to do with war."[4] Given this assumption, it is not difficult to understand Fenn's hesitation to use Indochinese agents.

There was no indication that Fenn's views changed over the next two months. However, at the instigation of the OSS in Kunming, Fenn queried "Jo-Jo," a Chinese GBT agent, about using Vietnamese "to go inside Indochina with radios." Jo-Jo replied, not surprisingly, that perhaps they could find some Chinese for the job. "Even if there were Annamites who could operate radios we shouldn't want to use them," Jo-Jo stated. "We formerly tried it on our own behalf, and even supplied them with arms. But when we agreed to recognize France as a power again, with de Gaulle as leader, we also agreed not to support the Annamites."[5]

As Fenn pondered the problem of finding suitable agents in the days following the Japanese coup, his mind flickered back to a story Frank Tan had told him some months earlier. According to Tan, an American pilot, lieutenant Rudolph Shaw, had been rescued by "some Annamites" when his plane went down in Tonkin. Evidently, Shaw had been escorted to Kunming by a man named Ho and his younger companion. Fenn had been particularly impressed by Ho's reported refusal of a monetary reward and by his desire to meet Chennault, "just for the honor." But Fenn had no luck following up on the story of the mysterious Ho. He was told that Shaw had already been flown home and that Ho and his companion had left. Although a bit disappointed, when Fenn heard the story in January 1945 he had no need to be overly concerned with access to the Vietnamese: In January the Japanese coup had not yet occurred, and the GBT network still thrived. After the coup, however, the story and the man named Ho gained importance in Fenn's mind.[6]

Meanwhile, with the loss of access to the French in Indochina, the OSS in Kunming also began looking for new avenues to gain access to information in the region. Although more restricted by bureaucratic decisions prohibiting involvement in Indochina than the GBT, the OSS had been working with Vietnamese agents on a limited basis for six months prior to the coup. Primarily responsible for these contacts was Major Austin Glass. As will be recalled, Glass's relationship with Fenn and the GBT was a bit strained, for although Glass continually praised the GBT, Fenn and Gordon believed he was undermining their network. Ironically, although Glass does not appear to have attempted any such thing, it was his work with Vietnamese agents, rather than any attempt at subverting GBT French agents, that would have provided the OSS with an intelligence advantage over the GBT. Glass's thirty years in Indochina and his fluency in both French and Vietnamese made him the ideal representative to procure Vietnamese operatives. In fact, in his OSS job description dated September 2, 1943, Glass was tasked with "procure[ing] agents in the field to enter Indo-China and keep[ing] in close contact with French *and native* underground organizations" (emphasis added).[7]

By the summer and early fall of 1944, Glass had managed to procure thirty-five Vietnamese agents. An agent known as "George," a prominent member of the Vietnamese community in Kunming, was sent with two other men to Tsingtsi, not far from Cao Bang. George was considered especially valuable because of his wide network of friends in Tonkin. Glass averred that George held a meeting in Indochina with a number of "friends" and briefed them on their duties and the kind of information to find. Glass also noted the difficulties encountered by agents, such as George, who participated in this network. For example, the agents were "obliged to travel by foot, being passed by the 'underground' from one point to another."[8]

Glass was even more impressed with "Jimmy," described as a "fearless" Tonkinese from a wealthy family. Educated in France, he had traveled extensively in Asia and, according to Glass, was "violently anti-Japanese and a strong Annamite nationalist." Evidently Jimmy was quite well known in Tonkin and could travel in the area only at considerable personal risk. Glass testified that Jimmy had "accomplished several dangerous missions," including one in which he took two Vietnamese women radio operators from Nanning to Lungchow and across the border into Tonkin to work "our [OSS] TR-1 [radio] set in the vicinity of Hanoi." The two women were described as "fully competent—speedy and accurate" by the OSS officer who trained them. While in Hanoi, Jimmy was able to "obtain samples of personal documents, French and native newspapers, magazines and books." With Jimmy's help, twelve Vietnamese recruits were sent into Indochina during July 1944. An additional group of twenty-one agents was sent into northern Vietnam in October. Also through Jimmy, contact was made with a new agent, designated as "Jean," whom Glass described as having "close relations with the native partisans in the mountainous regions of Hagiang and Yenbay in northern Tonkin."[9]

In October 1944 Glass wrote to his superior, Colonel Hall, inquiring about training for two more Vietnamese radio operators, reminding the colonel that the men had been waiting since August to begin "our course." He reported that the agents already working for him outside Kweihsien in southern China had begun producing information on October 13, adding that "first results appear interesting." From his brief letter, it is unclear exactly how much Glass knew about the political orientation of his agents. In his letter to Hall, Glass stated only that although he did not have the names of the two men awaiting training, they could be contacted through "Mssrs. Pham Viet Tu or Pham Minh Sinh."[10] Although Glass probably did not fully appreciate the connections of Pham Viet Tu (alias Pham Tuan) at the time, he was no ordinary agent.[11] He was the Viet Minh envoy to the French and U.S. missions in Kunming.[12]

Although the first contacts between the Viet Minh and the Americans had begun as early as December 1942, when the Viet Minh approached the American embassy for help in securing the release of Ho Chi Minh from prison in China, little had come of them.[13] This did not extinguish the hopes of the Viet Minh, however. In hopes of finding a sympathetic advocate in the United States, Pham Viet Tu evidently kept a close watch on the American news media and political process. On August 29, 1944, he wrote a letter to Kansas senator Arthur Capper thanking him for his "interest" in Indochina. In his letter Pham Viet Tu referred to an "inspirational message" recently published by Capper, "calling the attention of the world to the courageous opposition being given to the Japanese invaders by the people of Indochina." Although a little-known group during the war, the Viet Minh took great care to keep abreast of world events as they might pertain to Indochina at some point in the near future. Pham Viet Tu displayed his currency with world events, writing the senator: "Since you have taken this interest in our country, we feel that you would like to keep informed on Indochinese events and particularly on those movements in the country that is striving for the principles of freedom held in common by the United Nations in this war against tyranny." Although he promised that the Viet Minh would "double [their] efforts" against the Japanese because they were "greatly stimulated by the thought that the efforts in which [their] organization [were] engaged [had] been given such recognition [in Capper's publication]," the Viet Minh saw no tangible results from his correspondence.[14]

As had been the case in 1942, so it was again in October 1944: Pham Viet Tu had very little luck in dealing with either the Americans or the Free French in Kunming, both of whom found him and his organization rather inconsequential. He did, however, provide Glass with agents who, it can be assumed, were also members of the Viet Minh.[15] Glass met some of these agents in person, which led to one of his most intriguing statements: "Tonight [October 14, 1944]," he wrote, "I am meeting the most famous member of their race in China."[16] Modern historians might automatically assume this to have been Ho Chi Minh. However, in late September 1944 Ho Chi Minh had returned to the Viet Bac, the Viet Minh–liberated zone in northern Tonkin. Although Glass apparently did meet the man he called the "friendly Annamite,"[17] it remains unclear when and where this took place and who, exactly, Austin Glass met on the night of October 14, 1944.

Glass's planning and work with the Vietnamese was probably facilitated by an OSS memo written in October 1943, just one month after his own job description, directing him to "procure" Indochinese as well as French agents. The primary topic of the "Outline of a Plan for Indo-China" was the potential utilization of the Vietnamese. Section II of the document, "What We Have to Work with in Indo-China," stated:

> Fortunately, there exists a ready made weapon in the form of the Annamite Nationalist movement, one of the strongest and most violent organizations of its kind in all of Asia. This movement has been characterized in the past by numerous bloody uprisings, the use of terrorism as a political weapon and a well-organized, thoughtfully executed program of passive resistance and sabotage. . . . The Annamites are fearless fighters, and in 1918 when there were more than 50,000 Annamite troops on the Western front, they demonstrated qualities

described by an observer who knew them well as "courage, intelligence, endurance, discipline, resignation, avarice and a zeal for military decorations."[18]

With these characteristics in mind, Section III of the memo, entitled "What the Annamites Can Do for Us," discussed the specific value of the Indochinese for the Allied cause. Although the OSS author of the memorandum embellished certain aspects of the report, it is easy to understand why Glass, and others later on, would feel the use of Vietnamese to be an obvious advantage to the Americans. Section III argued:

> They can immobilize large numbers of Japanese troops by conducting systematic guerilla warfare in the difficult jungle country of Cochin China and numerous rubber plantations throughout all of Indo-China. The most fertile field for the recruitment of guerilla fighters is in the Red River delta where natural calamities, combined with over-population problems, have served to create an embittered and restless people. . . . The [Yen Bay] revolt [in 1930], like many others of its kind, was characterized by bomb throwing and guerilla warfare. The Annamite nationalists are familiar with all the tactics of disrupting lines of communications, ambush of small detachments and assassination of important leaders.[19]

The remaining sections of the document were equally instructive; they discussed various methods of turning the Vietnamese against the Japanese and the types of both subversive and overt propaganda that could be used in Indochina. Of specific interest was the statement that "the most effective propaganda line we can follow is to convince the Annamites that this war, if won by the Allies, will be the means through which they will gain their independence." But the author covered his own diplomatic and political backside with the caveat: "*Regardless of our own views* on the subject of whether or not there should be a free and independent Annamite state, this line would be the quickest method of turning the energies of the Annamite nationalist movement towards our own ends" (emphasis added). The plan encouraged the Vietnamese to kill as many Japanese as possible so they "wouldn't have to be killed somewhere else," thus speeding the Allied victory and the "freedom of the Annamites," which was in turn made to depend on the "number of Japanese they can assassinate."[20] Although the author laid out the potential benefits of utilizing the Indochinese in the war effort, he added that they needed training "on the art of sabotage, industrial and agricultural."

In addition, the "Plan for Indo-China" offered three suggestions on how the Vietnamese could be contacted to begin this valuable work on behalf of the Allies. The OSS could send propaganda information via radio broadcasts,[21] use the foreign intelligence service of the Kuomintang, or employ the Chinese communists. The OSS had already made numerous, often controversial, contacts with the Chinese communists in their mutual battle against Japan. It would not have been difficult for them to have gotten access to the CCP again to use as an intermediary to reach the Vietnamese communists. Of special long-term interest in the plan, however, was the information provided to the OSS on the "Annamite" communists.

> The Chinese communists have excellent connections among the Annamites. In 1931, when the Communist Party [in Vietnam] was at its height, it numbered 1,500 members with 100,000 affiliated peasants although the unofficial figures today are probably five times that amount. The leader of this Annamite communist movement was trained in Canton under [the Comintern agent Michael] Borodin in addition to his extensive schooling in Moscow and various European countries. His name, Nguyen-Ai-Quoc is known to all Annamites. Chao En-Lai, the Communist "ambassador" in Chungking would be the best contact in this connection.[22]

Although it would remain unknown to the OSS for quite some time, the "Nguyen-Ai-Quoc" they suggested courting for work against the Japanese in 1943, was the very same man, with a new alias, that Fenn began to seriously consider contacting for work as an agent in March 1945. Had Fenn realized this at the time, his relationship with Ho Chi Minh might have been very different.

Fenn's first mention of Ho Chi Minh came in one of his October 1944 reports. Fenn provided, among other things, a record of a conversation with General Chen, the military adviser to George Wou of the Chinese Fourth War Area, in which he explored the idea of working with the "Annamites." Chen dismissed the idea of using the Vietnamese because "none of the Annamites will furnish us help against the Japs without some expectation of help against the French, either now or later." Although seemingly adamant in his rejection, Chen qualified his earlier pronouncement: "Possibly some of the younger Communists might give such help. Their actions in FIC, as reported by Chinese agents, indicate a certain efficiency and are aimed largely against the Japs rather than French." But Chen qualified his statement yet again: "These communists may be in touch with Yenan [the base of the Chinese communists] and therefore a political problem would arise between the Americans and the Chinese if we should help them." "There is," added Fenn in his reporting of the conversation, "an Annamite named Hu Tze-ming [*sic*] who heads up the International Anti-Aggression Group (Anti-fascist) who might be used."[23] It is unclear whether or not either General Chen or Charles Fenn clearly connected the group of "younger communists" with the International Anti-Aggression Group and Ho Chi Minh.

By November 1944 Fenn had formed his own tentative opinion about the Vietnamese communists. He reported to the OSS that although the "Communist group seems to be the backbone of the so-called Revolutionary party, they lack good leaders and have had no direction as to the part they should play. Apparently they think they ought to have Russian guidance and that the Russians would not want them to be anti-Jap. They have liaison with Chinese Communists but are not much subject to their advice."[24] Fenn's relatively low opinion of the communists and their usefulness against the Japanese might well have prevented him from seeking out the man who had escorted an American pilot to Allied territory. Indeed it was the safe return of Lieutenant Shaw that seems to have secured Ho Chi Minh's future encounters with key members of the American community in Kunming. Fenn later called the rescue of Shaw the "magic key to open doors otherwise impregnable."[25]

The all-important rescue resulted when, during a reconnaissance mission, Shaw, an American pilot in the Fifty-first Fighter Group, made a forced landing in the vicinity of Cao Bang on November 11, 1944. In "From Kunming to Pac Bo," Vu Anh (alias Trinh Dong Hai), an ICP organizer in Kunming and the Viet Bac, recalled Shaw's arrival:

> One day, in Cao Bang, an organization for national salvation [unit] saved an American pilot [who] parachuted on our territory due to engine troubles. He was Lieutenant Shaw. The French and Japanese searched for him, but the revolutionaries protected him, and sent him to Pham Van Dong's office in the region of Nuoc Hai. Pham Van Dong sent him to Ho Chi Minh. Shaw was very well received and was very happy to meet Ho Chi Minh. He said that he had heard distorted propaganda concerning the Viet Minh, and it was not until then that he realised the truth.[26]

Vu Anh's account, written in 1962, undeniably embellished the truth. Although Shaw was probably very glad to meet Ho Chi Minh, since English-speaking Vietnamese in the jungles of northern Vietnam were rare, he could not, at that time, have attached any special significance to either the name or the man. It is also highly unlikely that Shaw had any knowledge whatsoever about the Viet Minh organization. He probably had been told, like most pilots, to be wary of the Vietnamese, who might turn him in to the French or Japanese authorities in order to collect the reward offered by the Japanese.[27] Thus, one could say that his favorable treatment by the cadres allowed him to "realise the truth" about the Vietnamese in general. He would soon discover a great deal more about the Viet Minh.

Shaw delivered a number of items while in Kunming, including a diary-style pamphlet entitled "The Real Indo China by First Lieutenant Shaw" and an undated letter to an unidentified colonel.[28] Although the pamphlet was allegedly written by Shaw, its authorship was immediately questioned by his superiors. An attached commentary from Chennault's office added that it was highly unlikely that Shaw had written the pamphlet or that even "the thoughts and ideas and their arrangement are his." "In fact," it went on, "it is hard to believe they are his at all. But the job is well done, and the pamphlet most revealing. . . . we [should] undertake to contact these people and do whatever we are able."[29] Officers in the Fourteenth Air Force concluded that members of the Viet Minh had ghostwritten the pamphlet—most probably the author was Ho Chi Minh himself—but regardless of its authorship Shaw's diary was very instructive. It provided telling details regarding Shaw's landing and stay with the Viet Minh and about their sophisticated manipulations of the situation, and it gave a basically accurate history of French Indochina.

In clear prose and immaculate handwriting, the diary wove together thoughts and facts, some of which could well have been Shaw's, with information that clearly did not originate with him. For example, the initial paragraphs in Shaw's diary explained his landing but also added important bits of information:

Since the beginning of the war against fascist Japan, I am probably the first airman of Allied armies to come to Indo-China, to live there a whole month, to learn something about the country and then to go back to my base, safe and sound. . . . Before taking my parachute, I set my machine in such a way that it should be entirely useless to the enemy when he gets it. As soon as I touched the ground a young Indo-chinese came

along smiling and warmly shaking both my hands and making signs to
me to follow him. I handed him 600 Indo-china dollars. He absolutely
refused to take the money and looked rather offended. I was surprised
by his attitude and thought that he considered the sum insufficient. It
was a great mistake on my part! What I first thought to be a greediness
is in reality a common virtue of the Indo-Chinese patriots. They help us
not for our money, but for love and friendship. They know that we are
fighting not only for America, but also for the freedom and democracy of
the world, hence for their country also. For that reason they consider it
is their patriotic duty to help us—their allies.[30]

The first Viet Minh cadre Shaw encountered did not speak English; however, with gestures he directed Shaw to a nearby hiding place. There Shaw
met a group of youths, and a sincere yet politically manipulative pattern of
dealing with Americans emerged. Although neither Shaw nor the youths
spoke the other's language, they began to communicate. Shaw described the
scene: The cadres said to him, "Viet Minh, America! Viet Minh, America!"
And Shaw, following their example, replied, "Viet Minh! Viet Minh!" His
diary recorded that the Viet Minh were "very pleased" with his response.
Shaw would learn to repeat this pattern at each new introduction, and each
time, the Viet Minh were "very pleased."

While hiding with the Viet Minh guerrillas, Shaw waited while first
French and then Japanese soldiers plundered his plane and searched the
woods and nearby villages for signs of him.[31] Shaw narrated his experience:

For 30 days, playing hide and seek with the French and the Japs, the
patriots brought me from one place of hiding to another. They did their
best to make me comfortable. Whenever and wherever they could the
villagers, men and women, boys and girls, hold secret meetings to
welcome me. When the speakers finished, I always replied with a brief
and simple speech: "Viet Minh! Viet Minh!" They then stood up and
said in chorus: "America! Roosevelt! America! Roosevelt!" The meetings
ended by an all round handshaking.[32]

Ten days later, Shaw received a letter from the Central Committee of the
Viet Minh welcoming him and telling him that "we have ordered our Cao
Bang Section to take all necessary measures to safeguard your person and to
accompany you to the Tonkin-China border." The Central Committee further entreated him to help build a strong friendship between the United

States and Vietnam.[33] This task would soon be made easier. Within a few days, Shaw reported, he met an English-speaking "patriot" who described his organization and explained that the safest route to Allied territory was unfortunately also the longest. Because few Vietnamese spoke English at the time and given Vu Anh's testimony that Shaw was taken to Ho Chi Minh soon after his arrival, it can be assumed that the Vietnamese patriot Shaw encountered was indeed Ho Chi Minh. Ho attempted to ease Shaw's fears, assuring him that he was "absolutely safe among us [the Viet Minh]." One can imagine how relieved Shaw must have felt, after an emergency landing in enemy-held territory and days spent communicating through nothing but hand gestures and slogans, to hear these soothing words in his own language. In his diary Shaw expressed his relief and then began to move past his daily experiences. "From this friend," he wrote, "I began to learn something of Indo-China."

In the next sixteen pages "The Real Indo-China" recounted the ugly history of French domination, with a precise chronology of Vietnamese opposition to French rule. It also related the collapse of the French in 1940 and life under the Japanese, including their use of the pro-Japanese party of Prince Cuong De.[34] It concluded that

> in short, the Indo-Chinese lot is a terrible lot. He enjoys no freedom, no happiness, no rights. He is crushed under inhuman exploitation and barbarous oppression. He lives in misery and ignorance! . . . Bent down under the double yoke of fascist tyranny, the Indo-Chinese know that they have either to fight for their life and freedom or to starve in slavery. They choose the first step.

Furthermore, the pamphlet laid out the origins and purpose of the Viet Minh and their position in relation to the Allies:

> How strong is Viet Minh, I do not know. But as far as I could see, it is very popular amongst the people. Everywhere I went the villagers gret [sic] me with the words "Viet Minh! Viet Minh!" and did everything to help the patriots; and this in spite of terror and repression.
>
>   In December, my Indo-Chinese friends brought me back to China. Before parting, they again and again asked me to give their best greetings to the army and the people of America. At the last handshaking they shouted: "Long live America! Long live Roosevelt! Long live General

Chennault!" And I shouted back: "Long live Indo-China! Long live Viet-Minh!" I am glad to be back and to be able to tell my country and her allies the real situation of Indo-China. . . .

I humbly think that, by democratic duty as well as by strategical interest, we must effectively help the anti-Jap, anti-fascist movement of Indo-China.

[Signed] R. Shaw[35]

Soon after his return to China, Shaw flew home to the United States. The story he told no doubt seemed unbelievable to many back at headquarters, but the facts of his forced landing and his safe return were verifiable. When asked who had taken care of him for a month in Japanese-occupied territory, the first words on his lips were probably "Viet Minh! Viet Minh!" His commanding general, Claire Chennault, wrote in his report to Wedemeyer that Shaw's "immediate welfare and ultimate escape" were due to "a native organization called The League for Indo China Independence." Chennault went on to say: "I am heartily in favor of maintaining good relations with any organization in French Indo China that will effectively aid in escape the US military personnel likely to require aid in that country, regardless of their local political affiliations." The inference in his concluding statement was clear. "It is noteworthy," he wrote, "that of three (3) rescues from French Indo China, the French are only directly involved in one, in which the Chinese also claim large credit."[36] Shaw's rescue involved neither the French nor the Chinese—only a seemingly very pro-American Indochinese group. For the Viet Minh, Shaw's rescue did indeed seem to be the "magic key."

Tasked with finding Vietnamese agents to work with, the Viet Minh seemed a logical avenue for Fenn to pursue. Fenn queried "Ravenholt," a war correspondent who had evidently taken down the story about Shaw's rescue, concerning Ho Chi Minh's whereabouts. Ravenholt reported that Ho was "still around" and often went to the Office of War Information (OWI) in Kunming to read "*Time* magazine and any other new literature they happened to have." Ho had begun frequenting the OWI in the summer of 1944, reading press accounts of the war and "chatting with available Americans."[37] The OWI, impressed by Ho's English, intelligence, and obvious interest in the Allied war effort, tried to acquire a visa for him to travel to San Francisco. From there, he would broadcast the news in Vietnamese.[38] Initial OSS reports stated that the OWI plan was dropped because of objections from the French consul.[39] David Marr concluded that, as with many

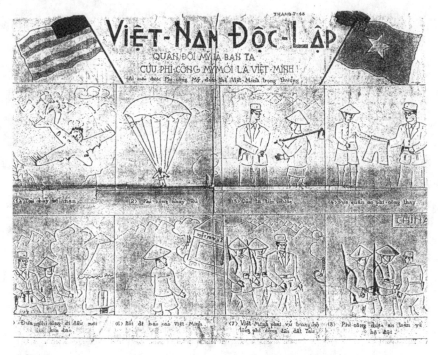

This Viet Minh hand-sketched pamphlet urged villagers to aid American pilots downed over Vietnam. *Courtesy of William Duiker.*

issues concerning Indochina, there was division within the U.S. State Department—the European section opposed the visa, the Far Eastern section supported it.[40] Needless to say, again, as with most issues concerning Vietnam, the European section prevailed; Ho did not receive his visa.

Ho Chi Minh's relationship with the OWI did make an impression on Fenn, however. Fenn remembered thinking that Ho's interest in American news and his involvement in Shaw's rescue "seemed to indicate a bias in our favor." Thus, a meeting was arranged for 11:00 AM on March 17, 1945. Ho arrived with a younger man, Pham Van Dong. Because Pham Van Dong did not speak English, the three conducted their conversation in French. In his diary Fenn remarked that Ho had "already met with Hall, Glass and de Sibour, but got nowhere with them." Fenn asked Ho what he had hoped to gain from the three OSS officers. "Only recognition of his group," Ho replied. Fenn wrote that he was "vaguely" aware that the Viet Minh was a communist group and asked Ho to talk about the issue, at which point Ho responded that the French labeled all Vietnamese who wanted independence as communists. Apparently satisfied, Fenn next explained the need for radio operators in Indochina. When asked what he would want in return, Ho responded "arms and medicines." Although the two men did not reach a complete agreement that day, Fenn recorded in his diary that he was "impressed by his [Ho's] clear-cut talk; [and] Buddha-like composure." Before their next meeting, scheduled for two days later, Fenn would have to get clearance for using Ho and his men. But, recalled Fenn, "I already felt sure he [Ho] was our man. Baudelaire felt the wings of insanity touch his mind; but that morning I felt the wings of genius touch mine."[41] Without a doubt, Ho Chi Minh was becoming adept at dealing with Americans, even those who were British-born.

In the next few days, Fenn's suspicions about Ho's political affiliation were confirmed by the French and the Chinese, both of whom labeled Ho a "long-standing rebel, anti-French, of course, and strictly communist." Although the assessment was more or less accurate, there was more to the man than such pigeonholing would indicate. Ho certainly could be considered a long-standing rebel: By 1945 when Fenn met him, Ho had been advocating independence for more than a quarter century. But although he wanted a Vietnam free of French domination, he was not strictly anti-French. He admired many of the outstanding qualities of French culture and still believed the French could play a role in helping develop Vietnam as a modern nation. Finally, to say that Ho was "strictly communist" oversimplified the man and his ideology. Although Ho Chi Minh and many in the higher echelons of the Viet Minh were communist, they merged Marxist philosophy with their own strong patriotic ideals and certainly could not be considered puppets of either the Soviets or the struggling Chinese communists. It would take some time before Fenn would begin to understand the complexities of Ho Chi Minh; however, for the immediate future Ho seemed like an excellent candidate to pursue intelligence work for the Americans. When Fenn presented the facts to Bernard and Tan and to Colonel Richard Heppner, his OSS commanding officer in Kunming, all three agreed to make use of Ho and his group.

This decided, Fenn, Bernard, and Tan sat down to decide how to best use Ho Chi Minh to accomplish their intelligence goals. They decided to send Ho back into Vietnam with one of the GBT Chinese radio operators. They also concluded that much could be gained by sending Tan along to conduct the training and collect information. The Americans incorrectly assumed that because Tan was racially Chinese, he would easily blend in with the large Chinese minority living in Tonkin. At Fenn's next meeting with Ho on March

20, the misperception was quickly corrected. Ho explained that as a Chinese *American* Tan would be easy to identify. He also expressed his reservations about taking in the GBT's local Chinese radio operator given the Vietnamese inclination "to be suspicious of the Chinese." To this, Fenn rebutted that there were "no Annamite radio operators."[42]

Ho acquiesced to the "inevitable" Chinese operator but still proposed an alternate arrangement. Instead of walking in with Tan, he wondered, could he not take along the Chinese agent, with a non-Chinese American officer, such as Fenn, to be dropped in later on? When Ho asked Fenn if he would be willing to be that American, Fenn replied that he would. "If you could fly us to the border, we'd then walk in," suggested Ho. "To elude the Japanese it would mean walking at night, which slows things down, so it would take us about two weeks to get to our base." Although Ho made clear that this was his "personal preference" and that among the Viet Minh "[a non-Chinese] American would be most welcome," in the end, he agreed to escort both the Chinese radio operator and Tan into Vietnam.[43]

At the same meeting, Pham Van Dong, who would be left behind in Kunming to liaise with the GBT, broached the question of supplies, especially "high explosives." Given the continued relationship of the GBT and the OSS with the French, Fenn was conscious of the potential diplomatic disaster that giving high explosives to the Vietnamese might cause. Therefore, he tried to soft pedal the issue, but he agreed they might later drop in light weapons, cameras, medicines, weather equipment, and further radio sets.

Before their meeting adjourned, Ho made one request of Fenn: He wanted to meet Chennault. Knowing that Ho had tried to visit Chennault once before and had been "politely shown the door," Fenn inquired about Ho's apparent determination to meet the Flying Tigers' commander. Ho is reported to have replied, "He's the Westerner we most admire. So I'd like to tell him so myself." Fenn reluctantly agreed to try and gain an appointment with the general but made Ho promise not to ask Chennault for anything, including recognition of the Viet Minh. The meeting proved remarkably easy to arrange. "Fortunately I knew Chennault well from having covered the Tigers' exploits as a war correspondent," Fenn remembered. "So out of channels I went to see him personally (another transgression which the OSS sniffer dogs got wind of) and explained the importance of playing along with this old man who had not only rescued one of the General's pilots but might well rescue more if we gained his future co-operation." Given Chennault's earlier statement that he was "heartily in favor of maintaining good relations" with those ready, willing, and able to help American pilots escape Indochina and given Fenn's personal approach, a date and time were soon set for the meeting.[44]

On March 29, Fenn, Bernard, and Ho arrived at Chennault's office. After a brief wait, the trio was ushered in. Fenn recorded the meeting in his diary:

> Chennault told Ho how grateful he was about the saved pilot. Ho said he would always be glad to help the Americans and particularly to help General Chennault for whom he had the greatest admiration. They exchanged talk about the *Flying Tigers*. Chennault was pleased the old man knew about this. We talked about saving more pilots. Nothing was said about the French, or about politics. I heaved a sigh of relief as we started to leave. Then Ho said he had a small favour to ask the general. "Here we go boys, hold your hats," was written all over Bernard's face. But all Ho wanted was the general's photograph. There's nothing Chennault likes more than giving his photograph. So he presses the bell and in comes Doreen [Chennault's secretary] again. In due course it's some other girl who produces a folder of eight-by-ten glossies. "Take your pick," says Chennault. Ho takes one and asks would the general be so kind as to sign it? Doreen produces a Parker 51 and Chennault writes across the bottom, "Yours Sincerely, Claire L. Chennault." And out we all troop into Kunming's sparkling air.[45]

Fenn characterized Chennault as "essentially the Southern gentleman" who "invariably treated Asians with courtesy," unlike so many Allied personnel in Asia. In the context of his military career, Chennault evidently assigned very little importance to this brief meeting with Ho Chi Minh. But for Ho and the Viet Minh, this seemingly innocent act would have significant repercussions later on when Ho combined a number of innocuous incidents into impressive propaganda about the special relationship between the Viet Minh and the Americans. That was in the future, however. For the moment, Fenn gave Ho Chi Minh the code name "Lucius," which he often abbreviated to "Luc," and Ho's work for the Americans formally began.

Bernard arranged with the Fourteenth Air Force for two L-5s, the small taxi planes then in use, to fly Ho Chi Minh, Tan, the Chinese radio operator Mac Shin, and their equipment to Ching-hsi on the Vietnamese border. By this time Mac Shin was an adept radio operator and an important member of the GBT. He communicated with relative ease in English and possessed a winning personality, described by Fenn as "a very clever adult who has somehow retained the open good natured delight of a child." Shin had been trained in the use of "all the weapons, including the Tommy-gun," and was "an excellent marksman with a .45."[46] He had even attended OSS parachute school—thus making him an unusually versatile and effective agent.[47]

When the L-5s were arranged, Fenn went to see Ho Chi Minh once again to inform him of the arrangements and to teach him the basics "about SI, SO, MO, and X2, and particularly about weather reports which were, indeed, almost the top of the list, since without them our planes couldn't fly." Bernard had prearranged for Ho and Shin to fly to Ching-hsi first. Tan would follow soon after with the equipment, including a generator, a transmitter, and various small arms, since Tan, rationalizing that "supplies give you face," insisted on taking a "load of stuff." At this last meeting before Ho's departure, he presented Fenn with one more request: He wanted six new Colt .45 automatic pistols in their original wrappings.[48] The seemingly insignificant quantity allowed Fenn to produce the pistols without great difficulty, but they, like Chennault's autographed photograph, would later produce highly significant results for Ho Chi Minh.[49]

In the days leading up to the departure of Tan, Shin, and Ho for Indochina, the OSS kept a close watch on Fenn and the GBT. Although Fenn had cleared the use of agent Lucius with Heppner, the OSS was still far from satisfied with its degree of control over either Fenn or the GBT. In fact, an OSS memo dated March 31, just two days after the meeting Fenn had privately arranged for Ho with Chennault, indicated serious displeasure with the GBT. The SI chief, Paul Helliwell, wrote: "At the present time Colonel Heppner feels that support to the G.B.T. group should be seriously limited, if not altogether eliminated and that we should go ahead with a purely OSS enterprise for penetration into FIC."[50]

The GBT had long been a frustration for the OSS. As each OSS attempt at a complete takeover of the GBT was thwarted, the OSS had become less and less inclined to work with them. However, the clear success of the GBT network and the lack of a better system for the OSS had prevented it from actually cutting its ties to the organization, although it had certainly threatened to do so many times. But by the end of March 1945, Helliwell and the OSS had concluded that controlling the GBT might soon be possible. By all appearances, the Japanese coup had destroyed the GBT network, and Helliwell believed that the "consequent disruption has made this outfit considerably more amenable, and it is possible that some arrangement can be worked out whereby G.B.T. can be utilized for penetration of certain FIC areas." Without their previously high level of productivity, the GBT might lose some, if not all, of their other sponsors, thus forcing them to bend to the will of the well-funded OSS. If the GBT network could be reestablished to the satisfaction of the OSS, however, Helliwell again advocated "a more or less general takeover." He concluded, "While I do not have the highest regard for the group as a whole, I do feel they have certain advantages [and] contacts which I should like to cash in on."[51]

Helliwell did not seem to comprehend the nature of the GBT or their determination to avoid any form of absolute takeover even though this might result in the loss of OSS supplies. Yet as chief of SI, his position in late March 1945 was a difficult one. Operation MEIGO had turned the situation in Vietnam on its head. The Allies still needed information, Helliwell believed the French in the area to be "completely unreliable," and it seemed that the irksome GBT might have outlived their usefulness. With all of this, he was still fully aware that theater headquarters was "extremely anxious" for him to "get an intelligence net set up in FIC at the earliest possible date." But to complicate matters even further, he still lacked firm orders from his superiors. "The whole FIC situation, quite frankly, is extremely confused," he explained. "We have had a multitude of conflicting directives from various quarters during the past two weeks. We are proceeding as rapidly as possible under the circumstances."[52] Even though the OSS had been advised that it "could not deal with native individuals or revolutionary groups,"[53] given the urgent need for intelligence, the complexity of the situation, and OSS distrust of the French in China, it is little wonder that the OSS approved Fenn's best option for getting his FIC net operational again: the use of the Vietnamese agent Ho Chi Minh.

While Fenn continued preparations for GBT/AGAS to use Ho Chi Minh, back in Kunming the situation was also changing. Three weeks earlier, on March 20, Wedemeyer had approved QUAIL, a major SI operation in Indochina, to "establish military intelligence nets in FIC and authorizing us to give arms and ammunition to anyone who would fight the Japanese." Although the directives from theater headquarters seemed clear enough, no immediate action was taken because on the same day "a message was received from Washington stating that we should not do anything about FIC." These were the same sort of mixed messages that Chennault was receiving at that same time with regard to aiding the French, then fleeing the Japanese in the wake of MEIGO. The two conflicting messages "created a muddle," Helliwell explained, "which prevented any further action from being taken."[54] Heppner also expressed his frustration, adding that: "The QUAIL project sat at Theater for three weeks without action. Theater would render no decision on GBT. Theater prohibited dealing with any native groups."[55]

On March 23 QUAIL was again given the go-ahead when General Marvin E. Gross, Chennault's acting chief of staff, "took the position that Washington had no authority to change a Theater directive . . . and decided that we could go ahead." Technically, the OSS could now move on QUAIL, but as Helliwell pointed out, "a dead agent is no good and . . . the mathematical chances of survival of agent personnel who simply go barging into FIC at this time are almost nil."[56] Thus, the OSS in Kunming sent an urgent wire to Washington requesting that "French-speaking personnel be moved to this theater on highest air priorities," and in flew Captain Archimedes Patti.[57]

On April 13, Patti, an OSS veteran of the Italian campaigns, arrived from Washington to take over as SI chief of the Indochina Desk and ultimately to "lead an OSS mission in Indochina." Before leaving for China, Patti had done his homework on the situation in Indochina. During his six months heading the Indochina Desk at OSS headquarters in Washington, Patti had developed plans, monitored correspondence, screened candidates for the proposed field team, and read the available accounts of the Indochinese situation, including an August 1944 letter to the American ambassador from the League for the Independence of Indochina. He also questioned friends such as Austin Glass about Vietnam. By late 1944 Patti had concluded that the league might well be an asset for an OSS mission in Indochina. He recalled bringing up the idea with OSS director Bill Donovan: "When I pressed the point of using Indochinese agents, Donovan's answer was, 'Use anyone who will work with us against the Japanese, but do not become involved in French-Indochinese politics.'"[58] Although not terribly pressing in late 1944, this issue would arise again almost as soon as Patti's plane touched the ground in Kunming.

Helliwell certainly hoped that after Patti assumed his duties in Kunming information procurement would improve. In the few days immediately preceding Patti's arrival Helliwell had become increasingly frustrated with the entire FIC situation. He expressed that frustration in his April 10 report:

Since receiving a Theater directive and getting the clarification which became necessary, this headquarters has had approximately two weeks to get the FIC net established. It is difficult to comprehend how it can be expected that a large flow of intelligence can be procured from an area in which all contact has been disrupted, in which Japanese troops are moving around without any precise knowledge on our part of their whereabouts, in which movement is extremely difficult under the best conditions, and in which a white man is extremely conspicuous, in a period of two months, much less two weeks. . . . As matters stand action is being taken at the most rapid rate consistent with intelligent planning and regard for security of personnel. The only further action that could be taken would be to put personnel into FIC completely blind, and in the opinion of this office such action would be the equivalent of signing a death warrant for all personnel involved.[59]

Helliwell's frustrations were echoed by his superior. Heppner pointed out that although the OSS had already sent "two officers and five native agents into FIC," and that "six GBT personnel with radio" were then on the "eastern border preparing to move across," in addition to a second OSS drop that was planned for Pleiku, the security in the area was clearly insufficient. His telegram to Chungking read:

It is not rpt [repeat] not clear to me how Theater can expect us or any other organization to go into a country in which [the] entire situation is badly confused in which greatest precautions must be taken to prevent pickup of agents and in which transportation is a problem of greatest difficulty and have a complete intelligence net functioning in two weeks. I do not feel warranted in dispatching American personnel into an area and unless directed otherwise by higher authority we shall operate on present basis namely that net in FIC will be built up as rapidly as is consistent with sound operation and security of personnel.[60]

Feeling pushed to rapidly produce information on Japanese activities in Indochina, both Heppner and Helliwell were happy to see Patti and to turn over Project QUAIL to him. QUAIL envisioned an intelligence network inside French Indochina with a main base inside Chinese territory at Szemao and a secondary one at Malipo. Because theater headquarters "continued to clamor" for intelligence that would allow the OSS to begin "harassing the Japanese along the Hanoi-Nanning-Canton corridor,"[61] the northeast section of Vietnam, including Hanoi and Haiphong, was targeted for special activity. QUAIL was an ambitious plan that was to eventually produce "operational stations located throughout Tonkin, Annam, Cochinchina and Cambodia, operated by twelve native teams. As soon as it was judged safe, the native teams were to be supervised by French-speaking US personnel who would enter Indochina for that purpose."[62]

Project QUAIL would allow the OSS to have more direct control over activities in Indochina. However, with QUAIL's emphasis on using Indochinese agents, one of Patti's first tasks was to find Vietnamese with whom to work. In the course of his April 14 meeting with Helliwell, Patti was given a tip on a possible agent by AGAS representative Major A. R. Wichtrich. "Wichtrich admitted," recalled Patti, "that AGAS had struck a deal with Mr. Ho to set up an air rescue operation in Indochina." Wichtrich also commented to Helliwell that "your man, Fenn, has had him in tow for several weeks." Helliwell admitted that he knew about Fenn's work with Ho. Indeed, even Patti, newly arrived in Kunming, knew about both Fenn and Ho Chi Minh, as well as about the GBT.[63]

Patti was quite impressed with the GBT's work since the onset of the war and with the limited resurgence of their network in the days following the Japanese coup. One incident in particular caught his attention. On March 20, British supply drops to the retreating French forces nearly caused an international incident among the Allies. According to the GBT, Chinese troops had observed a British airdrop to the French in the region of Mong Cai. Since the French had already departed Mong Cai, the Chinese soldiers picked up the supplies. "Within minutes GBT had received a radio message from the French that they had retreated to China and that the Japanese had occupied Tung Hing, Mong Cai, and Tien Yen. The French requested that all three locations be bombed." Archimedes Patti concluded that the role of the GBT was absolutely crucial at that moment. They realized that the French were "unwilling to risk exposing themselves to the Japanese by backtracking to Mong Cai" and did not want "the Chinese to collect the precious drop"; thus, they had "requested a bombing mission on the Chinese." "It was all too evident," stated Patti, "that the French were trying to dupe the Americans into bombing areas where Chinese troops were present, and it had been fortunate that GBT had been in radio contact with the intended victims."[64]

Patti also knew about Fenn's role in the GBT and had read his report on Ho's agreement to help the OSS and AGAS organize an intelligence network in Indochina. During his work in Washington, Patti had run across the name Ho Chi Minh and had basically decided to "look into the Vietnamese organization with a view to 'Project QUAIL.'" Patti remembered AGAS agent Wichtrich as being "visibly upset" at his decision, and both he and Helliwell took pains to assure Wichtrich that the OSS would not interfere with the AGAS operation and that "Ho's services to AGAS would benefit from our [OSS] SI support, both in funds and communications." Although Patti was concerned about the reaction of the French to OSS use of Vietnamese agents, Helliwell believed they should not discuss QUAIL with either the French or the American embassy staff. As the meeting broke up, Patti was set to begin preparations for the development of QUAIL: making a field inspection of Szemao and arranging a meeting with the Viet Minh leaders, especially Ho Chi Minh.[65]

As Patti began his quest to locate Ho Chi Minh, Frank Tan and Mac Shin were in Ching-hsi, preparing for what would be their two-week journey across the border south into Indochina. Ho had gone ahead of the two men and ordered twenty of his men back to act as escorts and to provide protection against any Japanese they might encounter and against the more prevalent danger, bandits. Tan, Shin, and their escorts set out early on the morning of April 15. Tan described his journey in his first message to GBT headquarters: "We set out dressed as border smugglers with all equipment carried in bamboo baskets so as to arouse normal suspicion of being illicit border traders. We walked parallel to the border until 15.00 hours, had our meal, waited until dark and then turned towards the border. This stretch of the journey was notorious for banditry so we unpacked and carried our arms while crossing the border."[66]

Eventually Ho joined the men for the last leg of the journey into the Viet Bac. It was a particularly difficult and dangerous journey for Tan. Although he had been in Indochina many times, he was unaccustomed to continuous hiking over such rough terrain. He remembered quitting at one point when his legs gave out from the overexertion, but Ho told him he had to go on—it was far too dangerous to stay put, and there was no other way to reach the Viet Minh–held territory.[67] Mac Shin also recounted the many difficulties of the long journey, especially the lack of food and water. Ho Chi Minh instructed them on the many uses of bamboo—to get water and to eat—and of the value of salt to replenish their bodies as they struggled onward. "Mac, remember, the salt is better than gold," Ho reminded him. The group was relieved when Shin was able to make radio contact with Fenn and the first airdrop of food arrived. In his postwar reflections, Shin credited Fenn with saving their lives—especially since they had already been forced to eat the horses that had carried Tan and Shin part of the way.[68]

Upon arriving at the rather unimpressive "headquarters"—a "mere hut in the entrance [to the cave at Bac Bo] by a waterfall"—Tan wrote:

I don't know how to classify VM. I guess they are what they are thru circumstances. The country where I am is very poor. They couldn't afford to pay taxes and still exist. As near as I can judge, this League is quite powerful and has several hundred followers. Before leaving Ching Hsi I was warned by the Chinese authorities that most of them are communists, and we ought to know what we are getting ourselves into.

He qualified his comments by adding, "But naturally they have to look at things from the Kuomintang point of view."[69]

With everyone safely across the border, the group continued on to the Viet Minh headquarters at Tan Trao (the new name given to Kim Lung by the Viet Minh). The group making this journey was much larger. Ho, Tan (whom the Viet Minh called Tam Xinh Shan to help protect his identity), and Shin (given the alias Nguyen Tu Tac) were joined by others from the Viet Minh, including "five radio operators who had finished a course on radio operations in China," "ten students who studied radio operation for intelligence work," "six persons to carry the transmitters," ten bodyguards—a majority of whom "had a lot of training in Gio Jio China and were at the rank of Lieutenant" and "were armed with 'tommies' and carbines"—and a contingent of young men specifically chosen to learn radio operation at Tan Trao. This last group included Nguyen Kim Hung and Trieu Duc Quang.[70]

Nguyen Kim Hung was a young student who was very impressed with both the words and deeds of Ho Chi Minh and eagerly awaited greater participation in the coming revolution. He was particularly affected by the organized nature of the march—which included radio transmission at both midday and in the evening—and by the warm reception the group received in marketplaces along the way. The people, he recalled,

> extended us a very warm welcome and they gave us, offered us, a lot of food. In the afternoon Ho Chi Minh asked Mr. Dang Tuan, who was logistic officer, and he told him to pay for all the things offered by the people. And the people replied that "These are our presents to you, our donations, they are free of charge, we don't get the money." Ho Chi Minh still said that we had some money and we can pay, and we understood that Ho Chi Minh was very concerned about some kind of suspicion that might arise that the liberation soldiers just take the things from the people.[71]

Trieu Duc Quang, a seventeen-year-old student, was also assigned to study radio operations with Mac Shin. Quang, who recalled putting revolutionary leaflets in the drawers of his classmates' school tables as one of his first activities in support of the Viet Minh, quit school after the March coup and joined the revolution with his father. Along with Nguyen Kim Hung, Trieu Duc Quang had developed an affection for both Tan and Shin and an ever-growing respect for Ho Chi Minh.

After the band's arrival at Tan Trao, Ho gave Tan a "typed account of the odyssey replete with details about the rugged topography, the dangers of night marching, the intricate system of local guides and porters along the route, the wild animals encountered," and so on. David Marr wrote that "clearly Ho wished to codify and supplement Tan's own impressions of the arduous walk from the border, in the hope that the radio reports Tan sent back to Kunming would create a favorable impression and result in increased Allied support to the Viet Minh."[72]

The account provided to Tan contains many similarities to Lieutenant Shaw's diary; both clearly place the Viet Minh center stage in the ongoing struggle against both the Japanese and the French. Nevertheless, Tan began putting Ho to work for the GBT; he was tasked with organizing an intelligence network of couriers while Mac Shin trained his students on radio operations, both "transmission and reception and also how to use the flashlights as a signal to communicate with planes."[73] Tan conveyed various details of the Viet Minh camp and guerrillas to Fenn:

> The gang all salute me and do everything they can to help us, and they worry if we can't eat their poor food. Mac is teaching them radio technique and says they all "love" him. They are very military-conscious and have military drill every day. The fact that we brought a sizeable amount of guns [reported as two rifles, three carbines, a Bren gun, and a few six-shooters] and ammo has really paid dividends. They say our weapons are much better than either the French or Japanese ones. Everyone has a gun of some sort in this country. I saw a 1904 Remington Rifle here. And a "flintlock" where you have to strike a spark and another where you light a match to set off a fuse and then the gun goes off—you hope. Some are like shotguns but you have to load them from the front—put in the shot and powder, then tamp. They you pull back a huge trigger and put a match head on the cap: looks like the guns the Pilgrims used to shoot turkeys with![74]

The first couriers from the Bac Bo brought a wealth of information from inside Indochina, including "letters, maps, documents, Japanese leaflets and other MO material."[75] Tan reported that the population was becoming even more anti-Japanese than anti-French in the wake of the coup.[76] In a letter of about the same time, Ho thanked Fenn for taking care of a group of Viet Minh he had sent to Kunming for training and for teaching them "other things necessary in our common fight against the Japs." Ho concluded his note by again extending an invitation to Fenn to visit the Viet Minh base camp and by asking Fenn to send his "respect to General Chennault."[77]

Again Ho demonstrated his calculated sincerity. Although his respect for
Chennault was no doubt genuine, Ho could only hope that should the innocent greeting reach the general, it might help keep the name Ho Chi Minh
alive in his memory, or at the very least that Chennault would attach a positive connotation to Ho's name should it come up in some other context.

After Tan's and Shin's arrival at Tan Trao, the quantity and quality of in-
telligence reports began to grow. "After some time," recalled Nguyen Kim
Hung, "among the air drops were a number of digital radio transmitters."
With these,

> Ho Chi Minh decided to establish three more radio stations. One
> station in Ha Giang, under the charge of Mr. Quy. Another station in
> Lang Son, under the charge of Mr. Lieu Minh. Another station was in
> Cao Bang under the charge of Mr. Bac. And I remember that the
> assignment that was given to those stations was to collect weather
> information twice a day for the Allied forces. And also to provide
> intelligence and information on where the Japs were stationed so that
> the Allied forces could attack. And also to find appropriate locations
> for air drops and landings.[78]

That Ho Chi Minh was the primary decision maker on where to establish
GBT/AGAS/OSS-sponsored radio stations is doubtful. His connection to
the Americans and the Allied war effort, however, seemed firm to the young
members of the Viet Minh and aided in the solidification of his control. But
even prior to the establishment of the net within Tonkin, agent Lucius had
begun producing reports for Fenn. On March 29, "Hoo" provided a scath-
ing report on the situation in French Indochina. Included, as in Shaw's
pamphlet, was a concise chronology and history of Vietnam since the
French "invasion." As part of his basis for the description of Vietnamese
anti-French activity, Ho remarked, "Beside the freedom to get drugged, to
get drunk, and to pay taxes, the Indo-Chinese have no other freedom." In
addition, Ho provided extensive information on the use of propaganda by
the Japanese and on Vietnamese attitudes toward both the Japanese and the
Allies. Special attention was given to the actions of the Viet Minh: their support of the peasantry, their actions against the Japanese, and their persecu-
tion by the French.[79]

"Besides propaganda and organizational work," Ho bragged, "[the] Vietminh pays much attention to educational questions. Despite unspeakable
difficulties, they organize secret evening schools to teach the peasant men

and women to read and to write. In places where the League is strong, illiteracy is almost liquidated." He was sure to point out, however, that their work went beyond the realm of self-help. At night, Viet Minh youths practiced guerrilla warfare with the weapons at hand—usually wooden guns and bamboo sticks. Due in part to this lack of weapons, resistance against the Japanese only rarely took on a violent nature. Most of the time resistance activities were more passive. For example, Ho explained that the cadres sometimes hid foodstuffs from the Japanese, only to encounter retaliation from the French, who, upon discovering "the hiding spots, took away all the rice, and punished the whole 'communist' village." While building up the Viet Minh in the eyes of those who would eventually read his report, Ho simultaneously castigated the French:

> The French shot dead Viet-minh men, then cut their heads off and hung
> them on a pole at the village cross-road. Viet-minh members often have
> their houses burned down, their properties confiscated, their family
> jailed and a high price put upon their head by the French. Where Viet-
> minh activity is suspected, the whole village is destroyed and its
> inhabitants arrested. . . . Jap and French spies, Chinese and Indo-
> Chinese traitors formed a perfectly organized network of informers.
> Underground communications are often cut off, and often Viet-minh
> workers have to spend several weeks to travel a short distance. Viet-
> minh activists often suffer hunger and cold and fever. In spite of all these
> and other difficulties, the Viet-minh people keep on working and
> growing, because they are deeply inspired by patriotism. They have
> courage, patience and a self-sacrificing spirit. They know what they are
> fighting, suffering and when need be, dying for.[80]

By all indications Ho Chi Minh was supremely confident about the eventual outcome of the war: the defeat of the Japanese and the victory of the Americans. As Ho waxed eloquent about the upcoming victory, he also posed a rhetorical question to his American readers: "Are the Allies really fighting for world freedom and democracy as they solemnly said in their official declarations? Or do they fight simply to save French selfish colonial interests?"[81] Fenn was moved by Ho's written words. And, just as Shaw had no doubt been, Tan was inspired as he conversed with this charismatic man long into the many nights they spent together in the jungles of northern Vietnam.

Both Frank Tan and Mac Shin stayed at Tan Trao for nearly four months. Although Ho was initially skeptical about taking Tan and Shin into

Vietnam, in one of his first letters to Fenn he commented that both men were getting along quite well. Tan's work in Tonkin quickly gained a great deal of importance. While there, he was involved in "gathering Japanese intelligence and concurrently (working with AGAS) expanding the escape and evasion net. He was also looking for certain Americans evading capture in the Tuyen-Quang, Thai Nguyen, Bac Can triangle—all in the heart of Ho's anti-Japanese operations."[82]

During their months together, Ho and Tan developed a particularly close friendship. With his elite schooling and American ways, Tan seemed on the surface very different from the much-older Vietnamese man. Yet they soon discovered that they had much in common. Both men had experienced discrimination at home—Ho under the French and Tan growing up Chinese in a very "white" section of Boston. Tan remembered his early days in Boston: "I soon began to sense that there was always a barrier, always a feeling that we were discriminated against by the whites." And both men experienced lost love. Not long before leaving China for the Viet Bac, Tan had been spurned by Gordon's beautiful young secretary. Disappointed and hurt, he confided in Ho, who in return told Tan about his own regrets at having to forget a young girl he was fond of when he left Vietnam to explore the world. "During the four months Mac Shin and I spent in the jungles with Ho, Giap and their cohorts," remembered Tan, "a friendship developed between all of us."[83]

Tan also reflected on the affection that emerged between Shin and Ho. "For Mac who was young and looked younger, Ho seemed to look on him as something of a son. He said that if Mac wanted to return after the war he would help him get settled on a nice piece of land, but leave it to Mac to find a nice wife." Both Tan and Shin experienced the kind, sympathetic demeanor that during Ho's lifetime endeared him, as the kind and gentle "Uncle Ho," to so many. Tan reminisced:

> As my relationship with Ho became closer, I began to see him as the man he was—a man who dedicated his life to win freedom for his people. He was a man who I felt was a lonely person, bereft and denied all the normal comforts and happiness of life. Such a sacrifice left him nothing but to think and act for one thing only. Hence, the inconsistency that caused some to describe him as a communist, or conversely as a patriot.[84]

Tran Trong Trung, one of the Viet Minh students who studied radio operations at Tan Trao, noticed the growing friendship from the Vietnamese perspective:

I also noticed that Mr. Mac Shin and Mr. Frank Tan were very fond of
Ho Chi Minh. And Mr. Mac Shin himself in the course of his instruction,
his radio lessons, he said that "Our Ho is a great man. This is a real
honor for you guys to be here with Ho Chi Minh, that's why you guys
have to try and master all these technologies so that you can best serve
Ho Chi Minh."

In looking back Tran Trong Trung compared the strong friendship among
them as a "kind of first love," which, he concluded "is [like] water that runs
deep."[85]

The appearance of Ho Chi Minh and his obvious relationship to Tan in
particular had caused quite a stir among his colleagues, some of whom had
even believed rumors that he was dead. The surprise of Ho's arrival was
compounded by their marvel at the equipment Tan and Shin brought along.
One of the Viet Minh couriers assigned to deliver letters to Fenn filled him
on the details: "[They had] all sorts of weapons [with them], better than
anything either the French or Japanese had." The relief at Ho's return was
marred only by concern for his seriously weakened physical condition. The
arduous trek that had made young Tan want to quit had pushed the fifty-
year-old Ho to the limits of his endurance. As he began to recover, Ho made
a move to consolidate his authority and influence by cleverly wielding the
seemingly insignificant mementos of his time in Kunming: the autographed
photograph of Chennault and the brand-new American Colt .45s. Fenn recorded the courier's story in his diary:

> When he got well enough he invited all the top leaders to a conference,
> not his own people, but rivals working for other groups, who had used
> his absence to push themselves forward. Ho told them he had now
> secured the help of the Americans including Chennault. At first nobody
> really believed him. Then he produced the photograph of Chennault
> signed "Yours sincerely." After this he sent for the automatic pistols and
> gave one to each of the leaders as a present. The leaders considered
> Chennault had sent these presents personally. After this conference there
> was never any more talk about who was the top leader.[86]

Tan added that the flight to the border in an American plane, Shin's ability to keep Ho in touch with the Americans via radio, and Ho's own arrival
carrying "powerful American weapons" had certainly seemed to "prove
American friendship" to many in attendance.[87] Soon after this conference,

Tan wired Kunming that Ho's "stock went up another ten points," when the GBT dropped in a load of OSS supplies—"radio sets, medicines, gadgets, weapons."[88] Needless to say, the messenger overestimated Ho's power both at the moment and in the long run. But although sincere in most of his early dealings with the United States, Ho Chi Minh's incredible ability to manipulate situations and the American role in them should not be overestimated.

Looking back at these crucial months after the coup, Fenn concluded that Ho became "the unquestioned leader of an overwhelmingly strong revolutionary party." At the time of the coup de main Ho "had been a leader of a party that was but one amongst many," Fenn went on to say. Ho was "unrecognized by the Americans, opposed by the French, shunned by the Chinese; with no weapons and no equipment. He was also, at that time, cut off from his group by a formidable 600 miles and no chance of flying any part of it." All of this changed, he believed, "largely thanks to the GBT."[89] By the beginning of May, Tan was routinely sending back intelligence from the Viet Minh base camp, especially MO material such as "Japanese newspapers, leaflets, notebooks and some pills the Japs were distributing to the Annamites as 'medicine.'"[90] In Kunming Viet Minh cadres were being trained by the GBT for future radio communications operations in Indochina. And although Fenn reported that he routinely sent the MO information he received off to OSS headquarters, by all indications he preferred to keep agent Lucius, and other Viet Minh cadre such as Pham Van Dong, for the GBT and AGAS.[91] Suspicious of Fenn's loyalty to the organization, OSS agents in Kunming, particularly Archimedes Patti, who were anxious to meet and use agent Lucius themselves, would have to find another way to meet the master of the moment—Ho Chi Minh.

7

The Relationship Deepens:
Ho Chi Minh and the Americans

As Frank Tan and Mac Shin settled into a routine in the Viet Minh base camp, the GBT intelligence network began to take shape once again. Charles Fenn and Harry Bernard received the reports in Kunming and passed information for the Flying Tigers on to AGAS. Fenn maintained his contact with the OSS and passed it MO material as well.[1] But the relationship between the OSS and the GBT had not improved, and Fenn was still not providing the OSS with what they wanted most: ready access to GBT personnel. New avenues of approach were opening up for the OSS, however. Within a few days of his April 13 arrival in Kunming, Archimedes Patti's inquiries about local Vietnamese exiles had attracted the attention of the Viet Minh.

Vuong Minh Phuong, one of the Viet Minh cadres then residing in Kunming, called on Patti in mid-April. Patti described Vuong Minh Phuong as a well-educated young man in his early thirties. Phuong reported his earlier contacts with Austin Glass and informed Patti of the others he knew in Kunming, including personnel at the OWI and the American consulate. The two men spent most of the day talking, and Patti quickly concluded that Phuong knew more about the OSS and AGAS than Patti knew about the Viet Minh. Indeed, although Patti was familiar with Phuong's name from various reports he had already read, he conceded that Phuong still knew more about him than he knew about Phuong. In what was becoming characteristic fashion for the Viet Minh, Phuong dressed up the truth about Viet Minh interactions with Chennault, AGAS, and the OSS. Patti reported: "With a touch of pride Phuong recounted how his colleagues in Indochina and China had been working 'very closely' with a number of General Chennault's and OSS's Americans, providing Japanese order of battle and target information. He alluded to OSS-AGAS operations in which the Viet Minh had contributed to the evasion and escape of 'many' Army and Navy flyers by giving them shelter and guiding them to safety."[2]

Without a doubt, stretching the truth was becoming a real asset for the Viet Minh. Just as Ho had expanded on the nature of his interactions with Chennault to consolidate his power among select rivals, Phuong now enhanced the Viet Minh's relationship with both the OSS and AGAS in hopes of further encouraging Patti to work with them and perhaps to give them what they wanted more than anything else: recognition by the United States as the "sole legal and authorized organization representing the people of Viet Nam"[3] in the fight against the Japanese. Although Phuong and Ho exaggerated the nature of their contact with the Americans, they did not lie about it; the substance of what they claimed was true. Both men were undoubtedly well aware that if they had been caught in an out-and-out lie, they and their messages would have been dismissed and they would have had very little chance of regaining credibility.

Although the wording of Phuong's request—for recognition as the "sole legal and authorized organization" in Vietnam—indicated a degree of legitimacy the OSS was neither prepared nor able to give at that time, the OSS had already acknowledged much of the substance. In a brief from early April, the OSS had declared that the Viet Minh "army" was the "nucleus of all the anti-Japanese forces in Indo-China with groups in various districts: Bac Kan, Thai Nguyen and Cao Bang."[4] Although this assessment—like the Viet Minh claims—was no doubt exaggerated, it does seem to have been an accurate presentation of what the OSS believed.

In the course of his conversation with Patti, Phuong described the Viet Minh as a political front that was also an "armed force, organized into guerrilla units and actively engaged in unorthodox warfare against the Japanese." He assured Patti that the Viet Minh were ready to fight side by side with the Americans against their common enemy.

In fact, the nucleus of the Viet Minh, the ICP, had declared in 1941 at the Eighth Enlarged Session of the Central Committee that "the watchword of the Party is first *to liberate the Indochinese people from the Japanese and French yoke.*"[5] For the next three years, however, the Viet Minh engaged in little more than empty rhetoric. In 1944 the Viet Minh founded the first Armed Propaganda Brigade for the Liberation of Viet Nam to begin the armed struggle for Vietnamese freedom. Ho Chi Minh's instructions to Vo Nguyen Giap, the former history teacher and top-ranking Viet Minh cadre, emphasized the importance of guerrilla warfare in this struggle. Ho advised Giap that they must "apply guerilla warfare; maintain secrecy, quickness of action and initiative (now in the east now in the west, arriving unexpectedly and departing without leaving any traces)."[6] At the ceremony founding the

Armed Propaganda Brigade on December 22, Giap exhorted the audience to take upon their shoulders the difficult mission of fighting two much stronger enemies: the Japanese and the French. His words undoubtedly inspired many of his listeners:

> We raise high the spirit of bravery and sacrifice, never afraid in spite of hardship, never giving up in spite of suffering. And although our heads may fall, and blood may flow, we will still not retreat. So great is the anger of the nation, so many are the tragic atrocities that await settlement of accounts. We will reveal clearly to the whole people that the way to life is the path of unity to prepare the armed uprising. The Liberation Army will show that it is a military unit of the people, of the country, going in the vanguard on the road to national liberation.[7]

Giap tied the upcoming struggle to Vietnam's history and tradition and asked the new Liberation soldiers to swear an oath of honor under the flag, including swearing "to sacrifice all for the Viet-nam Fatherland, to fight to the last drop of blood to destroy the Japanese and French fascists and Viet-namese traitors, to make Viet-nam an independent and democratic country, equal to other democratic nations in the world."[8] For the next two months, "using what few weapons they could get from the people or from raiding isolated French posts, armed propaganda teams began to harass the Japanese and the French in mountainous regions of North Vietnam."[9] Nevertheless, their exposure to combat against the Japanese was minimal. When the Japanese coup displaced the French, the Viet Minh became more vocal in their opposition to the Japanese. The "Viet Minh Summons to Fight the Japanese" in March 1945 decried the situation:

> Our blood boils
> Our stomach is empty
> Our belongings are plundered
> Our hearths are destroyed

> It is the Japanese who are responsible for all these disasters. There is only one way for us to save our lives; it is to prepare with all our compatriots to chase out the Japanese birds of prey.

The "Summons" chastised the people for "lament[ing] uselessly" and urged them to arm themselves with "clubs, spears, knives; expel the Japanese

brigands and recover control of your rice paddies and homes."[10] Truong
Chinh claimed in 1946 that the day following the coup,

> [Viet Minh] guerillas took the isolated posts in the High and Middle
> regions of North Vietnam by storm, disarmed a number of French
> soldiers and Bao An units to prevent their arms from falling into the
> hands of the Japanese; attacked the Japanese troops moving along the
> roads of Tuyen Quang, Thai Nguyen, Bac Kan and Cao Bang provinces,
> harassed them even in the chief town of Bac Can province, and launched
> sudden attacks against their base at Cho Chu.[11]

Although Truong Chinh's description was probably exaggerated, the Viet
Minh increasingly harassed the Japanese after the March coup. Years later
Tran Thi Minh Chau reminisced about the benefits of these early attacks:

> As a result of the attack[s], we killed the enemy as well as got the arms
> and supplies. Sometimes we got sufficient arms to equip the whole
> platoon. In Cao Bang Province, Mr. Vo Nguyen Giap launched attacks on
> the enemy post of Nga Ngun and Phai Cat. There we collected all the
> arms of the enemy. At that time, according to the policy of the Viet
> Minh, every locality where the conditions are good or favorable you
> could launch an attack on the enemy.[12]

In addition, Frank Tan sent messages to GBT headquarters reporting several of the same successful Viet Minh engagements as Truong Chinh had, including the attack on Bac Can and the ambush of a Japanese convoy near
Cho Chu. He concluded that "this Indian style stab in back fighting [is] just
down OSS alley."[13] Japanese sources also evidence at least some Viet Minh
guerrilla activity. In "Report of Measures Taken by Japanese Eighth Army in
FIC during 1945," written after the surrender, the Japanese author testified
that "the activities of [the] Viet-Nam Party in Northern Indo-China became
more and more vigorous, especially its disturbances of public security, aim-
ing to dispel Japanese forces in order to accomplish the full independence of
their people. . . . The Japanese army," the report continued, "was compelled
to continue to employ a considerable strength in painstaking work of sweeping Viet Minh partisans until the cessation of hostilities of August 15."[14]
    Although weak in comparison to European underground movements dur-
ing the war, the Viet Minh were organized and had a solid history of implor-
ing the people to stand up against the Japanese. By June the Japanese had

become sufficiently frustrated with Viet Minh harassment to order the Twenty-first Division (Japanese) into action against them. Historian Stein Tønnesson described the decision based on Japanese and Viet Minh sources:

> After an incident where a Japanese lieutenant had been killed in a Viet Minh ambush, the Japanese Army arrested four Viet Minh sympathizers in the nearest village and interrogated them. Afterwards they were released and asked to carry some letters to their leaders. The letters declared a general sympathy for the Viet Minh struggle for independence but urged the Viet Minh to cooperate with Japan against Britain and the USA. The Japanese had no intention of occupying the areas where the Viet Minh was active, one of the letters said, but if they continued to harass the Japanese Army, a company would be sent which would fight them to the death. The Viet Minh responded by publishing a summary of the letters in the clandestine press. Before long the Viet Minh problem was brought to the highest level in Hanoi. . . .
> Apparently the Japanese command in Hanoi concluded, at least for the time being, that it would be impossible to reach an understanding with the Viet Minh, because in June 1945, the Japanese 21st Division was ordered to fight the guerrillas.[15]

This activity had yet to occur, however, when the OSS R&A Branch informed Patti that it had "reports of Vietnamese active opposition to the Japanese in the area of Tuyen Quang–Thai Nguyen–Lang Son–Bac Can and that their operations smacked of paramilitary tactics."[16] With this in mind, after listening to Phuong reiterate much of the Viet Minh history and convinced of the Viet Minh's potential usefulness, Patti promised to discuss the viability of using the Viet Minh with his colleagues. He had, however, a request of his own: Patti wanted to meet with Ho Chi Minh.[17]

When Patti reported the substance of his conversation with Vuong Minh Phuong to Helliwell, Heppner, and Major Robert E. Wampler, chief of the SO Branch of the OSS in Kunming, all voiced the concern that any weapons provided to the Viet Minh for fighting the Japanese would be promptly turned against the French. The relatively uncooperative nature of both the French and the local Chinese, however, made the Viet Minh the OSS's best alternative for gaining the operatives necessary to establish the military intelligence networks in FIC envisioned in Project QUAIL. Moreover, Patti's information indicated that meeting with Ho Chi Minh was the best avenue toward gaining the agents he needed. When Patti and Vuong Minh Phuong next met, Phuong told Patti that he had sent a message to Ho and had set up a meeting in the border town of Ching-hsi.

At the end of April Patti left Kunming, combining a tour of OSS outposts along the Chinese border with his visit to Ching-hsi. After making arrangements with a Chinese communist intermediary, Patti and Ho Chi Minh finally met on April 27, 1945, in a small, out-of-the-way Chinese restaurant. The two men got along well from the start. Although from entirely different backgrounds, they shared many characteristics: both men possessed, and appreciated in others, a keen intelligence, and both were masters at the game of intrigue. Patti dropped lines that he instinctively knew would appeal to Ho: "I expressed my pleasure in meeting a man who had so many American friends in Kunming."[18] Ho briefly outlined the long list of grievances against French colonialism and gave Patti a series of pictures of victims of the 1945 famine, which had been aggravated by both French and Japanese actions.[19] Getting down to the business at hand, however, Ho offered suggestions of what his group might be able to accomplish for the Americans, but he asked for nothing directly, perhaps realizing how much the incessant demands of both the French and the Chinese irritated the Americans. Interestingly, in the course of describing the current organization and work of the Viet Minh, Ho told Patti that "AGAS and the Viet Minh were presently working to organize a clandestine operation in the interior to assist downed airmen, *but he considered that another matter*" (emphasis added).[20]

The AGAS mission Ho alluded to was undoubtedly the GBT mission that had taken Frank Tan and Mac Shin into the Viet Bac. Yet according to Patti's account, Ho did not mention the GBT, Tan, or his GBT contact and correspondent in Kunming, Charles Fenn. It seems plausible that this was a calculated omission on Ho's part. Each of the OSS men who spoke or wrote about their encounters with Ho Chi Minh commented that Ho knew much more about them personally and the Americans in general than they knew about him or the Viet Minh. If Ho knew of the animosity between the OSS and the GBT/Fenn, it was clearly in his best interest to shuffle all credit for Tan's information to AGAS (both Fenn and the GBT did work with AGAS, after all), omit his relationship with "troublesome" Fenn,[21] and entice this new OSS representative with what the Viet Minh could do for him.

For Patti, the possibilities for using the Viet Minh seemed promising. He had concluded, like Tan and Fenn before him, that Ho could be trusted. "Despite my studied objectivity and purposeful awareness of not allowing myself to become involved in the political aspects of the Indochina question," Patti reminisced, "Ho's sincerity, pragmatism, and eloquence made an indelible impression on me." At that meeting and in subsequent encounters, Patti reached a conclusion that would cause him to behave in the late summer of 1945 in ways that would seem questionable in retrospect, if not obviously at the time. "I saw," he wrote, "that his [Ho's] ultimate goal was to attain American support for the cause of a free Viet Nam and felt that desire presented no conflict with American policy." The future aside, in late April 1945, Patti was being pushed to obtain information from Indochina: G-2 (the military intelligence branch of the U.S. Army) wanted OSS operations in both Hanoi and Saigon, theater headquarters wanted intelligence on the arrival of Japanese combat units and the building of new military installations, and the MO office wanted a new propaganda campaign. "They wanted everything and they wanted it right away," noted Patti. "From a practical viewpoint, Ho and the Viet Minh appeared to be the answer to my immediate problem of establishing operations in Indochina."22

If Patti's planning succeeded, trained Viet Minh radio operators and operatives could staff Project QUAIL. At this point, the planning requirements for Operation CARBONADO intruded on Patti's concerns, placing a higher premium on accurate intelligence from within Vietnam and thus on his relationship with the Viet Minh. CARBONADO was the code name for a planned Allied offensive in southern China consisting of an "overland drive, along the Kweilen-Liuchow-Nanning line, to secure the Canton–Hong Kong area, thus opening major seaports in southern China to receive the armies from Europe and the Philippines."23 In fact, CARBONADO was a deception plan, intended to draw Japanese forces away from the actual targets of American offensive operations. This knowledge, of course, was restricted to the very highest levels of the chain of command, and the OSS was required to collect intelligence in support of CARBONADO with the same urgency as for a real operation. Indeed, Stein Tønnesson believed that QUAIL "might have played a significant role if CARBONADO had been carried out," and as operatives, "the Viet Minh guerrillas would have been able to render valuable assistance to the OSS in facilitating the planned Chinese entry into Tonkin under operation CARBONADO."24

The difficulties of supplying the army during CARBONADO necessitated first the capture of the tiny seaport at Fort Bayard. The seaport was sufficient for landing the envisioned "massive deliveries of supplies—at least one Liberty ship daily," but once inland, new supply problems would probably arise because of the poor quality of most roads in the area.25 The OSS would be responsible for the harassment of the enemy, including spearheading guerrilla, sabotage, and propaganda activities. QUAIL operatives would provide crucial intelligence on the disposition and movement of Japanese troops in Indochina with a close eye to preventing Japanese troops in Indochina from reinforcing the areas under attack. In preparation for the operation, the OSS was instructed to prepare demolition and guerrilla teams for work disrupting the Japanese corridor between Hanoi and Nanning. With so much potentially riding on CARBONADO, the need for accurate intelligence on Indochina was crucial.[26] When Heppner briefed Patti on CARBONADO in May, Patti had few options in looking for operatives in the area: He both liked and trusted Ho Chi Minh, and his relationship with the French was deteriorating.

By the end of 1945, many Frenchmen, and some Americans, would accuse Archimedes Patti of being anti-French.[27] He refuted this accusation in general and claimed that it was certainly not the case when he arrived in Kunming in April. From the beginning of his duties in China, Patti had been assailed with various requests from the French for supplies and information. He had assumed that French operatives would probably be involved in intelligence gathering in their colony and that he could work with them. As the urgency to gain intelligence on the Japanese in Vietnam mounted, the problem of working with the French came to a head. Patti met with General Sabattier in Szemao and witnessed firsthand the "wretched sight" of the defeated French army. Patti and the additional French-speaking staff he had requested spent ten days in the southern China town interviewing the French refugees—officers and noncommissioned officers, lower-ranking personnel, and a number of civilian officials and businessmen. Overall, he was unimpressed with their potential for carrying out immediate, successful operations.

Patti felt pity for the physical condition of the weary men, but his overall impression of the exiled French was not favorable. Patti described his conversations with the French refugees as "[eliciting] an unattractive picture of indifference, vengefulness, and selfish interest."[28] With more contact with different personalities, Patti's opinion of the French in China fell even more. Like Milton Miles before him, Patti's efforts to work with select French forces or individuals were constantly snagged by internal quarrels among the French. Indeed, even Sabattier and Alessandri, the two generals who linked up at Dien Bien Phu in their successful retreat from the Japanese coup, could not agree. Alessandri did not approve of Sabattier's plan to place a portion of his troops under Wedemeyer's control, and he disputed Sabattier's assumed role in the French military hierarchy in China. Furthermore, Patti and the new chief of the French intelligence unit in Kunming (M.5), Major Jean Sainteny,[29] quickly hit a sour note.

At this point, an individual offering an entirely different perspective of the events and personalities in question entered the story: OSS officer Lieutenant

René Défourneaux was assigned to work with the French. Perhaps it was his background that made Défourneaux less judgmental of the French; then again, the nature of his work did not put him in a position of dealing with the French hierarchy. Born and raised in France, Défourneaux immigrated to the United States in 1939 at the age of eighteen. In December 1942 he volunteered for service in the U.S. Army, where his fluency in French attracted the attention of the OSS. After completing his training, he was shipped to Europe in 1944, where he earned the Silver Star for his gallantry behind enemy lines in France.[30] Soon after his return from the European theater of operations, Défourneaux was again shipped out, this time to Asia. After additional training in India, he arrived in Kunming. By May he had settled into a series of routine and eminently tedious tasks. Thus, duty on the Indochina border interviewing escaped French soldiers seemed a pleasant change of pace.

Défourneaux easily passed among escapees as a "French friend" and rapidly gained their confidence. Défourneaux and his partner, Burley Fuselier, an intelligence specialist from the Fourteenth Air Force, circulated among the French identifying those with the "best information." They then escorted those men to Chennault's headquarters for further questioning. His work continued for a few weeks until "word got around," Défourneaux recalled, "that we two nosy fellows were not to be trusted and that all should stay clear." Défourneaux empathized with the plight of the French. He concluded: "The fact of the matter was that these wretched souls had been dealt a lousy hand by the events of the past few months and had not been given many options."[31]

At the end of May, one of the first joint OSS-French projects was beginning. Project PAKHOI involved Lieutenant Robert Ettinger (who had linked up with Sabattier's forces in March), Lieutenant James Jordan, and a number of agents provided by M.5. The goal was to report on Japanese troop dispositions and naval operations between Fort Bayard and Haiphong. A second agreement, concluded on June 1 by Sabattier and Wedemeyer, provided for 100 Vietnamese troops and ten to twelve European French officers to work under the control of the OSS. The men were to be placed in two teams, "Deer" and "Cat" under the direction of Major Allison Thomas and Captain Mike Holland, respectively. They would be trained at Ching-hsi for a sabotage mission in Indochina.[32]

Neither Alessandri nor Sainteny approved of Sabattier's agreement with Wedemeyer, and both resented the lack of French control and insight into Allied plans. Sabattier did not share the same reservations. Stein Tønnesson concluded that Sabattier was "probably correct" in maintaining that the pettiness often exhibited by many in the French intelligence community "contributed to throwing the OSS into the arms of the Viet Minh." "In Sabattier's view," wrote Tønnesson, "there was no danger in integrating and subordinating the French intelligence services into the command structure of the OSS." Indeed, Sabattier believed that "the Americans were like 'children' when it came to intelligence, and it would be very easy to gain quiet dominance of the activities of the OSS from within."[33]

Sabattier probably underestimated the ability of the OSS to maintain control, but his hypothesis was never tested. Although the French troops he promised arrived without incident, problems began immediately when their senior officer demanded that the OSS both pay and supply the men. The OSS had no intention of committing American resources to rebuilding the French. In fact, in his mid-May correspondence to Helliwell, Colonel John Whitaker, chief of SI in the China theater, stated that he and Major Quentin Roosevelt had "made clear" to the two French commanders who had called at OSS's Chungking headquarters that "OSS was interested in intelligence alone in FIC, and that no aid to the French could be envisaged beyond such arms and fire-power as we might need to protect American or joint intelligence missions."[34] Seeing the French demands as clearly exceeding their responsibility, the OSS refused. The French responded with a "sit-down strike." Simultaneously, Sainteny began demanding to be fully apprised of confidential Allied plans for the area and of orders issued to American personnel. To make matters worse, Sainteny and the French in both Ching-hsi and Kunming all seemed to receive their orders from different quarters. "The question for us was," recalled Patti, "with whom among the French were we to deal?"[35]

Patti characterized the American mood as one of "extreme exasperation," but indeed, the resentment seems to have gone much deeper than that. Patti's increasing disgust with the French could have been a product of his weariness and frustration with the failed attempts to combine efforts to gather intelligence. Perhaps the history lesson given him on the French role in Indochina by both Vuong Minh Phuong and Ho Chi Minh colored his attitude. Most probably it was a product of both, for Patti was clearly disenchanted with the French and increasingly taken with the enigmatic Ho. In his most telling remarks about the French, Patti wrote:

We Americans in the Pacific and Asia had one overriding goal—to defeat Japan—even if we had to go it alone, knowing that among our Allies were those who would willingly let someone else win the war while they prepared to reap the fruits of victory. . . . The French particularly, with their overriding desire for an early reoccupation of their colony, withheld critical political and military intelligence. They appropriated to themselves arms and supplies intended for Allied operations and wherever they could obstructed American attempts to function within Indochina. During the final months of the war, and continuing up to the present era, some of the French most deeply involved in impeding the war effort against Japan loudly proclaimed themselves mistreated, abused, neglected, and victims of "conspiracy"—quite in line with their studied policy of injured righteousness.[36]

Patti's sympathy for the Vietnamese and his disdain for the French would only grow. Unbeknownst to him, he already mirrored many of the sentiments of the first two Americans to have extensive contact with Ho, Frank Tan and Charles Fenn. Soon other Americans would join the ranks of Ho's admirers.

As Patti fumed about the French in late May, Ho Chi Minh's first intelligence reports arrived. Although accompanied, as usual, by Viet Minh political tracts, his report also gave "useful information identifying some units of the Japanese 37th Division, their location only a few days earlier, and the names of some senior officers." Several days later a second report provided "details of new Japanese construction and improvements to existing French-built defenses in the Cao Bang sector and on the road to Hanoi." Patti recalled that "the identification for the first time of units of the 38th Japanese Army and particularly elements of the 22nd Division in the Cao Bang border area aroused considerable interest in our Order of Battle Section and at Theater level."[37]

As the ability of the OSS, via the Viet Minh, to garner strategic information about the Japanese in Indochina increased, trouble brewed within the GBT. Although both Frank Tan and Mac Shin felt welcome in the Viet Bac and continued to train operatives and send back reports, a series of events left Charles Fenn, at the main office in Kunming, increasingly disturbed. These events were only tangentially related, yet combined, they eventually marginalized Fenn, the most important man to date in dealings with Ho Chi Minh and the Viet Minh. Fenn's problems began with AGAS. Fenn's and the GBT's relations with AGAS had always been positive. The GBT provided valuable information to that agency, and AGAS provided what support and funds they could. In fact, when difficulties had arisen between the OSS and the GBT, the GBT had transferred their services, including Fenn's, to AGAS in February 1945 with the mixed blessings of the OSS. However, Fenn's official capacity remained as the OSS liaison to AGAS, and of course to the GBT.

The routine in Kunming had become tedious for the energetic Fenn. With a burning desire to escape his desk Fenn planned to join Tan and Shin at the Viet Minh headquarters, as per his earlier agreement with Ho Chi Minh. However, when Fenn suggested to his AGAS superior, Major A. R. Wichtrich, that he parachute in "immediately," his request was denied. According to Fenn, Wichtrich rationalized that Fenn was "too essential" at headquarters to "be spared for such a mission." Fenn also learned that another AGAS agent, Lieutenant Dan Phelan, had already been assigned the mission. Not only would Phelan be the one to jump into Indochina, Wichtrich informed Fenn, but he would also be "staying around your [the GBT] camp for a week" to "pick up all the gen [general intelligence on Indochina]." However, Wichtrich assured Fenn, Phelan was "fairly knowledgeable already, since he's studied the lay-out pretty closely." Thus, AGAS disappointed and irritated Fenn three times with this one incident: (1) He was confined to his desk instead of the much more exciting mission of parachuting in to work with Ho; (2) he was saddled with something he detested, outsiders snooping around the GBT compound and operations; and (3) he did not like Dan Phelan. Fenn's reaction to Phelan's "pretty close study" of the "lay-out" was telling:

> Study is one thing, but attitude is something else. Phelan was so far to the right politically, that he even admitted he would rather have liaised with the French than with the Vietminh. What would Ho think about having such a reactionary officer foisted upon him? Another drawback to Phelan's character was that prevailing disease of snobbery, inherent in so many of both OSS and AGAS personnel who were all too often selected on the basis of family, wealth, education or social elitism.[38]

In Phelan's case, Fenn was both right and wrong in his analysis. Phelan did come from an elitist background; prior to his World War II duty he had been an official of the Chase Manhattan Bank and had lived and worked among the wealthy in New York.[39] There is no evidence, however, that he was chosen for his position based on connections alone. Phelan was "present almost everywhere in the world when the war broke. He had witnessed Italian guerrillas hanged by Mussolini, he participated in the disembarkation in the north region of France, and also took part in the greater war in the Philippines," recalled Tan.[40] Even Fenn added to his characterization of Phelan that he was "active, quick-witted, eager, good-humored and anxious to learn," which, Fenn determined, gave Phelan an overall "score above average." Although

Phelan was reluctant to undertake the mission into Tonkin and began his stint at the GBT camp by "grumbling to us [Fenn and Bernard] that Ho was a communist," he prepared for the mission as assigned.[41]

Fenn's loyalties were again put to the test when his Kunming Viet Minh contact, Pham Van Dong, came to query him about OSS policy. Dong complained to Fenn that he had heard the OSS was sending individuals into Indochina who worked closely with Frenchmen and who were "more anti-Annamite than anti-Japanese." Although this was certainly the case, at least with Lieutenant Ettinger, Fenn would have had no access to this information. Nonetheless, when asked by Dong about the OSS's "true policy," Fenn replied that "if operations were arranged through Tan, Bernard or myself, Ho could rely on their loyalty to him. But we couldn't be responsible for what OSS might do. AGAS were more reliable; but even they were basically anti-Communist." Fenn also informed Dong that Lieutenant Phelan, not he himself, would be the American dropped into Ho's headquarters. Phelan "was not my choice," stated Fenn, "and I wanted to warn Ho that he was sympathetic to the French. On the other hand he was essentially a pragmatist and I felt he would adapt when he learned the real score." Dong assured Fenn that the Viet Minh would welcome Phelan and expressed his regret that Fenn would not be allowed to join Tan in Tonkin.[42] Dong's apparent disappointment was no doubt genuine. The Viet Minh would certainly rather have had a pro-Ho American arrive, instead of one self-proclaimed to be both anticommunist and reluctant to drop in on the Viet Minh.

In mid-June Phelan parachuted into the stronghold of the Viet Minh, where he would spend the next several months. Upon landing he was met by Tan, who took him to Tan Trao and introduced him to Ho, Giap, and the Viet Minh around camp.[43] Phelan got along well with Tan and the others. Soon after his arrival Tan wired headquarters that "Phelan seems to be an okay guy." During his time with the Viet Minh, Phelan enjoyed lengthy conversations with Ho Chi Minh on several occasions. According to materials translated and given to Tan, Ho and the Viet Minh held Phelan in high regard, characterizing him as "very active like the devil, but as good as Buddha."[44] Soon he, like Fenn, Tan, and Patti, began to see the Viet Minh in a new light. A week after his arrival Phelan sent a message of a decidedly different tone to GBT headquarters: "You are misunderstanding Vietminh attitude. They are not anti-French merely patriots [who] deserve full trust and support."[45] Although Fenn was happy that harmony prevailed with the Americans working directly with Ho in Vietnam and was pleased with Phelan's change of heart, he was still disappointed at being left behind in

Kunming, where his job had become increasingly unpleasant. Two factors contributed to Fenn's difficulties and his eventual marginalization: his ongoing troubles with the OSS and the return of Laurie Gordon.

Although Fenn's assignment to work with the GBT was intended to ameliorate the strained relationship between the OSS and the GBT and to bring the group under OSS control, the rapport between the groups did not improve. Indeed, the OSS had taken to sending officers to GBT headquarters to "inspect overall prospects" by going through GBT files. One such officer was the man designated to head the Deer Team, Major Allison Thomas. In the light of Fenn's own postwar admissions, it is apparent that the OSS had good reason to be suspicious of both Fenn and the GBT. Fenn admitted that while he and Thomas were "having a preliminary coffee," Gordon's (and Fenn's in Gordon's absence) secretary, Helen Tong, "rapidly removed anything [from the files] we didn't want him [Thomas] to see." As always, Fenn and the GBT were determined to keep their most valuable assets, such as their list of agents, to themselves. A few days after Thomas's late-May visit, a courier brought a letter from Helliwell saying that the OSS was "finished with us [the GBT] unless we conformed to their requirements: we had three days to make up our minds." "Had we left everything in the files," Fenn added, "we might not have been given even shriving time!"[46]

The OSS had run out of patience with the GBT. On May 22 Helliwell provided his analysis of the GBT to Heppner. His frustration with the GBT and his distrust of Fenn are clear:

> The question of the ultimate destiny of the GBT Group has, I believe, reached the point that some definitive action must be taken. I have made efforts in numerous conversations with both Lt. Fenn and Mr. Bernard to get them to make some definite commitment as to whether or not they are willing to come under OSS control and as to when they will make a definite decision one way or the other. . . . By the admission of Lt. Fenn they are still providing information to the Chinese. Lt. Fenn states that they are not at present providing information to the French and the British as they have in the past, although in my opinion this statement may be open to question. It is the opinion of this branch that the situation with relation to intelligence activities in Indo-China has now developed to the point where we can afford to take a much firmer position with GBT.[47]

Whether Helliwell was primarily motivated by a quest for superior intelligence or by the desire to eliminate a rival organization is open to question.

In either case, by late May the OSS position in relation to Indochina was on firm footing: Patti had made a solid and profitable contact with Ho Chi Minh, and both the Deer and Cat teams were preparing for their own missions. Hence, Helliwell's recommendations concerning the GBT were more appropriate than they would have been a month earlier. He proposed giving the GBT a June 1 deadline to decide with whom their allegiances lay. If they agreed to put themselves "exclusively" under the control of the OSS, they would be required to use only OSS codes and ciphers and OSS communication facilities and to deliver intelligence and operational information "to OSS and OSS alone to be distributed as OSS [saw] fit," and the OSS would assume complete "control, supervision and approval of all GBT operations." If the GBT refused, in Helliwell's opinion, "all OSS equipment and personnel should immediately be retrieved from GBT and diverted to more profitable channels and . . . no further supply or support of any nature [should] be given to GBT."[48]

On May 28 Helliwell issued one further warning to the GBT: "This office has received instructions from higher authority that no further requisitions for supplies or for issuance of funds to GBT Group may be approved. . . . It is regretted that this step has now become necessary, but it is felt that sufficient time has elapsed for determination on the part of yourselves as to whether or not the foregoing status [absorption by the OSS] is acceptable."[49] Given the premium that all members of the GBT placed on the ability to act independently, their refusal to submit control of their network to the OSS should have come as no surprise to Helliwell or anyone else at OSS headquarters. The OSS's reaction to the rejection certainly did not surprise Fenn, although it surely irritated him. He wrote: "As per the ultimatum from Helliwell we received no further funds or supplies from OSS. The money we had on hand would carry us on for only two more weeks; and we had seven teams out in the field and were sending OSS a weekly average of nine pages of intelligence—probably as much as they got from all other sources."[50] In short, in Fenn's assessment, Helliwell and the OSS were more interested in securing their bureaucratic turf than in producing intelligence.

The loss of OSS support, however, was the least of Fenn's problems. By mid-May Gordon had finally returned from his trip to Washington. He arrived first in Chungking, where, faced with the OSS ultimatum, he decided to reject the offer, knowing he could still work with AGAS and the Fourteenth Air Force. He then headed back to GBT headquarters in Kunming. He was not happy with what he found. Fenn wrote of the encounter:

I was now mostly running the camp. The Ho operation and our seven
teams in southern China had all been organized by me. So when Gordon
had finished catching up on what we'd done, most of which he
disapproved of, he found himself at a loose end; and he couldn't bear to
be inactive! So frustration brought the inevitable outburst. "Charles,
look at it this way! I brought you into the group and made you more or
less a partner. Then I go away to get things straight with OSS and when
I get back I find everything's turned arse up! You've linked us up with
an Annamite group whose real interest is to kick out the French, who
happen to be my friends. One day they'll be killing some of those friends
and it's you I'll have to thank for it."[51]

Fenn defended his actions based on circumstances, replying that in the
wake of the Japanese coup, he had had few alternatives to the Vietnamese.
He also conveniently shuffled a bit of the blame onto the OSS. "You're a free
agent," Fenn told Gordon, "so you can afford to think of post-war Indochina, and take action accordingly. I have to do what I'm told—more or less.
So that's the way I've had to play it."[52]

Although Fenn's options were indeed limited in the wake of Operation
MEIGO and although he could rationalize approaching Ho Chi Minh,
Gordon's complaints about Fenn's actions were justified. Gordon was the undisputed founder and leader of the GBT, and Bernard, Tan, the headquarters
staff, and external authorities regarded him as such. He had allowed Fenn
into the group and had given him considerable latitude and power, but he
had also made his objections to using Vietnamese agents abundantly clear to
him. And although Bernard was technically second in command of the
group, Fenn's training and dominant personality had resulted in his taking
control of the GBT during Gordon's absence. Now that both men were again
on site, two strong personalities wrestled for allegiance and control. Given
the nature of the situation, Gordon was bound to prevail. Gordon promptly
wired Tan ordering him to return to Kunming. Although Fenn protested,
Gordon made his position clear: "I feel responsible for his welfare," Fenn recalled Gordon stating; "he'll get shot if he stays in that dicey set-up. Apart
from everything else, by working with anti-French Annamites, he's ruining
his prospects of getting a job with Texaco."[53]

Given the benefit of physical distance, Tan could resist Gordon's summons. Fenn, however, had the disadvantage of proximity, and quarrels
between the two men continued, with Bernard and the staff in the middle.
Gordon insisted that working with the Viet Minh was a serious mistake and

resented his perceived—and to a degree actual—loss of control. The situation did not improve, for Gordon soon also clashed with Wichtrich over AGAS control. Wichtrich found perhaps the only solution to the situation. According to Fenn's recollection of his dinner meeting with both Gordon and Wichtrich, Wichtrich counseled Gordon:

> Wedemeyer insists that all operations in his theater come under his command. This means military control of all units. You were offered a commission but refused it, on the grounds that you didn't want your outfit to be subject to outside interference. Also you object to our using men like Ho because you think he's anti-French—as well he may be. But Wedemeyer approves of your using him. And so do I. . . . If you won't run the show under our overall control, how about staying in as civilian advisor and running any activities that don't involve the Vietnamese?[54]

This solution worked for all parties. AGAS brought the GBT under its control, Fenn remained the OSS liaison to AGAS working with the GBT, and Gordon retained a strong voice in those aspects of the GBT that appealed to him without having to sanction operations with the Vietnamese or shoulder the financial burdens of his work without OSS funding.

With this new arrangement, Gordon and Fenn soon ironed out their disagreements. Gordon became immersed in plans for an insertion of French agents along the Indochinese coast via submarine and ceased work with the day-to-day operations of the network. Soon after Gordon's change in status to civilian adviser, Bernard resigned. Although he liked and had gotten along well with Fenn and AGAS, his primary loyalties had been to the GBT. With Gordon more or less out of the picture and Tan working in Vietnam, only Bernard remained, and he was tired. He had not returned home in more than three years and playing the middleman during Gordon and Fenn's disputes had taken a toll. Bernard's departure and the changes brought on by Gordon substantially changed Fenn's role. With Bernard gone Fenn had few like-minded persons with whom to work. His success up to this point had been in large part a result of the capable people with whom he worked, especially Bernard. Now Fenn was no longer effectively master of the GBT domain. Without this cachet and with the loss of his position in the Viet Minh base camp to Phelan, the chameleon Fenn became just one more in a long line of OSS agents.

Ho Chi Minh, ever the pragmatist, continued to write brief notes to Fenn. He concentrated the bulk of his efforts, however, on those with whom he had direct contact in Indochina: the men on the ground. Although initially Tan and Phelan were the only Americans with the Viet Minh, that would change dramatically in the summer of 1945 with the insertion of the Deer Team.

On May 16 Major Allison Thomas received his "Letter of Instructions" to commence work as SO Team Number 13, code-named "Deer." His primary mission was to interdict Japanese lines of communication, specifically the railroad and French colonial highways in the Hanoi-Ningming area. His secondary missions were to "work with guerrillas" and "indicate targets of opportunity for the air force." Furthermore, he was expected to provide weather reports for air drops and air force operations on an as-needed basis. Major Gerald W. Davis at Poseh was designated the primary contact person for the Deer Team.[55] Originally both the Deer and Cat teams were to train the Vietnamese troops and European officers provided in Sabattier's agreement with Wedemeyer, although Patti was also considering sending an OSS detachment to the Viet Minh–held area to train Ho Chi Minh's cadres. On May 27 Major Wampler sent a message to Davis further clarifying Thomas's job. Wampler had decided not to send Thomas or Holland (leader of Cat Team) into French Indochina but to keep them to work exclusively with Sabattier's Vietnamese troops. Still hopeful about their ability to cooperate with the French, theater headquarters had approved the use of one hundred "Annamites" and ten French officers for SO work in Indochina. Thomas and Holland would each be responsible for training fifty men.[56]

Wampler and Davis had every confidence in Thomas's ability to work with the French. Thomas, a Michigan native in his mid-twenties, had been drafted into the army in 1941. After training at Fort Benning, Georgia, he was recruited into the OSS. Thomas had served with distinction in the European theater, and in 1944 General Dwight D. Eisenhower had awarded him the Certificate of Merit for his counterintelligence work in occupied France. His citation read:

As counterintelligence officer of the Special Force Detachment, G-3 Section, Third United States Army, from 1 August 1944 to 1 October 1944, Major Thomas, through his extraordinary application and expert knowledge, was able to find hidden agents, uncover secret resistance groups, and determine whether operatives had been penetrated by the enemy. The success of his efforts made possible the utilization of armed French forces in direct support with the operations of the Third United States Army.[57]

In the spring of 1945, the OSS sent Thomas to China. There he found that success with the French resistance in the *métropole* did not necessarily result in equal success when dealing with the French from Indochina. The varying channels of communication among the multiple French agencies and commanders in China, along with the embarrassment that had resulted from not one but two routs at the hands of the Japanese (the initial invasion in 1940 and Operation MEIGO in 1945), had created an irritable and sensitive group of men determined to return to their colony with a show of force. Nevertheless, Thomas left in May for Poseh to meet the American members of his team and begin training the French personnel who would, in theory, participate in the Deer Team's SO work.

Thomas's second in command was Lieutenant René Défourneaux. Défourneaux approached the upcoming Deer Team mission with a mixture of excitement and apprehension. He eagerly anticipated what was described to him as a "very important mission," but he felt some trepidation about working with the team leader. Local gossip had presented a less-than-flattering picture of Thomas, and Défourneaux found himself wondering "what kind of team" he was joining. While Thomas traveled ahead from Kunming, Défourneaux and Cat Team leader Captain Holland proceeded overland with supplies. En route, other members of the Deer Team joined them. In addition to Thomas and Défourneaux, the Deer Team would eventually consist of Private First Class Henry Prunier, the interpreter, fluent in French and with a limited command of Vietnamese; Sergeant Alan Squires, the team photographer; Private First Class Paul Hoagland, the medic; Sergeant William Zielski, the radio operator; and Sergeant Lawrence Vogt, a weapons instructor. The much smaller Cat Team consisted of Holland and Sergeants John Stoyka and John Burrowes.

While the men of the Deer Team slowly made their way on foot toward the Indochina border, negotiations with the French in Kunming dragged on and the sit-down strike continued. Patti was becoming increasingly frustrated with the inaction. He asked Davis, the overall commander of both the Deer and Cat teams, to advise Thomas and Holland to reconsider the plan to use French troops for their missions and to think about another option. Although Patti still participated in talks with the French, he had not committed his energies solely to their demands. Since his meeting with Ho in late April, Patti had remained in contact with Viet Minh agents in Kunming, Poseh, and Ching-hsi. From these men he had learned a great deal about the "exploits of the Viet Minh" and the "wisdom" of Ho. "By mid-June," he recalled, "I had developed a certain rapport with select members of the Vietnamese community in Kunming."[58]

Patti reported to his OSS superiors, to theater headquarters, and to the American embassy on both the Viet Minh organization and their efforts against the Japanese. Although neither theater headquarters nor the embassy was pleased that Patti was working with Indochinese agents, which exceedingly irritated the French, the OSS could not ignore the reality of the situation. Patti, recognizing the "American penchant for substantive evidence," presented to Heppner a case file on the Viet Minh's accomplishments since the Japanese coup. Patti felt confident in his presentation of the facts, what he described as a "respectable box score": "[The Viet Minh had brought] six provinces in northern Tonkin under the military and administrative control of the Viet Minh, [had] an established Army of Liberation with self-defense and guerrilla units, an effective propaganda organization with limited press and radio capability, a political-social and military program, and that all-important ingredient, popular support from the Vietnamese people."[59]

Heppner decided to take Patti's data directly to Generals Wedemeyer and Gross, bypassing the American embassy altogether. From Chungking, the information was forwarded directly to Donovan in Washington. "After that," Patti (wrongly) boasted, "my activities and relationships with the Vietnamese were not questioned during my assignment in the China Theater."[60]

In the first week of June, Ho Chi Minh informed Patti that he had as many as 1,000 "well-trained" guerrillas who were at Patti's disposal for "any plan" he might have to fight the Japanese. Patti did not immediately take Ho up on his offer since, in the first two weeks in June, the Deer Team seemed to be making progress with the French. As part of the mission, twenty-five French troops were to be prepared to travel as an advance party with Thomas. Having only recently escaped the pursuit of the Japanese, the men were ill-clothed and poorly equipped, and Thomas decided to provide them with what extra uniforms, shoes, and equipment he could come up with. In addition, he ordered the men to shave the heavy beards they had grown during their escape from Indochina so they could "pass as Americans for the benefit of the local people." Défourneaux recalled that he transferred the equipment for the French troops to the FMM in Ching-hsi under cover of darkness because he "did not want the Chinese to know that we were arming the French." Meanwhile Thomas requested Chinese approval to set up a training area. The search for a staging area near the border proved frustrating to Défourneaux and the other Americans. They proceeded on foot from place to place, usually in the rain, seemingly without a plan, frequently without the company of Major Thomas.[61]

By midmonth the situation made even less sense to the men. On June 17 Défourneaux received a radio message, which he forwarded by runner to Thomas, ordering them to stop issuing material to the French. Unaware of the debates raging in Kunming, the men continued training the French without a clear understanding of their mission. Finally, the first week in July, new orders arrived, but only after a series of contradictory messages telling the team to travel first to Poseh and then to Ching-hsi. Défourneaux, Lieutenant Langlois (a French officer), and twenty-four "individuals," to be known collectively as Group Tersac, were to proceed overland to Indochina. The remainder of the American and French troops were to travel to Poseh for jump training with the intent of parachuting behind Japanese lines in Indochina. Thomas then departed, leaving his second to arrange the logistics of the march.

On July 8 Défourneaux met with the ranking French officer in Ching-hsi, Major Revole (also spelled Revol). Described as an "old colonial officer," Revole impressed both Thomas and Défourneaux with his insight.[62] Revole hinted to Défourneaux that the situation in Vietnam might be more complex than the Americans realized, commenting that "the Vietminh question was a factor to be seriously considered."[63] Revole counseled Thomas to "wait a minute" before heading into Tonkin, adding that a joint American-French mission had "no business going back there unless we know the Viet Minh are going to cooperate with us." Thomas was surprised by Revole's comments. At that point, he was quite ignorant about French Indochina. "About all I knew," Thomas wrote, "is that it was called French Indochina. I knew vaguely that it was a French colony and the missionaries came over first, followed by the French soldiers. I knew the French had rubber plantations, and they took profit out to France. That's about it." As Thomas recalled it, his exchange with Revole was the first time he heard the words "Viet Minh." When he asked Revole who the Viet Minh were, Revole told him "it was a guerrilla force that had been organizing in Tonkin for the last several months."[64] This information took Thomas by surprise. For the first two months of his tenure in China, Thomas had assumed he would work with the French, or French-led Vietnamese. "There was no idea in the beginning of contacting any Vietnamese guerrillas in place," Thomas testified, "We didn't know they were there."[65]

Although Thomas and Défourneaux were just "discovering" the Viet Minh in early July, they still believed they would be working with French troops, not Vietnamese guerrillas. However, by that time Captain Patti's patience with the French had reached its limit.[66] He had already concluded that using Ho's guerrillas was more realistic than waiting for the French to reach some sort of mutual accommodation with the Americans. When Patti approached Helliwell with his plan to use Ho's men, Helliwell, worried about the "political repercussions," continued to equivocate. Patti, however, was prepared and rationalized that the practical advantages simply outweighed the disadvantages. He pointed out:

> If we used Ho's unit at Cho Chu we would eliminate the problem of walking or transporting the French a distance of 25 miles to the border, plus the additional 150 miles to Hanoi. On existing jungle trails the actual distance would have been closer to 250 miles, ten to fifteen days' travel time. Other important considerations favoring the use of the Viet Minh base and personnel for the operation were that we would have local native support and excellent terrain cover.[67]

Thus, with Helliwell on board, Patti asked to parachute a small team headed by a senior American officer into Viet Minh territory, and Ho agreed.[68] In presenting his plan for the Deer Team, Patti was honest about the political orientation of the Viet Minh, admitting that they were "Marxist" but adding that their "immediate concern was to fight the Japanese."

Although the bloody battle for Okinawa had concluded with an American victory by the end of June, the specter of the invasion of the Japanese home islands still loomed large on the horizon. World War II seemed far from over. The offensive against the Japanese in southern China, CARBONADO, was still in the planning stages, and thus fighting the Japanese in Indochina, or at least preventing them from reinforcing the units in southern China during CARBONADO, seemed imperative. Therefore, regardless of his initial inclination to work with the French, Thomas agreed to Patti's plan to utilize Ho's men. Still harboring doubts however, "Thomas decided to make a personal reconnaissance of the situation before committing his team to Vietnamese or French participation."[69]

During the last few days before Thomas's entry into northern Vietnam, Défourneaux exchanged a series of messages with headquarters at Poseh. Although Défourneaux's contacts among the French community could produce only limited information regarding the Viet Minh, he had discovered enough by July 13 to recognize the potential importance of the Viet Minh and to be frustrated by his own lack of knowledge on this group. He wired Poseh: "Have possibility of contacting Chief Viet Minh. . . . I am working on angles to contact Viet Minh but need more info. Was left in dark for Pete's sake tell me something."[70] The response to his message alleviated some of his anxiety but indicated a serious lack of communication among OSS channels: "We have no info on Viet-Minh. You were not left in dark. We gave you all info we have." In his July 15 transmission to Poseh, Défourneaux requested his "views about F.I.C." be sent to Kunming.[71] While in Ching-hsi, the French consul told Défourneaux that Ho was a communist, "Moscow trained," and "ruthless, clever and very dangerous."[72] Although many different people were talking about the Viet Minh, there is no indication that Défourneaux's message was passed on to Thomas, who was due to jump into Indochina the next day.

On July 16 Thomas parachuted into the vicinity of the village of Tan Trao (Kim Lung) with two American members of his team, Prunier and Zielski. Three French envoys also accompanied him—an officer, Lieutenant Montfort, and two "representatives" of the French army, Sergeant Logos, a French Eurasian, and Sergeant Phac, a Vietnamese. Of the men, only Zielski had jumped before;[73] however, all of them reached the ground without injury. To the amusement of the Vietnamese, Thomas, Zielski, and Montfort did sustain minor bruises to their egos: All three landed in trees. The cadre who had been waiting for their arrival joked that "perhaps in America there was not a kind of tree which is as big as this Banyan tree here."[74]

The Viet Minh "welcoming committee" helped the men to the ground. "Everybody was real excited," Thomas reminisced. "We were glad to be on the ground all safe and sound."[75] Thomas then received a "welcoming salute" from what he estimated to be approximately 200 men.[76] The Viet Minh were armed with "French rifles, a few Brens, a few tommies, a few carbines, and a few stens," which made up, in Thomas's estimation "a very impressive reception committee."[77] In addition, Viet Minh veteran Vu Dinh Huynh recalled Thomas being "flabbergasted" when the Viet Minh returned to him "a wad of dollars that had fallen out during the parachute jump." "They were literally stunned," writes Vu Dinh Huynh. "All the more so because they knew that this restitution wasn't the work of primitive savages who knew nothing about the price of things, but from Resistance forces schooled in a number of languages and thus perfectly aware of the value of what had fallen from the sky."[78] Once on the ground, Thomas was asked to give a brief "welcome speech" consisting of a few "flowery sentences." He remembered the substance of it as: "Well, we're all together, fighting the war against the Japanese."[79] Thomas met Tan and Phelan, who conducted the men to their "new home," which had been especially prepared for the arrival of the Americans. Thomas wrote:

We first went under the archway of bamboo over which was a sign "Welcome to our American Friends." We then met Mr. Hoo, [sic] the Party Leader, who gave us a cordial welcome. They had killed a cow in our honor and gave us a case of Hanoi beer captured after a raid on a Jap convoy. Had a nice sleep in our comfortable bamboo hut—situated in the woods on a hill.[80]

Over the next two weeks Thomas toured the surrounding area while waiting for the remainder of the Deer Team to be dropped in. His diary is replete with compliments of Viet Minh hospitality. At each village he was met with tea and food, speeches and songs.[81] Although Thomas was unaware of the famine throughout Tonkin in 1945, the generosity of the villagers in providing him with such an abundance of food speaks in part to the peasants' esteem for the Americans but also to the ability of the Viet Minh to induce the people to part with their precious provisions.

Whereas the Americans were treated "royally," the French accompanying Thomas's mission were another matter. Although Thomas evidently felt comfortable with the French, prior to his jump he had received conflicting recommendations regarding the role of the French on the Deer Team. Patti had advised Thomas not to take Frenchmen with him into Indochina. In fact, Patti "cautioned" both Davis and Thomas "that the area was under Viet Minh control and French personnel would be unwelcome."[82] Fenn and GBT agent Simon Yu also warned against the dangers of including Frenchmen in an American mission into Indochina. Before leaving Poseh, Thomas had asked Yu about the situation in Indochina. Yu had advised Thomas that to go into Tonkin with any Frenchmen "would be a disaster, that the Viet Minh hated the French, [and] had absolutely no use for them."[83] Yu then reported his exchange with Thomas to Fenn at GBT headquarters, adding that "[a] French friend of his was actually in on the deal." Fenn next wired the information to Tan, stating that "although Thomas seemed okay, his team were pro-French and working with pro-French Annamites, and if Ho found we were co-operating with such, he would write us [GBT] off." Moreover, Fenn also advised Tan that if Thomas did arrive with Frenchmen, Tan should "be sure and have this Frenchman and any others arrested if only for their own safety."[84]

The situation was undoubtedly a confusing one for Thomas, who had become friends with many of the French personnel with whom he worked. One of them, the secretary of the French Consulate, reported that Thomas "was strongly shaken" by what he heard. He confided to the secretary that "the local authorities had repeated to him many times that if he tried to penetrate Indochina together with Frenchmen, the whole Indochina population would fight him."[85] But, of course, many of Thomas's French friends offered another view. As Patti recalled, "Thomas was being counseled by the French in the field that only they could be trusted to fight the Japanese, that the 'Annamite' would only cache any arms supplied them for a confrontation with the French."[86] Given such conflicting advice, Thomas can hardly be blamed for compromising and taking at least one man—disguised as an American—whom he knew and trusted, and who knew the territory, with him into the unknown jungles of Indochina.[87] Thomas clarified:

> I made the decision to have a French officer named Montfort parachute
> in with us, along with two of his Annamite soldiers. . . . The purpose of
> bringing Montfort was to see whether any Frenchman would be
> welcome. The French didn't believe they couldn't go in. They wanted to
> get in there in the worst way. They wanted the colony back. So they
> wanted to go in with us. The French were concerned that Montfort and
> these other two might be shot at when they were parachuting down if
> they looked like French soldiers. So they wore American helmets. . . .
> But we weren't trying to deceive Ho. . . . The only thing we were trying
> to do was prevent him and Phac and Logos from being killed when they
> came down from that airplane.[88]

When Thomas arrived with the three "French" in tow, they were immediately recognized. As Thomas pointed out, Phac and Logos were "Annamite soldiers" who clearly originated in the French colonial army, and Montfort did not speak any English.[89] Furthermore, their real identities were evidently exposed "almost immediately" after landing. Montfort was recognized by one of the Viet Minh cadres, a man who had served under him in the French colonial army, and Phac was identified first as pro-French and then as "a member of the pro-Chinese nationalist party, the VNQDD."[90] Thus, as Thomas, Prunier, and Zielski were being escorted through the bamboo archway, the French were being "rounded up" by the Viet Minh. Tan stepped in to help the situation. Looking back, Fenn deduced that it was only because of "Tan's amelioration" that the French were "treated amicably."[91]

Back in Kunming, Patti also had to deal with the results of the French inclusion in Thomas's jump.[92] On the morning of July 17 an M.5 officer visited Patti's office to announce that Lieutenant Montfort *and* Major Thomas had been captured by the Viet Minh. Patti, who had already been informed that the jump had been successful, tried to reassure the M.5 officer that all was well. It was then that the Frenchman revealed "with some embarrassment" that Montfort, Logos, and Phac were actually M.5 agents on a "special mission" to make contact with Ho Chi Minh.[93] Furthermore, the officer conceded to Patti, Montfort was "camouflaged as an American officer." Concerned for their safety, the French officer made clear to Patti that M.5 expected the OSS to "guarantee their safe return to French control with the least practicable delay."[94]

Although Thomas knew nothing of Patti's conversation in Kunming, he would have certainly concurred with its conclusion. In his brief wire to Davis at the Poseh headquarters on July 17, Thomas noted: "May have to eliminate French."[95] The next day he added: "After conference with Mr. Hoe [*sic*] Party Chief, imperative all rpt [repeat] all French and Annamese [from] Poseh be eliminated. Am returning Montfort, Phac and Logos soonest as L-5 strip almost completed."[96] Fenn was probably correct in his summation of the situation. He concluded: "Thomas soon weighed up the odds and decided to work with Ho rather than the French."[97] The facts of the matter must have seemed simple in the jungles of Tonkin: All of the Americans with the Viet Minh were treated as honored guests, and the Viet Minh cadre certainly seemed ready, willing, and able to participate in any mission against the Japanese in which the Allies wished to involve them. The French, however, were obviously unwelcome.

Although his decision to return Montfort, Logos, and Phac made perfect sense to Thomas on the ground in Vietnam, his dispatch caused a flurry of wires between Davis in Poseh and Wampler in Kunming. Davis was very concerned about Thomas's apparent rejection of the French, although he admitted that because of his location Thomas was the "best qualified" to decide on their use in conjunction with the Deer Team. He assailed Thomas with questions about the veracity of reports of Viet Minh actions against the Japanese and of their claims to want arms only to fight that enemy. He also made his opinion regarding the French abundantly clear, stating bluntly: "I believe that the best Jap fighters would be the French here." He advised Thomas:

> Consider that French will be bitterly disappointed if they are eliminated. Consider the opinions and advice of Montfort. The French are most firmly convinced that we will not fight any Japs if we use local Vietminh personnel. They are convinced that if we tell them that we are there to fight Japs[,] that we are using French because we have trained them and

know they are good fighters[,] that we will get cooperation from them and that you will be treated as the big chief.[98]

Davis further questioned Thomas's acceptance of the situation, asking: "Are people there exaggerating on importance of local target and length of time to walk to original area for selfish reasons?" Thomas had asserted in his July 17 wire that

plenty [of] well trained men here. Recommend new target to wit Thai Nguyen, Cao Bang Road. Now more important. Send rest of Americans soonest. When ready notify us and we will send weather. Send all arms and 1/3 demolitions. Set up training area here and permanent base and new dz [drop zone] near Chow Hu. Am staying here until hear from you on above. Would take 20 days to walk from here to our original advance base.[99]

Contrary to Thomas's request, Davis told Wampler that instead of sending the rest of the Deer Team right away, he was in fact suspending their departure for the immediate future. Moreover, Davis ordered Thomas to remain objective about both the French and the Vietnamese:

I direct that you keep an open mind until a decision is reached. Show the local people that you have not yet made a decision. You are the big American chief[,] impartial[,] wholly interested in fighting Japs. If you want to fight Japs and can do a good job perhaps can send another team to them. You have unlimited facilities available to you. You are the chosen representative of a huge and powerful nation. Treat these local chiefs with kindness but do not bow to them. After considering all angles send to me your considered opinions, recommendations and reasons for eliminating French and changing mission.[100]

Firmly convinced that working with the French was the best option, Davis advised Thomas to begin walking to the "original advance base" near Lang Son, optimistically predicting that "the French knowing the country and people will be of help and perhaps it will prove that in the area [in] which he is walking the French main body will be acceptable." Davis notified Wampler that "Thomas request for arms and Americans was his hasty decision to operate on new target without French." Nonetheless, Wampler remained more open-minded to the use of the Viet Minh instead of the

French, wiring Davis: "If you and Thomas decide that Vietminh Annamites are OK, then you have clearance from this headquarters to go ahead and use them." In fact, Wampler suggested that the Viet Minh might be able to prove their willingness to fight the Japanese by following American direction and attacking the original target: the Hanoi–Lang Son railroad.[101] Although he was willing to consider the usefulness of assaulting the Thai Nguyen–Cao Bang road at some later date, Wampler reiterated that the original target was still the first priority because of "overall Theater directive." Wampler concurred with Thomas, however, that Montfort, Logos, and Phac should be withdrawn from the mission. He added that he expected to receive "details of his [Thomas's] reasons" and a full report of his "extended conferences" with Ho Chi Minh.[102]

Although the issue of the three "Frenchmen" was settled,[103] they would remain in the Viet Bac for two weeks following the drop. It was apparent from the beginning that Montfort had to leave, but the status of Phac and Logos was less clear. Ho offered to allow both men to remain and to join the Viet Minh, Thomas remembered. However, Ho expressed serious doubt that the French would "release them." "That was true," concluded Thomas, "the French wouldn't."[104] This certainly may have been the case. Assuming that the men were part of an M.5 "secret mission," Montfort might have been reluctant to excuse the two men from duty. However, given the situation, it seems unlikely that a French prohibition was the reason they declined to join Ho's group. Montfort was the only Frenchman in an area controlled by the Viet Minh, inside Japanese-held territory, from which he was being involuntarily exiled, at that. Should Phac or Logos have chosen to join the Viet Minh and stay behind with them, there is little Montfort could have done to prevent it.

Patti reported that Phac "told his Vietnamese interrogators that he had accompanied Montfort in the hope that the Viet Minh would let him stay and fight the Japanese. They evidently had a different interpretation," concluded Patti, "and 'Sergeant' or 'Lieutenant' Phac was kept under close observation until his departure."[105] Phac certainly was no ordinary colonial foot soldier. According to Sainteny, Phac was a lieutenant in the French army and had left Indochina with Alessandri following the Japanese coup. After arriving in Yunnan, Phac renewed his contacts with several Vietnamese nationalists in Kunming. Just prior to his mission with Montfort, Phac had approached Sainteny about his willingness to meet with Nguyen Tuong Tam, a Vietnamese author and nationalist who had originally joined the Dai Viet Party at its inception in 1939 but who by 1945 was an important member of the VNQDD. Although Sainteny attached very little importance to this, he agreed to the meeting and left Phac free to make the necessary arrangements.[106] In view of Phac's apparent determination to gain recognition for the VNQDD at M.5, his sincerity in wishing to join Ho's forces must be questioned. Given the abundance of Viet Minh cadres in Kunming, the Viet Minh may have been well aware of Phac's maneuvering. And hence, they may also have been unwilling to have in their midst the apparently pro-French, pro-Chinese Phac.

Sergeant Logos was a bit less mysterious. During his two weeks in camp waiting to depart, Logos became friends with one of the Americans who had landed with him, Henry Prunier. Born in 1921 to a family of Franco-American descent, Prunier grew up in Massachusetts, attending first a Catholic prep school and then a small Catholic college in Worcester. Although he enlisted in the army in August 1942, he remained in school until called to active duty in June 1943. After basic training, Prunier was assigned to a Foreign Area (Far East) and "Annamese" language-studies program at the University of California, Berkeley. He remained in this army specialized training program from December 1943 until September 1944. While he was at Berkeley, the OSS recruited Prunier. In late 1944 he was sent to Washington for special testing and then on for additional OSS training. In March 1945 he landed in Kunming and in May was assigned to the Deer Team.[107]

Although Prunier studied Vietnamese for only nine months, the training was intensive, and he was able to use his language skills for very basic communication with the Vietnamese troops.[108] Thus, Prunier had two advantages in Tonkin: He could speak and understand simple Vietnamese, and having grown up in a French-speaking household, he spoke French fluently. After their July 16 jump into Kim Lung, Prunier and Logos became "quite friendly." Prunier's familiarity with Vietnamese and French allowed the two men to have many "interesting talks" about Vietnam, the war, and the Americans. Logos wondered, Prunier recalled, "why we Americans were involved with this rebel group called Vietminh." Prunier assured Logos that the Deer Team mission was "not political since we were only soldiers and that our goal was the same as the Vietminh to oust the Japanese."[109]

Prunier was sorry to see Logos depart, but he had little say in the matter. Ho had made his position on Montfort clear. Thomas had decided that his mission would be facilitated by the removal of the French, and after several days his headquarters had concurred.[110] To demonstrate his group's legitimacy and control of the area, Ho told Thomas, "The French think we are bandits. But to show you we're not, we will escort Montfort and the others back to the border."[111] On July 31, Montfort, Phac, and Logos left to join a group of twenty French refugees, "collected under the auspices of AGAS," at Tam Dao, a nearby resort village sixteen miles southwest of Thai Nguyen and twenty-eight miles northwest of Hanoi.[112]

The refugees had been waiting for AGAS to relocate them to China since the Viet Minh attack on July 16, 1945,[113] when a group of Viet Minh had attacked the Japanese garrison at Tam Dao, a tiny hill station manned by perhaps as few as nine Japanese soldiers. Outnumbered, the Japanese were routed, losing seven men in the fight.[114] Nguyen Huu Mui, a member of the Viet Minh who also worked with the Deer Team, was largely responsible for the decision to attack Tam Dao. Having recently been exposed to the Japanese for his revolutionary work in Vinh Yen, Nguyen Huu Mui had fled toward the hill station, where he believed he would have "the chance to go to fight the Japanese." Once there, he discovered that many of his comrades were reluctant to begin the fight because the Japanese "had all the modern weapons, and we had only rifles and each one had only ten bullets." Nguyen Huu Mui rationalized that since his cover was now blown, theirs would soon be as well, and that "if we didn't fight against them, they would kill us." The small band called upon a nearby "platoon in the name of Hoang Van Thai" for help, and the joint force organized their troops, cut the telephone lines, felled trees to block the road, and besieged the garrison.[115]

Although an insignificant contribution to the defeat of the Japanese, the attack on Tam Dao proved the Viet Minh willingness to engage the enemy when the battle seemed likely to end in their favor—one of the principle tenets of guerrilla warfare.[116] Donald Lancaster, a journalist in Vietnam during the war, wrote that the Viet Minh "displayed marked reluctance to incur casualties or to invite reprisals by attacking the Japanese and confined their contribution towards the victory to an attack on the hill station of Tam Dao."[117] However, even Sainteny acknowledged the psychological benefits to the Vietnamese of this small Viet Minh victory,[118] and the Japanese found it sufficiently annoying that they wired Tokyo that "the activities of the League are now becoming more and more flagrant. Just a few days ago, there was a large-scale surprise attack at Tam Dao by a band of persons connected with the movement."[119]

The Tam Dao attack also revealed the growing political awareness of the Viet Minh and the fact that they were not indiscriminately anti-French. After defeating the weak garrison, the Viet Minh liberated the Japanese "civilian concentration camp" at Tam Dao.[120] Nguyen Kim Hung recalled that their intention in attacking Tam Dao "was just to pound the Japanese and take away the weapons," but in doing so they also liberated the French prisoners. The Viet Minh were willing to help "the progressive French," whom Tran Trong Trung remembered as "mostly teachers and students from a school in Hanoi."[121] "Although the living condition of the local people was very low, and we experienced a lot of hardships and difficulties," Tran Trong Trung recalled, "Ho Chi Minh instructed us to do everything possible to improve the living conditions of these French people."[122]

Maurice and Yvonne Bernard, French professors residing at Tam Dao and among those "cared for" by the Viet Minh, provided a vivid account of the attack on Tam Dao and described in fulsome language their stay with the Viet Minh. In an open letter to their "friends in Hanoi," they attempted to correct what they believed were serious misimpressions of the Viet Minh, stating boldly: "The Viet Minh are not pirates and they do not hate the French; they are only men who detest fascism and wish to deliver their country from Japanese slavery."[123] Given the Viet Minh attitude toward the French, they could easily have left the colons open to possible Japanese reprisals after their victory. Yet "the Viet Minh helped French men, women, and children to escape to safety, caring for them until they could be picked up by Allied planes and evacuated to China," concluded noted historian Ellen Hammer.[124]

That the Viet Minh "liberated" the French civilians from the Japanese and turned them over to the Americans indicates that in early July 1945 the Viet Minh sought to demonstrate that they were not unilaterally anti-French and recognized that the path to American approval was to fight only their Japanese enemy while treating the French humanely. Although the victory at Tam Dao was not acknowledged by the American government, it was significant for the men on the ground at the time, especially Frank Tan, Dan Phelan, and Allison Thomas. It should be recognized, however, that with this maneuver the Viet Minh also succeeded in making more colons exiles from Vietnam. Although AGAS had arranged to fly out the French women and children, Lieutenant Montfort, accompanied by both Phac and Logos, led the remaining group of refugees from Tam Dao to the border and into China. On the day of their departure Thomas recorded in his diary, "Too bad they had to be sent away but these people dislike the French almost as much as they dislike the Japs."[125]

By his own admission, when he arrived at Kim Lung Thomas knew very little about either French Indochina or the Viet Minh. However, as is evident, he quickly discovered their attitude toward the French. The hospitality of the Viet Minh and his conversations with Tan and Phelan further convinced Thomas of the viability of joint OSS–Viet Minh actions, without the French.

During his stay with the Viet Minh, Thomas and Ho Chi Minh talked frequently—about politics, about their military mission, and about the Vietnamese "grievances" against the French. Ho explained to Thomas that he
"personally like[d] many French," but "most of his soldier's [sic] don't."[126]
As with Shaw, Fenn, Tan, and Phelan, Ho described the worst of French behavior to Thomas: The French had a monopoly on salt and alcohol and
"forced the people to buy opium" and to pay heavy taxes; they had "shot
and gassed many political prisoners"; they had built more "prisons than
schools"; and they had deprived the Vietnamese of freedoms considered
basic in American life: freedom of speech, of the press, and of assembly.
However, even long after the war, Thomas remained adamant that at the
time he did not know Ho was a communist:

> It was obvious he was well read and well educated. But bear in mind, I
> didn't know he was a Communist. I had no idea he spoke Russian, I had
> no idea he'd been to Russia. . . . I did feel he was very sincere. . . . He
> seemed like a man of iron determination. . . . Also bear in mind that I
> wasn't on a political mission. It was purely military. I was a little bit
> suspicious of Ho, because his troops used the clenched-fist salute. But I
> talked to Dan Phelan and Frankie Tan about it, and they both felt
> strongly that he was not a doctrinaire Communist, that he was a true
> patriot.[127]

Even though the relationship between the OSS and the GBT had strained
to the breaking point, on the ground Tan and Thomas, as well as the others,
got along well. Only days after Thomas's arrival Tan wired Fenn in Kunming: "Thomas is a great guy, already sold on the Vietminh and sending
wires to OSS that they should work only with Ho and not with the
French."[128] This in fact was true. Thomas questioned Ho directly about the
political orientation of the Viet Minh after his arrival and was assured that
the Viet Minh was composed of many different political parties. Ho added
that the Viet Minh "was working for the liberty and complete independence
of Indo-China from all foreign powers," Thomas remembered, and that
"after liberty had been achieved they would worry about politics."[129] Ho
had carefully skirted the issue—not lying, not presenting the whole truth—
as had become a Viet Minh pattern.[130] In the Deer Team's first official report
to Kunming, written only one day after his arrival, Thomas stated flatly:
"Forget the Communist Bogy. VML [Viet Minh League] is *not* Communist.
Stands for freedom and reforms from French harshness."[131]

Convinced that Ho and the Viet Minh were strongly pro-American—Ho told Thomas he would "welcome 10 *million* Americans"[132]—Thomas made a series of recommendations for the Deer Team mission. He reported that Ho allegedly had "3000 or more men under arms in Tonkin" and that he could provide Thomas with as many of them as he needed. Ho recommended, however, that Thomas use "not more than 100." He added "many are partially trained under a leader who was trained in guerilla warfare by the Navy in China."[133] Thomas also forwarded Ho's recommendation to change the target for Deer Team operations to the Thai Nguyen–Cao Bang road, listing the following reasons to make the change:

1. The airforce has disrupted the traffic on Hanoi-Langson road.
2. It has lost its importance since Nanning was taken.
3. The Japs are in much greater force in that area.
4. The VML Party are not as strong or as well armed in that area.
5. The Japs are constantly using the Thai-Nguyen-Bac Kan [road]. More so [than] Hanoi-Langson road.
6. Better area for training soldiers here.
7. The present area is completely controlled by the VML. No Japs penetrate.
8. This area is becoming static and from here we can take our men after they are trained and [move] south [to] operate on the RR to Lao-kay and eventually on the RR line Hanoi-Saigon, which is much more vital and important, or if necessary take our trained men and operate on the Hanoi-Langson road.[134]

As had become his style, in his rationale Ho incorporated elements of the truth (the Viet Minh were certainly strongest in the base area), items of interest to the Americans (the potential for disrupting the key railroad in Vietnam between Hanoi and Saigon), and points of particular benefit to him (the prospect of thoroughly training and equipping his soldiers in the Viet Bac.) Ho's rationale made sense to Thomas, who recommended to Poseh and Kunming that the change in the Deer Team's mission be made, that a "fairly permanent base" be set up in Kim Lung for training, and that the original target be postponed until the Deer Team had completed some training. Tønnesson commented: "Rather surprisingly, Thomas consented—with the approval of his superiors—to operate, temporarily, on the strategically much less important communication line favoured by Ho Chi Minh. Thomas thus postponed the mission he had been instructed to carry

out, which was an important ingredient in Carbonado."[135] Thomas may
have been influenced in making his decision by an intelligence report dated
July 8 on Japanese troop strength. The report placed 700 soldiers in Thai
Nguyen and 2,000 in Cao Bang, with an additional 2,500 troops at the mid-
way village of Bac Can—significant numbers for men hoping to fight the
Japanese.[136]

In addition, Thomas requested that the rest of the Deer and Cat teams,
including medical men, and arms and equipment be parachuted in as soon
as possible. He even sent a hand-drawn map depicting the best flight route
and drop zone to avoid "Jap held towns." Thomas also asked for a wide
range of miscellaneous equipment, including ten M-3s with silencers ("good
for Jap sentries & advance guards"); 100 mosquito nets; 100 "green fatigue
suits, small sizes, or camouflaged jungle suits and mechanics' caps (no khaki
clothes)"; five sets of complete maps of Indochina, described as "essential"
for patrols and "as gifts to party and military chiefs who need maps badly";
"plenty of picture magazines (*Life*), books, newspapers"; salt ("natives very
short of it"); and ten watches for "operational gifts to party and military
leaders." Thomas recommended getting part of the needed equipment from
the French. He advised, "Retake all equipment issued to French, as we need
all of it (including my .45 I gave to Langlois)."[137]

Although Thomas did not know it, the American equipment issued to
those Frenchmen intended for use with the Deer Team on June 11 had already been recalled. Lieutenant Défourneaux had been the unlucky bearer
of this news only a few days before Thomas made his suggestion. Unfortunately for Défourneaux, he had already made serious enemies among the
French in southern China. While working with and talking to the French
soldiers, he had discovered that they "planned to return to their colony, not
so much to fight the Japanese as to reestablish their control over that part of
the world which they considered theirs." Feeling it his duty, Défourneaux reported the information to his superiors. He believed the information stopped
there. However, shortly thereafter he was directed to instruct the French to
return the American equipment issued to them. He recalled the intensely un-
comfortable situation:

> When a circle of armed French officers slowly closed around me and
> pushed me against the wall, I knew that I was in a very precarious
> situation. I tried to tell them that I had nothing to do with the decision,
> but they were upset by the fact that I had ratted on them earlier. They
> really believed that only I could have told the U.S. Command that their

primary aim was the securing of their colony. . . . The fact that I was an American officer was immaterial. To them I was a Frenchman and I was a traitor.

Although Défourneaux's relations with the French were tense, he was disappointed to receive Thomas's news that the French must be excluded from the Deer Team mission. Although suspicious of French motives, he felt no better about the motives of the Viet Minh. In fact, Défourneaux was convinced that neither side really wanted to fight the Japanese. From his conversations with the French, and even with some Chinese in the area, he had formed a negative opinion of the Viet Minh and felt that working with them would be a mistake. As a junior officer, however, he decided to keep his opinion to himself. He recalled:

I felt that we were making a mistake as big as that of the French. . . . I felt that no one would be able to deal with the Vietminh successfully. They would not keep their promises because their main goal was not to chase the Japanese out of FIC, but to acquire as many weapons [as] they could and attempt to control the Tonkin. They knew that sooner or later the Japanese would leave Indochina, so why should [they] risk their lives for a forgone conclusion?[138]

Regardless of his personal feelings, Défourneaux and the men returned to Poseh as ordered. There Davis informed him that he and the rest of the Deer Team, as well as the Cat Team, would jump into Kim Lung on July 29. Davis suggested that in light of the Viet Minh attitude toward the French, as demonstrated by the recall of Montfort, he might want to consider assuming an alias, pointing out that with the French name "Défourneaux" he might experience the same sort of difficulties. With that, Défourneaux became Raymond Douglass. The team spent the next day preparing the gear that was to be dropped in with them. After having great difficulty finding the drop zone, the Deer and Cat teams jumped into what were to them the unknown jungles of northern Vietnam.

Ho, who was ill, could not be at the drop zone to greet the men, yet he still managed to benefit from the fact of their arrival. Lying on his sickbed, Ho told the local tribesmen to go to the clearing and wait for Americans to "fall from the sky." "We were very doubtful," one of the tribesmen recalled, "but we had faith in Uncle Ho, so we went. We waited most of the day and nothing happened. And then we looked up and there was an airplane, and from the airplane men came floating down. Everyone had to say that Uncle Ho was a genius. How could he have known such a thing would happen?"[139] Ho, of course, knew full well that the drop was planned. Thomas had told him of their planned arrival, and Viet Minh cadres had helped set up the drop zone and a visual sign (a white *T* formation on the ground) to guide the pilot. Perceptions, however, were everything, and once again Ho proved he was master of the moment.

As the Deer Team members got to their feet, they were greeted by Tan, Phelan, Zielski, and "Mr. Van," the alias of the moment for Vo Nguyen Giap. All members of the team landed without injury, and the Americans were escorted once again under the bamboo archway proclaiming "Welcome to Our American Friends." The team was not reunited with Thomas and Prunier until the following night; the two Americans were away on a reconnaissance mission of the Japanese fort at Cho Chu, which Thomas planned to attack but the war ended before he got the opportunity to do so.[140] Although wondering at the absence of their leader, the men were simply relieved to have finally landed in the place they were supposed to be, and they settled in for the night. Now that the Deer Team was "finally in place, ready and eager to do what it was created to do," Défourneaux found himself thinking about "our wasted efforts, our lack of direction and leadership."[141]

Although Défourneaux and others on the team harbored some resentment at what they perceived to be a lack of leadership, Thomas was largely impervious to the internal dissension. Over the next few days the men prepared to begin their training mission, stowing their supplies, selecting sites for their training ground and living quarters, and briefly touring the surrounding villages, in which the Americans were always warmly received. As the Deer Team settled into the area, others were leaving. Captain Holland's Cat Team left on July 31 to establish a base in another area. And Tan departed Indochina on an L-5 sent to retrieve him.

Tan had put off leaving as long as he could, ignoring Gordon's numerous summons to return to Kunming. However, with the Deer Team in place, the Cat Team beginning its mission, and Phelan remaining to work for AGAS, Tan no longer had a reason to stay in Indochina. Moreover, Tan and Ho had already "set up an intelligence network of native agents that amply replaced the French net lost by the Japanese coup." Tan was sad to leave behind the men he had come to regard as friends in Tonkin, specifically Ho Chi Minh. Ho also regretted Tan's leaving. Tan remembered Ho's final comment to him: "You will always have ways to get out to the world and so will the

French. But now that our association has ended, I won't have."[142] At the time, however, Tan did not fully appreciate the difficulties Ho Chi Minh would soon face. For although he looked fondly on Ho and the Viet Minh with whom he had worked, he was delighted to see his friends at GBT headquarters again.

Blissfully unaware of the tension between Gordon and Fenn and of Gordon's displeasure with his rendezvous with the Viet Minh, Tan immediately began to sing the praises of Ho and the Viet Minh. Gordon was not at the GBT compound when Tan arrived and Fenn warned him to "lay off this eulogy [for Ho] when they did meet." Fenn described Tan's enthusiasm for Ho as "irrepressible," and Tan was not anxious to mute his fervor for Gordon's benefit. "Laurie will have to face the facts," stated Tan. "The French in Indochina are as good as finished. When the war ends the Vietminh will certainly take over. And meanwhile Ho can do a lot to help us finish it!" Over the next months Tan would speak often about Ho Chi Minh and the Vietnamese desire for independence, and perhaps that is exactly what Ho counted on. In a letter to Fenn, written just before Tan's return to Kunming, Ho explained: "I want to write you a long, long letter to thank you for your friendship. Unfortunately I can't write much, because I am in bad health just now (not very sick, don't worry!). What I want to say, Mr. Tan will say it for me."[143] Although Tan did have much to say, in August 1945 there were few to listen.

As the last month of the war began, the Americans in Vietnam, unaware that Japan's defeat was imminent, settled into life with the Viet Minh. On August 1, the Americans witnessed the opening ceremony for the Viet Minh's newly built "communal house," complete with speeches and political skits, including one that depicted how the "Japs were wrecking their country" and another that portrayed the successful rescue of an American pilot.[144] During the team's first days in camp, they met many of the Viet Minh and a few villagers from the surrounding area. One person, however, was noticeably absent: Mr. Ho. On the day the team landed, Giap apologized for Ho's absence, telling the new Americans that the "Chief" of his group was ill. By August 3, Ho still had not emerged. Several of the team members, including Défourneaux and Paul Hoagland, decided to go into the nearby village to see Ho and to see if he needed help. Having been warned by the French about this "ruthless" and "dangerous" man, Défourneaux was surprised at Ho's appearance. Instead of a monster, Défourneaux discovered what seemed to be a frail old man hovering near death:

In the darkest corner of the room lay a pile of bones covered with yellow, dry skin. A pair of glassy eyes stared at us. The man was shaking like a leaf and obviously running a high fever. When my eyes had become accustomed to the darkness, I noticed the long scraggly goatee hanging from a pointed chin. . . . Hoagland took a quick look and said, "This man doesn't have long for this world."[145]

But Paul Hoagland was prepared.

Hoagland, born in Romulus, New York, had trained as a nurse at Willard State Hospital before World War II began. He had also had several years experience as a medic aboard the Swedish ship *The Gripsholm.*[146] Hoagland was recruited into the OSS in 1942 and reported for duty with the Deer Team in May 1944. After briefly examining Ho, Hoagland speculated that he was suffering from malaria, dengue fever, dysentery, or a combination of all three. He gave Ho quinine, sulfa drugs, and "other medicines." Over the next few days Hoagland "looked after him periodically."[147] Allison Thomas later commented that although Ho was "very sick," he was not sure that Ho "would have died without us."[148] Within ten days, Ho had more or less recovered and was again up and about camp.[149]

In addition to tending to Ho, Hoagland, who spoke French fluently, also trained Trieu Duc Quang as a medic. As well as becoming the "medical team for the company of Vietnam-USA soldiers," Quang and Hoagland also became good friends. At Hoagland's request to try some local cuisine, which Ho had told the cadre not to feed the Americans, the two medics "snuck out to a village at the foot of the hill to cook." "The first time we got away clean," reminisced Quang, "but the second time we were in a hurry and the rice was not well done. So we got this diarrhea."[150]

The camaraderie that developed between Quang and Hoagland was not unique to them. Tran Trong Trung, who was twenty-two years old, and Henry (Hank) Prunier, twenty-one, also built a friendship, communicating in French and Prunier's rudimentary Vietnamese. Trung had many questions for Prunier, including asking him who Roosevelt was, and the two spent much time talking. Trung taught Prunier "to sing the ballad of marching soldiers," which later became the national anthem of Vietnam, which no doubt endeared the young American to many more of the Vietnamese in camp.[151]

For the first six days in August, the Vietnamese and the Americans worked together building the training camp. While the Vietnamese concentrated on the construction of "buildings"—usually no more than four walls, a thatched roof, and a floor—the Americans focused on the interiors of their new home, cobbling together bunks, tables, and partitions. Within a week's time the training camp consisted of three barracks for the Vietnamese soldiers, one barracks for the OSS men, an assembly hall, a kitchen, a supply warehouse, an infirmary and radio "headquarters," a 150-yard shooting range, and an open training area. At the end of the training field stood a tall tree that was used as a flagpole to display the Viet Minh flag: a gold star centered upon a red background. The young Vietnamese men who came for military training (by the Americans) and political training (by the Viet Minh) were glad to be there. Défourneaux remembered they seemed happy simply to "be together without restraint, to talk among themselves and to learn from each other."[152] From the group of 110 assembled recruits, their field commander Dam Quang Trung[153] and the Deer Team chose 40 of the "most promising" young men to begin training immediately.[154] The eager recruits who would be working with the Deer Team were officially christened by Ho Chi Minh the Bo Doi Viet-My, the "Vietnamese-American Force."[155]

Except for William Zielski, who was kept busy with radio communications to and from Poseh and Kunming, all of the members of the Deer Team participated in the training of the Vietnamese. Thomas had brought with him U.S. Army field manuals, and instruction in American drill and in the use of American weapons began in earnest on August 9—three days after the dropping of the atomic bomb on Hiroshima. Unaware of the earth-shattering events that were taking place, the Deer Team proceeded to train this select group of Viet Minh recruits in preparation for guerrilla warfare against the Japanese.

The young recruits were trained to use M-1 carbines, Thompson submachine guns, Springfield rifles, bazookas, light machine guns, and Bren guns. Their instruction included triangulation, firing practice, and field cleaning of the weapons. The men were also instructed in the use of mortars and grenades. Drill was relatively intensive between August 9 and 15, beginning at 5:30 AM and ending at 5:00 PM. On August 10 they received an additional supply drop of weapons and ammunition to continue the training of the recruits. Certainly Vo Nguyen Giap was delighted with the additional materiel. The equipment parachuted into the Viet Bac in the Deer Team's three supply drops, combined with those "small arms crafted by the Viet Minh in their crude jungle weapons factories," created an army "sufficiently equipped to impress the people of the countryside." Giap recalled: "To see our new company standing in neat rows and armed with new rifles and shining bayonets filled us with jubilance and confidence." Giap's biographer, Cecil Currey,

Sergeant Larry Vogt (standing far left) and Lieutenant René Défourneaux (standing center) look on as members of the Viet Minh practice firing the M-1 carbine, August 16, 1945. *National Archives and Records Administration.*

added: "Giap made sure that his newly equipped units were seen by as many as possible."[156]

Both Thomas and Défourneaux were also impressed with the new units. Both men commented in their diaries on the enthusiasm of the young Vietnamese soldiers and on their rapid acquisition of most of the military skills.[157] Thomas and his second did not see eye-to-eye, however, on the validity of the mission as a whole. Whereas Thomas had recommended training the men at the base area and then, "once they were in the groove," attacking the Japanese at the more dangerous areas near Thai Nguyen and Lang Son,[158] Lieutenant Défourneaux disagreed with both the nature of the training and the overall premise of training the Viet Minh. About the nature of the training he wrote:

> We were training recruits for conventional warfare while contemplating guerrilla operations. The most important factor for a successful guerrilla operation is the knowledge of the terrain. This was certainly not within our range of expertise. The people we were training could operate

Major Allison Thomas looks on as Viet Minh soldiers practice grenade throwing on August 17, 1945. *National Archives and Records Administration.*

throughout Indochina without fear of being identified as other than natives. In no way could we, Occidentals, convince local people to take arms and resist an invading power. . . . All they needed from us were weapons, and training to use these weapons.

Défourneaux was even more critical of the concept of training the Viet Minh, whom he believed were communists, comparing their closed-fist salute, anthem, and behavior to that of French communists he had seen as a young man growing up in eastern France:

It was difficult for me to embrace the concept of giving military basic training to a bunch of natives who, thanks to their individual wits, had escaped the attentions of their Japanese colonial masters and managed to survive. . . . If these men were to be organized in regular platoons, companies, and battalion size units, although we were able to do it, we had no business being involved in the building of an armed force for the purpose of fighting "the Japanese."[159]

Although suspicious of their motivation, Défourneaux admitted that the Viet Minh were good military students and even that Ho Chi Minh himself was a "good conversationalist with a wide range of knowledge." As with most of his American guests, Ho spent at least part of his time discussing French transgressions in Vietnam and the desire of the Vietnamese to attain their freedom. He indicated to Défourneaux, as he had already to Thomas and Phelan, that he would even accept a "transition period during which the French would train and eventually turn over the responsibility of government to elected Indochinese."[160]

Thomas also recalled Ho mentioning a transition period of from five to ten years under French guidance. Even years after his mission in Vietnam, Thomas called special attention to the wires that he had sent to the French on Ho's behalf almost immediately after his arrival in Kim Lung. On July 17, Ho had asked Thomas to let the Americans in Kunming know that he was willing to talk with a high-ranking French officer, such as General Sabattier.[161] Patti described this attempt as Ho's seizing the "propitious moment," hoping that the French would be sufficiently impressed with the American presence in his camp that they might accord him a measure of respectability.[162] The Viet Minh five-point proposal asked that the French "observe in the political future of French Indo-China" the following items:

1. A parliament will be elected by universal suffrage. It will be the legislature for the country. A French governor will exercise the functions of president until our independence is assured. This president will choose a cabinet or a group of advisers accepted by the parliament. The precise powers of all these organs can be delineated in the future.

2. Independence will be given to this country in a minimum of five years and a maximum of ten.

3. The natural resources of the country will be returned to the inhabitants after a just compensation of the present holders. France will benefit from economic privileges.

4. All the liberties proclaimed by the United Nations will be guaranteed to Indo-Chinese.

5. The sale of opium is forbidden.[163]

As far as Patti could determine at the time, Ho's message went unanswered by the French. David Marr wrote: "The French prepared a conciliatory, if noncommittal, response but chose not to transmit it via OSS channels, apparently intending for Sainteny to present it personally to Ho."[164] But the time for wartime conciliation was rapidly coming to a close. On August 6 the assumptions on which our principals were operating were demolished by the atomic bomb that destroyed Hiroshima. At the Deer Team camp news of a possible surrender arrived via Dan Phelan.

The reaction among the soldiers was mixed. Although the men were excited at the prospect of returning home, they were also disappointed that the war might end before they had the opportunity to fight the Japanese directly. In his diary, Lieutenant Défourneaux wrote on August 11: "We still hope for some fight before it's over!" Défourneaux reported that all of the Deer Team members were "doing pretty well," under the circumstances, except for Sergeant Vogt. Vogt was unhappy with his training mission and made clear to the lieutenant that he "had volunteered to kill Japs, not to be a drill sergeant."[165] Thomas, however, was delighted with the news. In his August 15 diary entry, he wrote: "Wild hilarity to-day. 9 AM heard by our radio that negotiations for final surrender were almost finished."[166]

The major's happiness seemed to further underline his team's disappointment. "Three months earlier," clarified Défourneaux, "all had wanted to fight the Japanese, but now they felt that the Major was at fault for not having given them the opportunity." Overhearing Thomas rejoicing, the men "resented his attitude as their opportunities for combat shrank."[167] This very desire to fight the Japanese was one of the attributes that the Vietnamese admired. David Marr concluded: "The Vietnamese were fascinated by these strangers who dropped from the sky with tons of western equipment, maintained instant contact with great sources of power in the outside world, often insisted on walking around bare-chested (completely unlike the sartorially conscious French colonials), and showed every sign of wanting to kill 'Japs' the minute the training program was concluded."[168]

Although a Japanese surrender had seemed likely as early as August 10, neither the Americans nor the Vietnamese in the Viet Bac could be sure that the war was indeed over, so training continued over the next four days. But just as the Americans were winding up their war, the Viet Minh were laying new plans. From August 13 to 15, the ICP, the leading political party of the Viet Minh, held a "strategy conference" in the nearby village of Tan Trao. As delegates from as far away as southern Annam, Laos, and Thailand made their way to Tan Trao, there was excitement in the air as cadres who had not seen each other in years became reacquainted and as freedom from the Japanese invader seemed imminent. As a side note to the conference, the delegates were taken to the training camp to witness the training of the

The leader of the Deer Team, Allison Thomas, stands center. He is flanked on his left by Vo Nguyen Giap and on his right by Ho Chi Minh. Standing on Ho's right is René Défourneaux, the only member of the team to have serious concerns regarding the political affiliation of the Viet Minh. Squatting in front of Défourneaux is team photographer Alan Squires. Henry Prunier stands to Giap's left, and farthest to Giap's left is Paul Hoagland, who provided medicine to the ailing Ho Chi Minh. *Courtesy of René Défourneaux.*

Vietnamese-American Force. For most of the delegates, the members of the Deer Team were the first Americans they had ever seen.[169] Although not present initially at the conference because of illness, once again, Ho Chi Minh had quietly exhibited his apparent power and connections to the Americans.

Historian Stein Tønnesson cautioned against overemphasizing the impact of the Deer Team's presence at Tan Trao and pointed to the many factors already in play in bringing Ho Chi Minh to power in Vietnam—including his considerable reputation among some of the delegates as the prolific patriot Nguyen Ai Quoc, and the groundwork for the revolution that had already been laid by the party throughout the country. In Tønnesson's view, the American presence acted more to "boost the morale" than anything else.[170] However, all factors combined, and by the end of the conference, Ho's preference to launch "a general insurrection to seize power throughout the country" had prevailed. The following day, on August 16, the Viet Minh leadership "convened a so-called National People's Congress in Tan Trao" and approved, among other things a new national flag—a gold star upon a red field—and a new national anthem.[171]

As the first conference concluded on August 15 and as Thomas celebrated the news of the "forthcoming" surrender, he and Giap decided to break camp, go see Ho Chi Minh, and head toward Thai Nguyen. Just as Thomas and Giap were leaving for Ho's headquarters, Ho arrived in a sedan chair. Ho reported that the Japanese had given a "complete unconditional surrender" at noon. Thomas issued the arms the Deer Team had been using in training to the Viet Minh soldiers and informed both the trainees and the Americans that they would probably "move out" the next day. That night the Americans and the Vietnamese partied long into the night. "We shot our trip flares and our pyrotechnics before our troops," Thomas recorded. "They all shouted 'Hip Hip Horray.' We're a bunch of happy boys to-night. [We] Will be in pretty bad shape to leave to-morrow morning."[172] As the men drank and celebrated, Trieu Duc Quang talked with the Americans he had come to regard as friends. "Our American friends explained that peace has come and now I don't have to fight anymore," he recalled. "But," Trieu Duc Quang quickly added, "the Japanese were still in my country, and our country was still at war so we had to keep on fighting."[173] As the Deer Team and the Vietnamese-American Force celebrated the Allied victory, neither realized how soon they would be in battle with the Japanese.

8

On to Hanoi

Although told by Davis in Poseh to "sit tight until further orders,"[1] on August 16, 1945, the Deer Team and the Vietnamese-American Force left Tan Trao after a "send off before the National Delegates."[2] Both Thomas and Vo Nguyen Giap were anxious to leave for Thai Nguyen. Giap remembered the excitement that permeated the villages as news of the Japanese capitulation spread. "I received the order from the Central Committee to prepare for combat," Giap explained. "On August 16, with the Liberation Army I left Tan Trao to attack the Japanese at Thai Nguyen, which was the first town to be freed from the enemy's hands on our march to Hanoi."[3] Initially Giap and Thomas led the men as one unit over the difficult terrain between the training compound and their destination. However, on the morning of August 17 and again on August 18, the men split into two groups with Giap, Thomas, and a platoon of Viet Minh soldiers taking one route and Défourneaux and the remainder of the men—both American and Vietnamese (led by Dam Quang Trung)—taking another, more direct route to Thai Nguyen. Although the two groups were reunited at the end of each day, Thomas's decision not to stay with his men in order to accompany Giap only increased the hostility of some members of the Deer Team.

The four-day journey to Thai Nguyen was difficult; both Thomas's and Défourneaux's men traversed steep mountain paths and forded swollen streams, frequently walking in mud and rain. However, each night the men were provided with clean, dry sleeping quarters and a warm meal. Défourneaux remembered that along the way the Americans were greeted by curious villagers, some of whom offered the men beer and fruit.[4] Although Thomas's route was also difficult, Viet Minh veteran Nguyen Chinh reminisced about his pleasant conversations in French "as friends" with Thomas and about the major's smile and "no problem" response as he tolerated the heavy rains and picked off the green leeches. Thomas's experience was a bit different from the rest of the Deer Team's, perhaps because of his alternate route. As well as receiving provisions from the peasants, he was also greeted with jubilant smiles, clapping hands, and shouts of "Hip, hip, hoorah!" Local leaders came forward to welcome Thomas who in response reportedly answered:

> This is the first time we arrive in your country, but still we have got very good feelings and impressions about the scenic beauties and the people of this land. I hope that we will have more chances to visit your country, Vietnam, later on and it would be a great pleasure. But now, both you and we have to carry out the common duty of fighting against the Japanese and let us cooperate to fulfill our tasks, and we hope that the Vietnam-U.S. friendship will be long enduring.[5]

In addition to the welcome of the people, Thomas recalled seeing Viet Minh flags in the villages he passed through,[6] which he concluded was a clear indication of the strength of the Viet Minh in the area. "Those flags didn't just appear in a minute," Thomas deduced. "They had to be made sometime [earlier] and hidden away."[7] This was of course the case. The local villagers had been well prepared for the arrival of the Americans. "Some of our cadres, an advance team, had already talked to the people," stated Tran Trong Trung. "The duty of the local people was to keep secrets and organize the security activities, maintaining a guard in the whole area, and to appear to be very friendly to these people [the Americans]."[8]

Thomas could not help but be impressed by the warm reception that he and the Viet Minh received on their journey. It was also on the arduous trek to Thai Nguyen that Thomas got to know more about Giap:

> That walk through the mountains was when I was closest to Giap. I was about thirty at the time, and he was maybe three years older. At one point he told me that his wife and his sister-in-law had both died in French prisons. He had a very strong feeling against the French. He was an intense man, no question about it. The French called him a snow-covered volcano. He was always in control of himself, and obviously very bright and well educated. His troops looked up to him. I liked him.[9]

As Thomas's friendship with Giap developed, his relationship with his men deteriorated. Thomas's apparent disregard for the authority of head-quarters further rankled the members of the Deer Team. On August 19, after nearly two days without radio contact with Poseh because of the rain, Thomas received a series of messages sent on August 16, 17, and 18 ordering him not to accept the surrender of any Japanese in the area, to delay his trek to Hanoi until ordered to proceed, to keep all of his equipment, and to have the Americans travel alone, allowing only Vietnamese guides to accompany them. Furthermore, Davis ordered Thomas to obtain "accurate receipts" for the equipment he had already issued during the course of training. He was advised on August 18 that the Deer Team, as well as the Cat Team,[10] should proceed to Hanoi with the OSS equipment that would then be returned to an American base in China via truck. Equipment that the men could not carry would be "evacuated by air" when possible.[11]

By the morning of August 19, Thomas had already disobeyed three of the first four orders: He was well on the way to Hanoi, he was traveling with a large contingent of the Viet Minh, and on August 15, after hearing of the Japanese surrender, he had turned over most of the American weapons used in training to the Vietnamese-American Force. What made the situation even worse, Thomas appeared to his men not to care that he had disobeyed Poseh's orders. In his report on the Deer Team mission, Thomas admitted that the prohibition against accepting any Japanese surrenders[12] was "extremely disheartening" to him, "as we all felt that we had risked our lives in coming here and now when the going was to be easy we were not allowed to get in on the gravy."[13]

The members of the Deer Team were also concerned that Thomas, having already decided to help the Viet Minh take control of the town of Thai Nguyen, seemed far more concerned about the welfare of the Viet Minh than about that of his own men. As the Deer Team departed their bivouac on August 19, Défourneaux could not help but notice the "big red flag leading" the way. In addition, he was irritated that Major Thomas "was still in charge of the guerrillas," but he was even more disturbed that Giap "appeared to have full control over our leader." Défourneaux recorded his impressions in his diary on August 19:

He doesn't give a damn about us at all. He doesn't tell me anything, is always with Mr. Van [Giap]. Asks my approval only after [he has] decided to do something. Take[s] me aside to explain to me the situation, wrongly very often because he doesn't understand French. He deliberately disobeyed an order and let his team wonder [sic] around with[out] any interest on his part whatsoever. I stay with the boys and cannot help hear their conversations. They hate him, personally I hate him more and more every day. I feel like a PFC and not like an officer.[14]

By 7:00 PM on August 19, the men of the Deer Team had settled in for the night. Restless, Thomas left the room at 7:30 and went to "mix" with the Viet Minh leaders "to see what they will decide." Défourneaux and the others listened to the major's discussions with the Viet Minh with growing anxiety. That evening Défourneaux recorded what he had heard in his team diary. Thomas was, he wrote, "organizing the attack on T-G [Thai Nguyen]." He was "giving team equipment," including the "handy-talky and binoculars" to the Viet Minh. "I heard him give orders to platoon leaders who were to lead the attack," wrote Défourneaux. "The men and I could not sleep or relax."[15]

Viet Minh veteran Nguyen Chinh also felt Thomas played a large role in organizing the attack. The "operational plan was invented by the American friends," stated Chinh, "especially Mr. Thomas himself."[16] Thomas's diary does not clearly indicate his participation in the planning, although he did state in his official report that part of the rationale for leaving Tan Trao for Thai Nguyen was to "see what could be done in the way of 'action.'" He also included the plan for the following day: "The plan was for a group to go to the Provincial Governor and get the local guards to surrender, the Americans were to go to a safe house, and the remainder of the soldiers were to surround the Jap post."[17]

In the very early morning hours of August 20, the Deer Team was on the move again. The Americans, minus Thomas, traveled with about thirty Viet Minh guerrillas, and as was becoming the pattern, the Viet Minh's big red flag with a gold star led the way. It was a relatively short, easy trip—the final leg of the walk to Thai Nguyen took only an hour—but the men were both unclear and unhappy about the decision to leave in the day's wee hours. Deer Team member Henry Prunier recalled that although the war had already ended, "we walked in [to Thai Nguyen] at four o'clock in the morning [just] as though we were still in combat ourselves."[18] Upon their arrival, the Americans were surprised to find electric streetlights burning in the Vietnamese town, and they were relieved to quickly locate the comfortable "safe house," where they settled in for some much-desired sleep.

Thomas and Giap, who left an hour later than the men of the Deer Team, arrived in Thai Nguyen at about 5:00 AM. Their first stop was city hall. In accordance with the party policy decision of August 12, 1945, Giap sent an ultimatum to the Japanese asking for their surrender. But Nguyen Chinh remembered typing and sending two ultimatums that day: one from Giap and one in English signed by Thomas.[19] The surrender document, or documents, undoubtedly did little to convince the well-ensconced Japanese to hand their arms over to the Viet Minh. The generic "ultimatum" for all such occasions read in part:

Allison Thomas, standing with soldiers of Vo Nguyen Giap's ragtag army on August 20, 1945, just before embarking for Thai Nguyen, was later resented by some members of the Deer Team for choosing to march with the Vietnamese rather than accompanying his own men. Former members of the Viet Minh, however, had fond memories of Thomas's good nature and pleasant companionship on the journey. *National Archives and Records Administration.*

Japanese officers and men! The Japanese government has surrendered to the Allies. The Japanese troops are being gradually disarmed on all fronts. Before the landing in Indochina of the Allied forces, hand your arms over to the Viet Minh and to the Viet Nam Liberation Army. By doing so you will not only have your lives safeguarded but also contribute to the liberation of the Vietnamese people. The ultimate hour that is to decide your fate has come! Do not hesitate.[20]

The surrender, of course, was not that simple. The Japanese "were in a regular old French fort," Thomas recollected, "and they weren't about to surrender right away."[21] The party's August 12 "Call to Uprising" stated that Japanese troops who did not surrender "must be annihilated,"[22] and later that morning the "battle" for Thai Nguyen began.

Between 6:00 and 6:30 AM, firing broke out between the Japanese and the Viet Minh. At the safe house Défourneaux and the others were tense: "We

Soldiers of the Vietnamese-American Force, mostly armed with captured French weapons, in formation prior to the battle of Thai Nguyen. *National Archives and Records Administration.*

had no idea where the Major was, and we were alone between two antagonists." Although the men were dissatisfied about their inability to do what they had volunteered for during the war—fight the Japanese—with World War II already over, none of the Americans, save perhaps Thomas, wanted to participate in this battle. Thomas sent a message to the safe house, asking Défourneaux, Squires, and Zielski to join him with the Viet Minh. Although both Squires and Zielski went, Défourneaux did not. "I did not want to be involved with whatever he was doing," Défourneaux recalled, "and in the process get in trouble [with headquarters]."23

Sporadic firing continued throughout the day. That evening, Squires returned to the safe house. He told the men that Thomas had "assisted" in the surrender discussions between the Japanese and the Viet Minh. But the Japanese, believing that Thomas was French, refused to surrender to him. According to Squires, Thomas became quite agitated and tried to prove his nationality by producing his "identity card, a .38 bullet, and a little American flag." The Japanese, however, continued to believe that Thomas was a Frenchman—a logical conclusion given the time and place. The Japanese were accustomed to seeing Vietnamese soldiers led by French officers and had no reason to think that the Americans would be working with the Viet Minh. At that point, Squires told the men, Thomas admitted "that he shouldn't have been there." To Squires, Défourneaux, and the others, Thomas's behavior seemed inexplicable. "It seemed," recorded Défourneaux, "that he [was] going nuts. . . . When he talks, he starts laughing for no reasons—a laugh which give[s] the impression of his crazyness [sic]." Concerned and aggravated, Défourneaux sent the major a note telling him to "lay off" the Viet Minh and "worry about his team."[24]

In his own diary, Thomas recorded nothing of his purported exchange with the Japanese. But he had been ordered not to accept any Japanese surrenders. Given those circumstances, it would have been foolish for him to record these proceedings in an official diary. Thomas wrote that he was "kept informed of what was happening at all times by a party liaison man." By early in the evening, the 160 troops of the "Guard Indigene" (Indochinese troops which came under Japanese control after the coup) had capitulated to the Viet Minh.[25] The Japanese, however, still held out. Again on August 20, Défourneaux questioned Thomas's mental stability. He claimed to have overheard Thomas "clearly organizing the attack for the next morning with Mr. Van." But he had not conducted the planning session, according to Défourneaux, "like an intelligent officer would." Instead, he remembered Thomas sounding more like a "kid" playing war games.[26] The situation was no doubt unique for Thomas. Although he was accustomed to leading men in wartime, he was not in the habit of leading Vietnamese men in the postwar world. Any participation, no matter how brief, in the attack on Thai Nguyen was essentially disobeying orders. Thus, he had every reason to exhibit nervous laughter.

On August 21 the Deer Team again parted company and missions, with Thomas heading in one direction and his men another. Défourneaux and Zielski went in search of a more suitable house for the team. Although their current residence was pleasant enough, it was too small. They located a large, elaborate home and spent the first part of the day moving in. By early afternoon firing had resumed. Vogt and Zielski crawled out to see what was going on. Défourneaux and the others remained safely behind the walls. "The war is over," wrote Défourneaux, "why take a chance on getting bumped off now[?]" When the shooting had ceased, Thomas returned to check on the men. Seeing they were all safe, he reportedly regaled them with stories of the attack and the "fun" he was having—tales that Défourneaux angrily classified as "a big line of shit." Thomas returned to "whatever" he had been doing, giving Défourneaux and the others the distinct impression that he "was still directing the Viet Minh operation."[27]

Thomas's role in the battle can perhaps best be explained by examining the Viet Minh rationale for attacking. Stein Tønnesson looked at several different motivations for the clash, including the possibility that the fight was intended to enhance the image of the Viet Minh,[28] to be used as propaganda, or to allow Giap to test his forces. A further possibility is that the battle was "to impress the US Allies." Tønnesson wrote: "French services in China had received information that the Viet Minh intended to launch an attack on a major Japanese position in order to give the United States a pretext for helping them. . . . After all the preparations, both the Army commanders and the OSS advisers may have been reluctant to call the whole thing off merely because the Japanese had capitulated."[29]

Given Thomas's budding friendship with Giap as well as with Ho Chi Minh, he may have felt he had little to lose and much to gain by helping plan the attack. Although Thomas could play no official role at this stage, he could advise his new friends and rejoice in their success. When prodded years later about his relationship with Giap, Thomas grew defensive. "I was friendly with him," Thomas admitted, "and why shouldn't I be? After all, we were both there for the same purpose, fighting the Japanese. . . . it wasn't my job to find out whether he was a Communist or not. We were fighting a common enemy."[30] Although his official account of August 21 did not indicate his own participation on any level, years after the fact Thomas admitted that he had helped "somewhat in the planning of Thai Nguyen," adding that the battle was necessary "from Giap's perspective."[31] His 1945 report did indicate his relative proximity to the Viet Minh during the attack and also provided an excellent account of the weapons in their possession at Thai Nguyen:

> The Vietminh decided to launch a small attack to show the Japs how strong they were. About 3 PM "all hell" broke loose. The Vietminh fired for about 10 minutes with French rifles, French machine guns, Jap machine guns (that had been captured in previous engagements), British stens and brens (which the British had parachuted to the French here), grenades and weapons which we had given them which included bazookas, M-1s, and HE Anti-tank grenades. However, the Japs were well installed in their concrete fortifications and it is doubtful if any were even wounded at this time. But the townspeople were duly impressed by the "attack."[32]

The occasional fighting between the Japanese and the Viet Minh continued on August 22, 23, and 24. On the twenty-second Défourneaux wired Poseh: "We are now in Thai Nguyen. The Major is in the outskirts of the town. The remaining team is in the center of the town. Battle between Viet Minh and Jap Garrison started Monday [August] twenty, still going on. Street fighting day and night."[33] On August 23 Giap and "2 sections of troops" apparently departed for Hanoi, where events were unfolding very quickly. Despite Giap's absence, the Viet Minh attacked a number of other buildings, including the Japanese stables.[34] Although most sources maintain that Giap's lieutenants directed the attack,[35] Défourneaux believed Thomas was "in charge of the operations."[36] Whether or not he led the operation is open to speculation. However, in their final attack on August 25, the Viet Minh "liberated" a considerable supply of food and weapons from the Japanese, materiel that Thomas itemized and included in an attachment to his official report.[37] Finally, later in the afternoon, the Japanese agreed to a cease-fire. The Japanese would be allowed to keep their arms; however, they would be confined to their post and the Viet Minh would send food in to them.

Historian Douglas Pike described this brief battle for Thai Nguyen as especially significant. "General Giap led the new armed force into the first battle on 16 August 1945, an attack from Tan Trao, Tuyen Quang province, on Thai Nguyen town, which," Pike wrote, "marked the 'liberation' of Vietnam."[38] Stein Tønnesson observed the importance of the battle of Thai Nguyen in Vietnamese history but described it as being more a *pièce de théâtre* (play). In his evaluation, Tønnesson emphasized a number of crucial elements, including the facts that the local Viet Minh cadres were already negotiating with the Japanese garrison when Giap arrived, "preparing for a peaceful transfer of power"; that the deliberately arrogant nature of Giap's ultimatum foiled the negotiations; and that the much-heralded battle did not cost any lives.[39] There is some dispute about the loss of life during the battle, however. Thomas testified that six Japanese were killed "for certain," and several more wounded, but the exact number was "unverified." In addition, he claimed that three Viet Minh soldiers and five civilians were killed and that eleven Viet Minh and ten civilians were wounded in the six days of fighting.[40]

Nevertheless, on August 26 the town of Thai Nguyen celebrated its freedom from the Japanese. There was a parade in town, and "almost every building had a Vietminh flag waving." Thomas also noted that "the newly organized municipal government got under way" that day.[41] With the new government in place, the electricity, which had been cut off during the battle,

René Défourneaux, sitting on the bumper, and Allison Thomas, standing with a Viet
Minh member leaning against one of the "charcoal burner" buses that ran between Hanoi
and Thai Nguyen. Défourneaux often questioned the appropriateness of Thomas's
apparent sympathies with the Vietnamese. *National Archives and Records*

was restored, pleasing all of the Americans. While Thomas was in Thai
Nguyen, Ho Chi Minh arrived for a brief visit. He asked Thomas and the Deer
Team to accompany him to Hanoi, but a disappointed Thomas, ordered to
"stay put" by headquarters, reluctantly rejected Ho's request. During Ho's
visit he also reported on other Americans, telling Thomas that Dan Phelan
had recently flown out on an L-5 and that an American mission had arrived
in Hanoi.[42]

Disappointed at having to remain outside the capital city, the team welcomed a diversion for dinner that evening. While visiting the Catholic mission in town, Prunier, Hoagland, and Vogt met Father Pedro, a Dominican
priest from Spain, and invited him to join the Americans for their evening
meal.[43] Father Pedro spent three hours talking with Défourneaux that night
and an additional two hours with him the next day. Défourneaux was excited
to interview the priest and to learn more about Indochina. "The Major only
knew what the Vietminh wanted him to know, which was very little," complained Défourneaux, but Father Pedro, having lived in Tonkin since 1936,

simply "had better sources of information than we did."[44] The priest reiterated the history of the capitulation of France to the Japanese, the Japanese coup in March, and the Japanese use of propaganda with the Vietnamese people. Although Father Pedro did not realize it, his version of events corroborated much of what the Viet Minh had already told the OSS.

The Americans could very easily gain further confirmation of much of what Father Pedro told them. In fact, the Deer Team had a very recent example of probable Japanese propaganda. When Ho met Thomas at Thai Nguyen, he gave him a copy of two letters, which the Viet Minh had translated, allegedly sent from the Japanese garrisons at Thai Nguyen and Cho Chu to the "Viet Minh League." The letter from the Japanese army at Thai Nguyen, dated April 11, 1945, chastised the Viet Minh for "destroying the truce," disrupting communications between Thai Nguyen and Tuyen Quang, and creating fear among the population. The letter reminded the Viet Minh that the Japanese were responsible for freeing the Vietnamese from their French overlords and encouraged them to rethink the situation in the light of inevitable consequences:

> From the beginning, you did not understand our sincerity, and you always organize anti-Jap movement. You must consider carefully. Only Japan can help you realizing your hope. Hoping England or America to save Vietnam from the French hands, has the same sense as saving the Vietnam people from sunburn by throwing them into the fire.
>
> In order to keep peace and order in Tuyen-Quang and Thainguen, we are forced to use armed troups [*sic*] against your senseless activities. But before sending out our troops, we sent you this letter, asking you to stop immediately the destruction of roads between these two provinces. . . . If you don't listen to our advice, it will then happen heartbreaking things: the Yellow men killing the Yellow men, and you will find yourselves in miserable situation.[45]

The second letter, dated a month later, was an open proclamation to the populace surrounding Cho Chu that reprimanded the local Vietnamese for failing to understand the good intentions of the Japanese and cautioned them about the Viet Minh:

> Recently, the Japanese have driven the French out of Indo-China, and given independence back to Vietnam people. But that independence seems as shattered because of the Communist[s]. . . . But they

understand nothing about communism as published by the Russian Lenin. Such are the Communist[s] of Indo-China. Let them awake quickly![46]

Father Pedro confirmed Japanese attempts to get the Viet Minh involved in their fight against the Allies and the Viet Minh refusal to do so. He also explained that the Viet Minh continued to harass the Japanese regardless of their threats. Although Father Pedro complimented many aspects of the Viet Minh, he cautioned that their activities were primarily directed against the French and French collaborators, noting that their main activities were "stealing and killing."[47] After Father Pedro's visit, the Americans had few distractions in Thai Nguyen; the major wrote reports, and the men played cards and wandered about town, taking pictures and eating the ample food provided by the Viet Minh.[48] As the days became more and more monotonous, the men's thoughts centered on moving on to Hanoi and beginning their long trip home. The man who delayed their long-awaited homecoming was the head of the American Mercy Team in Hanoi, Captain Archimedes Patti.

A month prior to the Japanese surrender, the OSS had begun preparing for the rescue of "some twenty thousand American and Allied POWs and about fifteen thousand civilian internees in Japanese hands." The "commando-type" units responsible for carrying out those missions were known as "Mercy Teams." When news of the end of the war came, the OSS and the Fourteenth Air Force were ready, and the first Mercy Teams left for various parts of China on August 15. During the next seven days, additional teams were formed, including a team led by Patti, bound for Hanoi. Because of inclement weather, Patti did not leave Kunming until August 22. On that day, he flew out with the American members of his team, plus a small French contingent led by Jean Sainteny.[49]

Sainteny's battle to get aboard the American flight to Hanoi had been very difficult. Overall, the French in China were very unhappy with their lot. The war ended more quickly than they had anticipated, and although by mid-August there were a few Frenchmen participating in OSS units along the border, the French had been unable to reenter Indochina in significant numbers. Sainteny, hoping to reestablish a French presence at the earliest possible moment, requested permission to join the Mercy Team bound for Hanoi. By August 18 the OSS had learned that the French government had decided to "adopt a passive, diplomatic attitude toward the reoccupation of Indo-China"; Major Sainteny asserted he would represent the new "liberal" French policy in Hanoi.[50]

Sainteny's initial appeal to join the Mercy Team was rejected by Wedemeyer, who saw "no useful purpose in the French going to Hanoi on the Mercy Team flight," adding that "arrangements were being made for a French presence in Hanoi 'at the proper time.'"[51] Given his intense desire to reestablish a "victorious" French presence in Vietnam, an aggravated Sainteny lashed out at the Americans. Sainteny believed that the French "had been betrayed by the Americans and that General Wedemeyer personally has been hindering French activities in this theater [and had] not been honest with the French right from the beginning of negotiations."[52]

In addition to Wedemeyer's apparent snub, Sainteny also received the bad news that the French team he had attempted to infiltrate into Haiphong had been detained by the Japanese. The leader of the team, Captain Blanchard, did make contact with Lieutenant Colonel Kamiya, the former liaison officer between the Japanese military headquarters in Hanoi and the administrative offices of Admiral Decoux, but he was disappointed in the results. Instead of being permitted to reoccupy key offices, the French team was confined to transmitting messages related to the upcoming surrender ceremony and meteorological data to the French offices in Kunming. No doubt Sainteny was equally disturbed by the news that "Annamite leaders" in Kunming had "expressed the desire to bring Indo-China under status of an American protectorate"[53] and were hoping that the United States would intercede on their behalf with the United Nations to prevent the French "from their reoccupation of Indo-China" and to exclude the Chinese.[54]

In an attempt to placate the irate Frenchman, Patti and Wedemeyer agreed that Sainteny and his staff could go with the OSS Mercy Team provided they confined their activities to "humanitarian tasks in the French community."[55] Adding insult to injury, the French were to fall under "complete" U.S. command, and they could under no circumstances use the French flag as part of the mission.[56]

As Patti, Sainteny, and their staffs approached the Gia Lam airport outside Hanoi, tensions ran high. None of the men knew for certain what the Japanese response to their landing would be. Viewing the small tanks and antiaircraft guns on the airfield, Patti decided to drop in a reconnaissance party led by a native of Baltimore, Maryland, Captain Ray Grelecki. Although trained at Fort Benning and experienced in parachute drops, Grelecki was understandably uneasy about dropping in on the well-outfitted enemy below. Even though he was fully armed and in combat dress, he was obviously ill-prepared to meet a Japanese tank "with maybe a squad—ten or twelve Japanese—on the sides with their big bayonets" that came rolling toward him.[57]

When Patti's team landed at Gia Lam airport, they were greeted with cheers from a large contingent of POWs from the nearby prison camp. Americans wore the flag on the back of their uniforms to aid in their rapid identification by both the French and the Japanese. *Archimedes L. Patti, Papers, Special Collections, University of Central Florida, Orlando.*

Fortunately, the captain's party met no opposition and soon radioed Patti that it was safe to land. Patti recalled that a unit of fifty to sixty fully armed Japanese soldiers surrounded his plane. At about the same time, a large contingent of Indian (British) POWs from the nearby prison broke camp and cheered the arrival of the Allies.[58] The well-ordered and well-disciplined Japanese soldiers blocked the advance of the POWs but neither fired on them nor made hostile moves toward Patti's group. Patti then proceeded to conduct the business he had come for: checking on the status of the POWs and arranging for transport into Hanoi.

On the way into the city, the team passed numerous Viet Minh flags and large banners, printed in English, French, and Vietnamese, reading "Down with French Imperialism" and "Independence or Death!" Patti also recalled seeing a large "boisterous and hostile" crowd on the way to Hanoi.[59] "They had learned" he recalled, "that the French had arrived in an American plane under the protection of Americans." Once in Hanoi, Patti and his team set up their headquarters at the Hotel Métropole and were welcomed by a different sort of crowd: anxious and jubilant French residents who greeted Sainteny and the Americans with "joy and relief."[60] A number of the colons

The fifty to sixty fully armed Japanese soldiers who surrounded Patti's plane did not oppose the American landing, and afterward, in a very orderly manner, they loaded their gear on trucks for transport into Hanoi. *Archimedes L. Patti, Papers, Special Collections, University of Central Florida, Orlando.*

reportedly were terrified that "a group" who had killed "three or four of the Frenchmen" the night before would, as they had promised, return to kill again. Patti turned to Grelecki for his input. Grelecki noted, "This was my responsibility, it was a matter of the field and not an intellectual desk exercise. I am a field man, did about 150 pushups with one hand and I consider this fine person Patti as a desk man, they always had this belly on them." Grelecki decided to prepare the hotel for any possible attack and installed his 60 mm mortars on the roof. He also moved a number of the French women and children to another location. Nothing occurred, and the precautions ended up being just that, but Grelecki stated, "Candidly we were fully unprepared to go into Hanoi."[61]

The evening of their first night in Hanoi proved to be a busy one for Patti as well as for Grelecki. Patti received a number of visitors, including Le Trung Nghia, "representing the Hanoi City Committee," who welcomed Patti to the city and offered the services of his committee in facilitating the Americans' mission. He further questioned Patti about the arrival of the French, American attitudes, and Patti's knowledge of Ho Chi Minh. "In response to his questions," Patti recalled, "I assured him that no, I did not

Archimedes Patti and other Americans were impressed by the orderly demonstrations in Hanoi in which participants carried signs in English, as well as Vietnamese and French, denouncing colonialism and demanding independence. Patti commented: "From what I have seen these people mean business. The French will have to deal with them. For that matter we will all have to deal with them" (Patti to Indiv, NNNR61, September 2, 1945 [RG 226, Entry 154, Box 199, Folder 3373, NARA]). *Archimedes L. Patti, Papers, Special Collections, University of Central Florida, Orlando.*

anticipate the arrival of French troops; yes, there would be additional Americans coming shortly; yes, it was true that I had met President Ho Chi Minh; and no, the United States did not support colonialism."[62]

Although brief, the question-and-answer session produced answers that could be successfully manipulated by the Viet Minh in the future. Le Trung Nghia and many other Vietnamese who had not lived in or traveled to the Viet Bac may well have doubted Ho Chi Minh's connection to the powerful winners of World War II. Yet the senior American official to land in Hanoi admitted freely that he knew of and indeed had already met Ho. Furthermore, he told the Viet Minh exactly what they wanted to hear: More Americans—not Frenchmen—were on the way.[63]

Although most of the Vietnamese in Hanoi were thrilled with the possibility that there would not be an armed French return, the French population delighted in the prospect that there would soon be a French show of force. With Sainteny's delegation in the Hotel Métropole, the scene in the lobby soon resembled, noted Patti, "Grand Central Station at rush hour."[64] It was soon agreed among the Americans, the French, and the Japanese that the Americans and the French should be housed in separate quarters. Thus, Sainteny and his delegation were moved to the Governor-General's Palace.[65] From Patti's perspective the move improved his situation. "I was only too glad," he reminisced, "to be able to pursue my mission without the risk of public disorders or political entanglements."[66] Although Patti stated that Sainteny was "obviously pleased" to make the move, his satisfaction was short-lived. Over the next few days the opulent palace came to feel more like Sainteny's prison.[67]

On August 23, while Sainteny was moving to the Governor-General's Palace, Patti was busy with a host of visitors, including the president of the Bank of Indochina and the ranking Japanese officer in Hanoi, General Tsuchihashi Yuitsu. In his early-morning meeting with Tsuchihashi, Patti described the nature of his mission and emphasized the Japanese responsibility to maintain public order. In his wires for that day, Patti assured Kunming that the Japanese were not interfering in the Mercy Team mission and indeed had already released "287 British Indian POWs."[68] He was concerned, however, with their recent withdrawal of 50 million piastres and request for an additional 20 million, from the Bank of Indochina for "payment of expenses incurred in maintaining law and order plus the protection of the French."[69] The bank director echoed Patti's concern, fearing the Japanese would bankrupt the most important financial institution in the colony.

Vietnamese actions also prompted Patti to send a series of wires to Kunming on August 23. In at least three separate messages he expressed concern about additional French personnel arriving in Vietnam and the reactions of the Viet Minh. He began by stating, "Political situation critical. Vietminh strong and belligerent. Definitely out French, suggest no more French be permitted enter FIC and especially armed." Later in the day he added, "I repeat again that it will be most dangerous for armed Frenchmen to enter Indochina. Units are being formed to repulse the entry of armed French." The OSS office in Kunming, eager to withdraw their agents from the field, queried Patti about using French boats and crews to get the OSS team out of Pakhoi, where a QUAIL base had already been established. The Kunming office, respectful of Patti's take on the situation on the ground, also asked his opinion about a request from OSS agent Lucien Conein to use fourteen armed French personnel to get him to Hanoi. Patti's response was clear: "In view of the delicate political situation my recommendation is to stop our boys from proceeding to Hanoi with French personnel." He contrasted the

American delegation's freedom to circulate about Hanoi to Sainteny's position, which he described as "incommunicado at the government palace." Patti further warned that the Japanese were trying to stir up "5th column activities" using Vietnamese "as agents." In addition, "rumors are being spread," he cautioned, "that the French are coming from Laugson [*sic*] and by boat killing [Annamite] children and women. Vietminhs are recruiting a people's army to keep French out."[70]

Patti's perceptions of the tensions in Hanoi on that hot August day were accurate. In his memoirs, he portrayed the scene and the American role:

> This city of seeming normalcy and peacefulness was seething below the surface, and it obviously did not take much for it to erupt. Our OSS team had immediately become a center of Allied authority to which everyone with a cause or a desire for prestige brought himself to be heard. The French came to complain, make demands, and play conspiratorial games. The Vietnamese came to be seen with the Allies and acquire status in the eyes of their adversaries, creating an image of "insiders" with the American Mission.[71]

In an attempt to distance himself from the French, partly in recognition of the anti-French attitude among the Vietnamese and the image of the Hotel Métropole "as the rendezvous for many of the prominent French in Hanoi," Patti moved the American mission and its gear to the spacious Maison Gautier on August 24. There "the American flag was conspicuously displayed in the large reception room . . . signifying to all that this headquarters was an American installation, officiated by independent United States representatives with allegiance to none."[72]

Although the Americans wished to be viewed as "strictly neutral," they were not. Neither the French nor the Vietnamese regarded the Americans as impartial. At the Governor-General's Palace, Major Sainteny was increasingly unhappy in what he called his "golden cage." Sainteny had long deemed Patti and most of the OSS in Kunming anti-French and inimical to French aspirations. Soon after his arrival in Hanoi, Sainteny again complained to Patti, this time about the activities of an OSS agent already on his list of anti-French Americans: Major Allison Thomas. Remembering Thomas's role in having Montfort, Logos, and Phac removed from the Viet Minh headquarters in July, Sainteny was livid when he read Thomas's name in one of the local Hanoi newspapers in an article entitled "Viet Minh Fighting [in Collaboration] with U.S. Troops in Tonkin Will Soon Be Here to Oust the French Oppressors Who Last Year Starved 2 Million People." Luckily, neither Patti nor Sainteny knew the extent of Thomas's actions in Thai Nguyen. They certainly had no knowledge at that point that Thomas had attempted to help Giap gain the Japanese surrender at Thai Nguyen.

Patti listened to Sainteny's grievances and attempted to improve the situation by recommending that the Deer Team be withdrawn from Thai Nguyen and that other OSS teams working along and inside the Indochina border be recalled to Kunming. He advised Kunming of the newspaper headline and warned headquarters that the Vietnamese were excitedly awaiting Thomas's arrival "to stage [an] anti-French demonstration."[73] "I hoped to disassociate all our Americans from either the Viet Minh or the French causes," Patti wrote afterward. "But our teams were very loath to submit. Order and Theater policy seemed to matter little to them. They were in high spirits and the repeated messages ordering them to Kunming had little effect; they wanted to pursue their own paths to victory."[74]

In August 1945 no one was working harder to blaze a path to victory than the Viet Minh. When Patti arrived in Hanoi, there was substantial optimism among the Vietnamese that they might finally achieve the freedom for which they had worked so long. Three days before Patti's entrance, the Viet Minh had taken over the city without bloodshed, initiating what became known as the August Revolution.[75] As the revolution began, Giap had not yet arrived in Hanoi either. Years later he recalled, "Having thoroughly understood the Party's instructions, and taking advantage of the extreme demoralization of the Japanese forces, the consternation of the puppet government and the vacillation of the security troops, the local Party organizations and Viet Minh organizations immediately took the initiative to lead the people to seize power."[76]

While Giap was still marching on Thai Nguyen, the city of Hanoi erupted. On the morning of August 19, "tens of thousands of villagers" carrying "spears, machetes, knives, reaping hooks, and sickles" began marching toward the city to the "sound of drums, cymbals, and horns." Already in place were nearly "eight hundred self-defense unit members" under the direct control of the Viet Minh. Although ill-equipped, with only "about ninety firearms, as well as machetes, swords, spears, and knives," the cadres were excited at what the day might bring. The self-defense units assumed various positions throughout the city, while the largest group, perhaps as many as 200,000 people, filled the streets and square in front of the opera house. At 11:00 AM, Nguyen Huy Khoi gave a brief speech about the end of the war and the need to establish a Vietnamese "revolutionary people's government."[77]

After the oration at the opera house, the group marched on and successfully took over the palace of the Kham Sai (imperial delegate), the city hall, the hospital, the post office, and the treasury building. In some places, such as at the Kham Sai's Palace, they successfully seized the weapons of the civil guardsmen.[78] Although there were initial difficulties, they also succeeded in gaining control of the Civil Guard barracks. "Everywhere people were celebrating the victory, the bloodless taking of power," Vu Dinh Huynh said with obvious pride. "Everyone wanted to contribute something to the cause. We really had a marvelous group of intellectuals, and we were very proud."[79]

Although not everyone was pleased to see the Viet Minh assuming control, most ordinary Vietnamese were jubilant. David Marr wrote:

> The atmosphere on the streets of Hanoi was euphoric. Revolutionary change was symbolized that evening by people removing the black air-raid blinkers on all street lamps, giving a bright glow to the city for the first time in years. Viet Minh flags hung from hundreds of buildings. Thousands of citizens promenaded the sidewalks downtown, enjoying the new sense of freedom. People stopped to admire the new armed guards in front of public buildings, especially one proud sentinel in front of the Kham Sai's Palace who sported a belt of ammunition strung across his chest. They also marveled at the huge flag fluttering from the tall lightning rod on the Palace. . . . As one young participant ruminated, not in his wildest imagination could he have expected such a transformation in one day.[80]

When Prime Minister Tran Trong Kim heard about the events in Hanoi he felt "ambivalent." Kim, according to his nephew, Bui Diem,[81] would have been "amenable" to an "orderly, legitimate transfer of power," and he felt that the coup put him in a difficult position. However, the prime minister decided to resign from his post on August 19 anyway because, he told his nephew, "it appeared this new party had the backing of the Americans." "Clearly," added Bui Diem, "the United States was going to have a strong voice in determining the immediate future of Vietnam, and my uncle was not alone in believing that whoever had the Americans' confidence would be best placed to guide the nation during the postwar period."[82] Seeking to solidify their control of the city, the Viet Minh set about reestablishing order in Hanoi over the next few days.

Although the announcement to "launch the insurrection" had gone out via the radio transmitter left by Mac Shin earlier, it was only received by the

stations in Lang Son, Cao Bang, and Ha Giang.[83] Most uprisings were in
fact reactions by local committees to the evolving situation. In the outlying
regions of the north, Viet Minh representatives "marched on government
offices, detained mandarins, ransacked files, hung Viet Minh flags, talked
incessantly, collected whatever firearms were available and organized revolutionary committees." News of the events in Hanoi quickly spread south
into central Vietnam, and on August 23 an estimated 100,000 peasants
marched into Hue and cheered the formation of a Viet Minh liberation committee.[84] Although the commander of the Japanese garrison in Hue offered
the emperor protection, Bao Dai rejected the proposal. Marveling at the in-
credibly rapid "miracle" occurring, he placed his faith in the people and resigned himself to the fact that the proverbial Mandate of Heaven had
passed to the Viet Minh.[85] On the suggestion of a telegram from the "Patriotic Committee" in Hanoi,[86] the emperor, only recently "liberated" by the
Japanese, decided to renounce the imperial throne and become the "simple
citizen" Vinh-Thuy. On August 25 he announced his intention to abdicate to
the stunned members of the royal court, stating that he would "rather live
as a simple citizen in an independent nation than as the king of a subju-
gated nation."[87]

As Bao Dai was preparing to deliver what he believed would be his last
speech as emperor, Patti met with various members of the Vietnamese press
in Hanoi, one of whom passed along the news, then only a rumor, that the
emperor might abdicate the throne. The Vietnamese press representatives
arrived with a message for Patti: "We welcome the Americans to our country. We appreciate that Captain Patti has given us audience to hear our
grievances." Patti listened to what had become a familiar litany of French
abuses and excesses and issued a brief statement attempting to clarify the
American position:

> We Americans appreciate your warm welcome. Our job is purely a
> military one and please let that be firmly understood; our position and
> attitude is of a neutral nature. We are here for the sole purpose to pave
> the way for the forthcoming peace conferences designed to officially
> terminate hostilities. You are welcome to see me at any time, as is any
> person of any party and of any nationality.[88]

Although Patti believed that his words clearly established the American
role in Hanoi, his actions were easily misinterpreted by both the French and
the Vietnamese. The Vietnamese press account of the August 25 meeting

differed substantially from Patti's OSS "Daily Activities Report," which stressed American neutrality. In the Vietnamese account, Patti reportedly stated that

a) the French had no role in discussions between the Allies and the Japanese in Indochina; b) the Allies were not assisting or authorizing a French military return; c) the United States was well aware that Vietnam was a civilized country, "not barbaric as still thought by some"; and d) when the official Allied mission arrived to take the Japanese surrender, Vietnamese citizens ought to mount peaceful demonstrations demanding independence.[89]

"Enjoying his role as amateur plenipotentiary, Patti said too much," concluded David Marr. But "on the other hand, his Vietnamese listeners, desperately eager for American recognition, heard even more than Patti uttered."[90]

The events of August 26 further enhanced Patti's image as a tacit supporter of the Viet Minh. In the morning, Patti met briefly with four Viet Minh representatives, including Vo Nguyen Giap. Following the meeting, Giap invited Patti to step outside the American compound to be welcomed by "the people." The Americans watched as the "quasi-military" parade of civil guardsmen and self-defense teams marched past, followed by civilians carrying patriotic placards in English, Russian, and Chinese, all accompanied by a "fifty piece military band."[91] The assembled Americans and Vietnamese saluted the fluttering flags of the United States, the Soviet Union, Great Britain, China, and Vietnam and listened as their respective national anthems were played. Although Patti was impressed by the display, it held a deeper significance for the Vietnamese. As Giap prepared to leave, Patti remembered him commenting: "This is the first time in the history of Viet Nam that our flag has been displayed in an international ceremony and our national anthem played in honor of a foreign guest. I will long remember this occasion."[92] As reflected in his memoirs, the event clearly represented a significant moment for Patti as well. As Patti returned to work inside the compound, Giap spoke with reporters on scene, "conveying Patti's alleged remark that 'the independence of Vietnam is quite clear already; it simply needs to be consolidated.'"[93]

Whether or not Patti actually made the comment became irrelevant. It was reported that he had, and the paper's readership had only to admire the accompanying photos of Patti and Giap saluting the procession to assure themselves of his good will toward the new Vietnamese nation.

At the conclusion of the welcome "ceremony" for the Patti mission, the national anthems of both the United States and Vietnam were played as the Allied flags fluttered alongside the new Vietnamese standard. Giap, center in white suit, reportedly commented to Patti, on his right, that he would long remember the occasion as the first time the Vietnamese flag had been displayed and its national anthem played at an international ceremony. *Archimedes L. Patti, Papers, Special Collections, University of Central Florida, Orlando.*

Patti's activities for the day were only beginning, however. Upon his return to his quarters, he received an invitation to dine with Ho Chi Minh, who had recently arrived in Hanoi. Patti recalled being "pleased" to see Ho, but he was concerned at Ho's obvious physical weakness. After lunching with Ho, Giap, and several others, Patti and Ho were left alone to talk for the next two hours. They covered a wide variety of topics of the day, including the "uprisings" in Saigon and Hanoi, which Patti recalled being "glad to learn" more about, and the imminent arrival of the Chinese and British to accept the Japanese surrender north and south of the sixteenth parallel, respectively.[94] Patti proffered what had become his standard litany: He was "extremely limited" by his directive and had "no authority to become involved in French-Vietnamese politics." Ho responded that he understood perfectly, asking only that Patti not report his "whereabouts" to either the French or the Chinese, and adding with a smile: "Today we will talk as friends, not diplomats." Before leaving, Patti suggested that perhaps a meeting between Ho and Sainteny might prove fruitful. Although Ho expressed his doubts, he conceded that Patti "could use his best judgment in the matter."[95]

Over the next week, both the French and the Americans in Kunming questioned Patti's judgment, for this was only the first of several controversial and public appearances Patti made with Ho and other members of the Viet Minh.[96] Patti was much maligned for not maintaining his neutrality, and like Fenn, Tan, Phelan, and Thomas, his actions were misinterpreted by all sides. As reported in the daily activities reports and reiterated in his memoir, Patti received a long stream of visitors in Hanoi, most of whom made requests of one sort or another to the Americans. He had no personal connection to the long parade of individuals making demands, yet he did have a special relationship with the one man who seemingly did not agitate for his favors.

Patti and Ho Chi Minh had developed a friendly relationship in Kunming, and Ho proved to be a very cooperative agent. He provided what he promised to Patti and welcomed the Deer Team into his camp. Ho seemed to be the focus of great excitement in Hanoi, and he placed Patti on a perpetual pedestal. Moreover, Ho was, in many respects, the closest thing Patti had to a friend in the city. It should have surprised no one that the American dined with and listened to his eloquent friend, especially when the alternative was the very unhappy Major Sainteny in his "golden cage."[97] As this situation developed, however, it became increasingly difficult for Patti to maintain "strict neutrality."

Conversely, Patti should not have been even remotely surprised when the French, especially Sainteny, grew quite unhappy with him. On the evening of August 26, Patti brought up to Sainteny the possibility of meeting with Ho.[98] Sainteny readily agreed, and Patti sent a message to Ho, who assented to a meeting the next morning between Giap, then the minister of the interior for the Provisional Viet Minh Government, and Sainteny, "*if*" Patti recalled, "I accompanied him." Patti, having facilitated the meeting, and no doubt eager to participate in the proceedings, considered the condition trivial and happily agreed to accompany Giap to the Governor-General's Palace. Once again, Ho had skillfully manipulated the situation without making the American *feel* manipulated. Ho was no doubt well aware of the impression Patti's appearance at Giap's side would make—a Vietnamese delegate accompanied by an American officer, visiting a captive French official guarded by the defeated Japanese. The American and Viet Minh representative came and went at their own convenience, the Frenchman could do little more than sit and wait.

Sainteny's behavior at the meeting did not improve the image Patti had already formed of the French in relation to their colony.[99] As he remembered the exchange, Sainteny gave a "paternal lecture" to Giap on recent Vietnamese "behavior," while Giap, undoubtedly angered by his words, maintained "absolute self-control."[100] However, in his report to Kunming, Patti was more critical of the Vietnamese position, writing: "It was apparent from the start that French had [the] upper hand and that during course of negotiations Annamites lost considerable ground mainly due to their inferiority complex when confronted with a European." He also softened the nature of Sainteny's lecture, advising Helliwell that "Sainteny rebuked Annamese representative for having made known to world at large that people of Vietnam no longer desired presence of French in their country stating that such a declaration caused Allies much anxiety for safety of French hence keeping them out at this time."[101] All things considered, Sainteny felt optimistic about his meeting with Giap, noting that Giap was "visibly worried" about French reactions and was well aware of the "precariousness of their [Viet Minh] power."[102]

Events would soon show, however, the depths of Sainteny's self-delusion. Regardless of Giap's well-founded antagonism toward the French, Sainteny's failure to establish a good working relationship with the Viet Minh was also blamed on Patti. French historian Philippe Devillers asserted that the potential success of the conversation between Sainteny and Giap was undermined by Patti "and his compatriots," who "quickly interposed themselves and guaranteed the Viet Minh American support."[103]

Had this been true, the Viet Minh would have felt great relief. As it was, they had no such guarantee of American support and were still desperately looking for it. Late in the afternoon of August 28, French and Viet Minh representatives contacted Patti regarding the nationalization of the Bank of Indochina, the Yunnan railway, and other public utilities. The French, of course, were most unhappy with the concept and wanted the Americans to prevent any "nationalizations." The Viet Minh announced their intention to nationalize to Patti and hoped for the blessing of the American mission. When prodded for a "full explanation" of what the nationalization process would bring, the Viet Minh evaded the question, insisting that "the seizure of these utilities was within their democratic processes and national party platform." Perhaps sensing Patti's unease, Giap further insisted that "their movement was neither a Communist or Fascist revolution, but a democratic one based on American ideology."[104]

Although all of the buzzwords were in place, the information regarding the potential nationalization of these key enterprises disturbed Patti. The next day he transmitted the following message to Kunming:

> Provisional government groping in dark. After series of talks with leaders of provisional government I am convinced that they are not politically mature and being misled by Japanese agent-provocateur and red elements. They have no knowledge of meaning of terms such as nationalization, congressional assembly, liberalism, democracy, etc.; word[s] which they use quite freely, but during course of conversation they planned exactly opposite. . . . Provisional government is now preparing to requisition the Bank of Indo-China as it has already requisitioned the Yunnan Railroad from Lao Kay to Hanoi. It has similar plans for electric company, water works, and all transportation facilities. They call this "nationalization." They state "They are essential to the livelihood of new government." My comment—whole business has misleading misguided Soviet tinge assisted by well organized fifth column activity.[105]

The concept of nationalization, so contrary to the ideals of American capitalism, must have greatly disturbed the solidly Republican Patti. However, it must be noted that instead of proclaiming the Viet Minh purely communist, he alternately decried the intervention of the Japanese and immaturity of the Viet Minh, implicitly holding out hope for their political "education" at the feet of the world's democracies.

While Patti's message to Kunming seriously criticized the Viet Minh, their standing became even weaker as the wire was transmitted through channels. In his memorandum to the State Department, General Donovan passed on Patti's exact words, but Donovan's introductory paragraph confused the Viet Minh Provisional Government with the earlier government of Tran Trong Kim. Thus, the Viet Minh were reported not only as being "politically immature" and "misled by Japanese agents-provocateurs and communist elements" but also as being collaborators with the enemy.[106] The Viet Minh, of course, had no way of knowing about this distortion, and although they were deeply concerned about American opinion, the new Provisional Government of the Viet Minh had a potentially much larger problem literally on their doorstep.

On the same day as Giap's meeting with Patti, elements of the Chinese army "swarmed" across the Vietnamese border striking "fear and anger in the hearts of French and Vietnamese alike." Certainly Vietnamese fears were well founded both in ancient history (the 1,000 years of Chinese occupation) and in the more recent past. On August 11 and 12, Major Thomas had reported to Poseh from the Viet Bac that Chinese units attacked the Viet Minh in the "border area south of Tgingsi." Poseh passed on the message and confirmed for Kunming headquarters that a general in the "fourth war zone" had "launched [an] anti–Viet Minh campaign denouncing them as communists, bandist [bandits] etc."[107] The French also repeatedly expressed their fears about the impending arrival of the Chinese in Vietnam. On August 27 the French government requested transportation to evacuate French women and children to "points south [of the] 16 degree parallel of latitude in order to avoid Chinese occupation."[108]

The man in charge of the Chinese occupation and designated as Chiang Kai-shek's personal representative to accept the Japanese surrender in northern Vietnam was General Lu Han, commander of the First Army Group in the Ninth War Area. The generalissimo's government, like the American mission, routinely emphasized its purely military assignment in Indochina. Both Lu Han and Chiang, however, had other ideas in mind. According to historian King Chen, the Chinese government planned to "use the occupation as a means to secure more interests from the French through negotiations in Chungking and Paris." On the other hand, Lu Han, who was ardently anti-French "wanted to kick out the French from Vietnam." He had determined that the "only way" to make the French go was to settle in for a long period of Chinese occupation.[109] As August drew to a close, the French and the Vietnamese were unaware of Lu Han's intentions. Although fearful of the possibilities, they still had a window of time to prepare for the arrival of the Chinese troops in the cities. Traveling on foot from Yunnan, Lu Han's men would not enter Hanoi for another twelve days.[110] But, in the final days of the month, dramatic events continued to occur. On August 29 Ho asked Patti to visit him. He had two key announcements: First, the emperor would formally abdicate the following day, passing the symbols of power to the Viet Minh; and second, September 2 would become Independence Day for Vietnam. In preparation for the important day, Ho wanted Patti's opinion on an all-important document: Vietnam's Declaration of Independence.

Patti congratulated Ho and "wished him success" in his plans for independence. However, as he listened to the translator reading the Vietnamese Declaration of Independence he grew uneasy. The words sounded all too familiar: "All men are created equal; they are endowed by their Creator with certain unalienable rights; among these are liberty, life, and the pursuit of happiness." The opening lines, borrowed from the American Declaration of Independence, riveted his attention to the speaker. "I don't know why it nettled me," Patti admitted, "perhaps a feeling of proprietary right, or something equally inane." Ho may have sensed Patti's discomfort for he then asked, "Should I not use it?" Patti's next reaction was to feel "sheepish and embarrassed," at feeling "proprietary" over mere words. Recovered from his surprise, Patti then suggested a correction in the text. After asking the translator to reread the first section, Patti pointed out that the writer had transposed 'life' and 'liberty,' and "noted the difference in the order" of the two words. The next portion of their discussion is illuminating:

> Ho snapped to the point, "Why, of course, there is no liberty without life, and no happiness without liberty." He entered the correction himself and then pressed me for more, but I pleaded ignorance, which was the truth. I could not remember the wording of our Declaration. And I was becoming uncomfortably aware that I was participating—however slightly—in the formulation of a political entity and did not want to create an impression of participation.[111]

It was far too late, however, to eliminate the impression of American involvement. Ho, the master manipulator, had solicited exactly the reaction and participation that he wanted without seeming to do so. In a maneuver reminiscent of his meeting with Chennault, from whom he had elicited the eminently useful autographed photograph, at this point Ho did appear to have the tacit participation and approval of Vietnam's independence from the head of the American mission.[112]

Although Ho may have been genuinely interested in Patti's opinion of the new Vietnamese Declaration of Independence, it certainly was not the first time he had asked an American about the document. According to Lieutenant Dan Phelan, Ho had been thinking about the American Declaration of Independence for several months. Shortly after Phelan parachuted into Ho's base camp in May, the two men talked, among other things, about the American document. Phelan reminisced:

> He kept asking me if I could remember the language of our Declaration. I was a normal American, I couldn't. I could have wired up to Kunming and had a copy dropped to me, of course, but all he really wanted was the flavor of the thing. The more we discussed it, the more he actually seemed to know about it than I did. As a matter of fact, he knew more

about almost everything than I did, but when I thought his demands were too stiff, I told him anyway. Strange thing was he listened. He was an awfully sweet guy. If I had to pick out one quality about that little old man sitting on his hill in the jungle, it was his gentleness.[113]

Phelan, the AGAS agent so opposed to parachuting into the Viet Minh area at the outset, had instead become a friend and, inadvertently, a supporter of Vietnamese independence. Although Phelan did not provide the Viet Minh with a copy of the U.S. Declaration of Independence during his time in Tonkin, he did supply them with a copy of the U.S. Constitution and Bill of Rights, which, according to Défourneaux, were translated into French and Vietnamese with the help of a local priest.[114] Thus, the beginning of American involvement in the Vietnamese declaration was with Lieutenant Phelan in June, not with Captain Patti in August.

After finishing his conversation with Ho on August 29, Patti resumed his duties. In the days leading up to the Independence Day celebration, Patti met with Ho twice more. Although his meetings were apparently cordial, in his reports to Kunming Patti continued to express reservations about the Viet Minh. On the last day of the month, he wired Kunming: "Provisional govt is now clearly not a peoples govt, but a party govt. . . . in other words, the govt is composed strictly left wing element."[115] Patti did, nonetheless, deem the Viet Minh "fully in control," "well organized," and, as always, determined to maintain their independence "even at the cost of lives." "They feel they have nothing to lose," he added, "all to gain."[116]

Patti's opinions at that crucial time in Vietnam's history seem to have been in flux, for although he criticized the Provisional Government as a "party [government]," he could not bring himself to disparage its leader directly. Only two days later he cabled Kunming that Ho impressed him as a "sensible, well balanced, politically minded individual" whose demands were "few and simple." On the eve of Vietnam's Independence Day, Patti repeated Ho's "few and simple" requests of the outside world: to have "limited independence," to be granted "liberation from French rule," to "live as free people in [the] family of nations," to "deal directly with the outside world," and to be "permitted travel, particularly to America, particularly for education purposes and that America send technical experts to help them establish those few industries Indo-China is capable of exploiting." Patti added to his report that the next day the Vietnamese would be celebrating their Independence Day. "From what I have seen these people mean business," he reasoned; "the French will have to deal with them. For that matter we will all have to deal with them."[117]

On Sunday, September 2, Patti and his team joined thousands of Vietnamese in the streets of Hanoi waiting to see what would happen on this most auspicious day. Patti was undoubtedly impressed with the sights: In church vestments, Catholic priests who had that morning celebrated the Feast of Vietnamese Martyrs led their congregants in the streets; Buddhist monks and Cao Dai dignitaries came with their followers; colorfully dressed ethnic minorities and thousands of simply dressed peasants thronged the streets. Red flags fluttered on the slight breeze and highlighted the festooned city. Excitement was in the air, and people held animated conversations, speculating about what the day would bring. The best-trained, best-dressed, and best-equipped of the Viet Minh troops established an impressive presence in front of the flag-draped speakers' platform. Although they wore only mismatched uniforms and carried a wide variety of weapons, including spears and scimitars, the "people's militia" stood in formation. With the hot sun overhead, sharp whistle blasts pierced the air and brought the honor guard and military units to "rigid attention" as people appeared on the stage, all in Western suits and ties, save one. The crowd of roughly 400,000 people in Ba Dinh square waited to hear the man in a khaki tunic and sandals speak.[118] It was, Patti remembered, "a picturesque and awesome sight."[119]

Not all of the OSS agents in Hanoi agreed with Patti's assessment. Captain Lucien Conein had arrived in Hanoi only a few days after Patti, having just spent several months training French troops along the Indochina border.[120] After watching Giap's troops enter Hanoi after the battle of Thai Nguyen, Conein was clearly unimpressed. "If I'd had a battalion of troops," he said in an interview later, "I could have knocked off the whole goddamn bunch—not even a battalion, a *company* of troops." On September 2 he sat in the bar of the Hotel Métropole watching the crowd. Although he marveled at the spectacle, Conein also highlighted what he believed to be a complete lack of political or national awareness. "They had 'orchestra' leaders, you know, heading the cheering sections," he stated. "People didn't know what the hell they were doing. Something exciting was going on and everybody just came out to see what was happening. Somebody was going to make a big speech, but they didn't know who."[121]

Of course, Ho Chi Minh was the person they waited to hear. Although Conein discounted the notion that Ho was widely known, by September 2 many people had heard Ho's name used in conjunction with the idea of a "new" Vietnamese government. They did not know who he was personally, but the concept of a Vietnamese leader for a Vietnamese nation filled them with excitement and wonder. Even Bao Dai, having been invited to act as "supreme adviser" to the new government, reminisced that he had never even heard the name Ho Chi Minh before late August.[122]

Introduced as the "liberator and savior of the nation," Ho began speaking to the citizens, stopping after only one sentence to ask his "fellow countrymen" if they could hear him clearly. "It was a master stroke of oratory," Patti noted. "From that moment, the crowd hung on every word. . . . There was little doubt in our minds that he was reaching them."[123] Ho began his speech with words from the American Declaration of Independence, transitioned to the French Declaration of the Rights of Man and Citizen, and contrasted the values of both documents with the crimes perpetuated by the French colonialists. He disparaged the French for capitulating to the Japanese and praised the Viet Minh for their battle against the Japanese, determining that the Vietnamese had won their independence not as a grant from France but by helping defeat Japan. "Our people have broken the chains which for nearly a century have fettered them and have won independence for the Fatherland," Ho proclaimed. He then concluded with a statement reflecting his determination to prevail:

> For these reasons, we, members of the Provisional Government of the Democratic Republic of Viet Nam, solemnly declare to the world that Viet Nam has the right to be a free and independent country—and in fact it is so already. The entire Vietnamese people are determined to mobilize all their physical and mental strength, to sacrifice their lives and property in order to safeguard their independence and liberty.[124]

After the applause died down, each of the members of the new government took the oath of office. Vo Nguyen Giap then addressed the crowd on the practical matters of government, including a plan for elections and taxes. He implicitly appealed to the United States and China in particular for support of the fledging nation. "We have special affection for China and America," Giap told the crowd. The United States, he continued, "is a democratic country, which has no territorial ambitions, but has contributed particularly to the defeat of our enemy, Japanese fascism. Therefore we regard the U.S. as a good friend." As he prepared to conclude, Giap used a name that many peasants may not even have known but that his educated and international listeners certainly did: "Just as Mr. Roosevelt has said, oppression and cruelty have made us know what freedom means." Giap ended with the rousing statement:

Under the leadership of the Provisional Government and Chairman Ho
Chi Minh, our people will give all their wealth, their bones and blood to
build and beautify the fatherland, to make our beloved Vietnam bright,
and wealthy and powerful after so many years of misery and exhaustion.
Following the traditions of previous generations, our generation will
fight a final battle so that generations to follow will forever be able to
live in independence, freedom and happiness.[125]

After the starvation of the preceding year, nearly five years of Japanese occupation, and decades of colonial oppression, the masses present were stirred
by the words of Ho and Giap. Back at Tan Trao, Tran Thi Minh Chau "gathered people in the areas together" to listen to the Declaration of Independence. He recalled the villagers' excitement as they heard the Independence
Day speeches over a radio left by the Americans. Reportedly, they immediately recognized the voice of Ho Chi Minh, although they did not yet know
him by that name. "When people first heard his voice on the radio they cried
out 'Oh, this is the old man!'" "We explained to them," reminisced Tran Thi
Minh Chau, "that this was the voice of the President Ho Chi Minh and the
local people said 'No, no way! It must be the voice of the old man!'"[126]

In the days that followed, many more Vietnamese read, or heard about, the
text of their speeches and felt the rumblings of nationalistic pride. Future journalist and North Vietnamese Army colonel Bui Tin recalled his respect for Ho,
his prompt enlistment in the "first military class to be trained in Hanoi," and
his pride at being chosen to "stand guard with an American carbine at Bac Bo
Phu, the mansion where Ho worked."[127] Even those mandarins, such as
Duong Thieu Chi, who had grave reservations about the political underpin-
nings of the Viet Minh were proud of their compatriots. In her family history
Duong Van Mai Elliott wrote that numerous members of her "bourgeois" family, swept up in the excitement and promise of the August Revolution, began
working with the Viet Minh. She maintained, however, that Ho's use of the
American Declaration of Independence was lost on most of the Vietnamese
present in Ba Dinh Square. It was, she believed, not even intended for them.
Elliott concluded that the famous sentences were to "flatter the OSS delegation
in attendance and, through them, perhaps win support from the United
States."[128]

In fact, for many in the crowd on September 2, American support
seemed evident: Although not on the stage, OSS officials were present at
the ceremony, and two American P-38 Lightnings "swooped down low
over the crowd"—an event that Marr described as "immediately declared

One of the radios left by the OSS with the Viet Minh—similar to the one used by Nguyen Kim Hung and the local villagers to listen to Ho Chi Minh's Independence Day speech—is now on display at the Hanoi Vietnam Military History Museum. *Collection of the author.*

and believed by the people to represent a coordinated U.S. salute to the fledgling Vietnamese government."[129] The pilots, however, would have known nothing about Vietnam's Independence Day and were most probably conducting simple observations.

As the ceremonies concluded, Patti and the men with him slowly made their way through the crowd to the American headquarters at the Maison Gautier. In order to avoid any confrontations that might take place between the "jubilant Vietnamese" and the "disconsolate French," Patti invited the Americans in Hanoi to join his OSS team for a "quiet celebration of a Vietnamese 'Fourth of July' without fireworks." The crowd at OSS headquarters was substantial, since by September 2 the ranks of Americans in Hanoi had swollen considerably. An AGAS team consisting of six officers and enlisted men had entered the city a few days earlier. Additionally, Colonel Stephen Nordlinger, commander of the Civil Affairs, a military group known as G-5, had also arrived on a mission to care for Allied POWs[130]

U.S. soldiers shown raising the American flag over the Citadel in Hanoi as French liaison officers look on, September 1945. *National Archives and Records Administration.*

and gather information on Japanese war crimes. Including Patti's thirty OSS men, there were now fifty-nine Americans in Hanoi.[131]

The arrival of the additional Americans, especially Nordlinger, made Patti's life more difficult. Patti described Nordlinger, who was fluent in French, as a "World War I Francophile" who had too little to do in Hanoi and who "became an easy target of French pressure to release French POWs from the Citadel." It was, in fact, part of Nordlinger's job to "effect the release, rehabilitation, and eventual return to their homelands of French Foreign Legion prisoners of war," including the 5,000 prisoners confined at the Citadel. Because of his work with the French and his later efforts to aid Sainteny, Nordlinger became one of the few Americans in Vietnam that the much-aggrieved Jean Sainteny had anything good to say about.[132] Although Patti briefed Nordlinger on the complexities of the situation, the French, according to Patti, "exploited" his sympathy for them. Soon Nordlinger appeared to have become "antagonistic" toward the OSS mission and "a third element in troublemaking." Furthermore, Patti recalled, Nordlinger and his group "took umbrage at the restrictions I imposed on their pro-French anti–Viet Minh activities and, for the next months while I was in charge of the OSS mission, their well-intentioned but disruptive tactics were the source of many unpleasant exchanges between Hanoi and Kunming."[133]

Later in the month, General Philip E. Gallagher, chief of the U.S. Military Advisory and Assistance Group (USMAAG) working directly with Lu Han, echoed Patti's complaint. Writing to General Robert McClure, chief of staff for the China theater, Gallagher grumbled that Nordlinger had "extended his effort beyond that of merely helping the prisoners of war, in that he was carrying the torch wholly and completely for all the French in the area."[134] Nordlinger, however, avowed that he maintained complete neutrality while in Vietnam. In his own defense, Nordlinger explained that the French would never "have gone to Major [sic] Patti of the OSS since he was outspokenly anti-French politically," hence, they came to him because he was "sympathetic to their plight." There is no doubt that Nordlinger and his group provided considerable aid and comfort to the French sick and wounded, but that humanitarian work did not prevent him from investigating the political positions of the prisoners. As part of his reports, Nordlinger listed the names and occupations of those he looked after *and also* classified them—"Pro-Pétain and Germany," "Pro-Allies," "Opportunists," and so on—in accordance with his investigation on collaborators.[135]

As additional evidence of his neutrality, Nordlinger cited the "particularly close friendship" that he developed with Ho Chi Minh as the G-5 representative working to restore French medical supervision of the hospitals that had been taken over by the Viet Minh during the first days of the revolution.[136] Indeed, Ho Chi Minh also provided Nordlinger's group with their quarters and headquarters, as well as a staff of servants. Nordlinger recalled the "many cordial conversations on military and political matters" between himself and Ho Chi Minh and Ho's "eloquent pleas for American understanding of his position." In addition, "at Ho's request" Nordlinger "participated with him in various civic events for the care of the poor and undernourished" and requested and received "shipments of rice from the U.S. and elsewhere to feed his people in the countryside."[137] Although a lack of adequate food was clearly still a serious problem in northern Vietnam, Ho continued to master the moment: He managed to bring food to some of the hungry *and* to be seen with yet another powerful American "ally."

Similarly, Patti's team had also been moved by the plight of the hungry on Hanoi's streets. "We saw hundreds of children like that of all ages[;] it was almost like we saw the Holocaust," recalled Ray Grelecki. "So, [on] our own authority [we] cabled to our headquarters, because we had the aircraft, we had the food, we had the medical supplies and we organized that and brought in plane load after plane load of not only this but medical people."[138] Although often working toward similar goals and associating with and seemingly aiding Ho Chi Minh and the Viet Minh, Patti and Nordlinger continually questioned and commented on each other's neutrality. Yet the leader of the G-5 delegation was hardly the only American in Hanoi to comment on Archimedes Patti's reputation. Some of his harshest critics came from within the ranks of the OSS.

OSS officer Lucien Conein also exchanged mutual recriminations with Patti. Although Patti initially found Conein "trustworthy and not entirely in accord with French politics regarding Indochina,"[139] their relationship ended on a sour note with Conein stating point-blank, "I didn't like Patti. He was an arrogant Guinea [a disparaging term for those of Italian ancestry]. You'd never get the truth out of him."[140]

By September 1945, Conein, like Nordlinger, did sympathize with the French and was seemingly engaged in activities deemed undeniably pro-French. Evidently fearing that the French "civilian population in Hanoi might soon be slaughtered by the Viet Minh," Conein "embarked on a one-man crusade to rescue high French officials from both Japanese and Viet Minh retribution."[141] Nordlinger intervened to obtain the release of Sainteny after he was "seized by an angry crowd for flying the French tri-color in the front of his car."[142] Also reminiscent of Nordlinger, Conein met frequently with high-ranking members of the Viet Minh government, in his case, with Giap. "You didn't really *talk* to Giap. He talked to you," Conein remembered. "He had piercing eyes and you *knew* he was sincere; he *believed* in what he was saying. . . . He was really fantastic and personable. I liked him." Although his behavior indicated a different bias, Conein was, for the most part, in the same position as Patti. He was approached by all sides and was asked for answers at a time when he had no real answers to give. "All I wanted to do was get the hell out of there. The war's over. I wanted to go home. Yet Ho and Giap asked me to come see them. They were *very* interested in Americans and what Americans thought and what they would do for them. How the hell did I know what they would do for them? They wanted to hang all colonialists, that sort of thing."[143]

But it was not criticism from OSS men in the field that caused Patti the most trouble in September. Sainteny's mounting disgust and frustration with Patti had resulted in numerous wires to Kunming, Chungking, and

Calcutta complaining about his behavior.[144] In response Chungking wired
Patti's immediate superiors in Kunming to clarify the role of the OSS in
Hanoi, including a report "covering all personnel in Indo-China, their location, and what progress has been made towards evacuating them." Anxious
to settle worries in Chungking, Heppner instructed Patti to evaluate his activities carefully, stating flatly: "You will not rpt [repeat] not act as media-
tor, go between or arranger of meetings between French, Annamites or Chinese. Confine yourself to POW work and such other special things as are
directed by CCC or this Hqtrs."[145]

But Patti's mission included a wide range of possible duties grouped
under "special things." He maintained that his task to gather intelligence
necessitated his interaction with a variety of personalities, including members of the Viet Minh. His appraisal of the situation prior to and on Independence Day had only further irritated those inclined to want the return of Indochina to French "order." After watching the activities of Independence
Day and listening to a recent radio speech by General Jacques Leclerc declaring that there would be "no period of transition between the Japanese
surrender and the beginning of the French civil administration," Patti relayed his version of the situation to headquarters:

> Speech of General Leclerc over Radio Delhi has created unhealthy step
> among Annamese as well as French. From French point of view it has
> given them new spirit and hope that French forces will soon enter Indo-
> China and punish "these rebels." From Annamese point of view has
> caused apprehension creating spirit of preparation to fight to end in
> order to keep out the "foreigner." Tension once again high and slightest
> show of French belligerency certain [to] touch off powder keg which is
> now Indo-China.[146]

As time would tell, Patti's summation of the situation was basically accurate.
However, at that time, many at OSS headquarters were beginning to seriously question Patti's neutrality.[147] On September 4, he returned to Kunming to "give a report to headquarters." Patti recalled that the French were
delighted at his apparent recall, leaving the Americans in Hanoi under the
command of the more amenable Colonel Nordlinger.[148] OSS personnel soon
found themselves acting as armed guards for Nordlinger as he began moving
French prisoners from the Citadel to the hospital.

While Patti was in Kunming, gossip regarding his activities quickly
came to the forefront. Captain McKay of AGAS interrogated Patti's second,

Captain Grelecki, about the "real" OSS mission, adding that he had heard that Patti "even had a firing squad for necessary execution" of those he found guilty of war crimes. Grelecki repeated the official nature of Patti's mission again, but finally added "because of the implications made upon Capt. Patti, nothing further [should] be said, for any action taken by Capt. Patti may have been covered by instructions, and may be justified and warranted by reasons which he himself knew, and furthermore that Capt. Patti ought to be present to clarify any misunderstandings."[149] In Kunming Patti presented his own version of activities between his arrival on August 22 and September 5, adding that he had "no inkling of any friction whatsoever" between his office and the other Americans in Hanoi.[150]

Patti had little trouble defending his actions to his superiors or explaining Sainteny's interpretation of them. He had been recalled not for punishment but for further clarification of his operations and of U.S. policy toward Indochina. In fact, advised of the gossip among OSS, G-5, and AGAS personnel in Hanoi, Helliwell sent a clarifying message, noting in particular that the OSS was "charged with other missions by higher authority and Nordlinger will not concern himself in any way with these activities. . . . Capt. Patti returns soonest briefed in detail as to above matters and will discuss at length with Nordlinger."[151]

During the course of his discussions in Kunming, Patti recalled suggesting that the OSS be withdrawn from Vietnam—a proposal with which Heppner strongly disagreed. As Patti searched for guidance, Heppner summarized the problem: "The Indochina dilemma had always been American ambivalence with respect to French interests and American principles of democracy." When this ambivalence was combined with issues of personality—irascible Frenchmen bent on resuming their role as colonial masters and ingratiating Viet Minh constantly praising America and Americans—it is little wonder that the Viet Minh often found a receptive audience with members of the OSS. As he prepared to leave the conference, Patti, like most Americans on the ground in Vietnam, still had no clear idea of what American policy was. He was, however, conscious of his ability to give Ho "moral support, unofficially and discreetly, but nothing substantive."[152]

On September 9 Patti returned to Hanoi to resume command of the OSS mission. Over the next few days he would encounter a number of new challenges. The most serious of the issues facing the city of Hanoi was the arrival of Lu Han's troops to accept the Japanese surrender. Although the advance staff had arrived six days earlier, Hanoi was not prepared for Lu Han's "hordes." Many of the soldiers were poorly trained and loosely disciplined, and they descended on the city taking over homes and shops, demanding food and support from the Vietnamese residents. The Vietnamese citizens, with their historic distaste for the Chinese, were dismayed at their arrival and plundering. Fearful of repercussions, however, they could do little but watch.

The Provisional Government was also frustrated. In their earlier pleas to the Allies to control the Chinese, the Viet Minh had stressed the recent famine and the probable devastation of the local economy should the Chinese depend solely on the Vietnamese for food. In an attempt to stress the significance of the problem, Ho, who had already provided Patti with vivid photographs of Vietnamese famine victims, warned Patti: "Famine is imminent and should Chinese depend on Indo Chinese for their subsistence during occupation period they will all starve plus creating situation where Annamese will be forced to wage war upon Chinese to protect his livelihood and family."[153]

Aside from complaining, there was little the Viet Minh could do. In fact, the probable ruin of the economy was the least of Viet Minh worries. There was every possibility that the Chinese would refuse to deal with the Viet Minh and would place their own Kuomintang protégés in power.[154] The Viet Minh already had cause for alarm. When passing through Lang Son on their way to Hanoi, the Chinese forces forcibly disarmed the Viet Minh police. Ho warned the Americans that "repetition of these acts of disarmament . . . will be misconstrued as hostile acts against the existing government and the people of Vietnam will surely react."[155] As Patti watched the Chinese troops settle in, he received disturbing news about one of his own OSS officers: Lieutenant Ettinger had been arrested by the Viet Minh.

Although certainly displeased, Patti was not altogether surprised to hear that Ettinger was in some sort of trouble. As early as July Patti was receiving warnings of Ettinger's pro-French sentiments. At the OSS Pakhoi radio base, the commanding officer, Lieutenant James Jordan, wrote Patti that Ettinger's performance was not "particularly satisfactory," stating that Patti should have chosen a "more level-headed, better balanced person," for the assignment. Jordon added that Ettinger, among other things, continually disparaged American equipment for its inferiority to that of the French. During June and July Ettinger worked with French naval patrols capturing "sampans loaded with goods for Jap traffic from FIC" and "investigating sampan traffic" in the area. All seemed to be well until early August, when Jordan's criticism of Ettinger took on new weight. On August 9 Ettinger disobeyed a direct order to remain at the OSS base at Pakhoi,[156] and without "revealing himself" as an American officer, he set sail, along with a French captain and crew, on a French vessel flying French and American flags.[157] However, the situation became much more serious when he was detained aboard the French patrol boat *Crayssac* on September 4.

The *Crayssac* was no stranger to the potential dangers of sailing the waters near Haiphong. In May the *Crayssac* and its sister ship the *Frezouls* had been captured by the Japanese. They had eventually been released, and between August 16 and 21 both ships were again routinely patrolling the waters around Haiphong.[158] Their presence, coming so soon on the heels of the Japanese surrender, caused a frenzy in the city. The proud display of the French flag encouraged the French residents to hurry to "the docks to give the crews a frantic welcome." Looking at the scenario from both the French and the Vietnamese perspectives, David Marr wrote: "Just as the French looked to the sea for salvation, the Vietnamese perceived a grave threat from it." Sensing the possibility of a clash between the French and the Vietnamese, and in line with their directive to maintain order, the Japanese commanded the French to move to a "secluded anchor." By August 19 the *Crayssac*, tired of waiting at anchor, was "steam[ing] up the Bamboo Canal in the direction of Hanoi" but was turned back by gunfire from the local Viet Minh cadres. The Japanese promptly seized the ship for the second time in four months, sending the crew to Hanoi under armed guard.[159]

When the *Crayssac* set out again, this time with Ettinger on board, he reported that he was accompanying the ship on a "parliamentary expedition to Vachay and Hongay." There, on August 24 and 25, they met with the local Japanese and Viet Minh authorities, who had "from August 21 on," David Marr discovered, "worked openly in Haiphong [Province] setting up an office, arranging production of flags, and contacting the Civil Guard, the police, and youth groups established by the Japanese."[160] When the French unit and Ettinger arrived, they were given fresh food and water and obtained permission from the Viet Minh to take "wounded or sick personnel to the French civilian hospital of Hongay for emergency treatment." This became necessary when, according to Ettinger, on September 3 local fishermen asked the French ships to help chase away pirates looting a village. While battling the pirates, the French suffered one casualty.[161] Based on the earlier agreement, the patrol boats headed back to Hongay.

Having traveled during the night, the *Crayssac* docked at 6:55 AM on September 4 at the pier closest to the hospital. Ettinger and the *Crayssac*'s French commander, Lieutenant Vilar, went to the Hongay police station, and by 8:00 AM they had met with and secured the approval of the local Viet Minh "delegate" to take the wounded Frenchman to the hospital. At nine, Ettinger and Vilar, having completed their mission, bade the Viet Minh representative goodbye and set sail again. As they left port, the *Tigre*, a large tug controlled by the Vietnamese, hailed the French ship, which "obediently hove to." Ettinger and Vilar were asked to come ashore to visit with the delegate again but, "suspicious of a trap," they refused. The two men and the Viet Minh argued and debated for several hours. During this time, reported Ettinger, three tugs closed in on the *Crayssac*, and armed Viet Minh boarded the ship. They searched everyone, including Ettinger, and "removed" the ship's Vietnamese crew and all of the weapons and ammunition on board as part of what he considered general "looting." Although Ettinger and Vilar tried to remain with the ship, by 2:15 PM "direct threats to our lives" had resulted in their surrender and incarceration at the Hotel des Mines. Although Ettinger claimed to be "on a mission for the Allies," neither he nor Vilar had "papers or orders to substantiate their claims." The Viet Minh informed the two men that they were now prisoners of war.[162]

The next morning Ettinger and Vilar demanded, without success, to see their crew and to return to their ship. At 2:00 PM, Ettinger recalled, he presented his "AGO card," dog tags, and "AGAS flags" to the recently arrived Viet Minh commander, named Binh. Binh, Ettinger added, "recognized my being an American officer and agree[d] with me that Hanoi authorities should settle the affair." Arrangements were made between Binh and Ettinger to leave for Hanoi, but continued disagreements over the whereabouts of the crew and the necessity of accounting for all of the equipment on board the French ships derailed the plans, and Ettinger was returned to his "prison." The following day, September 6, a Chinese "delegation" entered the hotel. Ettinger convinced the Chinese soldiers that he was American and smuggled a letter to one of them to take to American authorities "in exchange for six packages of cigarettes." Although this letter would eventually gain his release, Ettinger was imprisoned by the Viet Minh for seven days. Ettinger was understandably angry at his incarceration and considered the Viet Minh little better than bandits. He completely discounted Cadre Binh's argument that "*Crayssac* and *Frezouls* intended to attack Hongay, since the French are determined to take FIC back through violence."[163] Although the Viet Minh probably did not fear the French vessels that had sailed so boldly into port, their fear of an armed French return was certainly well founded.

AGAS officer Lieutenant Burley Fuselier received Ettinger's smuggled letter, and on September 10 he arrived at the Hotel des Mines carrying a letter from Wedemeyer designating him as the American in charge of prisoners of war. Upon his arrival, Fuselier officially claimed Ettinger as a prisoner of war and accepted the Viet Minh report on their version of events. The Viet Minh maintained that they had mistaken Ettinger "for a Frenchman," since he was aboard a French ship, was participating with a French crew, and carried no orders to the contrary. They cited as evidence the *Crayssac*'s seven log books and navigational records, which asserted that the ship "had always been used by the French" and seemed to dispute Vilar's claim that the ship was at the disposal of the Allies. Furthermore, the Viet Minh commander added, the ship sported the French tricolor, it did not fly the required white flag that was "exacted by the rules" for humanitarian purposes, and the flag on the radio antenna was "similar to the American flag but had no stars in the blue square." Additionally, when searching the ship the Viet Minh found a Japanese flag, which they declared "proved that the French on this boat have illegally used the flags of other countries to reach more easily their wicked aims."[164]

In the weeks after the Provisional Government's assumption of power, independent Viet Minh councils were not yet under Hanoi's control. Although in Hanoi Ho and Giap were making every effort to impress the Americans, they were "as much a prisoner of the thousands of revolutionary committees emerging around the country as the directing authority," wrote Marr. And "although members also identified enthusiastically with the new central government, and particularly with its preparations to meet foreign threats, each committee had its own agenda."[165] Thus, Hanoi's lack of absolute control combined with the excitement of liberation, long-simmering hostility toward the French, and, probably, real doubts as to Ettinger's nationality all contributed to his arrest. In his report on Ettinger's liberation, Fuselier added that the Viet Minh "seemed to be very embarrassed by the fact that they had imprisoned an American officer and tried many times to explain the fact that this officer was in the company of French navy personnel, that he had been mistaken for a Frenchman."[166] The French, Ettinger stated, had specifically asked him to go along so that his "presence would prevent incidents by certifying the humanitarian purpose of the mission." Ettinger admitted that an American flag "had been made for emergencies" and that it was flying on the "radio antenna" to "indicate [the] presence of U.S. personnel on board." He stated explicitly that he always wore American uniforms and claimed to be an American officer and that he "never stated, hinted, or behaved in a way which might have made it appear otherwise."[167] The Viet Minh immediately released Ettinger to Fuselier, and on Tuesday evening, September 11, they arrived in Hanoi.[168]

The news of Ettinger's capture had caused a flurry of wires among OSS personnel. Although aware of his capture, OSS headquarters was initially unaware of the exact circumstances. Some reports erroneously stated that the "American on board" had been "released with his arms" and that only Frenchmen were being detained. However, on September 10 Patti received news from Kunming that "Ettinger disobeying orders proceeded to Hongay with French and the Party was captured." In order to gain his release Jordan sent an agent with a large amount of Chinese currency to "buy Ettinger."[169] Meanwhile, Lieutenant Commander Carleton Swift, who had joined Patti's Kunming staff in May, wired Patti that he should "attempt [to] corral Ettinger thru Viet Minh and return him [to Kunming] thru Hanoi." Although Ettinger felt misunderstood, OSS headquarters advised that their "previous directives [to him were] clearly and thoroughly understood. Ettinger's mission was to collect radios and receipts and keep out of trouble."[170]

Ettinger's meeting with Patti pitted two men in an argument neither could clearly win. Ettinger maintained that he had not disobeyed orders and had maintained his neutrality. Patti, so often accused of violating strict neutrality with his bias against the French, maintained that Ettinger had violated both American neutrality and direct orders; he placed Ettinger under house arrest and ordered him to refrain from communication with "French or even U.S. personnel" until after Patti had seen Colonel Helliwell. While awaiting transport to Kunming, Ettinger filed a wire directly to Kunming: "Coming back first plane with report. Did not disobey orders. Acted for the best and will prove it."[171] Ettinger was scheduled to fly out on September 16; until that time, Patti placed Ettinger in the custody of the commanders of the recently arrived Deer Team, Major Thomas and Lieutenant Défourneaux.[172]

The members of the Deer Team were delighted to finally reach Hanoi on September 9. Thomas, more than any of the others, deeply regretted being left behind in Thai Nguyen and missing the festivities surrounding Vietnam's Independence Day. He had maintained some contact with Giap, however. In late August Giap wrote a brief, hopeful letter to Thomas telling him that the Vietnamese-American Force had arrived in Hanoi.[173] He also sent Thomas "two bottles of champagne and a bottle of Scotch-Haigs" to help with the independence "celebrations" in Thai Nguyen. Once Thomas arrived in Hanoi, he was soon reunited with both Giap and Ho. Thomas was impressed by his first glimpse of the city. Viewing the flags "flying from almost every house" and the multilingual patriotic banners, Thomas claimed: "It was an extremely festive city for everyone except the French."[174]

The Deer Team promptly settled into a house the Viet Minh "had taken over" for them and "were able to visit Hanoi as tourists." "We were treated very well," remembered Henry Prunier of the week he spent there.[175] Some members of the Deer Team worked with the men they had trained in Tan Trao. Paul Hoagland went with Trieu Duc Quang to "some of the main hospitals in Hanoi like Bac Main, St. Paul hospitals to check the stock of medicine there for distribution to different units."[176] For most of the men, the time passed quickly. On September 15, the night before his departure for Kunming, Thomas was invited to a private dinner with Ho and Giap. Years later Thomas admitted that he remembered very little of that evening. However, one thing clearly stood out in his mind. "I asked Ho point-blank if he was a Communist. He told me, 'Yes. But we can still be friends, can't we?'"[177]

Thomas's interaction with the leaders of the Viet Minh in Hanoi reflected a change in Captain Patti's views. Thomas had been accused of disobeying orders for proceeding without authorization with the Viet Minh to Thai Nguyen. And in late August Patti had ordered Thomas to stay in Thai Nguyen because he thought Thomas was "not neutral," or at the very least would not be perceived as neutral because of his close association with the Viet Minh.[178] Reflecting on the situation, Thomas conceded years later, "of course we were supposed to be neutral at that point, but I guess I wasn't neutral."[179] Nonetheless, in mid-September 1945 Thomas was permitted to dine and visit freely with both Ho and Giap while Ettinger, against whom similar yet significantly different charges had been made, sat under house arrest. Evidently, whether the charges were of being too pro–Viet Minh or too pro-French mattered a great deal to Patti. Soon after Thomas's departure, the rest of the Deer Team also left Vietnam.

As the Deer Team left the city, another American entered the picture. On September 16, General Philip Gallagher arrived in Hanoi. Gallagher, chief of the USMAAG, was the American adviser attached to Lu Han's staff. Tasked with aiding in the disarmament and repatriation of Japanese troops in northern Indochina, Gallagher's role would soon become as controversial as that of Captain Patti. Warned by Patti to be "alert to French machinations," Gallagher delayed meeting with the French, preferring to speak directly with General Alessandri when he arrived rather than dealing with Sainteny,[180] whom Patti pointed out was still "without portfolio of any sort or even a basic political directive from Paris." Instead, on September 22 Gallagher, accompanied by Patti, met with Ho Chi Minh. Ho, Patti recalled, wanted to ask for American "advice" on a French proposal for a meeting between Ho and "a French representative in India." Ho had already consulted with Lu Han on the matter because the Chinese were the only ones in a position to provide his air transport to India. Although Lu Han made no immediate promises, he indicated that he might be able to arrange something in the next two weeks.[181]

Lu Han's relations with the Vietnamese Provisional Government were proving to be much friendlier than perhaps either side had anticipated. For although Lu Han, who had arrived in Hanoi on September 14 and met with Ho for the first time two days later, made numerous demands on the shaky Vietnamese economy, the demands were not an attempt to bring about the Provisional Government's collapse. Historian Peter Worthing concluded that "rather than seeking profit, the Chinese occupation command was trying to fund its mission, maintain order, and avoid the kind of violence and bloodshed that took place in the southern occupation zone."[182] Perhaps even more significant, in dealing with Ho Chi Minh directly, Lu Han gave de facto recognition to the very group Chungking had ordered him to "pay no attention to." Furthermore, Lu Han also sold a substantial stock of arms—American, French, and Japanese—to the Viet Minh.

Funds for this purchase were acquired in part during "Gold Week" which began on September 16. In his address to the people "On the Occasion of the 'Gold Week,'" Ho Chi Minh reminded the citizens that the new government was "badly in need of donations from the people, mainly from well-to-do families" to "devote to our most pressing and important task at present, which is national defense."[183] "Every Vietnamese felt patriotic, and wanted to do, or offer something," boasted Vu Dinh Huynh. "It's hard to say who gave the most. Those that had nothing but their wedding bands gave them up during 'Gold Week.'"[184] Historian Bernard Fall deduced that:

> The Chinese Nationalists, through their greed and shortsightedness, saw to it that the Communist take-over would be as painless and thorough as possible. When the Viet Minh held a "gold week," during which residents of North Viet-Nam were compelled to give their gold for the "purchase" of weapons from the Chinese, it was thoroughly successful and provided the nascent "Viet-Nam People's Army" (VPA) with 3,000 rifles, 50 automatic rifles, 600 submachine guns, and 100 mortars of American manufacture—plus the substantial French and Japanese stocks (31,000 rifles, 700 automatic weapons, 36 artillery pieces, and 18 tanks) that the Chinese were supposed to have secured but did not.[185]

As a "final humiliation" to the French, the Chinese "hung up Vietminh flags with their own and even marched arm in arm along the Hanoi streets with Giap's guerrillas."[186] In a memorandum for the president, General Donovan noted Lu Han's divergent policy and his open advocacy of an end to colonial rule. Lu Han was "at odds with the Kuomintang" and was thus "satisfied to support the Viet Minh," Donovan wrote, adding that the Chinese general had "just given wide distribution to a circular stating that the Allied powers have no territorial ambitions and favor eventual independence for all peoples according to the Atlantic Charter."[187] As the American attached to Lu Han's staff, Gallagher also contributed to this tacit recognition of the Provisional Government as Vietnam's legitimate government.

From the moment he stepped off the plane from Kunming, Gallagher had received contradictory information about the Viet Minh. Whereas Patti warned him to be wary of the French, Colonel Nordlinger recommended that the Viet Minh be disarmed immediately so they could no longer "terrorize" French civilians. Lieutenant Colonel John C. Bane, Nordlinger's intelligence officer, further briefed Gallagher that the Viet Minh were not only communist but were also sponsored by the Japanese. Moreover, Bane warned the general, the Viet Minh possessed a "menacing attitude" and constituted "a threat to good order as long as they are armed." Perhaps hoping to convince Gallagher—who might in turn persuade Lu Han, who had already vetoed the proposal to disarm the government troops—Bane included in his analysis the belief that the Viet Minh "would not prove to be a formidable organization if they were disarmed and Americans and Chinese were to indicate displeasure at their communistic background." If this were accomplished, he hypothesized, "a more democratic organization would probably evolve under new leadership and with the same following." Bane did admit that the Viet Minh had "been very friendly and helpful toward Americans."[188]

In a letter to General Robert McClure written soon after his arrival, Gallagher reiterated some of the mixed messages he was receiving. While conceding that Ho was an "old revolutionist and a political prisoner many times, a product of Moscow, a communist," he ended his note to McClure "confidentially, I wish the Annamites could be given their independence, but of course, we have no voice in this matter."[189]

As Gallagher maneuvered among the multiplicity of opinions, he became frustrated with Patti as well as with Nordlinger. In his correspondence with McClure he grumbled:

Patti talks too much, and he is ingratiating to the Annamites, the French, and the Japs. He explains he does this to get all the information he wants. He has got a great deal of information, and is pretty much in the know about what is going on. . . . he loves to appear mysterious, and

Archimedes Patti, seated center, with Vo Nguyen Giap on his right, clearly enjoyed his near celebrity status in Hanoi. Although he acknowledged that Patti was "in the know," General Philip E. Gallagher feared that Patti was "trying to build up an empire and appear important" (letter from Gallagher in Hanoi to McClure, in Kunming, September 20, 1945, cited in Drachman, *United States Policy toward Vietnam, 1940–1945*, 157). *Archimedes L. Patti, Papers, Special Collections, University of Central Florida, Orlando.*

is an alarmist. He always gets me into the corner of a room and whispers into my ear. When I enter a room, I expect to see him come out from under a rug. . . . I don't think much of him personally, believe he is trying to build up an empire and appear important.[190]

Although Gallagher could not speak for the U.S. government, he was now the highest-ranking American military authority in Hanoi, and his actions and words commanded the attention of many. Like Patti, Gallagher seemed to believe that he was following the directive of the late President Franklin Roosevelt. According to Gallagher's personal papers, "guidance on U.S. policy available" to him at the time "was apparently based on the concept that Indochina would ultimately come under a United States' Trusteeship."[191] Gallagher, again like Patti, consistently maintained that he was strictly neutral in his dealings with all parties. Regardless of what he believed, his actions further alienated the French. French historian Bernard Fall criticized Gallagher, claiming that although Gallagher and his staff "acted as if the French did not exist," their behavior toward Sainteny "could be explained on the basis of orders from Washington." However, Fall concluded, "their personal attitude of callousness toward the Frenchmen . . . exacerbated matters needlessly."[192]

French frustrations with the situation mounted as the date for the official Japanese surrender ceremony drew near. On September 28, beneath the flags of the Allied nations—American, Chinese, British, and Russian—arrayed in the Governor-General's Palace, General Tsuchihashi signed the official surrender document before a small crowd of American military officers, Chinese officers and civilians, and a sprinkling of Vietnamese witnesses. Conspicuously absent from the ceremony were the flags and representatives of France or the Vietnamese Provisional Government, for neither was recognized by General Lu Han as official participants in the war. Although Lu Han had invited Ho Chi Minh and members of his cabinet, Vietnam was not yet recognized by anyone as an independent nation, and Ho had no official status; hence, he chose not to attend "for reasons of health." Although General Alessandri was invited, he too shunned the ceremony because Lu Han refused to fly the French flag or seat Alessandri in the official section.[193]

Gradually, and often indirectly, Gallagher too was becoming identified as anti-French and sympathetic to the Vietnamese cause. Sainteny charged Gallagher with being "openly hostile" to the French and with delaying the return of peace to the area. He saw Gallagher as representative of a group of Americans who believed they were rising up against France's colonial past in the name of "the infantile anti-colonialism that blinded them."[194]

Much to the delight of many Frenchmen in Hanoi, Captain Patti received orders to return to Kunming on September 29, the day following the surrender ceremony. Although the French may have rejoiced, the Viet Minh did not. Patti's experience in Hanoi had been pleasant overall. The Vietnamese citizens of the city tended to welcome him with open arms. As Bui Diem recalled, "in a city plastered with slogans and banners denouncing imperialism, Major Patti's jeep, flying its American flag, was constantly mobbed by people who simply wanted to see and touch the representative of the United States of America."[195] He had also become a frequent guest of Ho Chi Minh, in whose company Patti spent his final evening in Hanoi. Giap joined the two men initially to express his "personal appreciation" of the Americans with whom he had worked and to wish Patti bon voyage. Patti recalled being "somewhat moved" during this "rare moment" when Giap "allowed his inner feelings or emotions to show." Patti spent the rest of the evening talking with Ho, who now considered him "a very special friend with whom he could confide." Patti wrote of that last meeting:

> For the second time that evening I was moved by the personal regard shown me. Both Giap and Ho knew that at best they could only expect from me understanding and sympathy. At the same time I knew they were taking advantage of this last evening to put themselves and their cause in the best possible light. Still, they were isolated from the communist world, they were surrounded by self-interested powers, and the few Americans within their view were the only ones with whom there was a rapport. Americans were the ones who understood the difficulty of achieving and maintaining independence. It was really this intangible rapport that the French in Indochina hated, despised, and fought in every way they possibly could.[196]

Patti had warned headquarters early in the month that "trouble seems to be brewing, and may break out after the armistice has been signed in Indo-China."[197] When Lieutenant Commander Carleton Swift assumed Patti's role as Hanoi station chief on September 30, all remained quiet. On October 1 Archimedes Patti left Hanoi, and the OSS was "turned over to War and State."[198]

The American experience in Hanoi during the heady days of Vietnamese independence was far different from their experience in Saigon. The exhilaration that enveloped the southern city with the news of the Japanese surrender evolved into euphoria as the expectation of becoming an independent nation spread across the land. As in Hanoi, the city of Saigon celebrated. But unlike its sister city, the jubilant atmosphere in Saigon soon turned deadly. Neither the bloodshed in Saigon nor the relative ease with which the Viet Minh took control of Hanoi was inevitable, however. There was one group in a position to have stopped both the struggle for power in Hanoi and the violence in Saigon: the Japanese.

9

"Cochinchina Is Burning . . ."

The situation in Saigon initially mirrored the euphoria witnessed in Hanoi with the end of World War II and the promise of independence. The few southern Viet Minh delegates who were able to make the long and difficult journey to Tan Trao in mid-August barely had time to return to the south before the August Revolution reached that area as well. Although most Vietnamese peasants in the southern region wished for independence from the French and the Japanese just as fervently as did their northern compatriots, the Viet Minh organization was not as strong in that region. This was due in part to the fact that the Central Committee in Saigon had only partially recovered from the "almost total disarray" into which it had fallen after the French violently suppressed the revolutionary uprisings in the south in 1940.[1] In addition, the location of the Viet Minh headquarters in the mountains of the north made it logistically impossible for the Viet Minh to exert as much influence and control on the population hundreds of miles from their mountain hideout as they did on those in the Viet Bac. In her memoir, Nguyen Thi Dinh recalled that she was unable to make contact with the Viet Minh until 1944 when the Viet Minh movement "became strong" in the south.[2] Excitement at the possibilities, however, was clearly in the air for most southerners. The difficulty for the south came not from a lack of enthusiasm or commitment to national independence but from too many groups hoping to lead the revolution.

The head of the ICP southern Regional Committee, Tran Van Giau, who had escaped from a French prison and worked to rebuild the party in the south, rejoiced at the news of the Japanese capitulation. However, at the meetings of the Uprising Committee on August 15, 1945, and the Regional Committee on August 17, 1945, he found they had more questions than answers: Should they act immediately or wait for instructions from the north? What would the Japanese do if they did attempt to seize power? After hearing

Highway 1
Railroad
River
(8-19) Selected dates of insurrection
during August Revolution

Cochinchina
(Southern Vietnam)

Tourane (Da Nang)

Quang Ngai
(8-28)

Qui Nhon

Kon Tum
(8-25)

Van Ninh

(8-24)
Ban Me Thuot

Nha
Trang
(8-19)

Cam Ranh Bay

Dalat
(8-25)

An Phuoc

(8-25)
Tay Ninh

Thu Dau Mot
Bien Hoa
(8-25)

(8-25) Saigon

Mekong R.

Long Xuyen
(8-25)

My Tho
(8-24) Vung Tau

Ben Tre
(8-25)

Can Tho
(8-26) Vinh Long

Soc Trang

Ca Mau

Mekong Delta

maps©Josh Weitzel

of the successful takeover of Hanoi, the ICP held a meeting with the well-organized Vanguard Youth, hoping to bring as many of them as possible under the Viet Minh banner. They endeavored to do the same with the United National Front, made up of religious groups as well as secular nationalists, including the Trotskyites. As they labored to develop a working coalition, the ICP decided to try a limited "test" of the Japanese attitude by taking control of Tan An Province on August 22 before making any attempt on Saigon. In Tan An, as in the northern region, the Japanese did not oppose the acts of the Viet Minh.[3] Had the Japanese forces chosen to, they could easily have crushed the Vietnamese revolutionaries and the August Revolution in the south would have stopped then and there. The Japanese role would become even more complex in the month to follow.

For the moment, however, the ICP laid plans for the capture of Saigon with guarded optimism that the Japanese would not interfere if not directly provoked. At 6:00 PM on August 24, Tran Van Giau spoke at a public meeting to announce the beginning of the revolution, and units of the Vanguard Youth began taking over important public buildings such as the treasury, the power plant, and local police stations. They did not attempt to enter buildings guarded by Japanese troops, thus leaving the airport, the Bank of Indochina, military posts, and the Governor-General's Palace under Japanese control.

Early the next morning "several hundred thousand peasants entered Saigon." By 9:00 AM, when "formal proceedings" celebrating the revolution began, "there may have been half a million rural and urban citizens swamping the downtown streets of Saigon, perhaps one-third of them armed with bamboo spears, pitchforks, machetes, and shotguns."[4] The celebration was much like the earlier one in Hanoi: Viet Minh flags waved in the breeze, people sang patriotic songs and chanted "Long Live Independent Vietnam," and the throngs of people paraded peacefully down the streets of the city. In the outlying areas smaller uprisings also took place. Some were led by small units of Viet Minh adherents, others by large groups of the people. Nguyen Thi Dinh remembered her role: "During the tumultuous uprising to seize Ben Tre province town, I was designated to carry the flag and leading [sic] thousands of people armed with knives, sticks, flags, bright red banners and placards, pouring into the province town. The mass of people marched at a brisk pace for tens of kilometers without stopping to rest, but felt neither tired nor hungry."[5]

Both the rural and urban scenes seemed to echo those in the north. Yet there were critical differences. In the north, Ho Chi Minh worried about the

Chinese-sponsored Nationalist organization, but he was already tacitly recognized by the Americans as the man in charge. Unfortunately for the southerners, there were no Allied representatives in Saigon to witness their triumph or its peaceful nature. And their alliance with the multiple groups contending for power was short-lived. By the time the Allies arrived, there would be bloodshed in Saigon.

Even prior to the Japanese surrender and the uprisings in the south, both the British and the Americans had been preparing contingents to enter Saigon. The British mission seemed clear: acceptance of the surrender of the Japanese in the south and repatriation of the enemy. The American mission was more ambiguous: the care and repatriation of the few American prisoners of war, the protection of the scant American property, and oversight of American "interests." In charge of these tasks was Detachment 404, also referred to as Operation EMBANKMENT, led by Lieutenant Colonel Peter Dewey.[6]

Since early August the OSS had been working on plans for the penetration of Saigon, including a plan to liaise with an invading French expeditionary force of two airborne divisions rumored to be in Madagascar preparing to be flown into French Indochina.[7] Except for contacting French representatives in case the rumor proved true, Dewey prepared for a purely American mission. By August 14 he had outlined eight intelligence objectives for Indochina, including the procurement of political and economic information, and requested thirteen personnel for the operation.[8] On August 15 the R&A branch further elaborated on EMBANKMENT's objectives, posing their own questions for Dewey's attention. The questions ranged from the status of ethnic groups and the Japanese attitude toward the Cao Dai to more-pointed questions regarding Indochina's "Status within the French Empire." Specifically, R&A asked Dewey to examine to what extent Vietnam would be given autonomy under what appeared to be the current French policy and whether or not there would be equal partnership in the "counsels of the Empire" as had been promised. Furthermore, they instructed Dewey to ascertain what "forces" would determine the Indochinese "attitude" in the months to come.[9] At least some in the OSS clearly believed, even after the ceasefire, that agents of Detachment 404 operating in Indochina would be focusing on the French and perhaps working directly with them.

Dewey seemed an excellent choice to head Detachment 404. The dashing young officer received his formative education in Switzerland and graduated from Yale with a double major in French language and history. Following his graduation he served as a secretary to Ambassador H. R. Wilson in Berlin and later worked in Paris for the *Chicago Daily News.* When the Germans attacked France, he served with the Polish Military Ambulance Corps, receiving two decorations for his service. In the summer of 1941 he was commissioned by the Office of the Coordinator of Inter-American Affairs to prepare a report summarizing French influences in Latin America, part of which he presented to General de Gaulle and other members of the Free French government in London. Dewey acted as a courier on his return to Latin America, delivering letters from de Gaulle's government-in-exile to the Free French in Latin and Central America. In July 1942 he joined the U.S. Army as a second lieutenant in the Air Corps and was sent to North Africa, where, between October 1942 and May 1943, he completed "eight or more intelligence missions," was decorated with the French Croix de Guerre, and became "well acquainted with many high ranking [French] persons."[10] Dewey joined the OSS in July 1943.[11] His most important operation with the OSS before being sent to French Indochina was Mission Etoile, a covert assignment on which Dewey led a team into southern France in August 1944. Etoile "sent back valuable intelligence on the eve of the Allied landing on the Riviera, then worked with the local resistance forces in capturing 400 Nazi prisoners and destroying three enemy tanks."[12] In July 1945 Dewey was chosen to head Operation EMBANKMENT.

The OSS "Basic Plan for Operation Embankment," warned: "Since U.S. policy towards Indo-China is suspected by the French of being contrary to the expressed policy of complete economic subjugation to France of F.I.C., or the *status quo anti-bellum* [*sic*], American observers will be regarded with suspicion."[13] Given the likelihood of French mistrust, Peter Dewey was an excellent choice of leaders: He spoke French fluently, had both lived and worked in France, had fought for France's freedom against the German onslaught, and had dealt with numerous members of the Free French government and military. In addition, he was overtly sympathetic to the Free French cause. In 1944 he wrote: "My personal feelings with respect to the French have always been that Americans can and must understand them. Our national security depends on an alliance resulting from an awareness of the facts."[14] Although Dewey prepared his team to arrive in Saigon the first week in September, he would not be the first American to enter the city.

On September 1, Lieutenant Emile R. Counasse of the OSS led the first contingent of EMBANKMENT into Saigon to negotiate with the Japanese command for the "release and exfiltration of the American prisoners of war and civilian internees." When they left Rangoon, his team consisted of three Americans, Captain Woolington and Sergeants Nardella and Hejna, and Paul, a Thai radio operator. At the refueling stop in Bangkok, Counasse's

team was joined by Captain Fitzsimmons, an ex-POW, and Major Pierce of
the British Army. While the Americans and Paul worked well together from
the start, problems soon developed between Counasse and the British officer.
Counasse reported:

> Upon arrival at Saigon Major Pierce started dictating the procedure to be
> followed to me. I informed him that I would be happy to work with him
> but would not work for him. He then severed himself from our group.
> Except for a glimpse of him a few days later, the last I saw of Major Pierce
> was when he was making a speech in front of the hotel to the French
> people after our arrival. Although he spoke very good French, Major
> Pierce made his speech to the glory of the British Empire in English.[15]

Thus, difficulties between the OSS and the British arose early on, but not
with Peter Dewey as would later be claimed. Although inter-Allied relations
were tense, the American mission was pleasantly surprised by their first interactions with the defeated enemy. The Japanese greeted the group at the
airport with "sticky courtesy" and proceeded to attend to all American requests with relatively little prodding.[16] From the airport the Americans were
taken to their new "headquarters" at the Continental Hotel, where they were
greeted "by what seemed to us to be half of the white population of Saigon"
who regarded the Americans as "manna from Heaven."[17]

While Hejna, Nardella, and Paul proceeded to set up their radio station,
Counasse, Fitzsimmons, and Woolington left for the POW camp, where they
found the prisoners to be in excellent spirits and reasonably good health. Although the bulk of Counasse's team's work over the next five days would
concentrate on preparing for and repatriating the prisoners, they could not
ignore the political situation around them.[18] Counasse and Nardella sent
back frequent reports to Dewey in Rangoon to brief him on the situation in
which he would soon find himself. On September 2, after first visiting the
POW camp, Counasse returned to the hotel to find the "Annamite population of Saigon in a huge demonstration":

> We were told there were between 30,000 and 40,000 people
> participating, and this was easy to believe after having seen them. They
> were all armed after a fashion. The leaders carried Japanese swords and
> Japanese pistols. A few others were armed with old flintlock shotguns,
> some Japanese rifles and a miscellaneous collection of old weapons. The
> majority of them had long bamboo poles sharpened on one end. They

had started marching about the middle of the morning, and continued throughout the day. There were banners stretched across the street in all parts of the city with slogans written in French, Annamese and English. Those in French and English had such sayings as: "Down with French Communism. Down with French Fascism. Down with French Nazism. Give us Liberty or Death. Independence or Death. Welcome to the Allied Legation. Welcome to the Deliverers." By the middle of the afternoon the demonstration was at its height but still very orderly.[19]

Although things seemed "orderly," the Vietnamese thoroughly irritated Counasse when they stopped him at gunpoint on his way back to the hotel. Aggravated, Counasse "drew his .32 pistol," and the guard who had stopped him immediately dropped his rifle and ran. Counasse commented that "had somebody been there with a stopwatch, he [the Vietnamese guard] would have won the 100 yard record." As Counasse continued to make his way toward the Continental, five more guards drew weapons; four dropped their rifles and ran, the fifth stood firm. However, "after about ten minutes [of] arguing," Counasse "convinced him that we were Americans and neutrals, [and] therefore had a right to pass where we wished."[20]

At the hotel things seemed more serious: The demonstration had turned into "a violent mob scene" and "several hundred"[21] French civilians had taken refuge in the hotel. Captain Fitzsimmons rushed to tell Counasse of the rumor that "the Annamites had declared their intention to kill every white man in Saigon that night, their next objective being the hotel." Counasse demanded protection from the Japanese, who immediately responded that they would place a guard outside each of the Americans' rooms but would not protect the hotel in general. Evidently, the Japanese considered themselves responsible only for the protection of Allied—American and British—personnel and property and not for the protection of the French citizens of Saigon. Thus, Counasse decided to "buy" the hotel and its annexes from the owner, who was delighted to sell. The Continental became American property, and the Japanese promptly obeyed Counasse's order to provide full protection. Counasse's French sources convinced him that his action and the subsequent protection provided by the Japanese prevented the French refugees from being "massacred." Counasse concluded that his acquisition of the hotel and the use of Japanese guards had "stopped" the Vietnamese "at their objective, the Continental Palace Hotel." That, in addition to the 1,000 Japanese who patrolled the streets of Saigon at Counasse's request, caused the "Annamites" to "quietly disappear" about 11:00 PM.[22]

When the streets had quieted down, Woolington, Hejna, and Fitzsimmons escorted ten French women home to "get their babies." En route, they were informed that two Americans were being held at the local police station by the Vietnamese. Although suspicious of the information, they proceeded to the jail to see for themselves. On the pretext that Americans might be held inside, the group gained admission and the right to inspect the cells. Although there were clearly no Americans there, Woolington, "being a doctor[,] was highly incensed at the condition of the [French] people and the way they were kept," and he demanded an explanation. Although the Vietnamese jailor tried to explain that the Vietnamese struggle for independence was similar to the American fight for independence, Woolington was not impressed. He lectured the man on prisoner protocol and wielded the mighty threat of Allied displeasure.

> Dr. Woolington answered that it was not democratic to beat helpless women and children, that we settle our differences peaceably, and that if the French women and children were not released immediately he would send word to the Americans, British, Russian and Chinese governments. He felt sure that troops of the United Nations would intervene. If the Annamites expected recognition as a republic they would have to amend their ways considerably. The jailor then stated that he wished to conform to U.S. standards, that he would release the prisoners immediately.[23]

The Americans left the jail with approximately 200 French women and children who were quartered at the Continental for the night. The male prisoners were released the next morning.

Thus far, both Counasse and Woolington had found that flourishing their status as American soldiers produced quick results with the Vietnamese. However, on September 3 confusion over Counasse's identity produced a situation that significantly altered his views of the situation. Having been (wrongly) informed by the Italian consul that ten American civilians were interned at My Tho, a town approximately forty-five miles from Saigon, Counasse and a small party, including two French women, set out.[24] A little over ten miles outside the city the road was barricaded and "about 100 to 150 Annamites armed with old flintlocks, shotguns and sharpened bamboo poles surrounded the barricade." Counasse and the men got out of the jeeps to confront the situation and were promptly disarmed, searched, tied with hands behind their backs, and deprived of their gold. Counasse reported:

The Annamites were a mob of savage barbarians, screaming at the top of their lungs. After we had been all tied up their leader approached us to find out who we were. I told him to look in my wallet for my AGO card, but it did no good as it was written in English and they couldn't read English. After much talking and arguing, finally the Italian Consul made them understand that they should look in one of his pockets for a pass explaining his identity . . . We were finally released after having been held prisoner for about two hours. I had been jabbed in my right leg with a sharp bamboo pole. They gave us what they thought was an apology, simply stating that it was their business and their patriotic duty to stop everyone and take prisoner or kill all Frenchmen who passed that point in the road.[25]

Counasse's group set out once again for My Tho, but they were stopped twice more. At each of the subsequent "stops" they had no trouble proving their identity and were neither abused nor detained for more than a few minutes. Nevertheless, given the setting sun, Counasse decided that they should return to Saigon and try to reach My Tho on another day. In his mission report Counasse wrote: "My feeling when I was a prisoner was: 'This can't happen to me. The war is over.'"[26]

Counasse's feelings were typical of those of other Americans treated with anything other than the deepest respect and reverence by the Vietnamese. By and large, as victors against two formidable enemies—the Germans and the Japanese—American soldiers expected to be treated as such in all instances. This expectation would later result in injury to one man of Detachment 404 and would prove fatal to another. Nevertheless, over the next few days Counasse and his team continued preparations for the evacuation of the POWs, mostly without incident. Although team reports were mostly positive about the Japanese role in preparing for the POWs' departure, Hejna concluded that the Japanese were to blame for the uprisings in Saigon. The demonstrations of September 2 were "staged" to "embarrass us and cause us to lose face in the eyes of the Japanese and Annamese," he wrote, adding, "I believe the Japanese are delighted with the state of affairs."[27] Other team members praised the Japanese attitude but continued to point out difficulties with the Vietnamese "drug-store revolution," although relations with the Vietnamese themselves were reported as "splendid."[28] Sergeant Nardella wrote: "Their [the Vietnamese] control at present is complete and it seems very incongruous that they should continue to loot and molest the French population after they have actually gained what they wanted in the first place."[29]

In the few days they were in Saigon, Detachment 404 attempted to compile for Dewey a list of the Vietnamese groups involved in the uprisings. Those categorized as the four major participants were the "Social Democrats who had formed the Vietminh," the Nationalist Party, the Communist Party, and the Cao Dai party. Singled out for special attention was the Cao Dai sect, which the Americans described as an "anti-white" religious group responsible for "all the terrorizing."[30] American reports conceded, however that "all of our information comes from the French civilians who are naturally prejudiced."[31]

On September 4 Counasse welcomed Peter Dewey and his staff to Saigon and passed along the information they had collected, including the troubling rumors that the Vietnamese were hoarding arms and ammunition in preparation for another demonstration. Informants reported that the Vietnamese were "storing guns and ammunition in caskets and graves, to be dug up at the appropriate time." According to local gossip, "they even had headstones on the graves to make them look realistic." Counasse did note that members of Detachment 404 had observed firsthand "several funerals accompanied by about twenty armed guards to the front and rear of each casket," but the sorting out of fact from fiction would be left to Dewey and his staff.[32]

One area of particular concern for Dewey was the source of the weapons carried by the Vietnamese. Counasse believed the Japanese were primarily to blame. In one of his first general summaries he reported: "The Japanese have seized British equipment parachuted into Saigon area before the armistice. They are selling these weapons, which are of all types, from sten guns to Webley automatics, to the Annamites who claim they intend to stage a revolution."[33] Gossip among French contacts tended to confirm these fears. Certainly the stories both fed French fears that the Japanese planned to actively support the Vietnamese bid for independence and further discredited both the defeated Japanese, who claimed to be cooperating, and the Vietnamese in control of the government, who welcomed the Allies. Furthermore, American reporter Harold Isaacs found that many of the Frenchmen he interviewed soon after Japan's surrender simply could not imagine the Vietnamese capable of an uprising against them and were convinced that the activities of early September could only be the work of the Japanese. In a conversation with a French police guard, Isaacs commented that the current situation seemed to him "a movement of Annamites who do not want the French back in the country." The Frenchman "jumped up and down with excitement," and retorted, "These people were all paid by the Japanese, armed by the Japanese, instigated by the Japanese. . . . It is a Japanese movement against the Allies, nothing else but that."[34]

In the days and months following the end of World War II and in the years since, a great deal of debate has gone on in political and military circles in France, the United States, and elsewhere regarding the relationship between the Japanese and the Vietnamese and whether or not the defeated Japanese provided weapons to various Vietnamese groups, in particular to the Viet Minh. Most sources tended to agree that the Vietnamese acquired some weapons from disaffected Japanese—the degree of aid claimed, however, varied considerably. Some reported that Japanese aid was often tentative when it came to supporting the internecine conflict among Vietnamese groups. For example, it was reported on September 8, 1945, that "some 15,000 Hoa Hao followers armed mostly with knives and other crude weapons, were bloodily put down by the Viet Minh–controlled Advance Guard Youth, reportedly supported by the local Japanese garrison."[35] More serious charges alleged that the Japanese armed Vietnamese prisoners recently freed from French prisons and "penal settlements"; those Vietnamese then utilized the weapons to "pillage the population" in the south.[36]

Whereas these charges alleged support among lower-echelon Japanese soldiers, historians David Marr and Stein Tønnesson both concluded that the Japanese commanders provided few arms to the Viet Minh. In late August, prior to the arrival of the Allies, Tran Van Giau, Pham Ngoc Thach, and Nguyen Van Tao represented the Viet Minh "Executive Committee in the first of five secret night meetings with Japanese dignitaries. . . . The most significant result of these secret meetings in Saigon was the transfer of a certain quantity of arms to the revolutionary authorities."[37] However, according to Tran Van Giau, who was interviewed by Marr in 1990, these armaments were primarily French weapons.

As a whole, Marr noted, although "some [Japanese] commanders prepared to turn over captured stocks of French weapons," there was "no readiness to accede to ultimatums, especially regarding Japanese weapons and equipment."[38] This is perhaps best exemplified by Field Marshal Terauchi Hisaichi, who clearly sympathized with the Viet Minh cause yet remained steadfast in his obedience to higher authorities. Tran Van Giau recalled his August 1945 conversation with the field marshal. "'You are defeated, now it is our turn to fight the white imperialists,'" Giau told Terauchi, "deliberately tossing in 'white' to exclude the Japanese." To this Terauchi replied that "orders from the Showa emperor forbade him to surrender Imperial Army weapons to anyone except the Allies," adding that "confiscated French equipment might be another matter. Then, in a remarkable gesture of support, Terauchi presented [Pham Ngoc] Thach with his short sword and gave

Giau a stunning silver revolver."[39] Jean Cédile, the French commissioner for
Cochinchina, accused the Japanese not only of giving moral support and
arms to the Viet Minh but of fighting *alongside* them as well. In an interview
with Peter Dunn he stated:

> One mustn't forget that these Japanese had in fact formed and armed
> some Vietnamese guerrillas. They armed and trained them against us.
> And that is why we very quickly found Vietnamese guerrillas fighting
> against us and in many places we even saw the Japanese commanding
> the Vietnamese commando troops. I'm not sure if the [Japanese]
> government knew anything about that; I am convinced that they must
> have had some inkling of it, but they always denied it when asked.[40]

Concern regarding the location of Japanese armaments and the possibility of Japanese deserters fighting with the Viet Minh was not confined to the
south. As early as August 12, OSS headquarters in Kunming received reports
that pro-Japanese partisans held the area from Lang Son to the Chinese
frontier, noting that "they are all armed and led by Jap non-coms and officers."[41] On August 18 Helliwell reported to his superiors in Chungking that
"well informed French and Annamese sources state that the Central Committee has been negotiating with local Japanese military authorities for purchase of arms and ammunition with intent of using them should either the
French or Chinese attempt to reoccupy their areas."[42] By the end of the
month, the report had been substantiated by a "high Thai official" and sent
on to Washington. The report claimed that "the giving of arms to the Annamese by the Japanese is part of the Greater East Asia policy and that the
Annamese can and will keep up guerrilla warfare for years. . . . The Annamese and Cochin Chinese superficially resemble the Japanese more than
any other Southeast Asiatics and the Japanese could melt into Annamese
guerrilla ranks."[43]

Estimates on the number of Japanese soldiers who "melt[ed] into" the
Vietnamese ranks vary. Historians Joseph Buttinger and William Duiker believed that only a few individuals deserted.[44] Stein Tønnesson concluded that
"several hundred deserted in order to continue the anti-European war as advisers to the Viet Minh, or to the armies of the Cao Dai and Hoa Hao sects."
David Marr concurred, adding that the number of desertions was particularly
high in the south.[45] Others estimated the numbers to be much higher. Cecil
Currey, John McAlister, and Murakami Hyoe believed the number of deserters to be between 1,500 and 4,500.[46] Most sources agreed that Japanese de-

serters were involved in training Viet Minh units and were especially useful in weapons instruction and in the establishment of facilities for the production and repair of small equipment and ordinance. Each of these deserters "was given a Vietnamese name and otherwise encouraged to blend in."[47] Both Currey and McAlister attributed an even more impressive role to the Japanese. According to Currey, Vo Nguyen Giap specifically enlisted "1,500 fanatically 'anti-white' Japanese military personnel who offered their services to him following Japan's surrender." As Currey described the fugitives:

> These soldiers were led by 230 noncommissioned officers and forty-seven gendarmes of the once-dreaded Japanese Kempeitai, all of whom were wanted for questioning by the Allies on charges of suspected war crimes. The entire group was commanded by Colonel Mukayama from the general staff of the 38th Imperial Army. Giap arranged for them all to receive Vietnamese citizenship and false identification papers. Mukayama became one of Giap's firm supporters and willingly served him when called upon.[48]

Casualty rates were apparently high among the Japanese deserters, and only "a few survivors arrived back in Japan quietly in the late 1950s."[49] What is certain is that at least some Japanese soldiers did desert and join the Viet Minh.[50] Post-surrender OSS intelligence reports estimated that most of the deserters were from the "middle ranks" and were not "acting under the direction of Tokyo or of any other high command" but were "self-seekers."[51] Their motivations, according to the OSS, had little to do with the GEACPS. Instead, the OSS reasoned that the Japanese deserted in increasing numbers because of increasingly difficult living conditions, low morale due to the expectation of a lengthy wait before being repatriated, increasing talk of war crimes, fear and disdain of the French, and a general "despair of [achieving a] decent life for many years."[52] However, in August and early September 1945, members of the OSS were more concerned with whether or not the Japanese were turning over weapons to the Vietnamese than they were with the possibility of Japanese deserters joining the ranks of the Viet Minh.

In Hanoi Patti noted that "three or four thousand Japanese dropped from sight into the clandestine pro-Asian movement,"[53] but he concentrated his attention on intelligence indicating that the Japanese were selling arms and ammunition as well as rice, furniture, and equipment to the Vietnamese. It seems likely that Patti's intelligence was correct. In an interview with David Marr, Resident Superior Nishimura Kumao recalled his suggestion to Viet

Minh representatives that "firearms might be available 'informally' from outlying Japanese units, even though officially all weapons had to be surrendered to the Allied representatives."[54] Patti warned the Japanese of their responsibility to maintain law and order and to turn all military equipment over to the proper Allied authorities. When charged with failing to do so, the Japanese promptly assured Patti that "severe disciplinary measures" would be taken against those violating the policy to safeguard the materiel. Nevertheless, information that "individual Jap soldiers were selling their arms to the Annamese" continued to reach OSS headquarters throughout the month.[55] Patti was not the only American officer in Hanoi to complain about the Japanese. General Gallagher wrote: "I am quite positive this turning over of weapons was a deliberate act on the part of the Japs to put into the hands of Annamites the necessary firearms to cause violence against the French, and to complicate Lu Han's problem."[56]

Clearly, some Japanese did provide—either through gift or sale—some weapons to the Viet Minh, but certainly not to the degree that the French, so fearful of the revolutions then sweeping the cities, asserted. This is corroborated by the "admission" of Viet Minh historian Truong Chinh, who wrote: "The second weakness in the August Revolution was the failure to fully disarm the Japanese troops at the hour of insurrection before the entry of the Allies into the country."[57] It is most likely that the vast majority of arms obtained by the Viet Minh from the Japanese were captured French weapons that were turned over to the revolutionaries by junior officers and enlisted men.

Although both Japanese weapons and deserters no doubt were causes for concern among the Allies, neither signified Japan's most crucial contribution to the revolutions sweeping both north and south. Much more important was the inaction of the Japanese high command as the Viet Minh assumed control of Hanoi and attempted to do the same with a coalition of parties in Saigon. Certainly the French and the British would have preferred it, and the Americans might have found their lives easier, had the Japanese maintained complete control of all buildings and facilities until the Allied arrival. The Japanese undoubtedly possessed the superior strength to do so, yet they yielded without a fight to the much weaker Viet Minh. This caused few significant problems in Hanoi, where the Chinese, designated to accept the surrender in the north, and the Americans proved willing to work with the Viet Minh. In Saigon the situation was much different, as Dewey was soon to find out.

The first days of Dewey's term in Saigon passed without incident. Although myriad rumors persisted, he and Counasse continued to see to issues surrounding the repatriation of the American POWs and received ample co-operation from the Japanese as well as the French population. As in Hanoi, the Viet Minh in Saigon continued to be encouraged by the presence of the Americans. On the day after Dewey's arrival the only newspaper then being published in Saigon printed a Hanoi news release from two days earlier. The headline read: "Two Representatives of the U.S. Advise Viet Nam to Resist Aggression to the Death." In the brief article the Americans were quoted as having advised the Vietnamese to "shed their last drop of blood in resistance to foreign aggression and to regain independence."[58]

Needless to say, Vietnamese officials welcomed any audience they could obtain with members of the American detachment. Early OSS reports from Saigon reiterated Vietnamese expressions of friendship toward the Allies (in particular the Americans and the British) and open pleas for American sup-port.[59] The arrival of the first British troops on September 6 only heightened Viet Minh awareness of their precarious hold on power. Although the Viet Minh hoped to establish good relations with the British, they had good rea-son to remain wary, fearing that Britain's role as a colonial power would re-sult in the occupation force's open support of a French return to power. The Viet Minh hoped the Americans might act as a counterbalance and prevent the seemingly imminent French return.

The British arrival in Saigon had already been delayed by the Ameri-cans—although not because of any desire to support the Vietnamese. British troops were originally scheduled to arrive in Saigon on September 2. How-ever, on August 20 General Douglas MacArthur suspended all reoccupation plans until after the official surrender ceremony in Tokyo Bay, initially set for August 28. Inclement weather delayed the signing until September 2, and thus, British troops were slower in arriving than anticipated. Many among the British and French would later conclude that "had it not been for MacArthur, British/Indian troops would have been in Saigon earlier, before the Viet Minh could have consolidated what power it had. And had not the Americans been fiercely opposing the French in their struggle to return to In-dochina, the same could be said for the occupation of Hanoi."[60]

Whether or not the presence of British troops in Saigon would have or could have prevented the independence parade and subsequent incidents of September 2 is debatable. What is certain is that in early September Ameri-cans on the ground in Saigon were not overly preoccupied with the arrival of the British or their overall intentions. Detachment 404, now headed by Dewey, set about finishing the job of dealing with prisoners of war, guarding American property, and acquiring intelligence. Meanwhile, other members of Dewey's team arrived in Saigon, including Private First Class George Wickes and Captain Frank White.

In August 1945 George Wickes was in Rangoon as a member of the SI branch of the OSS. He had studied Vietnamese at the Army Specialized Training Program and jumped at the chance to join the team headed for Saigon.[61] Wickes recalled that when he went to see Dewey to volunteer for the mission, the commander seemed unimpressed with his knowledge of Vietnamese. Instead, he tested Wickes's ability to speak French. Having been raised bilingual by his Belgian mother, Wickes passed with flying colors and soon was off to Saigon with an unofficial commission as a second lieutenant.

Unlike Wickes, Frank White was recruited by Dewey to participate in Operation EMBANKMENT. White, a former AP reporter, was signed on by the OSS in 1943 while he was working on the commanding general's staff at Fort Knox editing the *Armored Fort News* as well as the general's speeches. By July 1945 he was one of many men whose missions were over and who found themselves at a "holding camp" in Rangoon. From there, he flew with Wickes into Saigon. While in the southern city, White wrote most of the generic messages between Operation EMBANKMENT and its superiors. Dewey wrote most of his own dispatches, encoded by Wickes, and confided to few their contents.

After the departure of Counasse and his team, Dewey and the rest of Detachment 404 moved from the Continental Hotel to a villa on the outskirts of town formerly occupied by a Japanese admiral.[62] From there, Wickes sent messages written by White and Dewey to OSS headquarters detailing the activities of the team and the "political developments in southern Vietnam."[63] Occupied with his work at the villa, Wickes was initially unable to leave with any frequency. He was, however, routinely updated by the other members of the team, who "kept an eye on" the activities of the French, British, Vietnamese, Japanese, and Chinese. "They were all caught up in the intense atmosphere of intrigue that prevailed in Saigon and all talked about it when they returned to the villa," Wickes recalled. He added: "Colonel Dewey talked to me most of all, and I was impressed by his account of what was going on. . . . what impressed me most was his interpretation of the complicated political maneuverings of the different individuals and factions represented in Saigon, which he frequently explained to me."[64] Although Wickes was fascinated by Dewey's interactions with and accounts of the various political groups, the newly arrived British commander, General Douglas Gracey, was not.

Even before his arrival in the city, General Gracey was perturbed with the Americans for delaying the arrival of his occupation forces in Saigon.[65] Al-

Viet Minh troops holding American M-1 carbines stand guard by a jeep flying both the American and British flags. *National Archives and Records Administration.*

though the first troops had arrived on September 6 to a "rousing welcome from the local population—Annamite as well as French," the Advance Unit of the Twentieth Indian Division (Gurkhas) was further delayed and did not arrive until September 12.[66] Gracey and the main body of troops arrived the following day along with Brigadier M. S. K. Maunsell, the British Control Commission chief of staff. Although aware of the rumblings in the city, neither the British officers nor troops expected significant contact with the Vietnamese. The Gurkhas anticipated playing a primarily ceremonial role, and both Gracey and Maunsell expected to deal with the Japanese, not the Viet Minh.

In fact, although a small group of Viet Minh delegates were on the tarmac to greet Gracey as he descended from his plane, Maunsell recalled that neither he nor Gracey knew who the Viet Minh were. As the Viet Minh delegates started forward to speak, Gracey headed toward the senior Japanese officers, who promptly observed ceremonial formalities, saluting and bowing to Gracey. After concluding initial business with the Japanese, Gracey prepared to depart for central Saigon, whereupon the Viet Minh attempted once again to speak with him. Gracey, however, refused to acknowledge them and simply "waved them aside" and continued on to the heart of the city.[67]

The following day, Maunsell decided to tour Saigon and see for himself the state of things. He described the city as "fairly quiet, and half under the control of the Japanese 'who only acted when they felt like it.'" The Viet Minh "claim to control the city" was, in his opinion, "'a laugh'—they had no control." Maunsell declared after his tour that Saigon seemed to be a "completely and utterly quiescent city," informing Gracey that "if there was underlying dissent it was extremely difficult to recognize."[68] Yet in British official reports following the occupation, the situation in Saigon when British forces arrived was described as a Viet Minh "reign of terror against the French" in which "kidnapping, murder, looting and arson were all part of their technique."[69] In fact, British reports alleged that the Viet Minh government was "only vociferous on paper as regards democratic and even communistic plans . . . and quite incapable of keeping law and order." It further disparaged the Viet Minh as an "Annamite government army" that consisted of "a very large hooligan element out to make mischief, many of whom were criminals of the worst type."[70]

Certainly Viet Minh control over the city was tentative, by their own admission, but the description of Saigon as being under a Viet Minh "reign of terror" seems highly inconsistent with both the description of a "quiescent" city and the friendly advances made toward the British. It seems more likely that the Vietnamese groups were holding their collective breath to see whether the arrival of the British would indeed mean the automatic reestablishment of French rule.

Although Maunsell had found the city basically quiet that day, Gracey found himself in the position of reprimanding an unlikely group. Although he expected to deal with the Japanese and perhaps even with rogue Indochinese, he was not called upon to do so immediately after his arrival. Instead, historian Peter Dunn stated, "the activities of the OSS detachment were so blatantly subversive to the Allied command that within forty-eight hours of his arrival Gracey felt compelled to summon its chief, Lieutenant-Colonel Peter Dewey, to appear before him." In Dunn's opinion, Detachment 404 was in Saigon "only because the occupation was an Allied effort, and it only had two straightforward tasks"—to "watch over" American property and to "assist British Counter Intelligence Staff" in the collection of materials related to war crimes.[71]

This evaluation, however, is based on the British interpretation of Dewey's role. Along with the aforementioned tasks, Dewey was also charged with investigating the political situation, especially regarding Indochina's "status within the French Empire." By all accounts his reports were to be passed from OSS headquarters on to the State Department, which was facing its own inner turmoil regarding U.S. policy toward prewar Asian colonies and their European overlords. In fact, Dewey was specifically ordered *not to disclose* the full extent of his mission. Part 4 of the "Basic Plan for Operation Embankment" stated: "The mission should only reveal its activity with respect to X-2 [Counterintelligence], Prisoners of War, War Crimes, and the collection of documents and publications of such a nature as not to offend French susceptibilities."[72] Clearly, a full disclosure of his assignment to discover the exact nature of French plans for its colony—including whether or not the Vietnamese would be granted autonomy—would have offended the sensibilities of many colons.

The political nature of Dewey's intelligence gathering activities brought him into contact with a wide variety of people, including the Viet Minh and "perhaps other Vietnamese organizations."[73] From Gracey's perspective, Dewey's time "in and out of obscure alleyways and cafes in his dealings with the Communists and the Viet Minh" was at the very least highly inappropriate and a nuisance. Gracey also took issue with the maintenance of OSS headquarters at the villa, outside the "British area," and Dewey's rejection of "all suggestions that he was at risk out there."[74] Nevertheless, from the OSS commander's position the physical removal of the Americans from the European—colonial—sphere made perfect sense. It further distanced the United States from the taint of colonialism and facilitated the team's endeavors to independently read the political situation. Gracey's admonishment to stick to the tasks of aiding the Allies further irritated Dewey, who wired Coughlin that "at Gracey's request [we] must discontinue [our] assistance to [the] managers [of] American interests, [the] collection of documents, and war crimes investigation until [our] directive for this work and [the] presence of Embankment is clarified. Since [there is] no other US authority in Saigon, [I] consider this suspension [a] serious curtailment of US prerogative."[75]

Dewey's irritation was matched by Gracey's, who felt that in addition to everything else he had "caught him [Dewey] in a clumsy lie." According to Dunn, "Dewey had appeared and informed Gracey that he was charged with consular duties," of which Gracey had not been informed and Mountbatten had not approved. The report to the Foreign Office in London read in part: "I am afraid that what lies at the root of the matter is that OSS applies to go to places to fulfill one or more stated purposes only to engage in other activities which they do not disclose, which makes a very bad impression. There is nothing very sinister in undertaking Consular functions but there is no reason why Supreme Commander should not be consulted in the first instance."[76]

Although the exasperation of the British can be understood, from Dewey's perspective it was part of his job to be covert and to undertake relationships with various nationalities, relationships that could well have been described as consular in nature.[77] For the British, the most disturbing aspect of Dewey's behavior seems to have been his meetings with the Viet Minh—a group with whom Gracey did not know how to deal. Regardless of what may or may not have been Gracey's personal inclinations toward colonial peoples, in mid-September 1945 he was simply voicing his government's momentary indecision on how to deal with the Vietnamese. OSS director William Donovan sent a memorandum for the president outlining the situation as of September 14:

> There is considerable evidence that the British are handicapped by lack of a clear-cut policy toward the Annamese Government now controlling Saigon. The British at SEAC [Southeast Asia Command] are said not to have known that the French had lost authority which the SEAC directive was issued calling for cooperation with French in restoring Government functions. The British must now wait for a decision from the highest levels concerning the official policy to be adopted toward the Annamese. The Annamese on the other hand, although anxious to cooperate, are reluctant to advance currency to British occupation forces until assured that the British will not interfere with Annamese political aspirations.[78]

Although British policy had yet to be determined, Gracey's attitude indicated his lack of understanding of the strength of Vietnamese convictions. OSS reports noted what would become a frequent chain of events throughout the month. The beginning of the chain in the third week of September did not provoke serious violence on the part of the Vietnamese; later episodes would not be as peaceful. The chain began with the rearming of some of the French POWs, who "roamed the streets drunk, knocked down doors and looted Vietnamese and Chinese homes and stores," and when French residents, emboldened by the released POWs, "indiscriminately took revenge on any hapless Vietnamese who came their way." In retaliation the Vietnamese then "began using strong-arm tactics on fellow countrymen who still served the French." The British response was to order the Japanese to disarm the Vietnamese while simultaneously stating that the order "had no political implications." Next, the French seized the opportunity to begin "raising the tricolor," after so many months of its absence, over certain buildings and on cars. Radio

Saigon heightened tensions by announcing that the British would "maintain law and order until the arrival of French troops." Still hopeful, the Viet Minh used posters to exhort the population to "remain calm and avoid incidents," yet they also began to evacuate women and children from the city. In Hanoi the Vietnamese held a four-hour peaceful anti-British protest with "some speeches of minor consequence and a wide display of placards and banners denouncing the British attitude in the south."[79]

Over the next few days Gracey distributed leaflets to the Vietnamese population insisting on the strict maintenance of law and order and warning against attacks on the European population. His proclamation of September 19 reinstated the curfew established by the Japanese after the coup and threatened that criminals found guilty of sabotaging and pillaging either public or private property would be "summarily executed."[80] OSS reports noted the continuance of passive resistance in response to the British directives and the refusal of Vietnamese vendors to sell to the French in the markets.[81] Both Patti in Hanoi and Dewey in the south sent messages to Donovan advising the OSS that "if the British in the south and the Chinese in the north were running interference for the returning French we had better disassociate ourselves from that maneuver or be prepared to join the colonial interests in the Far East."[82]

As will be seen, neither Patti nor Dewey possessed an understanding of the changes that had taken place in American foreign policy circles since the death of Roosevelt in April. However, that aside, at the time both men continued to pursue their OSS assignments. Although Patti's intelligence work was not hindered, Dewey found his efforts to collect information among the Vietnamese becoming more difficult. Wickes recalled that "because he was well known to the French and the British, both of whom objected to his contacts with 'the enemy,' he could not very well meet with any Vietnamese without being observed."[83] Thus, in order to continue his mission, Dewey began to send Wickes to meet with the Viet Minh in his stead. Wickes remembered:

The streets were dark, there were still many former prisoners of war floating about, and I would dress as they did in order to escape notice. I would go to a house on a quiet street and there meet for perhaps two hours with three or four men who were obviously deeply committed to the liberation of their country. . . . they were leaders in the independence movement and wanted us to let Washington know that the people of Vietnam were determined to gain their independence from France.

During the war they had listened to Voice of America broadcasts which spoke of democracy and liberty, and they regarded the United States not only as a model but as the champion of self-government that would support their cause.[84]

Although Wickes expressed many of the same sentiments as those held by OSS officers in Hanoi, the situations were very different. Chinese relations with the Americans, combined with the early arrival of a strong American contingent and Ho Chi Minh's relatively firm control of Hanoi, made Patti's visits with the Viet Minh more or less acceptable to the Chinese, the official Allied power in charge of the north. The south, however, was quite another case. The vast differences between the governments of Chiang Kai-shek and Clement Attlee, British prime minister, and their need for American support influenced events, as did the tenuous control of the Viet Minh in the south and the fact that the French community in Saigon was larger, wealthier, and more vocal than that in Hanoi.

Some time later Wickes learned that French frustrations had mounted to the point that they had "put a price on" his head, although they had in fact mixed up Wickes and Dewey. Wickes does not believe he was ever in any real danger, but "clearly Dewey was persona non grata on account of his sympathy with the Vietnamese cause." Sympathy with the Vietnamese was not restricted to Wickes and Dewey but was felt by "all members" of the mission. "Our messages to Washington," Wickes recounted, "predicted accurately what would eventually happen if France tried to deny independence to Vietnam. This is only one of the many ironies of Saigon 1945."[85]

Although troublesome, the tensions between the OSS and their European Allies were the least consequential of the lot as September wore on. Among the French, British, and Vietnamese things were becoming much more hostile. British forces continued the process of assuming control from the Japanese. After taking over control of certain areas from the emperor's forces, the British proceeded to turn control of those areas over to the French. "A pattern," Dunn wrote, "which was followed until the British left Indochina, for the Japanese would not cooperate directly with the French."[86] In order to augment their manpower, the French continued rearming ex-POWs of the colonial forces. On September 21 Gracey proclaimed martial law. Patti recalled Dewey's anger at Gracey's behavior: "Dewey noted with considerable cynicism that although these measures were obviously targeted at the Vietnamese, Gracey had the gall to state publicly his 'firm intention' to see that the occupation would be conducted under peaceable conditions and 'with strict impartiality.'"[87] The release and rearming of the POWs fanned the passions of both the French and the Vietnamese. Although an OSS memorandum to the secretary of state had warned of the potential for French violence nearly two weeks earlier, the situation did not reach critical levels until September 22.[88]

On the night of September 21–22, Jean Cédile notified Gracey that his sources indicated the Viet Minh were preparing for a large-scale attack on the city. Cédile suggested that Gracey release and rearm the 1,400 French POWs then quartered just outside Saigon to aid the small British force. Cognizant that his 1,800 men might have serious difficulty should the rumors of a massive attack prove true, Gracey agreed with Cédile's plan, and in the early morning hours of September 22 he began the process. Although the former POWs were given instructions to rendezvous elsewhere and await orders, the men, "eager to prove their valor and loyalty" after so many months as captives of the Japanese, "gravitated instead toward the center of Saigon, where they pounced on any harmless Vietnamese who happened to be within reach."[89]

Meanwhile, members of Detachment 404 were meeting with the Viet Minh representative, Foreign Minister Pham Ngoc Thach. The Viet Minh Provisional Government in Saigon, like the one in Hanoi, requested that the OSS transmit its appeal for U.S. "moral" support to President Harry Truman[90] and informed the Americans of the Viet Minh intention to stage a peaceful demonstration "of several thousand Vietnamese" on the twenty-third. Warned that the demonstration was illegal under Gracey's orders and would probably produce bloodshed, Thach responded that the intent of the demonstration was to "provoke French and British reprisals 'causing many casualties'" and thus to bring world attention to the Vietnamese as "peaceful freedom-loving martyrs." Captain Herbert Bluechel, one of the members of the OSS team meeting with Thach, was "convinced that Thach at no time planned on having recourse to violence," adding, "I have reason to believe that he is appalled by the turn events have taken."[91] Nevertheless, "within hours," Patti recalled, "the plight of the Vietnamese in Saigon came to the attention of the world, not through a mass demonstration, but through an orgy of French violence."[92]

In the early morning hours of September 23, Cédile's forces moved rapidly across the city, retaking government buildings, reinstating the French flag, and killing or taking prisoner those Vietnamese who stood in their way. OSS sources quickly concluded that if the French POWs had been restrained, "strong action would not [have been] necessary, since the Annamese regime originally had planned passive resistance only."[93] Although headquartered in the north, Archimedes Patti summed up well the reaction of most Americans of the OSS:

> The French who had lived in fear for three weeks rejoiced. Their moment of victory had arrived, so also their moment of revenge. Instantly they reacted as one savage mob on the rampage. . . . They found many still unaware of the French coup and set upon them savagely with sticks and fists. In the orgiastic fit the French broke down doors to ferret out cowering "Annamites" from their homes or places of business to administer "a well-deserved and proper thrashing." For most victims the beatings were severe; some were maimed for life. In general, after the beatings, the victims were pushed and shoved into cars or trucks and sent off to the nearest jail for the crime of being Vietnamese. . . . The number of victims was reckoned, even conservatively, in the high hundreds and probably reached into the thousands.[94]

Dewey attempted to protest both the actions of the POWs and the inaction of the British military. Gracey refused to see him. Dewey next took his complaints to the French military and was warned by Cédile that "it was none of his business and that without a doubt the Americans were to blame for the state of affairs." Although both Gracey and Cédile were privately chagrined by the POWs' and colons' actions, they also viewed Dewey's skulking about meeting with Vietnamese groups as tacitly supporting Vietnamese actions and creating trouble. The following day, September 24, Gracey again declared Dewey "persona non grata"—this time adding an order for him to "leave Saigon as soon as possible."[95] Dewey had no choice but to make arrangements to leave Saigon. His departure was set for 9:30 AM September 26.

In hopes of preventing further violence, Gracey ordered that the POWs be disarmed and returned to their barracks and that many of the Vietnamese be released from jail. Unfortunately, Vietnamese hostility in reaction to the French actions could not be so easily contained: On the twenty-fourth they counterattacked, assailing the prison and freeing more of those recently jailed, attacking the airport, and cutting off electricity and water. The most violent actions occurred in the Saigon suburb of Cité Herault, where a Vietnamese mob took approximately 300 French and Eurasian civilians hostage and killed nearly half of them. There were many less-violent uprisings

throughout Saigon that night as Vietnamese groups reacted to the earlier aggression of the French and bid for control of the revolution. In an attempt to
maintain some semblance of Viet Minh authority over the movement, Giau
ordered a general strike, the evacuation of the Vietnamese population of
Saigon, and a blockade of the roads leading into and out of the city.[96] The
OSS reported their version of events to headquarters:

> The growing Annamese movement of passive resistance became an anti-
> white movement following circulation of reports that the British
> intended to help the French re-establish themselves in Indochina. When
> French former prisoners of war were armed and put to guarding bridges,
> this anti-white trend exploded. The situation quickly grew beyond the
> control of the nationalist Viet Minh Party, and the Annamese, professing
> their willingness to die in the cause of liberty, took up as their slogan—
> "Death to all Europeans."[97]

The OSS noted that Americans were not subject to the antiwhite movement
and were not classified as "Europeans" but were instead "considered to be a
separate people."[98]

American journalists were equally critical of the events in Saigon. In a
public interview an AP reporter added fuel to French resentment of what
they perceived to be the overall American attitude. He stated: "I am returning immediately to Hanoi to inform [the] American commission there on
what is happening in the south to avoid bloodshed in Tonkin. The French
are following [a] bad road and as for the British they have lost their heads to
have done what they have done."[99] On the evening of September 24, Dewey
sent his final report as head of Detachment 404. "Cochinchina is burning,"
he warned, "the French and British are finished here, and we ought to clear
out of Southeast Asia."[100]

Although neither Dewey nor his superiors were happy at his "dismissal"
from Saigon, there was little they could do to prevent it. In fact, notes regarding Dewey's removal had quickly traveled through the OSS chain directly to the State Department desk of Abbot Low Moffatt. OSS cables
pointed out that although Dewey was being withdrawn from Saigon "because the British had objections to his political and economic reporting,"
there could be no question as to Dewey's "superb job of objective reporting"
and the "high value of the information he had been sending." They also
pointed out that the secretary of state had "specifically requested OSS to develop intelligence in French Indochina," and should the State Department

Shortly before his death Captain Peter Dewey warned the OSS: "Cochinchina is burning, the French and British are finished here, and we ought to clear out of Southeast Asia" (Peter Dewey, final report as head of Detachment 404, quoted in Archimedes L. A. Patti, *Why Viet Nam? Prelude to America's Albatross* [Berkeley and Los Angeles: University of California Press, 1980], 320). *National Archives and Records Administration.*

wish that type of information flow to continue, a "competent successor" to Dewey had to be appointed.[101] OSS headquarters in Kandy, Ceylon, further advised Dewey to bring with him "written statements" absolving him from Gracey's charges. The cable clarified that Dewey was not being charged with anything, but it pointed out that the State Department was "interested" in his career.[102]

Given Dewey's aspirations toward a diplomatic career, his father's status as a former Illinois congressman, and the family's friendship with OSS director William Donovan, the attention was not unusual. Normally at this juncture, Dewey would have flown out and become another in a lengthening list of OSS agents who had completed their missions and were preparing to be discharged from the service. In Dewey's case, however, circumstances intervened.

Gracey's anger at Dewey was minimal compared to his fury at the Japanese for what he viewed as noncooperation with the Allies and possible complicity with the Vietnamese. Although he too dealt constantly with the rumors and innuendo about Japanese secret agents and fifth columnists, this time he severely reprimanded the Japanese commander for not maintaining order and threatened serious actions for noncooperation.[103] As events evolved, instead of disarming the defeated enemy, Gracey would soon begin to actively use Japanese troops to restore order in Saigon and to subdue the Vietnamese revolution. A Reuter's press release in London commented: "There are more than 4,000 fully armed Japanese troops in the city and 70,000 more in the country. . . . We depend on them—more than most of us like to think so—to meet that obligation [to maintain law and order].[104] In fact, during his four months in Saigon General Gracey "often ordered" Japanese forces to participate in "offensive operations," as well as "a variety of patrol, police, guard, and logistical duties."[105]

As Gracey worked to end the blockade of the city and restore order, members of the OSS continued to conduct their various duties. On September 25, an OSS mission headed by Captain Joseph Coolidge[106] left Saigon for Dalat to "assess the condition of considerable U.S. Missionary property" and to collect Japanese maps at the cartographic center. Although the Viet Minh allowed both British and American personnel to pass through the blockade around the city, Coolidge ran into trouble on his return. Coolidge's party consisted of himself, Lieutenant Varner, a number of Allied officers—including Frenchmen—and a few Vietnamese women. When the group encountered a Vietnamese roadblock on their return, the "mixed group of officers, all speaking French belligerently, tried to dismantle it. Mistaking them for Frenchmen, the Vietnamese tried to stop them." In the process, shots were fired, and Coolidge was wounded in the neck.[107] Although he was seriously injured, Coolidge's life was not in jeopardy. His wounding, however, was but a taste of the trouble to come.

Banished from Saigon by Gracey and unhappy about the Coolidge incident, Dewey nevertheless made his way to the airport on September 26. Though his flight was scheduled to leave at 9:30 AM for Kandy, he soon discovered that the plane would not land in Saigon until noon. With time on his hands, Dewey and team member Herbert Bluechel visited Coolidge in the hospital, returning to the airport shortly after noon. Informed that the plane had not yet arrived and that there would be a further delay, Dewey and Bluechel decided to return to OSS headquarters, only ten minutes away, for lunch.

Approximately 500 yards from the OSS house Dewey and Bluechel neared a familiar roadblock of two logs placed across the road to force an approaching vehicle to slow and make an *S* turn. Since the barricade did not totally block the road, Dewey did what he had already done that morning: He decelerated to navigate the obstacle. In those moments, a concealed machine gun fired from a distance of three yards. Dewey was hit in the head and died instantly.[108] Its driver dead, the jeep veered out of control, overturning on its right, thus protecting Bluechel, the passenger. Bluechel extricated himself from under Dewey's body and attempted to return fire. Finding his rifle jammed, he resorted to his Colt automatic. Bluechel estimated that about one minute elapsed before he was ready to defend himself. During that time, "though there were other armed Annamites present besides the machine gunner,"[109] no one attempted to attack Bluechel. He then started running toward the OSS house, turning occasionally to fire at the Vietnamese pursuing him. Although fired at several times, he was not hit.

The pursing Vietnamese then attacked the OSS house. At the time, only two other members of the OSS team and three lunch guests were present. Bluechel placed the occupants in strategic positions throughout the house. He ordered George Wickes to shout in Vietnamese that the occupants of the house were Americans. However, there was no change in the situation. "I do not believe," Wickes stated, "the annamites [*sic*] could hear me." It is impossible to know whether the attacking Vietnamese could not hear or would not listen.

Since the headquarters was situated at the north end of the Saigon golf course, the OSS team had an excellent range of vision and the Vietnamese had little cover during the initial attack, which lasted twenty to thirty minutes. Finding their position untenable, the Vietnamese moved to the other sides of the house, where more bushes and hedges provided cover. During a lull in the fighting four more OSS team members arrived at the house. One of them, Lieutenant Leslie Frost, was an especially welcome addition to the group: Bluechel wanted to send a message to the British Commission asking for assistance but had been unable to do so because the telephone wires had been cut. With the return of Frost, their radio operator, the team was able to wire OSS headquarters in Kandy, asking them to notify the British. At this point, forty-five minutes after the attack had begun, Bluechel ordered Captain Frank White to mobilize the nine Japanese soldiers charged with guarding the house. Although White placed the Japanese in strategic places around the house, they did not, for the most part, participate in the fight. By 3:00 PM, after more than two hours of firing, the Vietnamese were "forced to retire," reported Bluechel, "because of the accuracy of our fire." About ten minutes later, a "truck filled with [a] Japanese working party" passed in front of the house. Captain White stopped the truck and demanded that they accompany him as guards to recover the Dewey's body. However, when White arrived at the scene, he discovered that both Dewey's body and jeep had disappeared.[110]

As White and the French officer who had been lunching with him considered what to do next, they noticed a group of Vietnamese a bit further up the road in a jeep flying a Red Cross flag. Coming down the road from the airport was yet another jeep carrying Major Frank Rhoads, USAAF (U.S. Army Air Force), an officer in the Sanitary Corps, and two reporters, Downs and McClincy, they had just picked up. They too joined White's party. White's group approached the Vietnamese under a "flag" of truce.[111] White asked to speak to the Vietnamese in charge, and when the man was brought up White negotiated for an exchange: The Vietnamese could enter the now secured area of the golf course to pick up their wounded in exchange for Dewey's body. Throughout the conversation the Vietnamese "stoutly maintained that had he known that the Colonel was an American, he would never have allowed the shots fired. He had attacked the house, he said, because he believed that both French and British officers lived there, even though only an American flag was flown, and because we had killed so many of his men."[112]

The Vietnamese "chief" then discharged his men to collect the Vietnamese dead. In the ten minutes it took the men to return, the two reporters "plied" the leader with questions that "provoked from him lengthy and impassioned speeches on the indignities suffered by the Viet-Minh from the French. He also attacked the British at length, charging that the British, too, desired to 'dominate' the annamite [sic] people." As the Vietnamese soldiers returned with their dead, White could not help noticing that "the equipment on them, including cartridge boxes and canteens was Japanese." Nevertheless, their mission fulfilled, the Vietnamese commander prepared to depart to retrieve Dewey's body. At that moment, two platoons of the Thirty-first Gurkha Rifles charged down the road firing their weapons and "stampeding a large number of non-combatant annamites ahead of them." White continued, recalling the scene:

> Our position then—being in annamite hands with Gurkhas coming towards us—began to become awkward. This situation was further complicated by the two war correspondents. Apparently being unfamiliar with the disposition of Gurkha troops during combat, the two correspondents attempted to halt the oncoming troops in order to spare the non-combatant annamites caught between the lines. On agreement with Major Rhoads I broke off my negotiations with the annamites in an effort to try and prevent trouble between Downs and McClincy and the British Major commanding the Gurkhas. I was unsuccessful. The correspondents demanded that the Gurkhas retire while the civilians were cleared from the area. The Major refused. He told them his orders were to restore order "by the use of maximum force" and that was what he intended to do. The correspondents charged him with being a "murderer" if he continued. I finally managed to convince the correspondents that they were wasting their own and everyone else's time and they returned to OSS headquarters with me.[113]

White's mission thus thwarted, he reported the situation to Bluechel. Whether or not the Vietnamese commander "would have eventually carried out his pledge" to retrieve Dewey's body was, in White's estimation, "impossible to say." Regardless of the commander's intent, the Vietnamese were dispersed by the Gurkhas, and Dewey's body was still missing. Since in Bluechel's judgment "the area could not be adequately defended against a night attack," he ordered the Americans to gather their belongings and prepare to evacuate the house. The OSS team abandoned their headquarters at 5:15 PM, accompanied by a portion of the Gurkhas, leaving the Japanese to guard the house. By 5:40 Bluechel and the men now under his direction had "established themselves in suitable quarters" at the Continental Hotel. Bluechel personally notified Cédile of Dewey's death and missing body, and in turn, Cédile went to see General Gracey. Although neither man liked Dewey, both extended their regrets at Dewey's murder and ordered forces under their command to conduct a complete search for his body.[114]

Although fifty-five Japanese soldiers searched for Dewey's body from September 28 until October 15, they had little luck. On October 2 they did succeed in finding what was supposed to be the first burial place of Dewey's body. While digging in the "suspicious ground," the search party discovered a sword belt, pistol sack, and water bottle that were later confirmed by Bluechel to have been the property of Dewey. It was presumed that his body had been buried there on the day of his death and later moved. The British report detailing the Japanese party's efforts blamed the Viet Minh for both the shooting and the disappearance of the body, as well as for hindering the Japanese search.[115]

Almost every group in Saigon was blamed for Dewey's death at one time or another: The French charged the Viet Minh, the Viet Minh claimed a French conspiracy, and the British accused the Viet Minh and later Vietnamese agents of the Japanese. Although the men of the OSS clearly identified the shooter as Vietnamese, they did not believe the Vietnamese realized they were firing on Americans. Bluechel wrote:

> In view of the many instances of deference shown to me and other members of the OSS mission while moving through Annamite districts under protection of a displayed American flag . . . I am convinced that Major A. Peter Dewey, AC, 0–911947, was ambushed and killed through being mistaken of being a nationality other than American. If the jeep in which he was riding at the time of the incident had been displaying an American flag, I feel positive that the shots would not have been fired. . . . While it is true the Annamese fired on the OSS headquarters in spite of the fact an American flag was flying, yet by this time the fight was on and I do not believe the Annamese stopped to consider or to realize they were attacking American property. They were undoubtedly seeking revenge for the 5 Annamites hit during the course of my escape from the ambush, nothing but the force of arms could stop them.[116]

From the perspective of the men of Detachment 404, men who knew about Dewey's meetings with members of the Viet Minh and his sympathies with the Vietnamese cause, the absence of an American flag on Dewey's jeep as a contributing factor in his death became a central issue. Only a few days after his arrival in Saigon, General Gracey had ordered that only officers "of one-star rank or above ('flag rank') would be permitted to fly a flag on their cars. This was to denote rank, so no national flags were generally allowed." As the senior American then in Saigon, Dewey had protested the regulation, arguing that his work made it necessary for him to fly an American flag. Gracey warned Dewey that "his work should not take him to places where he found it necessary to seek protection under the American flag." The British firmly rejected the possibility that the absence of an American flag on the hood of the jeep contributed to Dewey's death, arguing instead that "it was extremely doubtful whether the flying of a flag or the painting of the U.S. flag on the Jeep would have had any deterrent effect on the attackers."[117] Later American investigations reached similar conclusions regarding the absence of a flag; however, even they could not agree on possible motivations. One report argued that the shooting of Dewey was "not by chance, but was intended,"[118] and a second contended that it was "highly unlikely that the Annamese had any idea of his identity at the time he was shot."[119]

New theories about the reasons for Dewey's death and leads about the possible whereabouts of his body continued to surface over the next two months. By November, Dewey's replacement, Lieutenant James Withrow reported that all leads thus far had produced "nothing of value." One scenario that seemed particularly plausible was also particularly frustrating for those hoping to solve the mystery of Dewey's missing body: In looking through British files relating to Dewey's death, Captain Robert Leonard discovered a memo discussing the discovery of a sketch of the front of Dewey's jeep together with a document containing a list of Vietnamese names at *kempeitai* headquarters in Cholon. Withrow wrote to India-Burma theater headquarters about the discovery:

> It is fairly well established that the Japs had several gangs of local persons, usually annaimits [*sic*], who they used for unofficial acts of terrorism. In so far as can be ascertained these gangs were available for hire by the highest bidder. If the act was committed by one of these, then the actual motivating force behind the killing could be anyone with a grievance against Col. Dewey or the United States.

Leonard's request for the sketch and a translation of the Vietnamese names was agreed to; however, two weeks later he was informed that regretfully the documents were missing and might in fact have been viewed as worthless and consigned to the trash bin.[120]

As the investigation in Saigon failed to produce any fruitful leads, the Dewey family became directly involved in the effort to find his body and repatriate it to the United States for burial. Devastated at their son's death, especially since the long, hard world war had already been fought and won, the Deweys searched for answers in Vietnam. Exactly where they looked to place blame for Peter's untimely death is open to speculation. Newspapers in the United States took decidedly different approaches to this peacetime casualty. Whereas the headline in a Washington paper decried Peter Dewey's death as the result of "rioting Annamites,"[121] his *New York Times* obituary presented a different picture, blaming not an angry mob but instead people who "mistook" Dewey for a French officer, their "oppressor." The *Times* further lamented the death of this young man it considered to be "a future leader" in light of his sympathy for "all those" subject to "foreign domination."[122]

Publicly blaming no one, Charles Dewey Sr., Peter's father, offered a reward for the return of his son's body, and Charles Dewey Jr., his brother, traveled to Saigon to help in the process.[123] Although neither effort bore fruit, the Dewey family was greatly moved by a letter they received from the Viet Minh soon after Charles Jr.'s return to Illinois. Dr. Pham Ngoc Thach expressed his regret at not seeing Charles Jr. while he was in Saigon to personally offer his condolences to the family and praised Peter Dewey, noting that "a good illuminating friendly smile was always on the Colonel's face. It was an illuminating light that came with the spirit of chivalry, and it was from the bottom of his heart, trying to understand us and with his great intelligence and his great sensitiveness for our cause."[124]

Thach assured the Deweys that the Viet Minh government was trying to locate the body and told them of its decisions to name the road on which Dewey was killed after him and to erect a monument on the spot. Charles Dewey Sr. drafted a reply thanking Thach for his letter. However, as he did not have an address, he sent it to Brigadier General John Magruder at the War Department and asked him to forward the letter on to the proper place in Saigon. Magruder returned the letter to the Deweys, explaining: "As much as we should like to accommodate you, the political situation in Indo-China is presently too volatile and the position of American forces there so delicate that to do so is to run the risk of misunderstanding and recrimination which our unit must avoid at all costs."[125]

Thach also wrote to Herbert Bluechel expressing his regret at both Dewey's murder and at having missed Bluechel, who departed for Washington in early October. Thach wrote: "I offer no excuses for this violence nor do I seek to justify it. More than anyone else, I regret it, but those directly responsible are they who have disregarded the rights of a free people, that is to say those who, in this century of the Great Democracy, Emancipator of humanity, seek to maintain the privileges of a colonizing nation." Thach clearly regarded the United States as Vietnam's only potential friend among the Western nations then in Saigon.[126]

Thach was not the only Viet Minh representative to express regret over the death of Peter Dewey. Ho Chi Minh was equally dismayed at the news that Vietnamese were responsible for an American officer's death. Ironically, on the same day that he had issued a "Message to Southern Compatriots," urging them to, among other things, "watch carefully" Frenchmen "captured in the war," but "also treat them generously,"[127] he met with General Gallagher to express his own sorrow and frustration at the death of the young American. Ho hypothesized that the incident "might have been staged for the benefit of French propaganda by French agents, but admitted it might have been the action of unruly elements of the Annamese." Ho further "assured" the general that such an event could occur in Hanoi "only over his dead body."[128] Ho also wrote a letter to Truman expressing his sorrow at Dewey's death and promising to search for the "culprits and severely punish them" as soon as possible, although he added, "it is impossible to investigate into the matter now, Saigon being still in the hands of the Franco-British troops."[129]

Without any clear leads to answer the myriad questions surrounding Dewey's death, the army was forced to close its investigation. He was posthumously cited for "exceptionally meritorious conduct" and given the Cluster to the Legion of Merit for "continuing his complex operations, without interruption to the steady flow of highly valued intelligence to Headquarters."[130] A further consequence of Dewey's death was the substantial scaling back of the American military presence in Saigon. As part of his report on the death of Dewey, Major F. M. Small advised that "it is unlikely in my opinion that military personnel will in the future be in a position to secure much valuable intelligence from French-Indochina. As soon as the situation reaches a point where elements of danger are in control, they should be replaced by civilian personnel operating under the cover of newspaper correspondents or others having legitimate business in the area."[131]

Of the original members of Detachment 404, both George Wickes and Frank White remained in Saigon until the first of December. Both men noted the increasing tension in the city. Although things were usually calm during the day, after dusk firing generally began. "Every night," Wickes recalled, "we could hear Vietnamese drums signaling across the river, and almost on the stroke of 12, there would be an outburst of gunfire and new fires breaking out among the stocks of tea, rubber, and tobacco in the dockyards." Increasing numbers of Japanese troops were used in conjunction with the Gurkhas and French troops in an effort to bring the city under control. Although that effort would be generally successful, the Americans still in Saigon "grew daily more sympathetic with the Vietnamese." "We no longer had any contact with representatives of the independence movement," Wickes stated, "but the French colonials we met made us increasingly pro-Vietnamese with their constant talk of how they had done so much for this country and how ungrateful the people were and how they would treat them once they regained control."[132] Both Wickes and White maintained, however, that although they empathized with the Vietnamese, their actions never went beyond a "statement of sympathy." But their presence in Saigon and their comments were enough to anger the French, who were growing increasingly tired of the American attitude. Finding its work difficult at best, Detachment 404 was phased out, and both White and Wickes left Vietnam for a brief time. They would, however, soon be reunited in Hanoi.

Although there were fewer and fewer American military personnel in Saigon, to many Vietnamese the American presence seemed to be growing in a most negative way. By November French troops arriving in the south appeared to be fully equipped by the U.S. government, including with American lend-lease trucks and jeeps that clearly bore American markings.[133] The United States, so long lauded by the Vietnamese as their possible savior from French colonialism, became increasingly lumped in with Vietnam's enemies in the south: the British, who seemed intent on handing Vietnam over to the French, who by all appearances intended to resubjugate the people, and the Japanese, once an enemy to the Allies and now their partner in denying the Vietnamese independence.[134] Given the increasing hostility of the situation, Peter Dewey's final dispatch from Saigon did seem prophetic: "Cochinchina is burning, the French and British are finished here, and we ought to clear out of Southeast Asia."[135]

Epilogue

The OSS mission in Saigon ended on a much different note than the one in Hanoi, although the leaders of both had been "recalled" in large part for offending America's European allies. The original team members of Detachment 404 were gradually withdrawn from the south, and the few new men sent in saw far less of the Vietnamese leadership and far more of the British and French, with whom they maintained better relations than had members of the Dewey mission. This was in large part due to the deteriorating situation in the south as the Vietnamese watched the British, French, Japanese, and Americans seemingly aid in the failure of their revolution.

The British, whom the Vietnamese had long feared were overly sympathetic to colonial interests, handed power back to the French south of the sixteenth parallel with the October 9 signing of the British-French Civil Affairs Agreement, which once again gave the French colonial authority over the administration of Vietnamese affairs. The French in Saigon became, especially with the arrival of growing numbers of French soldiers, progressively more arrogant as their position became stronger. The newly defeated Japanese, whose passivity had in fact allowed the revolution to briefly take hold and whose release of arms to the Viet Minh had altered the balance of power in the countryside, were frequently used in British and French attempts to sweep the revolutionaries out of Saigon and into the countryside, where it was hoped they would disperse. Reports to U.S. Army headquarters from October 1945 through February 1946 frequently mentioned Japanese soldiers engaged in action against the Vietnamese on behalf of the Allies, gave the numbers of casualties they both inflicted and endured, and noted British praise for their actions. Although reports of rogue Japanese soldiers fighting alongside the Viet Minh continued to emerge, these men were clearly the exception and not the rule. Overall, the Japanese fully cooperated with the British as they awaited repatriation, trial, or both.[1]

But for many Vietnamese, it was the American "support" of all three groups—British, French, and Japanese—that proved the most disappointing. On his return from Asia in 1947, journalist Harold Isaacs wrote:

It looked to them [people in other parts of Asia] very much as if the Americans were ready to allow the hated Japanese more relative self-government, freedom and independence, than they were willing to see granted to any of Japan's recent victims. Koreans, Annamites and Javanese considered themselves at least as capable as the Japanese of running their own affairs. After all it was not they but the Japanese who had plunged all of Asia and the world into the bitter agony of invasion and war. . . . And as a further shocking and cynical indignity, the victorious powers did not hesitate to use Japanese troops in this process wherever they lacked sufficient force of their own to suppress nationalist movements. This was not quite the picture people had of what American victory over Japan would mean in Asia.[2]

In addition, those Vietnamese who had closely followed the diplomatic rhetoric during the war had come to believe that the United States might stand by the principles of self-determination espoused in both the Atlantic Charter and the new United Nations Charter. But that hope was fading. In an early briefing, the Viet Minh had boasted of the order in the north and "the relations with the Allied disarmament mission [which were] pervaded with perfect understanding and outspokenness."[3] As late autumn approached and the familiar Americans left, this was less and less true. However, even in November 1945, the Vietnamese government's foreign policy statement reiterated their hopes that the ideals of the Atlantic Charter did pertain to Vietnam: "The victory of the Viet Nam nation will be insured by peaceable or forcible means, [proclaimed the Provisional Government] according to the attitude evinced by foreign powers, but always in accordance with the Atlantic Charter." It further emphasized their awareness of the public statements made during the war:

To consolidate the victory of Justice and Freedom, and to spare Humanity the plague of a new war, the Allied Powers had upheld and proclaimed humanitarian principles in the Atlantic, Teheran, San Francisco, Potsdam conferences—adopting liberty and equality of status as fundamental principles, and solemnly recognizing the right of peoples to decide themselves of their own fate. The third point of the Atlantic

Charter stipulated that the United Nations respect the right of all peoples to choose the form of Government under which they will live, and that they wish to see sovereign rights and self-government restored to those who have been forcibly deprived of them.[4]

Bui Diem, who joined the Viet Minh after the August Revolution, recalled that amid all the doubt and insecurity surrounding the arrival of the occupation forces, for Vietnamese, "one group of foreigners was universally admired—the Americans. That feeling was built on a gossamer hope that somehow the United States might yet save the situation."[5]

There were officials within the U.S. government who also hoped that an American anticolonial stance would carry over into the Truman administration. But after Franklin Roosevelt's death in April and after the war in Europe and in the Pacific had been won, the world had changed. The wartime exigencies that had resulted in OSS missions working with communist groups worldwide no longer existed; the disdain with which many regarded the defeated French had to be put aside as they regained their liberation and a reemerging world role; and the idealism for the future that oftentimes comes with the horrors of war was replaced by peacetime practicality.

Charles de Gaulle had first "threatened" Roosevelt's diplomats in March that the French might be "pushed" into the emerging Soviet sphere should American policy further alienate the French with talk of stripping away French colonial holdings. "If the public here comes to realize that you are against us in Indo-China," he flatly stated, "there will be terrific disappointment and nobody really knows to what that will lead." He then added for additional effect, "We do not want to become Communist; we do not want to fall into the Russian orbit, but I hope that you do not push us into it."[6] The French threat encouraged Roosevelt to keep more and more between himself and his closest aides his aspirations for French Indochina.

For Truman the possibility of France becoming part of the "Russian orbit" in the new peacetime world order was even more daunting. "During the last months of 1945 and throughout 1946," wrote Joseph Siracusa,

Franklin Roosevelt's policy towards Indochina became gradually transformed in the hands of Truman into a policy that attempted to accomplish two things simultaneously: first, to contribute towards the liberation and ultimate independence of the Indochinese people, *albeit now within a prescribed French framework*; and second, to coordinate Allied support against what was perceived as a Soviet threat to Western

Europe, a not unreasonable perception given Soviet activities in Eastern and Central Europe. [Emphasis added.]

In the case of the French, gaining their support against the Russians meant not alienating them with anticolonialist statements, and it meant "abandoning the colonial peoples if necessary." As history was written over the next few years, "American policy-makers systematically abandoned the Indochinese to the tender mercies of the French and in so doing sacrificed Vietnamese aspirations and dreams to the larger considerations of Cold War policy."[7]

As this policy emerged, some officials familiar with Asia attempted to steer it in a different direction. In September 1945 Patrick Hurley, the U.S. Ambassador to China, warned that "an opinion is steadily growing in Asia that America is supporting the imperialism of Britain, France and the Netherlands as against democracy."[8] This emerging sentiment came, of course, as no surprise to Hurley, for he had emphatically warned in the spring that:

> If American policy is not opposed to imperialism in Asia it is in conflict with the Hull policy. It is in conflict with the principles of the Atlantic Charter. It is in conflict with the principles of the Iran Declaration. It is in conflict with the policy to which all the nations including the imperialistic nations gave support when they were asking the United States to join the fight for liberty and democracy. It is in conflict with the policy that the United States invoked as our reason for the defeat and destruction of Japanese imperialism.[9]

Ambassador Hurley was not alone in his distress. State Department Asia specialists Abbot Low Moffat and Edwin F. Stanton stressed Indochina's importance as "a source of raw materials, a potential market for exports, and a strategic base in the Far East, and warned that a restoration of the prewar status quo would poorly serve American interests."[10] In 1946 Moffat visited Vietnam and met with Ho Chi Minh, believing erroneously that U.S. policy "was firm—not to help any colonial power return."[11] Moffat was impressed by both the country and the man and relayed Ho's lingering, generally positive image of the United States to his superiors. "Ho spoke of his friendship and admiration for the United States and the Americans he had known and worked with in the jungles, etc., and how they had treated the Annamese as equals," wrote Moffat, but his praise fell on deaf ears in Washington.[12] The die had already been cast. "Before I left, Ho gave me letters to President Truman and the secretary of state, the usual kind of stuff that he handed to everybody," recalled Moffat. "I brought them back and did what you'd expect me to do: I filed them away. Because our government was just not interested."[13] As has been seen, the United States had clearly decided its relationship with France was more important in the postwar world than ties to Vietnam or the little-known Vietnamese movement then in control.

Ho Chi Minh and other members of his government were obviously disappointed at what seemed to be the "handwriting on the wall." For although Ho continued to send telegrams to Truman "earnestly appealing" to the president and the American people to "interfere urgently in support of [Vietnam's] independence" and to push the French to "make the negotiations more in keeping with the principles of the Atlantic and San Francisco Charters,"[14] he was always answered by silent wires. He was not very surprised, for it had become clear that the wished for American support was just that, a wish. But he was still savvy enough, even long after friendly relations between the two countries had ceased, to capture the essence of American idealism when speaking with Americans. Controversial journalist Harrison Salisbury captured this ability well in his introduction to Ho Chi Minh's *Prison Diary* by quoting a question "often put to Americans who visited Hanoi in the interests of bringing the Vietnam war to an end. 'Tell me,' Ho would ask, 'is the Statue of Liberty still standing? Sometimes it seems to me it must be standing on its head.'"[15]

Many of the men involved on the ground in Vietnam would also come to believe that reason and American idealism had somehow been turned upside down in regard to U.S. policy and imperialism. But at the time, most of these men were unaware of official U.S. policy. They were both physically and officially far removed from governmental decision making and were ill-informed on America's postwar dilemmas; in fact, many in Washington would have argued that policy was in any case none of their affair as captains, majors, and even privates on the ground. These were the men of action, not those charged with developing the grand schemes, and their democratic ideals were often imbued with an anti-imperialism akin to that of Roosevelt and distant from the modern-day politics of Truman. In empathizing with the Vietnamese desire to escape the French colonial yoke and establish their own independence, the men on the ground were following what they believed to be a just course and—by extension of its very justness—an American course. As Carleton Swift noted, "Just viscerally, no American could object to national liberation."[16]

For their seemingly pro–Viet Minh words and actions, many of the men were vociferously criticized. Sainteny lashed out that the arrogant Americans were "blinded" by their "infantile anti-colonialism" and wondered how the OSS, "so rich in men of valor" could send to Hanoi "only second string underlings, incapable of evaluating the stakes and the incalculable results of the drama then taking place."[17] French author Françoise Martin pointed to the contradictions between "the liberal American attitude" exhibited by the OSS toward the Vietnamese and the mind-set in the United States, where the Native Americans were "murdered for their land" and "Blacks were oppressed."[18] But not all critics of the OSS have been French. Of the Dewey mission, historian Peter Dunn stated: "The sum total of its achievement was to have itself shot up and its leader killed. Had the wishes of certain factions of the OSS been satisfied, the terrible happenings in Indochina since 1975 might well have occurred years earlier."[19] Even former members of the OSS have at times disparaged the overall mission. "Alternately supporting the Vichy-French, Free French, Vietminh and other native groups," Charles Fenn observed, "OSS managed to infuriate even liberal French opinion while at the same time disillusioning the natives as to any real American understanding."[20]

Although blame was usually leveled at the OSS and at Americans in general, with particular emphasis on Patti and Dewey, those on the scene with the highest military ranks often came under the heaviest scrutiny. Even though there were few American military personnel still in Saigon, in Hanoi the American presence was much more prominent, and no one seemed to stand out more than General Philip Gallagher. On-the-scene reports from Hanoi continued to praise the Viet Minh control of the city, describing Ho as "politically a pure and simple nationalist," and displayed little sympathy for the French. Unlike in Saigon, where the French were forcefully reestablishing themselves, in Hanoi, one reporter wrote, the French "moved freely about the city, gathering disconsolately in patisseries, bars, and hotel lobbies, trying to talk each other out of the profound sense of humiliation and defeatism which grips them."[21] While the unhappy French blamed the United States for their lot, the Vietnamese still tended to view Americans positively, although they had many unanswered questions about apparent U.S. support for the French. With Patti's departure, much of their search for answers focused on Gallagher, who remained in Hanoi until mid-December 1945.

During that time, however, Gallagher observed a "cooling" of the Viet Minh attitude toward Americans, as it became more and more apparent that the American government would not recognize the independence of Vietnam and might even support the French return. "There has been a noticeable change in the attitude of the Annamites towards the Americans here in Hanoi since they became aware of the fact that we were not going to interfere and would probably help the French," noted Gallagher. "Some of our officers, who were previously welcomed with open arms at Viet Minh headquarters are now permitted to cool their heels indefinitely and are some times refused audiences with certain members of the Viet Minh government."[22] Nevertheless, Gallagher continued to meet with the Viet Minh because, according to his personal papers, "guidance on U.S. policy available" to him at the time "was apparently based on the concept that Indochina would ultimately come under a United States' Trusteeship,"[23] and, in his view, "there was no one else to deal with with any authority, or sense of responsibility."[24]

Gallagher's meetings with Viet Minh officials were often photographed, and what he believed to be innocuous comments were often embroidered and repeated in both Vietnamese and French circles. For many Frenchmen, Gallagher became the personification of the perceived American effort to deny France the rightful return of its colonial empire, for they too were largely ignorant of the shift in foreign policy since Roosevelt's death. Rumors about Gallagher's relationship with members of the Viet Minh and about his efforts to make a personal fortune in Vietnam circulated widely, although they contained little truth. Although Gallagher was not the only American believed to be asserting America's "economic imperialism" in Vietnam to the detriment of the French, he was the main topic of gossip. One story maintained that he had proposed to Ho that he could find the capital, materiel, and technicians to reconstruct and extend the country's railways and ports. The financing would come from none other than the Donovan group because, so the story went, "the French were finished but America was ready to help Vietnam." The tale maintained that the Viet Minh reacted "coldly" to Gallagher's "aggressive capitalism."[25] Although the general flatly denied the charges and there is no indication that the conversation ever occurred, the French continued to sense hostility toward them in his every move.

The French believed they saw solid proof of this enmity in mid-October. As Gallagher and Lu Han made preparations to transport some of the Chinese troops from Vietnam to Taiwan and Manchuria, they discovered that mines "sown in the harbor by the U.S. Army Air Forces" during the war had not been cleared. "Since sweeping the mines would open the harbor to French troop-ships and thus possibly lead to war between the French and the Vietnamese, neither General Gallagher nor General Lu Han wanted the harbor cleared."[26] Although the decision was made in the best interests of

Colonel Stephen Nordlinger, second from left, standing with Ho Chi Minh, on his left. Although criticized by Patti for being anti-Viet Minh, Nordlinger recalled his "cordial conversations" with Ho as well as "participating with him in various civic events for the care of the poor and undernourished." (Nordlinger, correspondence, letter to President Lyndon B. Johnson, March 18, 1968). *Courtesy of John Nordlinger.*

peace in northern Vietnam during the occupation period, it was often interpreted as nothing more than another anti-French maneuver. Another
episode involving Gallagher had, on the surface, nothing at all to do with
the French, yet it stirred more anger among the colons than almost any of
his activities to date. The incident occurred when General Gallagher "let
himself be persuaded to sing at the inaugural meeting" of the Vietnam-
America Friendship Association (VAFA).[27] This was, Joseph Buttinger
noted, "hardly a major act of anti-colonialism, but in the eyes of the
French, [it was] a betrayal by an ally whose support they considered vital
for the success of their cause."[28]

The VAFA was a joint venture between members of the Viet Minh and select members of the OSS.[29] Psychological warfare officer Robert Knapp
brought the idea to Carleton Swift, who had taken over Patti's position as
head of the OSS mission in Hanoi. The first draft "had a number of provisions" about commerce, politics, and economics, provisions that made Swift
nervous as he clearly recalled being told "not to get involved in politics."
"So," Swift recollected:

> I took a pencil and struck out anything to do with politics. And I struck
> out anything to do with commerce. I said, "Knapp is there anything
> left?" "Yes, we can study each other's language and each other's
> literature," [he said.] And that seemed to me, well how should I put it, a
> sentiment that an American could not say no to. So I signed off on my
> own authority.[30]

The VAFA drafted a constitution that designated the goals of the Association: (1) to "bring about a better understanding between Americans and
Vietnamese so as to promote sympathetic feelings"; (2) to translate and circulate publications from English into Vietnamese and vice versa for a "better understanding of the cultural aspects of the two nations"; (3) to organize
frequent lectures in both languages; (4) to hold Vietnamese and English language classes; and (5) to publish a monthly magazine—the *Vietnamese
American Friendship Association Review* (*VAFA Review*).[31] At the opening
ceremony, General Gallagher "thanked the Vietnamese for their reception
and expressed regrets that his and his companions' duties prevented them
from enjoying their stay in Hanoi more than they did." He concluded by en-
dorsing the earlier suggestion that the two countries exchange students to
promote greater cultural understanding. The *VAFA Review* reported: "A
burst of applause greeted General Gallagher's last words. He returned to his

seat with one more victory to his personal record: he had won 200 Viet-nam[ese] hearts, among which not a few belonging to the most attractive ladies in Hanoi."[32]

In this incident the French saw only blatant American support for the Vietnamese and were duly offended. Many Vietnamese in the audience also believed that the American presence was more than a courtesy. One Viet-namese attendee reminisced about the evening:

> I remember the red, white and blue flags that draped the hall of the one Friendship Society meeting I attended. The gathering was suffused with hope generated simply by the appearance of the two American officers, who looked so civilized and handsome in their uniforms that everyone, myself included, rushed to shake their hands. Throughout the affair, conversation revolved around the idea of an American trusteeship for Vietnam. And although neither Patti nor Gallagher said much of substance, it didn't matter. Their mere physical presence was encouragement enough.[33]

Upon his return to the United States, Gallagher briefed officials in Wash-ington and revealed his sympathy for Ho Chi Minh and other Viet Minh leaders. According to historian William Duiker, "he was impressed by their enthusiasm and their dedication as well as by their native ability. But he was skeptical of the capacity of the new government to carry out its responsibili-ties in the unstable conditions of the immediate postwar period."[34]

In Hanoi, Carleton Swift continued to report on VAFA meetings, pointing out the spontaneous growth of the meetings, which once reached "nearly 6000 attendees."[35] Swift had signed the VAFA charter "as a sign of good feeling," convinced that since "all of the teeth had been taken out of the first draft, not to sign such a harmless document would have looked un-Ameri-can." But Swift's actions were misinterpreted as being "political" in nature, and soon he too was reviled by many in the French community who saw him as little better than Patti. He spent one month in Hanoi before he was "kicked out" on French charges that he had "incited revolution and killed Frenchmen."[36]

Henry Prunier, the only member of the Deer Team still in Hanoi, did not join the association, mainly because the members, both Vietnamese and American, were not the same people he had known and worked with in the Viet Bac. Although initially withdrawn, Prunier was sent back to Hanoi to investigate Japanese war crimes, but without specific orders he spent most of his time wandering around the city speaking with both Vietnamese citizens and the local French. He remembers Hanoi as "festive" but also as "very tough at the time." He recalled that Hanoi was a city in the midst of rapid change: "The Japanese were still everywhere, the Chinese had arrived, there was a lot of hunger and a lot of young people on the streets."[37]

Prunier's experience in Hanoi, however, was different from that of most of the Americans there. Although the Vietnamese were particularly friendly toward him because he "had been with Ho and Giap at Tan Trao," Prunier, unlike most other members of the OSS, also made friends among the French community. He recalled in particular a French family, a mother and two daughters, who lived a short distance from the OSS house. Being a young man at the time, Prunier enjoyed spending his free time with the two young French women. Their father had been missing since the Japanese coup, and although a six-foot wall surrounded their home, they remained fearful and rarely left the compound. Both mother and daughters were glad for the company of the young American man, who offered not only a welcome diversion but also brought them a greater degree of "protection," and hence freedom, to move about Hanoi. The women held the typical French view of the situation; they explained to Prunier that the Viet Minh did "not amount to much" and optimistically predicted a rapid return of the French. Prunier was one of the few who sympathized openly with both the French and the Vietnamese desire for independence.[38] Because he was an American, both sides were interested in his reactions and interactions, but because he was only an enlisted man, he escaped the intense scrutiny given General Gallagher and OSS officers like Dewey and Patti.

As the men of the OSS returned home, resigned their commissions, and resumed their peacetime roles, the very organization to which most had felt such belonging was coming to an end. Donovan had been preparing for this eventuality, and just before the war's end he presented his view of the OSS's role: "The real job of OSS as an intelligence agency" he firmly believed, was "to produce strategic intelligence," which "boiled down to a simple formula: Intelligence which throws light on the capabilities and intentions of foreign powers, particularly our present and late enemies." This strategic intelligence would, in his view, "serve as a basis for decisions of national policy."[39] His planning aside, on October 1, 1945, the OSS—which had always been a temporary wartime agency—was abolished, months in advance of Donovan's anticipated phaseout.

Donovan hoped the precedent set by the OSS for intelligence activities would continue. In his considered opinion, "the cessation of hostilities did not eliminate the need for intelligence; peace merely changed the intelligence requirements."[40] Donovan was convinced that his OSS agents had performed well overall and had contributed significantly to the Allied victory. "We did not rely on the 'seductive blonde' or the 'phony mustache,'" he bragged. "The major part of our intelligence was the result of good old-fashioned intellectual sweat."[41] Thus, he proposed the creation of a permanent peacetime intelligence gathering agency based on the best characteristics of the OSS. After the conclusion of the European war he was more than ever convinced of this need, for he, like Truman, perceived the Soviet Union as a growing and tangible threat. In the summer of 1945 Donovan even went so far as to "advocate the maintenance of the European empires in Asia in order to prevent the Soviets from gaining influence"[42]—a stance that would have clearly separated him from his men in Vietnam had they been cognizant of it.

Although Donovan's dream of a peacetime intelligence agency would eventually come to fruition with the establishment of the Central Intelligence Agency, it would not be in 1945 and not under Donovan's control. "Wild Bill" Donovan returned to civilian life, and after October 1 the "OSS men" still in the field fell under the jurisdiction of the War Department's Strategic Services Unit (SSU). There they would complete their missions and await withdrawal.

The OSS had been targeted for criticism since the birth of its predecessor, the COI. With the end of the war that criticism continued, and debate over the organization's contributions to the overall war effort have continued to the present. Some critics charge the OSS with being too left wing, citing in particular the organization's dealings with known communists; others accuse it of just the opposite, right-wing political conservatism that ultimately hindered its ability in the field. The truth, of course, lies somewhere in the middle. Perhaps the fairest praise comes from this middle ground: "Despite some blemishes, [the OSS was] the embodiment of an American liberal ideology, characterized by humanitarianism, optimism, and generosity. . . . in contrast to the manipulative activities of the British and the brutality of the Soviets, American subversive warfare and central intelligence during World War II worked for the cause of morality"—at least as defined by the American exceptionalism of the 1940s.[43] Certainly many of the men and women of the OSS who worked diligently throughout the war would have agreed with this final assessment—especially those who served in Southeast Asia and believed that their revulsion at the excesses of colonialism justified their tentative support of nascent nationalist movements.

In particular, the role of the OSS in Vietnam has become a contentious issue since 1945. Arthur Dommen condemned OSS work in Indochina as "one of the most signal intelligence failures of World War II," citing as evidence Donovan's inability to satisfy Secretary of State Joseph Grew's request for information on Indochina in mid-1945.[44] Although this clearly indicated a problem in getting information to the highest levels—as we have seen, the GBT had been providing the OSS with information for months and Donovan should have been able to pull that intelligence—such a complete denunciation requires further explanation. Three factors must be considered before judging OSS operations in Indochina. First, with the Japanese coup in March there was an unavoidable and temporary lull in getting information flowing again from the colony. Second, Indochina had never been an area of primary governmental or military concern, and attention and resources were directed first and foremost to those areas deemed most important to the war effort; thus, there would naturally be less information on Indochina available at the very highest levels. And finally, Grew requested his information before Thomas jumped into Tonkin.[45] Had the request come after Thomas's arrival in Tonkin, a much greater supply of information would have been available.

Other critics have focused on the American role in the August Revolution. Some authors have claimed that the actions of the OSS, especially those of the Deer Team and Archimedes Patti, were instrumental in bringing the Viet Minh to power.[46] Others, especially among Vietnamese writers, have denied any positive role for the Americans in the 1945 revolution or have minimized them as mere pawns of Ho Chi Minh. By the first anniversary of the August Revolution, references to America's role in the victory over Japan had disappeared; instead, the Soviet Union was credited with "liberating the people subject to Japanese oppression." Of the August revolution, Truong Chinh wrote: "It [the Provisional Government] fooled not only the Chinese Nationalist forces that entered North Vietnam in September, 1945, but also the various American missions operating in the area, which were led to believe that Ho Chi Minh's regime consisted of old-fashioned nationalists and agrarian reformers."[47] Peter Dunn added: "It is no exaggeration to say that he [Ho Chi Minh] made the American officers dance to his tune with embarrassing ease; he simply had to trot out the 'anti-colonialism' tune."[48] To a degree, of course, this was true. "We had a great sensitivity toward the feelings of human dignity that [they] were struggling for, and the problems [the Vietnamese] had with French colonialism," remembered Swift.[49] By the 1980s the Americans' role in 1945 had come to be seen in even more negative terms. Of the OSS's early contacts with Ho, Ngoc An wrote:

This was an opportunity for the Americans to implement their planned infamy toward Indochina. Born from a neo-colonialist policy when Indochina was invaded by the Japanese, the US imperialists didn't help the French in their struggle against the Japanese, but instead had planned after the Allies' victory to convert Indochina into a satellite region under US influence. They perceived the Viet-Minh League as a nationalist organization that they could use to execute their strategy in turning our nation into a kind of neo-colony. . . . In coming to Vietnam, their purpose was to rescue the Allies' men. Also, they were studying as well as evaluating Vietnam's revolution status and its strength for the US long term planning aggression.[50]

None of these arguments, however, is entirely accurate. Perhaps Deer Team leader Allison Thomas and Vietnamese historian Duong Trung Quoc, summarized the American role best. Thomas mused:

People also say that as a result of our support, Ho came to power. I don't believe that for a minute. I'm sure Ho tried to use the fact that the Americans gave him some equipment. He led many Vietnamese to believe that we were allies. But there were lots of reasons why Ho came to power, and it wasn't because we gave a few arms for 100 men or less.[51]

To be sure, Thomas's interpretation might be regarded as self-serving, but the evidence supports it on balance: The Americans did not *bring* Ho Chi Minh to power. It must be remembered however, that what seemed like highly visible OSS support for the Viet Minh did play a significant, albeit symbolic, role in helping the Viet Minh *seize the opportunity presented them* with the sudden capitulation of the Japanese. "The presence of the OSS members after the surrender of the Japanese was exploited to the most by Ho Chi Minh," admitted Duong Trung Quoc. But, he continued,

I don't think of the exploitation in terms of military strength, but first of all in terms of the diplomatic motivation; public relations. To get some kind of legitimate status from the government within the country in terms of the other different political, social organizations in Vietnam as well as in the international arena.[52]

And although some members of the OSS seemed to represent official American support for an independent Vietnam, that was not their intent. In fact, those who had been most empathetic and friendly with Ho Chi Minh and the Viet Minh—Fenn, Tan, Phelan, Thomas, Prunier, Hoagland, and Wickes—went virtually unnoticed by the very harshest critics at that time, the French. In addition, it must be remembered that even Patti and Dewey, although highly visible in Hanoi and Saigon, respectively, were so far removed from the key decision makers that they were both uninformed about evolving American policy, *and* they carried no weight at those levels even if they had been privy to the discussions surrounding them. The men on the ground in Vietnam were not diplomats representing American foreign policy; they embodied something different.

The motivation of these young men—most were under thirty—tended to be rather straightforward. They were neither scouting out Vietnam for prospective business ventures nor attempting to make American policy. They were trained by the OSS to pursue effective action—even if that meant eschewing standard operating procedures—and were following the orders of their superiors to collect intelligence, rescue downed American pilots and POWs, investigate Japanese war crimes, and aid the respective occupation forces in disarming and repatriating the Japanese. In doing so, some worked with the Viet Minh in the field, training them to fight their mutual enemy; others, as they pursued their military duties, came into contact with the Viet Minh who controlled the government in Hanoi and with those who attempted to gain control in Saigon. In listening to and at times befriending members of the Viet Minh, the men appeared to represent American support for the Vietnamese cause.

And many of the men did sympathize with the Vietnamese desire for independence, although they certainly never claimed to represent the official views of the U.S. government. With the successful conclusion of World War II and the promise of a return to home and hearth and both the security and the boredom of daily life, some of the men took the additional opportunity to become involved in issues that both related to their jobs and interested them—including the fate of their new friends and their visions of themselves as liberators and as defenders of freedom. In the context of World War II this makes perfect sense; it is only in the era following 1965-1975 that America's early role in Vietnam has been imbued with hidden meanings.

The men of the OSS had spent considerable time fighting to end fascism and dictatorship and to bring freedom to the occupied nations in both Europe and Asia. The OSS had worked with communist groups in both Europe and Asia and at that time looked not to analyze their political views but to evaluate their potential for effective action against the enemy. "I was told he

[Ho] went to Moscow as a communist and that kind of thing, but so what?"
argued Grelecki, "the Soviet Union and we were allies."[53] Vu Dinh Huynh
also corroborated this perception of the young Americans with whom the
Viet Minh dealt: "I had the impression that at that moment the Americans
didn't care if we were communists or not. The only thing they cared about
was fighting the Japanese."[54] And it is only natural that many of the men on
the ground would have felt compassion for the Vietnamese fighting for freedom from both Japanese and French oppression, which some witnessed firsthand, especially when those same Vietnamese often demonstrated outright
admiration for and adherence to the values represented by the young Americans. In his observations of the interactions between Asians and Americans,
Harold Isaacs wrote:

> Some believed that the United States, if only out of enlightened self-
> interest, would stand by the [Atlantic] Charter and thereby guarantee
> their liberation from foreign rule. There was also another belief: that
> Americans were a different breed of men, practicing democrats who
> stood for and fought for and would deliver justice for everybody. Few
> Americans who came among the Indians, Burmese, Chinese, Koreans,
> Indochinese, and Indonesians in the various honeymoon periods of
> initial contact could fail to be affected and even a little exhilarated by
> the way they were set apart from all other Westerners as the bearers of
> the torch of liberty.[55]

Most of the Americans in Vietnam would have gladly placed themselves
in that category—as a "different breed of men," working to "deliver justice
for everybody." With the swagger and bravado of the newly victorious combining with their sincere conviction of the very rightness of American values,
the men on the ground became a symbol of hope, although an unintentional
one, for the Vietnamese—hope that the favorable reports written by Patti,
Swift, Dewey, Thomas, and others would somehow reach and impress the
highest levels of American government, and hope that the Americans would
prevent the return of colonialism to Vietnam and be a midwife at the birth of
their independence. The Vietnamese obviously overestimated the importance and power of the men they took every opportunity to impress. And at
times, the deference and admiration shown the young Americans encouraged them to play their "roles," both real and inferred, to the fullest.

A confidential "working paper" written in 1956 for the Council on Foreign
Relations offered a partial explanation of the actions of the young men of the

OSS: "Unfamiliar with the kind of loose, expansive, and irresponsible behavior that Americans sometimes indulge in, the French and Vietnamese could not be blamed for taking seriously, and as accurately reflecting the official position of the United States, what was only the braggadocio of a handful of isolated officers."[56] In his postwar analysis of the situation, OSS officer Carleton Swift summed up the situation from his viewpoint: "The circumstances were such that Patti and his team were drawn beyond a purely intelligence reporting role into representing American interests on the scene, a role that often fell to OSS. The mere presence of Americans willing to listen was a stimulation to the Vietnamese and proved anathema to the French."[57] Perhaps members of the OSS teams spoke their minds too frequently, but their partiality toward those seeking independence rather than toward those trying to deny it cannot be too heavily criticized. To many in that war-torn world, these young American soldiers were the embodiment of the values and idealism the United States had come to represent. Whether in Paris, Dachau, or Hanoi, Americans became the symbol of freedom and hope for the future.

The Americans on the ground found their words and actions taken very seriously by the Vietnamese and the French, both of whom saw U.S. support as a powerful element in determining the future of Indochina. But it must also be remembered that the Vietnamese, in particular Ho Chi Minh, were also important actors in this relationship. Many have written that Ho had an affinity for America and Americans because he always asked questions and had comments and was ready to engage in pleasant dialogue. Although this may be true, a more objective view is that he was simply a politically astute and polite host and had the social graces, especially on a one-on-one level, to make a visitor feel important. He could speak of French history and society, of his travels to the United States and of American history, and one would suspect the same, when the occasion presented itself, of Thailand, China or the Soviet Union. He knew how to use the rhetoric, even when sincere, that would appeal to the visitor of the moment. Vis-à-vis his relationship with the men on the ground, his conduct was both sincere and expedient—based on the hope that they might send back favorable reports that might help garner him U.S. recognition.

Part of this wish came true. The men did, overall, send back positive reports.[58] But the rest was a false hope that imbued both his own country and the Americans there with considerably more power than either of them had at the time. In fact, if not for the U.S. war in Vietnam, after the dust of 1945–1946 had settled, few would have looked back on the exchanges be-

tween the Americans and Viet Minh or questioned American motives and activities at all. The reports the Americans on the ground had filed would have
quietly settled into the dust, completely devoid of the controversy and
heartache that marks most things touching on the U.S. relationship with
Vietnam.

Years later, some historians still seek an answer to why OSS men "collaborated" with the Viet Minh. Stein Tønnesson outlined three probable reasons:

> First, the personnel who led the operations had been selected and had
> received their instructions while Roosevelt was still alive; they continued
> to implement his policy. Second, the OSS had its own momentum as a
> global institution; it had not been allowed to operate in the theaters of
> Admiral Nimitz and General MacArthur, but was welcomed in China. It
> was in the interest of the OSS to get as much done as possible in
> Wedemeyer's theatre; the OSS also, of course, cooperated with the
> Chinese communists. Third, getting accurate intelligence and carrying
> out effective subversive operations are the raison d'être of an
> organization like the OSS; information and cooperation had to be sought
> where they could be obtained most effectively.[59]

All three reasons are undoubtedly accurate, based on the reports and behavior of the men on the ground. But one additional factor came into play
with many of the men: the human factor—the human capacity for developing personal relationships with people of a variety of political stripes. The
first men on the ground, Frankie Tan, Dan Phelan, and Charles Fenn, all
formed a friendly rapport with Vietnamese individuals with whom they
worked, as did some members of the Deer Team, most specifically their
leader Allison Thomas. Both Henry Prunier and George Wickes also regarded certain Vietnamese with whom they worked as new friends. And the
situation was mutual; even after the "mission of the OSS team was ended,"
recalled Duong Trung Quoc, "the relationship between Viet Minh and OSS
still maintained, but in the context of the relationship between
individuals. . . . there was a lot of good, warm, feelings toward each other as
personalities, as persons."[60]

In the case of Archimedes Patti, Peter Dewey, and Carleton Swift, it
would be overstating the case to say that friendships developed. However, all
three of these men seemed to revel in the intellectual discourse they exchanged with members of the Viet Minh. Thomas, Tan, Fenn, and Patti continued to correspond with members of the Viet Minh even after they had

At the first OSS–Viet Minh reunion in Hanoi in 1995, Charles Fenn, left, and Vo Nguyen Giap reminisced about their experiences as young men in the heady days of August 1945. *Courtesy of Alyn Fenn.*

parted company, and Nordlinger wrote warm and encouraging letters to Ho Chi Minh in the late 1960s hoping that their positive relationship of the past might be used to ameliorate the situation in that turbulent decade.[61] Regarding Vietnamese individuals as friends, or at least as equals, may have encouraged the American men on the ground to sympathize more openly than policy makers in Washington, London, and certainly Paris would have liked, but at no time did any of the men perceive themselves to be acting contrary to American policy or misrepresenting their country's ideals.

Did these men provide the United States in 1945 with insights that might have helped avert the future war? Yes; as George Wickes stated, "our messages to Washington predicted accurately what would eventually happen if France tried to deny independence to Vietnam."[62] But did it matter in 1945? To that question the answer must be no; the political climate at the time simply dictated otherwise.

But the story of these men is valuable in and of itself, completely aside from any relationship to future wars. It speaks to a camaraderie in war—not just among fellow Americans but also among fellow combatants—that transcended nationality in the forging of a common if temporary purpose. Nguyen Chinh recalled missing Allison Thomas in particular because of his "marching with us, sharing with us, going through all his hardship and difficulty with us."[63] Their story also speaks to the altruistic nature of many of the young Americans of their era and to their belief in what the United States stood for, freedom and liberty, revering the legacy of Franklin Roosevelt. The OSS men in Vietnam were daring, confident, full of self-importance and the patriotic pride that came with victory. Although they were impatient to return home, they were far from real danger and could afford to be concerned with the welfare of others beyond the battlefield. They demonstrated, in most cases, the best qualities of the young of their generation: a solid conviction that the ideals for which they fought, often in both the European and Pacific theaters, really did apply.

Perhaps the OSS–Viet Minh relationship can best be illustrated by one of the last meetings between a member of the OSS (which had become the SSU) and Ho Chi Minh. Major Frank White arrived in Hanoi, having come from Saigon (via Shanghai), with George Wickes and their radio operator in the autumn of 1945. White recalled that the Saigon-based group had "almost no knowledge whatsoever of what was going on in Hanoi with their counterparts," and he was given only the brief orders to replace "the OSS team that had been withdrawn," to continue securing and updating information on the developing situation, and to "make contact with President Ho."[64] Soon after White and Wickes established themselves at the Hotel Métropole, White sent a note introducing himself to Ho Chi Minh and was invited to a meeting that afternoon.

White's conversation with Ho was not unlike those the Viet Minh leader had had with countless other Americans before him: Ho reiterated Vietnam's desire for independence, the atrocities and hardships resulting from French colonialism, and the deep respect the Vietnamese had for the United States and its people. Upon returning to his hotel, White found an invitation to a reception at Ho's governmental palace that evening. He arrived at the appointed place and time and soon discovered that he was surrounded by Chinese, British, and French colonels and generals, as well as the members of Ho's cabinet. Conscious of his rank and ill at ease, White stood back as the others assumed their places around the dinner table. As a newly appointed major and clearly the lowest-ranking man in the room, he expected to find his seat "well below the salt," but he was also ready to "slink away" if there were no empty chairs left.[65] When everyone else was seated, one seat remained— the chair next to President Ho Chi Minh. White recalled the evening:

> The dinner was a horror. The French confined themselves to the barest minimum of conversation and scarcely spoke to the Chinese, who quickly became drunk. . . . At one point I spoke to Ho very quietly. "I think, Mr. President, there is some resentment over the seating arrangement at this table." I meant, of course, my place next to him.
>
> Ho thought for a moment, then replied simply: "Yes, I can see that, but who else could I talk to?"[66]

Notes

INTRODUCTION

1. Quoted in William J. Duiker, *Ho Chi Minh* (New York: Hyperion, 2000), 278.

2. Corey Ford, *Donovan of OSS* (Boston: Little, Brown, 1970), 320.

3. Edmond Taylor, *Awakening from History* (Boston: Gambit, 1969), 346.

4. Ngo Vinh Long, *Before the Revolution: The Vietnamese Peasants under the French* (New York: Columbia University Press, 1991), v.

5. The following passage from *Le Monde*, quoted by Peter Dunn, illustrates the point well: "When we say: 'Ho Chi Minh is a Communist', the Vietnamese replies: 'Ho Chi Minh is my father in the rice-paddy, my brother in the maquis. Do you wish me to take up arms against my father and my brother?' When we say: 'But your father and your brother are fighting for Communism', the Vietnamese replies: 'I am fighting for my independence. My father and my brother are fighting for their independence. As for your Communism, I have no idea what you are talking about.'" Peter M. Dunn, *The First Vietnam War* (New York: St. Martin's, 1985), 23.

6. Huynh Kim Khanh, "The Vietnamese August Revolution Reinterpreted," *Journal of Asian Studies* 30, no. 4 (1971): 780.

7. General Gabriel Sabattier, among others, concluded that without the Japanese coup, the question of Indochina's postwar status would not have even been asked, and would certainly not have been asked in the way that it was in August 1945. General Gabriel Sabattier, *Le destin de l'Indochine: Souvenirs et documents, 1941–1951* (Paris: Librairie Plon, 1952), 360.

8. "The Implacable Man Named 'He Who Enlightens,'" *Life*, March 22, 1968, 22.

9. Robert Shaplen, *The Lost Revolution: The U.S. in Vietnam, 1946–1966* (New York: Harper Colophon, 1966), 34–35.

10. For a complete discussion on Ho Chi Minh and the Viet Minh, see Duiker, *Ho Chi Minh*; Robin W. Winks, "Getting the Right Stuff: FDR, Donovan, and the Quest for Professional Intelligence," in *The Secrets War: The Office of Strategic Services in World War II*, edited by George C. Chalou (Washington, DC: National Archives and Records Administration, 1992), 19–38.

11. Duiker, *Ho Chi Minh*, 135–136. See also Winks, "Getting the Right Stuff," 19–38.

12. William J. Donovan, "What Are We Up Against?" *Vital Speeches of the Day* 7, no. 13 (April 15, 1941): 389.

13. Jean Sainteny, *Histoire d'une paix manquée: Indochine, 1945–1947* (Paris: Librairie Fayard les Grandes Etudes Contemporaines, 1967), 107–108.

14. Austin Glass, "Comments on R&A/IBT Memos D-25, 26, 29, 30, 35 Dealing with Indo-China" (Records of the Office of Strategic Services, Record Group 226 [henceforth RG 226], Entry 19, Box 175, Document XL12971, National Archives and Records Administration [henceforth NARA], Washington, DC).

15. William J. Donovan, "A Central Intelligence Agency," *Vital Speeches of the Day* 12, no. 14 (May 1, 1946): 448.

CHAPTER 1
THE SITUATION ON THE GROUND: VIETNAM

1. Ngo Vinh Long et al., *Before the Revolution: The Vietnamese Peasants under the French*, trans. Ngo Vinh Long (New York: Columbia University Press, 1991), v.

2. Martin J. Murray, *The Development of Capitalism in Colonial Indochina (1870–1940)* (Berkeley and Los Angeles: University of California Press, 1980), 90.

3. Long, *Before the Revolution*, 138–139.

4. Murray, *The Development of Capitalism in Colonial Indochina*, 372–373.

5. Tam Lang, "I Pulled a Rickshaw," in *The Light of the Capital: Three Modern Vietnamese Classics*, translated by Greg Lockhart and Monique Lockhart (Oxford: Oxford University Press, 1996), 80.

6. Joseph Buttinger, *Vietnam: A Dragon Embattled*, 2 vols. (New York: Praeger, 1967), 1: 56–61.

7. Ibid., 1: 58–60.

8. Murray, *The Development of Capitalism in Colonial Indochina*, 380.

9. Ibid., 309–310.

10. Tran Tu Binh, *The Red Earth: A Vietnamese Memoir of Life on a Colonial Rubber Plantation*, translated by John Spragens Jr. (Athens: Ohio University Press, 1985), vii.

11. Ibid., 25–26.

12. Murray, *The Development of Capitalism in Colonial Indochina*, 372.

13. Jacques Dalloz, *The War in Indo-China, 1945–54*, 2nd ed. (Dublin, Ireland: Gill and Macmillan, 1990), 8.

14. Ibid., 8; William J. Duiker, *Sacred War: Nationalism and Revolution in a Divided Vietnam* (New York: McGraw-Hill, 1995), 15; Buttinger, *Vietnam*, 1: 46.

15. Tran Tu Binh, *The Red Earth*, 12.

16. Long, *Before the Revolution*, 139–140.

17. David Marr, *Vietnamese Tradition on Trial, 1920–1945* (Berkeley and Los Angeles: University of California Press, 1981), 8.

18. William J. Duiker, *Ho Chi Minh* (New York: Hyperion, 2000), 14–15.

19. Ibid., 22.

20. Ibid., 23.

21. Ibid., 27–37. See also Tran Dan Tien [Ho Chi Minh], *Glimpses of the Life of Ho Chi Minh, President of the Democratic Republic of Vietnam* (Hanoi: Foreign Languages Publishing House, 1958), 5. In this brief autobiography, written under the pseudonym of a fictitious historian, Tran Dan Tien, Ho Chi Minh mentioned his role in the uprising only briefly, stating: "The young Ho Chi Minh understood and suffered because of the misery of his compatriots. He worked secretly assuming the task of liaison."

22. In his own account, as "remembered" by his fellow Vietnamese seaman, Mai, Ho Chi Minh described his difficult jobs cleaning and bringing from the hold the foodstuffs necessary to feed the 700 to 800 persons aboard, adding that although exhausted at the end of the day he "read or wrote until 11 o'clock or midnight" while others played cards and slept. Tran Dan Tien, *Glimpses of the Life of Ho Chi Minh*, 5–7.

23. Quoted in Duiker, *Ho Chi Minh*, 45.

24. Tran Dan Tien, *Glimpses of the Life of Ho Chi Minh*, 9.

25. Ibid., 13, and Duiker, *Ho Chi Minh*, 51–60. According to "historian" Tran Dan Tien the name became so popular that the "French colonialists in Indochina acquired a new word: they called all Vietnamese patriots 'local Nguyen Ai Quoc.'" Tran Dan Tien, *Glimpses of the Life of Ho Chi Minh*, 26.

26. Tran Dan Tien, *Glimpses of the Life of Ho Chi Minh*, 13–14.

27. Ho Chi Minh, *Ho Chi Minh: Selected Articles and Speeches, 1920–1967*, edited by Jack Woddis (New York: International Publishers, 1970), 13.

28. Duiker, *Ho Chi Minh*, 64. In January 1924 Ho Chi Minh expressed his admiration for the recently departed Lenin in an essay in *Pravda*, calling Lenin the "most courageous" person in Russia. Ho Chi Minh, *Selected Works*, 4 vols. (Hanoi: Foreign Languages Publishing House, 1960), 1: 70.

29. Ho Chi Minh, "Lenin and the East," in Ho, *Selected Works*, 1: 140–141 (originally published in *Le Sifflet*, January 21, 1926).

30. Duiker, *Ho Chi Minh*, 131.

31. For coverage in more depth of Ho Chi Minh's activities in Siam, see Tran Dan Tien, *Glimpses of the Life of Ho Chi Minh*, 34–37; Hoang Van Hoan, *A Drop in the Ocean: Hoang Van Hoan's Revolutionary Reminiscences* (Beijing: Foreign Language Press, 1988); and Duiker, *Ho Chi Minh*, 150–167.

32. Duiker, *Ho Chi Minh*, 179–187.

33. Ho Chi Minh, "Appeal at the Founding of the Communist Party of Indochina, 1930," in *Ho Chi Minh: Selected Articles*, 27–28.

34. Quoted in Duiker, *Ho Chi Minh*, 217. For an interesting account of his time in Hong Kong, see Tran Dan Tien, *Glimpses of the Life of Ho Chi Minh*, 37–43.

35. Murray, *The Development of Capitalism in Colonial Indochina*, 161.

36. Quoted in Yevgeny Kobelev, *Ho Chi Minh* (Moscow: Progress, 1989), 118–119.

37. Ho Chi Minh, "The Party's Line in the Period of the Democratic Front (1936–1939)," in Ho Chi Minh, *Selected Works*, 3: 149–150.

38. Duiker, *Ho Chi Minh*, 240–248, quotations at 240, 245, 246.

39. Ibid., 249.

40. Huynh Kim Khanh, "The Vietnamese August Revolution Reinterpreted," *Journal of Asian Studies* 30, no. 4 (1971): 772.

41. Ho Chi Minh, "Letter from Abroad (1941)," in *Selected Works*, 2: 153.

42. Greg Lockhart, *Nation in Arms: The Origins of the People's Army of Vietnam* (Sydney: Allen and Unwin, 1989), 103.

43. Duiker, *Ho Chi Minh*, 258–264.

44. Minami Yoshizawa, "The Nishihara Mission in Hanoi, July 1940," in *Indochina in the 1940s and 1950s*, edited by Takashi Shiraishi and Motoo Furuta (Ithaca, NY: Cornell Southeast Asia Program, 1992), 21. France had basically ignored Japan's first protests in October 1938, and the border between China and Indochina remained open.

45. According to Japanese sources there were three other supply lines vital to the survival of Chiang Kai-shek's government: "the route to Longzhou via the Lang Son railroad, the route to Longzhou via Tien Yen and Lang Son, and the route to Longzhou via Mong Cai and Dongxing" (ibid., 22).

46. Shigemitsu Mamoru, *Japan and Her Destiny* (London: Hutchinson, 1958), 207. Shigemitsu added that Emperor Hirohito was disappointed in the army's defiance of the arrangements made with the French and "expressed grave concern that it should be the Army that had damaged Japan's fair name" (ibid.). See also Admiral Jean Decoux, *A la barre de l'Indochine: Histoire de mon gouvernement general (1940–1945)* (Paris: Librairie Plon, 1949), 120.

47. Hata Ikuhito, "The Army's Move into Northern Indochina," in *The Fateful Choice: Japan's Advance into Southeast Asia, 1939–194; Selected Translations from "Taiheiyo senso no michi: Kaisen gaiko shi,"* edited by James William Morley (New York: Columbia University Press, 1980), 157–162; Peter M. Dunn, *The First Vietnam War* (New York: St. Martin's, 1985), 53–56. See also Nicholas Tarling, "The British and the First Japanese Move into Indo-China," *Journal of Southeast Asian Studies* 21, no. 1 (March 1990): 35–65.

48. Yoshizawa, "The Nishihara Mission in Hanoi," 26. Indeed, it seems clear that Catroux was dismissed as governor-general because of his political views rather than over any particular failings in his negotiations with the Japanese. Arthur Dommen wrote that Catroux "made no secret of the fact that he intended to honor the Franco-British alliance and was in touch with British officials in Singapore." After leaving Indochina Catroux joined de Gaulle's government-in-exile in London. Arthur J. Dommen, *The Indochinese Experience of the French and the Americans: Nationalism and Communism in Cambodia, Laos, and Vietnam* (Bloomington: Indiana University Press, 2001), 48.

49. The text of the letter reads in part: "Concerning the procurement of special military facilities that Japan has requested, France notes that the Imperial Government of Japan intends to use the foregoing procurement solely for the purpose of resolving the conflict with Generalissimo Chiang Kai-shek, and consequently the aforementioned procurement is temporary and will be terminated with the resolution of the conflict, and that the above is applicable only to the Indochinese provinces along the China border." French ambassador Charles Arsene-Henry to Japanese foreign minister Matsuoka Yosuke, August 30, 1940, in Morley, *The Fateful Choice*, 301–302.

50. Foreign Minister Matsuoka Yosuke to Ambassador Arsene-Henry, August 30, 1940, in Morley, *The Fateful Choice*, 302.

51. In August 1944 troop strengths were slightly higher, at 40,490, including 11,790 in Tonkin, 7,660 in Annam, 19,800 in Cochinchina, and 1,240 in Cambodia. "Order of Battle/French Indo-China" (Records of the Office of Strategic Services, Record Group 226, [henceforth RG 226], Entry 140, Box 35, Folder 274, National Archives and Records Administration [henceforth NARA], Washington, DC). By late September the number of soldiers in Tonkin and Annam had decreased by 390 and 500, respectively. However, the number in Cochinchina had increased by 2,100 and that in Cambodia by 1,210. The enlargements were short-lived, however. By mid-October the number had decreased to its more usual figure, below 40,000 (39,105), with additional troops being withdrawn from Tonkin and Annam as well as from Cambodia and Cochinchina. Troops in Tonkin were dispersed throughout the region, with the largest strengths at Haiphong, Hanoi, and Bac Ninh. In Cochinchina 95 percent were stationed in and around Saigon. "O. B. in French Indo China" (RG 226 Entry 140 Box 35 Folder 273, NARA).

52. Decoux, *A la barre de l'Indochine*, 111–121; Stein Tønnesson, *The Vietnamese Revolution of 1945: Roosevelt, Ho Chi Minh and de Gaulle in a World at War* (London: SAGE, 1991), 37; André Gaudel, *L'Indochine française en face du Japon* (Paris: Susse, 1947), 92–93; Archimedes L. A. Patti, *Why Viet Nam? Prelude to America's Albatross* (Berkeley and Los Angeles: University of California Press, 1980), 74–75; Buttinger, *Vietnam*, 1: 236–238; Hata, "The Army's Move into Northern Indochina," 180–198; David Bergamini, *Japan's Imperial Conspiracy* (New York: Morrow, 1971), 728.

53. Buttinger, *Vietnam*, 1: 241; Dunn, *The First Vietnam War*, 60–63.

54. Dalloz, *The War in Indo-China*, 32.

55. Ho Chi Minh, report on Indochina for the OSS, March 29, 1945 (RG 226, Box 434, Document A-52494/L54540, NARA [henceforth Ho Chi Minh's March 29, 1945, report]); David Marr, *Vietnam 1945: The Quest for Power* (Berkeley and Los Angeles: University of California Press, 1995), 35–37.

56. I have corrected obvious typographical errors but have otherwise reproduced as written variant spellings and punctuations, as well as the telegraphic style of dispatches and the like.

57. Ho Chi Minh's March 29, 1945, report.

58. Joyce C. Lebra, ed., *Japan's Greater East Asia Co-Prosperity Sphere in World War II* (London: Oxford University Press, 1975), 71–72.

59. Yoshizawa, "The Nishihara Mission in Hanoi," 46.

60. Bergamini, *Japan's Imperial Conspiracy*, 812.

61. Marr, *Vietnam 1945*, 29–35; Buttinger, *Vietnam*, 1: 239–240; David Marr, "World War II and the Vietnamese Revolution," in *Southeast Asia under Japanese Occupation*, edited by Alfred W. McCoy (New Haven, CT: Yale University Southeast Asia Studies, 1980), 111–112.

62. The total population of the affected area was approximately 10 million people; thus, the projected death toll represented roughly 10 percent of the population. Marr, *Vietnam 1945*, 96–107; Marr, "World War II and the Vietnamese Revolution,"

113; Buttinger, *Vietnam*, 1: 240. See also Bui Minh Dung, "Japan's Role in the Vietnamese Starvation of 1944–45," *Modern Asian Studies* 29, no. 3 (1995): 573–618.

63. Tran Van Mai, "Who Committed This Crime?" in Long, *Before the Revolution*, 221.

64. Long, *Before the Revolution*, 221.

65. Ho Chi Minh, "Letter from Abroad," 153.

66. For a variety of interpretations of Zhang Fakui's motivations, see Hoang Van Hoan, *A Drop in the Ocean: Hoang Van Hoan's Revolutionary Reminiscences* (Beijing: Foreign Language Press, 1988), 193–202; Duiker, *Ho Chi Minh*, 270–276; and Peter Worthing, *Occupation and Revolution: China and the Vietnamese August Revolution of 1945* (Berkeley: Institute of East Asian Studies, University of California, 2001), 40–45.

67. "Comments on R&A/IBT Memos D-25, 26, 29, 30, 35 dealing with Indo-China" (RG 226, Entry 19, Box 175, Document XL12971, NARA). In his July 1945 report, OSS Glass went on to explain, "From 1939 to 1940 they were very bombastic and virulent in their criticism of the totalitarian dictators. But from the time that Marshal Pétain took power in 1940, French public opinion underwent a sudden metamorphosis and, at least outwardly, was solidly back of the octogenarian dictator of France. Beneath the surface, however, there was a strong cleavage of opinion; many people were secretly sympathetic towards the cause of the Free French, but did not necessarily admire or respect DeGaulle himself." Ibid.

CHAPTER 2
THE SITUATION ON THE GROUND: THE UNITED STATES

1. Robert Dallek, *Franklin D. Roosevelt and American Foreign Policy, 1932–1945* (Oxford: Oxford University Press, 1995), 3–4.

2. Ibid., 4.

3. Mark Twain, "A Greeting from the Nineteenth to the Twentieth Century," in *Mark Twain on the Damned Human Race*, edited by Janet Smith (New York: Hill and Wang, 1962), 5.

4. Albert J. Beveridge, "Speech in the Senate, 1900," in *Words That Made American History*, edited by Richard Current, John Garraty, and Julius Weinberg (Boston: Little, Brown, 1978), 1: 218–225.

5. Dallek, *Franklin D. Roosevelt and American Foreign Policy*, 8.

6. Ibid., 10–16.

7. U.S. Department of State, *Foreign Relations of the United States, 1938*, vol. 3, *The Far East* (Washington, DC: Government Printing Office, 1954), 591–597.

8. U.S. Department of State, *Foreign Relations of the United States, 1939*, vol. 3, *The Far East* (Washington, DC: Government Printing Office, 1955), 99–100, 115–116.

9. Quoted in Dallek, *Franklin D. Roosevelt and American Foreign Policy*, 230.

10. U.S. Department of State, *Foreign Relations of the United States, 1941*, July 24, 1941, in vol. 2, *Europe* (Washington, DC: Government Printing Office, 1959), 96.

11. Dallek, *Franklin D. Roosevelt and American Foreign Policy*, 275–276, 302.

12. Cordell Hull to William Leahy, January 20, 1942, in U.S. Department of State, *Foreign Relations of the United States, 1942*, vol. 2, *Europe* (Washington, DC: Government Printing Office, 1962), 124.

13. William Leahy to Cordell Hull, January 27, 1942, in U.S. Department of State, *Foreign Relations of the United States, 1942*, vol. 2, *Europe*, 124–126.

14. In Dallek, *Franklin D. Roosevelt and American Foreign Policy*, 324–325.

15. Quoted in ibid., 327.

16. Sumner Welles to Gaston Henry-Haye, April 13, 1942, in U.S. Department of State, *Foreign Relations of the United States, 1942*, vol. 2, *Europe*, 561.

17. Dallek, *Franklin D. Roosevelt and American Foreign Policy*, 341–342.

18. Quoted in Elliot Roosevelt, *As He Saw It* (New York: Duell, Sloan and Pearce, 1946), 74.

19. Quoted in ibid., 115.

20. Dallek, *Franklin D. Roosevelt and American Foreign Policy*, 329.

21. Ibid., 429.

22. Stalin quoted in ibid., 435; Roosevelt quoted in ibid., 429.

23. In his memoir, Air Marshal Nguyen Cao Ky recalled, "Even as a boy, listening with my father to the clandestine radio, I had believed that the promises of Roosevelt would come true, that when the war ended, Vietnam would be free. I could not have been more wrong." Nguyen Cao Ky, *Twenty Years and Twenty Days* (New York: Stein and Day, 1976), 16.

24. U.S. Department of State, *Cooperative War Effort*, Executive Agreement Series 236, Publication 1732 (Washington, DC: Government Printing Office, 1942), 4.

25. Cordell Hull, *The Memoirs of Cordell Hull*, 2 vols. (New York: Macmillan, 1948), 2: 1595. Gabriel Kolko argued that the "critical element in the first American position was that ultimate independence for the Vietnamese would not be something they might take themselves, and at no time did Washington express a belief in the intrinsic value of freedom for the Vietnamese, but [considered it] a blessing the world's Great Powers might grant at their own convenience." Gabriel Kolko, *The Politics of War: The World and United States Foreign Policy, 1943–1945* (New York: Random House, 1968), 608. See also Walter La Feber, "Roosevelt, Churchill, and Indochina: 1942–1945," *American Historical Review* 80 (December 1975): 1277–1295.

26. Hull, *Memoirs*, 2: 1597.

27. Mark Philip Bradley, "Franklin D. Roosevelt, Trusteeship, and U.S. Exceptionalism: Reconsidering the American Vision of Postcolonial Vietnam," in *The Transformation of Southeast Asia: International Perspectives on Decolonization*, edited by Marc Frey, Ronald W. Pruessen, and Tan Tai Yong (Armonk, NY: Sharpe, 2003), 198.

28. Quoted in Bradley, "Franklin D. Roosevelt, Trusteeship, and U.S. Exceptionalism," 199–200.

29. Quoted in Joseph M. Siracusa, "FDR, Truman, and Indochina, 1941–1952: The Forgotten Years," in *The Impact of the Cold War: Reconsiderations*, edited by Joseph M. Siracusa and Glen St. John Barclay (Port Washington, NY: Kennikat, 1977), 167.

30. International Colonial Exhibition, Paris, 1931, French Indo-China, *Le Laos* by R. Meyer (Hanoi: Imprimerie d'Extreme-Orient, 1930) as cited in Jacques Dalloz, *The War in Indo-China, 1945–54* (Dublin, Ireland: Gill and Macmillan, 1987), 10.

31. *La conference africaine Française, Brazzaville, 30 janvier 1944–8 février 1944* (Algiers: Commissariat aux Colonies, 1944), 35, quoted in Donald Lancaster, *The Emancipation of French Indochina* (London: Oxford University Press, 1961), 122–123.

32. William Roger Louis, *Imperialism at Bay: The United States and the Decolonization of the British Empire* (Oxford: Clarendon, 1997), 46. Ralph Bunche was one of many highly educated men recruited to work in the Research and Analysis Branch of the OSS. He handled "the subjects of colonial policy and administration, native problems, and race relations" within the British Empire, excluding India. Barry M. Katz, *Foreign Intelligence: Research and Analysis in the Office of Strategic Services 1942–1945* (Cambridge, MA: Harvard University Press, 1989), 8.

33. Robert Murphy, *Diplomat among Warriors* (New York: Doubleday, 1964), 168.

34. Hull, *Memoirs*, 2: 1597.

35. Bernard Fall, *The Two Viet-Nams: A Political and Military Analysis* (New York: Praeger, 1967), 58.

36. Gary R. Hess, "Franklin Roosevelt and Indochina," *Journal of American History* 59 (1972): 354.

37. Siracusa, "FDR, Truman, and Indochina," 167.

38. Hess, "Franklin Roosevelt and Indochina," 354. See also Peter A. Poole, *Eight Presidents and Indochina* (Malabar, FL: Krieger, 1978), 4–11.

39. Siracusa, "FDR, Truman, and Indochina," 166.

40. Dallek, *Franklin D. Roosevelt and American Foreign Policy*, 511–512.

41. U.S. Department of State, *Foreign Relations of the United States: The Conferences at Malta and Yalta* (Washington, DC: Government Printing Office, 1955), 770.

42. Hess, "Franklin Roosevelt and Indochina," 365. For a discussion of Anglo-American relations in the context of Indochina, also see John J. Sbrega, "'First catch your hare': Anglo-American Perspectives on Indochina during the Second World War," *Journal of Southeast Asian Studies* 14, no. 1 (1983): 63–78, and Christopher Thorne, "Indochina and Anglo-American Relations, 1942–1945," *Pacific Historical Review* 45 (1976): 73–96.

43. Dallek, *Franklin D. Roosevelt and American Foreign Policy*, 439.

44. Bradley F. Smith, *The Shadow Warriors: O.S.S. and the Origins of the C.I.A.* (New York: Basic Books, 1983), 332–333.

45. General Albert Wedemeyer, "Southwest Pacific: British-French-Dutch Accord on Imperialism," November 21, 1944 (RG 226, M1642, R90, F1355, NARA).

46. Quoted in U.S. Department of State, *Foreign Relations of the United States, 1943: China* (Washington, DC: Government Printing Office, 1956), 188. Although there were those in both the military and the government who championed the values of the Atlantic Charter, Gary Hess concluded: "The pledge of the Atlantic Charter to recognize the rights of people to self-determination, augmented by occasional assurances that this applied to all areas of the world, stood as the basic policy on imperialism, but for most areas of the colonial world that policy remained a vague and

platitudinous goal rather than a basis for specific policy and action." Hess, "Franklin Roosevelt and Indochina," 353.

47. Francis Patrick Duffy, *Father Duffy's Story: A Tale of Humor and Heroism, of Life and Death with the Fighting Sixty-ninth* (New York: Doran, 1919), 220–237.

48. William Donovan became one of the most decorated American soldiers in World War I, earning not only the Medal of Honor but also the Distinguished Service Cross and Purple Heart; the Distinguished Service Medal, Legion d'Honneur, Croix de Guerre avec Palme, and Silver Star from France; and the Croci de Guerra from Italy. For a more extensive biography of Donovan, see Cord Ford, *Donovan of OSS* (Boston: Little, Brown, 1970); Anthony Cave Brown, *The Last Hero: Wild Bill Donovan* (New York: Vintage, 1982); and Richard Dunlop, *Donovan, America's Master Spy* (Chicago: Rand McNally, 1982).

49. Dunlop, *Donovan, America's Master Spy*, 184.

50. Ibid., 184–190; Ford, *Donovan of OSS*, 80–83.

51. Quoted in Dunlop, *Donovan, America's Master Spy*, 193.

52. Quoted in ibid., 194. See also Dorothy Berg, "Notes on Roosevelt's 'Quarantine Speech,'" *Political Science Quarterly* 72, no. 3 (September 12, 1957): 405–433.

53. Joseph E. Persico, *Roosevelt's Secret War* (New York: Random House, 2001), 68.

54. Walter Karig, "The Most Mysterious Office in Washington," *Liberty*, January 3, 1942, 46.

55. William Donovan, "Our Spiritual Defense," *Vital Speeches of the Day* 7, no. 19 (June 28, 1941): 589–590.

56. Quoted in Persico, *Roosevelt's Secret War*, 77–82. See also Dunlop, *Donovan, America's Master Spy*, 243–274.

57. Persico, *Roosevelt's Secret War*, 80–82. For a fuller description of Donovan's relationship with William Stephenson, see Thomas F. Troy, *Donovan and the CIA* (Frederick, MD: University Publications of America, 1981), and Thomas F. Troy, *Wild Bill and Intrepid: Donovan, Stephenson, and the Origin of the CIA* (New Haven, CT: Yale University Press, 1996).

58. Ray S. Cline, *Secrets, Spies and Scholars: Blueprint of the Essential CIA* (Washington, DC: Acropolis, 1976), 2. Cline goes on to describe the presidential directive as both "revolutionary and farsighted" in its ability to transcend wartime necessity and serve the peacetime United States years later as the CIA.

59. Lawrence H. McDonald, "The Office of Strategic Services," *Prologue* 23, no. 1 (Spring 1991): 9.

60. Karig, "The Most Mysterious Office in Washington," 8.

61. Lawrence H. McDonald, "The OSS and Its Records," in *The Secrets War: The Office of Strategic Services in World War II*, edited by George C. Chalou (Washington, DC: National Archives and Records Administration, 1992), 83.

62. Troy, *Donovan and the CIA*, 136.

63. Katz, *Foreign Intelligence*, 8.

64. McDonald, "The Office of Strategic Services," 9. For a description of branches and their functions, see "Organizational Chart, OSS" (RG 226, Entry 154, Box 174, Folder 2023, NARA).

65. McDonald, "The OSS and Its Records," 83–95.

66. McDonald, "The Office of Strategic Services," 8; R. Harris Smith, *OSS: The Secret History of America's First Central Intelligence Agency* (Berkeley and Los Angeles: University of California Press, 1972), 29.

67. Katz, *Foreign Intelligence*, 196. Whereas Katz and most other authors find the work of the R&A Branch to have been quite effective, Nelson MacPherson provides a counterargument in "Reductio ad absurdum: The R&A Branch of OSS/London," *International Journal of Intelligence and Counterintelligence* 15, no. 3 (July 2002): 390–414.

68. Sun Tzu's *Art of War*, written in the fourth century B.C.E., discussed the need for secret agents and spies to spread false information and nurture fifth columnists to engage in subversive activities behind enemy lines as part of effective warfare. Sun Tzu, *The Art of War*, translated by Samuel B. Griffith (London: Oxford University Press, 1963), 39–44.

69. OSS operative Charles Fenn remembered many conversations with fellow officers who found his MO work questionable at best. Charles Fenn, interviews by author.

70. Ford, *Donovan of OSS*, 12.

71. Cline, *Secrets, Spies and Scholars*, 39–40.

72. Edmond Taylor, *Awakening from History* (Boston: Gambit, 1969), 319, 348.

73. Noel B. Poirier, "The Birth of Special Ops," *World War II* 17, no. 5 (January 2003): 64.

74. Max Corvo, "The OSS and the Italian Campaign," in *The Secrets War: The Office of Strategic Services in World War II*, edited by George C. Chalou (Washington, DC: National Archives and Records Administration, 1992), 193.

75. McDonald, "The OSS and Its Records," 95.

76. Brown, *The Last Hero*, 148. Stein Tønnesson, *The Vietnamese Revolution of 1945: Roosevelt, Ho Chi Minh and de Gaulle in a World at War* (London: SAGE, 1991), 196. In "A Different Kind of War," Admiral Milton Miles also concluded from his interactions with Donovan that Wild Bill was distinctly pro-European and did not really understand the situation in Asia: "Donovan, for reasons I shall never understand, aligned himself firmly with those who wished to preserve the prewar Asian status quo." Vice Admiral Milton E. Miles, USN, *A Different Kind of War: The Unknown Story of the U.S. Navy's Guerrilla Forces in World War II China* (New York: Doubleday, 1967), 191.

77. Brown, *The Last Hero*, 148. In his discussion of the Donovan-Stephenson relationship, Brown described both men in relation to their stance on empire: "There sprang up a rare relationship between Donovan, the anti-imperialist, and Stephenson, a principal representative of the world's leading imperial power." Ibid.

78. Brown, *The Last Hero*, 556–558. See also Dunlop, *Donovan, America's Master Spy*, 368, 440–443. Colonel Dewavrin's alias was "Passy."

79. Tønnesson, *The Vietnamese Revolution of 1945*, 196.

80. Ibid., 196.

81. William Donovan, "Memorandum for the President," July 10, 1944 (RG 226, M1642, R90, F1334-1335, NARA). Zinovi Petchkoff is also known as Pechkoff and

Pechkov. A de Gaulle appointee, Petchkoff did not represent the official French government; the title "ambassador" was bestowed by Chiang Kai-shek.

82. For a full discussion of issues relating to the division of theaters of operation in the Pacific, see Richard Aldrich, "Imperial Rivalry: British and American Intelligence in Asia, 1942–1946," *Intelligence and National Security* 3, no. 1 (January 1988): 5–55.

83. Brown, *The Last Hero*, 317. Brown went on to say that "the fervor with which [Roosevelt's] policy was prosecuted by OSS officers abroad depended in great measure upon the ethnic origins of the men concerned: White Anglo-Saxon Protestants tended to be much less fervent, for example, than officers of Jewish or Eastern European and Arabian origins." Although this may have held true in other areas, the ethnic background of OSS agents in Indochina was not the decisive factor in determining their stance on French colonialism or on the Vietnamese.

84. Bradley Smith, *The Shadow Warriors*, 320, 333.

CHAPTER 3

THE FIRST ON THE GROUND: MILES, MEYNIER, AND THE GBT

1. Charles Fenn, "Remembering Frank Tan," *Interchange* 12, no. 2 (Summer 2002): 10.

2. Texaco's official history reported that the corporation was proud to have aided in the World War II effort, citing the number of employees who served, the new products that were developed to aid the war effort, and the fact that 30 percent of Texaco products were dedicated to "war purposes." Marquis James, *The Texaco Story: The First Fifty Years, 1902–1952* (New York [?]:Texas Company, 1953), 70–79.

3. Archimedes L. A. Patti, *Why Viet Nam? Prelude to America's Albatross* (Berkeley and Los Angeles: University of California Press, 1980), 44.

4. Ibid., 44, 542. By all indications, at this early stage of the war U.S. intelligence had no connection with Gordon or his "mission."

5. Among American soldier-authors, Tai Li's reputation was mixed. For a most favorable view of Tai Li, see Vice Admiral Milton E. Miles, USN, *A Different Kind of War: The Unknown Story of the U.S. Navy's Guerrilla Forces in World War II China* (New York: Doubleday, 1967). In his memoir, *Why Viet Nam?* Archimedes Patti presented Tai Li in a more negative light. See also Charles Fenn, "Remembering Frank Tan," 10.

6. Patti, *Why Viet Nam?* 44.

7. Even after the Japanese attack on Pearl Harbor, Americans repatriated in 1943 testified that Westerners were able to move about with relative ease in French Indochina and could even acquire "passes" from the Japanese for travel throughout the country. "Repatriates" (RG 226, Entry 19, Box 657, Document A-19116, NARA).

8. Patti, *Why Viet Nam?* 44–45.

9. Ibid., 45; R. Harris Smith, *OSS: The Secret History of America's First Central Intelligence Agency* (Berkeley and Los Angeles: University of California Press, 1972), 325. Harry Bernard is listed as Paul Bernard in some sources.

10. Charles Fenn, memoir (unpublished).

11. Frank Tan, interviews by author. See also Fenn, memoir.

12. Marquis James wrote: "Texaco's 10 Norwegian-flag tankers were requisitioned by the Royal Norwegian Government in the Spring of 1940, shortly after the invasion of Norway, along with other Norwegian-flag vessels. Arrangements were made with the governmental authorities of Norway for Texaco to continue to operate these vessels." James, *The Texaco Story*, 74. Thus, Tan had the opportunity to both recognize and contact the friendly vessels.

13. Tan, interviews; Fenn, memoir; "Full Transcript of 1997 OSS/Viet Minh Meeting," courtesy of William Duiker. This transcript is of a 1997 meeting in which eight veterans of the OSS, six veterans of the Viet Minh, and twenty additional participants from the United States, Vietnam, and Europe took part in a roundtable meeting in Long Island, New York. The meeting, sponsored by the Fund for Reconciliation and Development, was a forum to enable the veterans from both sides to renew old friendships and share their common experiences from World War II. The transcript of that conference provides an excellent source to compare and contrast the veterans' reminiscences of a time when they were young men on the ground in Vietnam.

14. William Wainwright contended that members of the GBT sold fuel for a less altruistic reason: personal financial gain. See William H. Wainwright, "De Gaulle and Indochina, 1940–1945" (Ph.D. diss., Fletcher School of Law and Diplomacy, 1972).

15. Tan had a third close brush with the Japanese. In 1941, while working with German advisers near a mined rice field in northern Vietnam, Japanese officers spotted Tan, who was visiting friends, and ordered him to come across the minefield to them for questioning. He traversed the rice field without incident. The astonished Japanese ordered him to do it again, and when he was again successful, the "spooked" Japanese let him go. Tan, interviews.

16. "Full Transcript of 1997 OSS/Viet Minh Meeting," 20.

17. "French Indochina Report by G.B.T. Group," November 11, 1944 (RG 226, Entry 154, Box 115, Folder 2077, NARA).

18. Philippe Devillers, *Histoire du Viet-Nam de 1940 à 1952* (Paris: Seuil, 1952), 114; Fenn, memoir, 61, 72–73, 87.

19. "Report No. 8974–1124" (RG 226, Entry 19, Box 657, Document 54728, NARA).

20. R. Harris Smith, *OSS*, 251.

21. Miles, *A Different Kind of War*, 1–30; Claire Chennault, *Way of a Fighter: The Memoirs of Claire Lee Chennault* (New York: Putnam's Sons, 1949), 257.

22. R. Harris Smith, *OSS*, 197–198.

23. Bradley Smith, *The Shadow Warriors: O.S.S. and the Origins of the C.I.A.* (New York: Basic Books, 1983), 249–252.

24. Miles, *A Different Kind of War*, 117.

25. Bradley Smith, *The Shadow Warriors*, 132–133. Former OSS agent Carleton Swift, who worked with Archimedes Patti in Kunming in 1944 and replaced him in 1945 as head of the OSS mission in Hanoi, concurs with Smith's analysis. Swift stated that both Tai Li and the SACO teams were "basically useless.... since none of the SACO teams could be headed by an American, all intelligence went to the Chinese

first and overall, little of value was produced. After Donovan's deal and the end of the Miles-Tai Li arrangement, OSS began to produce real intelligence using their own radios and ciphers." Carleton Swift, interviews by author.

26. Chennault, *Way of a Fighter*, 257.

27. Miles, *A Different Kind of War*, 180–182.

28. "Secret War Diary, Section II—Intelligence" (Milton Miles Papers, Records of Naval Group China, Record Group 38 [henceforth RG 38], Box 42, Folder October 1943, NARA). OSS files contained the French source *Notabilities d'Indochine, 1943*, which provided a photograph with caption for both Mrs. Meynier's father and her uncle. Her father, Do Huu Thinh, was identified as the retired paymaster of the Treasury of Indochina and her uncle, Hoang Trong Phu, was identified as the "Venerable Councillor of the Tonkin Empire in 1937, Vice President of the Privy Council" (RG 226, OSS-P-9718 and OSS 112981, NARA). Although their positions would have provided the two men with opportunity and influence, their status as true political leaders cannot be substantiated. Their connections to elite Vietnamese society, however, was ample incentive to support Miles's use of Katiou Meynier in his developing intelligence network.

29. "Secret War Diary, Section II—Intelligence."

30. Miles, *A Different Kind of War*, 182–184. See also Patti, *Why Viet Nam?* 34–35.

31. "Log of Daily Events," August 28, 1943 (RG 38, Box 36, File 35.3, NARA).

32. Miles, *A Different Kind of War*, 182–184; "Secret War Diary" (RG 38, Box 42, Folder October 1943, NARA); "Log of Daily Events," August 28, 1943.

33. In mid-August, Naval Lieutenant Robert Larson wrote Miles inquiring on Robert Meynier's behalf as to whether Mrs. Meynier had left Cairo en route to Calcutta. Commander Meynier was anxious to get the information immediately because "the security of several agents are involved until she gets clear, and when done they must be notified at the earliest possible moment." Letter from Larson to Miles (RG 38, Box 36, File 35.3, NARA).

34. Miles, *A Different Kind of War*, 182–184.

35. "Secret War Diary."

36. "Log of Daily Events," August 28, 1943. See also Miles, *A Different Kind of War*, 185–186.

37. Miles, *A Different Kind of War*, 186–187.

38. Miles, "Memo. For Commanding General, C.B.I." October 17, 1943 (RG 38, Box 42, Files October 1943, NARA). Miles's information appears to have been based primarily on information from Katiou Meynier. Although he clearly did not possess a full understanding of the political nature of these groups, their existence can be substantiated in both William Duiker's biography of Ho Chi Minh (New York: Hyperion, 2000) and Nguyen Thi Dinh's memoir, *No Other Road to Take: Memoir of Mrs. Nguyen Thi Dinh*, translated by Mai V. Elliott (Ithaca, NY: Cornell University Press, 1976).

39. "Secret War Diary."

40. Miles, *A Different Kind of War*, 186–187.

41. Paula Martin [Katiou Meynier], "Propaganda Directed to Cochin China," October 16, 1943 (RG 38, Box 42, File October 1943, NARA).

42. Miles, *A Different Kind of War*, 184.

43. Larson to Miles, November 30, 1943 (RG 38, Box 36, File 35.3, NARA).

44. Major Hoffman to Miles, October 27, 1943 (RG 226, Entry 154, Box 191, Folder 3267, NARA).

45. Major Herbert Little, "Indo-China Mission," October 22, 1943 (RG 226, Entry 154, Box 191, Folder 3267, NARA).

46. "Indo China MO Unit," December 13, 1943 (RG 226, Entry 154, Box 191, Folder 3267, NARA).

47. Patti, *Why Viet Nam?* 36.

48. Miles, *A Different Kind of War*, 187–188. In a letter to Miles, Larson reported visiting with Father Bec in Algeria. According to Larson, French internecine politics continued to make Bec's situation difficult: "Father Bec too was considered a danger-ous character upon his return to Algeria. His whole trip had been hindered by Col. Emblanc." When Father Bec arrived in Algeria, he "found the French Military Mis-sion under Col. Escarra was indeed an organization closely bound in opposition to anything and anyone who was on the wrong side of the fence in China. Father Bec had nothing to do for more than two months." Larson to Miles, September 22, 1944 (RG 38, Box 35, Folder 35.3, NARA).

49. Ronald Spector, *Advice and Support: The Early Years of the U.S. Army in Viet-nam, 1941–1960* (New York: Free Press, 1985), 25.

50. Miles, *A Different Kind of War*, 189.

51. Ibid., 311.

52. Ibid., 424–425. Although Miles overestimated the success of Admiral Halsey's raid, it was a significant achievement. Halsey sank forty-four ships that day, includ-ing the French cruiser *La Motte-Piquet* (the largest vessel present). The mission was a disappointment, however, as Halsey's goal was to sink two Japanese battleships that were mistakenly reported to be in the area. Stein Tønnesson noted an even greater long-term significance: "This raid contributed more than anything else to arouse Japanese fears of [an Allied] invasion" of French Indochina. Stein Tønnesson, *The Vietnamese Revolution of 1945: Roosevelt, Ho Chi Minh and de Gaulle in a World at War* (London: SAGE, 1991), 190–196. See also Louis Allen, Ju-dith Stowe, and Thanatphong Smitabhindu, "The Japanese Coup of 9 March 1945 in Indo-China," in *1945 in South-East Asia* (London: London School of Economics and Political Science, 1985), 1–29.

53. Patti, *Why Viet Nam?* 36.

54. Spector, *Advice and Support*, 25–26.

55. Miles, *A Different Kind of War*, 159–174; R. Harris Smith, *OSS*, 242–285; Corey Ford, *Donovan of OSS* (Boston: Little, Brown, 1970), 267–272. Although relieved of his OSS command, Miles continued on in China with the U.S. Navy, engaging in many of the same types of activities. At a January 1945 staff meeting called by Gen-eral Wedemeyer "to outline the Generalissimo's desires with reference to coordination of clandestine and quasi-military activities in the China Theater, including China and French Indo-China," Miles maintained that he was deputy to Tai Li, the chief of op-erations of Naval Group China. Furthermore, Miles stated that "the Navy Group is

not involved in any clandestine or quasi-military operations . . . because we are straight military." The situation became even more interesting when Wedemeyer pressed for clarification, asking specifically whether Naval Group China was involved in intelligence and guerrilla activities, which he defined as "units that are not in the usual or regular military organizations, for example, small bands that are sent out to accomplish a specific mission, such as sabotage and counter-sabotage activities." Miles admitted that indeed they were engaging in such activities, using American personnel and equipment, but that they were "under General Tai Li" and operated "by direct orders from the Generalissimo." Miles remained a strong advocate for the Nationalist Chinese and a close personal friend to both Tai Li and Chiang Kai-shek throughout and after the war. "Minutes of Conference: Clandestine and Quasi-Military Activities," January 24 1945 (RG 226, Entry 154, Box 174, Folder 3022, NARA).

56. Larson, "Propaganda and the War in Indo-China," 1944 (RG 226, Entry 154, Box 199, Folder 3276, NARA).

57. Ibid.

58. Ibid.

59. Larson to Wight, March 26, 1944 (RG 38, Box 35, File 35.3, NARA).

60. Ibid.

61. Ibid.

62. Ibid.

63. Wight to Larson, March 27, 1944 (RG 38, Box 35, File 35.3, NARA).

64. Letters from Larson to Wight, February through June 1944 (RG 38, Box 35, File 35.3, NARA).

65. Larson probably misunderstood the name of Mullen's organization. The Air Ground Aid Service was the China-based group mostly responsible for pilot rescue.

66. Larson to Wight, June 1944 (RG 38, Box 35, File 35.3, NARA).

67. Ibid.

68. Patti, *Why Viet Nam?* 36. See also untitled memo regarding Indochina (RG 226, Entry 154, Box 199, Folder 3373, NARA).

69. Robert Meynier proceeded to North Africa, where French politics continued to plague him. Larson reported that "Commander Meynier found that his recall was at the direct instigation of General DeGaulle who was afraid that he, Commander Meynier, would fly the coop and join up completely with the Americans.... There are indications that the British and the French are working contrary to some American interests in the Far East and Commander Meynier characteristically refuses either to work for the English or against the Americans. However, he fears he may be forced to do so. It was because of that fear that he asked me the question concerning American citizenship. In case he is ordered to work with the English and French against us he wants nothing more than to become an American citizen, by desertion from the French Navy if necessary." Larson to Miles, September 22, 1944.

70. Miles, *A Different Kind of War*, 191.

71. Larson, "Propaganda and the War in Indo-China."

72. "GBT Report," November 25, 1944 (RG 226, Entry 140, Box 35, Folder 272, NARA).

73. "Log of Daily Events" (RG 38, Box 35, File 35.3, NARA).

74. "Gordon and His BGT [*sic*] Group" (RG 226, M1642, Roll 88, Frames 1116-1117, NARA).

75. Ibid.

76. David Marr, *Vietnam 1945: The Quest for Power* (Berkeley and Los Angeles: University of California Press, 1995), 272.

77. Bernard Fall, "La politique americaine au Viet-Nam," *Politique Etrange*, July 1955, 308-309. French historian André Gaudel made even more impressive claims. He wrote: "Grace à ces informations, quatre croiseurs, cinq destroyers, huit transports, six pétroliers, trios escorteurs, deux cargos et treize autres bâtiments, soit 41 navires, jurent coules ou gravement endommages, entre le 14 octobre 1944 et le 9 mars 1945, tandis que 1.800 hommes de troupes ennemis périssaient au cours de ces attaques." André Gaudel, *L'Indochine française en face du Japon* (Paris: Susse, 1947), 136.

78. Cecil B. Currey, *Victory at Any Cost: The Genius of Viet Nam's Gen. Vo Nguyen Giap* (Washington, DC: Brassey, 1997), 84.

79. Robert Shaplen, *The Lost Revolution: The U.S. in Vietnam, 1946-1966* (New York: Harper Colophon, 1966), 34. For a slightly different version, also see Shaplen, "The Enigma of Ho Chi Minh," *Reporter*, January 27, 1955, 11-19.

80. Untitled document regarding Austin Glass (RG 226, Entry 92A, Box 26, Folder 391, NARA); Marr, *Vietnam 1945*, 281.

81. Untitled document regarding Austin Glass (RG 226, Entry 92A, Box 26, Folder 391, NARA).

82. Robert Hall, untitled memo (RG 226, Entry 154, Box 199, Folder 3373, NARA).

83. R. Harris Smith, *OSS*, 260-261.

84. "The Gordon Plan" (RG 226, M1642, Roll 88, Frames 1108-1113, NARA).

85. OSS reports from October 1944 agreed that the French Resistance was in need of money and equipment. Major H. C. Faxon to Colonel Robert Hall, "Resume of Discussion with French Military Mission," October 5, 1944 (RG 226, Entry 154, Box 199, Folder 3373, NARA). One report elaborated further: "The French are false—even the officials. When they talk with the Japanese they hope for a Japanese victory but as soon as they turn their backs they think only of the victory of the Anglo-Saxons. The French can furnish a powerful fifth column for the Allies in case they decide to attack French Indochina." "Notes from a Secret Japanese Document," October 4, 1944 (RG 226, Entry 16, Box 1130, Document A-44281, NARA).

86. In March 1945, the OSS reported four confirmed POW camps in Saigon housing at least 1,959 Allied prisoners, including 209 Americans. "P.O.W. Camps French Indo-China," March 7, 1945 (RG 226, Entry 154, Box 199, Folder 3381, NARA).

87. "The Gordon Plan."

88. Ibid., Frames 1110-1111, 1118-1123.

89. Ibid., Frame 1115.

90. "French Indochina Report by G.B.T. Group" (RG 226, Entry 154, Box 115, Folder 2077, NARA).

91. Ibid. See also Admiral Jean Decoux, *A la barre de l'Indochine: Histoire de mon gouvernement general (1940-1945)* (Paris: Librairie Plon, 1949), 318.

92. Marr, *Vietnam 1945*, 272.

93. "Gordon and His BGT [*sic*] Group."

94. Tønnesson, *The Vietnamese Revolution of 1945*, 197.

95. Patti, *Why Viet Nam?* 66.

96. Cordell Hull, *The Memoirs of Cordell Hull*, 2 vols. (New York: Macmillan, 1948), 2: 1598.

97. Untitled memo on GBT (RG 226, Entry 154, Box 149, Folder 2552, NARA).

CHAPTER 4

THE CHAMELEON: CHARLES FENN

1. Charles Fenn, *Ho Chi Minh: A Biographical Introduction* (New York: Charles Scribner's Sons, 1973), 9.

2. Charles Fenn, memoir (unpublished), 1–7; Fenn, interviews by author.

3. Fenn to Major Little, "Indo-China MO Mission," October 30, 1943 (RG 226, Entry 139, Box 138, Folder 1864, NARA).

4. Fenn to Lieutenant Colonel Jacques de Sibour, "Operations for 1944" (RG 226, Entry 154, Box 149, Folder 2552, NARA). Interestingly, in his plan for MO work in French Indochina, written in October 1943, MO chief de Sibour assigned Fenn to handle "Recruiting and Distributing of Material." According to Fenn's first reports, he was only chosen for MO work in the China-Burma-India theater in December 1943. Fenn to Little, "Indo-China MO Mission," October 30, 1943, and Fenn to de Sibour, "Operations for 1944."

5. "China-Burma-India Theatre Operation II, MO in Support of the 14th Airforce" (RG 226, Entry 139, Box 148, Folder 2015, NARA).

6. Fenn, memoir, 26–32. Fenn's Chinese agents were able to blend in with the southern Chinese and Tonkin Chinese, who routinely crossed the border as agents for either the Kuomintang or the Japanese. The various agents passed between the borders with relative ease because they had "at their disposal large sums of money as well as special goods such as soap, piece goods, crepe rubber, etc." From Ilion, October 5, 1944 (RG 226, Entry 140, Box 35, Folder 273, NARA). See also "French Indo-China—Japanese Secret Services," March 18, 1944 (RG 226, Entry 154, Box 199, Folder 3276, NARA).

7. Fenn recorded in his diary Coughlin's view of Indochina: "You got Annam here in the north, Tonkin in the south, and Cambodia and Laos over here in the west. They call the whole shebang 'French Indochina' or simply FIC. When the French folded up in Europe the Japs walked in and took the lot. We couldn't do a thing about it until last year when we had a few plans for bombing and strafing. But we pretty soon found out there was practically no intelligence on weather, defenses or targets. The French Military Mission operating in China keep up certain contacts with a few Free French inside. But it's only courier stuff, and mostly useless by the time we get it." Fenn, memoir, 42. As is obvious from the above, the head of the OSS for the Far East demonstrated an ignorance of geography in "FIC" and had obviously completely disregarded the Meynier network and their potential.

8. "Operations for 1944" (RG 226, Entry 154, Box 149, Folder 2552, NARA). See also Fenn, memoir, 42.

9. Lungchow was mentioned frequently in late-1944 OSS reports in relation to trade and espionage along the China-Indochina border. For example: "The mercury and coins are brought over by Chinese coolies, men and women from Lungchow and Tsinsi districts. The goods are carried to the nearest Annamite markets or to frontier posts.... the collecting and forwarding of these commodities is done in China with the help of the authorities at the frontier in Lungchow and at Tsinsi." "Japanese Espionage System in the Cao Bang Area," November 22, 1944 (RG 226, Entry 154, Box 1136, NARA).

10. Fenn to Colonel Robert Hall, "Gordon-Bernard Liaison," September 28, 1944 (RG 226, Entry 154, Box 191, Folder 3267, NARA). See also Fenn, memoir, 43–50.

11. Fenn, memoir, 51.

12. Fenn to Hall, "Gordon-Bernard Liaison."

13. Quoted in Fenn, memoir, 52.

14. Fenn to Hall, "Report No. 2," October 13, 1944 (RG 226, Entry 154, Box 191, Folder 3267, NARA). See also Fenn, untitled memo regarding the GBT (RG 226, Entry 154, Box 149, Folder 2552, NARA).

15. Fenn to Hall, "Report No. 2"; and Fenn, interviews. See also Philippe Devillers, *Histoire du Viet-Nam de 1940 à 1952* (Paris: Seuil, 1952), 115.

16. Quoted in Fenn, memoir, 85–86.

17. Quoted in ibid.

18. British Ministry of Information and Political Warfare Executive, "Plan of Political Warfare against Japan," 1944 (RG 226, Entry 139, Box 138, Folder 1864, NARA). The author's opinion of the French bears mentioning. Of the "psychological attitudes" of the French, the writer began: "The average Frenchman, whether official or unofficial, is in Indo-China to make money. His main pre-occupation is how soon he can save enough to take his family with him back to France and there buy a 'propriété,' preferably with a small vineyard.... He is in a hurry to get back to France, and the aim is held to justify almost any means."

19. Major H. C. Faxon to Colonel Robert B. Hall, "Resume of Discussion with French Military Mission re: Suggested Training Plan in Indo-China," October 5, 1944 (RG 226, Entry 154, Box 199, Folder 3373, NARA).

20. R. P. Leonard to Major Harley C. Stevens, "Proposed Means of Disseminating Propaganda in Indo-China," May 16, 1944 (RG 226, Entry 139, Box 138, Folder 1863, NARA).

21. R. P. Leonard, "Determinating [*sic*] a Policy for MO Operations in Indochina," May 1944 (RG 226, Entry 139, Box 138, Folder 1863, NARA).

22. Ibid.

23. B. M. Turner, "Comments re: Memorandum of Mr. Leonard," May 23, 1944 (RG 226, Entry 139, Box 138, Folder 1863, NARA).

24. Ibid.

25. Major Herbert S. Little, "Indo-China—Additional Rumor Themes," July 22, 1943 (RG 226, Entry 154, Box 199, Folder 3276, NARA).

26. "Outline of MO Objectives and Operations in Indo-China," 1943 (RG 226, Entry 154, Box 149, Folder 2552, NARA).

27. Quoted in Fenn, memoir, 74. See also "Outline of MO Objectives and Operations in Indo-China," 1943.

28. Fenn, memoir, 75. See also "Outline of MO Objectives and Operations in Indo-China," 1943.

29. Fenn to de Sibour, untitled report on Indochina (RG 226, Entry 154, Box 149, Folder 2552, NARA).

30. Ibid.

31. Full text of Fenn's report (RG 226, Entry 154, Box 203, Folder 3438, NARA).

32. Fenn to de Sibour, untitled report on Indochina.

33. Quoted in Fenn, memoir, 87–88. Although elements of Lan's story are perhaps apocryphal, they do demonstrate his ability to connect with and report on Allied prisoners. Unfortunately, his narrative cannot be substantiated.

34. For Fenn's discussion of civil resistance in French Indochina and the disposition of resistance fighters throughout the region, see Charles Fenn, "Civil Resistance in F-I-C, Disposition of Combat and Sabotage Groups as of September 1st, 1944" (RG 226, Entry 154, Box 191, Folder 3267, NARA).

35. Charles Fenn, "Report No. 2" (RG 226, Entry 154, Box 191, Folder 3267, NARA). See also Fenn, memoir, 54–55.

36. Fenn, memoir, 66. See also Fenn, "Report No. 2."

37. Quoted in Fenn, memoir, 67. See also Fenn, "Report No. 2." Fenn believed that a hostile French military officer, "Captain Jourdan," was "responsible for the torchlight round-up which faced Marshall," as well as the "hounding of an American pilot to death" earlier in the same locality. Fenn to Hall, "Report No. 3," October 22, 1944 (RG 226, Entry 154, Box 191, Folder 3267, NARA).

38. In his follow-up report, Glass suggested that a "more judicious distribution of explanatory leaflets should be made available" to help enlist more help from the Vietnamese. He remarked that such activity might "prevent the recurrence of former regrettable incidents." Major Austin Glass, "A Report on the Situation in the Field (French Indochina)" (RG 226, Entry 92A, Box 26, NARA).

39. Quoted in Fenn, memoir, 70. See also Fenn to Hall, "Report No. 2."

40. Fenn to Hall, "Report No. 2." See also Fenn, memoir, 54–70. In his interaction with the local populace and the Japanese, Pop was much more practical than Fenn. In fact, Fenn's offer to give the peasant a picture of himself at GBT headquarters was shockingly irresponsible. Had such a photograph been discovered it would have endangered not only Pop but the network itself.

41. Fenn, memoir, 88; Fenn to Hall, "Report No. 3"; René Défourneaux, correspondence with author, December 1999.

42. Fenn to Hall, "Report No. 2."

43. Quoted in Fenn, memoir, 77.

44. Fenn to Hall, "Report No. 3."

45. John Costello, *The Pacific War, 1941–1945* (New York: Morrow, 1982), 522–523, 671; Gerhard L. Weinberg, *A World at Arms: A Global History of World War II* (Cambridge: Cambridge University Press, 1994), 640–641.

46. Quoted in Fenn, memoir, 89–90.

47. Both Gordon's and Fenn's egos were also pricked by what they assumed to be a deliberate slight. OSS wires to GBT headquarters were repeatedly addressed to "Gordon and Glass" instead of "Gordon and Fenn." These memos, which may simply have been carelessly or ignorantly addressed, were viewed as an insult to Fenn's position and as falsely promoting the work of Austin Glass, whom both Gordon and Fenn felt had been sent to Indochina to compete with them. Fenn, memoir, 82; Fenn, interviews.

48. Glass, untitled report on GBT (RG 226, Entry 92A, Box 26, Folder 391, NARA).

49. Fenn, memoir, 98–109.

50. Fenn to Hall (RG 226, Entry 154, Box 149, Folder 2552, NARA).

51. Fenn, memoir, 119. Charles Fenn speculated as to the rationale for Bird's advice. He concluded that either Bird liked both Fenn and the GBT and felt that they would be better served by AGAS, or disliked them and wanted rid of the lot.

52. "Gordon-Bernard-Tan Group" (RG 226, Entry 92A, Box 26, Folder 391, NARA).

53. Stein Tønnesson, *The Vietnamese Revolution of 1945: Roosevelt, Ho Chi Minh and de Gaulle in a World at War* (London: SAGE, 1991), 197.

54. Fenn for Heppner, "Det. 202 Communications," February 2, 1945 (RG 226, Entry 154, Box 191, Folder 3267, NARA); Fenn, memoir, 135–136; Fenn, interviews.

55. Fenn, memoir, 136–150. See also Archimedes L. A. Patti, *Why Viet Nam? Prelude to America's Albatross* (Berkeley and Los Angeles: University of California Press, 1980), 43. The United Nations War Crimes Commission reported that "several instances of illegal executions of American airmen were discovered" in French Indo-China. By 1948 only four cases, involving the deaths of eleven American airmen executed shortly after capture by the Japanese, had been "completed with success." United Nations War Crimes Commission, *History of the United Nations War Crimes Commission and the Development of the Laws of War* (London: His Majesty's Stationery Office, 1948), 386.

56. Quoted in Fenn, memoir, 148–150.

57. "Gordon-Bernard-Tan Group" (RG 226, Entry 154, Box 199, Folder 3373, NARA).

58. One example of the strained OSS-GBT relations was Bernard's February 1945 requests for supplies for an operation already approved by General Wedemeyer, requests that consistently went unanswered. H. V. Bernard to Lieutenant Colonel J. B. de Sibour, "Pleiku Scheme," February 27, 1945 (RG 226, Entry 154, Box 203, Folder 3453, NARA).

59. Patti, *Why Viet Nam?* 45; Fenn, *Ho Chi Minh*, 76; Fenn, memoir, 151–155; Fenn, interviews.

CHAPTER 5
ENDINGS AND BEGINNINGS

1. Louis Allen, Judith Stowe, and Thanatphong Smitabhindu, "The Japanese Coup of 9 March 1945 in Indo-China," in *1945 in South-East Asia* (London: London School of Economics and Political Science, 1985), 7. See Asagumo Shimbunsha, *Sittan: MEIGO sakusen* (Tokyo: Defence Agency, 1969).

2. Allen, Stowe, and Smitabhindu, "The Japanese Coup of 9 March 1945 in Indo-China," 8.

3. Kiyoko Kurusu Nitz, "Japanese Military Policy towards French Indochina during the Second World War: The Road to the *Meigo Sakusen* (9 March 1945)," *Journal of Southeast Asian Studies* 14 (September 1983): 337.

4. Allen, Stowe, and Smitabhindu, "The Japanese Coup of 9 March 1945 in Indo-China," 10–11.

5. Japanese Dispatch no. H-166390, January 6, 1945, decoded by Ultra (the term for encrypted World War II intelligence discovered through American or British cryptanalysis) and reprinted in Pacific Strategic Intelligence Section, Commander-in-Chief United States Fleet and Chief of Naval Operations, "Recent Political Developments in French Indo-China" ("Magic" Documents, Record Group 457 [henceforth RG 457], Entry 900, Box 17, Document SRH-095/PSIS 400–6, NARA).

6. Bernard Fall, *The Two Viet-Nams: A Political and Military Analysis* (New York: Praeger, 1967), 55.

7. Allen, Stowe, and Smitabhindu, "The Japanese Coup of 9 March 1945 in Indo-China," 6.

8. Stein Tønnesson, *The Vietnamese Revolution of 1945: Roosevelt, Ho Chi Minh and de Gaulle in a World at War* (London: SAGE, 1991), 198–220.

9. In November 1944 Zinovi Petchkoff, chief of the FMM in China, informed the French chargé in Paris that "the resistance" was considered to be "representing France in Indo-China" and that the French army was "the resistance." Furthermore, it was "ready to do all it [could] at any time to assist in Allied landings." "Indochina: French Plans" (RG 226, Roll 90, OSS#42671, NARA).

10. Pacific Strategic Intelligence Section, Commander-in-Chief United States Fleet and Chief of Naval Operations, "Recent Political Developments in French Indo-China."

11. Allen, Stowe, and Smitabhindu, "The Japanese Coup of 9 March 1945 in Indo-China," 18–19.

12. In his memoir, Decoux wrote: "Après la libération de la métropole, la radio française devait, jour après jour, poursuivre ses declarations menaçantes et agressives. J'ai évoque, d'autre part, les graves imprudences qui se commettaient quotidiennement en Indochine, sous le signe de la Résistance." Jean Decoux, *A la barre de l'Indochine: Histoire de mon gouvernement general (1940–1945)* (Paris: Librairie Plon, 1949), 335.

13. The full text of Decoux's observation follows: "Tout au milieu, j'ai fait, comme à Hanoi, dresser un imposant mat de pavillon, où flottent nos couleurs. Cette vue me soutient et m'exalte. Sous mon gouvernement général, le pavillon de la France flotte

ainsi librement, depuis cinquante-six mois, d'un bout à l'autre de l'Indochine."
Ibid., 328.

14. The full text of Decoux's statement is as follows: "Ainsi, l'atmosphère demeurait-elle normale. Nous étions cependant à moins de quarante-huit heures du coup de force et les Japonais allaient, une fois de plus, montrer dans l'exécution de leur acte abominable contre l'Indochine, la maîtrise et le machiavelisme consommés, qui les caractérisent dans de semblables occasions." Ibid., 326.

15. Decoux's racial attitudes are exemplified in his description of Ambassador Matsumoto. He wrote: "M. Matsumoto me parait préoccupé et quelque peu nerveux, chose rare chez un Asiatique." Ibid., 328.

16. F. C. Jones, *Japan's New Order in East Asia: Its Rise and Fall, 1937–45* (London: Oxford University Press, 1954), 397.

17. As had been typical of the Japanese-French relationship for the preceding five years, both sides continued to step to their own music. For example, Decoux recalled Matsumoto stating: "Le général de Gaulle a récemment exprimé l'espoir de voir bientot l'Indochine reprendre sa place dans la communauté française." Decoux shrewdly answered that "qu'une telle déclaration n'a rien que de très naturel." For the full text of Matsumoto's queries and Decoux's responses, see Decoux, *A la barre de l'Indochine*, 328–329.

18. Although Decoux was reviled as a traitor in the years following the war, his sincere affection for the colony cannot be doubted. His words are a testament to his fondness for French Indochina: "Un silence de mort plane sur tout le Gouvernement général. La cérémonie des couleurs s'est faite comme d'habitude, au coucher du soleil; le pavillon national a été rentre a l'heure règlementaire, avec la cérémonial *accoutume*." Ibid., 333.

19. André Gaudel, *L'Indochine française en face du Japon* (Paris: Susse, 1947), 149.

20. Decoux, *A la barre de l'Indochine*, 331. For the complete texts of the aide-mémoire, see ibid., 330.

21. Gaudel reported that the director of the Bank of Indochina in Saigon and his assistant director had already been arrested by 7:10. Gaudel, *L'Indochine française en face du Japon*, 153.

22. Ibid., 149–150. One can only speculate as to how Captain Robin became lost. He is listed as the commissioner-general of the Commissariat-General of Franco-Japanese Relations in the March 31, 1944, report "Who's Who in Japan and the Japanese Occupied Territories" (RG 226, Box 747, Document 68830, NARA), prepared by the Intelligence Division of the Far Eastern Bureau, British Ministry of Information, New Delhi. Given his position as the highest-ranking member of the Commissariat-General of Franco-Japanese Relations, it seems safe to assume that after more than a year in that position, he would have been—or at least should have been—familiar with the location of Japanese military headquarters.

23. Pacific Strategic Intelligence Section, Commander-in-Chief United States Fleet and Chief of Naval Operations, "Military and Political Plans for the Southern Pacific Area Formulated by the Japanese Prior to 14 August 1945" (RG 457, Document SRH-089/PSIS 400-28, NARA).

24. Allen, Stowe, and Smitabhindu, "The Japanese Coup of 9 March 1945 in Indo-China," 28.

25. Gaudel, *L'Indochine française en face du Japon*, 151.

26. Ibid., 150–151.

27. Claude de Boisanger, *On pouvait éviter la guerre d'Indochine: Souvenirs, 1941–1945* (Paris: Librairie d'Amerique et d'Orient, 1977), 110.

28. Japanese Dispatch no. H-171978, March 10, 1945, in Pacific Strategic Intelligence Section, Commander-in-Chief United States Fleet and Chief of Naval Operations, "Recent Political Developments in French Indo-China" (RG 457, Entry 900, Box 17, Document SRH-095/PSIS 400-6, NARA).

29. David Marr, *Vietnam 1945: The Quest for Power* (Berkeley and Los Angeles: University of California Press, 1995), 67–68.

30. Marr, *Vietnam 1945*, 54–69; Gaudel, *L'Indochine française en face du Japon*, 152–153.

31. Jones, *Japan's New Order in East Asia*, 397.

32. Shigemitsu Mamoru, *Japan and Her Destiny* (London: Hutchinson, 1958), 298, 330.

33. Pacific Strategic Intelligence Section, Commander-in-Chief United States Fleet and Chief of Naval Operations, "The Aftermath of Japanese Occupation of French Indo-China (March–May 1945)" (RG 457, Document SRH-100/PSIS 400-14, NARA).

34. International Military Tribunal for the Far East, *Court Papers, Journal, Exhibits, and Judgments of the International Military Tribunal for the Far East*, compiled and edited by R. John Pritchard and Sonia Zaide (New York: Garland, 1981), 15,292–15,296; Marr, *Vietnam 1945*, 59–60; Gaudel, *L'Indochine française en face du Japon*, 176–181; J. Lee Ready, *Forgotten Allies*, vol. 2, *The Asian Theatre* (Jefferson, NC, and London: McFarland, 1985), 198. See also Archimedes L. A. Patti, *Why Viet Nam? Prelude to America's Albatross* (Berkeley and Los Angeles: University of California Press, 1980), 74–75.

35. Marr, *Vietnam 1945*, 61. See also Gaudel, *L'Indochine française en face du Japon*, 176–181.

36. Gaudel, *L'Indochine française en face du Japon*, 143–144.

37. Ibid., 170; Tønnesson, *The Vietnamese Revolution of 1945*, 238.

38. Gaudel provided a vivid account of the fall of these two garrisons. Gaudel, *L'Indochine française en face du Japon*, 181–182.

39. Tønnesson, *The Vietnamese Revolution of 1945*, 239.

40. Ready, *The Asian Theatre*, 198; Marr, *Vietnam 1945*, 60; Tønnesson, *The Vietnamese Revolution of 1945*, 238–239.

41. "Apart from some native guides no natives were taken along, not even the *congai*—private soldiers' mistresses." Ready, *The Asian Theatre*, 198.

42. Ibid.

43. Gaudel, *L'Indochine française en face du Japon*, 171.

44. Quoted in Ellen J. Hammer, *The Struggle for Indochina* (Stanford, CA: Stanford University Press, 1954), 40.

45. Marr, *Vietnam 1945*, 60–61.

46. Ultra, "Attitude of the Indo-Chinese Natives," April 27, 1945 (RG 457, Box 16, Document SRS1650/1128, NARA).

47. There are numerous French accounts of the "fall" of Indochina and the French-Vietnamese experience. One of the most intriguing is the story of Madame Louise Maria Mariet, the wife of Jacques Mariet, the adjutant chief at the French army post at Bao Ha. In the turmoil following the Japanese coup, Jacques Mariet was forced to evacuate with his men toward China. Unable to take his wife with him, he left her in the care of a local mandarin (later assassinated by the Viet Minh), Nguyen Dinh Van. Madame Mariet was hidden from both the Japanese and the "hostile" elements of the local population for more than two years after the coup. According to Lieutenant Henri Michel, the author of the account, she was the last of the French who escaped the Japanese coup to be "recovered." She was "liberated" by the French on November 7, 1947, at the age of fifty-one. Although she regarded Michel, the French lieutenant who "rescued" her and delivered her back into the French community, as her knight in shining armor, Michel maintained that it was actually Nguyen Dinh Tan (the son of the mandarin initially charged with Madame Mariet's care) who was her savior. Tan, a disgruntled member of the Viet Minh, arranged for the necessary hiding places for Madame during her "stay" in the highlands and provided Michel with the information and aid that resulted in her safe return. Henri Michel, "Du 9 mars au 7 novembre 1947: Le calvaire et la libération de Louise Maria Mariet au pays Thai; Reddition de Nguyen-Dinh-Tan," courtesy of René J. Défourneaux.

48. Quoted in Frances Fitzgerald, *Fire in the Lake: The Vietnamese and the Americans in Vietnam* (Boston: Little, Brown, 1972), 63.

49. Quoted in William H. Elsbree, *Japan's Role in Southeast Asian Nationalist Movements, 1940 to 1945* (Cambridge, MA: Harvard University Press, 1953), 100–101.

50. Ready, *The Asian Theatre*, 198; Tønnesson, *The Vietnamese Revolution of 1945*, 239. J. Lee Ready had a different timetable and account of Alessandri's travails in mid-March 1945. Ready wrote: "Captain Guy de Cockborne led the battalion against the enemy at the village of Ban Na Ngha on the 25th, and at the end of a very mean fight indeed, the Japanese withdrew, leaving 150 dead behind. On the 28th, with all the legionnaires united, the column cautiously approached Meos Pass, and the scouts soon alarmed Alessandri. The Japanese were waiting with about six battalions supported by mortars and mountain artillery. For two days the 1st and 2nd Battalions threw themselves against the position and in return staved off Japanese counter charges, until Captain Roger Gaucher broke through with his 1st Battalion. He and his men then held the flanks while the rest of the column rushed over the bridges and through the pass. The column had lost only about 80 killed and wounded in this supposed Japanese trap. The Japanese were not about to give up, though, and while Alessandri was marching northwards, a three-battalion Japanese force was digging in ahead of him at Dien Bien Phu. The French garrison at this airfield had fled, and it joined Gaucher's men to hold a blocking position, so that the column could bypass the Japanese. This tactic worked, but the blocking troops suffered heavily, and the 2nd Battalion ran into an enemy force and also had a disastrous battle on its hands. The

Japanese trap failed, but the column that continued the march was far different from that which had started." Ready, *The Asian Theatre*, 198–199.

51. Tønnesson, *The Vietnamese Revolution of 1945*, 238–239; Marr, *Vietnam 1945*, 60–61; Jacques Dalloz, *The War in Indo-China, 1945–54* (Dublin, Ireland: Gill and Macmillan, 1987), 44.

52. Although Gaudel recorded that the resistance continued until April 9, a U.S. intelligence report stated that "organized resistance was abandoned about 7 April when fresh Japanese troops arrived from the South." Pacific Strategic Intelligence Section, Commander-in-Chief United States Fleet and Chief of Naval Operations, "The Aftermath of Japanese Occupation of French Indo-China (March–May 1945)."

53. Marr, *Vietnam 1945*, 61. See also Gaudel, *L'Indochine française en face du Japon*, 171–172. Gaudel wrote that the Chinese were "profoundly moved" by the French who crossed the border at Muong-la. These men entered China emaciated and ragged, but "in good order and singing." Ibid., 172.

54. For a comprehensive discussion of Sabattier's retreat to China, as well as complete statistics on the northern garrison strengths prior to MEIGO and their demise during the coup, see General Gabriel Sabattier, *Le destin de l'Indochine: Souvenirs et documents, 1941–1951* (Paris: Librairie Plon, 1952), 151–218 and 382–451.

55. Marr, *Vietnam 1945*, 61.

56. Ronald Spector, *Advice and Support: The Early Years of the U.S. Army in Vietnam, 1941–1960* (New York: Free Press, 1985), 31.

57. Quoted in Patti, *Why Viet Nam?* 64.

58. Spector, *Advice and Support*, 34.

59. Claire Lee Chennault, *Way of a Fighter: The Memoirs of Claire Lee Chennault* (New York: G. P. Putnam's Sons, 1949), 342.

60. Memo from Colonel Bird to Colonel Heppner, April 25, 1945 (RG 226, Entry 154, Box 199, Folder 3373, NARA).

61. Even prior to the March 7 meeting with the president, Ambassador Hurley was not particularly inclined to provide substantial aid to the French. In April Hurley met in London with the French ambassador, René Massigli, stating that "although he deplored the dangers facing the French Indo-Chinese forces, he thought it wise for America not to redirect any materials from the principal theatre of operations." In response to Massigli's rebuttal that French needs were "small," Hurley countered, "You do not realize how limited American resources in China are." Pacific Strategic Intelligence Section, Commander-in-Chief United States Fleet and Chief of Naval Operations, "The Aftermath of Japanese Occupation of French Indo-China (March–May 1945)."

62. Tønnesson, *The Vietnamese Revolution of 1945*, 219–220.

63. Chennault, *Way of a Fighter*, 342.

64. Pacific Strategic Intelligence Section, Commander-in-Chief United States Fleet and Chief of Naval Operations, "The Aftermath of Japanese Occupation of French Indo-China (March–May 1945)."

65. Spector, *Advice and Support*, 40. See also Patti, *Why Viet Nam?* 88; "Report of the Summers Mission in FIC" (RG 226, Entry 148, Box 14, Folder 200, NARA).

66. "Report of the Summers Mission in FIC."

67. Ibid. Archimedes Patti recalled, "Major Summer's team had held its ground while the radios, codes, and special equipment were destroyed and had then dispersed northward. Helliwell and Davis asked me to look for them. I found them on 2 May after several daylight reconnaissance flights over mountainous trails and jungle terrain. They were on the Chinese side of the border at Chengtung (Keng Tung) and safe, after suffering severe hardships wandering through the jungle." Patti, *Why Viet Nam?* 88.

68. "OSS Activities in French Indo-China," April 10, 1945 (RG 226, Entry 154, Box 199, Folder 3373, NARA).

69. R. Harris Smith, *OSS: The Secret History of America's First Central Intelligence Agency* (Berkeley and Los Angeles: University of California Press, 1972), 328. Smith erroneously reported that Ettinger jumped into French Indochina on March 15; this is not corroborated by OSS reports.

70. "Policy in French Indochina" (RG 226, Entry 154, Box 199, Folder 3373, NARA).

71. Ibid.

72. War Department, "MAGIC—Diplomatic Summary, 26 February 1945" (RG 457, Box 14, Document 1068) and "MAGIC—Diplomatic Summary, 28 February 1945" (RG 457, Box 14, Document 1070, NARA).

73. Nitz, "Japanese Military Policy towards French Indochina during the Second World War," 341. Some French historians contend that the Japanese intentionally created a "racial war." French historian Philippe Devillers wrote: "Le Viet-Nam, on pouvait l'espérer alors, pourrait être libre sans être pour cela hostile à la France. La haine? Elle est le fruit empoisonné de la Kempeitai et des activists japonais. Elle a été semée par ceux qui voulaient créer entre Blancs et Jaunes en général, entre Français et Vietnamiens en particulier, un mur impenetrable de méfiance et d'hostilité pour pouvoir mieux dominer l'Asie." Devillers supported his argument with data collected in Nha Trang in November 1945. His reports concluded that 74 percent of the population remained pro-French, while the number of anti-French never exceeded 15 percent of the population. Philippe Devillers, *Histoire du Viet-Nam de 1940 à 1952* (Paris: Seuil, 1952), 129.

74. Cordell Hull, *The Memoirs of Cordell Hull*, 2 vols. (New York: Macmillan, 1948), 2: 1595.

75. Shigemitsu, *Japan and Her Destiny*, 330.

76. Tønnesson, *The Vietnamese Revolution of 1945*, 170.

77. Shigemitsu, *Japan and Her Destiny*, 330. Shigemitsu's contentions aside, there seems little doubt that Japan's Greater East Asia policy was simply calculated rhetoric, especially with regard to the question of independence for European colonies. As part of their negotiations with Chiang Kai-shek in 1940, the Japanese were willing to offer the Chinese the occupation of Tonkin "as part of the price for a deal." Thailand would be "presented with" Cambodia—hardly evidence of Japan's sincerity regarding local aspirations. Elsbree, *Japan's Role in Southeast Asian Nationalist Movements*, 17.

78. Nitz, "Japanese Military Policy towards French Indochina during the Second World War," 339.

79. War Department, "Magic—Diplomatic Summary, 1 March 1945" (RG 457, Box 14, Document 1071, NARA). These sentiments were repeated on March 3, 1945: "It is planned to abrogate the protective agreement between Annam, Cambodia, etc., and France, and to make them independent. They look forward to this with an unfaltering attitude." War Department, "Magic—Diplomatic Summary, 3 March 1945" (RG 457, Box 14, Document 1073, NARA). See also War Department, "Magic—Diplomatic Summary, 5 March 1945" (RG 457, Box 14, Document 1075, NARA).

80. War Department, "Magic—Diplomatic Summary, 1 March 1945."

81. The Yasutai, also called the Yasu Butai, was formed in January 1945 by five Japanese colonels for "the sole purpose" of preparing for Operation MEIGO. Tønnesson, *The Vietnamese Revolution of 1945*, 241, 251.

82. Bao Dai, *Le dragon d'Annam* (Paris: Plon, 1980), 99–100; Kiyoko Kurusu Nitz, "Independence without Nationalists? The Japanese and Vietnamese Nationalism during the Japanese Period, 1940–45," *Journal of Southeast Asian Studies* 15 (March 1984): 126.

83. In his memoirs Bao Dai explained that even he was surprised that the Japanese selected him instead of Prince Cuong De to "rule" the newly independent Vietnam. Indeed, it seems that the Japanese supreme adviser, Yokoyama Masayuki, took great pains to assure Bao Dai that although Prince Cuong De had been important in Japan's wartime goals, he, Bao Dai, was the most qualified man to sit on the imperial throne in an "independent" nation. Bao Dai recalled the ambassador's words: "Nous voulons redonner 'l'Asie aux Asiatiques.'... C'est une longue enterprise. Le Prince Cuong-De fut l'instrument de nos buts de guerre vis-à-vis des Français; mais aujourd'hui c'est à Votre Majesté seule qu'il convient d'apporter la conclusion." Bao Dai, *Le dragon d'Annam*, 101–102.

84. Evidently Cuong De's son was "murdered" in Indochina in early 1942. Untitled document (RG 226, Entry 16, Box 1036, NARA).

85. Patti, *Why Viet Nam?* 515–518. See also Nitz, "Independence without Nationalists?" 110–120 and 128–129. In her memoir, Nguyen Thi Dinh recounts: "In these years, the pro-Japanese movement was very active in the countryside, trying to recruit people into their organization. The pro-Japanese people came to gauge my attitude and to persuade me [to join their movement]. Even though I had not succeeded in reestablishing contact [with the revolution] and did not know what the standpoint and policy of the revolution at that juncture was, I resolutely repeated to the villagers the things that Bich and the other brothers had told me before: The Japanese are cruel fascists.... Don't listen to their lies and deceptions." Nguyen Thi Dinh, *No Other Road to Take: Memoir of Mrs. Nguyen Thi Dinh*, translated by Mai V. Elliott (Ithaca, NY: Cornell University Press, 1976), 35.

86. Untitled document (RG 226, Entry 16, Box 1036, NARA).

87. War Department, "Magic—Diplomatic Summary, 4 June 1945" (RG 457, Box 14, Document 1166, NARA). See also Tønnesson, *The Vietnamese Revolution of 1945*, 283. For a more extensive discussion of Phan Boi Chau, Prince Cuong De, and the

Vietnamese Restoration League (Phuc Quoc), see David Marr, *Vietnamese Tradition on Trial, 1920–1945* (Berkeley and Los Angeles: University of California Press, 1981). See also Bui Minh Dung, "Nominal Vietnamese Independence Following the Japanese Coup de Force on 9 March 1945," *Japan Forum* 6, no. 2 (October 1994): 233–234.

88. Japanese Dispatches nos. H-172107, H-175605, and H-178505, decoded by Ultra and reprinted in Pacific Strategic Intelligence Section, Commander-in-Chief United States Fleet and Chief of Naval Operations, "The Aftermath of Japanese Occupation of French Indo-China (March–May 1945)."

89. For a more comprehensive discussion of this event, see David Chandler, "The Kingdom of Kampuchea, March–October 1945: Japanese Sponsored Independence in Cambodia in World War II," *Journal of Southeast Asian Studies* 17, no. 1 (March 1986): 80–93.

90. Tønnesson, *The Vietnamese Revolution of 1945*, 283.

91. According to the GBT report, this statement was signed by the ministers of home affairs, finance, justice, public works, education, and economic affairs and approved by Bao Dai. GBT, "Indochina Intelligence Report: Proclamation of Bao Dai," May 3, 1945 (RG 226, Entry 140, Box 40, Folder 314, NARA). See also Devillers, *Histoire du Viet-Nam de 1940 à 1952*, 124–125.

92. Bui Minh Dung, "Nominal Vietnamese Independence," 235.

93. In fact, according to his memoir, Bao Dai never believed the propaganda of the Japanese. He avows that although impressed with their rapid progress after the 1868 Meiji Restoration, he always regarded them with suspicion. "Ayant suivi avec curiosité et inquietude les manoeuvres nippones durant les années qui ont précédé Pearl Harbor, je nourris a l'égard des Japonais une certaine méfiance.... Je ne suis pas dupé du machiavelisme des Japonais" (Bao Dai, *Le dragon d'Annam*, 100–103).

94. Translated by the War Department, "Magic—Diplomatic Summary, 29 March 1945" (RG 457, Box 14, Document 1099, NARA).

95. According to an OSS intelligence report, Tran Trong Kim was allowed to travel to Japan in 1944 to meet with Prince Cuong De and discuss the leadership of a "new government." Untitled intelligence memo (RG 226, Entry 16, Box 1036, NARA).

96. Tønnesson, *The Vietnamese Revolution of 1945*, 282. See also Vu Ngu Chieu, "The Other Side of the 1945 Vietnamese Revolution: The Empire of Viet-Nam (March–August 1945)," *Journal of Asian Studies* 45, no. 2 (February 1986): 300–316.

97. Bui Minh Dung, "Nominal Vietnamese Independence," 236.

98. Vu Ngu Chieu, "The Other Side of the 1945 Vietnamese Revolution," 294–316; Bao Dai, *Le dragon d'Annam*, 106–108; Devillers, *Histoire du Viet-Nam de 1940 à 1952*, 126. See also Shiraishi Masaya, "The Background to the Formation of the Tran Trong Kim Cabinet in April 1945: Japanese Plans for Governing Vietnam," in *Indochina in the 1940s and 1950s*, edited by Takashi Shiraishi and Motoo Furuta (Ithaca, NY: Cornell Southeast Asia Program, 1992), 113–141.

99. Quoted in Bui Minh Dung, "Nominal Vietnamese Independence," 244.

100. Georges Boudarel and Nguyen Van Ky, *Hanoi: City of the Rising Dragon* (Lanham, MD: Rowman and Littlefield, 2002), 78.

101. Duong Van Mai Elliott, *The Sacred Willow: Four Generations in the Life of a Vietnamese Family* (Oxford: Oxford University Press, 1999), 103–104.

102. Elliott, *The Sacred Willow*, 105.

103. Ultra, "Political," March 25, 1945 (RG 457, Box 15, Document SRS-1617, NARA).

104. David Marr, "World War II and the Vietnamese Revolution," in *Southeast Asia under Japanese Occupation*, edited by Alfred W. McCoy (New Haven, CT: Yale University Southeast Asia Studies, 1985), 135.

105. Elliott, *The Sacred Willow*, 111.

106. Vu Ngu Chieu, "The Other Side of the 1945 Vietnamese Revolution," 297.

107. Marr, *Vietnamese Tradition on Trial*, 371.

108. American commentary on Japanese Dispatches nos. H-172107, H-175605, and H-178505, decoded by Ultra and reprinted in Pacific Strategic Intelligence Section, Commander-in-Chief United States Fleet and Chief of Naval Operations, "The Aftermath of Japanese Occupation of French Indo-China (March–May 1945)."

109. Bui Minh Dung, "Nominal Vietnamese Independence," 234–235.

CHAPTER 6

AFTER THE COUP DE MAIN: MARCH AND APRIL 1945

1. In his Ph.D. dissertation, William Wainwright stated that there were a few survivors of the "Gordon-Lan network" who "kept the liaison open in the hills of Tonkin where they took refuge with the Vietminh partisans." William H. Wainwright, "De Gaulle and Indochina, 1940–1945" (Ph.D. diss., Fletcher School of Law and Diplomacy, 1972), 127. Although a very intriguing possibility, this does not seem likely. By all indications Gordon was not in favor of working with the Vietnamese, and his French agents most probably would not have been aware of the location of the Viet Minh sanctuary. Furthermore, as will be seen, in their 1945 propaganda Ho Chi Minh and the Viet Minh made ample use of their brief involvement with the Americans and their lack of brutality toward the French after the coup. It seems highly unlikely that the Viet Minh would have sheltered Gordon's agents and never taken any credit for doing so—or at the very least would not have used the GBT agents to gain access to Allied personnel and supplies. In addition, by all accounts, the first GBT agent to enter the Viet Minh area was Frankie Tan, who made no mention of encountering any other GBT agents, at least one of whom he presumably would have known.

2. Charles Fenn, memoir (unpublished), 156; Fenn, *Ho Chi Minh: A Biographical Introduction* (New York: Charles Scribner's Sons, 1973), 76.

3. Fenn used as an example the downing of two American planes: "The Japs proudly exhibited the remains of two American bombers which they had brought down. The Annamites lost the point completely. They examined with admiration these products that were so obviously superior." Charles Fenn, "French Indo-China—Intelligence of Special Interest to M.O." (RG 226, Entry 154, Box 203, Folder

3438, NARA). Of course, it could also be argued that the Vietnamese in 1945 had simply never seen a bomber up close and were merely curious.

4. Ibid.

5. Quoted in Fenn, memoir, 146.

6. Ibid., 148–151; Fenn, *Ho Chi Minh*, 73.

7. Untitled memo regarding Austin Glass (RG 226, Entry 92A, Box 26, Folder 391, NARA).

8. "A Report on the Situation in the Field," February 7, 1945 (RG 226, Entry 92A, Box 26, NARA).

9. Ibid.

10. Ibid.

11. An August 1944 OSS report listed Pham Viet Tu as chairman of the seven-member Independence League of Indochina in Kunming. He was described as a young man, in his early thirties, from Hanoi, who "[spoke] French fluently and formerly wrote for the native press (*'Ami du Peuple'* and *'Le Monde'*) in Hanoi." Although the report tried to sort out an identity for the Independence League, the author clearly did not have a coherent idea of who the Viet Minh were or what they stood for in the wider picture. "The Nationalist Movement in Indochina" (RG 226, Entry 140, Box 35, Folder 273, NARA). Historian Stein Tønnesson, however, pointed out that it was difficult to distinguish between the Viet Minh and the Viet Nam Revolutionary League since "at the outset in 1941 and again after the Liuchow Congress of March 1944, the two organizations actually tried to amalgamate." Stein Tønnesson, *The Vietnamese Revolution of 1945: Roosevelt, Ho Chi Minh and de Gaulle in a World at War* (London: SAGE, 1991), 137.

12. For an enlightening account of the meetings between Pham Viet Tu and the Free French and of his discussions with the Americans, see Tønnesson, *The Vietnamese Revolution of 1945*, 136–137.

13. Ronald Spector, "'What the Local Annamites Are Thinking': American Views of Vietnamese in China, 1942–1945," *Southeast Asia* 3, no. 2 (1974): 741–742. Spector noted that at the same time the Viet Minh approached the Americans regarding Ho's imprisonment, Secretary of State Cordell Hull cabled the embassy about a recent article in a Chinese newspaper describing the establishment of a "Pro-Allied Provisional Government of Indo-China." According to Archimedes Patti, Ho had worked with "several associates" to have the article planted in a Chungking daily newspaper in order to embarrass the Kuomintang. The article appeared on December 18, 1942, and was "promptly picked up by the United Press for relay to New York and Washington." Archimedes L. A. Patti, *Why Viet Nam? Prelude to America's Albatross* (Berkeley and Los Angeles: University of California Press, 1980), 47. See also William J. Duiker, *Ho Chi Minh* (New York: Hyperion, 2000), 283–285.

14. Letter to the Honorable Arthur Capper, U.S. Senate, from Pham Viet Tu, Chairman, Vuong Minh Phoung, Member, and Tong Minh Phuong, Member, for the Independence League of Indochina, August 29, 1944 (RG 226, Entry 140, Box 35, Folder 273, NARA). Capper, a five-term liberal Republican, was a seasoned newspaper man, owning both the *Topeka Daily Capital* and *Capper's Weekly*.

15. According to Vu Anh, an important member of the Indochinese Communist Party, "most of our comrades lived in Kunming" during World War II. He added that "among those who carried on the struggle in Kunming at that time, [Phung Chi] Kien [killed in 1941] and I excepted, there were Hoang Van Hoan, then Pham Van Dong and Vo Nguyen Giap"—all important members of the Viet Minh during World War II. Vu Anh, "From Kunming to Pac Bo," in *Days with Ho Chi Minh*, Hoai Thanh, et al. (Hanoi: Foreign Languages Publishing House, 1962), 163–164.

16. Letter to Colonel Hall from Major Glass, October 14, 1944 (RG 226, Entry 154, Box 199, NARA).

17. Patti, *Why Viet Nam?* 46; Fenn, *Ho Chi Minh*, 76–77.

18. "An Outline of a Plan for Indo-China," October 20, 1943 (RG 226, Microfilm no. 1642, Roll 57, NARA).

19. Ibid.

20. Ibid. This OSS memo came close to establishing an early form of "body count." If followed to its logical conclusion, the argument basically states that the more Japanese the Vietnamese killed, the sooner they would receive their freedom. Thus, it was clearly in the best interest of the Vietnamese to attack Japanese outposts whenever possible.

21. The plan noted that the Japanese had handed out "thousands of radio sets" and had sent out propaganda broadcasts "in Annamite from Hainan." It also observed that prior to the Japanese distribution, there were still "many" radios among the Vietnamese population, "evidenced by the fact that Radio Saigon gave many broadcasts daily in the Annamite tongue." Ibid.

22. Ibid. Interestingly, six months later an OSS-produced review of political movements in Indochina failed to mention either the communists or Nguyen Ai Quoc. It instead concentrated on groups deemed pro-Japanese, such as the Cao Dai religious group and the "Trotskiist" group in Cochinchina. "Analytic outline of political movements in Indochina during the first stage of Japanese occupation" (RG 226, Entry 16, Box 959, NARA).

23. Charles Fenn to Colonel Robert Hall, "Report No. 3," October 22, 1944 (RG 226, Entry 154, Box 191, Folder 3267, NARA).

24. Fenn, "French Indo-China—Intelligence of Special Interest to M.O."

25. Fenn, *Ho Chi Minh*, 73.

26. Vu Anh, "From Kunming to Pac Bo," 179–180.

27. Tran Thi Minh Chau, who marched to Tan Trao with Ho Chi Minh, Frank Tan, and Mac Shin, acknowledged the problem from the Viet Minh perspective. "It was very hard for us to get all these messages and instructions down to local people, to tell them not to do any harm to the Americans. Ho Chi Minh knew how hard it was for these people to tell one Westerner from the other, so he said to us, come on, forget the instructions and just come down and talk to them, don't just send papers. We agreed later on to instruct all the American pilots that they have got to say the password 'Viet Minh' when they were shot down in the area.... When we had that play featuring a downed American pilot saying Viet Minh, of course, we had a local man, Vietnamese playing that role. Later on we found out that it was very hard for

Americans to pronounce 'Viet Minh' in the right way. So, Uncle Ho asked us to come and meet Americans and ask them to pronounce the word 'Viet Minh' their way and our actors just imitate it, so that local people will know how Americans pronounce the word Viet Minh." "Full Transcript of 1997 OSS/Viet Minh Meeting," courtesy of William Duiker, 19.

28. Although the letter did not have a specific addressee, its contents remain interesting. Obviously the Viet Minh believed they had favorable relations with an important colonel in Kunming. The letter read: "Dear Colonel, On the occasion of the first day of a new year, we have the honor of wishing you a happy and victorious year. We take this opportunity to thank you sincerely for the expression of friendship you have been so kind as to offer us. May we, through your generous efforts, look forward to the Government and the Army of the United States of America providing us with effective assistance in fighting and vanquishing our common enemy, facist [sic] Japan. Please allow us, dear Colonel, to express our highest esteem, The National Committee of the League for Indo-China Independence." Letter accompanying correspondence between Major General Claire Chennault and Commanding General, USF China Theater, January 2, 1945 (RG 226, Entry 148, Box 14, Folder 212, NARA).

29. Ibid.

30. Lieutenant Rudolph Shaw, "The Real Indo-China" (RG 226, Entry 148, Box 14, Folder 213, NARA).

31. The diary entry claimed that 600 French soldiers surrounded a neighboring forest to look for Shaw. Ibid.

32. Ibid.

33. Letter to Mr. Rudolph C. Shaw from the Central Committee of the League for Indo China Independence (Viet Nam Doc Lap dong Minh abr. Viet Minh), November 27, 1944 (RG 226, Entry 148, Box 14, Folder 212, NARA).

34. The pamphlet also provided remarkably accurate statistics on Vietnam's geography and natural and human resources.

35. Shaw, "The Real Indo-China."

36. Correspondence between Major General Claire Chennault and Commanding General, USF China Theater, January 2, 1945 (RG 226, Entry 148, Box 14, Folder 212, NARA).

37. Fenn, memoir, 156.

38. The need for improved propaganda aimed at the Vietnamese from the United States was pointed out by Milton Miles in his earlier initiatives. According to Miles's "Secret War Diary," Madame Meynier, the Princess of SACO, "insisted that our propaganda directed toward Indo-China from our short-wave radio stations in America is direct evidence that we Americans don't know anything about the Indo-China situation or that the people writing the propaganda and delivering the messages over the radio are too long out of the country to be of much value in this work." Milton Miles, "Secret War Diary," October 15, 1943 (RG 38, Box 42, October 1943, NARA).

39. OSS report, "The Nationalist Movement in Indo-China" (RG 226, Entry 140, Box 35, Folder 273, NARA). See also Duiker, *Ho Chi Minh*, 283, and Patti, *Why Viet Nam?* 46–48, 57.

40. David Marr, *Vietnam 1945: The Quest for Power* (Berkeley and Los Angeles: University of California Press, 1995), 280.

41. Fenn, *Ho Chi Minh*, 76–77; Fenn, memoir, 158.

42. This was, of course, incorrect. Given the difficult relationship between Fenn and Glass and Fenn's frequent difficulties with the OSS, it can be assumed that he was not up-to-date on Glass's by all indications successful use of Vietnamese radio operators.

43. Fenn, *Ho Chi Minh*, 76–77; Fenn, memoir, 160–161.

44. Fenn, *Ho Chi Minh*, 75; Fenn, memoir, 161; Fenn, interviews by author. Peter Dunn presented a much more pessimistic view of Ho Chi Minh and the Viet Minh's efforts to aid Allied pilots. Dunn wrote: "One of the main arguments projected is that the OSS supported Ho Chi Minh because of the potential assistance his people could render in returning downed Allied crews. However, a vastly greater number of American flyers were cared for and returned at great risk by the French than by the Communists, who for thirty years have viewed American fliers as little more than bargaining chips." Peter M. Dunn, *The First Vietnam War* (New York: St. Martin's, 1985), 34.

45. Fenn, *Ho Chi Minh*, 79.

46. "Full Transcript of 1997 OSS/Viet Minh Meeting," 19.

47. Mac Shin moved to the United States after the war and became a millionaire dealing in real estate.

48. Fenn, memoir, 176. There is some controversy as to who exactly gave Ho Chi Minh the six Colt .45s. Cecil Currey wrote that Colonel Paul Helliwell, head of the SI branch in Kunming, provided Ho with the guns and 20,000 rounds of ammunition. Curry wrote: "Intrigued by this small, intense Asian, Helliwell reported the contact [during which he provided the .45s] to his superiors. They authorized additional contacts and increased aid." Cecil B. Currey, *Victory at Any Cost: The Genius of Viet Nam's Gen. Vo Nguyen Giap* (Washington, DC: Brassey's, 1997), 85. Likewise, French historian Bernard Fall claimed that Ho made "several contacts in the winter of 1944–45 with Colonel Paul Helliwell" and concluded that Helliwell had provided Ho with the pistols. Bernard Fall, *The Two Viet-Nams: A Political and Military Analysis* (New York: Praeger, 1967), 100. News correspondent Robert Shaplen also claimed Helliwell provided the weapons. Robert Shaplen, *The Lost Revolution: The U.S. in Vietnam, 1946–1966* (New York: Harper Colophon, 1966), 38. It seems more likely, however, that Fenn provided the guns. There is no evidence that Helliwell and Ho met or negotiated for the Colt .45s. But Helliwell probably did approve the request for the pistols, as Fenn held no sway over the officer in charge of OSS supplies. This fits the recollection of OSS officer Archimedes Patti as well as of Fenn himself. Patti wrote that "Helliwell authorized the issuance from OSS stock of six new Colt .45 automatic pistols and several rounds of ammunition to an AGAS representative for delivery to Ho Chi Minh." Patti, *Why Viet Nam?* 545. Fenn wrote: "As AGAS had none in stock we got these [the Colt .45s] from OSS. I rather think this is how it came about that an OSS officer later reported supplying Ho." Fenn, *Ho Chi Minh*, 79. (Fenn was probably referencing a letter Helliwell wrote to Bernard Fall in 1954 in which Helliwell seemingly admitted to giving Ho Chi Minh the pistols, although he

never mentions his own role. Helliwell wrote, "The only arms or ammunition which were ever given by OSS/China to Ho were six .38 caliber revolvers." Fall, *The Two Viet-Nams*, 100.)

49. Fenn, *Ho Chi Minh*, 79; Fenn, memoir, 164–167, 172–176.

50. Paul Helliwell to Lieutenant Colonel Willis Bird, March 31, 1945 (RG 226, Entry 154, Box 199, Folder 3373, NARA).

51. Ibid.

52. Ibid.

53. Paul Helliwell, "OSS Activities in French Indo-China," April 10, 1945 (RG 226, Entry 154, Box 199, Folder 3373, NARA).

54. Ibid.

55. Heppner, memo to Bird, April 10, 1945 (RG 226, Entry 154, Box 199, Folder 3373, NARA). See also SI Branch, "The Quail Project: Draft Proposal for a Major OSS Secret Intelligence Operation in French Indo China," February 26, 1945 (RG 226, Entry 154, Box 168, Folder 2904, NARA); SI to Lieutenants Ambelang and Pye, March 9, 1945 (RG 226, Entry 154, Box 199, Folder 3375, NARA); "Status of Operations Proposed from 1 January 45 to 31 March 45," March 30, 1945 (RG 226, Entry 154, Box 185, Folder 3170, NARA).

56. Helliwell, "OSS Activities in French Indo-China."

57. Patti, *Why Viet Nam?* 7, 29–30.

58. Ibid.

59. Helliwell, "OSS Activities in French Indo-China."

60. Heppner, memo to Bird.

61. Patti, *Why Viet Nam?* 68.

62. Tønnesson, *The Vietnamese Revolution of 1945*, 309; untitled document re French Indochina (RG 226, Entry 148, Box 14, Folder 200, NARA).

63. Patti, *Why Viet Nam?* 66–67.

64. Ibid.

65. Ibid., 67–68.

66. Quoted in Fenn, *Ho Chi Minh*, 79. See also Fenn, memoir, 188.

67. Frank Tan, interviews by author.

68. "Full Transcript of 1997 OSS/Viet Minh Meeting," 18–20.

69. Frank Tan, GBT "Indochina Intelligence Report," May 10, 1945, and May 12, 1945 (RG 226, Entry 140, Box 40, Folder 314, NARA); Fenn, *Ho Chi Minh*, 79–80.

70. "Full Transcript of 1997 OSS/Viet Minh Meeting," 31–32. Ho Chi Minh assigned Dao Van Anh as commander of the march, and Dang Tuan, the logistical officer. Ibid., 32.

71. Ibid., 32–33.

72. Marr, *Vietnam 1945*, 228–229; Tan, interviews. Having done extensive research, Marr concluded that "Ho always enjoyed role-playing; this is not the only example of Ho writing about himself and his movement as if he were someone else"; unfortunately, Marr does not offer an example to elucidate this statement. Marr, *Vietnam 1945*, 229.

73. "Full Transcript of 1997 OSS/Viet Minh Meeting," 33.

74. Tan, GBT "Indochina Intelligence Report," May 10, 1945; Fenn, memoir, 206. According to Tan, in addition to his report, he sent two rolls of film to GBT headquarters in Kunming. Tan's accompanying text explained that "one of them shows our group of 20 boys all armed to the teeth with our weapons plus some of their own ancient arsenal. In one snap you'll see the village 'meeting house.' One group is being taught to read, another about maps, a third about Vietminh principles." Tan, GBT "Indochina Intelligence Report." Although many similar photographs have materialized from the Deer Team mission in the summer of 1945, Tan's photos have not yet emerged.

75. Fenn, memoir, 200.

76. Tan, GBT "Indochina Intelligence Report," May 10, 1945.

77. Fenn, *Ho Chi Minh*, 80; Fenn, memoir, 205.

78. "Full Transcript of 1997 OSS/Viet Minh Meeting," 34.

79. Ho Chi Minh, OSS report, March 29, 1945 (RG 226, Box 434, Document A-52494/L54540, NARA); untitled report on French Indochina (RG 226, Entry 16, Box 1429, Document 124840, NARA).

80. Ho Chi Minh, OSS report, March 29, 1945.

81. Ibid.

82. Patti, *Why Viet Nam?* 126. According to Fenn's recollections, Ho had "alerted his group to be on the look out for downed pilots." He asked that the pilots wear "native clothes" beneath their uniforms with a thousand piastres distributed here and there to pay for food and other expenses if they were shot down. If downed, the pilots were to remove and bury their uniforms and shoes. "The sign to and from the Vietminh would be to raise the left foot and scratch the ankle.... from now on it would not be safe to contact any French since those pro-Ally had nearly [all] been put behind bars or had fled into China." Fenn, memoir, 200. Although Ho's information regarding the imprisonment of the pro-Allied French was correct, it was also clearly in his long-term best interest to have any downed pilots looking for Viet Minh to save them, instead of Frenchmen.

83. Tan, interviews; "Full Transcript of 1997 OSS/Viet Minh Meeting," 21; Fenn, *Ho Chi Minh*, 81; Fenn, memoir, 167.

84. "Full Transcript of 1997 OSS/Viet Minh Meeting," 21.

85. Ibid, 37.

86. Fenn, *Ho Chi Minh*, 81.

87. Quoted in Fenn, memoir, 226; Tan interviews.

88. Tan, GBT "Indochina Intelligence Report."

89. Fenn, *Ho Chi Minh*, 82.

90. Fenn, memoir, 204.

91. In his memoir Fenn wrote that "the indefatigable Betty M. [McDonald, later married to Richard Heppner] cornered me with a new scheme for MO work in all the main Indochina cities; and would I kindly introduce her to this Annamite name[d] Pham [Van Dong] who was still around some place? When I obliged she tried to wean him away from GBT to work directly with OSS. But Pham of course wasn't interested." Fenn, memoir, 190. Although Pham had been liaising with Fenn for several

weeks at that point, given the Viet Minh determination to develop a close relationship with the Americans, it is improbable that he would have turned down any American offer point-blank. One can only speculate as to the type of "introduction" Fenn made between Betty M. and Pham Van Dong. Fenn stated that he also sent Betty M. the MO material provided by Tan—she wanted Japanese "postal wrappings" and names of Japanese officers so "they could send letter bombs" to them—a ploy that purportedly "had quite some success in blowing off hands of Japanese officers." Ibid., 204–205.

CHAPTER 7
THE RELATIONSHIP DEEPENS: HO CHI MINH AND THE AMERICANS

1. By early May 1945, both the quantity and quality of GBT reports to the OSS had improved. For example, on May 1, the GBT reported on the Japanese release of Vietnamese political prisoners in Hanoi and Yen Bay and on Japanese propaganda regarding Vietnamese independence. By May 8 the GBT had produced an extensive report on the fall of Hanoi during the Japanese coup in March, including the preferential treatment accorded Indochinese soldiers in the French colonial army. The report also reproduced local newspapers, including one that added the headline "What Is Independence? Only Real Independence When No Foreign Power in Indochina." The following day the GBT account stated that most Indochinese realized the "empty promises" of the Japanese, adding that "Japs no longer veil their feeling of superiority and complete control in attitude to natives. Before, they tried to show politeness and equality." GBT Group, "French Indochina Intelligence Reports," May 2, 8, and 9, 1945 (RG 226, Entry 140, Box 40, Folder 314, NARA).

2. Archimedes L. A. Patti, *Why Viet Nam? Prelude to America's Albatross* (Berkeley and Los Angeles: University of California Press, 1980), 69.

3. Ibid., 70.

4. "French Colonial and Guerrilla Forces," early April 1945 (RG 226, Entry 19, Box 1575, Document #A-58339, NARA).

5. Vo Nguyen Giap, *People's War, People's Army* (New York: Praeger, 1967), 74.

6. "Instructions by Ho Chi Minh for Setting Up of the Armed Propaganda Brigade for the Liberation of Viet Nam, December, 1944," in *Vietnam: The Definitive Documentation of Human Decisions*, edited by Gareth Porter, 2 vols. (Stanfordville, NY: Earl M. Coleman, 1979), 14.

7. "Speech by Comrade Van (Vo Nguyen Giap) at the Ceremony Founding the Viet-Nam Liberation Armed Propaganda Brigade, December 22, 1944," in Porter, *Vietnam*, 14–17.

8. Ibid.

9. Huynh Kim Khanh, "The Vietnamese August Revolution Reinterpreted," *Journal of Asian Studies* 30, no. 4 (1971): 774.

10. "Viet Minh Summons to Fight the Japanese," March 1945, in *Conflict in Indo-China and International Repercussions: A Documentary History, 1945–1955*, edited by Allan B. Cole (Ithaca, NY: Cornell University Press, 1956), 16.

11. Truong Chinh, *Primer for Revolt: The Communist Takeover in Viet-Nam* (New York: Praeger, 1963), 10. Several months later, Allison Thomas reported that the Viet Minh "hindered the Japs in many other ways. They destroyed bridges, dug craters in roads, put barricades across roads, and the people of Cho Chu burned down their entire village and left the ruins to the Japs." Although Thomas saw the results of the destruction, his report must be questioned since his sources regarding the causes of the ruin were Viet Minh partisans. Major A. K. Thomas, "The Vietminh Party or League," September 16, 1945 (RG 226, Entry 154, Box 199, Folder 3377, NARA).

12. "Full Transcript of 1997 OSS/Viet Minh Meeting," courtesy of William Duiker, 45.

13. Quoted in H. V. Bernard to Col. Richard Heppner, "Operations in Tonkin," June 9, 1945 (RG 226, Entry 154, Box 191, Folder 3267, NARA).

14. "Report of Measures Taken by Japanese Eighth Army in FIC during 1945," in *International Military Tribunal for the Far East, Court Papers, Journals, Exhibits, and Judgments of the International Military Tribunal for the Far East*, compiled and edited by R. John Pritchard and Sonia Zaide, 10 vols. (New York: Garland, 1981), 7179.

15. Stein Tønnesson, *The Vietnamese Revolution of 1945: Roosevelt, Ho Chi Minh and de Gaulle in a World at War* (London: SAGE, 1991), 349. Ultra messages for July 7 noted that the Japanese had been "obliged to take measures against the anti-French and anti-Japanese group known as the Indo-China Independence League.... about 20 June a large military force was employed in carrying out the first stage of the subjugation." "Magic Diplomatic Summary," July 15, 1945 (RG 457, Box 18, Document 1207, NARA). See also "Magic Diplomatic Summary," July 22, 1945 (RG 457, Box 18, Document 1214, NARA).

16. Patti, *Why Viet Nam?* 67. In his evaluation of Viet Minh actions against the Japanese, Stein Tønnesson concluded, "Various contemporary and independent sources confirm that there was a fair number of incidents, and the Viet Minh clearly was a nuisance to the Japanese." Tønnesson, *The Vietnamese Revolution of 1945*, 349.

17. Patti, *Why Viet Nam?* 68–71. Although Ho and Patti were clearly not yet acquainted, Lancaster gave Laurie Gordon credit for establishing the "initial contact between the Viet Minh leader and American and French intelligence officers." Donald Lancaster, *The Emancipation of French Indochina* (London: Oxford University Press, 1961), 116.

18. Patti, *Why Viet Nam?* 83–84.

19. The packet of three-by-five black-and-white pictures labeled "Given to me by Ho at our first meeting in April 1945" is located in the Archimedes L. Patti Papers, Special Collections, University of Central Florida, Orlando.

20. Patti, *Why Viet Nam?* 83–84.

21. According to Fenn, interviews by author, his repeated clashes with members of the OSS had resulted in the less-than-flattering adjective being often connected to his name.

22. Patti, *Why Viet Nam?* 83, 86.

23. Ibid., 98.

24. Tønnesson, *The Vietnamese Revolution of 1945*, 309, 349.

25. Vice Admiral Milton E. Miles, USN, *A Different Kind of War: The Unknown Story of the U.S. Navy's Guerrilla Forces in World War II China* (New York: Doubleday, 1967), 467.

26. Although plans for CARBONADO were maintained until the very end of the war, Japanese evacuation from the initial invasion areas (Kweilin and Liuchow), and of course the decision to use the atomic bombs to end the war, made the plan obsolete. For a favorable account of CARBONADO, see General Albert C. Wedemeyer, *Wedemeyer Reports!* (New York: Henry Holt, 1958), 332–337. For a more negative review from a naval commander's point of view, see Miles, *A Different Kind of War*, 493–498.

27. Although Patti denied charges of being anti-French, his overall view, present in his memoir and commentary on the American role in Vietnam, is reminiscent of Roosevelt's. Patti wrote: "Their lack of foresight and determination to resist left Japan in undisputed strategic control of Southeast Asia and exposed China's soft underbelly. Both the Generalissimo and Wedemeyer were sorely disappointed with the French." Patti, *Why Viet Nam?* 100.

28. Ibid., 90.

29. Sainteny replaced Lieutenant Commander Flichy as head of M.5 in early May.

30. His citation read in part: "Lieutenant Défourneaux was parachuted into France, in civilian clothes, as an organizer and director of French resistance forces. By exercising tact and diplomacy, he successfully organized resistance forces and led them in sabotage activities. Bridges were destroyed and German convoys were harassed by a series of ambushes, forcing them to turn back or to change their routes. Lieutenant Défourneaux took an active part in the reception and distribution of arms and munitions with which to supply the resistance forces and procured and delivered valuable intelligence information to the United States Army." René J. Défourneaux, *The Winking Fox: Twenty-two Years in Military Intelligence* (Indianapolis: Indiana Creative Arts, 1997), 105.

31. Ibid., 125–126.

32. General G. Sabattier, *Le destin de l'Indochine: Souvenirs et documents, 1941–1951* (Paris: Librairie Plon, 1952), 455–456; "Detachment 202 Communications," message from Heppner to Buxton, June 4, 1945 (RG 226, Entry 154, Box 199, Folder 3374, NARA). In addition to Deer and Cat teams, there was an additional OSS mission bound for French Indochina. The six-member Cow Team, led by Captain Zachariah Ebaugh, met up with Thomas and Holland at Ching-hsi on June 10. Whereas Thomas and Holland were slated to train French troops, Ebaugh's team was designated to build a Chinese outfit. By July 27 the Cow Team fielded 134 men—the Chinese officers among the group had been provided with radio, tactical, and medical training in addition to weapons training and classes in English and sketching—and departed Ching-hsi for the border. Operations in Vietnam, against pro-Japanese villages near Ha Long, began on August 1. On August 2 Ebaugh recorded the "First Allied victory on FIC" with the capture of two "pro-Jap villages." Ebaugh sent word out to the "village head-men" in the area to report to him and hand in their weapons, and within a

week he reported to Poseh that "village head-men came from as far away as thirty miles to pledge their cooperation to us" and that "all of the people were eager to cooperate with the Americans." On August 8 Ebaugh agreed to coordinate attacks against the Japanese with Hwong Kwong Win, the local "leader of 'The FIC Allied Revolutionary Army.'" Ebaugh reported that he was "impressed" by Hwong and his "well disciplined and well run" outfit whose "aim was independence" for French Indochina. Although an attack was planned on "Lang Dink bridge," the alliance was never tested. On August 15 Cow was ordered to cease operations and on the sixteenth, to turn over their weapons to the Chinese Nationalists and return to Poseh. Cow Team documents (RG 266, Entry 154, Box 211, Folder 3591, NARA).

33. Tønnesson, *The Vietnamese Revolution of 1945*, 318.

34. Colonel John Whitaker to Lieutenant Colonel Paul Helliwell, "French Proposal for Joint Intelligence FIC," May 14, 1945 (RG 226, Entry 154, Box 174, Folder 3013, NARA). The two commanders who visited Whitaker were Commandant Gourvest, former head of the Chungking office of the Section de Liaison Française en Extreme-Orient, and Commandant de Courseulles, the head in May 1945.

35. Patti, *Why Viet Nam?* 88–109; "Notes of Meeting between Maj. Sainteny of F.M.M. and Capt. Patti, O.S.S." (RG 226, Entry 154, Box 199, Folder 3374, NARA).

36. Patti, *Why Viet Nam?* 88–109.

37. Ibid., 102.

38. Charles Fenn, memoir (unpublished), 214.

39. R. Harris Smith, *OSS: The Secret History of America's First Central Intelligence Agency* (Berkeley and Los Angeles: University of California Press, 1972), 330.

40. "Full Transcript of 1997 OSS/Viet Minh Meeting," 51.

41. Fenn, memoir, 214.

42. Ibid., 214–215. See also Charles Fenn, *Ho Chi Minh: A Biographical Introduction* (New York: Charles Scribner's Sons, 1973), 81.

43. Cecil B. Currey, *Victory at Any Cost: The Genius of Viet Nam's Gen. Vo Nguyen Giap* (Washington, DC: Brassey's, 1997), 89.

44. "Full Transcript of 1997 OSS/Viet Minh Meeting," 51. Tan recollected, "Dan Phelan was looked upon [by the Viet Minh at Tan Trao] as a most sympathetic friend and a good person." Ibid., 21.

45. Quoted in Fenn, *Ho Chi Minh*, 81; Fenn, memoir, 235. Fenn credited Phelan's change of heart as a result of "1) his basic common sense and judgement; 2) Ho's convincing personality; 3) the infectious enthusiasm of Ho's disciples." Fenn, memoir, 235.

46. Fenn, memoir, 214–215; also in Fenn, interviews.

47. Helliwell, "G.B.T. Group," May 22, 1945 (RG 226, Entry 154, Box 203, Folder 3453, NARA).

48. Ibid.

49. Lieutenant Colonel Paul Helliwell, memorandum to GBT Group, May 28, 1945 (RG 226, Entry 154, Box 199, Folder 3373, NARA).

50. Fenn, memoir, 218.

51. Ibid., 219–220.

52. Ibid.

53. Ibid.

54. Ibid., 330–335.

55. Special Operations Branch APO 627, "Letter of Instructions" to Major Thomas, May 16, 1945 (RG 226, Entry 154, Box 199, Folder 3377, NARA).

56. Wampler to Chow [message code], May 27, 1945 (RG 226, Entry 154, Box 199, Folder 3377, NARA).

57. "Certificate of Merit to Major Allison K. Thomas" (RG 226, Box 116, Folder 2501, NARA).

58. Patti, *Why Viet Nam?* 124–125.

59. Ibid. Patti based his assessment on reports from Austin Glass as well as on reports by the GBT network and, of course, Viet Minh claims. A May 1945 report from "French Battalion Commander A. Reul, who led the repression of the Viet Minh in the northern highlands until March 1945" also confirmed Viet Minh areas of control and small clashes with Japanese columns. Tønnesson, *The Vietnamese Revolution of 1945,* 350.

60. Patti, *Why Viet Nam?* 125. As will be seen, Patti's actions were indeed questioned by many before his departure from Vietnam.

61. Défourneaux, *Winking Fox,* 140–148. Défourneaux described the situation as becoming increasingly frustrating for the men, who were anxious to fight the Japanese and tired of what seemed like aimless wandering along the difficult terrain of southern China, all too often in rain and mud. Furthermore, he believed that one result of this experience was the team's loss of respect for Major Thomas. For example, he wrote: "But unlike the three of us, who were straining under the load of our gear, he [Thomas] was riding a horse and a coolie trotting behind, carrying his equipment. I do not believe he knew that we saw him. Right then our leader lost the confidence and the respect of the rest of the team." Ibid., 148. See also Major René J. Défourneaux, "Deer Team Diary," courtesy of Défourneaux.

62. Fenn and the GBT had also formed a positive opinion of Revole. In his report to Hall, Fenn described Revole as "straightforward, clear-thinking" and "long Fighting French." Charles Fenn to Colonel Robert Hall, "Report No. 3," October 22, 1944 (RG 226, Entry 154, Box 191, Folder 3267, NARA).

63. Défourneaux, *Winking Fox,* 153; also in Défourneaux, "Deer Team Diary." Défourneaux added: "Up to that time no one on the American side had acknowledged the existence of this factor." *Winking Fox,* 153. Although unknown to Défourneaux, Ho Chi Minh and the Viet Minh were certainly well known by many Americans, including Patti and Fenn. "Viet Minh" had also become an increasingly familiar term among the OSS SI and SO officers in Kunming.

64. Major Allison Thomas, "Welcome to Our American Friends," in *Strange Ground: Americans in Vietnam, 1945–1975; An Oral History,* edited by Harry Mauer (New York: Henry Holt, 1989), 30–38. In his memoir, Jean Sainteny wrote that in early July Revole met with a representative of the Viet Minh in Tra-linh and with another cadre in Kunming. Revole's impression of the Viet Minh was favorable, according to Sainteny, and he believed that the French and the Viet Minh might be able to

undertake a joint military action against the Japanese in Indochina. Jean Sainteny, *Histoire d'une paix manquée: Indochine 1945–1947* (Paris: Librairie Fayard les Grandes Etudes Contemporaines, 1967), 68.

65. Thomas, "Welcome to Our American Friends," 31.

66. Stein Tønnesson asserted that "apparently the OSS had planned to have the Viet Minh and French compete with each other—if they could not cooperate." Tønnesson, *The Vietnamese Revolution of 1945*, 313.

67. Patti, *Why Viet Nam?* 126.

68. Charles Fenn recalled that Ho agreed to the drop on the condition that no Frenchmen would take part. Fenn, memoir, 237. Patti does not record any conditions attached to Ho's acceptance.

69. Patti, *Why Viet Nam?* 126–127.

70. Message to V.Q.P., July 13, 1945, copies of original courtesy of René Défourneaux.

71. Message from V.Q.P., July 13, 1945; message to V.Q.P., July 15, 1945; copies of originals courtesy of René Défourneaux.

72. Défourneaux, *Winking Fox*, 163–164.

73. In March 1945, General Eisenhower had awarded Zielski the Distinguished Service Cross for "extraordinary heroism in connection with military operations against an armed enemy from 17 July 1944 to 9 September 1944." Zielski's exploits in France had certainly prepared him for anything he might encounter in occupied Vietnam. Parachuted into the Brest peninsula to make contact with the French resistance, Zielski discovered that "the enemy had liquidated most of the Maquis groups in the vicinity of Brest, he and his companions entered the city by concealing themselves in empty wine barrels, placed among full casks being delivered to the German garrison. Despite his constant peril, First Sergeant Zielske [*sic*] maintained radio contact with London and transmitted important intelligence and operational information. In addition, he executed the extremely hazardous mission of a night reconnaissance through, and to a point thirty miles behind, the enemy lines for the purpose of securing information on the activities of the German garrison at Vrest [*sic*]." U.S. Army, Distinguished Service Cross citation, March 10, 1945 (RG 226, Entry 92A, Box 118, Folder 2553, NARA).

74. Tran Thi Minh Chau added that "the Banyan tree now has become some sort of a historic relic." "Full Transcript of 1997 OSS/Viet Minh Meeting," 46.

75. Thomas, "Welcome to Our American Friends," 29.

76. Deer Team radio message, July 17, 1945 (RG 226, Entry 154, Box 199, Folder 3372, NARA).

77. "Deer Team Report #1, 17 July 1945, Kumlung [*sic*], Tonkin, FIC" (RG 226, Entry 154, Box 199, Folder 3377, NARA); Patti, *Why Viet Nam?* 127.

78. Quoted in Georges Boudarel and Nguyen Van Ky, *Hanoi: City of the Rising Dragon* (Lanham, MD: Rowman and Littlefield, 2002), 86.

79. "Deer Team Report #1"; Thomas, "Welcome to Our American Friends," 29.

80. Allison Thomas, diary, Giap Papers, Cecil B. and Laura G. Currey Archive of Military History, Forsyth Library Archives, Fort Hays State University, Hays, Kansas (henceforth Giap Papers); Allison Thomas, interviews by author.

81. Thomas, diary. For example, on July 19 Thomas wrote: "Armed guard on one side, women and children on one side, men on the other. Chief of Village gave us a welcome speech and presented us with bananas, eggs, ducks and chickens." On July 22: "Saw some of the 'Man' people.... we were invited in for tea." On July 28: "Went to village of Ban—where we were royally greeted and saw a marching demonstration of 30 soldiers."

82. Patti, *Why Viet Nam?* 550.

83. Thomas, "Welcome to Our American Friends," 31.

84. Fenn, memoir, 227, 237; Frank Tan, interviews by author.

85. Tønnesson, *The Vietnamese Revolution of 1945*, 313.

86. Patti, *Why Viet Nam?* 550.

87. Lieutenant Montfort (and possibly Sergeants Logos and Phac) was with Thomas and the other Deer Team members during the training of the French troops in southern China in June. On at least one occasion, while Thomas went ahead, Montfort acted as a guide in the border region for Défourneaux and the Deer Team personnel. Défourneaux, *Winking Fox*, 147; Défourneaux, "Deer Team Diary."

88. Thomas, "Welcome to Our American Friends," 32. Although Thomas admitted that he made the decision to include Montfort, he also maintained: "The Americans in Poseh got real chummy with the French, and of course they couldn't understand why I was opposed to sending all these Frenchmen in." Ibid. It is possible that officials in Poseh tried to convince Thomas to take more than Montfort with him although there is no direct evidence to support this hypothesis.

89. Thomas added that even if the Viet Minh cadre had not recognized Montfort and Phac, the Viet Minh would soon have known their true identities anyway because he would have told them. Ibid., 33. See also "Full Transcript of 1997 OSS/Viet Minh Meeting," 34.

90. Patti, *Why Viet Nam?* 128. See also Thomas, "Welcome to Our American Friends," 32–33.

91. Fenn, memoir, 227; Tan, interviews.

92. Jean Sainteny described the initial Deer Team mission in a different way. He claimed that the French provided arms and training to the Viet Minh for their fight against the Japanese as part of the July 16 "Franco-American" mission. "Le 16 jailed une mission franco-americaine d'encadrement, composée du lieutenant Montfort, des sergents Logos et Phac et de trois Americains, était parachutée auprès du Comité Directeur du Viet-Minh.... Par contre, ils [les Viet Minh] nous reclamaient de l'armement et des instructeurs français pour continuer leurs actions contre l'occupant." Sainteny, *Histoire d'une paix manquée*, 69.

93. Patti, *Why Viet Nam?* 127–128. Patti wrote that M.5 asked Gordon to set up the meeting with Ho and that through Gordon's contacts, Major Revole, the M.5 agent in Ching-hsi, arranged for Lieutenant Montfort to join Thomas (Patti, *Why Viet Nam?* 128). Given Gordon's excellent relations with the French it is certainly plausible that M.5 approached him on this matter. However, Gordon's only, and best, immediate contact with Ho Chi Minh was Frank Tan, who was also apparently under orders from Fenn to have the Frenchman arrested when he landed in Kim Lung. Given Tan's

sympathies for Ho by this time and given that he was already ignoring Gordon's summons to return to Kunming, Tan is more likely to have arranged the subsequent detention than the initial meeting. If indeed Gordon facilitated Montfort's jump with Thomas and Tan advised the lieutenant's arrest, then the GBT was working at cross-purposes and was doomed even without Bernard's departure.

94. Ibid., 128.

95. Deer Team radio message, NR13, July 17, 1945 (RG 226, Entry 154, Box 199, Folder 3377, NARA).

96. Deer Team radio message, NR14, July 17 1945 (RG 226, Entry 154, Box 199, Folder 3377, NARA).

97. Fenn, memoir, 227.

98. Message from Chow to Wampler, NR141, July 18, 1945 (RG 226, Entry 154, Box 199, Folder 3377, NARA).

99. Deer Team radio message, NR141.

100. Message from Chow to Wampler, NR141; Message from Wampler to Chow, NR0664, July 19 1945 (RG 226, Entry 154, Box 199, Folder 3377, NARA).

101. Feeling that the inspiration for an attack on the road linking Thai Nguyen and Cao Bang was not Thomas's, Wampler wrote: "Suggest that Thomas clarify his position to you and to Kunming with regard to Vietmenh [*sic*] leaders. The proof of Vietmenh to assist would be for them to change their plans from their target to ours. Query if Vietmenh will comply with our target mission." Message from Wampler to Davis, NR0709, July 19, 1945 (RG 226, Entry 154, Box 199, Folder 3377, NARA).

102. Message from Chow to Wampler, NR144, July 19, 1945, and messages from Wampler to Chow, NR0692 and NR0659, July 19, 1945 (RG 226, Entry 154, Box 199, Folder 3377, NARA). Although unknown to Thomas or Davis, the destruction of the Hanoi–Lang Son railroad was part of Project QUAIL and the envisioned Operation CARBONADO.

103. In his message to Wampler on July 20, Thomas reiterated, "all the French and Annamese at Poseh will have to be eliminated *or we will have to go back*" (emphasis added). Thomas to Wampler, July 20, 1945 (RG 226, Entry 154, Box 199, Folder 3377, NARA).

104. Thomas, "Welcome to Our American Friends," 33; "Deer Team Report #1."

105. Patti, *Why Viet Nam?* 128.

106. Sainteny, *Histoire d'une paix manquée*, 63–64.

107. Henry Prunier, interviews by author, and correspondence.

108. Although Allison Thomas stated that Prunier's Vietnamese was "so rudimentary that it was useless—so you could not really call him our linguist," both Prunier and Défourneaux felt that Prunier's skills were sufficient for the task assigned him. While in Tonkin, Prunier was tasked with basic communication with the troops the Deer Team trained—primarily giving instructions in the use of various weapons and in military drill. Défourneaux gave the instruction in English, and Prunier translated into Vietnamese. Défourneaux stated that according to his observations, the soldiers fully understood Prunier's instructions. Correspondence from Allison Thomas to Cecil Currey, Giap Papers, Box 8, File 108; Thomas, interviews; Prunier, interviews; René Défourneaux, interviews by author.

109. Prunier, interviews. Prunier added: "We [members of the Deer Team] were not familiar with the ultimate goal of Ho to get the French out as well. Even though we had an inkling to this fact."

110. Thomas was clearly irritated by Davis's earlier wire urging him to "keep an open mind." Thomas wired Davis that his comments were "an insult to his [Thomas's] intelligence" and again reiterated that "French operations [in] that area [were] absolutely impossible." In his communication to Wampler, Davis added that Montfort had confirmed Thomas's assertion that the French could not remain. Message from Davis to Wampler, July 23, 1945, NR48 (RG 226, Entry 154, Box 199, Folder 3377, NARA).

111. Quoted in Thomas, "Welcome to Our American Friends," 33.

112. Patti, *Why Viet Nam?* 128, 550.

113. In Bert Cooper, John Killigrew, and Norman LaCharite's book *Case Studies in Insurgency and Revolutionary Warfare: Vietnam, 1941–1954* (Washington, DC: Special Operations Research Office, 1964), 96–97, the battle at Tam Dao is dated July 17, 1945. A French eyewitness account has the first shot fired on July 16. Maurice and Yvonne Bernard, one-time teachers at the Lycée Albert-Sarraut, "Lettres aux amis d'Hanoi" (RG 226, Entry 140, Box 52, NARA). Patti, however, recorded the date of the liberation as July 4. *Why Viet Nam?* 128.

114. Cooper, Killigrew, and LaCharite claimed that five hundred Viet Minh attacked Tam Dao (*Case Studies in Insurgency and Revolutionary Warfare*). See also Lancaster, *The Emancipation of French Indochina*, 116. Cooper, Killigrew, and LaCharite, and Lancaster, as well as Vo Nguyen Giap and Philippe Devillers, claimed there were forty Japanese soldiers at the fort. Giap, *People's War, People's Army*, xxxv; Philippe Devillers, *Histoire du Viet-Nam de 1940 à 1952* (Paris: Seuil, 1952), 133. David Marr, *Vietnam 1945: The Quest for Power* (Berkeley and Los Angeles: University of California Press, 1995), 234, concluded there were nine Japanese soldiers present.

115. "Full Transcript of 1997 OSS/Viet Minh Meeting," 56.

116. When Allison Thomas visited with General Giap in Hanoi in 1990 he inquired about Tam Dao. Although Giap had been the overall military commander at that time, he told Thomas in 1990 that he "played no part in this sqirmkish [*sic*]." Allison Thomas, diary, Giap Papers.

117. Lancaster, *The Emancipation of French Indochina*, 116. A number of other historians concurred, including Joseph Buttinger, who noted: "The Vietminh never dreamed of sacrificing its precious troops in the hopeless and ultimately unnecessary task of fighting the Japanese. Minor clashes between Japanese troops and Vietminh units were of course hardly avoidable, but the only incident of any scope was an attack by 500 Vietminh partisans on the post at Tam Dao." Joseph Buttinger, *Vietnam: A Dragon Embattled.* 2 vols. (New York: Praeger, 1967), 1: 299. Stein Tønnesson noted that "the Viet Minh leaders did not want to waste arms and manpower on premature fighting. Plans for armed attacks against Japanese units were seen in connection with the expected Allied invasion, and up to August 1945 all Japanese-Viet Minh incidents were very limited in scale." Tønnesson, *The Vietnamese Revolution of 1945*, 350.

118. "Le fait d'armes de cette action anti-japonaise fut la destruction de la faible garnison de Tam-Dao, anéantie après un long siège par des bandes du Viet-Minh très

supérieures en nombre. Les officers français qui furent, par la suite, parachutés dans la Haute Region, tels que le lieutenant Montfort et l'adjudant-chef Dulery, confirmerent l'impression de leurs comarades americains sur les sentiments de 'résistance' du Viet-Minh et sur la sympathie dont ils furent entourés par les 'maquisards' indigenes." Sainteny, *Histoire d'une paix manquée*, 117.

119. "Magic Diplomatic Summary," August 2, 1945 (RG 226, Box 18, Document 1225, NARA).

120. David Marr deduced that there was no "concentration camp." Instead, several hundred European civilians simply continued to reside in the resort town. They fled during the course of the fighting. Marr, *Vietnam 1945*, 233–234.

121. "Full Transcript of 1997 OSS/Viet Minh Meeting," 35, 37.

122. Ibid., 37.

123. The Bernards said of their enlightening sojourn with the Viet Minh: "Notre exode nous a mis en contact avec ces hommes remarquables et c'est une de nos plus grandes joies." Maurice and Yvonne Bernard, "Lettre aux amis d'Hanoi" (RG 226, Entry 140, Box 52, Folder 416, NARA).

124. Ellen J. Hammer, *The Struggle for Indochina* (Stanford, CA: Stanford University Press, 1954), 42.

125. Thomas, diary.

126. "Deer Team Report #1."

127. Thomas, "Welcome to Our American Friends," 33–34.

128. Fenn, memoir, 240.

129. Thomas, correspondence in Giap Papers.

130. Cecil Currey wrote: "That they chose not to emphasize their dedication to communism is an illustration of their willingness to be all things to all people in their effort to further their goals." Currey, *Victory at Any Cost*, 92.

131. "Deer Team Report #1." In a 1991 letter to Cecil Currey (then in the process of writing his book on Giap, *Victory at Any Cost*), Thomas wrote: "I regret that I first reported that Ho was not a communist. It made no difference as Hq already knew he was a communist, but I was not briefed about him before the jump. I relied on what both Phelan and Frank Tan (GBT) told me about Ho." Thomas to Currey, Giap Papers, Box 1, File 1.

132. Thomas, interviews.

133. Currey found that after the 1945 New Year's holidays, Giap had expanded his "army" to company size. Headquartered in the caves at Cao Bang, his company consisted of 40 Viet Minh cadres and 500 Montagnard guards "who devoted themselves to learning how to build an army." Currey, *Victory at Any Cost*, 80–84.

134. "Deer Team Report #1."

135. Tønnesson, *The Vietnamese Revolution of 1945*, 313.

136. "Deer Team Report #1."

137. Ibid.

138. Défourneaux, *Winking Fox*, 157–158; and Défourneaux, "Deer Team Diary."

139. Quoted in William Broyles Jr., *Brothers in Arms: A Journey from War to Peace* (New York: Knopf, 1986), 108. On his return journey to Vietnam in 1984, Vietnam

War veteran Marine Lieutenant William Broyles visited the famous headquarters of Ho Chi Minh at Tan Trao. While there he met "Mr. Su," a Tay tribesman who had taken care of Ho in August 1945. Mr. Su described for Broyles seeing the Americans of Deer Team drift to the ground.

140. Message from Davis to Wampler, August 1, 1945 (RG 226, Entry 154, Box 199, Folder 3377, NARA).

141. Défourneaux, *Winking Fox*, 139.

142. Tan, interviews.

143. Fenn, memoirs, 241; Fenn, *Ho Chi Minh*, 82; quotation from Ho in letter to Fenn reprinted in *Ho Chi Minh*, 82. In addition, Tan, interviews.

144. Thomas, diary; also in Défourneaux, *Winking Fox*; Défourneaux, "Deer Team Diary."

145. René J. Défourneaux, "A Secret Encounter with Ho Chi Minh," *Look*, August 9, 1966, 32–33.

146. Perhaps Hoagland met Austin Glass, who was repatriated aboard the *Gripsholm* in 1942.

147. Défourneaux, "A Secret Encounter with Ho Chi Minh," 32. With the change in America's relationship with Vietnam after 1945, the story of Ho's recovery also changed. Mr. Su, the Tay tribesman with whom William Broyles spoke in 1984, told him that the very ill Ho Chi Minh had been given "modern medicine" by *a Russian* in 1945. Broyles, *Brothers in Arms*, 104.

148. Broyles interview with Thomas, in Broyles, *Brothers in Arms*, 104.

149. Défourneaux, one of the only Americans who worked closely with Ho Chi Minh and did not develop a friendship and affection for him, commented in 1998 that it was too bad Hoagland had saved Ho's life in 1945. "What ever Hoagy gave him unfortunately it worked!" René Défourneaux, correspondence.

150. "Full Transcript of 1997 OSS/Viet Minh Meeting," 53–54.

151. Ibid., 43.

152. Défourneaux, *Winking Fox*, 167.

153. Dam Quang Trung was a founding member of the People's Army in 1944 and a member of the Party Central Committee. When Allison Thomas met with him in 1990, Dam Quang Trung was a three-star general. Thomas correspondence in Giap Papers. Chu Van Tan, who was the minister of defense in the first Democratic Republic of Vietnam, also "received instruction from the OSS" Deer Team. James William Gibson, *The Perfect War: Technowar in Vietnam* (Boston: Atlantic Monthly Press, 1986), 48.

154. Allison Thomas's September 1945 report on the Deer Team mission states that Ho Chi Minh provided 200 recruits of whom 100 were chosen for training. Défourneaux stated that there were 40 soldiers. Défourneaux, *Winking Fox*, 168–169. Pictures of the soldiers in formation with the Americans show about 40 Vietnamese soldiers. Major A. K. Thomas, "Report on the Deer Mission" (RG 226, Entry 154, Box 199, Folder 3377, NARA). Also reprinted in U.S. Congress, Senate, Committee on Foreign Relations, *Hearings before the Committee on Foreign Relations on Causes, Origins, and Lessons of the Vietnam War* (92nd Cong., 2nd sess., 1972).

155. Ngoc An, "Bo Doi Viet-My," *Tap Chi Lich Su Quan Su* (November 1986), translated for Allison Thomas, Giap Papers.

156. Currey, *Victory at Any Cost*, 92.

157. David Marr commented: "The Americans were impressed by how quickly the Vietnamese learned, not realizing that many of the trainees had previously spent long hours dry firing and disassembling and assembling captured French weapons." Marr, *Vietnam 1945*, 364.

158. Thomas, "Report on the Deer Mission."

159. Défourneaux, *Winking Fox*, 169–171.

160. Ibid., 173.

161. Message from Davis to Wampler, NR148, July 20, 1945 (RG 226, Entry 154, Box 199, Folder 3377, NARA).

162. Patti, *Why Viet Nam?* 126.

163. "Vietnamese Aide-memoire Transmitted to the United States through an Agent of the Office of Strategic Services, July 1945," reprinted in Cole, *Conflict in Indo-China and International Repercussions*, 17.

164. Marr, *Vietnam 1945*. Jean Sainteny claimed that he had arranged with Gordon to invite Ho Chi Minh for talks. Sainteny, *Histoire d'une paix manquée*, 57–58. However, Sainteny and Ho did not meet until October 1945. Given that the proposed meeting should have been relatively simple to arrange—after all, Frank Tan was by then quite familiar with Ho—the accuracy of his statement must be questioned.

165. Défourneaux, *Winking Fox*, 177; also in Défourneaux, "Deer Team Diary."

166. Thomas, diary.

167. Défourneaux asserted that the problem had actually begun prior to the August celebrations: "Before leaving Kunming the Major had said that he would not risk anyone's life, he would only fool around until the war was over. Our men had heard him, they remembered, and resented his attitude." Défourneaux, *Winking Fox*, 179. See also Défourneaux, "Deer Team Diary."

168. Marr, *Vietnam 1945*, 365.

169. Ibid., 362–364. Trieu Duc Quang, of the Vietnamese-American Force, recalled that part of their duties was "providing security protection" for the conference. "Full Transcript of 1997 OSS/Viet Minh Meeting," 54.

170. Tønnesson, *The Vietnamese Revolution of 1945*, 413–416.

171. William J. Duiker, *Ho Chi Minh* (New York: Hyperion, 2000), 304–306.

172. Thomas, diary.

173. "Full Transcript of 1997 OSS/Viet Minh Meeting," 54.

CHAPTER 8
ON TO HANOI

1. Davis to Wampler and Helliwell, NR197, August 16, 1945 (RG 226, Entry 154, Box 199, Folder 3377, NARA).

2. Allison Thomas, diary, Giap Papers. Défourneaux recalled that prior to their departure on August 16, Major Thomas gave a brief speech before the assembled delegates. René Défourneaux, *The Winking Fox: Twenty-two Years in Military Intelligence* (Indianapolis: Indiana Creative Arts, 1997), 181. Henry Prunier recalled "the sixty or so people" meeting at Tan Trao watching the "Americans working with the Viet Minh" troops who "had been outfitted with American fatigues, [and] American light weapons and were carrying our weapons." "Full Transcript of 1997 OSS/Viet Minh Meeting," courtesy of William Duiker, 63. Trieu Duc Quang remembered the situation a bit differently: "The commander of the company, Mr. Quang Trung, read the ten oaths, and a lot of people from the Congress, which was just over, came out of the meeting place and greeted us. He was not aware that the Congress was going on and he marched through it. We didn't wear any kind of American uniform, but we were carrying only American weapons." Ibid., 71.

3. Hoai Thanh et al., *Days with Ho Chi Minh* (Hanoi: Foreign Languages Publishing House), 225.

4. Major René J. Défourneaux, "Deer Team Diary," courtesy of Défourneaux; Défourneaux, *Winking Fox*, 181–183.

5. "Full Transcript of 1997 OSS/Viet Minh Meeting," 42.

6. There were other OSS units that had completely different experiences. One unit operating with the French near the border sent the following message to Kunming: "Natives and partisans patrolling all trails and frontier. The Vietnam[ese] very active in Tonkin. Their principal is Indochina for Indo-Chinese and are against French. The American flag doesn't protect us here; we are white and therefore enemies." Bellevue to Indiv, NR63 (RG 226, Entry 154, Box 199, Folder 3375, NARA).

7. Major Allison Thomas, "Welcome to Our American Friends," in *Strange Ground: Americans in Vietnam, 1945–1975; An Oral History*, edited by Harry Mauer (New York: Henry Holt, 1989), 36. See also Thomas, diary. Viet Minh veteran Nguyen Huu Mui recalled the reaction of the villagers to Thomas and the other Americans: "On the way we saw a lot of people coming and approaching us to admire, to look at us. The people were very pleased to see our army very well equipped, and everyone looked very in shape. They were wondering why there were a number of American soldiers, who look very French, and they wondered why? Mr. Van [Giap] explained to the people that they were American comrades in arms, who are here to assist us in fighting the Japanese, and they come from the Allied Forces. And the people were very happy." "Full Transcript of 1997 OSS/Viet Minh Meeting," 57.

8. "Full Transcript of 1997 OSS/Viet Minh Meeting," 42.

9. Thomas, "Welcome to Our American Friends," 36.

10. Although the Cat Team did not become involved with the Viet Minh training or their battle at Thai Nguyen, their experience was just as exciting. In mid-August, the three members of the team, Captain Mike Holland, Sergeant John Burrowes, and Sergeant John Stoyka, were captured by the Japanese. The loosely guarded men planned their escape, but only Stoyka was successful. Luckily, villagers who were members of the Viet Minh helped him reach the Deer Team, by then in Thai Nguyen. Holland and Burrowes were released unharmed to Patti in Hanoi on August 31. Stoyka and the members of the Deer Team were convinced that Stoyka's escape "was the reason why

the Japanese had not killed Mike and Burrowes." Défourneaux, *Winking Fox*, 195. See also Défourneaux, "Deer Team Diary"; "Activities Report," August 31, 1945 (RG 226, Entry 154, Box 199, Folder 3376); Chow to Wampler, August 16, 1945; Indiv and Swift to Chow; and Chow to Indiv, NR215, September 2, 1945 (all in RG 226, Entry 154, Box 199, Folder 3377, NARA).

11. Davis to Wampler, August 16, 1945; Helliwell and Wampler to Davis, August 16, 1945; Wampler to Thomas, August 17, 1945; and Helliwell and Wampler to Davis, August 18, 1945 (all in RG 226, Entry 154, Box 199, Folder 3377, NARA).

12. Thomas had originally suggested that the Viet Minh be allowed to "accept Japanese prisoners and weapons for subsequent transfer to the proper authorities." This idea was rejected by OSS headquarters in China. David Marr, *Vietnam 1945: The Quest for Power* (Berkeley and Los Angeles: University of California Press, 1995), 370.

13. Major A. K. Thomas, "Report on Deer Team Mission" (RG 226, Entry 154, Box 199, Folder 3377, NARA). Acknowledging Thomas's disappointment, Archimedes Patti added: "Major Thomas was a fine young officer but understandably unsophisticated in the way of international power struggles." Archimedes L. A. Patti, *Why Viet Nam? Prelude to America's Albatross* (Berkeley and Los Angeles: University of California Press, 1980), 136.

14. Défourneaux, "Deer Team Diary."

15. Défourneaux, "Deer Team Diary." See also Défourneaux, *Winking Fox*, 184.

16. "Full Transcript of 1997 OSS/Viet Minh Meeting," 60.

17. Thomas, "Report on Deer Team Mission." See also Thomas, diary. For a discussion of the battle of Thai Nguyen, see also Marr, *Vietnam 1945*, 422–424.

18. "Full Transcript of 1997 OSS/Viet Minh Meeting," 63.

19. Ibid., 60.

20. "Ultimatum" sent by the Viet Nam Liberation Army to the Japanese troops in Indochina, in *Breaking Our Chains: Documents of the Vietnamese Revolution of August 1945* (Hanoi: Foreign Languages Publishing House, 1960), 81. Nguyen Chinh remembered that the surrender document that he typed mentioned the Americans as well: "We the Liberation Army and the Vietnam-America troops, commanded by the Viet Minh organization, already encircled tightly this garrison. We demand the troops inside the garrison accept the following conditions." "Full Transcript of 1997 OSS/ Viet Minh Meeting," 60.

21. Thomas, "Welcome to Our American Friends," 36.

22. Vo Nguyen Giap, "Call to Uprising," August 12, 1945, reprinted in *Vietnam: The Definitive Documentation of Human Decisions*, edited by Gareth Porter, 2 vols. (Stanfordville, NY: Earl M. Coleman, 1979), 1: 56–57.

23. Défourneaux, *Winking Fox*, 185 and Défourneaux, "Deer Team Diary."

24. Défourneaux, "Deer Team Diary."

25. Thomas, "Report on Deer Team Mission."

26. Défourneaux, "Deer Team Diary."

27. Ibid.

28. Greg Lockhart found this—that the battle was intended to enhance the image of the Viet Minh—the most compelling argument. He wrote that the fighting was

"hardly essential to the seizure of power. The 'battle' for Thai Nguyen was thus an armed propaganda operation which the Liberation Army mounted to enhance its own image, and to reinforce the effect of less militarized demonstrations in the rest of the country." Greg Lockhart, *Nation in Arms: The Origins of the People's Army of Vietnam* (Sydney: Allen and Unwin, 1989), 137.

29. Tønnesson, *The Vietnamese Revolution of 1945*, 386.

30. Thomas, "Welcome to Our American Friends," 34–35.

31. Allison Thomas, interviews by author. Tran Thi Minh Chau, whose elder brother was killed at Thai Nguyen, stated that "the Americans were not involved in the fight," but, probably in reference to the use of American weapons and Thomas's "participation," he clarified that "you could provide us technology and advice, but not be directly involved, because I don't think it was the duty of the American friends." "Full Transcript of 1997 OSS/Viet Minh Meeting," 74.

32. Thomas, "Report on Deer Team Mission." On August 23 Thomas reported a Viet Minh attack on the "Villa Gautier where the Jap Secret police were living." Although the Japanese soldiers had already fled, Thomas noted that the "prizes of war were considerable, consisting in part of guns, documents, gasoline, and several cases of TNT (French)."

33. Message from Daniel to Chow, August 22, 1945, copy courtesy of René Défourneaux.

34. Thomas, diary. See also Défourneaux, "Deer Team Diary."

35. Cecil B. Currey, *Victory at Any Cost: The Genius of Viet Nam's Gen. Vo Nguyen Giap* (Washington, DC: Brassey's, 1997), 96.

36. Défourneaux, "Deer Team Diary."

37. On the first anniversary of the August Revolution, the ICP general secretary, Truong Chinh, reevaluated the Viet Minh's lack of success in acquiring Japanese weapons, using the battle of Thai Nguyen as his example: "This failure to completely disarm the Japanese troops was due to the subjective conditions of the August Revolution.... What happened was that in many regions, immediately after the insurrectional forces had occupied a town, either by a sudden attack from outside or by an inner uprising, the Japanese entrenched themselves; and while they had enough supplies and munitions to hold out for a long time, our troops merely encircled them and, for want of good tactics, failed to destroy their fortifications (as for example, the seizure of Thai Nguyen); whatever the case, it must be admitted that with more promptitude and boldness, we should have been able to disarm the Japanese troops from the very beginning of the insurrection." Truong Chinh, *Primer for Revolt: The Communist Takeover in Viet-Nam* (New York: Praeger, 1963), 39.

38. Douglas Pike, *PAVN: People's Army of Vietnam* (Novato, CA: Presidio, 1986), 32. Pike added that the month following the battle for Thai Nguyen, "the Vietnam Liberation Army was renamed the Vietnam National Defense Army."

39. Tønnesson, *The Vietnamese Revolution of 1945*, 385–386.

40. Thomas, "Report on Deer Team Mission."

41. Ibid., and Thomas, diary. See also Défourneaux, "Deer Team Diary."

42. According to his diary, Thomas did not know that it was Captain Patti who led the American mission in Hanoi until August 30. Thomas, diary.

43. Father Pedro's name is also listed as Perez and Prieto.

44. Défourneaux, "Deer Team Diary."

45. "Jap Army at THAINGUYEN to the VML," April 11, 1945 (RG 226, Entry 140, Box 52, Folder 416, NARA).

46. "Proclamation of Chief of Jap Gendarmerie, Cho Chu," May 27, 1945 (RG 226, Entry 140, Box 52, Folder 416, NARA).

47. "Report Following the Interview of a Dominican Priest at Tai Nguyen" (RG 226, Entry 140, Box 52, Folder 416, NARA).

48. The Americans continually noted the generosity of the Viet Minh, who provided chicken, duck, or some other type of meat to accompany their daily rice, fruit, vegetables, and beer. Thomas, "Report on Deer Team Mission"; Thomas, diary; Défourneaux, "Deer Team Diary." Providing such relative luxury for the Americans may have prompted Ho Chi Minh's letter to Dan Phelan on August 17 (or 18). In his correspondence, Ho apologized for a request of 20,000 piastres to ransom an American pilot from "overseas Chinese bandits." He explained that "the going of our armed boys with Major Thomas (and the staying too long of the French) drained rather heavily on our local purse." David Marr, *Vietnam 1945*, 372. Although the Viet Minh accompanying Thomas no doubt added an additional expense, the provisions afforded the Americans surely accounted for a large percentage of the monies spent.

49. Patti, *Why Viet Nam?* 141. Cecil Currey stated that Sainteny parachuted into Tonkin on August 28. Currey, *Victory at Any Cost*, 100.

50. Helliwell to Davis and Coughlin, August 18, 1945 (RG 226, Entry 154, Box 199, Folder 3373, NARA).

51. Patti, *Why Viet Nam?* 144. Jacques Dalloz presented the situation from a French perspective: Sainteny, he wrote, "decided to go to Hanoi as soon as he could, but the ill-will of the local authorities and particularly of Major Patti, chief of the OSS for the north of Indo-china, was obvious." Jacques Dalloz, *The War in Indo-China, 1945–54* (Dublin, Ireland: Gill and Macmillan, 1987), 56.

52. Helliwell to Washington, August 20, 1945 (RG 226, Entry 154, Box 199, Folder 3373, NARA).

53. There have been numerous scholarly debates on whether or not the Viet Minh would have accepted an American "protectorate" or "trusteeship." For example, historian Gary Hess maintained that they most probably would have done so, whereas historian Robert Brigham contended the opposite, arguing that the Viet Minh would not have considered an American trusteeship as a viable option. Given the history between the two countries since 1945, it is impossible to reach an indisputable answer. However, the OSS contention that the Provisional Government was interested in a protectorate is probably inaccurate. The OSS reports stated that the Vietnamese believed one possible solution to their problems might be "placing Indochina under a protectorate status" of the United States. However, they cite "Annamite Kuomintang Representatives" as the source of this request on behalf of the Provisional Government. Helliwell to Washington, August 20, 1945.

54. Helliwell to Davis and Coughlin, August 18, 1945. This message was transmitted to the head of the OSS, General Donovan in Washington, who then sent it on to the secretary of state on August 22. "Memorandum for the Secretary of State," August 22, 1945 (RG 226, Microfilm #1642, Roll 21, Frames 886–889, NARA).

55. Jean Sainteny discussed his frequent displeasure with Patti and the Americans in his memoir, *Histoire d'une paix manquée: Indochine 1945–1947* (Paris: Librairie Fayard les Grandes Etudes Contemporaines, 1967), 77–80.

56. Helliwell to Davis and Coughlin, August 18, 1945.

57. "Full Transcript of 1997 OSS/Viet Minh Meeting," 81. Grelecki was awarded the Soldier's Medal "for heroic actions and services during the period from 22 August 1945 to 18 September 1945, when he was the executive administrative officer of a Prisoner of War humanitarian trip to French Indochina, with the mission of locating Prisoner of War camps in the area and bringing medical attention, affection, comfort and aid to allied POWs." Ibid., 79.

58. In his daily "Activities Report," Lieutenant Grelecki listed "approximately 280 Annamite Jap prisoners" as breaking camp "upon the sight of the descending parachutes." "Activities Report," August 22, 1945 (RG 226, Entry 154, Box 199, Folder 3376, NARA).

59. Patti, *Why Viet Nam?* 156. The Vietnamese presence in the streets was regarded by some in Kunming as troublesome. Several wires on August 23 reported that "there is trouble with Annamite Revolutionists in Hanoi," or "Annamites in Hanoi apparently causing local disturbances." Davis to Indiv and Fisher, August 23, 1945; Indiv to Coughlin and Parker, August 23, 1945 (both in RG 226, Entry 154, Box 199, Folder 3376, NARA).

60. Patti, *Why Viet Nam?* 153–156.

61. "Full Transcript of 1997 OSS/Viet Minh Meeting," 81.

62. Patti, *Why Viet Nam?* 156–157. Using Patti as a source, Jacques Dalloz interpreted Patti's presence differently: "When, on 22 August, he [Sainteny] finally reached the capital of Tongking, he realized that there had been a revolution. This revolution did not frighten Patti. The major was well placed to participate in the demonstrations organized by the new power which he thereby seemed to be guaranteeing.... Denying Sainteny any role other than a humanitarian one, he put the Hanoi authorities on guard against colonialism and advised them to trust the United States." Dalloz, *The War in Indo-China*, 56.

63. This was, in fact, true. By the following day, August 23, an AGAS representative and "additional personnel" were to fly into Hanoi with radios and equipment. Indiv to Davis and Fisher, August 23, 1945 (RG 226, Entry 154, Box 199, Folder 3376, NARA).

64. Patti, *Why Viet Nam?* 157.

65. French historians have placed Sainteny in a much more proactive position, insisting that Sainteny was angling to be housed in the Governor-General's Palace from the start. "Sainteny, jouant au bluff, va s'installer directement au Gouvernement Général, prend contact avec les civils français, obtient du Commandement japonais la libération des prisonniers de guerre." Philippe Devillers, *Histoire du Viet-Nam de 1940 à 1952* (Paris: Seuil, 1952), 151.

66. Patti, *Why Viet Nam?* 157.

67. A few days later Sainteny asked Patti to send the following wire to General Alessandri in Kunming: "Entire French military under Major Sainteny have been placed in confinement within grounds of Governor General's Palace. They may not circulate beyond a certain line or demarcation within the palace grounds, nor will they be permitted to see visitors except Patti." Patti for Sainteny, NR011, August 25, 1945 (RG 226, Entry 154, Box 199, Folder 3373, NARA).

68. Indiv to Coughlin and Parker, August 23, 1945.

69. Patti to Indiv, NR3, August 23, 1945 (RG 226, Entry 154, Box 199, Folder 3373, NARA).

70. "Activities Report," August 23, 1945; Patti to Indiv, #21408, August 23, 1945; Patti to Indiv, #21409, August 23, 1945; Indiv to Patti, NR4, August 23, 1945; Patti to Indiv, NR5, August 23, 1945. The next day Patti again wired Kunming: "I insist it most dangerous to individuals and policy to have French accompany US personnel." Patti to Indiv, August 24, 1945 (all in RG 226, Entry 154, Box 199, Folder 3376, NARA).

71. Patti, *Why Viet Nam?* 162.

72. "Activities Report," August 24, 1945.

73. Patti to Indiv, 25 August 1945 (RG 226, Entry 154, Box 199, Folder 3376, NARA).

74. Patti, *Why Viet Nam?* 171, 173.

75. Huynh Kim Khanh provided an excellent chronology of the insurrections of the August Revolution. Huynh Kim Khanh, *Vietnamese Communism, 1925–1945* (Ithaca, NY: Cornell University Press, 1982), 326.

76. Vo Nguyen Giap, *People's War, People's Army* (New York: Praeger, 1967), 84.

77. Marr, *Vietnam 1945*, 393–401. Marr's book provides the definitive account of the 1945 August Revolution.

78. Ibid., 397. While Marr indicated that the weapons were acquired from Vietnamese guards ("Apparently lacking clear orders from their officers and convinced by Viet Minh sympathizers in their ranks that they would not be ill treated, the guardsmen dumped their rifles in a big pile and walked away"), Cecil Currey included Japanese soldiers among those who forfeited weapons: "Like a wave cresting on a beach, the crowd flowed into the compound and captured it. Men and women of all ages marched into the barracks of the Japanese soldiers and seized their entire stock of weapons, distributing them to frantically reaching hands." Currey, *Victory at Any Cost*, 100.

79. Quoted in Georges Boudarel and Nguyen Van Ky, *Hanoi: City of the Rising Dragon* (Lanham, MD: Rowman and Littlefield, 2002), 87.

80. Marr, *Vietnam 1945*, 401. In his memoirs, Bao Dai repeated local gossip that the Japanese *kempeitai* were responsible for the new Viet Minh flag. "On y a acclame l'indépendance, 'Doc Lap,' et arboré un nouveau drapeau, rouge à étoile jaune, qu'on dit avoir été confectionné par la Kampetai." Bao Dai, *Le dragon d'Annam* (Paris: Plon, 1980), 117, 401.

81. Bui Diem was the South Vietnamese ambassador to the United States from 1967 to 1972.

82. Bui Diem, *In the Jaws of History*, with David Chanoff (Boston: Houghton Mifflin, 1987), 34–35.

83. Nguyen Kim Hung, trained by Mac Shin, sent the message on Ho Chi Minh's instruction. "I was a new guy so I could only do it very slowly," he recalled. "So, the radio communication was waiting for several days until after August 19th when the power was handed over. And I think it was August 20th that we got a message from Kunming [with whom they were still in contact], that message was in French." It said, "The battle is now seized. Also there's a wish of good luck in there, and goodbye." "Full Transcript of 1997 OSS/Viet Minh Meeting," 35–36.

84. David Marr, "Vietnam: Harnessing the Whirlwind," in *Asia—The Winning of Independence*, edited by Robin Jeffrey (New York: St. Martin's, 1981), 199.

85. With perhaps a note of sarcasm, the emperor waxed poetic in his memoir: "Leur incontestable succes n'est pas le signe qu'ils ont reçu mandat du ciel? Le peuple possedé un instinct très sur qui, dans les heures historiques, le conduit toujours vers ceux qui ont mission de le guider." Bao Dai, *Le dragon d'Annam*, 119.

86. The telegraph read: "Devant la volonté unanime du peuple vietnamien prêt a tous les sacrifices pour sauvegarder l'indépendance nationale, nous prions respectueusement Votre Majesté de bien vouloir accomplir un geste historique en remettant ses pouvoirs." Ibid., 118.

87. Ibid., 115–123. In an interview on September 10 with Sergeant William Borrowes of the OSS, Bao Dai stated that he had "voluntarily abdicated and was not coerced by the Provisional Government." William Burrowes, "Interview with Bao Dai," September 19, 1945 (RG 226, Entry 140, Box 52, Folder 416, NARA). The empress, however, expressed fear for her life and sent her sister to tell the Allied Commission that both she and the emperor were pro-French. "Fears of Empress Nam Phuong," September 23, 1945 (RG 226, Entry 19, Box 270, Document A-613352, NARA).

88. "Activities Report," August 25, 1945. Sainteny maintained that the Americans were all too easily convinced by the "propaganda offensive" of the Viet Minh. Sainteny, *Histoire d'une paix manquée*, 100.

89. Marr, *Vietnam 1945*, 485.

90. Ibid., 486.

91. The OSS mission photographer captured the parade on film for OSS headquarters. One of his photos shows the armed guard and jeep that brought Giap to the American headquarters. The photographer noted, "The weapons are American made, presumably weapons that were air dropped to our men in the field, captured by the Japs, and later sold to the Viet Nam[ese]" (RG 226, Entry 154, Box 199, Folder 3376, NARA; for photos, see RG 226, Entry 154, Box 199, Folder 3373, NARA).

92. Patti, *Why Viet Nam?* 198–199.

93. Marr, *Vietnam 1945*, 486. Years later, even Americans writing about Patti's relationship with the Viet Minh asserted his open support for Giap and Ho. For example: "Moreover, the American Office of Strategic Services (OSS) was openly supporting the forces of Vietnamese independence: when the OSS's Captain Patti accompanied Jean Sainteny to Hanoi in the wake of the Viet Minh takeover, he was

greeted as a friend." Martin Shipway, *The Road to War: France and Vietnam, 1944–1947* (Providence, RI: Berghahn Books, 1996), 137.

94. Although the coordinates were wrong, Giap knew as early as August 15 that the British and the Chinese would soon occupy Vietnam. In his diary entry for that day, Major Thomas wrote: "As we get the terms the British occupy south of 13 degree latitude and the Chinese North, which the VML don't like because the Chinese have their own party to setup." Thomas, diary.

95. Patti, *Why Viet Nam?* 200–201.

96. On September 1, OSS headquarters warned Patti to avoid "arranging conferences and mediating between French and Annamites... since this action puts the U.S. right in the middle." Davis to Heppner, September 1, 1945 (RG 226, Entry 154, Box 199, Folder 3373, NARA).

97. Even without the full story, Donald Lancaster wrote: "Indeed, so persuasive did the Viet Minh prove that Patti is reported to have adopted their cause with a zeal which shocked and offended the captive French community." Donald Lancaster, *The Emancipation of French Indochina* (London: Oxford University Press, 1961), 125.

98. In his memoir Sainteny claimed that Laurie Gordon had offered to serve as an intermediary between Sainteny and Ho earlier, but the events surrounding the rapid end to the war got in the way. Sainteny, *Histoire d'une paix manquée*, 69.

99. Perhaps one of the best examples of Patti's growing disdain for the French in Indochina is evidenced by a minor incident late in August, when Sainteny complained to Kunming about insufficient food at the Governor-General's Palace. When questioned about the grievance by OSS headquarters, Patti retorted that Sainteny and his group, who had been "eating like kings until the Annamese servants could no longer stand serving Frenchmen," had gone "one whole day" with only American K rations. He had, Patti informed Kunming, intervened on their behalf with the management of the Hotel Métropole, and Sainteny's group were fed in the kitchen of the palace. This would have to do, Patti added, "because Annamese spirit of Independence will not be subdued by French appetite for luxury." Patti to Indiv and Swift, September 1, 1945 (RG 226, Entry 154, Box 199, Folder 3376, NARA).

100. Patti, *Why Viet Nam?* 208–209. The official "Activities Report" for August 27 provides a far less colorful description of the meeting. In addition, on the morning of the meeting, Patti watched as "well over 5,000 paraded by [his] window shouting Independence and 'Chase out the French.'" Patti to Indiv, NR19, August 27, 1945 (RG 226, Entry 154, Box 199, Folder 3373, NARA).

101. Patti to Indiv, NR023, August 27, 1945 (RG 226, Entry 154, Box 199, Folder 3373, NARA).

102. Sainteny described his treatment in Hanoi and his frequent displeasure with Patti in his memoir, *Histoire d'une paix manquée*, 98–114.

103. Devillers, *Histoire du Viet-Nam de 1940 à 1952*, 151. A number of American writers have accepted this conclusion. One example reads, "Sainteny was apparently hamstrung by the Viet Minh with Patti's tacit approval." W. Macy Marvel, "Drift and Intrigue: United States Relations with the Viet-Minh, 1945," *Millennium* 4, no. 1 (1975): 17.

104. "Activities Report," August 28, 1945.

105. Patti to Indiv, NR36, August 29, 1945 (RG 226, Entry 154, Box 199, Folder 3376, NARA).

106. "Memorandum for the Secretary of State," August 31, 1945 (RG 226, Microfilm #1642, Roll 21, Frames 842–843, NARA).

107. Wampler to Chow, August 11, 1945; Chow to Wampler, August 12, 1945 (both in RG 226, Entry 140, Box 52, Folder 416, NARA).

108. Patti to Indiv, NR19, August 27, 1945.

109. King Chen, "China and the Democratic Republic of Vietnam 1945–54" (Ph.D. diss., Pennsylvania State University, 1962), 103–104. For a thorough discussion of the Chinese role in the August Revolution, see Peter Worthing, *Occupation and Revolution: China and the Vietnamese August Revolution of 1945* (Berkeley: Institute of East Asian Studies, University of California, 2001). Joseph Buttinger added that for the Chinese "the end of the war signaled the end of French rule in Vietnam. The sentiments of the Americans stationed in the China theater of war were in tune with these expectations." Joseph Buttinger, *Vietnam: A Dragon Embattled*, 2 vols. (New York: Praeger, 1967), 1: 280.

110. David Marr wrote that this was one reason that China theater headquarters spurned General Alessandri's request for a fleet of planes to transport French troops into Tonkin. "Aside from real shortages of China Theater aircraft and fuel, Wedemeyer knew that Chiang Kai-shek had no intention of allowing French troops to arrive ahead of his own units, most of whom would be required to walk overland to Hanoi or Haiphong." Marr, *Vietnam 1945*, 478.

111. Patti, *Why Viet Nam?* 223–224.

112. Some sources give Patti an even larger role. For example, one author wrote that Patti "even helped draft the Declaration of Independence." Dalloz, *The War in Indo-China*, 56.

113. Quoted in Robert Shaplen, "The Enigma of Ho Chi Minh," *Reporter*, January 27, 1955, 13. See also Shaplen, *The Lost Revolution: The U.S. in Vietnam, 1946–1966* (New York: Harper Colophon, 1966), 29; Charles Fenn, *Ho Chi Minh: A Biographical Introduction* (New York: Charles Scribner's Sons, 1973), 82. In both Shaplen's article and his book, Phelan, anxious to protect his identity, is referred to as "John."

114. Défourneaux, *Winking Fox*, 174.

115. Patti to Indiv, NR48, August 31, 1945 (RG 226, Entry 154, Box 199, Folder 3376, NARA).

116. Patti to Commanding, CCC, Info Indiv, NR60, September 1, 1945 (RG 226, Entry 154, Box 199, Folder 3376, NARA).

117. Patti to Indiv, NNNR61, September 2, 1945 (RG 226, Entry 154, Box 199, Folder 3373, NARA).

118. Marr, *Vietnam 1945*, 529–535. The Vietnamese organizers estimated the size of the crowd to be roughly 1 million. American aerial photographs placed the number between 500,000 and 600,000. David Marr, however, concluded that given the population of Hanoi at that time (200,000), "and assuming an equivalent number of people arrived from nearby provinces," it is "unlikely that the crowd exceeded 400,000."

Although far less than the original estimate, "this would still have been the largest gathering ever seen in Hanoi." Marr, *Vietnam 1945*, 530.

119. Patti, *Why Viet Nam?* 248–252. Vu Dinh Huynh recalled his struggle to find the appropriate clothes for Ho to wear on Independence Day. His two suits were not suitable for the occasion, and he "categorically refused" to wear either a tie or leather shoes. "Make me anything, but make sure it is very simple. No wool, no leather. Make it simple and easy, practical; and especially not expensive or elegant," Vu Dinh Huynh recalled Ho saying to him. He added, "I ended up basing the suit on what Stalin wore in photographs." Quoted in Boudarel and Nguyen Van Ky, *Hanoi*, 88–89.

120. Lucien Conein was born in Paris but grew up in the United States. At the beginning of World War II he enlisted in the French army. After France's defeat and the entry of the United States into the war, he joined the OSS. His fluency in French made him an obvious candidate to be dropped behind enemy lines in France. In Indochina he was known as Lieutenant Laurent. Neil Sheehan, *A Bright Shining Lie: John Paul Vann and America in Vietnam* (New York: Random House, 1988), 9; R. Harris Smith, *OSS: The Secret History of America's First Central Intelligence Agency* (Berkeley and Los Angeles: University of California Press, 1972), 352. For additional insight into Conein's later exploits in Vietnam, see Kenneth Conboy and Dale Andrade, *Spies and Commandos: How America Lost the Secret War in North Vietnam* (Lawrence: University Press of Kansas, 2000), 1–30.

121. Lucien Conein, interview by Cecil Currey, Giap Papers; Currey, *Victory at Any Cost*, 99–104.

122. In Bao Dai's account of his journey to Hanoi to join the new Vietnamese government as a "simple citizen," he stated that "apparently, he had never been more popular" among the people than at this moment of "sacrifice." Bao Dai, *Le dragon d'Annam*, 120, 127.

123. Patti, *Why Viet Nam?* 250.

124. "Declaration of Independence of the Democratic Republic of Viet Nam," in *Breaking Our Chains*, 96. See also, Ho Chi Minh, *Selected Works*, 4 vols. (Hanoi: Foreign Languages Publishing House, 1961), 3: 17–21.

125. "Speech by Vo Nguyen Giap," September 2, 1945, in Porter, *Vietnam*, 1: 66–71. For Giap's recollections of the heady days of August and Independence Day see, Vo Nguyen Giap, *Des journées inoubliables* (Hanoi: Editions en Langues Etranges, 1975), 9–34.

126. "Full Transcript of 1997 OSS/Viet Minh Meeting," 48. Most probably, the villagers heard the speech read over the radio at some time after the celebration in Ba Dinh square.

127. Bui Tin, *Following Ho Chi Minh: Memoirs of a North Vietnamese Colonel* (Honolulu: University of Hawaii Press, 1995), 4, 16.

128. Duong Van Mai Elliott, *The Sacred Willow: Four Generations in the Life of a Vietnamese Family* (Oxford: Oxford University Press, 1999), 120–126.

129. Marr, *Vietnam 1945*, 537. More than two decades later, Americans writing about Vietnam also misinterpreted the event. Theodore White wrote that two U.S. Air Force planes "buzzed the crowd to add glory to the ceremony." Theodore H. White,

"Indo-China—The Long Trail of Error," in *Vietnam: Anatomy of a Conflict*, edited by Wesley R. Fishel (Itasca, IL: F. E. Peacock, 1968), 17.

130. Nordlinger's team consisted of twenty-two officers and men. His duties are listed as "sort out prisoners of war, prepare nominative list [of] their nationality, info on vital statistics, and prepare their evacuation... hospitalize prisoners, rehabilitate them and entertain them while awaiting repatriation." Patti to Indiv for Swift, NR59, September 1, 1945 (RG 226, Entry 154, Box 199, Folder 3376, NARA).

131. Patti to Commanding Officer, NR58; Patti to Indiv for Swift, NR59, September 1, 1945 (both in RG 226, Entry 154, Box 199, Folder 3376, NARA).

132. "Cet homme [Nordlinger], à l'encontre de ses compatriotes arrivés avant lui saura se cantonner dans sa mission et attirera sur lui et sur l'uniforme qu'il porte la reconnaissance et la sympathie de tous ceux qui l'approcheront." Sainteny, *Histoire d'une paix manquée*, 108. Joseph Buttinger also singled Nordlinger out: "Nordlinger, incidentally, was the only prominent American in Vietnam against whom the French leveled no political accusations." Buttinger, *Vietnam*, 1: 340. Nordlinger and Sainteny corresponded briefly in the late 1960s as part of Nordlinger's efforts to contact Ho Chi Minh and to discover information on the fate of American pilots begin held as POWs in North Vietnam. Colonel Stephen Nordlinger, correspondence, courtesy of John Nordlinger.

133. Patti, *Why Viet Nam?* 239–240.

134. Gallagher to McClure, September 20, 1945, cited in Edward R. Drachman, *United States Policy toward Vietnam, 1940–1945* (Rutherford, NJ: Fairleigh Dickinson University Press, 1970), 143.

135. Nordlinger, September 26, 1945, documents courtesy of John Nordlinger.

136. Nordlinger, correspondence with Edward Drachman, cited in Drachman, *United States Policy toward Vietnam, 1940–1945*, 144–146. In his interview with Drachman, Nordlinger added that Ho Chi Minh presented him with an embroidered bird as a gift just prior to his departure.

137. Nordlinger, correspondence, letter to President Lyndon B. Johnson, March 18, 1968.

138. "Full Transcript of 1997 OSS/Viet Minh Meeting," 85.

139. Patti, *Why Viet Nam?* 113.

140. Cecil Currey interview with Lucien Conein, Giap Papers. Conein had his share of critics as well. His initial OSS service report—for consideration as one of the participants in an OSS drop behind enemy lines in France—stated that he demonstrated a "complete lack of any leadership qualifications and it is extremely doubtful whether he would develop any during training." "Jedburgh Board Report" (RG 226, Entry 128, Box 9, Folder 67, NARA).

141. R. Harris Smith, *OSS*, 352.

142. Nordlinger, correspondence, October 2004.

143. Cecil Currey interview with Lucien Conein, Giap Papers; Currey, *Victory at Any Cost*, 96–87. Conein left Vietnam in 1945 and soon was busy "running undercover agents in and out of East European countries." He became an agent for the CIA and in 1954 was recruited by Lieutenant Colonel Edward Lansdale for a variety of operations

in Vietnam with the Saigon Military Mission. Up until October 9, 1955, Conein's tasks included organizing a "stay-behind resistance network" in North Vietnam that carried out "systematic sabotage of North Vietnam's utility, transportation, and port facilities" and developing a paramilitary organization primarily made up of remnants of the Dai Viet party. Conein left Hanoi with the last French troops in 1955. Conein's activities were just as varied in the South. It was his OSS training, Neil Sheehan asserted, that "made him one of the more useful members of a special action group Lansdale organized to pull off 'dirty tricks' on Diem's behalf during the height of the fighting with the Binh Xuyen in Saigon." Conein then became involved in bringing a number of officers in the "Vietnamese National Army over to [Ngo Dinh] Diem's side." After Lansdale left, Conein stayed on as the CIA liaison officer to Diem's Ministry of the Interior. As the political climate changed in Saigon, so did the nature of Conein's activities. In 1963, he "accomplished the act that is one of the highest professional aspirations for a man of Conein's calling—setting up a successful *coup d'état.*" By his own admission, Conein carried Ambassador Henry Cabot Lodge's "quiet assurances" of US support to the generals responsible for the overthrow and murder of President Diem and his brother. Currey, *Victory at Any Cost,* 251–216, 243; Sheehan, *A Bright Shining Lie,* 9, 136, 139, 179.

144. For a lengthy discussion of Sainteny's opinions of Patti in conjunction with Vietnamese Independence Day, see Sainteny, *Histoire d'une paix manquée,* 98–106.

145. Davis to Indiv, NR4, September 2, 1945; Heppner and Indiv to Patti, September 3, 1945 (both in RG 226, Entry 154, Box 199, Folder 3373, NARA).

146. Patti to Indiv relay to Gallagher for Info, NR63, September 3, 1945 (RG 226, Entry 154, Box 199, Folder 3373, NARA).

147. Although most accused Patti of oversympathizing with the Viet Minh and blatantly disregarding the French, there was at least one contradictory complaint. In his September 15 report, Lieutenant Colonel John C. Bane of the OSS wrote: "Captain Patti, it has been stated by several American officers, has handled his contacts with Japanese and Annamese rather badly. I have very incomplete information to the effect that he was overly patronizing toward Japs and Annamese." (RG 226, Entry 154, Box 199, Folder 3373, NARA).

148. "Activities Report," September 4, 1945; Patti, *Why Viet Nam?* 264–270. Even before Patti touched down in China, Grelecki had wired him about new directives from Major Shingledecker of the G-5 from Kunming, emphasizing that all American personnel came under Nordlinger and would engage in work and send messages only as approved by him. Shingledecker added that theater headquarters "had sent OSS for initial purpose only [POW activities and humanitarian work]" and that OSS personnel "would leave this area shortly." Grelecki to Indiv for Patti, NR79, September 4, 1945 (RG 226, Entry 154, Box 199, Folder 3373, NARA).

149. "Activities Report," September 5, 1945.

150. Patti, "Activity Report, Hanoi Detachment," September 5, 1945 (RG 226, Entry 154, Box 174, Folder 3015, NARA).

151. Mayer and Helliwell to Nordlinger and Bernique, NR6678, September 7, 1945 (RG 226, Entry 154, Box 199, Folder 3373, NARA).

152. Patti, *Why Viet Nam?* 265–268.

153. "Activities Report," August 31, 1945; Patti to Indiv, NR61, September 2, 1945 (RG 226, Entry 154, Box 199, Folder 3373, NARA).

154. The oft-repeated fear that "Chungking has prepared a puppet government with which to present the Annamese upon arrival" was passed on through Patti and OSS headquarters to the secretary of state by September 6, 1945. Memo to secretary of state (RG 226, Microfilm 1642, Roll 21, Frame 8–9, NARA).

155. Parrot for Gallagher and Davis Chungking, NR6611, September 6, 1945 (RG 226, Entry 154, Box 199, Folder 3373, NARA).

156. In his later operational report, Ettinger claimed that he had not disobeyed orders by joining the French ship but had sent Patti a message that he evidently did not receive. Ettinger to Indiv, September 17, 1945 (RG 226, Entry 154, Box 199, Folder 3375, NARA).

157. Jordan to Patti, July 15, 1945 (RG 226, Entry 154, Box 199, Folder 3376, NARA); Jordan to Indiv, August 9, 1945 (RG 226, Entry 154, Box 199, Folder 3375, NARA).

158. Sainteny, *Histoire d'une paix manquée*, 45, 80, 92–92.

159. Marr, *Vietnam 1945*, 403.

160. Ibid., 404.

161. Ettinger reported that fifty-four pirates were killed in the twelve-minute engagement, during which a French lieutenant, de Beaucrops was injured by a "pirate bullet." Lieutenant Robert Ettinger to CO, OSS Det, Hanoi, FIC—"Info Indiv," September 12, 1945 (RG 226, Entry 154, Box 174, Folder 3015).

162. Capt. John D. Wilson, "French Indo-China: Arrest of French Patrol Boat *Crayssac* at Hongay on 2 Sept. 1945," November 28, 1945 (RG 226, Entry 19, Box 372, NARA); Ettinger to CO, OSS Det, Hanoi, FIC—"Info Indiv."

163. "Report of Bui Manh Phu, Chief of the Administrative Service of the Revolutionaries Committee in Hongay to the Commander of the 4th Zone in Haiphong," quoted in Wilson, "French Indo-China: Arrest of French Patrol Boat Crayssac at Hongay on 2 Sept. 1945." The Viet Minh claims about the log books, navigational records, and flags were all substantiated by Ettinger, who found the arguments irrelevant.

164. Ibid.

165. Marr, *Vietnam 1945*, 402.

166. "Account of AGAS Officer in Hanoi," quoted in Wilson, "French Indo-China: Arrest of French Patrol Boat Crayssac at Hongay on 2 Sept. 1945."

167. Ettinger to CO, OSS Det, Hanoi, FIC—"Info Indiv."

168. Ettinger to CO, OSS Det, Hanoi, FIC—"Info Indiv." Fuselier tried to take Vilar with him to Hanoi as well, but Vilar would not leave without his ship. Although the Viet Minh agreed to release Vilar, they would not release the ship. Thus, Vilar remained in Hongay when Fuselier and Ettinger departed. René Charbonneau and José Maigre asserted that Vilar was killed by the Viet Minh a few days after Ettinger's departure. René Charbonneau and José Maigre, *Les parias de la victoire: Indochine-Chine, 1945* (Paris: France-Empire, 1980), 369.

169. Another OSS report indicated that another agent was sent to "ransom Ettinger with 250,000 CN." Mims to Indiv, September 15, 1945; Loy to Mims to Indiv and Swift, September 10, 1945 (both in RG 226, Entry 154, Box 199, Folder 3375, NARA). Regardless of these plans, no money was exchanged for Ettinger's release.

170. Bernique to Indiv and Patti, September 9, 1945; Indiv and Swift to Patti and Mims, September 10, 1945; Mims to Indiv and Swift, September 12, 1945 (all in RG 226, Entry 154, Box 174, Folder 3015, NARA).

171. Patti for Ettinger to Indiv, NR113, September 14, 1945 (RG 226, Entry 19, Box 372, NARA).

172. Ettinger to CO, OSS Det, Hanoi, FIC—"Info Indiv."

173. Giap wrote: "If the French come, we will fight. Hanoi will not rest until it is the capital of a free country. We are waiting for you.... even now I am returning for dinner with three American friends. The Chinese may fight us but we have a solid heart. Vietnam will be independent." Letter from Giap to Thomas, Giap Papers.

174. Thomas, diary; Thomas, "Welcome to Our American Friends," 36–37.

175. "Full Transcript of 1997 OSS/Viet Minh Meeting," 64.

176. Ibid., 55.

177. Thomas, diary; also in Thomas, "Welcome to Our American Friends," 36–37.

178. Chow to Indiv, NR215, September 2, 1945 (RG 226, Entry 154, Box 199, Folder 3377, NARA).

179. Thomas, interviews.

180. Sainteny's image had recently taken a considerable beating when Lu Han had unceremoniously evicted him from the Governor-General's Palace so that he could set up his own official headquarters in the prestigious building.

181. All quotations in this paragraph from Patti, *Why Viet Nam?* 290–293, 343.

182. Worthing, *Occupation and Revolution*, 100.

183. Ho Chi Minh, "On the Occasion of the 'Gold Week,'" in *Selected Works*, 3: 26–27.

184. Quoted in Boudarel and Nguyen Van Ky, *Hanoi*, 87.

185. Bernard Fall, *The Two Viet-Nams: A Political and Military Analysis* (New York: Praeger, 1967), 65.

186. Fenn, *Ho Chi Minh*, 91.

187. Donovan, "Memorandum for the President," September 27, 1945 (RG 226, Microfilm 1642, Roll 31, Frames 608–610, NARA).

188. John C. Bane to CCC, September 14, 1945 (RG 226, Entry 154, Box 199, Folder 3373, NARA).

189. "Letter from Maj. Gen. Philip E. Gallagher in Hanoi to Major General R. B. McClure, Kunming, September 20, 1945," reprinted in Porter, *Vietnam*, 1: 77–78. Cecil Currey and Gabriel Kolko interpreted Gallagher's words and behavior as disapproving of the Viet Minh and their bid for independence. Currey, *Victory at Any Cost*, 103; Gabriel Kolko, *The Politics of War: The World and United States Foreign Policy, 1943–1945* (New York: Random House, 1968), 610. Bernard Fall, on the other hand, saw Gallagher as completely ignoring the French mission in favor of establishing strong, friendly relations with the Provisional Government.

Bernard Fall, "La politique americaine au Viet-Nam," *Politique Etrange*, July 1955, 313–314.

190. Letter from Gallagher in Hanoi to McClure, Kunming, September 20, 1945, cited in Drachman, *United States Policy toward Vietnam, 1940–1945*, 157.

191. Gallagher made his papers available to Bert Cooper, John Killigrew, and Norman LaCharite for their book *Case Studies in Insurgency and Revolutionary Warfare: Vietnam, 1941–1954* (Washington, DC: Special Operations Research Office, 1964), 111–112.

192. Fall, *The Two Viet-Nams*, 69.

193. Patti to Indiv, September 29, 1945 (RG 226, Entry 154, Box 199, Folder 3373, NARA); Patti, *Why Viet Nam?* 360–362; Devillers, *Histoire du Viet-Nam de 1940 à 1952*, 151–153.

194. Sainteny, *Histoire d'une paix manquée*, 137.

195. Bui Diem, *In the Jaws of History*, 38.

196. Patti, *Why Viet Nam?* 369.

197. "Memoranda for Secretary of State James Byrnes from O.S.S. Director William J. Donovan," September 5 and 6, 1945, in Porter, *Vietnam*, 1: 71–72.

198. Ibid., 364.

CHAPTER 9
"COCHINCHINA IS BURNING..."

1. William J. Duiker, *Ho Chi Minh* (New York: Hyperion, 2000), 246–248.

2. Nguyen Thi Dinh, *No Other Road to Take: Memoir of Mrs. Nguyen Thi Dinh*, translated by Mai V. Elliott (Ithaca, NY: Cornell University Press, 1976), 36.

3. David Marr, *Vietnam 1945: The Quest for Power* (Berkeley and Los Angeles: University of California Press, 1995), 454–458.

4. Ibid., 460.

5. Nguyen Thi Dinh, *No Other Road to Take*, 36.

6. Although Peter Dewey was in fact a major, he gave himself an unofficial commission, called at the time "Mexican commissions," to give himself better leverage in his dealings with higher-ranking British and French officers in Saigon. Those of all nationalities in Saigon often referred to Major Dewey as a lieutenant colonel. Dewey also "upgraded the rank of the officers on the mission so that they could deal with French and British colonels and generals. All of this was of course unofficial, but the OSS was a very informal organization that readily disregarded inconvenient Army rules and regulations." George Wickes, memoir (unpublished). Such unofficial field promotions were common in the OSS during the war.

7. Memo from Major Amos Moscrip to Colonel Coughlin, "Activities in French Indo China," August 10, 1945; Moscrip to Major Dewey, "Operation Embankment," August 12, 1945 (both in RG 226, Entry 110, Box 25, Folder 284, NARA).

8. Dewey's intelligence objectives included the following categories: "physical and geographic (communications, air fields, harbor installations, public utilities), political

(indigenous and external), economic, military (French military and naval activity), War Crimes, Japanese activity, Collection of material (pertinent documents, movie films, publications), and Intelligence activity (ascertain extent of French, Allied and enemy intelligence activities)." Dewey, "Progress Report for 13–14 August: Operation Embankment" (RG 226, Entry 110, Box 25, Folder 284, NARA).

9. "R&A Objectives for French Indochina Mission," August 15, 1945 (RG 226, Entry 110, Box 25, Folder 284, NARA).

10. R. Harris Smith, *OSS: The Secret History of America's First Central Intelligence Agency* (Berkeley and Los Angeles: University of California Press, 1972), 338. The list of Frenchmen Dewey interacted with included Generals de Gaulle, Giraud, Leclerc, and Petchkoff and a number of ministers of the Free French government-in-exile.

11. Major A. Peter Dewey, "The Account of My Experience as a Member of OSS prior to Mission Etoile" (RG 226, Entry 92, Box 603, Folder 6, NARA); "Captain Albert Peter Dewey, AC," undated (RG 226, Entry 92A, Box 29, Folder 421, NARA).

12. R. Harris Smith, *OSS: The Secret History of America's First Central Intelligence Agency* (Berkeley and Los Angeles: University of California Press, 1972), 338; Anthony Cave Brown, *The Last Hero: Wild Bill Donovan* (New York: Vintage Books, 1982), 587–594.

13. "Basic Plan for Operation Embankment," undated (RG 226, Entry 110, Box 25, Folder 284, NARA).

14. Dewey, "The Account of My Experience as a Member of OSS prior to Mission Etoile."

15. Lieutenant Emile R. Counasse, "Embankment Operation-Saigon," September 1–6, 1945 (RG 226, Entry 110, Box 25, Folder 284, NARA).

16. Ibid. The Americans reported that Major Pierce was not as lucky in his dealings with the Japanese. According to Counasse, the British officer exhibited little tact or diplomacy and immediately insulted the Japanese, who then proceeded to give Pierce "as little cooperation as they could and still be on the safe side." Ibid.

17. "General Summary of Counasse Operation in Saigon," September 2, 1945 (RG 226, Entry 110, Box 25, Folder 284, NARA); Emile R. Counasse, "Saigon Mission" (RG 226, Entry 148, Box 124, Folder 2151, NARA). Counasse added: "It is quite difficult to go around because as soon as the Americans appear on the scene they are mobbed and cheered. Various civilians who cannot be brushed off are hindering us with complaints."

18. The last of the American prisoners of war were evacuated on September 5.

19. Counasse, "Saigon Mission."

20. Ibid.

21. Counasse, "Embankment Operation-Saigon." In a later report Counasse stated that there were "at least 1,000 people in the halls and lobby who had taken refuge from the mob on the streets." Counasse, "Saigon Mission."

22. Counasse wrote that "all the pertinent information" was from three Frenchmen. Counasse, "Embankment Operation-Saigon," "General Summary of Counasse Operation in Saigon," and "Saigon Mission."

23. Counasse, "Saigon Mission."

24. For a full discussion of the revolution in My Tho and its subsequent history, see David W. P. Elliott, *The Vietnamese War: Revolution and Social Change in the Mekong Delta* (New York: East Gate Books, 2002), 65–114.

25. Counasse, "Saigon Mission." See also "Report on Operation Embankment by Sgt Nardella" (RG 226, Entry 110, Box 25, Folder 284, NARA).

26. Counasse, "Saigon Mission."

27. Sergeant Hejna, "General Summary of Counasse Operation in Saigon" (RG 226, Entry 110, Box 25, Folder 284, NARA).

28. Nardella elaborated: "On the whole the Annamites too are extremely anxious to cultivate good will with the United States and hence they were very courteous and not at all inimical to us." "General Summary of Counasse Operation in Saigon"; "Report on Operation Embankment by Sgt Nardella" (RG 226, Entry 110, Box 25, Folder 284, NARA).

29. "Report on Operation Embankment by Sgt Nardella."

30. Ibid. On September 4 Nardella concluded: "French civilians are walking the streets again unmolested but the situation is still very tense and if the Kowdists [*sic*] can do it, it is very possible that they might continue their terroristic activities."

31. Counasse, "General Summary of Counasse Operation in Saigon."

32. Counasse, "Saigon Mission." Counasse and his team left with the American POWs, who were evacuated on September 4, 5, and 6, 1945.

33. Counasse, "General Summary of Counasse Operation in Saigon."

34. Harold R. Isaacs, *No Peace for Asia* (Cambridge, MA: M.I.T. Press, 1947), 135. Isaacs also wrote: "The insurgents, one heard endlessly from Frenchmen in high place and low, were nothing but a handful of agitators and paid terrorists, tools of the Japanese who stood momentarily between the benevolent French and the great mass of the people who yearned only to have the French return and desired only to till their lands in the peace assured by French rule." Ibid., 141; see also 152–155.

35. Donald Lancaster, *The Emancipation of French Indochina* (London: Oxford University Press, 1961), 137. See also John T. McAlister Jr., *Viet Nam: The Origins of Revolution* (New York: Knopf, 1969), 206.

36. Lancaster, *The Emancipation of French Indochina*, 129. Nguyen Cao Ky asserted that the Viet Minh acquired "large supplies of arms and ammunition" that the Japanese had left behind. Nguyen Cao Ky, *Twenty Years and Twenty Days* (New York: Stein and Day, 1976), 18. Peter Harclerode also concluded that "large quantities of weapons" were obtained from the Japanese. Peter Harclerode, *Fighting Dirty: The Inside Story of Covert Operations from Ho Chi Minh to Osama Bin Laden* (London: Cassell, 2001), 78.

37. Stein Tønnesson, *The Vietnamese Revolution of 1945: Roosevelt, Ho Chi Minh and de Gaulle in a World at War* (London: SAGE, 1991), 392.

38. Marr, *Vietnam 1945*, 377.

39. Quoted in ibid., 458. John McAlister also wrote that the Viet Minh in Saigon received weapons via Terauchi's office. "Lt. Gen. Numata Takazo, chief of staff to Count Terauchi, the Japanese commander, conceded that arms had been supplied to

the Vietnamese after the capitulation, without specifying which group. It seems clear from subsequent events that it was not the Trotskyites or imperial government." McAlister, *Viet Nam*, 204. By mid-December 1945, the Strategic Services Unit of the War Department, the new name for the by then defunct OSS, maintained the Vietnamese were "operating in groups ranging in size from one to two hundred, and have arms which the Japanese took from the French and turned over to them." Strategic Services Unit Report A-640813, December 15, 1945 (RG 226, Entry 154, Box 174, Folder 3015, NARA).

40. Quoted in Peter M. Dunn, *The First Vietnam War* (New York: St. Martin's, 1985), 46–47.

41. Belleview to Helliwell, August 12, 1945. See also Belleview to Indiv and MMF, August 23, 1945 (both in RG 226, Entry 154, Box 199, Folder 3375, NARA).

42. Helliwell to Davis and Coughlin, August 18, 1945 (RG 226, Entry 154, Box 199, Folder 3373, NARA). A later report stated that the Japanese consul general "apparently turned down" the Viet Minh request for the Japanese army's weapons. (RG 457, SRS1782, 6 September 1945, Number 1260, NARA).

43. "The Political Situation in Indo-China," August 31, 1945 (RG 226, Entry 19, Box 223, Document A-60805/XL15126, NARA). See also Ellen J. Hammer, *The Struggle for Indochina* (Stanford, CA: Stanford University Press, 1954), 101.

44. Joseph Buttinger, *Vietnam: A Dragon Embattled*, 2 vols. (New York: Praeger, 1967), 1: 328; William J. Duiker, *The Communist Road to Power in Vietnam*, 2nd ed. (Boulder, CO: Westview, 1996), 119.

45. Tønnesson, *The Vietnamese Revolution of 1945*, 363; Marr, *Vietnam 1945*, 543.

46. McAlister, *Viet Nam*, 251–252; Cecil B. Currey, *Victory at Any Cost: The Genius of Viet Nam's Gen. Vo Nguyen Giap* (Washington, DC: Brassey's, 1997), 126; Murakami Hyoe, *The Years of Trial, 1919–52* (Tokyo: Japan Culture Institute, 1982), 221–222. Murakami stated that among the "four thousand Japanese officers and men" who deserted was Colonel Nakagawa, commander at Lang Son. In his work on the Asian nature of the Vietnamese war against the French, Christopher Goscha also estimated that roughly 5,000 Japanese soldiers deserted and joined the Viet Minh. Christopher E. Goscha, "Allies tardifs: Les apports techniques des deserteurs japonais au Viet Minh (1945–1950)" (unpublished), courtesy of the author.

47. Marr, *Vietnam 1945*, 543. See also Bernard Fall, *The Two Viet-Nams: A Political and Military Analysis* (New York: Praeger, 1967), 75; McAlister, *Viet Nam*, 252. Murakami stated that former Japanese soldiers were particularly important after Mao Tsetung's victory in China in 1949. "Once Chinese aid to the Ho Chi Minh forces began, truck transport over the steep mountainous areas between the two countries was almost entirely the work of former Japanese soldiers." Murakami, *The Years of Trial, 1919–52*, 223–224. See also Kiyoko Kurusu Nitz, "Independence without Nationalists? The Japanese and Vietnamese Nationalism during the Japanese Period, 1940–45," *Journal of Southeast Asian Studies* 15 (March 1984): 108–133.

48. Currey, *Victory at Any Cost*, 126. John McAlister made similar findings: "Those who did join were part of a group known as the 'Japanese Organism for Collaboration and Aid for the Independence of Viet Nam,' which was headed by Lieutenant Colonel

Mukayama, who with his principal assistant, Major Oshima, was located at Thai Nguyen, in the Viet Minh mountain-base area. Although Japanese groups were located at other strategic spots, the one at Thai Nguyen, comprising about 1,500 combatants and 600 technicians and workers, accounted for almost half the largest estimate of the total number of deserters." McAlister, *Viet Nam*, 251–252. One may only speculate as to when Giap's "recruiting" of the Japanese in Thai Nguyen might have occurred. Giap left Thai Nguyen for Hanoi without a victory on August 23, only a few days after the initial "assault" on the city. The ceasefire was reached by his subordinates only on August 25. Initial American impressions of the defeated enemy did not indicate that a wholesale desertion of the Japanese garrison took place at that time. Members of the Deer Team first encountered the Japanese during a shopping and sightseeing venture in Thai Nguyen on September 1. Although the Japanese had originally been confined to their post, their detention lasted only briefly, and they were allowed to walk about town without their arms. Both Thomas and Défourneaux recalled the Japanese soldiers' surprise when, during one of their strolls in town, they ran into the seven Americans of the Deer Team. "They looked at us, and we looked at them," recollected Thomas, "And neither of us said a word." By September 5 the number of Japanese in town had increased substantially. Thomas noted in his diary entry for that day that there were "about 1000 Japs in town—coming down from Bac Kan. They sure look like rough customers." Allison Thomas, diary, Giap Papers. Défourneaux also noted the Japanese demeanor, describing them as men "who strutted arrogantly in full uniform, alone and in small groups, and in cases of officers with a sword dangling at their side." Major René J. Défourneaux, "Deer Team Diary," courtesy of Défourneaux. Défourneaux wrote that even though the small group of American men represented the victor, the Japanese who passed them "gave us cruel stares or with disdain looked straight ahead." Défourneaux, *The Winking Fox: Twenty-two Years in Military Intelligence* (Indianapolis: Indiana Creative Arts, 1997), 192–193.

49. Marr, *Vietnam 1945*, 543. McAlister asserted: "Before the end of 1946 nearly half of them [Japanese deserters] had either been killed or captured or had given themselves up, which left a hard core of some 560 in the south, of whom the largest number, 220, were concentrated around Tay Ninh.... Because of the small percentage of Japanese activists with the Vietnamese and their concentration in homogenous groups at key locations, the press and intelligence reports that they were almost exclusively agents of the Kempeitai seem to be substantiated." McAlister, *Viet Nam*, 215–216.

50. From October 1945 through February 1946 former OSS agents reporting in their new roles as SSU agents occasionally mentioned the presence of Japanese soldiers leading the Vietnamese forces ("an undetermined number of Japanese deserters reportedly in well-entrenched positions were reinforcing the Annamites."), conducting espionage activities or training "stay-behind" agents. "Situation in Saigon," October 18, 1945 (RG 226, Entry 140, Box 52, Folder 416, NARA); "Military, Political and Economic Information," November 8, 1945 (RG 226, Entry 19, Box 334, Document A-62914, NARA); "General Situation: Saigon," November 23, 1945 (RG 226, Entry 19, Box 346, Document A-63322, NARA); "Saigon," December 15, 1945 (RG 226, Entry

154, Box 174, Folder 3015, NARA); "Saigon," December 29, 1945 (RG 226, Entry 200, Box 1, Folder 2, NARA); "Saigon" (RG 226, Entry 200, Box 1, Folder 5, NARA); "Saigon," February 28, 1946 (RG 226, Entry 200, Box 1, Folder 5, NARA). In addition, in March 1946 French headquarters reported that five Japanese deserters were among the men captured during a raid on Bac Lo and the "dead bodies of three Japanese, including an officer" were "found at the point where the operation was carried out." U.S. Department of Defense, *The Pentagon Papers: The Defense Department History of United States Decisionmaking on Vietnam*, 8 vols. (Boston: Beacon Press, 1971), 1: 18.

51. "Saigon," December 27, 1945 (RG 226, Entry 19, Box 372, Document A-64221, NARA). See also Dunn, *The First Vietnam War*, 158–161.

52. Radio wire Saigon to Singapore, February 17, 1946 (RG 226, Entry 200, Box 1, Folder 5, NARA). See also Donald G. Gillin and Charles Etter, "Staying On: Japanese Soldiers and Civilians in China, 1945-1949," *Journal of Asian Studies* 42, no. 3 (May 1983): 497–518.

53. Archimedes L. A. Patti, *Why Viet Nam? Prelude to America's Albatross* (Berkeley and Los Angeles: University of California Press, 1980), 341.

54. Ibid., 382.

55. Patti to Commander, CCC, Info Indiv, September 1, 1945; CCC to SI, R&A, Intelligence, September 29, 1945 (both in RG 226, Entry 154, Box 199, Folder 3373, NARA). Patti, *Why Viet Nam?* 301–306. In his book on the OSS, Bradley Smith wrote that there was a "general sale or gift of arms by the Japanese to the Annamites." Bradley F. Smith, *The Shadow Warriors: O.S.S. and the Origins of the C.I.A.* (New York: Basic Books, 1983), 327. See also Buttinger, *Vietnam*, 1: 277; George K. Tanham, *Communist Revolutionary Warfare: From the Vietminh to the Viet Cong* (New York: Praeger, 1967), 9. King Chen wrote that although the Japanese "burned some arms rather than let them fall into the Viet Minh hands, in other sections of Vietnam the Japanese did give their equipment to the Viet Minh." King Chen, "China and the Democratic Republic of Vietnam 1945-54" (Ph.D. diss., Pennsylvania State University, 1962), 68. John McAlister concluded that "the Japanese appear not to have required payment for weapons and their generosity seems to have been motivated by political purposes. But as a vanquished armed force the Japanese had few alternatives in late 1945, and the tie with the Viet Minh served to maximize what power remained to them." In his estimation, as of early March 1946 the Viet Minh had almost 32,000 weapons from three sources, all corresponding in some way to Japanese aid: "1) from stocks of the Guard Indochinoise allegedly with the help of the Japanese; 2) from stocks of the French Colonial Army obtained with Japanese help; and 3) from Japanese army stocks, some ceded directly, others received through the Chinese." McAlister, *Viet Nam*, 246–247, 254.

56. Letter from Gallagher USMAAG to his commanding general in China, Robert McClure, reprinted in Edward R. Drachman, *United States Policy toward Vietnam, 1940–1945* (Rutherford, NJ: Fairleigh Dickinson University Press, 1970), 105–106. See also "Allied Land Forces—French Indochina, September 1945—February 1946" (Sir Douglas Gracey Papers [henceforth Gracey Papers], Box 4, File 2, Liddell Hart Centre for Military Archives, King's College London, Strand, London).

57. Truong Chinh, *Primer for Revolt: The Communist Takeover in Viet-Nam* (New York: Praeger, 1963), 37.

58. "Political Activities in Saigon," September 7, 1945 (RG 226, Entry 16, Box 1670, Document A-60808a, NARA).

59. For example, OSS dispatch for Helliwell, September 7, 1945 (RG 226, Entry 134, Box 208, Folder 1306, NARA).

60. Dunn, *The First Vietnam War*, 124.

61. In addition to George Wickes and Henry Prunier, twenty-seven other Americans studied Vietnamese at the Army Specialized Training Program. Of that class, Prunier recalled, "around 10 ended up in Vietnam." "Full Transcript of 1997 OSS/ Viet Minh Meeting," courtesy of William Duiker, 67.

62. Prior to EMBANKMENT's departure for Saigon, Dewey had made clear his intention not to live with other Allied troops in the city. Instead, he preferred to live on American property if at all possible. His first choice was the Texaco home outside the city. Dewey to Moscrip, August 25, 1945 (RG 226, Entry 110, Box 25, Folder 284, NARA).

63. Wickes, memoir. Wickes noted: "These reports would now make interesting reading and should be available under the U.S. Freedom of Information Act, but to date all attempts to obtain copies have been frustrated. I know they still exist, for I once met an American Foreign Service officer who had read them and who was able to discuss the situation in Saigon in 1963 knowledgeably and with great interest. That was in 1963, yet in 1997, over half a century after we sent our reports, they are still inaccessible." Wickes, memoir. Wickes is one of many, including many professional historians, who have failed to locate the missing dispatches from Saigon 1945. Although some do survive, they are not those written by Dewey or White and encoded and sent by Wickes detailing their views on the political situation—especially Dewey's and Wickes's meetings with the Viet Minh.

64. Wickes, memoir.

65. General Douglas Gracey commanded the Twentieth Indian Division (Gurkhas) from 1942 until 1946. For his efforts in Saigon he was awarded the Citoyen d'Honneur of Saigon, the Grand Cross Royal Order of Cambodia, the Commander Legion of Honour, and the French Croix de Guerre avec Palme (Gracey Papers, Box 5, File 1).

66. "Allied Land Forces—French Indochina, September 1945–February 1946" (Gracey Papers, Box 4, File 7). The Viet Minh in Saigon subjected Gurkha troops to routine propaganda professing Indian-Vietnamese friendship and urging them to remember their own colonial status and to refuse to aid the "British imperialists" in subjugating a fellow colonized people. Untitled propaganda document (Gracey Papers, Box 4, File 20).

67. Dunn, *The First Vietnam War*, 152.

68. Quoted in ibid., 154. The OSS evaluation of the city was similar but with a different view of the Viet Minh control: "Armed Japanese patrol the streets and the Annamite government is in control." "Political Situation in Saigon," September 16, 1945 (RG 226, Entry 19, Box 260, Document A-61092, NARA).

69. "Allied Land Forces—French Indochina, September 1945–February 1946" (Gracey Papers, Box 4, File 7).

70. Ibid. (Gracey Papers, Box 4, File 8).

71. Dunn, *The First Vietnam War*, 155.

72. "Basic Plan for Operation Embankment."

73. Wickes, memoir. See also Patti, *Why Viet Nam?* 276–277, 310–311.

74. Dunn, *The First Vietnam War*, 155. See also Wickes, memoir.

75. Dewey to Coughlin, September 14, 1945 (RG 226, Entry 110, Box 25, Entry 284, NARA).

76. Quoted in Dunn, *The First Vietnam War*, 156.

77. The secretary to the Swiss consul in Saigon (and former secretary to the U.S. consul) and U.S. Air Force Major Frank Rhoads later gave sworn statements that Peter Dewey was not engaging in consular duties. Statements dated September 25, 1945 (RG 226, Entry 110, Box 25, Folder 277, NARA).

78. Memorandum for the president, September 17, 1945 (RG 226, Microfilm 1642, Roll 31, Frames 601–602, NARA).

79. Patti, *Why Viet Nam?* 309–310. See also "Political Situation," September 17, 1945 (RG 226, Entry 19, Box 258, Document A-61141, NARA).

80. "Proclamation N. 1," September 19, 1945, was distributed in Vietnamese as "Thong Cao So 1" (RG 226, Entry 148, Box 124, Folder 2151, NARA).

81. "General Political Situation" (RG 226, Entry 19, Box 270, Document A-61292, NARA).

82. Patti, *Why Viet Nam?* 310.

83. Wickes, memoir; Dunn, *The First Vietnam War*, 155.

84. Wickes, memoir.

85. Ibid. Archimedes Patti argues that Peter Dewey "had become persona non grata" with Gracey much earlier. According to Patti, months prior to the Japanese surrender Gracey had been presented with the plans for Operation EMBANKMENT, calling for an American force of fifty officers and enlisted men "trained and equipped for special OSS-AGAS operations," which he rejected as part of the British occupation force. Only after Heppner contacted Mountbatten directly was a much smaller team of Americans agreed upon and was planning for Operation EMBANKMENT allowed to proceed. Patti argued that Gracey was sufficiently annoyed at being overruled that he "flagged" Dewey's British file and that Dewey "had become persona non grata" before ever entering French Indochina. Patti, *Why Viet Nam?* 270–272.

86. Dunn, *The First Vietnam War*, 203.

87. Patti, *Why Viet Nam?* 315; Buttinger, *Vietnam*, 1: 330.

88. The memorandum cautioned the secretary of state that "SEAC plans for French Indo-China endorse aggressive French military action against the Annamese as a part of overall SEAC pacifying operations in Southeast Asia.... The French will undoubtedly resume their pre-war suppression methods against the Annamese under the guise of restoring order for SEAC." "Memorandum for the Secretary of State," September 10, 1945 (RG 226, Microfilm 1642, Roll 31, Frames 599–600, NARA).

89. Patti, *Why Viet Nam?* 316; and Captain Herbert J. Bluechel, "Political Aims and Philosophy of the Viet Minh Government of French Indo-China, and Their Attitude toward America and Americans" (RG 226, Entry 110, Box 25, Folder 284, NARA).

90. The appeals, included as part of a more general OSS "Memorandum for the President and the Secretary of State," resembled those already sent by Ho Chi Minh. It praised the United States for having fought to defend "the liberty of the world" and reiterated the support of the Vietnamese people for an independent nation, concluding: "The Annamese firmly rely on the sympathy on the part of American proponents of justice and liberty." "Memorandum for the President," September 25, 1945 (RG 226, Microfilm 1642, Roll 31, Frames 604–605, NARA). See also "Full Transcript of 1997 OSS/Viet Minh Meeting," 85.

91. Bluechel, "Political Aims and Philosophy of the Viet Minh."

92. Patti, *Why Viet Nam?* 316. See also Marr, *Vietnam 1945,* 541.

93. "Memorandum for the Secretary of State," September 27, 1945 (RG 226, Microfilm 1642, Roll 57, Frames 670–673, NARA).

94. Patti, *Why Viet Nam?* 317. See also Frank White, interviews by author. Frank White described General Gracey as "a *pukka sahib* of the old Indian army" who "would tolerate no nonsense from natives; he cleared them from the government buildings in the heart of Saigon, leaving them in the suburbs for the incoming French to mop up—a task that a French general estimated would take 'about a month.'" Frank White, quoted in Wesley R. Fishel, ed., *Vietnam: Anatomy of a Conflict* (Itasca, IL: F. E. Peacock, 1968), 17. Gracey's rendering of the situation was far milder. He referred to the POWs' behavior as "rough handling and a few unnecessary reprisals" that were "natural under the circumstances" and "over-emphasized by various Press correspondents" (Gracey Papers, Box 4, File 8).

95. Patti, *Why Viet Nam?* 317.

96. Ibid., 319–320; Department of Defense, *United States–Vietnam Relations, 1945–1967,* 12 vols. (Washington, DC: Government Printing Office, 1971), 1: 4; Department of Defense, *The Pentagon Papers,* 1: 45; Marr, *Vietnam 1945,* 541; Memorandum for the Secretary of State, September 27, 1945 (RG 226, Microfilm 1642, Roll 21, Frames 775–776, NARA). The Provisional Government argued that in the wake of the "treacherous" French assault, "nationalists outside Saigon rapidly organized a stubborn resistance. Bitter and murderous street fighting is going on, together with a non-collaboration movement the result[s] of which, both for [the] Indochinese as well as [the] world economy, are incalculable. Provisional Government of the Republic of Vietnam, "Declaration of the Foreign Office," September 1945 (RG 226, Entry 19, Box 352, NARA). British reports noted in part: "Hooligan reaction was barbaric. Several French nationals, men, women and children, mostly half-caste, or loyal Annamites, were murdered most foully, including some who had spent their lives in excellent service to the Annamites." "This phase, was one of rioting and bloodshed; the actions of the mob were typical of those of all savages" (Gracey Papers, Box 4, File 8).

97. "Memorandum for the Secretary of State," September 28, 1945 (RG 226, Microfilm 1642, Roll 57, Frames 670–673, NARA).

98. Bluechel, "Political Aims and Philosophy of the Viet Minh."

99. Quoted in Patti to Indiv, September 29, 1945 (RG 226, Entry 154, Box 199, Folder 3373, NARA).

100. Quoted in Patti, *Why Viet Nam?* 320.

101. Don S. Garden, Chief, Southeast Asia Sec., to Chief, SI, "Activities of Lt. Col. Peter Dewey," September 27, 1945 (RG 226, Entry 92A, Box 29, Folder 421, NARA).

102. Moscrip to Dewey, Kandy #1013, September 25, 1945 (RG 226, Entry 110, Box 25, Folder 277, NARA).

103. "Allied Land Forces South East Asia Weekly Intelligence Review," for week ending October 5, 1945 (RG 226, Entry 19, Box 329, Document XL24212, NARA); Patti, *Why Viet Nam?* 318–319; Dunn, *The First Vietnam War*, 203–205. See also Gracey Papers, Box 4, File 8, Louis Allen, "Studies in the Japanese Occupation of South-East Asia 1942–1945. 'French Indochina' to 'Vietnam.' Japan, France and Great Britain, Summer 1945," *Durham University Journal* 64, no. 2 (March 1972): 120–132.

104. News Bulletin, "Situation in Saigon," September 30, 1945 (RG 226, Entry 140, Box 52, Folder 416, NARA).

105. Marr, *Vietnam 1945*, 542. Gracey's papers list the first use of Japanese soldiers under British command as occurring on September 16, 1945 (Gracey Papers, Box 5, File 5. See also Gracey Papers, Box 4, File 8 for further details of Japanese actions while under British command).

106. Estimates of Coolidge vary considerably. In 1943 his cousin, Captain Harold Coolidge, wrote a glowing letter to help aid in Joseph's OSS security clearance. Harold J. Coolidge, Capt. AUS, RE: Joseph Coolidge, September 10, 1943 (RG 226, Entry 92, Box 387, Folder 53, NARA). Counasse, however, had nothing but complaints concerning Coolidge's behavior, referring to him in one report as "Capt. Screwball." Although Counasse declared him a "continuous thorn in everyone's side and absolutely useless" and recommended that Dewey have Coolidge recalled "immediately," Dewey kept him as part of Detachment 404. There is no indication that Dewey had problems with him. Counasse, "Embankment Operation-Saigon."

107. Herbert Bluechel, "Trip to Dalat by Captain Coolidge and Lieutenant Varner," September 25, 1945 (RG 226, Entry 110, Box 25, Folder 277, NARA). See also Patti, *Why Viet Nam?* 320, 564. Although Coolidge was immediately taken to a British hospital and treated, the Americans decided to remove him, greatly perturbing the British. "The Americans flew a special Skymaster hospital plane complete with Lt. Col. Surgical specialist, Major Medical specialist and Capt. Pathologist to remove a wounded American officer from our care, and also an appendicitis case. This dramatic incident was accompanied by much clicking of cameras, and one had the impression that our Allies were convinced they had saved their colleagues from a terrible fate" (Gracey Papers, Box 4, File 7).

108. Over the years, accounts of Dewey's death have been embellished. One author wrote: "For Dewey was known to have favoured the claim of the Provisional Executive Committee to represent the Government of Vietnam and to have disapproved of the reckless manner in which the French had regained administrative

control in Saigon, and over the cry of 'I am American' with which he tried to deter his assailant, appeared to represent a claim to benefit from some invidious if unspecified apartheid." Lancaster, *The Emancipation of French Indochina*, 132–133. Ellen Hammer wrote that Dewey called out the same phrase, only in French. In her view: "Saigon was in the grip of an indiscriminate xenophobia and snipers did not stop to look at the cut of the uniforms or the markings on the equipment of the white men at whom they shot." Hammer, *The Struggle for Indochina*, 119.

109. Bluechel, "Political Aims and Philosophy of the Viet Minh."

110. Affidavits of Herbert Bluechel, George Wickes, Harold Varner, and Frank White (RG 226, Entry 110, Box 25, Folder 277, NARA). Affidavits state that one Japanese soldier, stationed on the roof, fired twice into a clump of bushes.

111. The "flag" was in this case a carbine with a white handkerchief tied to it.

112. Affidavit of Captain Frank White (RG 226, Entry 110, Box 25, Folder 277, NARA). See also Gracey Papers, File 5, Box 1.

113. Affidavit of Captain Frank White.

114. Affidavit of Captain Herbert Bluechel; Affidavit of Captain Frank White; Affidavit of T/5 George Wickes; Affidavit of Lieutenant Herbert [*sic*] Varner; Affidavit of Lieutenant Leslie Frost; Affidavit of Major Frank Rhoads (all in RG 226, Entry 110, Box 25, Folder 277, NARA); From Kandy to OSS (RG 226, Entry 134, Box 208, Folder 1306, NARA); "Siege of Saigon," *Newsweek*, October 8, 1945, 57; "Chas. Dewey's Son Killed in Saigon Riot," *Chicago Herald America*, September 27, 1945. A less favorable account of Gracey's reaction to Dewey's death reads: "Gracey, on the other hand, remarked that Dewey 'got what he deserved.'" James S. Olson and Randy Roberts, *Where the Domino Fell: America and Vietnam 1945 to 1990* (New York: St. Martin's, 1991), 24.

115. Lieutenant G. T. Manaki, Chief of Indo-China Dept. to Brigadier General J. A. E. Hirst D.S.O., Commander of Allied Land Forces (RG 226, Entry 110, Box 25, Folder 277, NARA).

116. Bluechel, "Political Aims and Philosophy of the Viet Minh" and Bluechel, "Comments on Report Published by the Allied Control Commission, Saigon, Concerning the Events of 26 September 1945," September 30, 1945 (RG 226, Entry 110, Box 25, Folder 277, NARA); White, interviews. In a second affidavit, Bluechel reiterated his belief that the presence of an American flag on the jeep would have prevented trouble. As evidence, he reported on his trips in and out of the city the day before Dewey's death. As Bluechel and Wickes approached villages with roadblocks, they mounted the American flag on a short rod on the radiator. As they approached the nearby houses and shops, unarmed Vietnamese ran out to open the barricades for them, smiling and saluting at the two Americans. The same procedure repeated itself at every barricade they encountered that day. Affidavit of Captain Herbert Bluechel (RG 226, Entry 110, Box 25, Folder 277, NARA).

117. Dunn, *The First Vietnam War*, 153–154. See also Bluechel, "Comments on Report."

118. Captain Robert P. Leonard, "Shooting of Lieutenant Colonel Dewey," October 20, 1945. See also "Investigation of Death of Lt. Col. Dewey," undated (both in RG 226, Entry 110, Box 25, Folder 277, NARA).

119. Major F. M. Small, October 25, 1945 (RG 226, Entry 110, Box 25, Folder 277, NARA); and Small, "Investigation of Death of Major Peter Dewey," undated (RG 226, Entry 190, Box 588, Folder 0472, NARA).

120. Capt. Robert P. Leonard to Lieutenant-Colonel Cass, Commanding Officer, November 10, 1945. See also Lt. Herbert Bluechel to Strategic Services Officer, India-Burma Theatre, undated; Capt. Robert Leonard to Lt. James Withrow, November 26, 1945 (all in RG 226, Entry 110, Box 25, Folder 277, NARA). See also Philippe Devillers, *Histoire du Viet-Nam de 1940 à 1952* (Paris: Seuil, 1952), 160–161.

121. Alongside an official military photograph of Dewey, the Washington newspaper ran the partially correct caption "Annamite Riot Casualty: Col. Peter Dewey, Washington, DC, was killed by machine gun fire when rioting Annamites besieged US headquarters near OHI, Saigon, Indo-China. Another American officer wounded during the rioting was rescued by Japanese troops." September 27, 1945 (RG 226, OSS-P-74, NARA).

122. Arthur Krock, "The Late A. Peter Dewey," *New York Times*, October 3, 1945.

123. By mid-October the reward had not helped in producing Peter Dewey's body, so his father informed the army that he wished to increase the amount (5,000 piastres) offered in hopes of obtaining results. Both American and British officials rejected the senior Dewey's request, fearing that it would create a "very real danger to white officers." Furthermore, they concluded: "Annamites now have nothing to lose by producing body, and would gain some United States appreciation by doing so." Headquarters United States Forces India-Burma Theater from Kandy US, October 23, 1945. See also Commanding Officer, S.S.U., from Col. Frank Milani, Adjutant General, October 24, 1945 (both in RG 226, Entry 110, Box 25, Folder 277, NARA).

124. Pham Ngac Thach to Charles Dewey Sr., October 16, 1945; Charles Dewey Sr. to Brigadier General John Magruder, December 23, 1945; Brigadier General John Magruder to Charles Dewey Sr., December 27, 1945 (RG 226, Entry 190, Box 588, Folder 0472, NARA).

125. Pham Ngac Thach to Charles Dewey Sr., October 16, 1945; Charles Dewey Sr. to Brigadier General John Magruder, December 23, 1945; Brigadier General John Magruder to Charles Dewey Sr., December 27, 1945 (RG 226, Entry 190, Box 588, Folder 0472, NARA).

126. Thach added: "We rely actually on the United States to put an end to the machiavellian plot of the Anglo-French just as we rely on the United States for the external development of our country." Dr. Pham Ngoc Thach to Herbert Bluechel, October 15, 1945 (RG 226, Entry 148, Box 124, Folder 2151, NARA).

127. Ho Chi Minh, "Message to Southern Compatriots," September 26, 1945, *Selected Works*, 4 vols. (Hanoi: Foreign Languages Publishing House, 1961), 3: 31. Ho went on: "We must show to the world, and to the French people in particular that we want only independence and freedom, that we are not struggling for the sake of individual enmity and rancour."

128. "Memorandum for the Record: General Gallagher's Meeting with Ho Chi Minh," September 29, 1945, in Gareth Porter, ed. *Vietnam: The Definitive Documentation of Human Decisions*, 2 vols. (Stanfordville, NY: Earl M. Coleman, 1979), 1:

80–81. See also Ronald Spector, *Advice and Support: The Early Years of the U.S. Army in Vietnam, 1941–1960* (New York: Free Press, 1985), 68.

129. "The President of the Provisional Government of the Republic of Viet-Nam to the President of the United States of America," September 29, 1945 (RG 226, Entry 19, Box 350, Folder 27710, NARA). Reportedly Ho Chi Minh also met with Dewey's mother while in Paris in 1946 to express his condolences. "Full Transcript of 1997 OSS/Viet Minh Meeting," 95.

130. "Citation for the Cluster to the Legion of Merit" (RG 226, Entry 92A, Box 29, Folder 421, NARA).

131. Small, "Investigation of Death of Major Peter Dewey."

132. Wickes, memoir.

133. "Popular Sentiment in Saigon Regarding Americans," November 27, 1945 (RG 226, Entry 19, Box 348, Document RB-29109, NARA); White, interviews.

134. One State Department report noted: "It must also be recognized that the moral and political validity of the Allied position has been significantly compromised by the deliberate use of Japanese troops to maintain order and to take interim general responsibility for the areas which they had conquered and from which they were supposedly being expelled in disgrace." "United States Policy toward the Netherlands Indies and Indochina," November 20, 1945 (Philippine and Southeast Asia Division, 1944–1952, Record Group 59, Microfilm C0014, Reel 6, NARA).

135. Quoted in Patti, *Why Viet Nam?* 320.

EPILOGUE

1. Throughout 1946 and 1947 the Allies continued to try to execute Japanese soldiers for their activities in French Indochina during the war. For example, the *London Times* reported in February 1947 the execution of thirteen members of the *kempeitai*, as well as the imprisonment of twenty-seven others, for war crimes committed in Saigon. "Thirteen Japanese Condemned to Death," *London Times*, February 17, 1947.

2. Harold R. Isaacs, *No Peace for Asia* (Cambridge, MA: M.I.T. Press, 1947), 239.

3. "A Rapid Survey of the Vietnamese Situation since the Establishment of the Republic," October 1945 (RG 226, Entry 140, Box 53, Folder 422, NARA).

4. "Foreign Policy of the Provisional Government of the Republic of Viet Nam," November 20, 1945 (RG 226, Entry 154, Box 174, Folder 3015, NARA).

5. Bui Diem, *In the Jaws of History*, with David Chanoff (Boston: Houghton Mifflin, 1987), 38.

6. Quoted by U.S. Ambassador Jefferson Caffery to the Secretary of State, March 13, 1945, in U.S. Department of State, *Foreign Relations of the United States, 1945*, vol. 6, *China* (Washington, DC: Government Printing Office, 1962), 300.

7. Joseph M. Siracusa, "FDR, Truman, and Indochina, 1941–1952: The Forgotten Years," in *The Impact of the Cold War Reconsiderations*, edited by Joseph M. Siracusa

and Glen St. John Barclay (Port Washington, NY: Kennikat, 1977), 173–174. See also Peter A. Poole, *Eight Presidents and Indochina* (Malabar, FL: Krieger, 1978), 12–22.

8. Quoted in George C. Herring, "The Truman Administration and the Restoration of French Sovereignty in Indochina," *Diplomatic History* 1 (1977): 102–113.

9. Quoted in Siracusa, "FDR, Truman, and Indochina, 1941–1952," 172.

10. Herring, "The Truman Administration and the Restoration of French Sovereignty in Indochina," 102–113.

11. Abbot Low Moffat, "Welcome to Our American Friends," in *Strange Ground: Americans in Vietnam 1945–1975; An Oral History*, ed. Harry Mauer (New York: Henry Holt, 1989), 38.

12. Quoted in U.S. Department of Defense, *United States–Vietnam Relations, 1945–1967*, 12 vols. (Washington, DC: Government Printing Office, 1971) 1: 13.

13. Moffat, "Welcome to Our American Friends," 42.

14. "President Ho Chi Minh Vietnam Democratic Republic, Hanoi to the President of the United States of America, Washington, DC," February 28, 1946 (RG 226, Entry 140, Box 53, Folder 427, NARA).

15. Harrison Salisbury, "Introduction," in Ho Chi Minh, *The Prison Diary of Ho Chi Minh*, translated by Aileen Palmer (New York: Bantam Books, 1971), ix.

16. "Full Transcript of 1997 OSS/Viet Minh Meeting," courtesy of William Duiker, 91.

17. Jean Sainteny, *Histoire d'une paix manquée: Indochine 1945–1947* (Paris: Librairie Fayard les Grandes Etudes Contemporaines, 1967), 137, 107–108.

18. Françoise Martin, *Heures tragiques au Tonkin* (Paris: Berger-Levrault, 1948), 154.

19. Peter M. Dunn, *The First Vietnam War* (New York: St. Martin's, 1985), ix.

20. Charles Fenn, *Ho Chi Minh: A Biographical Introduction* (New York: Charles Scribner's Sons, 1973), 84.

21. Harold R. Isaacs, "Indo-China: Freedom—Or We Burn the House," *Newsweek*, December 3, 1945, 44–46.

22. Gallagher, correspondence cited in Edward R. Drachman, *United States Policy toward Vietnam, 1940–1945* (Rutherford, NJ: Fairleigh Dickinson University Press, 1970), 132.

23. Gallagher made his papers available to Bert Cooper, John Killigrew, and Norman LaCharite for their book *Case Studies in Insurgency and Revolutionary Warfare: Vietnam 1941–1954* (Washington, DC: Special Operations Research Office, 1964), 111–112.

24. Gallagher, correspondence cited in Drachman, *United States Policy toward Vietnam, 1940–1945*, 136.

25. Philippe Devillers, *Histoire du Viet-Nam de 1940 à 1952* (Paris: Seuil, 1952), 202. According to one source, although Gallagher's offer was rebuffed, "certain members of his mission allegedly realised fruitful profits in the trade of arms, machinery, and munitions." W. Macy Marvel, "Drift and Intrigue: United States Relations with the Viet-Minh, 1945," *Millennium* 4, no. 1 (1975): 19. Gallagher was not the first American to be accused of trying to assert American economic interests in Vietnam.

On October 15 *Le Monde* reported that Archimedes Patti offered "economic advantages to the Viet-Minh in return for the independence of Vietnam." Quoted in Marvel, "Drift and Intrigue," 19.

26. Ronald Spector, *Advice and Support: The Early Years of the U.S. Army in Vietnam, 1941–1960* (New York: Free Press, 1985), 68–69.

27. In October 1995 the Vietnam-America Friendship Association, now known as the Vietnam-USA Society, celebrated its fiftieth anniversary with a reunion in Hanoi of former Viet Minh and seven of the Americans who had worked with them in 1945. Prominent among the Vietnamese present was Vo Nguyen Giap. The Americans present were Charles Fenn, Ray Grelecki, Henry Prunier, Mac Shin, Carleton Swift, Frank Tan, and Allison Thomas. Carol Brightman, "Our Men in Hanoi," *Indochina Interchange* 5, no. 4 (December, 1995): 1, 17–19. Tara McAuliff, "Vietnam-USA Society Celebrates Its 50th Anniversary," *Indochina Interchange* 5, no. 3 (September 1995): 6–7.

28. Joseph Buttinger, *Vietnam: A Dragon Embattled.* 2 vols. (New York: Praeger, 1967), 1: 341; Bernard Fall, *The Two Viet-Nams: A Political and Military Analysis* (New York: Praeger, 1967), 69; Fall, "La politique americaine au Viet-Nam," *Politique Etrange*, July 1955, 314. See also U.S. Congress, Senate, Committee on Foreign Relations, *The United States and Vietnam: 1944–1947* (92nd Cong., 2nd sess., 1972); General G. Sabattier, *Le destin de l'Indochine: Souvenirs et documents, 1941–1951* (Paris: Librairie Plon, 1952).

29. Boudarel wrote that the VAFA was formed "under the aegis of Prince Vinh Thuy and General Gallagher." Georges Boudarel and Nguyen Van Ky, *Hanoi: City of the Rising Dragon* (Lanham, MD: Rowman and Littlefield, 2002), 92.

30. "Full Transcript of 1997 OSS/Viet Minh Meeting," 90.

31. "Constitution of the Vietnam-American Friendship Association," October 1945, in Gareth Porter, ed., *Vietnam: The Definitive Documentation of Human Decisions*, 2 vols. (Stanfordville, NY: Earl M. Coleman, 1979), 1: 82–83. See also Senate, Committee on Foreign Relations, *The United States and Vietnam: 1944–1947*.

32. *V.A.F.A. Review*, November 1945, 1–2, 5.

33. Bui Diem, *In the Jaws of History*, 39.

34. William J. Duiker, *The Communist Road to Power in Vietnam*, 2nd ed. (Boulder, CO: Westview, 1996), 5; Department of Defense, *United States–Vietnam Relations, 1945–1967*, 8: 53–55.

35. OSS officials were not pleased with the early news that the VAFA was "organized under OSS supervision" and warned that if such activity was going on "without specific theater organization it must be stopped immediately." Furthermore, they noted: "If Swift has submitted himself to such ill advised action you should recall him at once and take the necessary steps to clear our people from any political action." Heppner and Indiv to Magruder and 154, October 24, 1945, copy courtesy of Carleton Swift.

36. "Full Transcript of 1997 OSS/Viet Minh Meeting," 86; Carleton Swift, interviews by author. Although withdrawn from Hanoi, Swift proceeded to Canton, where he became Deputy Chief.

37. Henry Prunier, interviews by author. Regardless of Prunier's impression of the streets, David Marr described the accomplishments of the Provisional Government: "It was already apparent by late September that Ho Chi Minh's government enjoyed tremendous popularity, and that most villages were responding to official requests to form revolutionary councils, self-defense units, literacy classes, and welfare committees. This promising beginning made it possible for the government to levy taxes, expand the army, and establish a wide-range of specialized institutions from weapons factories to counter-intelligence teams, from broadcasting stations to theatrical troupes." David Marr, *Vietnamese Tradition on Trial, 1920–1945* (Berkeley and Los Angeles: University of California Press, 1981), 410.

38. Prunier, interviews. See also Raymond P. Girard, "City Man Helped to Train Guerrillas of Ho Chi Minh," *Worcester (Mass.) Evening Gazette*, May 14/15, 1968.

39. "Improvement of OSS Intelligence," August 2, 1945 (RG 226, Entry 154, Box 116, Folder 2097, NARA).

40. Quoted in Thomas F. Troy, *Donovan and the CIA* (Frederick, MD: University Publications of America, 1981), 287.

41. Quoted in Corey Ford, *Donovan of OSS* (Boston: Little, Brown, 1970), 148.

42. Stein Tønnesson, *The Vietnamese Revolution of 1945: Roosevelt, Ho Chi Minh and de Gaulle in a World at War* (London: SAGE, 1991), 312.

43. Bradley F. Smith, *The Shadow Warriors: O.S.S. and the Origins of the C.I.A.* (New York: Basic Books, 1983), 331.

44. Arthur J. Dommen, *The Indochinese Experience of the French and the Americans: Nationalism and Communism in Cambodia, Laos, and Vietnam* (Bloomington: Indiana University Press, 2001), 166.

45. Correspondence between General Donovan and Acting Secretary of State Joseph Grew, July 14, 1945 (RG 226, Microfilm 1642, Roll 112, Frames 1032–1039, NARA).

46. For example, John McAlister claims that the Americans gave 5,000 weapons to the Viet Minh during World War II, weapons that were subsequently used against the French. John T. McAlister Jr. and Paul Mus, *The Vietnamese and Their Revolution* (New York: Harper Torchbooks, 1970), 161. See also Marvel, "Drift and Intrigue," 26.

47. Truong Chinh, *Primer for Revolt: The Communist Takeover in Viet-Nam* (New York: Praeger, 1963), xviii, 12.

48. Dunn, *The First Vietnam War*, 50.

49. "Full Transcript of 1997 OSS/Viet Minh Meeting," 69.

50. Ngoc-An, "Bo Doi Viet-My," *Lich Su Quan Su* 10 (October 1986): 18–20, 31. Translation of article by Dr. Van T. Nguyen for Allison Thomas.

51. Major Allison Thomas, "Welcome to Our American Friends," in *Strange Ground: Americans in Vietnam, 1945–1975; An Oral History*, edited by Harry Mauer (New York: Henry Holt, 1989), 35.

52. "Full Transcript of 1997 OSS/Viet Minh Meeting," 76.

53. Ibid., 84.

54. Boudarel and Nguyen Van Ky, *Hanoi*, 86.

55. Isaacs, *No Peace for Asia*, 232.

56. Buttinger, *Vietnam*, 1: 630.

57. Carleton Swift, "Intelligence in Recent Public Literature: Review of *Why Viet Nam? Prelude to America's Albatross*," courtesy of Carleton Swift.

58. Historian Huynh Kim Khanh wrote that "until several months later, US officers on the scene continued, in public and private reports, to espouse the cause of Vietnamese independence. American officers and journalists sometimes spoke at Viet Minh rallies, supporting Vietnamese independence and the Viet Minh Front ('the liberator of the Vietnamese people') and reports to the State Department and military headquarters sided with the Vietnamese." Khanh, *Vietnamese Communism, 1925–1945* (Ithaca, NY: Cornell University Press, 1982), 318.

59. Tønnesson, *The Vietnamese Revolution of 1945*, 312.

60. "Full Transcript of 1997 OSS/Viet Minh Meeting," 76. These fond recollections were, in some cases, passed down to children of the participants. For example, Thomas recalled trying to visit his "aide-de-camp and interpreter" years later in Vietnam. He was disappointed to discover that the man had already died, but he was deeply touched to find that the man's son had a framed picture of the Deer Team on his living room wall. Allison Thomas, interviews by author.

61. Vo Nguyen Giap wrote chatty letters to Thomas in Lansing, Michigan, until November 1946; Ho Chi Minh wrote to Tan for several months after Tan left the Viet Bac and returned to Kunming. Stephen Nordlinger reminisced about his work in Vietnam in 1945 in his letter to Ho Chi Minh and asked if they might work together to get information back to American families about three American pilots who had become prisoners of war in 1968. He even offered to return to Hanoi if that might facilitate the situation. Nordlinger also wrote to President Lyndon Johnson offering his services in searching for a peaceful solution to the American war in Vietnam. His congressman, Richard Ottinger (New York, Twenty-fifth District) further encouraged Ambassador-at-Large Averell Harriman to take advantage of Nordlinger's personal connections to Ho. Colonel Stephen Nordlinger, correspondence, courtesy of John Nordlinger.

62. George Wickes, memoir (unpublished).

63. "Full Transcript of 1997 OSS/Viet Minh Meeting," 61.

64. Ibid., 96, 101.

65. Ibid., 97.

66. Frank White, interviews by author. See also "The Implacable Man Named 'He Who Enlightens,'" *Life*, March 22, 1968, 24; R. Harris Smith, *OSS: The Secret History of America's First Central Intelligence Agency* (Berkeley and Los Angeles: University of California Press, 1972), 358–360.

Bibliography

PRIMARY SOURCES

Oral Interviews and Correspondence

Défourneaux, René. September 1998–November 2000.

Fenn, Charles. December 1998–October 2001.

Prunier, Henry. November 1998–February 1999.

Swift, Carleton. November 1998–June 2001.

Tan, Frank. December 1998–December 2000.

Thomas, Allison. December 1998–February 1999.

White, Frank. December 1998–April 2000.

Wickes, George. September 1998–January 1999.

Manuscript and Record Collections

Giap Papers. Cecil B. and Laura G. Currey Archive of Military History. Forsyth Library Archives. Fort Hays State University, Hays, Kansas.

Sir Douglas Gracey Papers. Liddell Hart Centre for Military Archives. King's College London.

Milton Miles Papers. Naval Group China. Record Group 38. National Archives and Records Administration. Washington, DC.

Philippine and Southeast Asia Division, 1944–1952. Record Group 59. National Archives and Records Administration. Washington, DC.

Records of the Office of Strategic Services. Record Group 226. National Archives and Records Administration. Washington, DC.

"Magic" Documents. Record Group 457. National Archives and Records Administration. Washington, DC.

Archimedes L. Patti Papers. Special Collections. University of Central Florida, Orlando, Florida.

Unpublished Primary Sources

Défourneaux, Major René J. "Deer Team Diary." Courtesy of the author.

Fenn, Charles. Memoir. Courtesy of the author.

Full Transcript of 1997 OSS/Viet Minh Meeting. Courtesy of William Duiker.

Michel, Henri. "Du 9 mars au 7 novembre 1947. Le calvaire et la libération de Louise Maria Mariet au pays Thai. Reddition de Nguyen-Dinh-Tan." Courtesy of René J. Défourneaux.

Nordlinger, Colonel Stephen. Correspondence. Courtesy of John Nordlinger.

Swift, Carleton. "North Indochina in the Far East Scene of 1945." Lecture at the University of Maryland, September 19, 1996. Copy courtesy of the author.

Wickes, George. Memoir. Courtesy of the author.

PUBLISHED PRIMARY SOURCES

Bao Dai. *Le dragon d'Annam.* Paris: Plon, 1980.

Beveridge, Albert J. "Speech in the Senate, 1900." In *Words That Made American History,* edited by Richard Current, John Garraty, and Julius Weinberg, 2 vols., 1: 218–225. Boston: Little, Brown, 1978.

Boisanger, Claude de. *On pouvait éviter la guerre d'Indochine: Souvenirs, 1941–1945.* Paris: Librairie d'Amerique et d'Orient, 1977.

Breaking Our Chains: Documents of the Vietnamese Revolution of August 1945. Hanoi: Foreign Languages Publishing House, 1960.

Brigham, Robert. "OSS and Viet Minh Veterans Meet in the U.S." *Indochina Interchange,* December 1997, 6–7.

Broyles, William Jr. *Brothers in Arms: A Journey from War to Peace.* New York: Knopf, 1986.

Bui Diem. *In the Jaws of History.* With David Chanoff. Boston: Houghton Mifflin, 1987.

Bui Tin. *Following Ho Chi Minh: Memoirs of a North Vietnamese Colonel.* Honolulu: University of Hawaii Press, 1995.

Buttinger, Joseph. "An Eyewitness Report on Vietnam." *Reporter,* January 27, 1955.

Chennault, Claire Lee. *Way of a Fighter: The Memoirs of Claire Lee Channault.* New York: G. P. Putnam's Sons, 1949.

Decoux, Admiral Jean. *A la barre de l'Indochine: Histoire de mon gouvernement general (1940–1945).* Paris: Librairie Plon, 1949.

Défourneaux, René J. "A Secret Encounter with Ho Chi Minh." *Look,* August 9, 1966, 32–33.

———. *The Winking Fox: Twenty-two Years in Military Intelligence.* Indianapolis: Indiana Creative Arts, 1997.

Donovan, William J. "A Central Intelligence Agency." *Vital Speeches of the Day* 12, no. 14 (May 1, 1946): 446–448.

———. "Discarding Transient Emotionalism." *Vital Speeches of the Day* 2, no. 13 (March 23, 1936): 397–398.

———. "Is America Prepared for War?" *Vital Speeches of the Day* 6, no. 5 (December 15, 1939): 155–157.

———. "Our Spiritual Defense." *Vital Speeches of the Day* 7, no. 19 (June 28, 1941): 589–590.

———. "The Struggle in Asia." *Vital Speeches of the Day* 21, no. 12 (April 1, 1955): 1135–1138.

———. "What Are We Up Against?" *Vital Speeches of the Day* 7, no. 13 (April 15, 1941): 386–389.

Duffy, Francis Patrick. *Father Duffy's Story: A Tale of Humor and Heroism, of Life and Death with the Fighting Sixty-ninth.* New York: George H. Doran, 1919.

Elliott, David W. P. *The Vietnamese War: Revolution and Social Change in the Mekong Delta.* New York: East Gate Books, 2002.

Elliott, Duong Van Mai. *The Sacred Willow: Four Generations in the Life of a Vietnamese Family.* Oxford: Oxford University Press, 1999.

Fenn, Charles. *Ho Chi Minh: A Biographical Introduction.* New York: Charles Scribner's Sons, 1973.

———. "Remembering Frank Tan." *Interchange* 12, no. 2 (Summer 2002): 10–11.

Ho Chi Minh. *Ho Chi Minh: Selected Articles and Speeches, 1920–1967.* Edited by Jack Woddis. New York: International Publishers, 1970.

———. *The Prison Diary of Ho Chi Minh.* Translated by Aileen Palmer. New York: Bantam Books, 1971.

———. *Selected Works.* 4 vols. Hanoi: Foreign Languages Publishing House, 1960–1962.

Hoai Thanh et al. *Days with Ho Chi Minh.* Hanoi: Foreign Languages Publishing House, 1962.

Hoang Van Hoan. *A Drop in the Ocean: Hoang Van Hoan's Revolutionary Reminiscences.* Beijing: Foreign Language Press, 1988.

Hull, Cordell. *The Memoirs of Cordell Hull.* 2 vols. New York: Macmillan, 1948.

International Military Tribunal for the Far East. *Court Papers, Journals, Exhibits, and Judgments of the International Military Tribunal for the Far East.* Compiled and edited by R. John Pritchard and Sonia Zaide. 10 vols. New York: Garland, 1981.

Isaacs, Harold R. "Indo-China: Freedom—Or We Burn the House." *Newsweek*, December 3, 1945, 44–46.

———. *No Peace for Asia.* Cambridge, MA: M.I.T. Press, 1947.

———. "Saigon: French Island in a Sea of Rebellion." *Newsweek*, November 26, 1945, 54.

"Japanese Executed." *London Times*, March 20, 1947.

Krock, Arthur. "The Late A. Peter Dewey." *New York Times*, October 3, 1945.

Miles, Vice Admiral Milton E., USN. *A Different Kind of War: The Unknown Story of the U.S. Navy's Guerrilla Forces in World War II China.* New York: Doubleday, 1967.

Miles, Wilma Jerman. *Billy, Navy Wife*. Chevy Chase, MD: Murray E. Miles and Charles H. Miles, 1999.

Moffat, Abbot Low. "Welcome to Our American Friends." In *Strange Ground: Americans in Vietnam 1945–1975; An Oral History*, edited by Harry Mauer, 42–46. New York: Henry Holt, 1989.

Murphy, Robert. *Diplomat among Warriors*. New York: Doubleday, 1964.

Mus, Paul. *Le Viet Nam chez lui*. Paris: Centre d'Etudes de Politique Etrangère, 1946.

Nguyen Cao Ky. *Twenty Years and Twenty Days*. New York: Stein and Day, 1976.

Nguyen Thi Dinh. *No Other Road to Take: Memoir of Mrs. Nguyen Thi Dinh*. Translated by Mai V. Elliott. Ithaca, NY: Cornell University Press, 1976.

Patti, Archimedes L. A. *Why Viet Nam? Prelude to America's Albatross*. Berkeley and Los Angeles: University of California Press, 1980.

Porter, Gareth, ed. *Vietnam: The Definitive Documentation of Human Decisions*. 2 vols. Stanfordville, NY: Earl M. Coleman, 1979.

Roosevelt, Elliott. *As He Saw It*. New York: Duell, Sloan and Pearce, 1946.

Sabattier, General G. *Le destin de l'Indochine: Souvenirs et documents, 1941–1951*. Paris: Librairie Plon, 1952.

Sainteny, Jean. *Histoire d'une paix manquée: Indochine 1945–1947*. Paris: Librairie Fayard les Grandes Etudes Contemporaines, 1967.

Sheean, Vincent. *This House against This House*. New York: Random House, 1946.

Sheldon, George. "Status of the Viet Nam." *Far Eastern Survey* 15, no. 25 (1946): 373–377.

Shigemitsu Mamoru. *Japan and Her Destiny*. London: Hutchinson, 1958.

Stetler, Russell, ed. *The Military Art of People's War: Selected Writings of General Vo Nguyen Giap*. New York: Monthly Review Press, 1970.

Sun Tzu. *The Art of War*. Translated by Samuel B. Griffith. London: Oxford University Press, 1963.

Tam Lang. "I Pulled a Rickshaw." In *The Light of the Capital: Three Modern Vietnamese Classics*, 51–120. Translated by Greg Lockhart and Monique Lockhart. Oxford: Oxford University Press, 1996.

Taylor, Edmond. *Awakening from History*. Boston: Gambit, 1969.

———. *Richer by Asia*. 2nd ed. New York: Time-Life Books, 1964.

"Thirteen Japanese Condemned to Death." *London Times*, February 17, 1947.

Thomas, Major Allison. "Welcome to Our American Friends." In *Strange Ground: Americans in Vietnam, 1945–1975; An Oral History*, edited by Harry Mauer, 28–37. New York: Henry Holt, 1989.

Tran Dan Tien [Ho Chi Minh]. *Glimpses of the Life of Ho Chi Minh, President of the Democratic Republic of Vietnam*. Hanoi: Foreign Languages Publishing House, 1958.

Tran Tu Binh. *The Red Earth: A Vietnamese Memoir of Life on a Colonial Rubber Plantation*. Translated by John Spragens Jr. Athens: Ohio University Press, 1985.

Tran Van Mai. "Who Committed This Crime?" In *Before the Revolution: The Viet-namese Peasants under the French*, by Ngo Vinh Long et al., translated by Ngo Vinh Long, 220–276. New York: Columbia University Press, 1991.

Truong Chinh. *Primer for Revolt: The Communist Takeover in Viet-Nam*. New York: Praeger, 1963.

Twain, Mark. *Mark Twain on the Damned Human Race*. Edited by Janet Smith. New York: Hill and Wang, 1962.

United Nations. War Crimes Commission. *History of the United Nations War Crimes Commission and the Development of the Laws of War*. London: His Majesty's Stationery Office, 1948.

U.S. Congress. Senate. Committee on Foreign Relations. *Hearings before the Committee on Foreign Relations on Causes, Origins, and Lessons of the Vietnam War*. 92nd Cong., 2nd sess., 1972.

———. Committee on Foreign Relations. *The United States and Vietnam: 1944–1947*. 92nd Cong., 2nd sess., 1972.

U.S. Department of Defense. *The Pentagon Papers: The Defense Department History of United States Decisionmaking on Vietnam*. 8 vols. Boston: Beacon Press, 1971.

———. *United States–Vietnam Relations, 1945–1967*. 12 vols. Washington, DC: Government Printing Office, 1971.

U.S. Department of State. "Declaration by United Nations, Washington, January 1, 1942, and Declaration Known as the Atlantic Charter, August 14, 1941." *Cooperative War Effort*, Executive Agreement Series 236, Publication 1732 (1942): 4.

———. *Foreign Relations of the United States, 1938*. Vol. 3, *The Far East*. Washington, DC: Government Printing Office, 1954.

———. *Foreign Relations of the United States, 1939*. Vol. 3, *The Far East*. Washington, DC: Government Printing Office, 1955.

———. *Foreign Relations of the United States, 1941*. Vol. 2, *Europe*. Washington, DC: Government Printing Office, 1959.

———. *Foreign Relations of the United States, 1942*. Vol. 2, *Europe*. Washington, DC: Government Printing Office, 1962.

———. *Foreign Relations of the United States, 1943: China*. Washington, DC: Government Printing Office, 1956.

———. *Foreign Relations of the United States, 1943*. Vol. 3, *The British Commonwealth, Eastern Europe, the Far East*. Washington, DC: Government Printing Office, 1963.

———. *Foreign Relations of the United States, 1944*. Vol. 3, *The British Commonwealth, Europe*. Washington, DC: Government Printing Office, 1965.

———. *Foreign Relations of the United States, 1944*. Vol. 6, *China*. Washington, DC: Government Printing Office, 1967.

Vo Nguyen Giap. *Des journées inoubliables*. Hanoi: Editions en Langues Etranges, 1975.

———. *People's War, People's Army*. New York: Praeger, 1967.

Wedemeyer, General Albert C. *Wedemeyer Reports!* New York: Henry Holt, 1958.

SECONDARY SOURCES

Books and Articles

Aldrich, Richard. "Imperial Rivalry: British and American Intelligence in Asia, 1942–1946." *Intelligence and National Security* 3, no. 1 (January 1988): 5–55.

Allen, Louis, Judith Stowe, and Thanatphong Smitabhindu. "The Japanese Coup of 9 March 1945 in Indo-China." In *1945 in South-East Asia*, 1–29. London: London School of Economics and Political Science, 1985.

———. "Studies in the Japanese Occupation of South-East Asia 1942–1945. 'French Indochina' to 'Vietnam.' Japan, France and Great Britain, Summer 1945." *Durham University Journal* 64, no. 2 (March 1972): 120–132.

Appy, Christian G. *Patriots: The Vietnam War Remembered from All Sides*. New York: Viking, 2003.

Barnet, Richard. *Intervention and Revolution: The United States and the Third World*. New York: World, 1968.

Beasley, W. G. *Japanese Imperialism, 1894–1945*. Oxford: Clarendon, 1987.

Bergamini, David. *Japan's Imperial Conspiracy*. New York: Morrow, 1971.

Bodard, Lucien. *The Quicksand War: Prelude to Vietnam*. Boston: Little, Brown, 1967.

Boudarel, Georges, and Nguyen Van Ky. *Hanoi: City of the Rising Dragon*. Lanham, MD: Rowman and Littlefield, 2002.

Bradley, Mark Philip. *Imagining Vietnam and America: The Making of Postcolonial Vietnam, 1919–1950*. Chapel Hill: University of North Carolina Press, 2000.

Brightman, Carol. "Our Men in Hanoi." *Indochina Interchange* 5, no. 4 (December 1995): 1, 17–19.

Brown, Anthony Cave. *The Last Hero: Wild Bill Donovan*. New York: Vintage, 1982.

Bui Minh Dung. "Japan's Role in the Vietnamese Starvation of 1944–45." *Modern Asian Studies* 29, no. 3 (1995): 573–618.

———. "Nominal Vietnamese Independence Following the Japanese Coup de Force on 9 March 1945." *Japan Forum* 6, no. 2 (October 1994): 231–249.

Buttinger, Joseph. *Vietnam: A Dragon Embattled*. 2 vols. New York: Praeger, 1967.

Chalou, George C., ed. *The Secrets War: The Office of Strategic Services in World War II*. Washington, DC: National Archives Trust Fund Board, 1992.

Chandler, David. "The Kingdom of Kampuchea, March–October 1945: Japanese Sponsored Independence in Cambodia in World War II." *Journal of Southeast Asian Studies* 17, no. 1 (March 1986): 80–93.

Charbonneau, René, and José Maigre. *Les parias de la victoire: Indochine-Chine, 1945*. Paris: France-Empire, 1980.

Cline, Ray S. *Secrets, Spies and Scholars: Blueprint of the Essential CIA*. Washington, DC: Acropolis, 1976.

Cole, Allan B., ed. *Conflict in Indo-China and International Repercussions: A Documentary History, 1945–1955*. Ithaca, NY: Cornell University Press, 1956.

Conboy, Kenneth, and Dale Andrade. *Spies and Commandos: How America Lost the Secret War in North Vietnam.* Lawrence: University Press of Kansas, 2000.

Conroy, Hilary, and Harry Wray. *Pearl Harbor Reexamined: Prologue to the Pacific War.* Honolulu: University of Hawaii Press, 1990.

Cooper, Bert, John Killigrew, and Norman LaCharite. *Case Studies in Insurgency and Revolutionary Warfare: Vietnam, 1941–1954.* Washington, DC: Special Operations Research Office, 1964.

Costello, John. *The Pacific War, 1941–1945.* New York: Morrow, 1982.

Currey, Cecil B. *Victory at Any Cost: The Genius of Viet Nam's Gen. Vo Nguyen Giap.* Washington, DC: Brassey's, 1997.

Dallek, Robert. *Franklin D. Roosevelt and American Foreign Policy, 1932–1945.* Oxford: Oxford University Press, 1995.

Dalloz, Jacques. *The War in Indo-China, 1945–54.* Dublin, Ireland: Gill and Macmillan, 1987.

Deacon, Richard. *Kempei Tai: The Japanese Secret Service Then and Now.* New York: Morrow, 1994.

Dennis, Peter. *Troubled Days of Peace: Mountbatten and South East Asia Command, 1945–46.* New York: St. Martin's, 1987.

Devillers, Philippe. *Histoire du Viet-Nam de 1940 à 1952.* Paris: Seuil, 1952.

Dewey, A. Peter. *As They Were.* New York: Beechhurst, 1946.

Dommen, Arthur J. *The Indochinese Experience of the French and the Americans: Nationalism and Communism in Cambodia, Laos, and Vietnam.* Bloomington: Indiana University Press, 2001.

Dommen, Arthur J., and George W. Dalley. "The OSS in Laos: The 1945 Raven Mission and American Policy." *Journal of Southeast Asian Studies* 22, no. 2 (September 1991): 327–346.

Drachman, Edward R. *United States Policy toward Vietnam, 1940–1945.* Rutherford, NJ: Fairleigh Dickinson University Press, 1970.

Duiker, William J. *The Communist Road to Power in Vietnam.* 2nd ed. Boulder, CO: Westview, 1996.

———. *Ho Chi Minh.* New York: Hyperion, 2000.

———. *Sacred War: Nationalism and Revolution in a Divided Vietnam.* New York: McGraw-Hill, 1995.

Dunlop, Richard. *Donovan, America's Master Spy.* Chicago: Rand McNally, 1982.

Dunn, Peter M. *The First Vietnam War.* New York: St. Martin's, 1985.

Duus, Peter, Ramon H. Myers, and Mark R. Peattie, eds. *The Japanese Wartime Empire, 1931–45.* Princeton, NJ: Princeton University Press, 1996.

Elsbree, Willard H. *Japan's Role in Southeast Asian Nationalist Movements, 1940 to 1945.* Cambridge, MA: Harvard University Press, 1953.

Fall, Bernard. *Last Reflections on a War.* New York: Doubleday, 1967.

———. "La politique americaine au Viet-Nam." *Politique Etrange,* July 1955, 299–322.

———. *The Two Viet-Nams: A Political and Military Analysis.* New York: Praeger, 1967.

Ferrier, Sergeant David J. "ONI and OSS in World War II." *World War II Fact Sheet.* Washington, DC: Navy and Marine Corps WWII Commemorative Committee, Navy Office of Information, 1995.

Fishel, Wesley R., ed. *Vietnam: Anatomy of a Conflict.* Itasca, IL: F. E. Peacock, 1968.

Fitzgerald, Frances. *Fire in the Lake: The Vietnamese and the Americans in Vietnam.* Boston: Little, Brown, 1972.

Ford, Corey. *Donovan of OSS.* Boston: Little, Brown, 1970.

Ford, Corey, and Alastair MacBain. *Cloak and Dagger: The Secret Story of the OSS.* New York: Grosset and Dunlap, 1946.

Frey, Marc, Ronald W. Pruessen, and Tan Tai Yong, eds. *The Transformation of Southeast Asia: International Perspectives on Decolonization.* Armonk, NY: Sharpe, 2003.

Gaudel, André. *L'Indochine française en face du Japon.* Paris: Susse, 1947.

Gibson, James William. *The Perfect War: Technowar in Vietnam.* Boston: Atlantic Monthly Press, 1986.

Gillin, Donald G., and Charles Etter. "Staying On: Japanese Soldiers and Civilians in China, 1945–1949." *Journal of Asian Studies* 42, no. 3 (May 1983): 497–518.

Girard, Raymond P. "City Man Helped to Train Guerrillas of Ho Chi Minh." *Worcester (Mass.) Evening Gazette,* May 14/15, 1968.

Goodman, Grant K. *Imperial Japan and Asia—A Reassessment.* New York: East Asian Institute, Columbia University, 1967.

Goscha, Christopher E. "Allies tardifs: Les apports techniques des deserteurs japonais au Viet Minh (1945–1950)." Unpublished article, courtesy of the author.

Hammer, Ellen J. *The Struggle for Indochina.* Stanford, CA: Stanford University Press, 1954.

Harclerode, Peter. *Fighting Dirty: The Inside Story of Covert Operations from Ho Chi Minh to Osama Bin Laden.* London: Cassell, 2001.

Herring, George C. "The Truman Administration and the Restoration of French Sovereignty in Indochina." *Diplomatic History* 1 (1977): 97–117.

Hess, Gary R. "Franklin Roosevelt and Indochina." *Journal of American History* 59 (1972): 353–368.

Hesse d'Alzon, Claude. "Le coup de force japonais, ou le temps de la Dislocation (Mars 1945)." In *L'armée française d'Indochine pendent la Seconde Guerre Mondiale, 1939–1945,* edited by P. Isoart, 119–130. Paris: Presses Universitaires de France, 1982.

Hood, Steven J. *Dragons Entangled: Indochina and the China-Vietnam War.* Armonk, NY: Sharpe, 1992.

"The Implacable Man Named 'He Who Enlightens.'" *Life,* March 22, 1968, 22–31.

Isoart, Paul, ed. *L'Indochine française, 1940–1945.* Paris: Presses Universitaires de France, 1982.

James, Marquis. *The Texaco Story: The First Fifty Years, 1902–1952.* New York: Texas Company, 1953.

Jamieson, Neil L. *Understanding Vietnam.* Berkeley and Los Angeles: University of California Press, 1995.

Jones, F. C. *Japan's New Order in East Asia: Its Rise and Fall, 1937–45.* London: Oxford University Press, 1954.

Kamm, Henry. *Dragon Ascending: Vietnam and the Vietnamese.* New York: Arcade, 1996.

Karig, Walter. "The Most Mysterious Office in Washington." *Liberty,* January 3, 1942, 8–9, 45–46.

Katz, Barry M. *Foreign Intelligence: Research and Analysis in the Office of Strategic Services, 1942–1945.* Cambridge, MA: Harvard University Press, 1989.

Khanh, Huynh Kim. "The Vietnamese August Revolution Reinterpreted." *Journal of Asian Studies* 30, no. 4 (1971): 761–782.

———. *Vietnamese Communism, 1925–1945.* Ithaca, NY: Cornell University Press, 1982.

Kobelev, Yevgeny. *Ho Chi Minh.* Moscow: Progress, 1989.

Kolko, Gabriel. *The Politics of War: The World and United States Foreign Policy, 1943–1945.* New York: Random House, 1968.

———. *The Roots of American Foreign Policy: An Analysis of Power and Purpose.* Boston: Beacon Press, 1969.

Krebs, Gerhard, and Christian Oberlander. *1945 in Europe and Asia: Reconsidering the End of World War II and the Change of the World Order.* Monographien aus dem Deutschen Institut fur Japan Studien der Philipp-Franz von Siebold-Stiftung 19. Munich: Iudicium, 1997.

La Feber, Walter. "Roosevelt, Churchill, and Indochina: 1942-1945." *American Historical Review* 80 (December 1975): 1277-1295.

Lacouture, Jean. *Vietnam: Between Two Truces.* New York: Vintage, 1966.

Lamb, David. *Vietnam, Now.* New York: Public Affairs, 2002.

Lancaster, Donald. *The Emancipation of French Indochina.* London: Oxford University Press, 1961.

Lattimore, Eleanor. "Indo-China: French Union or Japanese 'Independence.'" *Far Eastern Survey,* no. 14 (May 23, 1945): 132–134.

Lebra, Joyce C. *Japanese-Trained Armies in Southeast Asia.* New York: Columbia University Press, 1977.

———. *Japan's Greater East Asia Co-Prosperity Sphere in World War II: Selected Readings and Documents.* London: Oxford University Press, 1975.

Lockhart, Greg. *Nation in Arms: The Origins of the People's Army of Vietnam.* Sydney: Allen and Unwin, 1989.

Long, Ngo Vinh, et al. *Before the Revolution: The Vietnamese Peasants under the French.* Translated by Ngo Vinh Long. New York: Columbia University Press, 1991.

Louis, William Roger. *Imperialism at Bay: The United States and the Decolonization of the British Empire.* Oxford: Clarendon, 1997.

MacPherson, Nelson. "Reductio Ad Absurdum: The R&A Branch of OSS/London." *International Journal of Intelligence and Counterintelligence* 15, no. 3 (July 2002): 390-414.

Marr, David. "Vietnam: Harnessing the Whirlwind." In *Asia—The Winning of Independence,* edited by Robin Jeffrey, 163-207. New York: St. Martin's, 1981.

———. *Vietnam 1945: The Quest for Power*. Berkeley and Los Angeles: University of California Press, 1995.

———. *Vietnamese Tradition on Trial, 1920–1945*. Berkeley and Los Angeles: University of California Press, 1981.

———. "World War II and the Vietnamese Revolution." In *Southeast Asia under Japanese Occupation*, edited by Alfred W. McCoy, 104–131. New Haven, CT: Yale University Southeast Asia Studies, 1985.

Martin, Françoise. *Heures tragiques au Tonkin*. Paris: Berger-Levrault, 1948.

Marvel, W. Macy. "Drift and Intrigue: United States Relations with the Viet-Minh, 1945." *Millennium* 4, no. 1 (1975): 10–27.

McAlister, John T. Jr. *Viet Nam: The Origins of Revolution*. New York: Alfred A. Knopf, 1969.

McAlister, John T. Jr., and Paul Mus. *The Vietnamese and Their Revolution*. New York: Harper Torchbooks, 1970.

McAuliff, Tara. "Vietnam-USA Society Celebrates Its 50th Anniversary." *Indochina Interchange* 5, no. 3 (September 1995): 6–7.

McDonald, Lawrence H. "The Office of Strategic Services." *Prologue* 23, no. 1 (Spring 1991): 7–22.

———. "The OSS and Its Records." In *The Secrets War: The Office of Strategic Services in World War II*, edited by George C. Chalou, 78–102. Washington, DC: National Archives and Records Administration, 1992.

Melton, H. Keith. *OSS Special Weapons and Equipment: Spy Devices of WWII*. New York: Sterling, 1991.

Military History Institute of Vietnam. *Victory in Vietnam: The Official History of the People's Army of Vietnam, 1954–1975*. Translated by Merle L. Pribbenow. Lawrence: University Press of Kansas, 2002.

Morley, James William, ed. *The Fateful Choice: Japan's Advance into Southeast Asia; Selected Translations from "Taiheiyo senso e no michi: Kaisen gaiko shi."* New York: Columbia University Press, 1980.

Murakami Hyoe. *The Years of Trial, 1919–52*. Tokyo: Japan Culture Institute, 1982.

Murray, Martin J. *The Development of Capitalism in Colonial Indochina (1870–1940)*. Berkeley and Los Angeles: University of California Press, 1980.

Myers, Ramon H., and Mark R. Peattie. *The Japanese Colonial Empire, 1895–1945*. Princeton, NJ: Princeton University Press, 1984.

Ngoc-An. "Bo Doi Viet-My." *Lich Su Quan Su* 10 (October 1986): 18–20, 31.

Nitz, Kiyoko Kurusu. "Independence without Nationalists? The Japanese and Vietnamese Nationalism during the Japanese Period, 1940–45." *Journal of Southeast Asian Studies* 15 (March 1984): 108–133.

———. "Japanese Military Policy towards French Indochina during the Second World War: The Road to the *Meigo Sakusen*." *Journal of Southeast Asian Studies* 14 (September 1983): 328–353.

O'Donnell, Patrick K. *Operatives, Spies, and Saboteurs: The Unknown Story of the Men and Women of WWII's OSS*. New York: Free Press, 2004.

Olson, James S., and Randy Roberts. *Where the Domino Fell: America and Vietnam, 1945 to 1990.* New York: St. Martin's, 1991.

Persico, Joseph E. *Roosevelt's Secret War.* New York: Random House, 2001.

Piccigallo, Philip R. *The Japanese on Trial: Allied War Crimes Operations in the East, 1945–1951.* Austin: University of Texas Press, 1979.

Pike, Douglas. *PAVN: People's Army of Vietnam.* Novato, CA: Presidio, 1986.

Poirier, Noel B. "The Birth of Special Ops." *World War II* 17, no. 5 (January 2003): 62–65.

Poole, Peter A. *Eight Presidents and Indochina.* Malabar, FL: Krieger, 1978.

Quinn-Judge, Sophie. *Ho Chi Minh: The Missing Years.* Berkeley and Los Angeles: University of California Press, 2002.

Ready, J. Lee. *Forgotten Allies: The Military Contribution of the Colonies, Exiled Governments, and Lesser Powers to the Allied Victory in World War II.* 2 vols. Jefferson, NC: McFarland, 1985.

Roosevelt, Kermit. *War Report of the O.S.S.* New York: Walker, 1976.

Sbrega, John J. *Anglo-American Relations and Colonialism in East Asia, 1941–1945.* New York: Garland, 1983.

———. "'First Catch Your Hare': Anglo-American Perspectives on Indochina during the Second World War." *Journal of Southeast Asian Studies* 14, no. 1 (1983): 63–78.

Schlesinger, Arthur M. Jr. *The Bitter Heritage: Vietnam and American Democracy, 1941–1966.* Boston: Houghton Mifflin, 1966.

"Siege of Saigon." *Newsweek,* October 8, 1945, 57.

Shaplen, Robert. "The Enigma of Ho Chi Minh." *Reporter,* January 27, 1955, 11–19.

———. *The Lost Revolution: The U.S. in Vietnam, 1946–1966.* New York: Harper Colophon, 1966.

Sheehan, Neil. *A Bright Shining Lie: John Paul Vann and America in Vietnam.* New York: Random House, 1988.

Sheldon, George. "Status of the Viet Nam." *Far Eastern Survey* 15, no. 25 (1946): 373–377.

Shipway, Martin. *The Road to War: France and Vietnam, 1944–1947.* Providence, RI: Berghahn, 1996.

Shiraishi Masaya. "The Background to the Formation of the Tran Trong Kim Cabinet in April 1945: Japanese Plans for Governing Vietnam." In *Indochina in the 1940s and 1950s,* edited by Takashi Shiraishi and Motoo Furuta, 113–141. Ithaca, NY: Cornell Southeast Asia Program, 1992.

———. "La politique officielle japonaise a l'égard de l'Indochine jusqu'en mars 1945: Le maintien de statu quo." In *L'armée française d'Indochine pendent la Seconde Guerre Mondiale, 1939–1945,* edited by P. Isoart, 119–130. Paris: Presses Universitaires de France, 1982.

Silverstein, Josef, ed. *Southeast Asia in World War II: Four Essays.* New Haven, CT: Yale University Southeast Asia Studies, 1966.

Siracusa, Joseph M. "FDR, Truman, and Indochina, 1941–1952: The Forgotten Years." In *The Impact of the Cold War Reconsiderations,* edited by Joseph M. Siracusa and Glen St. John Barclay. Port Washington, NY: Kennikat, 1977.

Siracusa, Joseph M., and Glen St. John Barclay, eds. *The Impact of the Cold War Reconsiderations.* Port Washington, NY: Kennikat, 1977.

Smith, Bradley F. *The Shadow Warriors: O.S.S. and the Origins of the C.I.A.* New York: Basic Books, 1983.

Smith, R. Harris. *OSS: The Secret History of America's First Central Intelligence Agency.* Berkeley and Los Angeles: University of California Press, 1972.

Spector, Ronald. *Advice and Support: The Early Years of the U.S. Army in Vietnam, 1941–1960.* New York: Free Press, 1985.

——. "Allied Intelligence and Indochina, 1943-1945." *Pacific Historical Review* 51, no. 1 (1982): 23-50.

——. "'What the Local Annamites Are Thinking': American Views of Vietnamese in China, 1942-1945." *Southeast Asia* 3, no. 2 (1974): 741-751.

"A Study in Intransigence." *Life*, March 22, 1968, 21-31.

Tanham, George K. *Communist Revolutionary Warfare: From the Vietminh to the Viet Cong.* New York: Praeger, 1967.

Tarling, Nicholas. "The British and the First Japanese Move into Indo-China." *Journal of Southeast Asian Studies* 21, no. 1 (March 1990): 35-65.

Thorne, Christopher. "Indochina and Anglo-American Relations, 1942-1945." *Pacific Historical Review* 45 (1976): 73-96.

Titarenko, M. "The Rout of Japanese Militarism as a Factor That Promoted Popular Revolutions in China, Korea and Vietnam." *Far Eastern Affairs* 1 (1986): 26-43.

Tønnesson, Stein. *The Vietnamese Revolution of 1945: Roosevelt, Ho Chi Minh and de Gaulle in a World at War.* London: SAGE, 1991.

Tran My-Van. "Japan and Vietnam's Caodaists: A Wartime Relationship (1939-45)." *Journal of Southeast Asian Studies* 27, no. 1 (1996): 179-193.

Troy, Thomas F. *Donovan and the CIA.* Frederick, MD: University Publications of America, 1981.

——. *Wild Bill and Intrepid: Donovan, Stephenson, and the Origin of the CIA.* New Haven, CT: Yale University Press, 1996.

Truong Buu Lam. *Colonialism Experienced: Vietnamese Writings on Colonialism, 1900–1931.* Ann Arbor: University of Michigan Press, 2000.

U.S. Air Force Historical Division. *Brief History of 51st Fighter Group, 1940–1954.* Maxwell Air Force Base, AL: Research Studies Institute, 1955.

U.S. Department of the Army. *Minority Groups in North Vietnam.* Washington, DC: Government Printing Office, 1972.

U.S. Joint Chiefs of Staff. *History of the Indochina Incident, 1940–1954.* Washington, DC: Historical Division Joint Secretariat, Joint Chiefs of Staff, 1971.

Vu Ngu Chieu. "The Other Side of the 1945 Vietnamese Revolution: The Empire of Viet-Nam (March–August 1945)." *Journal of Asian Studies* 45, no. 2 (February 1986): 293-328.

Weinberg, Gerhard L. *A World at Arms: A Global History of World War II.* Cambridge: Cambridge University Press, 1994.

White, Theodore H. "Indo-China—The Long Trail of Error." In *Vietnam: Anatomy of a Conflict,* edited by Wesley R. Fishel, 13–28. Itasca, IL: F. E. Peacock, 1968.

Wilhelm, Maria. *The Fighting Irishman: The Story of "Wild Bill" Donovan.* New York: Hawthorn, 1964.

Worthing, Peter. *Occupation and Revolution: China and the Vietnamese August Revolution of 1945.* Berkeley: Institute of East Asian Studies, University of California, 2001.

Yoshizawa, Minami. "The Nishihara Mission in Hanoi, July 1940." In *Indochina in the 1940s and 1950s,* edited by Takashi Shiraishi and Motoo Furuta, 9–54. Ithaca, NY: Cornell Southeast Asia Program, 1992.

Young, Marilyn B. *The Vietnam Wars, 1954–1990.* New York: HarperCollins, 1991.

Theses and Dissertations

Chen, King. "China and the Democratic Republic of Vietnam 1945–54." Ph.D. diss., Pennsylvania State University, 1962.

Evans, Edward Taylor. "Vietnam in Turmoil: The Japanese Coup, the OSS, and the August Revolution in 1945." Master's thesis, University of Richmond, 1991.

Murakami Sachiko. "Japan's Thrust into French Indochina, 1940–1945." Ph.D. diss., New York University, 1981.

Wainwright, William H. "De Gaulle and Indochina, 1940–1945." Ph.D. diss., Fletcher School of Law and Diplomacy, 1972.

Index